The New York Times
Everyday Reader's
Dictionary
of
Misunderstood,
Misused,
Mispronounced
Words

The New York Times

Everyday Reader's Dictionary of Misunderstood, Misused, Mispronounced Words

Edited by Laurence Urdang

QUADRANGLE BOOKS

 A New York Times Company

Foreword

In the (good) old days, dictionaries seldom bothered defining the common words of a language—words like *the*, *a*, *and*, *but*, *for*—because "everyone knew what they meant" and it seemed only useful to list and define those words whose meanings were somewhat obscure. Today, when the acknowledged function of dictionaries has changed, in keeping with modern linguistic and lexicographical theory, to become "a description of the lexicon of a language," the shorter the dictionary, the greater the proportion of space devoted to the listing, pronouncing, and defining of the "words everyone knows."

The Everyday Reader's Dictionary of Misunderstood, Misused, Mispronounced Words contains what must be a selection based on personal choice: it doesn't pretend to contain *every* word that people are likely to misunderstand, misuse, or mispronounce and it probably contains words that are quite familiar to some users.

Some of the words have been chosen because they have appeared in popular newspapers and magazines and I thought they were uncommon enough to be included—words like *obsecrate*, *neoteric*, *nugatory*, *splenetic*, *hegemony*, *exiguous*, and *flagitious*. Others, words like *lestobiosis*, *lyncean*, *renifleur*, *fuliginous*, *ochlesis*, *oscitant*, and *nimiety*, have been included because their meanings are readily applied in ordinary writing and speaking yet the words themselves are seldom seen or heard. It seemed rather fun to include these.

By and large, technical and scientific words have been omitted with the two exceptions of anatomical terms and diseases because it was felt that so much conversation and writing centers on these subjects.

The editor would welcome, for future editions of this work, receiving comments on entries and, particularly, on omissions, though the latter should be accompanied by documentary evidence of their use.

Not a succedaneum for satisfying the nympholepsy of nullifidians, it is hoped that the haecceity of this enchiridion of arcane and recondite sesquipedalian items will appeal to the oniomania of an eximious Gemeinschaft whose legerity and sophrosyne, whose Sprachgefühl and orexis will find more than fugacious fulfillment among its felicific pages.

L.U., March, 1972

Pronunciation Key

Vowels

a	act, tan
ā	made, stay
ä	art, calm
e	pen, ever
er	air, various
ē	see, neat
ēr	here, clear
i	pig, brick
ī	might, hide
o	pot, bottom
ō	own, coal
ô	paw, bought
oi	foil, joy
o͝o	hook, foot
o͞o	pool, food
ou	out, powder
u	cup, touch
ur	third, urn
ə	(unstressed syllables only) above, mother

Consonants

b	baby, nab
CH	church, pitcher
d	door, weed
f	for, offer
g	gain, leg
h	high, behind
j	judge, hedge
k	keep, quick
l	lily, nail
m	man, balm
n	night, banner
p	pepper, step
r	red, berry
s	see, sister
SH	shoe, fish
t	tea, meet
th	thin, thistle
TH	then, heather
v	voice, have
w	win, owing
y	yellow, yet
z	zebra, hazel
ZH	treasure, azure

Stress (follows syllables)

′   main stress (əbāt′)

′   secondary stress (ban′təmwāt′)

Foreign Sounds

KH	*German* ach, *Scottish* loch
N	(nasalization) *French* bon, vin
Y	*French* tu, *German* über

aard·vark (ärd′värk), *n.* an African anteater.

Aaron's rod (er′ənz), (in the Bible) a staff, marked with the name Aaron, that blossomed. Numbers 17: 8.

ab·a·cus (ab′əkəs, əbak′əs), *n., pl.* **ab·a·cus·es, ab·a·ci** (ab′əsī, ab′əkī, abak′ī). **1.** a frame having several rows of beads strung across it on stiff wires: used in the orient as a calculating device and in some elementary schools for teaching arithmetic. **2.** a square slab at the top of an architectural column.

ab·a·lo·ne (abəlō′nē), *n.* a large, edible snail, common in California, whose shell is a source of mother-of-pearl.

à bas (äbä′), *French.* down with, as *A bas la tyrannée*! (Down with tyranny!).

a·bate (əbāt′), *v.* **1.** to diminish or cause to moderate or lessen. **2.** *Law.* **(a)** to stop an action. **(b)** to put an end to (a nuisance). —**a·bate′ment,** *n.*

ab·a·tis, ab·at·tis (ab′ətē, ab′ətis), *n., pl.* **ab·a·tis,ab·at·tis**(ab′ətēz,əbat′ēz) or **ab·a·tis·es, ab·at·tis·es.** a barricade of felled trees with sharpened branches directed toward an advancing enemy.

a·bat·jour (əbä′zHo͞or), *n.* an aperture, as a skylight, or a device, as a reflector, for directing light into a room or building.

ab·at·toir (abətwär′), *n.* a slaughterhouse.

ab·di·cate (ab′dəkāt), *v.* to give up or renounce, formally and voluntarily, an office or responsibility. —**ab·di·ca′tion,** *n.*

ab·duct (abdukt′), *v.* to kidnap. —**ab·duc′tion,** *n.*

ab·duc·tor (abduk′tər), *n.* **1.** a kidnapper. **2.** a muscle that controls movement away from the body. See also **adductor.**

a·be·ce·da·ry (ābēsē′dərē), *n. pl.* **a·be·ce·da·ries.** a book arranged in alphabetical order.

ab·er·rant (aber′ənt), *adj.* deviating; differing, in some characteristics, from others of the same class. —**ab·er′rance,** *n.*

ab·er·ra·tion (abərā′sHən), *n.* **1.** a wandering away, esp. from normal behavior, thought processes, etc. **2.** (in astronomy) apparent displacement of a heavenly body caused by the observer's motion.

a·bet (əbet′), *v.* to help or aid. —**a·bet′tor,** *n.*

ab·hor (abhôr′), *v.* to hate; detest. —**ab·hor′rence,** *n.* —**ab·hor′rent,** *adj.*

ab in·it·i·o (äb init′ēō, ab inisH′ēō), *Latin.* from the beginning.

ab intra (äb in′trä, ab in′trə), *Latin.* from within.

ab·i·o·gen·e·sis (ab′ēōjen′isis), *n.*

1

generation of living organisms from inanimate matter, as the laboratory creation of a virus from a complex protein molecule.

ab·ir·ri·tant (abir′ətənt), *n.* a soothing drug or medication.

ab·ject (ab′jekt′, abjekt′), *adj.* so low as to be hopeless; utterly humiliated.

ab·jure (abjoŏr′), *v.* to withdraw from formally; renounce; retract. See also **adjure.**

ab·la·tion (ablā′sHən), *n.* a wearing away, as of a glacier by erosion or the nose cone of a rocket by the heat of high-speed reentry into the atmosphere.

ab·le·gate (ab′ləgāt), *n.* a papal envoy to newly appointed cardinals or civil dignitaries.

ab·lu·tion (əbloŏ′sHən), *n.* a ritual or ceremonial washing or cleansing.

ab·ne·gate (ab′nəgāt′) *v.* to deny oneself (something); renounce. —**ab·ne·ga′tion,** *n.*

ab·o·ma·sum (abəmā′səm), *n., pl.* **ab·o·ma·sa** (abəmā′sə), the fourth of the four stomachs of a ruminant. See also **rumen, reticulum, omasum.**

ab·o·rig·i·nal (abərij′inəl), *adj.* **1.** pertaining to aborigines; primitive. —*n.* **2.** an aborigine.

ab·o·rig·i·ne (abərij′ənē), *n.* an original, primitive native of a region. [from Latin *ab origine* 'from the beginning']

a·bor·ti·cide (əbôr′tisīd), *n.* destruction of a fetus in the uterus.

a·bor·ti·fa·cient (əbôr′təfā′sHənt), *n.* **1.** a drug that causes abortion. —*adj.* **2.** tending to cause abortion.

a·bou·li·a (əboŏ′lēə), *n.* See **abulia.**

ab o·vo (äb ō′wō, ab ō′vō), *Latin.* from the beginning; literally, from the egg.

ab·re·act (ab′rēakt′), *v.* to remove a psychological complex by abreaction.

ab·re·ac·tion (ab′rēak′sHən), *n.* removal of a pyschological complex by expressing, by word or act, a repressed experience.

ab·ro·gate (ab′rəgāt), *v.* to repeal, abolish, or annul. —**ab·ro·ga′tion,** *n.*

ab·scess (ab′ses), *n.* a collection of

pus in the tissues of the body, usually caused by an infection.

ab·scond (abskond′), *v.* to run away suddenly and secretly, in order to avoid legal action.

ab·sinthe (ab′sin*th*), *n.* a bitter, aromatic liqueur prepared from wormwood and tasting of licorice.

absolute zero, the lowest temperature that could occur in nature; the temperature (−273°C) at which particles whose motion constitutes heat would be at rest.

ab·so·lu·tion (absəloŏ′sHən), *n.* release from consequences, obligations, or penalties, esp. from the penal consequence of sin.

ab·solve (abzolv′), *v.* to grant absolution to.

ab·sor·be·fa·cient (abzôr′bəfā′-sHənt), *n.* **1.** a substance that causes absorption. —*adj.* **2.** causing absorption.

ab·stain (abstān′), *v.* to refrain from indulging one's passions or appetites, as *to abstain from eating meat.*

ab·ste·mi·ous (abstē′mēəs), *adj.* moderate in eating and drinking.

ab·sten·tion (absten′sHən), *n.* the practice of being abstinent.

ab·sterge (absturj′), *v.* to cleanse by wiping or washing. —**ab·ster′gent,** *adj., n.*

ab·sti·nent (ab′stinənt), *adj.* refraining from indulging one's desire for something, esp. for alcoholic drinks. —**ab′sti·nence,** *n.*

abstract art, a form of 20th-century art that appeals to an emotional appreciation of color, shape, texture, material and their interrelations rather than to realistic or concrete representations.

ab·struse (abstroŏs′), *adj.* difficult to understand.

a·bu·li·a (əbyoŏ′lēə), *n.* a mental disorder characterized by loss of will power. Also spelled **aboulia.**

a·bys·mal (əbiz′məl), *adj.* like an abyss; unfathomable; profound; immeasurable. —**a·bys′mal·ly,** *adv.*

a·byss (əbis′), *n.* an immeasurably deep space. —**a·byss′al,** *adj.*

ac·a·dem·ic (akədem′ik), *adj.* **1.** pertaining to an advanced institution of learning. **2.** unrealistic; impractical; theoretical. **3.** conventional; conforming to set rules and traditions; not imaginative or innovative.

a cap·pel·la (ä käpel′lä), (of singing) without musical accompaniment. Also **alla cappella.**

ac·a·ri·a·sis (akarī′əsis), *n.* infestation by mites.

a·car·i·cide (əkar′isīd), *n.* a substance that kills mites.

ac·ci·den·tal (ak′siden′təl), *n.* a sign put before a musical note to show a change of pitch.

ac·claim (əklām′), *v.* **1.** to applaud. —*n.* **2.** acclamation.

ac·cla·ma·tion (akləmā′sHən), *n.* **1.** a shout, applause, or other demonstration of assent or approbation. **2.** spontaneous approval or adoption of a measure by oral vote, applause, etc., in place of a formal ballot.

ac·cli·mate (əklī′mit, ak′ləmāt), *v.* to acclimatize.

ac·cli·ma·tize (əklī′mətīz′), *v.* to accustom or adapt to a new climate or environment.

ac·cliv·i·ty (əkliv′itē), *n.* an upward slope (from the observer's point of view). See also **declivity.**

ac·co·lade (akəlād′), *n.* praise; commendation for quality.

ac·cord·ant (əkôr′dnt), *adj.* in conformity; agreeing.

ac·cost (əkôst′), *v.* **1.** to approach with a greeting. **2.** to approach brazenly. **3.** (of prostitutes) to solicit for sexual purposes.

ac·cou·ter, ac·cou·tre (əkōō′tər), *v.* to equip or furnish.

ac·cou·ter·ments, ac·cou·tre·ments (əkōō′tərmənts), *n. pl.* (rarely used in sing.) nonessential features that superficially characterize and identify something.

ac·cred·it (əkred′it), *v.* to approve the credentials of (a school, individual, etc.) —**ac·cred·i·ta′tion,** *n.*

ac·cre·tion (əkrē′sHən), *n.* an increase by natural growth, esp. by addition of external parts.

ac·cru·al (əkrōō′əl), *n.* accretion; act or process of accruing.

ac·crue (əkrōō′), *v.* to happen or result as a natural growth.

ac·cul·tu·ra·tion (əkul′cHərā′sHən), *n.* the adoption of the culture of another social group. —**ac·cul′tu·rate,** *v.*

a·cer·bic (əsur′bik), *adj.* sharp; harsh. Also, **a·cerb′.** —**a·cer′bi·ty,** *n.*

ach·ro·mat·ic (akrəmat′ik), *adj.* (of a camera or telescope lens) corrected for chromatic aberration.

a·cid·u·lous (əsid′jələs), *adj.* having a sour, harsh, caustic disposition or expression. Also **a·cid′u·lent.**

ac·o·lyte (ak′əlīt), *n.* an attendant or assistant.

a·cou·asm (əkōō′azm), *n.* an imagined ringing in the head.

a·cous·tics (əkōō′stiks), *n.* the science of hearing or of sound. —**a·cous′tic,** *adj.*

ac·rid (ak′rid), *adj.* bitter, sharp, or irritating to taste or smell.

ac·ri·mo·ny (ak′rəmōnē), *n.* bitterness or sharpness of disposition or nature. —**ac·ri·mo′ni·ous,** *adj.*

ac·ro·ceph·a·ly (akrəsef′əlē), *n.* a malformation in which the head is somewhat pointed. Also **hypsicephaly.** —**ac·ro·ce·phal′ic,** *adj.*

ac·ro·lith (ak′rəlith), *n.* a sculptured figure having the head and extremities carved in stone and the rest usually of wood.

ac·ro·meg·a·ly (akrəmeg′əlē), *n.* abnormal enlargement of the head and the extremities due to dysfunction of the pituitary gland. —**ac·ro·me·gal′ic,** *adj.*

ac·ro·nym (ak′rənim), *n.* a pronounceable word made up from the initial letters or parts of words in a phrase, title, company name, or the like: *Nabisco* from *Na*(*tional*) *Bis*(*cuit*) *Co*(*mpany*); *radar* from *ra*(*dio*) *d*(*etecting*) *a*(*nd*) *r*(*anging*).

ac·ro·pho·bi·a (akrəfō′bēə), *n.* a dread of being in or looking down from high places.

ACTH, adrenocorticotropic hormone; a hormone, secreted by the pituitary gland, which stimulates the adrenal cortex to generate cortisone.

ac·ti·nism (ak'tinizm), *n.* the property of radiation to produce chemical changes.

ac·tion·a·ble (ak'sHənəbəl), *adj.* furnishing sufficient ground for legal action.

ac·tiv·ist (ak'təvist), *n.* one who takes an energetic, active part in political or social causes.

ac·tu·ar·y (ak'cHōōe'rē), *n.* an expert on life expectancy and the statistics of insurance. —**ac·tu·ar'i·al,** *adj.*

ac·u·men (ak'yəmən), *n.* keen perception; penetrating insight.

a·cu·mi·nate (əkyōō'mənit), *adj.* tapering to a point.

ac·u·punc·ture (ak'yəpuNGk'cHər), *n.* a practice, developed in China, in which delicate needles are inserted into the tissues to cure illness.

ad·age (ad'ij), *n.* a saying, proverb, or maxim.

ad·a·mant (ad'əmənt), *adj.* obstinately firm despite appeal; unyielding.

ad·den·dum (əden'dəm), *n., pl.* **ad·den·da** (əden'də). something to be added; appendix.

ad·duce (ədōōs', ədyōōs'), *v.* to present as evidence.

ad·duc·tor (əduk'tər), *n.* a muscle that controls movement of parts toward one another or to a common center. See also **abductor.**

a·de·no·vi·rus (ədē'nōvī'rəs), *n.* a cold-like virus which irritates the upper respiratory tract and the lymph nodes.

a·deph·a·gous (ədef'əgəs), *adj.* gluttonous; having a voracious appetite.

a·dept (ədept'), *adj.* **1.** skilled; proficient. —*n.* **2.** one who is skilled or proficient.

a·di·aph·o·re·sis (ā'dēafərē'sis), *n.* lack of perspiration.

a·di·aph·o·ret·ic (ā'dēafəret'ik), *n.* **1.** a drug that prevents perspiration; antiperspirant. —*adj.* **2.** preventing perspiration.

ad in·fi·ni·tum (ad'infinī'təm), *Latin.* to infinity; limitlessly.

ad in·ter·im (ad' in'tərim), *Latin.* for the time being.

ad·i·po·pex·i·a (ad'əpōpek'sēə), *n.* lipopexia. Also **ad·i·po·pex·is** (ad'-əpōpek'sis).

ad·i·pose (ad'ipōs), *adj.* fatty; consisting of or resembling fat. —**ad·i·pos'i·ty,** *n.*

ad·join (əjoin'), *v.* to be next to or in contact with.

ad·journ (əjurn'), *v.* to put off or postpone. —**ad·journ'ment,** *n.*

ad·ju·di·cate (əjōō'dəkāt), *v.* to pronounce judgment upon. —**ad·ju·di·ca'tion,** *n.*

ad·junct (ad'juNGt), *n.* something added to another but not necessarily a part of it.

ad·jure (əjōōr'), *v.* to command, entreat, or order, usually with appeal to God, or the invocation of a curse; beseech. See also **abjure.** —**ad·ju·ra'tion,** *n.*

ad·ju·vant (aj'əvənt), *adj.* **1.** contributory; auxiliary, as *an adjuvant drug.* —*n.* **2.** something that helps or assists.

ad lib (ad' lib'), to the extent of one's wishes; freely.

ad·re·nal (ədrē'nl), *adj.* located near the kidneys.

ad·sci·ti·tious (ad'sitisH'əs), *adj.* supplemental; additional; unessential.

ad·um·brate (adum'brāt), *v.* to foreshadow; give a faint shadow of; outline. —**ad·um·bra'tion,** *n.*

ad va·lo·rem (ad'vəlōr'əm, vəlôr'-əm), *Latin.* according to the value (applied to import duties based on the declared value of merchandise).

ad·ven·ti·tious (advəntisH'əs), *adj.* accidentally or casually acquired; added from another source.

ad·verse (advurs', ad'vurs), *adj.* antagonistic; hostile; unfavorable; unfortunate. See also **averse.**

ad·ver·si·ty (advur'sitē), *n.* an unfortunate, calamitous, or distressful state or occurrence.

ad·vo·cate (ad'vəkit), *n.* one who defends a cause; one who defends another in a court; an intercessor.

ae·gis (ē′jis), *n.* protection; sponsorship.

ae·on (ē′on), *n.* See **eon.**

aer·o·bic (erō′bik), *adj.* living in air (applied to an organism).

aer·o·stat (er′əstat′), *n.* a lighter-than-air craft; balloon or dirigible.

aes·the·sia (esthē′zнə), *n.* See **esthesia.**

aes·the·sis (esthē′sis), *n.* See **esthesis.**

aes·thete, es·thete (esthēt′), *n.* a lover of beautiful things, esp. to the scornful exclusion of practicalities.

aes·thet·ic, es·thet·ic (esthet′ik), *adj.* concerning or having sensitivity toward beauty or toward what is beautiful.

aes·ti·val (es′təvəl), *adj.* See **estival.**

aes·ti·vate (es′təvāt), *v.* See **estivate.**

aet., Abbrev. for **anno aetatis suae.**

ae·the·re·al (ithēr′ēəl), *adj.* See **ethereal.**

ae·ti·ol·ogy (ētēol′əjē), *n.* See **etiology.**

af·fa·ble (af′əbəl), *adj.* having a kind, benevolent manner; hence, easy and pleasant to talk to or deal with. —**af·fa·bil′i·ty,** *n.* —**af′fa·bly,** *adv.*

af·fec·ta·tion (afəktā′sнən), *n.* a striving to produce an effect, esp. with an artificiality of manner or behavior. —**af·fect′ed,** *adj.*

af·fer·ent (af′ərənt), *adj.* (in physiology) carrying to or toward or inward, as a nerve carrying an impulse to a center. See also **efferent.**

af·fil·i·ate (əfil′ēit), *n.* a company or corporation owned partly or wholly by another.

af·fin·i·ty (əfin′itē), *n.* an attraction for a person or thing; sense of relationship.

af·flu·ent (af′lōōənt), *adj.* **1.** wealthy. —*n.* **2.** a tributary stream. —**af′flu·ence,** *n.*

af·for·est (əfor′ist), *v.* to convert bare or cultivated land into a forest. —**af·for·es·ta′tion,** *n.*

Af·ri·kaans (afrikäns′), *n.* a language, resembling Dutch, spoken in South Africa.

Af·ri·kan·der (afrikän′dər), *n.* a native of South Africa born of white European parents.

Af·ro (af′rō), *n., pl.* **Af·ros.** a large bushy hairdo, sometimes worn by blacks and other people with kinky hair.

af·ter·burn·er (af′tərburnər), *n.* a device in the exhaust system of a jet or internal combustion engine to increase its power.

af·ter·care (af′tərker), *n.* the treatment of a patient during convalescence.

af·ter·ef·fect (af′tərəfekt), *n.* an effect produced or felt after the removal of a stimulus.

af·ter·im·age (af′tərim′ij), *n.* an image seen after the removal of a stimulus; for example, staring at a red light produces a green afterimage.

a·ga·ve (əgā′vē), *n.* a genus of American plants grown for economic or ornamental purposes.

a·gen·da (əjen′də), *n. pl., sing.* **a·gen·dum** (əjen′dəm). things to be done, usually listed in a formal manner for a meeting.

a·gent pro·voc·a·teur (äzнän′ prōvokätur′), *pl.* **a·gents pro·voc·a·teurs.** a police or political spy who provokes suspicious people to perform an illegal action that will get them arrested.

ag·glom·er·ate (əglom′ərit), *n.* **1.** (in geology) rock composed of angular volcanic fragments. **2.** any collection or accumulation of miscellaneous materials. —**ag·glom·e·ra′tion,** *n.*

ag·glu·ti·nate (əglōō′tnāt), *v.* (in linguistics) to form and express grammatical relationships by the continued addition of strings of meaningful elements, as in Turkish. —**ag·glu·ti·na′tion,** *n.* —**ag·glu′ti·na·tive,** *adj.*

ag·gran·dize (əgran′dīz), *v.* to enlarge, broaden, or increase in wealth, power, rank, or honor. —**ag·gran′dize·ment,** *n.*

ag·i·o (aj′ēō), *n., pl.* **ag·i·os.** a fee charged by money brokers for exchanging coin for paper currency or one currency for another.

ag·it·prop (aj′itprop′), *n.* agitation

and propaganda. [from Russian *Agit-propbyuro, agit(atsiya) prop(aganda) byuro*]

ag·nate (ag′nāt), *adj.* a kinsman whose relationship is traceable only through males; any male relation on the father's side. See also **cognate.** —**ag·na′tion,** *n.*

ag·nos·tic (agnos′tik), *n.* one who denies knowledge of God. —**ag·nos′ti·cism,** *n.*

ag·o·ra·pho·bi·a (ag′ərəfō′bēə), *n.* a dread of being in open spaces.

a·grar·i·an (əgrer′ēən), *adj.* concerning land, esp. public or agricultural land.

ag·ri·ol·ogy (agrēol′əjē), *n.* the comparative study of the customs of uncivilized man.

ag·ro·bi·ol·ogy (ag′rōbiol′əjē), *n.* the study of the biology of crops in relation to soil. —**ag·ro·bi·o·log′i·cal,** *adj.*

a·grol·o·gy (əgrol′əjē), *n.* soil science. —**ag·ro·log′i·cal,** *adj.*

a·gron·o·my (əgron′əmē), *n.* the study of soil science in relation to crop management. —**ag·ro·nom′ic,** *adj.*

a·gryp·ni·a (əgrip′nēə), *n.* sleeplessness; insomnia.

ai·lu·ro·phile (īlo͞or′əfīl), *n.* one who is fond of cats; a cat fancier.

ai·lu·ro·phil·i·a (īlo͞or′əfil′ēə), *n.* love of cats.

ai·lu·ro·phobe (īlo͞or′əfōb′), *n.* one who fears cats.

ai·lu·ro·pho·bi·a (īlo͞or′əfō′bēə), *n.* dread of cats.

air·brush (er′brusн), *n.* an atomizer used to spray paint.

air·foil (er′foil), *n.* any surface on an aircraft for controlling or aiding its motion.

air·speed (er′spēd), *n.* the speed of an aircraft with respect to the air through which it is flying. See also **groundspeed.**

ait (āt), *n.* a small island in a river or lake.

à jour (ä zнo͞or′), (of decorative objects) pierced to let through light, as a screen.

a·kim·bo (əkim′bō), *adj., adv.* (of the arms) bent outward at the elbow when the hands are on the hips, as *she stood, arms akimbo, and demanded to know why I'd come.*

a·la (ā′lə), *n., pl.* **a·lae** (ā′lē), (in zoology and botany) a wing or wing-like part.

a·lac·ri·ty (əlak′ritē), *n.* liveliness; readiness; cheerful willingness.

al·a·nine (al′ənēn), *n.* an amino acid discovered to be present in a 1970 meteorite.

a·lar·ums (əlar′əmz) **and excursions,** a stage direction used in early modern English theater (15th and 16th century) to call for the sound effects of a battle, with trumpets, clash of arms, etc.

a·late (ā′lāt), *adj.* (in botany and zoology) having alae.

a lat·ti·ci·nio (ä lät′tēchē′nyô), *Latin.* (of ornamental glass) having the transparent body decorated with embedded lines or bands of opaque, milky-white glass.

Al·bi·on (al′bēən), *n.* an old, poetic name for Britain.

al·cal·de (alkal′dē), *n.* (in Spain and S.W. U.S.) a mayor with authority as a justice of the peace.

al·che·my (al′kəmē), *n.* medieval chemistry concerned chiefly with transmuting baser metals into gold. —**al·chem′i·cal,** *adj.*

a·le·a·to·ry (ā′lēətôrē), *adj.* depending on a contingent event; uncertain; dependent on luck.

a·lex·i·a (əlek′sēə), *n.* inability to read because of aphasia.

al·fres·co (alfres′kō), *adv., adj.* out of doors; in the open air.

al·go·rithm (al′gəriтнm), *n.* a method for computing or for solving a particular problem.

al·ien·ate (āl′yənāt), *v.* to estrange; ward off; keep at a distance, esp. someone who was formerly a friend or close associate.

al·ien·a·tion (ālyənā′sнən), *n.* derangement; insanity, esp. legal insanity.

al·ien·ist (āl′yənist), *n.* an expert in the study of mental disease.

al·i·ment (al′əmənt), *n.* nourishment; food. —**al·i·men′ta·ry**, *adj.*

alimentary canal, the system of organs in the body through which food passes.

al·i·quant (al′əkwənt), *adj.* (of a number) not dividing evenly into a larger number as 6 *is an aliquant part of* 16. See also **aliquot.**

al·i·quot (al′əkwət), *adj.* (of a number) dividing evenly into a larger number as 6 *is an aliquot part of* 18. See also **aliquant.**

al·ka·hest (al′kəhest), *n.* the universal solvent sought by alchemists.

al·ka·li (al′kəlī), *n.* a chemical that neutralizes acids. —**al′ka·line,** *adj.*

al·ka·lize (al′kəlīz), *v.* to change (an acid) into an alkali.

al·la cap·pel·la (äl′lä käpel′lä). See **a cappella.**

al·lege (əlej′), *v.* to assert, declare, or affirm. —**al·le·ga′tion,** *n.*

al·leged (əlejd′), *adj.* **1.** stated to be as maintained (used in journalism to avoid possible libel action for declaring a person a criminal, as *the alleged killer.* **2.** supposed; questionable, as *an alleged cure for cancer.*

al·le·go·ry (al′əgôrē), *n.* a story, drama, or other treatment in which the subject is not mentioned but is represented symbolically. —**al·le·gor′i·cal,** *adj.* —**al·le·gor′i·cal·ly,** *adv.*

al·lele (əlēl′), *n.* a form of gene causing hereditary variation. Also **al·lel·o·morph** (əlē′ləmôrf, əlel′əmôrf).

al·ler·gen (al′ərjən), *n.* something that produces an allergic reaction. —**al·ler·gen′ic,** *adj.*

al·ler·gy (al′ərjē), *n.* an abnormal reaction resulting from sensitivity toward a germ or substance. —**al·ler′gic,** *adj.*

al·li·a·ceous (al′ēā′sHəs), *adj.* smelling or tasting of garlic, onions, or the like.

al·lit·er·a·tion (əlit′ərā′sHən), *n.* the repetition of the same sound at the beginning of two or more words in a phrase, verse of poetry, etc., as *Tippecanoe and Tyler, too.* —**al·lit′er·a·tive,** *adj.*

al·loch·tho·nous (əlok′thənəs), *adj.* not native to the region where found. See also **autochthonous.**

al·lop·a·thy (əlop′əthē), *n.* the principle of treating disease by using agents that produce effects different from the symptoms of the disease treated. See also **homeopathy.** —**al·lop′a·thist, al′lo·path,** *n.*

al·lo·trope (al′ətrōp), *n.* one of the two or more forms in which an element exists, as *Diamond is an allotrope of carbon.* —**al·lo·trop′ic,** *adj.*

al·lot·ro·py (əlot′rəpē), *n.* a property of certain chemical elements to exist in more than one form, as *Carbon exhibits allotropy.*

al·lude (əlood′), *v.* to refer casually or indirectly. —**al·lu′sion,** *n.*

al·lu·vi·um (əloo′vēəm), *n., pl.* **al·lu·vi·ums, al·lu·vi·a** (əloo′vēə). sedimentary deposit of a river or flood.

Al·ni·co (alnē′kō), *n.* a trademark for an alloy used in making permanent magnets.

al·o·pe·cia (aləpē′sHə), *n.* baldness.

Al·pha Cen·tau·ri (al′fə sentô′rē), the first-magnitude star nearest the sun (4.3 light-years).

alpha particle (al′fə), a positively charged particle; the nucleus of the helium atom.

al·tru·ism (al′trooizm), *n.* benevolent and unselfish regard for others. —**al′tru·ist,** *n.* —**al·tru·is′tic,** *adj.*

a·mal·gam (əmal′gəm), *n.* a mixture, esp. a silver-mercury mixture used as a dental filling.

a·man·u·en·sis (əman′yooen′sis), *n., pl.* **a·man·u·en·ses** (əman′yooen′sēz). a secretary who can write rapidly enough to record dictation; one employed to copy what another has written.

am·a·ranth (am′əranth), *n.* an imaginary flower that never fades or withers. —**am·a·ran′thine,** *adj.*

am·ba·gious (ambā′jəs), *adj.* not straightforward; devious; circumlocutory; roundabout.

am·bi·ance, am·bi·ence (ämbyäns′, am′bēəns), *n.* atmosphere; environment, as *an ambience of mystery.*

am·bi·ent (am'bēənt), *adj.* surrounding; encompassing, as *the ambient air was redolent with perfume.*

a·mel·io·rate (əmēl'yərāt), *v.* to improve or make better. —**a·mel·io·ra'tion,** *n.* —**a·mel'io·ra·tive,** *adj.*

a·mend (əmend'), *v.* to change for the better; improve. See also **emend.**

American plan, a system of paying for both hotel rooms and meals at one fixed rate.

a·merce (əmurs'), *v.* to punish by an arbitrary fine not provided for by statute; mulct. —**a·merce'ment,** *n.*

a·mi·cus cu·ri·ae (əmē'kəs kyŏor'ıē) (in law) a disinterested person who volunteers or is invited to advise the court in a proceeding. [*Latin,* a friend of the court']

a·mi·no acid (əmē'nō, am'ənō), a class of organic chemical compounds from some of which proteins are constructed.

am·nes·ty (am'nistē), *n.* **1.** a general or conditional pardon for a crime or for a class of offenses. —*v.* **2.** to grant amnesty to; pardon.

am·ni·ot·ic fluid (amnēot'ik), the fluid in which an unborn fetus floats.

a·moe·ba, a·me·ba (əmē'bə), *n., pl.* **a·moe·bae** (əmē'bē), **a·moe·bas.** a one-celled, microscopic animal. —**a·moe'bic, a·me'bic,** *adj.*

a·mok (əmuk'), *adv. used chiefly in the expression* **run amok**: to run about wildly, attacking everyone indiscriminately.

a·mor·al (āmôr'əl, amôr'əl), *adj.* having no moral sense; unable to distinguish between moral and immoral quality or behavior.

a·mor·phous (əmôr'fəs), *adj.* having no distinct shape or structure.

a·mour-propre (ämŏor'prôpr'), *n.* self-respect.

am·pere (am'pēr), *n.* a measure of amount of electric current: one volt acting through a resistance of one ohm. See also **ohm, volt.** —**am·per·age** (am'pərij), *n.*

am·per·sand (am'pərsand), *n.* the name for the symbol '&'.

am·phet·a·mine (amfet'əmēn), *n.* a drug which stimulates the central nervous system, used in treatment of depressive states.

am·phi·bol·o·gy (amfəbol'əjē), *n.* the use of ambiguous or quibbling phrases or statements. Also, **am·phib'o·ly.**

am·phig·e·an (amfij'ēən), *adj.* extending around the earth in approximately the same latitudes, as certain botanical species.

am·phi·gor·y (am'fəgôrē), *n.* a meaningless hodge-podge; a nonsensical parody. —**am·phi·gor'ic,** *adj.*

am·pho·ra (am'fərə), *n., pl.* **am·phoras, am·pho·rae** (am'fərē). a tall, two-handled vessel, usually made of clay and having a pointed base for insertion into a stand or the ground, used by the Greeks and Romans for storage of grain, honey, wine, etc.

am·yl·ase (am'əlās), *n.* an enzyme capable of splitting up starches.

a·nab·a·sis (ənab'əsis), *n., pl.* **a·nab·a·sis.** a military expedition. See also **katabasis.**

an·a·bat·ic (anəbat'ik), *adj.* (of a wind) rising upward because of local heating. See also **katabatic.**

an·a·bi·o·sis (an'əbīō'sis), *n.* reanimation; recovery to consciousness after seeming death. —**an·a·bi·ot'ic,** *adj.*

a·nab·o·lism (ənab'əlizm), *n.* constructive metabolism, a process in which a substance is transformed into another which is more complex or more highly organized and energetic. See also **catabolism.** —**an·a·bol'ic,** *adj.*

a·nach·ro·nism (ənak'rənizm), *n.* a person or event misplaced in time, as if a Shakespearian character were to quote Lincoln. See also **parachronism, prochronism.** —**a·nach·ro·nis'tic,** *adj.*

A·nac·re·on·tic (ənak'rēon'tik), *adj.* pertaining to the praise of love and wine.

a·nad·ro·mous (ənad'rəməs), *adj.* denoting fish, like the salmon, that swim from the sea up a fresh-water river to spawn. See also **catadromous.**

an·aer·obe (aner′ōb), *n.* an organism able to live without air or oxygen or unable to live in their presence. —**an·aer·ob·ic** (an′erob′ik), *adj.*

an·a·glyph (an′əglif), *n.* **1.** a picture printed in two, slightly overlapping colors so that, when viewed through lenses with corresponding colors, it appears to be three-dimensional. **2.** any form of carving in low relief.

an·a·gram (an′əgram), *n.* the re-arrangement of the letters of a word or sentence to form a new word, as *ward* from *draw* or *stare down* from *don't swear.*

an·a·lects (an′əlekts), *n., pl.* (rarely used in sing.) selected passages or extracts from the writings of one or more authors.

an·a·lep·tic (anəlep′tik), *adj.* restorative; invigorating; giving strength during convalescence.

an·al·ge·sic (anəljē′zik), *n.* **1.** any drug that relieves pain. —*adj.* **2.** serving to remove pain. —**an·al·ge·si·a** (anəljē′zēə), *n.*

an·a·log, an·a·logue (an′əlôg), *n.* something bearing a resemblance or proportion to another thing or things: an electric wire as an analog of a nerve. —**a·nal·o·gy** (ənal′əjē), *n.* —**a·nal·o·gous** (ənal′əgəs), *adj.*

analog computer, a computer that uses properties of known physical processes (like the voltage, amperage, resistance of electric current) to solve mathematical problems. See also **digital computer, hybrid computer.**

a·nal·o·gy (ənal′əjē), *n.* a likeness between two things in certain respects; something partially similar to another.

an·am·ne·sis (anəmnē′sis), *n., pl.* **an·am·ne·ses** (anəmnē′sēz). reminiscence of the past; esp. of a previous existence of the soul. —**an·am·nes·tic** (anəmnes′tik), *adj.*

an·a·mor·phic (anəmôr′fik), *adj.* having or making unequal magnifications along two perpendicular axes.

an·a·mor·phism (anəmôr′fizm), *n.* a change under the earth's surface which changes simple minerals into complex ones. See also **katamorphism.**

an·a·mor·pho·sis (anəmôr′fəsis), *n.* an image distorted so as to appear natural when reflected in a curved mirror or viewed from a certain angle.

an·ar·chy (an′ərkē), *n.* absence of government or law in a society; political and social disorder. —**an·ar′chic,** *adj.*

an·ash·er (an′əsHər), *n.* a blend of fine marijuana from India.

an·as·tig·mat (ənas′tigmat, an′əstig′mat), *n.* a lens that corrects astigmatism. —**an·as·tig·mat′ic,** *adj.*

a·nath·e·ma (ənath′əmə), *n.* a person or thing hated, loathed, or detested.

an·chor·ite (aNG′kərit), *n.* a hermit; recluse.

an·cil·lar·y (an′səlerē), *adj.* auxiliary; subordinate; extra.

an·dro·cen·tric (an′drōsen′trik), *adj.* dominated by males, as *an androcentric culture.*

an·droc·ra·cy (androk′rəsē), *n.* rule by males. —**an·dro·crat·ic** (an′drōkrat′ik), *adj.*

an·drog·y·nous (androj′ənəs), *adj.* exhibiting both male and female sexual characteristics.

an·dro·sphinx (an′drəsfiNGks), *n.* a sphinx with the head of a man.

an·e·cho·ic (an′ekō′ik), *adj.* (of a recording studio, etc.) having echoes reduced to a minimum.

an·e·mom·e·ter (anəmom′ətər), *n.* an instrument for measuring the speed of wind.

an·er·oid (an′əroid), *adj.* noting a kind of barometer consisting of a box containing a partial vacuum and having a flexible diaphragm on one side to which a pointer is attached. The pointer, when calibrated, indicates the atmospheric pressure.

an·eu·rysm (an′yərizm), *n.* dilatation of an artery caused by a weakening of its wall through disease.

an·frac·tu·ous (anfrak′cHŌŌəs), *adj.* having turnings and windings. —**an·frac·tu·os′i·ty,** *n.*

an·gi·na pec·to·ris (anjī′nə pek′

təris), a condition characterized by intense pain below the sternum caused by lack of blood supply to the heart.

angst (äNGst), *n.* dread; anxiety; anguish.

ang·strom unit (aNG'strəm), a unit of length used to express electromagnetic wave lengths, equal to one tenth of a millimicron.

an·i·mad·ver·sion (an'əmadvur'-ZHən), *n.* criticism; censure; adverse comment.

an·i·mal·cule (anəmal'kyo͞ol), *n.* a microscopic animal.

an·i·mism (an'əmizm), *n.* the belief that inanimate objects, like natural phenomena, possess souls or consciousness.

an·i·mos·i·ty (anəmos'ətē), *n.* active ill-will or enmity.

an·i·mus (an'əməs), *n.* **1.** animosity; hostility; antagonism. **2.** an animating spirit.

ankh (aNGk), *n.* a cross with a loop on top: an ancient Egyptian symbol of life.

an·ky·lo·sis (aNGkəlō'sis), *n.* the consolidation of articulating joints, forming a stiff joint.

an·nals (an'əlz), *n.* (*used as pl.*) **1.** a yearly record of events. **2.** historical records.

an·neal (ənēl'), *v.* to toughen (as glass or metal) by heating and gradually cooling.

an·no ae·ta·tis su·ae (än'nō ītä'tis so͞o'ī), *Latin.* in the year of his age; aged. *Abbrev.*: **aet.**

an·nul (ənul'), *v.* to abolish; invalidate; cancel. —**an·nul'ment,** *n.*

an·nu·lar (an'yələr), *adj.* having a ring-like form.

an·ode (an'ōd), *n.* **1.** a positive electrode, emitting positive ions in a cell, etc. **2.** the positive pole of a battery. **3.** a positive plate in an electron tube.

an·o·dize (an'ədīz), *v.* to coat a metal with a protective film.

a·nom·a·ly (ənom'əlē), *n.* **1.** variation from the common form. **2.** an irregularity or incongruity. **3.** (in astronomy) the angular distance of a planet

from its perihelion. —**a·nom'a·lous,** *adj.*

an·o·mie (an'əmē), *n.* the condition of an uprooted race, of individuals, or of their society, characterized by a breakdown of accepted values.

an·o·rex·i·a (anərek'sēə), *n.* an abnormal, often psychological inability to eat.

an·ox·em·i·a (an'oksē'mēə), *n.* lack of oxygen in the blood.

an·ox·i·a (ənok'sēə), *n.* lack of sufficient oxygen in the blood.

An·schluss (än'sHlo͞os), *n.* annexation, as the forced union of Austria and Germany in 1938.

Ant·a·buse (an'təbyo͞os), *n.* a trade name for the drug disulfiram, used in the treatment of alcoholism by creating unpleasant reactions when combined with liquor.

An·tar·es (anter'ēz), *n.* a red supergiant star of the first magnitude in the constellation of Scorpius.

an·te·bel·lum (an'tēbel'əm), *adj.* before the war, especially the American War between the States.

an·te·di·lu·vi·an (an'tēdilo͞o'vēan), *adj.* before the (Biblical) flood; hence, ancient, antiquated.

an·te par·tum, pertaining to the period before childbirth. See also **post partum.**

an·te·pe·nult (an'tēpē'nult), *n.* **1.** the third from the last syllable of a word, as *te* in *antepenult.* **2.** the third from the last in any series. —**an·te·pe·nul'ti·mate,** *adj.*

an·te·ri·or (antē'rēər), *adj.* situated in or near the front. See also **posterior.**

an·thro·po·cen·tric (an'thrəpōsen'trik), *adj.* assuming man to be the focal point of the universe. —**an·thro·po·cen'trism,** *n.*

an·thro·po·mor·phic (an'thrəpōmôr'fik), *adj.* ascribing human form and attitudes as to a god. —**an·thro·po·mor'phism,** *n.*

an·thro·poph·a·gi (anthrəpof'əjī), *n. pl.* cannibals.

an·thro·pos·co·py (anthrəpos'kəpē), *n.* See **physiognomy.**

an·thro·pos·o·phy (an'thrəpos'əfē), *n.* a philosophy emphasizing study of the nature of man, based on the teachings of Rudolf Steiner. —**an·thro·po·soph'i·cal, an·thro·po·soph'ic,** *adj.*

an·ti·bi·ot·ic (an'tēbīot'ik), *n.* a substance, as penicillin, produced by mold or fungi, that inhibits the growth of bacteria or other microorganisms.

an·ti·bo·dy (an'tibodē), *n.* a protein in blood plasma, that reacts to overcome bacterial toxins and viruses.

an·ti·cryp·tic (an'tēkrip'tik), *adj.* concealing an animal from its prey. See also **procryptic.**

an·ti·cy·clone (an'tēsī'klōn), *n.* the circulation of winds round an area of high barometric pressure; clockwise in the Northern Hemisphere; counterclockwise in the Southern Hemisphere. See also **cyclone.** —**an·ti·cy·clon'ic,** *adj.*

an·ti·fer·ro·mag·net·ic (an'tēfer'ōmagnet'ik), *adj.* pertaining to a substance the magnetic moments of whose adjacent atoms point in opposite directions at low temperatures. See also **diamagnetic, ferromagnetic, paramagnetic.**

an·ti·he·ro (an'tēhērō), *n.* in literature, etc., a created central figure who lacks all heroic attributes and noble qualities.

an·ti·his·ta·mine (an'tēhis'təmēn), *n.* any of certain medicines used in the treatment of allergies. See also **histamine.**

an·ti·knock (an'tēnok), *adj.* pertaining to substances added to internal combustion engine fuel to minimize knock.

an·ti·mat·ter (an'tēmatər), *n.* matter composed of antiparticles.

an·ti·par·ti·cle (an'tēpärtikəl), *n.* an elementary particle that annihilates a corresponding particle of the same mass upon collision.

an·tip·a·thy (antip'əthē), *n.* a settled aversion; a basic repugnance. —**an·ti·pa·thet'ic,** *adj.*

an·tip·o·des (antip'ədēz), *n. pl.* places diametrically opposite on the globe.

—**an·tip·o·de·an** (antip'ədēən), *adj., n.*

an·tith·e·sis (antith'əsis), *n., pl.* **an·tith·e·ses** (antith'əsēz). complete contrast or opposite. —**an·ti·thet·ic** (antəthet'ik), **an·ti·thet'i·cal,** *adj.*

an·ti·trust (an'tētrust'), *adj.* opposing the formation of commercial trusts that would tend to create monopolies.

an·ti·ven·in (an'tēven'in), *n.* an antitoxin formed in blood following repeated injections of venom; hence, an antitoxic serum obtained from this blood.

an·to·no·ma·sia (an'tənəmā'ZHə), *n.* the use of a title or epithet, instead of a name, to identify a person. —**an·to·no·mas·tic** (an'tənəmas'tik), *adj.*

a·part·heid (əpärt'hīt), *n.* the policy of racial segregation in the Republic of South Africa.

ap·a·tet·ic (ap'ətet'ik), *adj.* (of animals) assuming colors that afford camouflage.

ap·a·thet·ic (apəthet'ik), *adj.* having or showing mental or emotional indifference.

ap·a·thy (ap'əthē), *n.* an absence or lack of emotion, interest, or concern.

a·per·i·ent (əpēr'ēənt), *adj.* **1.** laxative. —*n.* **2.** a laxative food or medicine.

a·pha·sia (əfā'ZHə), *n.* impairment or loss of speech or the power to understand written or spoken language.

a·pha·si·ac (əfā'zēak), *n.* **1.** Also, **a·pha·sic** (əfā'zik). a person suffering from aphasia. —*adj.* **2.** losing the power of speech, or the ability to understand written or spoken language.

a·phe·li·on (əfēl'yən, afēl'yən), *n., pl.* **a·phe·li·a** (əfēl'yə, afēl'yə). the point of a planet's or comet's orbit farthest from the sun. See also **perihelion.**

aph·o·rism (af'ərizm), *n.* a short, pithy maxim embodying a general truth. —**aph·o·ris'tic,** *adj.*

aph·ro·dis·i·ac (af'rōdiz'ēak), *n.* an agent, as a drug, arousing sexual excitement.

a·pi·ar·y (ā′pēere), *n.* a place for keeping bees. —**a′pi·a·rist,** *n.*

ap·i·cal (ap′əkəl), *adj.* pertaining to the tip or apex.

ap·i·cul·ture (ap′əkulcHər), *n.* beekeeping.

a·poc·a·lyp·tic (əpok′əlip′tik), *adj.* prophesying total destruction or great disasters.

apo·o·ca·tas·ta·sis (ap′ōkətas′təsis), *n.* restitution or reestablishment. —**ap·o·cat·a·stat·ic** (ap′ōkatəstat′ik), *adj.*

a·poc·o·pe (əpok′əpē), *n.* omission of the last letter or syllable of a word.

a·poc·ry·phal (əpok′rəfəl), *adj.* of doubtful authenticity; false.

ap·o·dic·tic (apədik′tik), *adj.* incontrovertible; incontestable.

a·pod·o·sis (əpod′əsis), *n., pl.* **a·pod·o·ses** (əpod′əsēz). the consequence clause in a conditional sentence, beginning with '*then*'. See also **protasis.**

ap·o·gee (ap′əjē), *n.* **1.** the point where the moon or an earth satellite is furthest from the earth. See also **perigee. 2.** the climax, as of a career.

ap·o·logue (ap′əlog), *n.* a moral fable.

ap·o·mix·is (apəmik′sis), *n.* any of several kinds of asexual reproduction. —**ap·o·mic·tic** (ap′əmik′tik), *adj.*

ap·o·pemp·tic (apəpemp′tik), *adj.* pertaining to dismissal or departing.

a·poph·y·ge (əpof′əjē), *n.* (in architecture) a curve joining the base to the shaft of a column. Also, **hypophyge.**

a·pos·ta·sy (əpos′təsē), *n.* a rejection of one's religion, allegiance, party, principles, etc.

a·pos·tate (əpos′tāt), *n.* **1.** one who rejects his faith, allegiance, party, principles, etc. —*adj.* **2.** characterized by apostasy.

a pos·te·ri·o·ri (ā′ postē′rēôr′ē), **1.** proceeding from effect to cause. **2.** based upon observation. See also **a priori.**

ap·os·tol·ic delegate (ap′əstol′ik), a papal representative in a country where no diplomatic relations with the Vatican exist. See also **nuncio.**

ap·o·thegm (ap′əthəm), *n.* a pithy saying; maxim. —**ap·o·theg·mat·ic** (ap′əthegmat′ik), *adj.*

a·poth·e·o·sis (əpoth′ēō′sis, ap′əthē′əsis), *n.* the raising of a person to be a god or an ideal.

ap·o·tro·pa·ic (ap′ətrəpā′ik), *adj.* having power to ward off evil.

ap·pel·lant (əpel′ənt), *n.* (in law) one who appeals, esp. to a higher court.

ap·pel·late (əpel′it), *adj.* (in law) pertaining to or reviewing appeals, as a court.

ap·per·ceive (apərsēv′), *v.* (in psychology) to be conscious of perceiving. —**ap·per·cep·tion** (ap′ərsep′sHən), *n.*

ap·pe·tence (ap′ətəns), *n.* intense natural desire; craving.

ap·pos·ite (əpoz′it), *adj.* pertinent; appropriate; suitable.

ap·pur·te·nance (əpur′tənəns), *n.* something subordinate to another thing; accessory; appendage.

a pri·o·ri (ā′ prēôr′ē), **1.** proceeding from cause to effect. **2.** not based on observation; nonanalytic. See also **a posteriori.**

ap·te·ri·um (aptēr′ēəm), *n., pl.* **ap·te·ri·a** (aptēr′ēə), the part of a bird's body having no feathers. See also **pteryla.**

aq·ui·cul·ture (ak′wəkulcHər), *n.* the cultivation of plants in a solution, not soil; hydroponics.

a·rach·noid (ərak′noid), *adj.* **1.** like a spider's web. **2.** like a spider or other member of the same class. **3.** the membrane forming the middle of three coverings of the spinal cord and brain. See also **dura mater, pia mater.**

ar·bi·trage (är′bəträzH), *n.* the buying and selling simultaneously of securities in different places to profit by the different prices. —**ar·bi·tra·geur** (är′bəträzHur′), *n.*

ar·bit·ra·ment (ärbit′rəmənt), *n.* arbitration; the deciding of a dispute by an agreed authority.

ar·bo·re·al (ärbôr′ēəl), *adj.* **1.** pertaining to trees. **2.** living in trees.

ar·cane (ärkān'), *adj*. obscure; secret; esoteric.

ar·che·type (är'kətīp), *n*. a prototype from which copies are made; original pattern or model. —**ar·che·ty'pal, ar·che·typ'i·cal,** *adj*.

ar·chi·tec·ton·ic (är'kətekton'ik), *adj*. pertaining to architecture esp. the principles of architecture.

ar·ci·fin·i·ous (är'səfin'ēəs), *adj*. having a border that forms a natural barrier, as from invasion.

ar·col·o·gy (ärkol'əjē), *n*. a combination of the fields of architecture and ecology. —**ar·col'o·gist,** *n*.

ar·cu·ate (är'kyōoit), *adj*. curved or bent like a bow.

are (er, är), *n*. a unit of area measurement equaling 100 square meters.

ar·e·ca nut (ar'əkə, ərē'kə), the nut of a palm growing in tropical Asia, esp. the betel palm.

ar·e·na·ceous (arənā'sHəs), *adj*. sandy. Also **ar'e·nose.**

a·rête (ərāt'), *n*. a sharp ridge of a mountain.

ar·got (är'gō, är'gət), *n*. a slang belonging to a group or class, esp. the private language of thieves.

ar·id (ar'id), *adj*. **1.** dry or parched. **2.** unimaginative; sterile; dull.

ar·ith·man·cy (ar'*ith*mansē), *n*. prophecy by numbers, esp. the number of letters in names.

arithmetic progression, a series of numbers obtained by adding a constant number to the preceding number. See also **geometric progression, harmonic progression.**

Ar·ma·ged·don (är'məged'n), *n*. scene of the final battle between good and evil, esp. the battle on the Day of Judgment.

ar·mip·o·tent (ärmip'ətənt), *adj*. strong in arms; possessing powerful weapons.

ar·mo·man·cy (är'məmansē), *n*. prophecy by the shoulders of animals.

ar·mor·ist (är'mərist), *n*. an expert in heraldry.

ar·rack (ar'ək), *n*. any of various spirituous liquors distilled from molasses, rice, etc.

ar·raign (ərān'), *v*. to accuse as before a court or tribunal. —**ar·raign' ment,** *n*.

ar·rant (ar'ənt), *adj*. absolute; complete, as *an arrant idiot.*

ar·rhyth·mi·a (əriTH'mēə), *n*. a disturbance in the rhythm of the heartbeat. —**ar·rhyth'mic,** *adj*.

ar·rière-pen·sée (äryer'päNsā'), *French*. a hidden motive.

ar·ri·viste (ar'ēvēst'), *n*. one who has acquired success or money by dubious methods.

ar·ro·gate (ar'əgāt), *v*. to seize without right.

ar·roy·o (əroi'ō), *n*. a small watercourse, dry except after rain.

ars gra·ti·a ar·tis (ärz grä'tēə är'tis), *Latin*. art for art's sake.

ars lon·ga, vi·ta brev·is (ärz loNG'gə vē'tə brev'is), *Latin*. art is long, life is short.

Art Dec·o (dek'ō). See **moderne.** Also, **Art Dec·o·ra·tif** (dek'ərätef'), **Art Dec·or** (dekôr').

ar·tel (ärtel'), *n*. (in the U.S.S.R.) a workers' cooperative.

ar·te·ri·o·scle·ro·sis (artēr'ēōsklerō'sis), *n*. a disease characterized by thickening of the artery walls. See also **atherosclerosis.** —**ar·te·ri·o· scle·rot'ic,** *adj*.

ar·ti·fact, ar·te·fact (är'təfakt), *n*. anything made by man.

ar·ti·fice (är'təfis), *n*. a trick or wile.

Art Nou·veau (nōovō'), a style of the late 19th and early 20th centuries, characterized by highly stylized patterns of vines and entwined flowers.

as·bes·to·sis (as'bestō'sis), *n*. a condition of the lung caused by inhaling asbestos dust.

as·cend·er (əsen'dər), *n*. (in lowercase letters) the part extending upward above the top of an "x" of the same size and typeface. See also **descender.**

as·cet·ic (əset'ik), *n*. **1.** one who practices severe self-denial, as for religious reasons. —*adj*. **2.** austere; self-denying. —**as·cet'i·cism,** *n*.

a·sep·sis (əsep'sis), *n*. absence of sepsis as in wounds. —**a·sep'tic,** *adj*.

Ashcan School, a group of artists of the early 20th century in America who painted scenes of city life in a sardonic style.

Ash·ke·na·zim (äsнkənä′zim), *n. pl.* Jews of central and eastern Europe or their descendants.

ash·lar (asн′lər), *n.* a square-cut building stone; such stones collectively.

as·i·nine (as′ənīn), *adj.* stupid; silly; idiotic.

a·skance (əskans′), *adv.* 1. with disapproval or mistrust. 2. obliquely; sidewise.

a·so·ma·tous (əsō′mətəs), *adj.* bodiless; incorporeal.

as·par·tic acid (əspär′tik), an amino acid, recently identified in a meteorite, used in the preparation of culture media.

as·per·i·ty (əsper′ətē), *n.* 1. sharpness of manner. 2. unevenness of surface.

as·perse (əspurs′), *v.* 1. to slander or attack with damaging charges. 2. to spatter. —**as·per′sion,** *n.*

as·sev·er·ate (əsev′ərāt), *v.* to affirm earnestly; aver. —**as·sev·er·a′tion,** *n.*

as·si·du·i·ty (asədoo′ətē), *n.* constant perseverance; industry.

as·sid·u·ous (əsid′yooəs), *adj.* persevering; constant; unremitting.

as·sig·na·tion (asəgnā′sнən), *n.* an arrangement to meet; esp. a secret lovers' meeting.

as·sim·i·la·ble (əsim′ələbəl), *adj.* that may be assimilated.

as·sim·i·late (əsim′əlāt), *v.* 1. to take in; absorb; understand fully. 2. to digest and convert (food) for absorption into the system. 3. to adapt or adjust; become like. See also **dissimilate.**—**as·sim·i·la′tion,** *n.*—**as·sim′i·la·tive,** *adj.*

as·suage (əswāj′), *v.* to relieve; ease; soothe.

as·ter·oid (as′təroid), *n.* any of the thousands of minor planets revolving round the sun between the orbits of Mars and Jupiter.

as·then·ic (asтhen′ik), *adj.* relating to or denoting a physical type characterized by a tall, narrow, lean build. See also **athletic, pyknic.**

as·tig·ma·tism (əstig′mətizm), *n.* a defect of vision resulting from irregular curvature of the cornea.

as·tra·pho·bi·a (astrəfō′bēə), *n.* an abnormally intense fear of thunder and lightning.

as·tro·gate (as′trəgāt), *v.* to navigate a spacecraft in space. —**as·tro·ga′tion,** *n.*

as·tro·man·cy (as′trəmansē), *n.* prophecy by means of the stars.

as·tro·naut (as′trənôt), *n.* one who has traveled beyond the earth's atmosphere. Also **cosmonaut.**

as·tro·nau·tics (astrənô′tiks), *n.* the science of space travel.

as·tro·phys·ics (astrəfiz′iks), *n.* the branch of astronomy dealing with the physical properties of celestial bodies. —**as·tro·phys′i·cist,** *n.*

at·a·rax·i·a (atərak′sēə), *n.* a calm and tranquil state free from anxiety. —**at·a·rac′tic, at·a·rax′ic,** *adj.*

at·a·vism (at′əvism), *n.* a reappearance of a characteristic belonging to a remote ancestor. —**at·a·vis′tic,** *adj.*

at·e·lier (atəlyā′), *n.* a craftsman's workshop or an artist's studio.

ath·er·o·scle·ro·sis (atн′ərōsklərō′sis), *n.* a form of arteriosclerosis characterized by fatty substances in the intima. See also **arteriosclerosis.** —**ath·er·o·scle·rot′ic,** *adj.*

ath·let·ic (athlet′ik), *adj.* relating to or denoting a physical type characterized by a sturdy, well-proportioned build. See also **asthenic, pyknic.**

at·las (at′ləs), *n., pl.* **at·lan·tes** (atlan′tēz). a male figure serving as a supporting column. See also **caryatid.**

at·ra·bil·i·ous (atrəbil′ēəs), *adj.* morose; gloomy; sad.

a·tri·um (ā′trēəm), *n.* either of the two heart chambers that receive blood from the veins.

at·ro·phy (at′rəfē), *n.* 1. a withering away of an organ in the body. —*v.* 2. to waste away, as from lack of use. —**a·troph·ic** (ətrof′ik), *adj.*

at·ta·ché (atasHā′), *n.* a diplomatic official employed in a technical capacity on the staff of an embassy, as *a military attaché.*

at·ten·u·ate (əten′yo͞oāt), *v.* **1.** to make slender or thin. **2.** to reduce in force or value. —*adj.* **3.** slender; tapering. —**at·ten·u·a′tion,** *n.*

at·ti·tu·di·nize (atəto͞o′dəniz), *v.* to pose; strike an attitude.

at·tra·hent (at′rəhənt), *adj.* drawing to; attracting.

at·trite (ətrit′), *v.* to wear away as by harassment or by friction. —**at·tri′tion,** *n.*

a·typ·i·cal (ātip′ikəl), *adj.* deviating from type; not typical; irregular.

au con·traire (ō kəntrer′) *French.* on the contrary.

au cou·rant (ō ko͞oräN′), *French.* up-to-date; aware of the latest trends, news, etc.

au·di·ent (ô′dēənt), *adj.* hearing; listening.

au·di·o·phile (ô′dēəfil), *n.* an enthusiast in listening to high-fidelity sound reproduction of recorded or broadcast music.

au·dio-vis·u·al (ô′dēōvizH′o͞oəl), *adj.* simultaneously involving hearing and sight.

au fait (ō fe′), *French.* versed, expert, or knowledgable in something.

au·gur (ô′gər), *n.* **1.** a soothsayer or prophet. —*v.* **2.** to foretell the future. —**au·gu·ry** (ô′gyərē), *n.*

au·gust (ôgust′), *adj.* majestic; noble; very eminent.

au na·tu·rel (ō natərel′), *French.* **1.** naked. **2.** cooked simply. **3.** uncooked.

au·re·ole (ôr′ēōl), *n.* **1.** a halo. **2.** the sun's corona during a total eclipse.

aus·cul·tate (ôs′kəltāt), *v.* to examine internal organs by listening to them through a stethoscope. —**aus·cul·ta′tion,** *n.*

aus·pi·cious (ôspisH′əs), *adj.* favorable; propitious; predicting success.

au·toch·tho·nous (ôtok′thənəs), *adj.* pertaining to the original inhabitants or plants of a region. See also **alloch·thonous.**

au·to·clave (ô′tōklāv), *n.* an apparatus for sterilization by steam at high pressure.

au·toc·ra·cy (ôtok′rəsē), *n.* **1.** government by one absolute ruler. **2.** a state so governed. —**au·to·crat·ic** (ô′tə-krat′ik), *adj.*

au·to·da·fé (ô′tōdäfā′), *n., pl.* **au·tos-da-fe.** the public burning of heretics condemned by the Spanish Inquisition. [literally, act of faith]

au·to·e·rot·ic (ô′tōərot′ik), *adj.* producing sexual excitement without another person. —**au·to·er·o·tism** (ô′tōer′ətizm), *n.*

au·to·mate (ô′təmāt), *v.* to introduce the use of automatic devices to processes formerly either performed or controlled by people. —**au·to·ma′tion,** *n.*

au·tom·a·ton (ôtom′əton), *n., pl.* **au·tom·a·ta. 1.** a mechanical figure or device which moves itself. **2.** a person who acts mechanically.

au·to·nom·ic nervous system (ôtə-nom′ik), the nervous system that controls the involuntary functions of the heart, blood vessels, etc.

au·ton·o·my (ôton′əmē), *n.* **1.** self-government; independence. **2.** a self-governing community. —**au·ton′o·mous,** *adj.*

au·to·nym (ô′tənim), *n.* one's real name; an author's own name.

au·to·troph (ô′tətrof), *n.* a microorganism using carbon dioxide as its source of carbon. See also **hetero·troph.** —**au′to·troph·ic,** *adj.*

au·tres temps, au·tres moeurs (ōtrə täN′ ōtrə murs′), *French.* other times, other customs.

aux·e·sis (ôgzē′sis, ôksē′sis), *n.* induction of cell division, esp. by the influence of a chemical agent. See also **merisis.**

aux·o·car·di·a (ôk′sōkär′dēə), *n.* enlargement of the heart.

a·vant-garde (ä′väNgärd′), *adj.* **1.** characterized by unorthodox and experimental treatment of visual, literary, or musical material. —*n.* **2.** the radical group in these fields.

av·a·tar (avətär′), *n.* **1.** an incarnation, in Hindu mythology, of a god. **2.** the manifestation or display of an attitude or principle.

a·ver (əvur'), *v.* **1.** to declare with confidence; to affirm strongly. **2.** (in law) to assert as a fact. —**a·ver'ral,** *n.*

a·verse (əvurs'), *adj.* having a feeling of repugnance; opposed; disinclined. See also **adverse.** —**a·ver·sion** (əvur'zHən), *n.*

a·vi·an (ā'vēən), *adj.* pertaining to birds.

a·vi·ar·y (ā'vēerē), *n.* a large cage, or building, containing cages for housing birds.

a·vi·cul·ture (ā'vəkulcHər), *n.* the breeding or keeping of birds.

av·i·ga·tion (avəgā'sHən), *n.* aerial navigation.

a·vi·on·ics (ā'vēon'iks), *n.* the science and application of electronics in aviation.

a·vun·cu·lar (əvuNG'kyələr), *adj.* **1.** pertaining to or characteristic of an uncle. **2.** kind; cheerful.

ax·i·om (ak'sēəm), *n.* a generally accepted principle or proposition; a self-evident truth. —**ax·i·o·mat'ic,** *adj.*

ax·on (ak'son), *n.* a nerve fiber of the neuron which transmits impulses away from the cell. Also **neurite.** See also **neuron.**

a·zon·ic (āzon'ik), *adj.* not local; not restricted to a particular zone.

az·y·gous (az'əgəs), *adj.* not forming one of a pair, as a leaf or a bodily organ.

Bab·bitt (bab′it), *n.* a complacent person who conforms unthinkingly to middle-class standards.

Ba·bel·ize (bā′bəlīz, bab′əlīz), *v.* to make confused or unintelligible.

Ba·bin·ski's reflex (bəbin′skēz), a reflex upward movement of the great toe, caused by stroking the sole of the foot.

bab·ka (bäb′kə), *n.* a sweet-flavored yeast cake, spongy in texture and made with raisins.

ba·boon·er·y (baboo͞o′nərē), *n.* uncouth or stupid behavior.

ba·bush·ka (bəboo͝osh′kə), *n.* a woman's scarf, worn as a head covering with the ends tied under the chin.

bac·ca·lau·re·ate (bakəlô′ēit), *n.* **1.** a bachelor's degree. **2.** a religious service at a university or other educational institution.

bac·cha·nal (bäkənäl′), *n.* **1.** a drunken reveler. **2.** a drunken orgy or feast.

bac·chant (bak′ənt), *n.* a devotee of Bacchus the ancient Greek god of wine; a drunken reveler.

Bac·chic (bak′ik), *adj.* pertaining to Bacchus the ancient Greek god of wine; riotously drunk.

bac·cif·er·ous (baksif′ərəs), *adj.* bearing or yielding berries.

bac·ci·form (bak′səfərm), *adj.* shaped like a berry; coccoid.

bac·civ·or·ous (baksiv′ərəs), *adj.* feeding on berries.

bac·il·lar·y (bas′əlerē), *adj.* **1.** shaped like a rod or bacillus. **2.** pertaining to or produced by bacilli.

ba·cil·lus (bəsil′əs), *n.* any of various rod-shaped bacteria producing spores in the presence of free oxygen.

back bench, any of the seats reserved for backbenchers. See also **front bench.**

back·bench·er (bak′ben′chər), *n.* any member of the British House of Commons who does not sit on the front benches reserved for those holding ministerial posts and for opposition party spokesmen.

back·lash (bak′lash), *n.* any sudden or violent reaction, esp. one against a movement of reform, etc.

back·sheesh (bak′shēsh), *n.* See **baksheesh.**

back·ward·a·tion (bakwərdā′shən), *n.* a fee paid by a seller of stock on the London Stock Exchange to the buyer in compensation for its deferred delivery.

bac·te·ri·a (baktēr′ēə), *n. pl., sing.* **bac·te·ri·um** (baktēr′ēəm), any of numerous microscopic organisms found in organic matter and causing putrefaction, fermentation, disease, etc.

bac·te·ri·cide (baktēr′isīd), *n.* something capable of destroying bacteria.

bac·te·ri·ol·o·gy (baktēr′eol′əjē), *n.* the science or study of bacteria.

bac·te·ri·ol·y·sis (baktēr/ēol/isis), *n.* the destruction or dissolution of bacteria.

bac·te·ri·o·phage (baktēr/ēəfāj), *n.* a virus that attacks certain bacteria.

bac·te·ri·os·co·py (baktēr/ēos/kəpē), *n.* the examination of bacteria under a microscope.

bac·te·ri·o·sta·sis (baktēr/ēəstā/sis), *n.* the inhibition of the growth of bacteria without destroying them.

bac·te·ri·o·stat (baktēr/ēəstat), *n.* anything that inhibits the growth of bacteria.

bac·ter·oid (bak/təroid), *n.* **1.** any of the rod-like or branched organisms found in the root nodules of nitrogen-fixing plants. —*adj.* **2.** resembling bacteria. Also **bac·te/ri·oid.**

bac·te·roi·des (baktəroi/dēz), *n., pl.* **bac·te·roi·des.** any of a number of rod-like bacteria found in man and animals.

ba·cu·li·form (bəkyoō/ləfərm/), *adj.* shaped like a rod.

bac·u·line (bak/yəlin), *adj.* pertaining to the cane or rod or its use as a means of punishment.

ba·di·geon (bədij/ən), *n.* a substance used to repair superficial defects in woodwork or masonry.

bad·i·nage (badənäzH/), *n.* light, playful repartee or banter; teasing; raillery.

ba·gasse (bəgas/), *n.* the residue left after making sugar from sugar cane or beets.

bag·a·telle (bagətel/), *n.* **1.** an unimportant trifle; something of little value. **2.** a short, light piece of music. **3.** a game, similar to billiards, played on an oblong board with a cue and balls.

ba·gel (bā/gəl), *n.* a hard roll shaped like a doughnut, made of leavened dough that has been boiled before baking.

bagn·io (ban/yō), *n.* **1.** a brothel. **2.** an Oriental prison for slaves. **3.** a public bath or bathing house.

ba·guette (baget/), *n.* **1.** a gem cut in a rectangular shape; this shape. **2.** (in architecture) a small molding.

ba·hu·vri·hi (bähoōvrē/hē), *n.* a compound noun or adjective comprising two parts, the first, which is adjectival, describing the second, which is substantival, as *fairminded, redeye.*

bail·iff (bā/lif), *n.* **1.** a minor officer employed by some U.S. courts. **2.** (in Britain) an officer employed by a sheriff to serve writs, make arrests, etc. **3.** (in Britain) the overseer or manager of an estate or farm.

bail·i·wick (bā/ləwik), *n.* **1.** the area in which a bailiff has jurisdiction. **2.** one's sphere of interest, skill, authority, or responsibility.

bain-ma·rie (ban/mərē/), *n., pl.* **bains-marie** (ban/mərē/). a vessel containing hot water inside which another vessel, usually containing food, is placed for heating.

ba·kla·va (bäkləvä/), *n.* a pastry, originating in Near Eastern countries, made of thin dough filled with nuts and honey.

bak·sheesh, back·sheesh (bak/-sHēsH), *n.* (in Eastern countries) a gratuity, tip; alms.

bal·a·cla·va (baləklä/və), *n.* a close-fitting woolen covering for the head and ears.

bal·a·lai·ka (baləlī/kə), *n.* a Russian musical instrument, similar to a guitar, having a triangular shaped body.

balance of payments, the difference between a country's total payments to foreign nations and its total income from them.

balance of power, the distribution of forces among two or more countries to prevent any one of them from becoming the dominant power.

balance of trade, the difference in monetary value between a country's imports and exports.

bal·a·noid (bal/ənoid), *adj.* having the shape of an acorn.

bal·a·ta (bal/ətə), *n.* a gum obtained from the latex of the bully tree, used in making golf balls, machinery belts, etc.

ba·laus·tine (bəlôs/tin), *n.* the dried flowers of the pomegranate used in the preparation of medicines.

bal·brig·gen (balbrig′ən), *n*. a cotton fabric used in underwear and hosiery.

bal·co·net (balkənet′), *n*. a railing outside a window giving the effect of a balcony.

bal·da·chin (bal′dəkin), *n*. **1.** a silk fabric embroidered with gold or silver threads. **2.** a canopy carried over an important person or sacred object in religious processions. **3.** a canopy over an altar, etc.

bal·der·dash (bôl′dərdasн), *n*. a meaningless or nonsensical verbal hodgepodge.

bal·dric (bôl′drik), *n*. a belt, often ornamented, worn over one shoulder to support a sword, etc.

ba·leen (bəlēn′), *n*. whalebone.

bale·ful (bāl′fəl), *adj*. having a deadly or malicious influence; harmful; pernicious.

Balkan frame, a frame over a bed for supporting a broken limb in a splint in traction.

Bal·kan·ize (bôl′kənīz), *v*. to split up a large region or country into small, relatively impotent and often mutually conflicting states. —**Bal·kan·i·za′tion,** *n*.

bal·let·o·mane (balet′əmān), *n*. a lover of the ballet.

bal·lis·tic (bəlis′tik), *adj*. pertaining to the study of the motion of projectiles.

bal·lis·to·car·di·o·graph (bəlis′-tōkär′dēəgraf), *n*. a device used in medicine to ascertain cardiac output. —**bal·lis·to·car′di·o·gram,** *n*.

bal·lot·tine (bal′ətēn), *n*. a dish of meat, poultry, or fish, prepared as a kind of galantine, usually served hot.

bal·ly·hoo (bal′ēhoō), *n*. exaggerated or blatant publicity on behalf of a cause; clamor; outcry.

bal·ma·caan (balməkän′), *n*. a short overcoat for men, usually of rough wool, and with raglan shoulders.

bal·ne·al (bal′nēəl), *adj*. pertaining to baths or bathing.

bal·ne·ol·o·gy (balnēol′əjē), *n*. the science or study of the therapeutic use of baths and bathing.

bal·op·ti·con (balop′tikon), *n*. an apparatus used for projecting images of objects by reflected light.

bal·us·ter (bal′əstər), *n*. one of a series of upright supports for a banister.

bal·us·trade (bal′əstrād), *n*. a banister with its supporting row of balusters.

ba·nal (bā′nəl, bənal′), *adj*. lacking originality; trite; commonplace; stereotyped.

ba·naus·ic (bənô′sik), *adj*. of practical use only; utilitarian; functional.

ban·deau (bandō′), *n*. a band or ribbon worn around the forehead for ornamentation or for binding the hair.

ban·de·ril·la (bandərē′ə), *n*. a barbed, decorated dart used by banderillos in bullfighting.

ban·de·ril·le·ro (bandəreer′ō), *n., pl.* **ban·de·ril·le·ros** (bandəreer′ōs). (in bullfighting) an assistant to the matador, who sticks banderillas in the back of the bull's neck.

ban·dog (ban′dog′), *n*. any dog kept chained, esp. a mastiff or bloodhound.

ban·do·leer (bandəlēr′), *n*. a belt worn over the shoulder having small pockets or loops for holding cartridges. Also **ban·do·lier′.**

ban·dy (ban′dē), *v*. to exchange; pass from one to another; convey to and fro.

bane (bān), *n*. a cause of death or disaster; a curse.

Ban·ga·lore torpedo (baнGəlôr′), a metal pipe containing an explosive mixture and used for making gaps in barbed wire, detonating mines, etc.

banns (banz), *n*. a proclamation, esp. one given in church, of an intended marriage.

ban·tam·weight (ban′təmwāt′), *n*. a boxer whose maximum weight for his class does not exceed 118 pounds.

ban·ter (ban′tər), **1.** *n*. light, playful teasing. —*v*. **2.** to speak in a teasing or playful manner; make fun of.

ban·zai (bänzī′), *interj., n*. a Japanese patriotic cry or cheer of triumph. [literally, (*may you live*) 10,000 *years*]

bar·ag·no·sis (baragnō′sis), *n.* lack or loss of ability to judge the weight of an object. See also **barognosis.**

bar·bi·tal (bär′bital), *n.* a hypnotic drug.

bar·bi·tu·rate (bärbicH′ərāt), *n.* any of a group of organic compounds used as sedatives or hypnotics.

bar·bi·tur·ism (bärbicH′ərizm), *n.* poisoning resulting from excessive use of barbiturates.

bar·ca·role, bar·ca·rolle (bär′kərōl), *n.* a Venetian boat song or a piece of music in imitation of this.

bar·chan (bärkän′), *n.* a sand dune formed in the shape of a crescent, with the ends pointing away from the direction of the wind.

bar·es·the·sia (bäristhē′zHə), *n.* the ability to perceive pressure.

bar·ghest (bär′gest), *n.* an evil spirit appearing as an omen of death or misfortune.

Bar·me·cid·al (bärmisī′dəl), *adj.* providing an illusion of plenty or abundance; illusory.

bar mitz·vah (bärmits′və), **1.** a ceremony marking the formal admittance of a boy as an adult member of the Jewish community. **2.** the boy himself.

barn (bärn), *n.* a unit used for measuring cross-sectional areas of atomic nuclei. 10^{-24} sq. cm.

bar·og·no·sis (barognō′sis), *n.* the ability to judge variations in weight of an object. See also **baragnosis.**

bar·o·gram (bar′əgram), *n.* a graph traced by a barograph.

bar·o·graph (bar′əgraf), *n.* a barometer which records automatically.

ba·rom·e·ter (bərom′itər), *n.* an instrument which indicates relative changes in atmospheric pressure.

bar·on·et (bar′ənit), *n.* (in England) a member of a hereditary order below a baron and above a knight.

ba·roque (bərōk′), *n.* an extravagant style in European art and architecture, often characterized by elaborate and even grotesque ornamentation, prevalent in the seventeenth and early eighteenth centuries.

bar·o·ther·mo·graph (barəthur′-

məgraf), *n.* an instrument that automatically records atmospheric pressure and temperature.

bar·o·ther·mo·hy·gro·graph (bar′-əthur′məhī′grəgraf), *n.* an instrument that automatically records atmospheric pressure, temperature, and humidity.

bar·o·trau·ma (barətrô′mə), *n. pl.* **bar·o·trau·ma·ta** (bar′ətrô′mətə), **bar·o·trau·mas.** injury to the eardrum caused by a change in atmospheric pressure.

bar·ra·tor (bar′ətər), *n.* one who commits barratry.

bar·ra·try (bar′ətrē), *n.* **1.** a fraudulent or negligent action by the captain or crew of a ship at the expense of the owners. **2.** frequent instigation of quarrels and lawsuits, considered as an illegal action. **3.** traffic in ecclesiastical promotions or offices of state.

bar·rel·house (bar′əlhous), *n.* a vigorous, rough and crude style of jazz.

bar·rio (bär′ryô), *n.* (in Spain and Spanish-American countries) one of the sections into which a town or city is divided.

ba·sal (bā′səl), *adj.* relating to or constituting the base; basic; essential; minimal.

ba·salt (bəsôlt′), *n.* a dark-colored, dense, igneous rock of volcanic origin, often found in the form of hexagonal columns.

bash·i·ba·zouk (basH′ēbəzook′), *n.* a member of an irregular force of mounted troops in the Ottoman Empire.

bas·i·lar (bas′ələr), *adj.* relating to, growing from, or situated at, the base. Also **bas′i·lar·y.**

ba·sil·ic (bəsil′ik), *adj.* pertaining to a king; regal; royal.

ba·sil·i·ca (bəsil′ikə), *n.* an early Christian or medieval church.

bas·i·lisk (bas′əlisk), *n.* **1.** a mythical reptile said to have a fatal breath and glance. **2.** a small lizard of tropical America.

bas-re·lief (bärəlēf′), *n.* a kind of sculpture in which the projecting parts stand out only slightly from the surrounding surface. Also **bas·so·ri·lie·vo** (bas'ōrəlē'vō).

bastard title. See **half title.**

bas·ti·na·do (bastənä'dō), *n.*, *pl.* **bas·ti·na·does.** a blow or a beating with a stick, esp. as applied to the soles of the feet as a method of punishment.

bas·tion (bas'chən), *n.* a fortress or strongpoint.

bath mitz·vah, bas mitz·vah (bäs mits'və), **1.** a ceremony marking the formal admittance of a girl as an adult member of the Jewish community. **2.** the girl herself. See also **bar mitzvah.**

ba·thos (bā'thos), *n.* **1.** a descent from the sublime to the ludicrous or from the exalted to the commonplace. **2.** sentimentality; pathos lacking sincerity.

bath·y·al (bath'ēəl), *adj.* pertaining to the ocean depths.

bath·y·met·ric (bathəmet'rik), *adj.* pertaining to the measurement of depths of water in oceans, seas and lakes. —**ba·thym'e·trist,** *n.* —**ba·thym'e·try,** *n.*

bath·y·pe·lag·ic (bath'əpəlaj'ik), *adj.* pertaining to the deeper parts of an ocean.

bath·y·scaphe (bath'iskāf), *n.* a submersible sphere used for exploring the depths of the ocean. Also **bath·y·scaph** (bath'əskaf), **bath·y·scape** (bath'əskāp).

bath·y·sphere (bath'isfēr), *n.* a spherical diving chamber for deep-sea observation.

ba·tik, bat·tik (bətēk', bat'ik), *n.* a method of preparing fabrics for hand-dyeing by coating with wax the parts which are not to be dyed.

ba·tiste (bətēst'), *n.* a fine, usually sheer fabric of plain weave.

bat·man (bat'mən), *n.* the soldier servant of a British army officer.

ba·tra·chi·an (bətrā'kēən), *adj.* pertaining to the vertebrate amphibians, as frogs, toads, etc.

bat·tol·o·gize (bətol'əjīz), *v.* to repeat words or phrases excessively in speech or writing.

bat·tol·o·gy (bətol'əjē), *n.* the constant, tiresome repetition of words in speech or writing.

baud (bôd), *n.* a measure, equivalent to one unit per second, used in telegraphy to ascertain the speed of signaling.

Bau·haus (bou'hous), *adj.* pertaining to a school of design established in Germany in 1918 which emphasized chiefly the functional aspect of design.

bau·xite (bôk'sīt), *n.* a rock, the chief ore of aluminum.

ba·var·dage (bavardazh'), *n.* foolish or nonsensical talk.

bawd (bôd), *n.* a prostitute; a woman who keeps a brothel.

bawd·y (bô'dē), *adj.* indecent; obscene; salacious.

bay·ou (bī'oo), *n.* a creek, tributary, or outlet of a river, etc.

ba·zoo·ka (bəzoo'kə), *n.* a portable rocket launcher, for destroying tanks and other armored vehicles.

bea·dle (bē'dəl), *n.* **1.** an official who supervises ceremonial processions at British universities. **2.** a minor parish official.

bear·ish (ber'ish), *adj.* marking or tending toward a decline in stock exchange prices; economically unfavorable, occasioning investors' cautious retreat. See also **bullish.**

beat generation, those who matured after World War II, and who, through disillusionment, rejected traditional moral standards and sought refuge in mysticism and the relaxation of social tensions.

beat·nik (bēt'nik), *n.* one who rejects traditional standards and adopts unconventional behavior, dress, etc.

beau geste (bōzhest'), *pl.* **beaux gestes** (bōzhest'), a graceful or conciliatory gesture, esp. one intended only for effect.

beau monde (bō mônd'), the world of fashionable society.

be·di·zen (bidī'zən), *v.* to ornament or dress gaudily or vulgarly.

be·guile (bigīl'), *v.* to deceive or influence by trickery; charm; captivate.

be·gum (bē'gəm), *n.* a Muslim woman or widow of high rank.

be·hav·ior·ism (bihā'vyərizm), *n.* a theory in psychology that emphasizes the importance of the objective study of facts of behavior and actual responses.

be·he·moth (bihē'məth), *n.* a huge and powerful animal or man.

be·laud (bilôd'), *v.* to bestow lavish praises upon, esp. with the aim of causing ridicule.

bel·dam (bel'dəm), *n.* an old woman; a hag.

be·lea·guer (bilē'gər), *v.* to beset with troubles; annoy; afflict.

bel-es·prit (belesprē'), *n.*, *pl.* **beaux-es·prits** (bōzesprē'). a witty or intellectually gifted person.

be·lie (bilī'), *v.* to give a false impression of; prove false; contradict.

bel·li·cose (bel'əkōs), *adj.* aggressive; quarrelsome; warlike.

bel·lig·er·ent (bəlij'ərənt), *adj.* **1.** aggressive; hostile; waging war. —*n.* **2.** a nation in a state of war. —**bel·lig'er·ence,** *n.*

bell·weth·er (bel'weᴛʜər), *n.* one who takes the lead or initiative, as a male sheep which leads the flock, usually carrying a bell round its neck.

bel·o·man·cy (bel'əmansē), *n.* foretelling the future by the use of arrows.

bel·o·noid (bel'ənoid), *adj.* shaped like a needle or stylus.

be·lu·ga (bəloo'gə), *n.* the white sturgeon.

be·muse (bimyooz'), *v.* to bewilder; confuse; stupefy.

be·mused (bimyoozd'), *adj.* bewildered, confused; preoccupied; lost in thought.

bench warrant, a warrant issued by a judge or court for the apprehension of an accused or guilty person.

bends (bendz), *n. pl.* See **decompression sickness.**

bend sinister, a diagonal band running across an escutcheon from top left to bottom right, supposedly a sign of bastardy.

ben·e·dic·tion (ben'idik'sʜən), *n.* **1.** the conferring of a blessing in a formal manner. **2.** a special service in the Roman Catholic Church.

ben·e·fac·tor (ben'əfak'tər), *n.* one who gives help to others; one who provides financial assistance for a cause, institution, etc.

be·nef·ic (bənif'ik), *adj.* doing or causing good.

ben·e·fice (ben'əfis), *n.* an ecclesiastical office or living held by an Anglican clergyman; the revenue derived from this.

be·nef·i·cent (bənef'isənt), *adj.* doing or producing good; kindly; generous. —**be·nef'i·cence,** *n.*

be·nev·o·lent (bənev'ələnt), *adj.* characterized by a desire to do good; showing good will; well-wishing. —**be·nev'o·lence,** *n.*

be·night·ed (binī'tid), *adj.* **1.** ignorant, backward. **2.** overtaken by darkness or night.

be·nign (binīn'), *adj.* **1.** kindly; well disposed; gentle. **2.** (of a tumor, etc.) not malignant; mild.

be·nig·nant (binig'nənt), *adj.* kind, gracious; beneficial.

be·nig·ni·ty (binig'nitē), *n.* kindness; goodness.

ben·ny (ben'ē), *n. Slang.* any amphetamine tablet, esp. Benzedrine.

ben·thos (ben'thos), *n.* the animals and plants that live at the bottom of the sea.

be·queath (bikwēth'), *v.* to give, leave, or dispose of by will; transmit; pass on to.

be·quest (bikwest'), *n.* something bequeathed; a legacy.

be·rate (birāt'), *v.* to scold; chide angrily; rebuke.

ber·dache (bərdasʜ'), *n.* an American Indian tribesman who adopts the clothing and duties of a woman.

be·reave (birēv'), *v.* to deprive, esp. by death; leave destitute; make disconsolate; rob.

be·reft (bireft'), *adj.* deprived; destitute.

be·rhyme (birīm'), *v.* to commemorate in verse.

berm (burm), *n.* a path or edge alongside a road, canal, etc.

23 **bicameral**

ber·serk (bursurk′), *adj.* in a murderous rage; frenziedly destructive.
be·seech (bisēcH′), *v.* to plead urgently; implore; appeal humbly.
be·seem (bisēm′), *v.* to be worthy, suitable, or fitting.
be·smirch (bismurcH′), *v.* to detract from the good name of; sully or tarnish.
be·sot (bisot′), *v.* to make intoxicated; stupefy with drink.
be·speak (bispēk′), *v.* to suggest; signify; indicate.
be·spoke (bispōk′), *adj.* (in Britain) (of clothing) custom-made.
bes·tial (bes′cHəl), *adj.* cruel; inhuman; barbarous.
bes·ti·al·i·ty (bēs′cHēal′itē), *n.* **1.** bestial behavior or character. **2.** gratification of brutish or animal instincts, appetites, etc. **3.** sexual relations between a human being and an animal.
bes·ti·ar·y (bes′cHēerē), *n.* a collection of moralizing stories using animals as the characters.
be·ta·tron (bā′tətron), *n.* a device that accelerates electrons to high energy by varying a magnetic field.
be·tel nut (bē′təl), the areca nut, chewed by people of Southeastern Asia.
bête noire (bāt nwär′), *pl.* **bêtes noires** (bāt nwärz′). a person or thing regarded with particular loathing or fear.
be·think (bithiNGk′), *v.* to consider, think or reflect; recall; resolve or determine.
be·tide (bitīd′), *v.* to happen; come to pass.
be·times (bitīmz′), *adj.* early; soon.
bê·tise (betēz′), *n.* a stupid or foolish remark or act.
be·to·ken (bitō′kən), *v.* to signify, portend; be an indication or evidence of; show.
bev·a·tron (bev′ətron), *n.* (in physics) a device for accelerating protons to very high energies.
bey (bā), *n.* **1.** a provincial governor under the Ottoman Empire. **2.** a title of respect given to high-ranking Turkish dignitaries.

bez·el (bez′əl), *n.* a groove in a setting for holding a gem.
bhang, bang (baNG), *n.* the leaves and stalks of Indian hemp used as a narcotic or an intoxicant.
bhees·ty, bhees·tie (bē′stē), *n.* (in India) a water-carrier.
bi·a·ly (bēä′lē), *n.* a roll made of white flour and flavored with onion.
bi·an·nu·al (bīan′yōōəl), *adj.* **1.** occurring twice a year. **2.** (sometimes) occurring every two years. See also **biennial.**
bi·be·lot (bib′lō), *n.* a small decorative object having esthetic value or prized for its rarity.
bib·li·o·clast (bib′lēəklast), *n.* one who destroys books.
bib·li·og·o·ny (bib′lēog′ənē), *n.* the production and publication of books.
bib·li·o·klept (bib′lēəklept), *n.* one who steals books.
bib·li·ol·a·try (bib′lēol′ətrē), *n.* an exaggerated respect for the Bible.
bib·li·o·man·cy (bib′lēəmansē), *n.* prophecy or divination from verses chosen from the Bible at random.
bib·li·o·ma·ni·a (bib′lēəmā′nēə), *n.* excessive zeal for acquiring books.
bib·li·op·e·gy (bib′lēop′əjē), *n.* the art of book-binding.
bib·li·o·phage (bib′lēəfāj), *n.* a person with a passion for reading.
bib·li·o·phile (bib′lēəfīl), *n.* a book-lover; one who is fond of collecting books. Also **bib·li·oph′i·list.**
bib·li·o·phobe (bib′lēəfōb), *n.* one who distrusts or dreads books.
bib·li·o·pole (bib′lēəpōl), *n.* a dealer in books, esp. rare books. Also **bib·li·op′o·list.**
bib·li·o·taph, bib·li·o·taphe (bib′lēətaf), *n.* one who hoards books.
bib·li·o·the·ca (bib′lēəthē′kə), *n.* a library.
bib·li·o·ther·a·py (bib′lēəther′əpē), *n.* the use of reading as a means of psychiatric therapy.
bib·u·lous (bib′yələs), *adj.* given to alcoholic drinking.
bi·cam·er·al (bīkam′ərəl), *adj.* having or consisting of two branches or charibas, as a legislative body.

bi·cen·ten·ni·al (bī′senten′ēəl), *adj.*
1. lasting 200 years. **2.** occurring
every 200 years. —*n.* **3.** a 200th anniversary. Also, *chiefly Brit.*, **bi·cen·
te·nar·y** (bīsen′tənerē).

bi·cip·i·tal (bīsip′itəl), *adj.* possessing two heads.

bi·cor·po·ral (bīkôr′pərəl), *adj.* possessing two bodies, divisions, etc.

bi·di·rec·tion·al (bī′direk′sHənəl),
adj. operating or functioning in two
different directions.

Bie·der·mei·er (bē′dərmī′ər), *adj.*
denoting or relating to a style of interior decoration, furnishing, etc.,
found in German-speaking countries
in the 19th century and characterized
by ebony inlays and veneers of fruit-
wood used in a simplified style resembling French Empire.

bi·en·ni·al (bīen′ēəl), *adj.* occurring
every two years; lasting two years.
See also **biannual.**

bi·fa·cial (bīfā′sHəl), *adj.* having two
faces; having opposite surfaces alike.

bi·fid (bī′fid), *adj.* separated by a cleft
into two parts.

bi·flex (bī′fleks), *adj.* having a bend
at two different places.

bi·fo·cal (bīfō′kəl), *adj.* (of spectacle
lenses) having two parts one above
the other, the lower for near and the
upper for distant vision.

bi·form (bī′fôrm), *adj.* having or
combining the forms of two different
kinds of individual; hybrid.

bi·fur·cate (bī′fərkāt), *v.* **1.** to divide
into two parts or branches. —*adj.* **2.**
divided into two parts; split; forked.

big·a·mist (big′əmist), *n.* one who
commits the crime of marrying a
second time while still legally married. —**big′a·my,** *n.*

big bang theory, a theory that the
universe began with an enormous
explosion and is still expanding. See
also **steady state theory.**

big·gin (big′in), *n.* a silver coffee pot
with a separate container for holding
the coffee while it is being heated.

big·ot (big′ət), *n.* a person prejudiced
against any belief or opinion different
from his own.

bi·jou·te·rie (bēzHoo′tərē), *n.* a collection of jewelry.

bi·lat·er·al (bīlat′ərəl), *adj.* of or relating to two sides or parties; symmetrical; two-sided.

bil·bo (bil′bō), *n. pl.* **bil·boes.** an iron
bar with sliding cuffs used for fastening the ankles of prisoners.

bil·let-doux (bilēdoo′), *n. pl.* **bil·lets-
doux** (bilēdooz′), a love letter.

bil·lings·gate (bil′iNGzgāt), *n.* coarse
or abusive language.

bi·lo·ca·tion (bī′lōkā′sHən), *n.* being
in two places simultaneously.

bim·a·nous (bim′ənəs), *adj.* two-
handed.

bi·men·sal (bīmen′səl), *adj.* happening once every two months.

bi·mes·tri·al (bīmes′trēəl), *adj.* **1.**
happening every two months. **2.** lasting two months.

bi·na·ry (bī′nərē), *adj.* pertaining to
a system of numbers having 2 as its
base.

binary star, (in astronomy) a double
star system in which two stars orbit
a common center of gravity.

bin·au·ral (bīnôr′əl), *adj.* pertaining
to, using, or adapted for two ears.

binaural broadcasting, a system of
radio broadcasting designed to
achieve a stereophonic effect.

bi·o·as·say (bī′ōəsā′), *n.* **1.** a means
of calculating the relative strength of
a substance by testing its effect on an
organism. —*v.* **2.** to test in such a way.

bi·o·as·tro·nau·tics (bī′ōastrənô′-
tiks), *n.* the study of the effects of
space travel upon animal and plant
life.

bi·o·de·gra·da·ble (bī′ōdigrā′dəbəl),
adj. noting a substance, esp. a household cleaner, that is easily disposed
of by bacterial decomposition, thus
reducing pollution.

bi·o·dy·nam·ics (bī′ōdīnam′iks), *n.*
the study of living organisms in relation to their activity.

bi·o·e·col·o·gy (bī′ōēkol′əjē), *n.* the
study of the interrelationship between living organisms and their environment.

bi·o·gen·e·sis (bī′ōjen′isis), *n.* the

evolution of living forms from other living forms.

biological sociology, 1. the study of the development of social behavior in correlation with the study of living organisms. **2.** the study of social behavior treated as a phenomenon deriving from physiological structure. Also **biosociology.**

bi·o·lu·mi·nes·cence (bī′ōlōō′-mənes′əns), *n.* the generation of light by living organisms. —**bi·o·lumi·nes′cent,** *adj.*

bi·ol·y·sis (bīol′isis), *n.* the destruction or dissolution of a living organism.

bi·o·mass (bī′ōmas′), *n.* the amount of living matter in a given plane or cubic unit of habitat.

bi·o·med·i·cine (bī′ōmed′isin), *n.* medicine concerned with the relationship of body chemistry and function. —**bi·o·med′i·cal,** *adj.*

bi·om·e·try (bīom′itrē), *n.* the study of the probable length of human life. —**bi·o·met′ric,** *adj.* —**bi·o·me·tri′cian,** *n.*

bi·o·mor·phic (bī′ōmôr′fik), *adj.* (in fine arts) producing or evoking images of living organisms.

bi·on·ics (bīon′iks), *n.* the study of certain functions of man and animals and the application of the findings derived therefrom to the designing of computers.

bi·o·nom·ics (bīənom′iks), *n.* See **ecology.**

bi·on·omy (bīon′əmē), **1.** See **physiology. 2.** See **ecology.**

bi·o·phys·ics (bī′ōfiz′iks), *n.* the study of the application of the methods of physics to biological problems.

bi·op·sy (bī′opsē), *n.* the removal of tissue, cells, etc., from a living body for examination.

bi·o·psy·chic (bī′ōsī′kik), *adj.* relating to or denoting the interaction of biological and psychological phenomena.

bi·o·so·cial (bī′ōsō′sHəl), *adj.* relating to or denoting the interaction of biological and social phenomena.

bi·o·so·ci·ol·o·gy (bī′ōsō′sēol′əjē), *n.* See **biological sociology.**

bi·o·sphere (bī′əsfēr), *n.* that part of the world in which living organisms can exist.

bi·o·stat·ics (bī′ōstat′iks), *n.* the study of living organisms in relation to their function and structure.

bi·o·syn·the·sis (bī′ōsin′thisis), *n.* the formation of chemical compounds by a living organism.

bi·o·tech·nol·o·gy (bī′ōteknol′əjē), *n.* the study of the relationship between human beings and machines.

bi·ot·ic (bīot′ik), *adj.* relating or pertaining to life.

biotic potential, the capacity of an organism or species to reproduce and survive in an optimum environment.

bi·o·type (bī′ətīp), *n.* a group of organisms sharing genetic characteristics.

bip·ar·ous (bip′ərəs), *adj.* giving birth to offspring in pairs.

bi·par·ti·san (bīpär′tizn), *adj.* representing, agreed upon, or supported by two parties, esp. political parties.

bi·par·tite (bīpär′tīt), *adj.* **1.** having two parts or divided into two. **2.** shared by two.

bi·ped (bī′ped), *n.* **1.** an animal with two feet. —*adj.* **2.** having two feet. Also **bi·ped·al** (bī′pedəl).

bi·pod (bī′pod), *n.* a two-legged stand or support.

bi·pro·pel·lant (bī′prəpel′ənt), *n.* a rocket propellant consisting of fuel and oxidizer which are kept separate until they are ignited in the combustion chamber.

bi·ra·mous (bīrā′məs), *adj.* having or divided into two branches. Also **bi·ra·mose** (bīrā′mōs).

bird·ie (bur′dē), *n.* (in golf) one stroke under par on a hole. See also **bogey, eagle.**

bi·sect (bīsekt′), *v.* to divide or cut into two, usually equal, parts; split into two; fork.

bi·sex·u·al (bīsek′sHōōəl), *adj.* **1.** having both male and female reproductive organs. **2.** (of people) sexually attracted to both sexes. —*n.* **3.** one having the reproductive organs of both sexes. **4.** one who is sexually attracted to both sexes.

bis·sex·tile (bīseks′til), *adj.* having or denoting February 29, the extra day of a leap year.

bis·sex·tus (bīseks′təs), *n.* February 29th considered as the extra day added every four years to the Julian calendar.

bi·sym·met·ri·cal (bīsimet′rikəl), *adj.* denoting or having two planes of symmetry at right angles to each other.

biv·ou·ac (biv′ōōak), *n.* **1.** a temporary encampment, esp. a military one, providing very little protection. —*v.* **biv·ou·acked, biv·ou·ack·ing. 2.** to sleep or rest in such an encampment.

black powder, an explosive composed of saltpeter, sulfur, and powdered charcoal, used in fireworks, etc.

Black Shirt, a member of a fascist organization wearing a black shirt as a distinctive part of its uniform.

blanch (blanCH), *v.* (in cookery) to scald or parboil in order to whiten or skin.

blanc·mange (bləmänj′), *n.* a jelly-like pudding made with milk, cornstarch, and gelatin, and flavored with rum, vanilla, etc.

blan·dish (blan′disH), *v.* to seek to influence with flattering words; coax; cajole; flatter. —**blan′dish·ment,** *n.*

blan·quette (bläNket′), *n.* a stew of veal, lamb, or chicken prepared in a white sauce, served with cooked onions, mushrooms, etc.

blas·pheme (blasfēm′), *v.* to speak about God or sacred things without respect or reverence; curse; revile; swear.

blas·phe·mous (blas′fəməs), *adj.* uttering or containing profane language; irreverent.

blas·phe·my (blas′fəmē), *n.* an impious or profane utterance about God or sacred things; irreverent attitude towards anything considered sacred; abusive speech.

bla·tant (blā′tnt), *adj.* flagrantly obvious; disagreeably noisy; conspic-

uous in a vulgar or offensive manner.

blath·er·skite (blaTH′ərskīt), *n.* one given to blustering or empty talk.

Blau·e Rei·ter (blou′rī′tər), a group of artists employing free form and unconventional colors, active in Munich in the early 20th century.

blench (blenCH), *v.* to flinch; shy away through lack of courage; quail.

blight (blīt), *n.* **1.** a disease that causes plants to wither. **2.** a pernicious or malignant influence. —*v.* **3.** to cause to wither. **4.** destroy; shatter.

blithe (blīTH), *adj.* **1.** joyful; cheerful; glad. **2.** carefree; heedless of responsibility.

blood count, the number of blood cells in a given volume of blood.

blous·on (blōōzön′), *n.* a woman's blouse-like outer garment drawn in at the waist.

blow·out (blō′out′), *n.* See **flameout.**

blowz·y (blou′zē), *adj.* **1.** having a coarse reddish-colored complexion. **2.** untidy in appearance; unkempt; sluttish.

blue laws, a number of rigorous, puritanical laws designed to regulate morals, forbidding such activities as dancing, drinking, etc.

blue·nose (blōō′nōz′), *n.* a prudish, censorious or puritanical person.

blue-ribbon jury, a jury consisting of better educated or more intelligent people selected to try especially difficult or complex cases.

blue-sky law, any law providing for the regulation of the sale of securities.

blue·stock·ing (blōō′stokiNG), *n.* a woman who devotes herself to scholarly or literary pursuits.

B'nai B'rith (bənä′ brith′), a Jewish organization which promotes the educational and cultural improvement of Jews.

boat·el (bōtel′), *n.* a hotel at or near the waterside with docking space, providing accommodation for people traveling by boat.

bo·cage (bōkäzH′), *n.* (in the arts) a decorative pattern consisting of foliage, trees, branches, etc.

boc·cie (bocH′ē), *n.* a kind of lawn

bowling played by Italians in a narrow court.

bock beer, a variety of strong, dark beer.

bo·de·ga (bôтнe′gä), *n.* (in Spanish America) a grocery store.

bod·kin (bod′kin), *n.* a sharp, slender instrument for making holes in leather, cloth, etc.

boff (bof), *n.* (in the theater) a humorous remark or saying which causes the audience to laugh.

bo·gey (bō′gē), *n.* (in golf) one stroke over par on a hole. See also **birdie, eagle.**

bog·gle (bog′əl), *v.* to be dismayed or alarmed; shrink from; hesitate; waver.

bo·gie (bō′gē), *n.* the rear wheel assembly unit of a truck.

bo·gus (bō′gəs), *adj.* **1.** sham; not genuine; false. —*n.* **2.** (in printing) matter set by a compositor which duplicates material already supplied.

Bo·he·mi·an (bōhē′mēən), *n.* a person, esp. one with artistic pretensions, who scorns conventional social behavior.

boil·er·mak·er (boil′lərmākər), *n.* whiskey drunk with beer as a chaser.

boite (bwat), *n.* a night-club.

bo·la (bō′lə), *n.* (in South America) a missile consisting of a length of cord with two or more heavy balls at each end, thrown so as to entangle the legs of cattle, etc.

bo·lide (bō′līd), *n.* a large meteor; a fireball.

bo·lo (bō′lō), *n.* a heavy, machete-like knife with a single cutting edge used in the Philippines.

Bol·she·vik (bōl′sнəvik), *n.* **1.** a member of the extreme wing of the Russian Social-Democratic party which seized power in 1917. **2.** a member of a Communist party in any other country. —**Bol′she·vism,** *n.*

bo·lus (bō′ləs), *n.* (in medicine) a large pill, usually in the form of a sphere.

Bo·marc (bō′märk), *n.* a type of U.S. surface-to-air missile.

bom·bast (bom′bast), *n.* pompous or pretentious language. —**bom·bas′tic,** *adj.*

Bombay duck, a small fish used when dried as a relish with curries, etc. Also **bummalo.**

bombe (bom, bomb), *n.* a frozen dessert made in a round mold and consisting of ice cream, mousse, etc.

bom·bé (bombā′), *adj.* (of furniture) curving or bulging outward.

bo·na fi·de (bō′nəfīd), in good faith; without intention to deceive.

bon·ho·mie (bon′əmē), *n.* kindliness; good nature; joviality.

bon mot (bôn′ mō′), *pl.* **bons mots** (bôn′mōz′). an apt or clever remark; a witty saying.

bon·ny·clab·ber (bon′ēklab′ər), *n.* thick, sour milk.

bon·sai (bon′sī), *n. pl.* **bon·sai. 1.** a potted plant, usually a tree, which has been dwarfed by special methods of cultivation, pruning, etc. **2.** the art of growing such plants, developed in Japan.

bon vi·vant (bôn vēväɴ′), one who takes pleasure in good food and drink; an epicure.

boon·docks (bōōn′doks), *n.* an uninhabited area, esp. one overgrown with vegetation; any remote area, esp. in the countryside.

boon·dog·gle (bōōn′dogəl), *n.* **1.** trivial or useless work, carried out to give the appearance of being busy. —*v.* **2.** to perform such work.

boot·less (bōōt′lis), *adj.* of no avail; fruitless; useless.

bo·rax (bô′aks), *n.* cheap or shoddy merchandise, esp. furniture.

bor·del·lo (bôrdel′ō), *n.* a brothel.

bor·de·reau (bôrdərō′), *n. pl.* **bor·de·reaux** (bôr′dərōz′). a detailed note, esp. one listing documents.

bo·re·al (bôr′ēə), *adj.* pertaining to the north or the north wind.

borscht (bôrsнt), *n.* a Russian soup of beef stock flavored with cooked beets.

borscht circuit, (in theatrical use) the nightclubs and other entertainments in the Catskill Mountains, considered as a Jewish resort area.

bor·stal (bôr′stəl), *n.* (in England) a reformatory for young delinquents.

bos·cage (bos′kij), *n.* a thicket; a growth of trees or shrubs.

bos·ket (bos′kit), *n.* a thicket or grove. —**bosk·y** (bos′kē), *adj.*

bot·an·o·man·cy (bot′ənəmansē), *n.* prophecy based on examination of plants.

bot·te·ga (bōtā′gə), *n. pl.* **bot·te·gas, bot·te·ghe** (bōtā′gē). the studio of an artist of repute where students and apprentices learn.

bot·u·lin (bocH′əlin), *n.* the toxin produced by botulinus, the cause of botulism.

bot·u·li·nus (bocHəlī′nəs), *n. pl.* **bot·u·li·nus·es.** the bacterium, *Clostridium botulinum*, which secretes botulin.

bot·u·lism (bocH′əlizm), *n.* acute food poisoning caused by the presence of botulin in food.

bou·chée (bōōshā′), *n.* a small, cup-shaped piece of puff pastry used as a receptacle for an hors d'oeuvre, etc.

bouf·fant (bōōfänt′), *adj.* full, puffed out, as a skirt, sleeves, etc.

bouil·la·baisse (bōōlyəbäs′), *n.* a kind of soup or stew made of various kinds of fish.

bou·le·var·dier (bōōl′əvärdēr′), *n.* a man-about-town who frequents fashionable places.

bou·le·ver·se·ment (bōōlversmän′), *n.* a turning upside down; upset.

bound·en (boun′dən), *adj.* under an obligation; morally obliged.

bou·quet (bōōkā′), *n.* the distinctive aroma of a wine.

bou·quet gar·ni (bōkā′ gärnē′), a selection of herbs, tied in a cloth bag, used for flavoring soups, sauces, stews, etc.

bour·geois (bōōrzHwä′), *n. pl.* **bourgeois. 1.** a member of the middle class, esp. a merchant or businessman. **2.** one whose outlook is supposedly determined chiefly by private property interests. —*adj.* **3.** consisting of or belonging to the middle class. **4.** conventional or limited in outlook; lacking in taste.

bour·geoi·sie (bōōr′zHwäzē′), *n.* the middle class, esp. as contrasted with the proletariat or wage earners.

bouse, bowse (bous, bouz), *n.* a spree; a drinking bout.

bou·stro·phe·don (bōōstrəfē′dən), *n.* writing in which alternate lines read in opposite direction.

bou·tique (bōōtēk′), *n.* a small shop that sells fashionable clothes or luxury items.

bo·va·rism (bō′vərizm), *n.* a distortedly magnified opinion of one's own abilities; conceit.

bo·vine (bō′vīn), *adj.* resembling an ox; sluggish, stolid, or dull.

Bow bells (bō), the bells of the church of St. Mary-le-Bow, in the East End of London: the only true Cockneys are traditionally those born within sound of them.

bowd·ler·ize (bōd′lərīz), *v.* to expurgate (a book, play, etc.) prudishly, by omitting passages considered indecent or immodest.

bo·yar (bōyär′), *n.* a member of the old Russian nobility, abolished by Peter the Great. Also **bo·yard′.**

bra·ce·ro (brəser′ō), *n. pl.* **bra·ce·ros.** a Mexican laborer who does seasonal farmwork in the U.S.

bra·chyl·o·gy (brəkil′əjē), *n.* brevity of speech; a concise means of expression.

brack·ish (brak′isH), *adj.* having a slightly salty flavor.

brad·y·aux·e·sis (brad′ēôgzē′sis), *n.* (in an organism) the growth of a part at a slower rate than the whole. See also **isauxesis, tachyauxesis.** —**brad·y·aux·et′ic,** *adj.*

brad·y·car·di·a (brad′ikär′dēə), *n.* an abnormally slow pulse rate.

brad·y·ki·net·ic (brad′ikinet′ik), *adj.* moving very slowly; having a slow rate of motion.

brad·y·tel·ic (brad′itel′ik), *adj.* having a slower rate of evolution than normal for a specific group, species, etc. See also **horotelic, tachytelic.**

brag·ga·do·ci·o (bragədō′sHēō), *n.* **1.** one who boasts; a braggart. **2.** empty boasting.

brag·gart (brag′ərt), *n.* a boastful or bragging person.

Braille (brāl), *n.* a system that enables the blind to read, using combinations of raised dots as symbols.

brain·storming (brān′stôrm′iNG), *n.* a technique in which a group of people hold a spontaneous discussion in order to stimulate creative thinking, develop new ideas, etc.

brain·wash·ing (brān′wosH′iNG), *n.* a forcible, systematic method of indoctrination used to undermine a person's political or religious beliefs and to compel him to accept contrary ones.

braise (brāz), *v.* to cook slowly in a little liquid in a closed pan.

bran·dish (bran′disH), *v.* to shake or wave in a menacing or ostentatious manner.

bran·dreth (bran′dri*th*), *n.* **1.** a wooden railing or fence around a wall. **2.** a three-legged stand of iron placed over a fire.

bran·ni·gan (bran′əgən), *n.* a squabble or brawl; a spree.

brash (brasH), *adj.* reckless, impetuous, rash; impudent; tactless.

brass·age (bras′ij), *n.* a charge levied by a mint to cover the cost of coining money.

bras·sard (bras′ärd), *n.* an armlet or badge worn on the upper arm; a piece of armor worn to protect the arm.

bras·se·rie (bras′ərē′), *n.* a restaurant, saloon, etc., providing food or alcoholic drinks.

brat·tle (brat′l), *n.* **1.** a clattering or rattling noise. —*v.* **2.** to make such a noise.

brat·wurst (brat′wərst), *n.* a sausage made of pork, spices, etc.

bra·va·do (brəvä′dō), *n.* an ostentatious display of courage; a swaggering pretense of bravery.

bra·vu·ra (brəvyŏŏr′ə), *n. pl.* **bra·vu·ras.** a display of brilliance or daring in the performance of something.

bray (brā), *v.* to crush or pound into fine pieces or powder.

bra·zen (brā′zən), *adj.* **1.** made of brass. **2.** resembling brass in color,

sound, etc. **3.** shameless; insolent; impudent.

bread (bred), *n.* (Slang) money.

break bone fever. See **dengue.**

brec·ci·a (brecH′ēə), *n.* a rock consisting of sharp fragments of older rock embedded together in a matrix.

breech delivery, a birth in which the baby's posterior or feet are presented first.

breeches buoy, a life buoy fitted with canvas breeches and moving on a rope, enabling a person to be hauled from a ship to shore or to another ship.

bre·telle (britel′), *n.* an ornamental shoulder strap.

bre·vet (brəvet′), *n.* a commission granting a military officer higher rank without extra pay.

Brie (brē), *n.* a variety of soft, white, self-ripening cheese originated in France.

bri·gand (brig′ənd), *n.* a bandit who lives by robbing travelers, esp. in forests and mountains.

brig·and·age (brig′əndij), *n.* the work of brigands; robbery; plunder.

brink·man·ship (briNGk′mənsHip), *n.* the art of following a dangerous course of action to the limits of safety in order to achieve one's ends.

bri·oche (brē′ōsH), *n.* a roll or sweet bun made from eggs and yeast.

bri·quette, bri·quet (briket′), *n.* a block of compressed coal dust used for fuel.

bri·sance (brizäns′), *n.* the power of high explosive to shatter.

bris·ket (bris′kit), *n.* the breast of an animal, esp. that part lying nearest the ribs and considered as a cut of meat.

broach (brōcH), *v.* **1.** to introduce or mention for the first time. **2.** to break the surface of water from below.

broad-spec·trum (brôdspek′trəm), *adj.* denoting an antibiotic that is effective against a number of organisms.

bro·cade (brōkād′), *n.* a heavy fabric having an elaborate raised pattern in silver or gold.

broc·a·tel, broc·a·telle (brok'ətel'), *n.* a kind of brocade having a pattern woven in high relief.

bro·chette (brōsHet'), *n.* a small spit or skewer used in cooking.

bro·gan (brō'gən), *n.* a coarse, strongly made shoe, esp. one reaching to the ankle.

brogue (brōg), *n.* 1. a strongly made, comfortable shoe, often with decorative perforations. 2. English spoken with a pronounced Irish accent.

bro·mide (brō'mīd), *n.* 1. a trite or platitudinous remark. 2. a tiresome or boring person.

Bronze Age, a period in human culture, occurring between the Stone Age and the Iron Age, characterized by the use of bronze tools and weapons.

brook (brŏok), *v.* to put up with, bear, tolerate.

Brook Farm, a farm in West Roxbury, Massachusetts, the scene of an experiment in communistic living during 1841–7.

broth·el (broTH'əl), *n.* a house for prostitution.

brou·ha·ha (brŏohä'hä), *n.* uproar, hubbub, turmoil.

bruit (brŏot), *v.* to spread a rumor.

bru·lé (brŏolā'), *n.* a forest region destroyed by fire.

bru·mal (brŏo'məl), *adj.* occurring in winter; wintry.

brume (brŏom), *n.* mist; fog.

brum·ma·gem (brum'əjəm), *adj.* gaudy, cheap, and inferior.

brunch (brunCH), *n.* a meal taken late in the morning combining both breakfast and lunch.

brusque (brusk), *adj.* having a curt or abrupt manner; rough; blunt.

brus·que·rie (brus'kərē), *n.* a display of brusque manners.

brut (brŏot), *adj.* (of champagne) very dry.

brux·ism (bruk'sizm), *n.* the grinding of teeth, esp. during sleep.

bubble chamber, an apparatus containing heated liquid designed to make visible the paths of ionizing particles as a row of bubbles.

bu·bon·ic plague (byŏobon'ik), a virulent form of plague characterized by the growth of inflammatory swellings called buboes.

buc·cal (buk'əl), *adj.* relating to the cheek, the sides of the mouth or the mouth itself.

buc·ca·ro (bŏokär'ō), *n.* a kind of unglazed pottery.

buc·co·lin·gual (buk'əliNG'gwəl), *adj.* relating to the cheek and tongue.

bu·cen·taur (byŏosen'tôr), *n.* the state barge formerly used by the doge of Venice for the ritual of wedding the state to the Adriatic Sea.

Buch·man·ism (bŏok'mənizm), *n.* the principles and beliefs of the Moral Re-Armament Movement, formerly the Oxford Group, which advocated strict observance of high moral standards both publicly and privately.

buck·a·roo (buk'ərŏo'), *n.* a cowboy.

bucket shop, a broker's establishment which speculates fraudulently against its customers' interests.

buck·eye (buk'ī'), *n.* a work of art, esp. a painting, produced as a saleable commodity and generally lacking intrinsic worth.

buck·ram (buk'rəm), *n.* a durable, plainwoven cotton cloth used for binding books, making interlinings, etc.

bu·col·ic (byŏokol'ik), *adj.* relating to shepherds or the countryside; pastoral; rural.

Bud·dhism (bŏod'izm), *n.* a religion of southern and eastern Asia, teaching that suffering is an essential characteristic of life and that liberation can be achieved only through enlightenment and self-purification.

budg·er·i·gar (buj'ərēgär), *n.* a small parakeet of Australia.

buff·er (buf'ər), *n.* a unit designed to store computer data until these can be fed into their appropriate unit for processing.

buffer state, a small state lying between two powerful states, esp. one which by its position lessens the risk of conflict between them.

buf·fet[1] (buf'it), v. to strike with the hand; push against or strike repeatedly.

buf·fet[2] (bəfā'), n. **1.** a china cupboard or sideboard; a counter or bar for refreshments. **2.** a meal set out on a table, etc., usually offering a choice of dishes to be eaten informally.

bu·lim·i·a (byōōlim'ēə), n. a morbid and constant hunger; an unnatural craving for food.

bull (bōōl), n. a document issued by a pope.

bul·la (bōōl'ə), n., pl. **bul·lae** (bōōl'ē). a seal attached to a papal bull.

bul·lion (bōōl'yən), n. gold and silver considered as bulk, and not as manufactured articles.

bull·ish (bōōl'isн), adj. (in a stock market, etc.) marked by, conducive to or tending toward a rise in prices, occasioning investors' optimism. See also **bearish.**

bully tree, any of various tropical American trees which yield balata.

bum·boat (bum'bōt), n. a small boat used to ferry provisions to ships lying in harbor.

bum·ma·lo (bum'əlō), n. See **Bombay duck.**

bump·tious (bump'sнəs), adj. excessively and unpleasantly self-assertive.

Bund (bōōnd), n. a pro-Nazi organization in the U.S. before World War II.

Bun·des·rat (bōōn'dəsrät), n. **1.** the upper chamber of the parliament of the German Federal Republic. **2.** the federal council of Switzerland.

Bun·des·tag (bōōn'dəstäg), n. the lower chamber of the parliament of the German Federal Republic.

bung (buнg), n. a plug or stopper for the hole in a wooden barrel.

bung·start·er (buнg'stärtər), n. a hammer for removing a bung.

bun·ko (buнg'kō), n. pl. **bun·kos.** a confidence trick or swindle in a gambling game, etc.

bunko steerer, a swindler, esp. one who entices a victim into a gambling game in which he will be cheated.

bun·kum (buнg'kəm), n. deceitful speechmaking by a politician calculated to impress his constituents.

bur·geon (bur'jən), v. to expand quickly; flourish.

bu·rin (byōōr'in), n. a steel cutting tool used for engraving metal, marble, etc.

burke (burk), v. to murder, as by smothering, so as to leave no traces of violence.

bur·nish (bur'nisн), v. **1.** to polish by friction so as to make smooth and shiny. **2.** (in engraving) to rub (the dots of a halftone) so as to flatten and enlarge them.

bur·noose, bur·nous (bərnōōs'), n. a hooded cloak worn by Arabs.

burn·out (burn'out'), n. the stage in the flight of a rocket engine when the propellant fuel ceases to provide power.

bur·sar (bur'sər), n. an official at a university, etc., having charge of financial matters. —**bur·sar·i·al** (bərser'ēəl), adj.

burse (burs), n. a small receptacle as a pouch, purse, etc.

bus·by (buz'bē), n. a tall fur cap with a bag hanging down from the top, worn by certain British Army regiments.

bus·kin (bus'kin), n. **1.** a high shoe with thick soles worn by actors in ancient Greek drama. **2.** tragedy; the tragic style of acting.

byte (bīt), n. a unit of machine-readable information equal to eight bits.

ca·bal (kəbal′), *n.* a small group of persons engaged in secret plotting, as against a government, etc.

cab·a·la (kab′ələ, kəbä′lə), *n.* an esoteric theosophical system based on a mystical interpretation of the Scriptures.

cab·a·lism (kab′əlizm), *n.* the doctrines or the interpretation of the cabala. —**cab′a·list,** *n.*

cabinet wine, a German wine of good quality.

cab·o·chon (kab′əsʜon), *n.* a rounded, polished but not faceted precious stone.

ca·bo·clo (kəbô′klo͞o, kəbô′klo), *n.* a Brazilian Indian.

ca·boo·dle (kəbo͞o′dl), *n.* the whole collection; the lot.

cab·o·tage (kab′ətij), *n.* **1.** navigation or trade restricted to coastal waters. **2.** the restriction of air transport within a country's borders to that country's aircraft.

ca·can·ny (käkan′ē), *n.* (in Britain) a work slowdown by employees in a factory, etc., in order to reduce production.

cac·cia·to·re (kaᴄʜətôr′ē), *adj.* (of an Italian dish) containing or prepared with tomatoes, mushrooms, herbs, etc. Also **cac·cia·to′ra.**

cach·a·lot (kasʜ′əlot), *n.* See **sperm whale.**

cache (kasʜ), *n.* **1.** a hiding place for treasure, stores, etc. **2.** something so hidden.

cache·pot (kasʜ′pot), *n.* a decorative container for concealing a flower pot.

ca·chet (kasʜā′), *n.* a mark or sign of approval or distinction, esp. as conferred by a person in authority.

ca·chex·i·a (kəkek′sēə), *n.* general poor health accompanied by emaciation as the result of chronic disease.

cach·in·nate (kak′ənāt), *v.* to laugh noisily or excessively.

ca·chou (kəsʜo͞o′), *n.* a pill eaten to sweeten the breath.

ca·cique (kəsēk′), *n.* the head man of an Indian tribe in Mexico or the West Indies.

cac·o·de·mon (kak′ədē′mən), *n.* a demon or evil spirit.

cac·o·ë·thes (kak′o͞eē′*th*ēz), *n.* an insatiable desire; mania.

cac·o·gen·ic (kak′əjen′ik), *n.* See **dysgenics.**

ca·cog·ra·phy (kakog′rəfē), *n.* **1.** inartistic or illegible handwriting. See also **calligraphy. 2.** bad spelling. See also **orthography.**

ca·col·o·gy (kakol′əjē), *n.* defective speech.

ca·coph·o·ny (kəkof′ənē), *n.* harshness or discordance in sound. See also **euphony.** —**ca·coph′o·nous,** *adj.*

ca·cu·mi·nal (kəkyo͞o′mənl), *adj.* articulated with the tip of the tongue turned up to touch the roof of the mouth under the hard palate. Also **cerebral, retroflex.**

ca·das·tral (kədas′trəl), *adj.* of or pertaining to property boundaries, land divisions, etc.

ca·das·tre, ca·das·ter (kədas′tər), *n.* an official register of property, giving details of ownership, etc.

ca·dence (kā′dns), *n.* 1. the beat or measure of any rhythmical motion. 2. (in music) a sequence of chords showing the end of a section or phrase.

ca·dent (kā′dnt), *adj.* having rhythm or cadence.

ca·den·tial (kāden′sнəl), *adj.* denoting or relating to a cadence in music.

ca·den·za (kəden′zə), *n.* an elaborate, ostentatious passage for a solo instrument or voice in a concerto, aria, etc.

ca·dre (kä′drə), *n.* a nucleus of skilled people who train others in an expanding organization, military unit, etc.

ca·du·ce·us (kədoo′sēəs), *n.* the symbolic staff carried by Mercury as herald of the gods, now used as a symbol for medicine.

ca·du·ci·ty (kədoo′sitē), *n.* 1. senility. 2. the quality of being transitory; impermanence.

cae·cum (sē′kəm), *n., pl.* **cae·ca** (sē′kə). See **cecum.**

cae·no·gen·e·sis (sē′nəjen′isis), *n.* See **cenogenesis.**

ca·fard (kafar′), *n.* a mood of melancholy or deep depression.

ca·fé au lait (kaf′ā ō lā′), coffee with hot milk in equal proportions.

ca·fé brû·lot (kaf′ā broolō′), black coffee flavored with sugar, lemon, spices, and brandy, ignited briefly before being drunk.

caf·tan, kaf·tan (kaf′tən, käftän′), *n.* a coat-like garment with long sleeves and tied at the waist.

ca·hier (kayā′), *n.* a report of the proceedings, transactions, etc., of an official body.

Cai·no·zo·ic (kī′nəzō′ik), *n.* See **Cenozoic.**

cairn (kern), *n.* a heap of stones serving as a landmark, memorial, etc. Also **carn.**

cais·son disease (kā′sən). See **decompression sickness.**

cai·tiff (kā′tif), *n.* 1. a contemptible or cowardly person. —*adj.* 2. base; despicable.

ca·jole (kəjōl′), *v.* to coax or persuade with flattery; deceive with false promises. —**ca·jol′er·y,** *n.*

cakes and ale, the pleasures of life; enjoyment of material things.

cak·ra·var·tin, chak·ra·var·tin (cнuk′rəvär′tin), *n.* (in Indian philosophy) one who rules the world perfectly, bringing justice and peace to all.

cal·a·boose (kal′əboos), *n.* a prison; jail.

cal·a·man·co (kal′əmanG′kō), *n.* a woolen, glossy fabric brocaded in the warp so as to produce a pattern on one side only, common in the 18th century.

cal·a·thi·form (kal′əthəfôrm), *adj.* shaped like a cup.

calced (kalst), *adj.* having shoes on the feet; shod.

cal·car·e·ous (kalker′ēəs), *adj.* consisting of or containing calcium carbonate; chalky.

cal·ci·fi·ca·tion (kal′səfikā′sнən), *n.* the action of changing into lime, esp. by the deposition of lime salts in tissue.

cal·ci·fy (kal′səfī), *v.* to make hard, as by the deposition of calcium salts; make or become intransigent or unyielding.

cal·ci·mine (kal′səmīn), *n.* a white or tinted wash for distempering walls, ceilings, etc.

cal·cine (kal′sīn), *v.* to change into calx through the action of heat.

calc-tu·fa (kalk′too′fə), *n.* See **tufa.** Also **cal·tuff** (kal′tuf).

cal·cu·lous (kal′kyələs), *adj.* pertaining to or caused by a calculus or small stone.

cal·cu·lus (kal′kyələs), *n., pl.* **cal·cu·li** (kal′kyəlī). 1. (in mathematics) a systematic method of calculation using a special symbolic notation. 2. a stony mass sometimes found in the kidneys, gall bladder, etc., and usually made up of layers of mineral salts.

cal·de·ra (kalder′ə), *n.* a large crater formed by the collapse of the center of the cone of a volcano.

cal·e·fa·cient (kal′əfā′sHənt), *n.* a medicinal substance producing a feeling of warmth.

cal·e·fac·tion (kal′əfak′sHən), *n.* the act of heating; the state of being heated.

cal·e·fac·to·ry (kal′əfak′tərē), *adj.* producing heat.

cal·en·dar (kal′əndər), *n.* a list of motions for consideration; agenda.

ca·les·cent (kəles′ənt), *adj.* increasing in heat.

Cal·i·ban (kal′əban), *n.* a man showing brutal and bestial characteristics.

cal·i·ber (kal′əbər), *n.* 1. the internal diameter of a hollow cylinder, esp. of the barrel of a gun. 2. degree of merit or importance.

cal·i·brate (kal′əbrāt), *v.* to ascertain or check the graduations of (an instrument, etc.).

cal·i·cle (kal′ikəl), *n.* a cup-like shape, esp. as found in corals.

cal·i·duct (kal′idukt), *n.* a pipe used for conveying a means of heating, as hot air or water.

cal·i·pash (kal′əpasH), *n.* an edible greenish-colored gelatinous substance lying beneath the upper shell of a turtle.

cal·i·pee (kal′əpē), *n.* an edible, yellowish-colored gelatinous substance attached to the lower shell of a turtle.

ca·liph, ca·lif, ka·lif, ka·liph (kā′lif, kal′if), *n.* a religious or civil ruler in Muslim countries.

cal·iph·ate (kal′əfāt), *n.* the rank, office, or area of jurisdiction of a caliph.

cal·is·then·ics (kal′isthen′iks), *n.* physical exercises designed to develop bodily strength and grace of movement.

calk (kôk), *n.* an attachment to a shoe designed to prevent slipping on ice, snow, etc. Also **cal·kin** (kô′kin, kal′kin).

cal·let (kal′it, kä′lit), *n.* (in British dialect) 1. a prostitute; a woman of loose morals. 2. a shrewish, sharp-tongued woman.

cal·lig·ra·phy (kəlig′rəfē), *n.* the art of fine handwriting; penmanship. See also **cacography.**

cal·li·pyg·i·an (kal′əpij′ēən), *adj.* having well-formed buttocks.

cal·los·i·ty (kəlos′itē), *n.* the condition of being callous.

cal·lous (kal′əs), *adj.* unfeeling; insensitive; hardened; brutal.

cal·low (kal′ō), *adj.* lacking maturity; inexperienced.

cal·lus (kal′əs), *n.* 1. a piece of skin which has become thick or hard. 2. a substance issuing from the ends of broken bone, which helps to join them.

cal·ma·tive (kal′mətiv, kä′mətiv), *adj.* 1. tending to calm or soothe. —*n.* 2. that which calms or soothes; a sedative.

cal·o·re·cep·tor (kal′ōrisep′tər), *n.* a receptor which is stimulated by heat.

cal·o·res·cence (kal′əres′əns), *n.* incandescence resulting from the absorption by a body of radiation with a frequency less than that of visible light.

ca·lor·ic (kəlôr′ik), *adj.* relating to calories or to heat.

ca·lor·i·fa·cient (kəlôr′ifā′sHənt), *adj.* pertaining to heat-producing foods.

cal·o·rif·ic (kal′ərif′ik), *adj.* producing heat.

cal·o·rim·e·ter (kal′ərim′itər), *n.* an instrument which measures quantities of heat.

cal·o·rim·e·try (kal′ərim′itrē), *n.* the measurement of heat.

ca·lotte (kəlot′), *n.* 1. a skullcap, esp. as worn by Roman Catholic clerics. 2. a small dome.

calque (kalk), *n.* the borrowing by one language from another of a construction in which the structure remains the same but the meaningful elements are replaced by those of the native language.

cal·trop (kal′trəp), *n.* a spiked iron ball used to obstruct the passage of cavalry. Also **cal·throp** (kal′*th*rop), **cal·trap** (kal′trap).

cal·u·met (kal′yəmet), *n.* an ornamented ceremonial pipe used by North American Indians. Also **peacepipe**.

ca·lum·ni·ate (kəlum′nēāt), *v.* to malign; accuse falsely; spread malicious reports about. —**ca·lum·ni·a′ tion,** *n.*

cal·um·ny (kal′əmnē), *n.* a false statement; a malicious report intended to injure another's reputation. —**ca·lum′ni·ous,** *adj.*

calve (kav), *v.* **1.** (of a mass of ice) to become detached; break up. **2.** to split off a division or other corporate unit from a conglomerate.

cal·vi·ti·es (kalvisH′ēēz), *n.* the state of being bald.

cal·vous (kal′vəs), *adj.* bald.

calx (kalks), *n., pl.* **calx·es, cal·ces** (kal′sēz). lime.

cam (kam), *n.* an irregularly shaped disk or cylinder used for changing rotary into reciprocating motion, etc.

ca·ma·ra·de·rie (kam′ərä′dərē), *n.* loyalty and goodwill among comrades or friends.

cam·ber (kam′bər), *v.* **1.** to curve upward in the middle. —*n.* **2.** a slight curving or arching upward.

cam·bi·on (kam′bēən), *n.* the offspring of an incubus and a succuba.

cam·bist (kam′bist), *n.* one who deals in bills of exchange; one versed in foreign exchange.

Cam·bri·an (kam′brēən), *adj.* relating to the oldest geologic period, characterized by the preservation of many fossils in rocks.

ca·mel·o·pard (kəmel′əpärd), *n.* a giraffe.

Cam·em·bert (kam′əmber), *n.* a strong-smelling, soft-ripening, rich cheese.

cam·e·o (kam′ēo), *n.* **1.** a method of engraving in relief upon a gem, stone, etc. **2.** the gem or stone engraved in this way. **3.** a short piece of detailed polished writing, dramatic scene, etc., which gives a vivid presentation of its subject.

cam·er·al (kam′ərəl), *adj.* of or relating to a judicial or legislative chamber.

ca·mi·no re·al (kämē′nô reäl′), *pl.* **ca·mi·nos re·a·les** (kämē′nôs reä′les), (in Spanish) a highway or main road.

cam·i·on (kam′ēən), *n.* a wagon or truck used for carrying heavy loads.

ca·mise (kəmēz′), *n.* a loose-fitting shirt or gown.

cam·i·sole (kam′isōl), *n.* a woman's underbodice.

cam·let (kam′lit), *n.* a kind of hardwearing, waterproof cloth.

ca·mou·flet (kam′əflā′), *n.* a bomb, mine, etc., exploded underground, which makes a cavity but does not break the surface.

cam·ou·fleur (kam′əflur), *n.* one who disguises objects by the use of camouflage.

camp (kamp), *n.* **1.** exaggeration or extravagance in gesture or style, speech or writing, etc., esp. when inappropriate to the surroundings, context, etc. **2.** one who possesses these qualities. —*adj.* **3.** of or relating to these qualities or to one who possesses them. —*v.* **4.** to make an ostentation or flamboyant display, often in self-parody.

cam·pa·ni·le (kam′pənē′lē), *n.* a bell tower, esp. one separated from surrounding buildings.

cam·pa·nol·o·gy (kam′pənol′əjē), *n.* the technique or art of bell ringing or of making bells.

cam·pan·u·late (kampan′yəlit), *n.* shaped like a bell.

camp·er (kam′pər), *n.* a portable accommodation unit, carried on a pickup truck and used for camping, etc.

cam·pes·tral (kampes′trəl), *adj.* pertaining to the countryside.

cam·pim·e·ter (kampim′itər), *n.* an apparatus for testing the field of vision of the human eye.

camp·y (kam′pē), *adj.* extravagant or exaggerated in speech, gesture, etc., esp. as implying homosexual tendencies.

can·a·pé (kan′əpē, kan′əpā), *n.* a

piece of bread or toast topped with anchovies, caviar, or some other spread.

ca·nard (kənärd′), *n.* a false report or rumor; a hoax.

can·dent (kan′dənt), *adj.* heated to a white-hot state.

can·des·cent (kandes′ənt), *adj.* glowing, esp. as a result of intense heat; incandescent.

can·did (kan′did), *adj.* outspoken; sincere; frank; unreserved; straightforward.

can·dor (kan′dər), *n.* frankness; forthrightness; sincerity in speech or action.

can·na·bis (kan′əbis), *n.* a preparation of Indian hemp smoked as a drug; hashish.

can·nel·lo·ni (ka′nəlō′nē), *n. pl.* cylindrical pieces of pasta filled with meat or cheese. Also **can·ne·lons** (kan′əlonz).

can·ni·bal·ize (kan′əbəlīz), *v.* to dismantle (a machine, motor vehicle, etc.) in order to provide spare parts for use elsewhere.

can·non·ade (kan′ənād′), *n.* continuous, heavy artillery fire.

can·ny (kan′ē), *adj.* cautious; prudent; knowing; shrewd.

can·on (kan′ən), *n.* an established set of rules, principles, etc., regarded as inviolate.

ca·non·i·cal (kənon′ikəl), *adj.* orthodox; recognized; standard.

can·on·ize (kan′ənīz), *v.* **1.** to include within a canon, esp. of sacred writings. **2.** to treat as holy or sacrosanct.

Ca·no·pic jar (kanō′pik), a vase used by the ancient Egyptians to hold the entrails of a deceased person.

ca·no·rous (kənôr′əs), *adj.* pleasant sounding; melodious.

can·tan·ker·ous (kantaNG′kərəs), *adj.* ill-natured; quarrelsome.

can·thar·i·des (kan*th*är′idēz), *n.* See **Spanish fly.**

can·thus (kan′*th*əs), *n.* either of the angles formed by the junction of the upper and lower eyelids.

can·ti·cle (kan′tikəl), *n.* a hymn or song of praise.

can·ti·le·na (kan′tlē′nə), *n.* a simple melody.

can·ti·lev·er (kan′təlev′ər), *n.* a beam or member projecting from a vertical support and secured firmly only at one end.

can·til·late (kan′təlāt), *v.* to intone or chant. —**can·til·la′tion,** *n.*

canting arms, a coat of arms with a rebus-like heraldic device that makes a punning allusion to the name of the owner.

can·tle (kan′tl), *n.* **1.** a slice or portion. **2.** the rear part of a saddle, usually projecting upward.

can·to (kan′tō), *n., pl.* **can·tos.** one of the main divisions of a long poem.

can·tor (kan′tər), *n.* an official in a synagogue who leads the singing or sings the solo parts.

caou·tchouc (kou′CHŌŌk), *n.* the natural milky juice of rubber trees, a highly elastic solid substance; rubber.

ca·pa (kä′pə), *n.* the red cloak carried by a bullfighter.

cap-a-pie (kapəpē′), *adj.* from head to foot. Also, **cap-à-pié.**

ca·par·i·son (kəpar′isən), *n.* **1.** an ornamental covering for a horse. —*v.* **2.** to dress or deck out in a sumptuous or ornate fashion.

ca·pe·a·dor (kä′pēədôr′), *n.* one who assists a matador by waving his red cloak at the bull in order to distract it.

cap·il·lar·i·ty (kap′ilar′itē), *n.* the action by which the surface of a liquid in contact with a solid is raised or lowered, depending on surface tension and the forces of cohesion and adhesion.

cap·il·lar·y (kap′əlerē), *adj.* **1.** relating to or occurring in a tube having a very small bore. —*n.* **2.** one of the tiny blood vessels connecting arteries with veins.

cap·i·tal·ism (kap′itəlizm), *n.* an economic system based on the ownership by private individuals of the means of production, distribution, and exchange.

cap·i·tal·ist (kap′itəlist), *n.* one who

makes use of his wealth for business ventures.

cap·i·tal·is·tic (kap/itəlis/tic), *adj.* relating to or practicing capitalism.

cap·i·ta·tion (kap/itā/sHən), *n.* a method of assessment or enumeration by the head.

ca·pi·teux (kapētoo/), *adj. French.* (of wine) heady.

ca·pit·u·lar (kəpicH/ələr), *adj.* relating to an ecclesiastical chapter.

ca·pit·u·late (kəpicH/əlāt), *v.* to surrender on agreed terms; surrender unconditionally. —**ca·pit·u·la/ tion,** *n.*

cap·o·ral (kap/ərəl), *n.* a variety of coarse tobacco.

ca·pote (kəpōt/), *n.* a long hooded cloak.

cap·puc·ci·no (kap/ooCHē/nō), *n.* expresso coffee served with milk and sometimes cream.

ca·pric·ci·o (kəprē/CHēō), *n., pl.* **ca· pric·ci·os, ca·pric·ci** (kəprē/CHē). a frolic, caper, or prank.

ca·price (kəprēs/), *n.* a sudden whim or fancy; an abrupt and unpredictable change. —**ca·pri·cious** (kəprisH/əs), *adj.*

cap·ri·ole (kap/rēōl), *n.* a spring, leap, or caper.

cap·si·cum (kap/səkəm), *n.* common garden pepper.

cap·stan (kap/stən), *n.* a winch for moving heavy weights by winding a cable around a vertical drum which is rotated by hand or mechanically.

cap·tious (kap/sHəs), *adj.* characterized by a tendency to find faults; hard to please; critical.

cap·ti·vate (kap/təvāt), *v.* to enchant; to enthrall by some special charm; to appeal irresistibly.

car·a·van·sa·ry (kar/əvan/sərē), *n.* (in the East) an inn with a courtyard providing accommodation for caravans. Also **car·a·van·se·rai** (kar/- əvan/sərī).

car·a·vel (kar/əvel), *n.* a small, two- or three-masted vessel, used by the Spanish and Portuguese during the 15th and 16th centuries.

car·bine (kär/bīn), *n.* a short rifle,

esp. as formerly used by mounted troops.

Car·bon·if·er·ous (kar/bənif/ərəs), *adj.* of a period occurring from 270 million to 350 million years ago, noted for its vegetation, from which modern coal is mined.

car·boy (kär/boi), *n.* a large container, usually of glass and protected by basketwork, for holding corrosive acids, etc. See also **demijohn.**

car·bun·cle (kär/buNGkəl), *n.* **1.** a local inflammation of the skin resulting in the discharge of pus and sloughing of dead tissue. **2.** a rounded, unfaceted garnet.

car·ca·net (kär/kənet), *n.* an ornamental jeweled circlet or neckband.

car·cin·o·gen (kärsin/əjin), *n.* a substance which produces cancer. —**car· cin·o·gen/ic,** *adj.*

car·ci·no·ma (kar/sənō/mə), *n., pl.* **car·ci·no·mas, car·ci·no·ma·ta** (kar/sənō/mətə). a malignant tumor; a cancer.

car·da·mom (kär/dəməm), *n.* the aromatic seed of various Asian plants used as a spice or condiment and in medicine. Also **car/da·mum.**

car·di·ac (kär/dēak), *adj.* **1.** relating to the heart. **2.** relating to the anterior portion of the stomach.

car·di·al·gi·a (kär/dēal/jēə), *n.* **1.** heartburn. **2.** See **cardiodynia.**

car·di·ec·to·my (kär/dēek/təmē), *n.* **1.** excision of the heart. **2.** excision of the cardiac portion of the stomach.

car·di·o·dyn·i·a (kär/dēōdin/ēə), *n.* pain in or near the heart.

car·di·oid (kär/dēoid), *n.* a mathematical curve in the shape of a heart.

car·di·ol·o·gy (kär/dēol/əjē), *n.* the study of the heart and its functions.

car·di·o·meg·a·ly (kär/dēōmeg/əlē), *n.* pathological enlargement of the heart.

car·di·o·vas·cu·lar (kär/dēōvas/ kyələr), *adj.* relating to or affecting the heart and blood vessels.

card punch. See **key punch.**

cark·ing (kär/kiNG), *adj.* **1.** disturbed; worried; anxious. **2.** penny-pinching; stingy; miserly.

car·min·a·tive (kärmin′ətiv, kär′-mənātiv), *n.* a drug which relieves flatulence.

car·mine (kär′min, kär′mīn), *n.* a rich crimson color.

carn (kärn), *n.* See **cairn.**

car·nage (kär′nij), *n.* the killing of large numbers of people; massacre.

car·nal (kär′nl), *adj.* **1.** worldly; unspiritual. **2.** pertaining to the desires of the flesh; sensual.

car·ne·ous (kär′nēəs), *adj.* resembling or having the color of flesh.

car·net (kärnā′), *n., pl.* **car·nets** (kärnāz′). a customs license permitting a motor vehicle to be taken from one country to another.

car·ni·fi·ca·tion (kär′nəfəkā′sHən), *n.* the conversion into flesh of other tissue.

car·nose (kär′nōs), *adj.* relating to flesh; fleshlike.

ca·rot·id (kərot′id), *n.* either of the two main arteries in the neck.

carp (kärp), *v.* to find fault unreasonably; complain in a querulous manner.

car·pal (kär′pəl), *adj.* of or relating to the wrist.

car·pe di·em (kär′pe dē′em), *Latin.* enjoy the present; get the most out of life while ignoring the future.

car·phol·o·gy (kärfol′əjē), *n.* See **floccillation.**

car·poph·a·gous (kärpof′əgəs), *adj.* fruit-eating.

car·re·four (kar′əfŏŏr), *n.* a junction or crossroads; public square.

car·rel, car·rell (kar′əl), *n.* a small alcove in library reserved for individual study.

car·ri·on (kar′ēən), *n.* dead and rotting flesh.

carte blanche (kärt blansH′), *pl.* **cartes blanches** (kärts blansH′). full and unconditional power of action.

car·tel (kärtel′), *n.* an organization of business interests designed to regulate output and prices.

car·tel·ist (kär′telist), *n.* a member of a cartel.

car·tel·ize (kär′təlīz), *v.* to form into a cartel.

car·ti·lag·i·nous (kär′tlaj′ənəs), *adj.* relating to or resembling cartilage.

car·to·gram (kär′təgram), *n.* the presentation of statistics on a map base.

car·to·man·cy (kär′təmansē), *n.* fortune-telling or divination by the use of playing cards.

car·touche, car·touch (kärtōōsH′), *n.* an oblong or oval design enclosing characters representing a sovereign's name, as on ancient Egyptian monuments.

car·vel-built (kär′vəlbilt′), *adj.* (of a ship) built with the planks meeting flush at the seams and not overlapping. See also **clinker-built.**

car·y·at·id (kar′ēat′id), *n., pl.* **car·y·at·ids, car·y·at·i·des** (kar′ēat′idēz). (in architecture) a draped female figure serving as a supporting column. See also **atlas.**

cas·ca·bel (kas′kəbel), *n.* a projection behind the breech of a muzzleloading cannon.

ca·se·ate (kā′sēāt), *v.* to be converted into a cheeselike substance. —**ca·se·a′tion,** *n.*

ca·se·fy (kā′səfī), *v.* to turn into or become like cheese.

ca·sern (kəsurn′), *n.* an army barracks.

cash·ier (kasHēr′), *v.* to dismiss with ignomy from a position of responsibility, esp. in military service.

casque (kask), *n.* a head covering resembling a helmet in shape.

cas·sa·tion (kasā′sHən), *n.* cancellation; abrogation; annulment.

cas·sol·ette (kas′əlet′), *n.* a receptacle in which individual portions of food are cooked and then served; a casserole.

cas·sou·let (kas′əlā′), *n.* a stew, originally French, made of white beans, pork, garlic sausage, etc.

cas·tel·lan (kas′tlən), *n.* the warden or governor of a fort or castle.

cas·tel·la·ny (kas′tlā′nē), *n.* **1.** the office or dominion of a castellan. **2.** the land belonging to a castle.

cas·tel·lat·ed (kas′tlā′tid), *adj.* having turrets and battlements like a castle.

cas·ti·gate (kas'təgāt), *v.* to chastise, punish, or reprove severely.

cas·tra·me·ta·tion (kas'trəmətā'sHən), *n.* the art of planning or the act of setting up a military camp.

cas·tra·to (kasträ'tō), *n.* (formerly) a male singer castrated in boyhood to preserve his soprano or contralto voice.

cas·u·al·ism (kazH'ōōəlizm), *n.* a philosophical doctrine holding that all events occur by chance.

cas·u·ist (kazH'ōōist), *n.* one skilled in the application of general moral rules to specific cases, esp. one who reasons speciously or dishonestly.

cas·u·is·tic (kazH'ōōis'tik), *adj.* relating to casuists or casuistry; specious or intellectually dishonest.

cas·u·ist·ry (kazH'ōōistrē), *n.* the application of general moral rules to specific cases, esp. dishonestly or speciously.

ca·sus bel·li (kä'sōōs bel'lē), *pl.* **ca·sus bel·li**. *Latin.* an event which leads to or justifies a declaration of war.

ca·tab·o·lism, ka·tab·o·lism (kətab'əlizm), *n.* destructive metabolism; a process in which a complex substance is transformed into a simpler one. See also **anabolism.** —**cat·a·bol'ic,** *adj.*

cat·a·chre·sis (kat'əkrē'sis), *n.* the misuse or wrong use of words.

cat·a·clysm (kat'əklizm), *n.* a violent change or upheaval, esp. one involving sweeping political or social changes.

cat·a·clys·mic (kat'əkliz'mik), *adj.* relating to, resulting from, or having the effect of a cataclysm.

ca·tad·ro·mous (kətad'rəməs), *adj.* denoting fish, like the eel, that swim from a fresh-water river down to the sea to spawn. See also **anadromous, diadromous.**

cat·a·falque (kat'əfalk), *n.* a raised platform on which the coffin of a dead person is laid.

cat·a·lep·sy (kat'əlepsē), *n.* a physical condition associated with a mental or nervous disorder and characterized by complete muscular rigidity, loss of sensation, etc. Also **cataleptic seizure.**

ca·ta·logue rai·son·né (kat'əlog rezənā'), *pl.* **ca·ta·logues rai·son·nés** (kat'əlogz rezənā'), a catalog with annotations on or detailed descriptions of the items listed.

ca·tal·y·sis (kətal'isis), *n.*, *pl.* **ca·tal·y·ses** (kətal'isēz). an increase in the rate of a chemical reaction by the introduction of a substance which does not itself undergo permanent change.

cat·a·lyst (kat'əlist), *n.* a substance which brings about catalysis.

cat·a·lyze (kat'əlīz), *v.* to subject to or act upon by catalysis.

cat·a·mite (kat'əmīt), *n.* a boy kept for taking part in homosexual activities.

cat·am·ne·sis (kat'amnē'sis), *n.*, *pl.* **cat·am·ne·ses** (kat'amnē'sēz). the medical history of a sick person.

cat·a·pha·sia (kat'əfā'zHə), *n.* a disorder of speech marked by constant repetition of a word or phrase.

cat·a·pho·re·sis (kat'əfərē'sis), *n.* the action of passing medicinal substances through living tissue in the direction of a positive electric current; electrophoresis.

cat·a·phract (kat'əfrakt), *n.* **1.** an armed warship of ancient Greece. **2.** a Roman soldier in mail.

cat·a·pla·sia, kat·a·pla·sia (kat'əplā'zHə), *n.* degeneration of cells or tissues or reversion to a more primitive form.

cat·a·plasm (kat'əplazm), *n.* a poultice.

ca·tas·ta·sis (kətas'təsis), *n.*, *pl.* **ca·tas·ta·ses** (kətas'təsēz). that part of a play immediately preceding the climax. See also **catastrophe, epitasis, protasis.**

ca·tas·tro·phe (kətas'trəfē), *n.* the decisive point in a play, esp. a tragedy. See also **catastasis, epitasis, protasis.**

ca·tas·tro·phism (kətas'trəfizm), *n.* the theory that important geological alterations in the structure of the earth were caused by catastrophes rather than by gradual development.

cat·a·to·ni·a, kat·a·to·ni·a (kat′ətō′-nēə), *n.* a mental disorder marked by catalepsy.

catch·ment (kaCH′mənt), *n.* something which collects water, as a reservoir; the water thus collected.

cat·e·che·sis (kat′əkē′sis), *n.* oral instruction in the doctrines of Christianity. —**cat·e·chet·i·cal** (kat′əket′-ikəl), *adj.*

cat·e·chism (kat′əkizm), *n.* a manual of instruction in the doctrines of Christianity, esp. in question and answer form. —**cat′e·chist**, *n.*

cat·e·chize (kat′əkīz), *v.* to teach doctrines, esp. those of Christianity, by means of question and answer.

cat·e·chu·men (kat′əkyōō′mən), *n.* one who is receiving instruction in the basic elements of Christianity.

cat·e·gor·i·cal (kat′əgôr′ikəl), *adj.* without qualification; unconditional; absolute.

ca·te·na (kətē′nə), *n., pl.* **ca·te·nae** (kətē′nē). a connected series of related things, esp. extracts from the writings of the fathers of the church.

cat·e·nar·y (kat′ənerē), *n.* a curve formed by a cord hanging freely from two fixed points.

cat·e·nate (kat′ənāt), *v.* to connect in a series; link together.

ca·thar·sis, ka·thar·sis (kəthär′sis), *n.* **1.** (in medicine) purging; evacuation. **2.** the relieving of emotions through the effects of tragic drama.

ca·thar·tic (kəthär′tik), *adj.* **1.** relating to catharsis. —*n.* **2.** a purgative medicine.

cath·e·ter (kath′itər), *n.* a tube designed to drain fluids from the body, esp. urine from the bladder.

cathode ray tube (kath′ōd), a vacuum tube in which cathode rays in the form of spots or lines can be observed on a fluorescent screen.

cath·o·lic (kath′əlik), *adj.* **1.** relating to the Christian church as a whole. **2.** of general or universal interest. **3.** broad-minded or liberal in tastes, views, etc.

cat's-paw (kats′pô′), *n.* one used by another as a tool; a dupe.

cau·cus (kô′kəs), *n., pl.* **cau·cus·es** (kô′kəsiz), *n.* **1.** a meeting of persons belonging to a political party to nominate or elect candidates, decide on policy, etc. —*v.* **2.** to come together in a caucus.

cau·dal (kô′dl), *adj.* relating to, or situated at or near the tail.

cau·dle (kô′dl), *n.* a warm drink for invalids made from wine, brandy, etc., mixed with bread, gruel, eggs, sugar, and spices.

cau·sa·tion (kôzā′sHən), *n.* the act of causing; cause; the relationship between cause and effect.

cause cé·lè·bre (kôz səleb′rə), *pl.* **causes cé·lè·bres** (kôz səleb′rəz). any event that creates widespread interest, esp. a famous trial.

cau·se·rie (kōzərē′), *n.* a chat; an informal discussion.

caus·tic (kôs′tik), *adj.* having a corrosive effect; biting or sarcastic.

cau·ter·ize (kô′tərīz), *v.* to burn with a hot iron, esp. in order to sear or destroy tissue. —**cau′ter·y**, *n.*

ca·vate (kā′vāt), *adj.* hollowed out so as to form a cave, etc.

ca·ve·at (kā′vēat), *n.* a legal notice to a court to suspend proceedings temporarily.

ca·ve·at emp·tor (kā′vēat emp′tôr). the principle that the buyer of goods buys at his own risk unless the goods are covered by a warranty.

ca·ve ca·nem (kä′we kä′nem), *Latin.* beware of the dog.

cav·il (kav′əl), *v.* **1.** to raise trivial objections; quibble; find fault unnecessarily. —*n.* **2.** an irritating and pointless objection.

cav·i·ta·tion (kav′itā′sHən), *n.* the formation of partial vacuums in a flowing liquid in areas of very low pressure.

ca·vo-re·lie·vo (kä′vōrilē′vō), *n., pl.* **ca·vo-re·lie·vos.** a kind of sculpture in relief in which the highest points are beneath the level of the original surface. See also **intaglio.**

ce·cum, cae·cum (sē′kəm), *n., pl.*

ce·ca, cae·ca (sē′kə). (in anatomy) a cavity open at one end, esp. the beginning of the large intestine.

cede (sēd), *v.* to give up, surrender, or yield.

ce·dil·la (sidil′ə), *n.* a mark placed under a letter, usually indicating a sibilant pronunciation.

ceil (sēl), *v.* to overlay with wood or plaster, as the ceiling of a room, etc.

cel·a·don (sel′ədon), *n.* a porcelain having a light green glaze.

cel·a·ture (sel′əcнōōr), *n.* the process of embossing metal.

cel·e·brant (sel′əbrənt), *n.* the priest who officiates at the Eucharist.

ce·ler·i·ty (səler′itē), *n.* rapidity; speed.

celestial mechanics, the application of Newton's law of gravitation and the laws of dynamics to the movements of celestial bodies.

celestial navigation, navigation by observation of the position of celestial bodies.

ce·li·ac disease, coe·li·ac disease (sē′lēak), a nutritional disorder in young children marked by poor digestion, diarrhea, etc.

cel·i·ba·cy (sel′əbəsē), *n.* the state of being unmarried, esp. as the result of a religious vow.

cel·i·bate (sel′əbət), *n.* **1.** one who does not marry, esp. as the result of a religious vow. —*adj.* **2.** unmarried.

cel·lar·et, cel·lar·ette (sel′əret′), *n.* a cabinet or cupboard in which bottles of wine are stored.

ce·lo·scope (sē′ləskōp), *n.* a device used in medicine for examining body cavities. Also **ce·li·o·scope** (sē′lēəskōp).

ce·lot·o·my (səlot′əmē), *n.* See **herniotomy.**

Cel·si·us (sel′sēəs), *n.* See **centigrade.**

cel·ure (sel′yər), *n.* a decorated canopy for a bed, throne, etc.

ce·men·ti·tious (sē′mentisн′əs), *adj.* having the properties of cement.

cen·a·cle (sen′əkəl), *n.* the room in which the Last Supper was held.

ce·nes·the·sia (sē′nisthē′zнə), *n.* See **coenesthesia.**

ce·no·bite (sē′nəbīt), *n.* a member of a religious group living a communal life.

ce·no·gen·e·sis, cae·no·gen·e·sis (sē′nəjen′isis), *n.* (in biology) the introduction, in the development of an individual, of characteristics which differentiate it from the earlier phylogeny of its race or stock. See also **palingenesis.**

cen·o·taph (sen′ətaf), *n.* a tomb or monument erected as a memorial to a deceased person who is buried elsewhere.

Ce·no·zo·ic (sē′nəzō′ik), *adj.* relating to the present or tertiary geological era, marked by the evolution of mammals. Also **Cainozoic.**

cense (sens), *v.* to perfume with a censer; burn incense near.

cen·ser (sen′sər), *n.* a receptacle for holding burning incense.

cen·sure (sen′sнər), *n.* **1.** strong condemnation or disapproval. —*v.* **2.** to blame or condemn; criticize severely.

cen·te·nar·y (sen′tənerē), *adj.* **1.** relating to a period of 100 years. —*n.* **2.** a centennial.

cen·ten·ni·al (senten′ēəl), *adj.* **1.** relating to or marking the completion of 100 years. —*n.* **2.** a 100th anniversary.

center of gravity, that point of a body at which it will balance if supported.

cen·tes·i·mal (sentes′əməl), *adj.* relating to or characterized by a division into hundredths.

cen·ti·grade (sen′təgrād), *adj.* relating to a thermometer in which a scale of 100 equal degrees is fixed between the freezing point and boiling point of water.

cen·ti·gram (sen′təgram), *n.* 1/100th of a gram.

cen·ti·li·ter (sen′təlē′tər), *n.* 1/100th of a liter.

cen·ti·me·ter (sen′təmē′tər), *n.* 1/100th of a meter.

cen·ti·me·ter-gram-sec·ond (sen′təmē′tərgram′sek′ənd), *adj.* relating to the system of measurement in which the centimeter, gram, and second are the basic units of length, mass, and time, respectively. *Abbrev.:* **cgs.**

cen·trif·u·gal (sentrif′yəgəl), *adj.* proceeding or acting in a direction away from the center.

cen·tri·fuge (sen′trəfyoōj), *n.* an apparatus which uses centrifugal force to separate substances having different densities.

cen·trip·e·tal (sentrip′itl), *adj.* proceeding toward or acting upon the center.

cen·tu·ple (sen′təpəl), *adj.* a hundredfold; one hundred times as great.

ce·phal·ic (səfal′ik), *adj.* relating to the head.

ceph·a·lo·pod (sef′ələpod), *n.* a class of mollusks including the squid, octopus, etc., having tentacles on the head.

ce·ra·ceous (sərā′sHəs), *adj.* resembling wax in appearance or feel.

ce·ram·ic (səram′ik), *adj.* relating to the manufacture of products from clay, etc.

ce·rat·ed (sēr′ātid), *adj.* covered with wax.

cer·a·tin (ser′ətin), *n.* See **keratin.**

cer·a·toid (ser′ətoid), *adj.* horny; resembling horn.

cer·e·bel·lum (ser′əbel′əm), *n.,* *pl.* **cer·e·bel·lums, cer·e·bel·la** (ser′-əbel′ə). part of the hindbrain which coordinates movement and helps balance.

cer·e·bral (ser′əbrəl), *adj.* **1.** relating to the cerebrum. **2.** See **cacuminal.**

cerebral palsy, a kind of paralysis caused by injury to the brain.

cer·e·brate (ser′əbrāt), *v.* to think; use one's mind.

cerebrospinal meningitis (ser′-əbrōspī′nl), inflammation of the meninges of the brain and the spinal cord.

cer·e·brum (ser′əbrəm), *n.* the larger, anterior part of the brain concerned with conscious and voluntary mental processes.

cere·cloth (sēr′klôth′), *n.* a wax-coated, waterproof cloth, used as a winding sheet.

cere·ment (sēr′mənt), *n.* usually *pl.* a cerecloth used as a shroud for the dead.

ce·rif·er·ous (sərif′ərəs), *adj.* producing wax.

ce·ro·graph (sēr′əgraf), *n.* an engraving on a wax surface. —**ce·rog′ra·phy,** *n.*

ce·ro·plas·tic (sēr′əplas′tik), *adj.* relating to modeling in wax.

cer·ti·o·ra·ri (sur′sHēərer′ē), *n.* a writ issued by a higher court calling up for review of the records of the proceedings of a lower court.

ce·ru·le·an (səroō′lēən), *adj.* deep blue; resembling the blue of the sky.

ce·ru·men (siroō′mən), *n.* a waxy secretion from the glands of the external ear.

cer·ve·lat (sur′vəlat), *n.* a smoked sausage made of pork and beef. Also **cer′ve·las.**

cer·vi·cal (sur′vikəl), *adj.* relating to the cervix or the neck.

cer·vine (sur′vīn), *adj.* relating to deer; deerlike.

cer·vix (sur′viks), *n.,* *pl.* **cer·vix·es, cer·vi·ces** (sur′visēz). the neck or any part resembling a neck, esp. the narrow outer end of the uterus.

ces·sion (sesH′ən), *n.* the act of yielding something to another; surrender.

ce·ta·cean (sitā′sHən), *adj.* **1.** belonging to a marine mammal family including whales, dolphins, etc. —*n.* **2.** a cetacean mammal.

ce·te·ris pa·ri·bus (set′əris par′ibəs), *Latin.* other things being equal.

ce·tol·o·gy (sētol′əjē), *n.* the branch of zoology that deals with whales.

cha·bouk, cha·buk (cHä′boŏk), *n.* a whip used in eastern countries to inflict corporal punishment.

cha·cun à son goût (sHakoōnasôn-goō′), everyone to his own taste.

chad (cHad), *n.* the paper removed when holes are perforated in a card or tape.

chae·toph·o·rous (kitof′ərəs), *adj.* bristly; having bristles.

chaff (cHaf), *n.* strips of metal dropped by aircraft to confuse enemy radar systems. Also **window.**

cha·grin (shəgrin′), *n*. **1.** disappointment, vexation. —*v*. **2.** to cause disappointment or vexation to.

chak·ra·var·tin (chukrəvär′tin), *n*. See **cakravartin**.

chal·ced·o·ny (chalsed′ənē), *n*. a translucent variety of quartz, often pale blue or gray in color.

chal·cog·ra·phy (kalkog′rəfē), *n*. the technique of engraving on copper or brass.

chal·co·lith·ic (kal′kəlith′ik), *adj*. relating to or characteristic of the Copper Age.

chal·lah (khä′lə), *n*., *pl*. **chal·lahs, chal·loth** (khälôt′). a kind of Jewish bread containing eggs.

chal·lis (shal′ē), *n*. a soft woolen or cotton fabric.

chal·one (kal′ōn), *n*. a secretion of the endocrine glands that tends to depress activity.

cha·lyb·e·ate (kəlib′ēit), *adj*. (of a mineral spring, etc.) impregnated with salts of iron.

cha·made (shəmäd′), *n*. (formerly) a signal sounded on a drum calling an enemy to a truce or parley.

cham·ber·lain (chām′bərlin), *n*. an attendant upon a king or noble in his bedchamber; an official in charge of a royal household; a treasurer.

cham·fer (cham′fər), *n*. an oblique surface cut into the corner of a board, usually at an angle of 45°; a groove.

cham·paign (shampān′), *n*. an expanse of open country.

cham·per·ty (cham′pərtē), *n*. a device whereby a party who promotes litigation illegally shares in the proceeds.

cham·pi·gnon (shampin′yən), *n*., *pl*. **cham·pi·gnons**. a mushroom.

champ·le·vé (shänləvā′), *n*. a technique for making jewelry and other small objects in which enamel is fused onto designs on a metal base.

chan·cel (chan′səl), *n*. the area around the altar of a church, reserved for the clergy, choir, etc.

chan·cel·ler·y (chan′sələrē), *n*. the building or room in which the office of a chancellor is situated.

chan·cel·lor (chan′sələr), *n*. (in some countries) a title of various high-ranking officials, as judges, finance ministers, etc.

chan·cre (shang′kər), *n*. a sore or ulcer caused by syphilis.

chan·croid (shang′kroid), *n*. a soft venereal sore.

chan·dler (chand′lər), *n*. **1.** one who deals in naval stores or provisions. **2.** one who makes or sells candles.

chan·dler·y (chand′lərē), *n*. the warehouse, storeroom, or business of a chandler.

change·ling (chānj′ling), *n*. a child substituted for another in infancy; a strange or ugly child, esp. one supposedly left by fairies.

cha·no·yu (chä′nôyōō′), *n*. a Japanese tea ceremony.

chan·son (shan′sən), *n*., *pl*. **chan·sons**. a song, esp. as sung in French cabaret or music-hall.

chan·son de geste (shänsôn də zhest′), *pl*. **chan·sons de geste** (shänsôn də zhest′). a medieval French epic poem.

chan·son·nier (shänsənyā′), *n*., *pl*. **chan·son·niers** (shänsənyāz′). a nightclub entertainer who combines singing with telling stories, jokes, etc.

chan·teuse (shäntōōz′), *n*., *pl*. **chan·teu·ses** (shäntōōz′). a woman who sings in night clubs, etc.

chant·ey (shan′tē), *n*. a song sung by sailors at work.

chan·ti·cleer (chan′təklēr), *n*. a rooster or cock.

Chan·til·ly (shantil′ē), *n*. See **mousseline**.

chap·ar·ral (chapəral′), *n*. a dense thicket, esp. a growth of dwarf, evergreen oaks.

cha·pa·ti (chəpat′ē), *n*., *pl*. **cha·pa·ti** (chəpat′ē), **cha·pa·tis** (chəpat′ēz), **cha·pa·ties** (chəpat′ēz). a kind of Indian flat bread made of a dough of flour and water.

chap·book (chap′bŏŏk), *n*. a small book containing popular tales, ballads, etc.

cha·peau (shapō′), *n*., *pl*. **cha·peaux** (shapōz′). a hat.

chapel

chap·el (CHap′əl), *n.* a printing house or the association of employees belonging to it.

chap·fall·en (CHap′fôlən), *adj.* crestfallen; downcast; dejected.

chap·let (CHap′lit), *n.* **1.** a garland intended to be worn on the head. **2.** a string of beads.

chap·tal·i·za·tion (sHap′təlizā′sHən), *n.* the addition of sugar to wine before or during fermentation in order to increase the alcoholic content. —**chap′tal·ize,** *v.*

char-à-banc (sHar′əbaNG), *n., pl.* **char-à-banc, char-à-bancs.** a motor coach, esp. an open one, formerly used for sightseeing tours.

char·ac·ter·y (kar′iktərē), *n.* the use of symbols or characters to convey meaning; such symbols collectively.

char·cu·te·rie (sHärko͞otərē′), *n., pl.* **char·cu·te·ries** (sHärko͞otərēz′). (in France) a butcher's shop specializing in pork.

char·cu·tier (sHärko͞otēā′), *n., pl.* **char·cu·tiers** (sHärko͞otēāz′). a butcher who specializes in pork.

char·gé d'af·faires (sHärzHā′ dəfer′), *pl.* **char·gés d'af·faires** (sHärzHāz′ dəfer′). an official in charge of an embassy during the ambassador's absence.

char·i·ly (CHer′əlē), *adv.* cautiously; carefully.

cha·ris·ma (kəriz′mə), *n., pl.* **cha·ris·ma·ta** (kəriz′mətə). an outstanding quality in a person that gives him influence and authority over others.

cha·riv·a·ri (sHəriv′ərē′), *n.* See **shivaree.**

char·la·tan (sHär′lətn), *n.* one who fraudulently claims to have exceptional powers of some kind.

char·la·tan·ism (sHär′lətnizm), *n.* the practices of a charlatan. Also **char′la·tan·ry.**

char·nel (CHär′nl), *n.* a place where dead bodies are kept.

char·nu (sHarny′), *adj.* (of a wine) full-bodied.

char·rette, char·ette (sHəret′), *n.* an attempt to meet the deadline set for some task by an all-out effort.

char·ta (kär′tə), *n., pl.* **char·tae** (kär′tē). **1.** a piece of paper impregnated with medicine for external use. **2.** Also **char·tu·la** (kär′CHələ). a piece of paper folded to hold powdered medicine.

char·ta·ceous (kärtā′sHəs), *adj.* resembling paper.

char·tist (CHär′tist), *n.* a stock market official who makes forecasts by means of charts and graphs.

char·treuse (sHärtro͞oz′), *n.* a liqueur, usually pale green or yellow in color, made by Carthusian monks.

char·tu·lar·y (kär′CHəlerē), *n.* a collection or register of title deeds, etc.

char·vet (sHär′vā), *n.* a soft fabric in silk or rayon.

char·y (CHer′ē), *adj.* cautious; careful; wary; timid; frugal or sparing. —**char′i·ness,** *n.*

Cha·sid (hä′sid), *n., pl.* **Cha·sid·im** (häsid′im). See **Hasid.**

chas·ten (CHā′sən), *v.* **1.** to inflict punishment upon; chastise; discipline. **2.** calm; subdue; restrain.

chas·tise (CHastīz′), *v.* to punish or discipline by beating.

chas·u·ble (CHaz′yəbəl), *n.* a sleeveless outer vestment worn by a celebrant of mass.

chat·e·laine (sHat′lān), *n.* **1.** the mistress of a castle or large country house. **2.** a girdle or clasp for holding a large bunch of keys.

cha·ton (sHatôn′), *n.* an imitation gem made from paste.

cha·toy·ant (sHətoi′ənt), *adj.* **1.** having a changing luster or color. **2.** (of a jewel, etc.) reflecting a single beam of light when cut in a convex form.

chat·tel (CHat′l), *n.* a movable possession or item of property.

chauf·fer (CHô′fər), *n.* a small, portable stove.

chau·vin·ism (sHō′vənizm), *n.* excessive or blind patriotism; jingoism. —**chau′vin·ist,** *n.*

cheap-jack (CHēp′jak), *n.* a peddler, hawker, etc., who sells cheap goods.

ché·chia (sHäsH′yä), *n.* a close-fitting hat with a tassel, worn in the Middle East.

Ched·dar (CHed′ər), *n.* a hard, smooth cheese, yellow or white in color.

chee·cha·ko (CHēCHä′kō), *n.* a newcomer; a naive or inexperienced person; a greenhorn.

cheese-par·ing (CHēz′perinG), *adj.* miserly; mean; parsimonious.

chef-d'oeu·vre (sHedoō′vrə), *n.*, *pl.* **chefs-d'oeu·vres** (sHedoō′vrə). a masterpiece in literature or art.

chei·li·tis (kīlī′tis), *n.* an inflammation that affects the lips.

che·la (kē′lə), *n.*, *pl.* **che·lae** (kē′lē). a nipper- or pincer-like organ of certain crustaceans.

che·loid (kē′loid), *n.* See **keloid.**

che·lo·ni·an (kilō′nēən), *adj.* relating to or belonging to turtles.

chem·ic (kem′ik), *adj.* relating to alchemy.

chemical warfare, warfare using poisonous or corrosive gases.

chem·i·cul·ture (kem′əkul′CHər), *n.* hydroponics.

che·mig·ra·phy (kəmig′rəfē), *n.* the making of engravings with the use of chemicals.

chem·i·lum·i·nes·cence (kem′ə-loō′mənes′əns), *n.* light produced by chemical reaction at low temperatures. —**chem·i·lu·mi·nes′cent,** *adj.*

che·min de fer (sHəman′dəfer′), a card game similar to baccarat.

che·mise (sHəmēz′), *n.* a woman's one-piece, loose-fitting undergarment; a loose, straight-hanging dress.

chem·i·sette (sHemizet′), *n.* a woman's garment worn over a low-cut bodice.

chem·o·ki·ne·sis (kem′ōkinē′sis), *n.* an increase in activity in an organism as a result of a chemical substance.

chem·o·pause (kem′əpôz), *n.* the stratum or boundary lying between the chemosphere and the ionosphere.

chem·o·pro·phy·lax·is (kem′ōprō′-fəlak′sis), *n.* prophylaxis by the means of some chemical agent. —**chem·o·pro·phy·lac′tic,** *adj.*

chem·o·re·cep·tion (kem′ōrisep′-sHən), *n.* physiological response to a chemical stimulus.

chem·o·re·cep·tor (kem′ōrisep′tər),

n. any sense organ stimulated by chemical means.

chem·o·re·flex (kemərē′fleks), *n.* a reflex brought about by a chemical stimulus.

chem·o·sphere (kem′əsfēr), *n.* a stratum of the atmosphere in which the most intense chemical activity takes place.

chem·o·sur·ger·y (kem′ōsur′jərē), *n.* the use of a chemical agent to effect a result usually obtained by surgery, as the removal of tissue, etc.

chem·o·syn·the·sis (keməsin′*th*isis), *n.* the synthesis of organic compounds by means of energy resulting from chemical reactions. —**chem·o·syn·thet′ic,** *adj.*

chem·o·tax·is (kemətak′sis), *n.* the attraction or repulsion to chemical agents shown by a cell or organism. —**chem·o·tac′tic,** *adj.*

chem·o·ther·a·py (kemə*ther*′əpē), *n.* the use of chemical agents in the treatment of a disease. Also **chem·o·ther·a·peu·tics** (kem′ə*ther*′əpyoō′-tiks). —**chem·o·ther·a·peu′tic,** *adj.*

che·mot·ro·pism (kimō′trəpizm), *n.* growth or movement in plants and other organisms in response to the presence of chemical stimuli.

chem·ur·gy (kem′ərjē), *n.* a branch of applied chemistry which is concerned with the industrial utilization of organic substances derived from farm products.

che·nier (sHin′yər), *n.* a clump of oak trees growing on a hillock in marshy or swampy regions.

che·nille (sHənēl′), *n.* a fabric having a raised pile, used in the manufacture of bedspreads, etc.

cher·chez la femme (sHershā′ la fam′), *French.* look for the woman (as the cause of trouble, etc.).

che·root (sHəroōt′), *n.* a cigar cut square at each end.

cherry picker, any of various kinds of crane with a jointed boom for lifting loads vertically.

cher·so·nese (kur′sənēz), *n.* a peninsula.

chert (CHurt), *n.* a rock resembling

chervil

flint and composed of microcrystalline quartz.

cher·vil (CHur′vil), *n.* a herb with aromatic leaves, belonging to the parsley family and used to flavor salads, soups, etc.

che·val glass (sHəval′), a full-length mirror suspended on a frame so that it can be tilted.

cheval screen, a fire screen supported at the ends and mounted on legs.

che·vee (sHəvā′), *n.* **1.** a carving on a gem stone, having a figure in relief on a hollowed out background. **2.** a smooth gem, the surface of which forms a slight depression.

chev·ret (sHəvrā′), *n.* a variety of French cheese made from goat's milk.

chev·rette (sHəvret′), *n.* a thin variety of kidskin.

chev·y (CHev′ē), *v.* to chase; run after; annoy; worry; nag; harass.

chez (sHā), *prep. French.* at or to the home of; with; in.

chi·a·ro·scu·ro (kēär′əskyŏŏr′ō), *n.* (in painting) the treatment or arrangement of light and shade in a picture in order to create a general effect. Also **chi·a·ro·o·scu·ro** (kēär′-ŏŏskyŏŏr′ō).

chi·bouk, chi·bouque (CHibŏŏk′), *n.* a Turkish tobacco pipe having a long stem.

chi·cane (sHikān′), *n.* deceit; chicanery.

chi·can·er·y (sHikā′nərē), *n.* trickery by the use of subterfuge or sophistry; sharp practice.

chi·chi (sHē′sHē′), *adj.* elegant or fashionable in an ornate or pretentious manner.

chick·pea (CHik′pē′), *n.* a plant bearing edible seeds, looking like peas, eaten in S. Europe and Latin America. Also **garbanzo.**

chic·le (CHik′əl), *n.* a gum obtained from the latex of the sapodilla and used in making chewing gum.

chide (CHīd), *v.* to reprove, scold, or rebuke; voice disapproval; worry; harass.

chig·oe (CHig′ō), *n.* a flea of the Caribbean region and Africa, the female of which burrows under the skin of man and animals. Also **chig·ger** (CHig′ər), **jigger.**

child·bed (CHīld′bed′), *n.* the condition of a woman in labor.

chil·i·arch (kil′ēärk), *n.* (in ancient Greece and Rome) an officer in charge of a thousand men.

chil·i·asm (kil′ēazm), *n.* the doctrine that Christ will return to reign on earth for a thousand years.

chil·i con car·ne (CHil′ē kon kär′nē), a Mexican dish made from meat, chilies, peppers and beans.

chi·me·ra (kimēr′ə), *n.* **1.** a mythological monster commonly shown as having a lion's head, a goat's body and a serpent's tail. **2.** any imagined horror or morbid fancy. **3.** (in biology) an organism having tissues of genetically different kinds.

chinch·y (CHin′CHē), *adj.* miserly, stingy, or cheap.

chine (CHīn), *n.* the backbone of an animal.

chi·noi·se·rie (sHēnwoz′ərē′), *n.* a style of decoration or ornamentation characterized by imitations of supposedly Chinese motifs.

chintz·y (CHint′sē), *adj.* tawdry; cheap; gaudy.

chirk (CHurk), *v.* to make a strident or shrill sound.

chi·rog·ra·phy (kīrog′rəfē), *n.* handwriting or penmanship. —**chi·ro·graph′ic,** *adj.*

chi·ro·man·cy (kīr′əmansē), *n.* divination by examining the palm of the hand.

chi·rop·o·dy (kīrop′ədē), *n.* the treatment of corns, bunions, and other foot ailments. —**chi·rop′o·dist,** *n.*

chi·ro·prac·tic (kīrəprak′tik), *n.* a system of treatment involving the manipulation of the spinal column, based on the theory that disease is caused by the malfunction of nerves. —**chi′ro·prac·tor,** *n.*

chirr (CHur), *v.* to make the trilling sound characteristic of a grasshopper or cricket.

chi-square (kī'skwer), *n.* (in statistics) the sum of the quotients, the result of dividing the square of the difference between the observed and expected values of a quantity by the expected value.

chi·tin (kī'tin), *n.* a horny, organic substance forming part of the outer integument of some insects and crustaceans.

chit·ter (CHit'ər), *v.* to chirp or twitter.

chlo·ro·phyll (klôr'əfil), *n.* the green coloring substance of plants and leaves associated with the production of carbohydrates by photosynthesis. —**chlo·ro·phyl'lous**, *adj.*

chlo·ro·sis (klôrō'sis), *n.* a diseased condition in plant tissues marked by a tendency to turn yellow.

chlor·prom·a·zine (klôrprom'əzēn), *n.* a drug used to depress the central nervous system and prevent nausea and vomiting.

chok·er (CHō'kər), *n.* a short necklace that fits tightly round the throat.

cho·le·cys·ti·tis (ko'lisistī'tis), *n.* inflammation of the gall bladder.

chol·e·lith (kol'əlith), *n.* a gallstone.

cho·les·ter·ol (kəles'tərōl), *n.* a sterol found in egg yolk, meat, and dairy fats, the main ingredient of the plaques which clog arteries, leading to atherosclerosis.

cho·les·ter·ol·e·mi·a (kəles'tərōlē'-mēə), *n.* a condition in which an abnormal amount of cholesterol is present in the blood.

cho·li, cho·lee (CHō'lē), *n.* a short blouse worn by women in India.

chon·dral (kon'drəl), *adj.* relating to cartilage.

chon·drule (kon'drōōl), *n.* a rounded mass often found in meteoric stones.

choo·ra (CHōōr'ə), *n.* a kind of single-edged Indian dagger.

chop·log·ic (CHop'loj'ik), *n.* an excessively complicated or specious way of reasoning.

cho·ra·gus (kərā'gəs), *n., pl.* **cho·ra·gi** (kərā'jī), **cho·ra·gus·es.** one who officiates at an entertainment, festival, etc. Also **cho·re·gus** (kərē'gəs).

cho·re·a (kərē'ə), *n.* a nervous disorder characterized by involuntary, spasmodic movements.

cho·re·o·graph (kôr'ēəgraf), *v.* to compose choreography for; work as a choreographer.

cho·re·og·ra·pher (kôr'ēog'rəfər), *n.* one who creates dance movements for stage dances, esp. ballet.

cho·re·og·ra·phy (kôr'ēog'rəfē), *n.* the art of composing and arranging techniques, movements, etc., for dances, esp. ballet.

cho·rog·ra·phy (kərog'rəfē), *n.* the technique of systematically mapping a region or district.

choroid coat (kôr'oid), a vascular membrane lining the eyeball.

chor·tle (CHôr'tl), *v.* to laugh or chuckle triumphantly or gleefully.

chouse (CHous), *v.* **1.** to cheat or swindle. —*n.* **2.** a fraud; swindle.

chow-chow (CHou'CHou), *n.* mixed pickles in mustard sauce.

chres·tom·a·thy (krestom'əthē), *n.* a selection of excerpts from literary works, esp. in a foreign language. —**chres·to·math'ic**, *adj.*

chrism (krizm), *n.* consecrated oil used in certain sacraments.

Christian Science, a religion based on a particular interpretation of the Scriptures and including the practice of spiritual healing.

Chris·to·cen·tric (kristəsen'trik), *adj.* based exclusively on the doctrines of Jesus Christ.

Chris·to·gram (kris'təgram), *n.* a symbolic representation of Christ.

Chris·tol·o·gy (kristol'əjē), *n.* that branch of theology concerned with the nature, person and work of Jesus Christ.

Chris·toph·a·ny (kristof'ənē), *n.* an appearance of Christ on earth after the time of his Resurrection.

chro·mat·ic (krōmat'ik), *adj.* **1.** relating to color. **2.** (in music) modifying the normal scale by the use of accidentals.

chro·mat·i·cism (krōmat'isizm), *n.* (in music) the use of chromatic tones.

chro·ma·tic·i·ty (krōmətis'itē), *n.* the quality of a color as characterized by

chromatics

its dominant wavelength and its purity considered together.

chro·mat·ics (krōmat′iks), *n.* the science of colors. Also **chro·ma·tol·o·gy** (krōmətol′əjē).

chro·ma·tog·ra·phy (krōmatog′-rəfē), *n.* a method of separating mixtures into their constituent parts through preferential adsorption by a solid such as clay.

chrom·hi·dro·sis (krō′midrō′sis), *n.* the secretion of colored sweat.

chro·mo·gen (krō′məjən), *n.* a substance, as a microorganism, which produces pigmented compounds when oxidized.

chro·mo·gen·ic (krōməjen′ik), *adj.* producing pigment.

chro·mo·some (krō′məsōm), *n.* any of several thread-shaped bodies found in the nucleus of living cells and carrying the genetic code.

chro·mo·sphere (krō′məsfēr), *n.* **1.** a gaseous envelope surrounding the photosphere of the sun. **2.** a similar envelope surrounding a star. —**chro·mo·spher′ic,** *adj.*

chron·o·gram (kron′əgram), *n.* an inscription, sentence, etc., in which certain letters express a date or period through their value as Roman numerals.

chron·o·graph (kron′əgraf), *n.* an instrument for recording and measuring the exact moment of an event or very short time intervals.

chro·nom·e·ter (krənom′itər), *n.* an instrument for measuring time with great accuracy.

chron·o·pher (kron′əfər), *n.* an electrical apparatus used to broadcast time signals.

chron·o·scope (kron′əskōp), *n.* an instrument for making precise measurements of very short intervals of time.

chrys·a·lis (kris′əlis), *n.* the pupa of a butterfly.

chrys·el·e·phan·tine (kris′eləfan′-tin), *adj.* containing or composed of gold and ivory.

chrys·o·graph (kris′əgraf), *n.* a manuscript written in ink containing

gold or silver in powdered form.

chrys·o·prase (kris′əprāz), *n.* a green-colored chalcedony used in jewelry.

chtho·ni·an (*th*ō′nēən), *adj.* (in mythology) relating to the gods and spirits of the underworld. Also **chtho′nic.**

chuck·a·luck (CHuk′əluk), *n.* a betting game played with three dice.

chuff·y (CHuf′ē), *adj.* boorish; ill-mannered.

chum (CHum), *n.* **1.** bait cut small and thrown into the water to attract fish. —*v.* **2.** to fish by throwing such bait into the water.

church invisible, the whole of Christianity both in heaven and on earth.

church militant, those Christians constantly active in the fight against evil.

church suffering (in Roman Catholic doctrine) the souls of people in purgatory.

church triumphant, those Christians in heaven who have been victorious in the fight against evil.

church visible, the whole body of Christian believers on earth.

church·ward·en (CHurcH′wôrdn), *n.* a tobacco pipe with a long stem.

chu·rin·ga (CHŌŌriNG′gə), *n., pl.* **chu·rin·ga, chu·rin·gas.** a carved wooden object regarded as sacred by Australian aborigines.

churl (CHurl), *n.* an ill-mannered or surly person. —**churl′ish,** *adj.*

chur·ri·gue·resque (CHŌŌr′ēgə-resk′), *adj.* relating to a style of Baroque architecture that flourished in Spain and Spanish America. Also **chu·ri·gue·res·co** (CHŌŌr′ēgeres′kô).

chut·ney (CHut′nē), *n.* a pickle or relish of Indian origin made from fruits, herbs and spices.

chutz·pa (KHŌŌt′spə), *n.* insolence; audacity; impudence.

chyle (kīl), *n.* lymph containing emulsified fats formed from chyme in the small intestine.

chyme (kīm), *n.* the semiliquid mass of partially digested food formed by gastric secretion.

ci·bo·ri·um (sibôr′ēəm), *n.*, *pl.* **ci·bo·ri·a** (sibôr′ēə). **1.** a vaulted canopy placed over a high altar. **2.** a vessel or chalice for holding Eucharistic bread or wafers.

cic·a·trix (sik′ətriks), *n.*, *pl.* **cic·a·tri·ces** (sikətrī′sēz). **1.** the scar that forms on a wound which has healed. **2.** a mark left on a stem by a fallen leaf.

cic·a·trize (sik′ətrīz), *v.* to heal by the formation of a cicatrix.

cic·e·ro·ne (sisərō′nē), *n.*, *pl.* **cic·e·ro·nes, cic·e·ro·ni** (sisərō′nē), a guide who escorts tourists or sightseers.

ci·cis·be·ism (CHē′CHizbā′izm), *n.* the practice of keeping a cicisbeo.

ci·cis·be·o (CHē′CHēzbe′ô), *n.*, *pl.* **ci·cis·be·i** (CHē′CHēzbe′ē). (formerly in Italy) the escort or lover of a married woman.

ci-de·vant (sēdväN′), *adj. French.* former; one-time.

cil·i·a (sil′ēə), *n.*, *sing.* **cil·i·um** (sil′-ēəm). any minute, hair-like processes, esp. eyelashes.

cil·i·ar·y (sil′ēer′ē), *adj.* relating to a ring of tissue in the eye or to cilia.

cil·ice (sil′is), *n.* a hairshirt.

cin·cho·na (sinkō′nə), *n.* any of several trees whose barks yield quinine and other alkaloids.

cin·chon·ism (sin′kənizm), *n.* an illness due to excessive use of one of the cinchona alkaloids.

cin·cho·nize (sin′kənīz), *v.* to administer quinine to.

cinc·ture (sinGk′CHər), *n.* something which encircles; a girdle or belt.

cin·e, cin·é (sin′ē), *n.* a motion picture.

cin·e·aste (sin′east′), *n.* an enthusiast for motion pictures, esp. in their artistic and technical aspects.

cin·e·mat·ics (sinəmat′iks), *n.* the art or technique of motion-picture making.

cin·e·ra·di·og·ra·phy (sin′ərā′dē-og′rəfē), *n.* the technique of filming motion pictures through a fluoroscope.

cin·e·rar·i·um (sinərer′ēəm), *n.*, *pl.*

cin·e·rar·i·a (sinərer′ēə). a place where the ashes of the cremated dead are deposited.

cin·e·rar·y (sin′ərere), *adj.* pertaining to or intended for ashes, esp. those of cremated bodies.

cin·er·a·tor (sin′ərātər), *n.* an incinerator.

ci·ne·re·ous (sinēr′ēəs), *adj.* ash-colored; resembling or consisting of ashes.

cin·quain (sinGkān′), *n.* a group of five, esp. a five-line poem.

cinque (sinGk), *n.* the number five in cards or dice.

cin·que·cen·tist (CHinG′kwiCHen′-tist), *n.* a writer or artist of the cinquecento period.

cin·que·cen·to (CHinG′kwiCHen′tō), *n.* the 16th century, esp. with reference to Italian art or literature.

cinque·foil (sinNGk′foil), *n.* (in architecture) a decorative design consisting of a rounded form divided into five lobes radiating from a common center.

cir·ca (sur′kə), *prep., adv.* about (used for approximate dates). *Abbr.*: **ca, c.**

cir·ca·di·an (surkədē′ən), *adj.* relating to a cycle occurring at about 24-hour intervals.

cir·ci·nate (sur′sənāt), *adj.* rounded or ring-shaped.

cir·clet (sur′klit), *n.* a small circle or ring.

cir·cu·lus (sur′kyələs), *n.* a concentric circle on the scale of a fish showing the growth of the scale.

cir·cum·am·bi·ent (surkəmam′-bēənt), *adj.* encircling; encompassing.

cir·cum·am·bu·late (surkəmam′-byəlāt), *v.* to go around; approach indirectly.

cir·cum·ba·sal (surkəmbā′səl), *adj.* surrounding or encircling the base.

cir·cum·bend·i·bus (surkəmben′-dəbəs), *n.*, *pl.* **cir·cum·bend·i·bus·es.** an indirect or roundabout way; circumlocution.

cir·cum·flex (sur′kəmfleks), *adj.* characterized or shown by the mark ^, as used in French and other languages to indicate changes in vowel sound.

cir·cum·flu·ent (sərkum′flo͞oənt), *adj.* flowing around.

cir·cum·flu·ous (sərkum′flo͞oəs), *adj.* 1. circumfluent. 2. entirely surrounded by water.

cir·cum·fuse (surkəmfyo͞oz′), *v.* to surround or cover, as with a liquid.

cir·cum·gy·ra·tion (sur′kəmjīrā′-sнən), *n.* a circular movement.

cir·cum·ja·cent (surkəmjā′sənt), *adj.* surrounding or encircling; lying all around.

cir·cum·lo·cu·tion (sur′kəmlōkyo͞o′-sнən), *n.* excessive use of words to express an idea; an evasive or round-about way of speaking.

cir·cum·lu·nar (surkəmlo͞o′nər), *adj.* around the moon.

cir·cum·nu·tate (surkəmno͞o′tāt), *v.* (of a plant) to grow in an irregular circular movement.

cir·cum·scribe (surkəmskrīb′), *v.* 1. to draw a line around. 2. to delimit or mark off; constrain with limits; confine.

cir·cum·so·lar (surkəmsō′lər), *adj.* around the sun.

cir·cum·val·late (surkəmval′āt), *adj.* 1. encircled by or as if by a rampart. —*v.* 2. to encircle or surround with or as with a rampart.

cir·cum·vent (surkəmvent′), *v.* 1. to outwit, evade, get the better of. 2. to avoid or by-pass. —**cir·cum·ven′ tion,** *n.*

cir·cum·vo·lu·tion (sur′kəmvəlo͞o′-sнən), *n.* 1. an act or instance of turning or revolving around. 2. a winding or bending around; sinuosity.

cir·cum·volve (surkəmvolv′), *v.* to wind about or around; rotate.

cire per·due (sēr′ perdo͞o′). See **lost-wax process.**

cirque (surk), *n.* a basin in a mountain forming a circular space like an amphitheater.

cir·rho·sis (sirō′sis), *n.* a disease of the liver caused by an excess of connective tissue.

cir·ro·cu·mu·lus (sir′ōkyo͞o′myə-ləs), *n.* a cloud form consisting of

small rounded patches at high altitudes.

cir·ro·stra·tus (sir′ōstrā′təs), *n.* a cloud form having the appearance of a thin, whitish veil and found at high altitudes.

cir·rus (sir′əs), *n.* a cloud form consisting of wispy white strips and found at high altitudes.

cis·al·pine (sisal′pīn), *adj.* on this (the Italian) side of the Alps.

cis·at·lan·tic (sisatlan′tik), *adj.* on this side of the Atlantic.

ci·se·le (sēzəlā′), *adj.* (of velvet) having a pattern in relief.

cis·lu·nar (sislo͞o′nər), *adj.* lying between the earth and the moon.

cis·mon·tane (sismon′tān), *adj.* on this side of the mountains.

cit·ri·cul·ture (si′trəkul′cнər), *n.* the cultivation of citrus fruits.

cit·y·scape (sit′ēskāp), *n.* a panoramic or broad view of a large city, as *a cityscape of London.*

civil death, the legal status of a person who has been deprived of civil rights.

civil disobedience, a refusal on moral grounds to obey certain laws or an attempt to influence government policy, characterized by the use of non-violent techniques.

civil rights, a citizen's right to personal liberty as established by the U.S. constitution.

clad·ding (klad′iнg), *n.* the technique of bonding one metal to another, usually to prevent corrosion.

clair·voy·ance (klervoi′əns), *n.* the power of seeing things beyond the natural limits of the senses. —**clair· voy′ant,** *adj., n.*

cla·mant (klā′mənt), *adj.* noisy; urgent; pressing.

clam·jam·fry (klamjam′frē), *n.* (in British dialect) ordinary people collectively; mob; rabble.

clan·des·tine (klandes′tin), *adj.* held or conducted in secrecy; surreptitious.

clang·or (klaнg′ər), *n.* a resounding clanging sound or series of such sounds.

claque (klak), *n.* a group of persons

hired to applaud a theatrical performance, etc. —**cla·queur** (klakur′), *n.*

clas·tic (klas′tik), *adj.* disintegrating into fragments; consisting of detachable pieces; fragmental.

clau·di·cant (klô′dəkənt), *adj.* lame; having a limp.

clau·di·ca·tion (klôdəkā′sнən), *n.* a limp.

claus·tral (klô′strəl), *adj.* cloister-like; cloistral.

claus·tro·phil·i·a (klôstrəfil′ēə), *n.* a morbid desire to be confined in a small place.

claus·tro·pho·bi·a (klôstrəfō′bēə), *n.* an abnormal dread of closed or narrow spaces. —**claus′tro·phobe,** *n.*

cla·vate (klā′vāt), *adj.* having the shape of a club.

clav·i·form (klav′əfôrm), *adj.* having the shape of a club; clavate.

cla·vus (klā′vəs), *n., pl.* **cla·vi** (klā′vī). a headache causing intense pain, found in some forms of hysteria.

clear text. See **plain text.**

clem·ent (klem′ənt), *adj.* mild; gentle; merciful.

clep·sy·dra (klep′sidrə), *n., pl.* **clep·sy·dras, clep·sy·drae** (klep′sidrē). an apparatus for measuring the passage of time by the regulated flow of water.

clep·to·bi·o·sis (klep′tōbīō′sis), *n., pl.* **clep·to·bi·o·ses** (klep′tōbīō′sēz). a mode of existence in which one species steals food from another. —**clep·to·bi·ot′ic,** *adj.*

clep·to·ma·ni·a (kleptəmā′nēə), *n.* See **kleptomania.**

clere·sto·ry (klēr′stôr′ē), *n.* a part of the interior of a building which rises above adjacent rooftops or the ground and is perforated with a series of windows.

cler·i·hew (kler′ihyo͞o), *n.* a four-line piece of verse having a usually humorous character.

cler·i·sy (kler′isē), *n.* learned or educated people collectively; intelligentsia.

cle·ro·man·cy (klēr′əman′sē), *n.* divination by casting lots.

clev·is (klev′is), *n.* a U-shaped metal fastening, to which a bolt or hook (clevis pin) can be attached.

cli·ché (klēsнā′), *n.* a hackneyed, trite, or stereotyped phrase or expression.

cliff-hang·er (klif′haNGər), *n.* a story, esp. a serial, which depends for its effect on crude melodramatic suspense.

cli·mac·ter·ic (klīmak′tərik), *n.* a period in life leading to decreased sexual activity in men and to menopause in women.

cli·mac·tic (klīmak′tik), *adj.* relating to or forming a climax.

cli·mat·ic (klīmat′ik), *adj.* relating to climate.

cli·ma·tol·o·gy (klīmətol′əjē), *n.* the study of climates and climatic conditions.

clink·er-built (kliNG′kərbilt), *adj.* (of ships) having boards or planks which overlap. See also **carvel-built.**

cli·nom·e·ter (klīnom′itər), *n.* an instrument for measuring the amount of slope on an inclined plane.

clin·quant (kliNG′kənt), *adj.* glittering with tinsel.

clique (klēk), *n.* a small exclusive circle of people, esp. with identical interests; coterie. —**cli′quish,** *adj.*

clith·ral (klīth′rəl), *adj.* (of a classical temple) covered by a roof. See also **hypethral.**

clo·a·ca (klōā′kə), *n., pl.* **clo·a·cae** (klōā′kē). 1. a sewer. 2. the terminal part into which intestinal, urinary, and generative canals open in birds, amphibians, fishes, and mammals. —**clo·a′cal,** *adj.*

cloche (klôsн), *n.* 1. a glass cover, usually bell-shaped, placed over plants to protect them from frost. 2. a woman's close-fitting, brimless hat.

cloi·son (kloi′zən), *n.* a thin strip of metal dividing off the colored areas in cloisonné enamels.

cloi·son·né (kloizənā′), *n.* a colored decoration made of enamels in which the colored areas are divided off by thin metal strips secured to a metal groundwork.

clo·que (klōkā'), *n.* a fabric with a quilted pattern or a raised design in relief. See also **matelassé.**

closed shop, a factory, etc., in which union membership is an essential condition of employment or in which the employer must ask a particular labor union to provide employees. See also **open shop.**

clo·ture (klō'CHər), *n.* (in a legislature) the ending of a debate by calling for a vote or gaining a two thirds majority vote. Also **closure** (klōzHər).

cloud chamber, an apparatus for determining the paths of ionizing particles.

clowd·er (klou'dər), *n.* a group of cats.

cloy (kloi), *v.* to satiate or become distasteful through excess; surfeit.

clyp·e·ate (klip'ēāt), *adj.* having the shape of a rounded shield.

cly·sis (klī'sis), *n.* **1.** the giving of an enema. **2.** the administration of intravenous solutions in order to provide nourishment, remove pain, etc.

clys·ter (klis'tər), *n.* an enema.

co·ac·tive (kōak'tiv), *adj.* obligatory; compulsory.

co·ad·ju·tant (kōaj'ətənt), *adj.* **1.** providing mutual assistance. —*n.* **2.** an assistant.

co·ad·ju·tor (kōaj'ətər), *n.* an assistant, esp. to a bishop or other church dignitary.

co·ad·ju·tress (kōaj'ətris), *n.* a female assistant. Also **co·ad·ju·trix** (koaj'ətriks).

co·ag·u·late (kōag'yəlāt), *v.* to thicken; congeal; curdle. —**co·ag·u·la'tion,** *n.*

co·a·li·tion (kōəlisH'ən), *n.* a joining together, esp. a temporary alliance between political parties.

co·ap·ta·tion (kōaptā'sHən), *n.* a fitting together of separate parts.

co·ax·i·al (kōak'sēəl), *adj.* having the same axis. Also **co·ax·al** (kōak'səl).

co·cain·ism (kōkā'nizm), *n.* a morbid condition caused by excessive consumption of cocaine.

coc·coid (kok'oid), *adj.* berry-shaped. See also **bacciform.**

coc·cyx (kok'siks), *n.*, *pl.* **coc·cy·ges** (koksī'jēz). a small bone forming the base of the spine.

coch·le·a (kok'lēə), *n.* a spiral-shaped cavity of the inner ear.

coch·le·ate (kok'lēit), *adj.* having the shape of a snail shell.

cock·a·lo·rum (kokəlôr'əm), *n.* a conceited or pretentious little man.

cock·a·trice (kok'ətris), *n.* a mythical serpent with a deadly glance, hatched by a serpent from a cock's egg.

cock·boat (kok'bōt), *n.* a small boat, esp. one used as a tender to a larger vessel.

cock·loft (kok'lôft), *n.* a small attic or garret.

cock·ney (kok'nē), *n.*, *pl.* **cock·neys.** **1.** a native of the East End district of London. **2.** the dialect spoken there.

co·cotte[1] (kōkot'), *n.* a prostitute.

co·cotte[2] (kōkot'), *n.* a kind of small, round casserole.

co·dex (kō'deks), *n.*, *pl.* **co·di·ces** (kō'disēz). a manuscript book of the Scriptures or ancient classics.

cod·i·cil (kod'isəl), *n.* a supplement or appendix, esp. a modificatory addition to a will.

cod·i·fy (kod'əfī), *v.* to put (laws, etc.) in the form of a code; arrange systematically.

coe·la·canth (sē'ləkan*th*), *n.* a primitive form of fish found off the coast of Southern Africa.

coe·lan·a·glyph·ic (silan'əglif'ik), *adj.* (of a sculpture or carving) carried out in cavo-relievo.

coe·li·ac disease (sē'lēak). See **celiac disease.**

coe·lo·stat (sē'ləstat), *n.* a telescope fitted with an adjustable mirror used to reflect the light of a star, etc., into the telescope. See also **siderostat.**

coe·nes·the·sia, ce·nes·the·sia (sē'nist*hē*'zHə), *n.* the general sense of body consciousness derived from the aggregate of organic sensations.

co·erce (kōurs'), *v.* to force; compel by force; constrain. —**co·er'cive,** *adj.*

co·e·ta·ne·ous (kōitā'nēəs), *adj.* of the same age; coeval.

co·e·val (kōe′vəl), *adj.* of the same period, age or duration; contemporary.

cof·fle (kof′əl), *n.* a train of men, as convicts, slaves, etc., or animals, fastened together.

coff·ret (kô′frit), *n.* a small chest or coffer.

co·gent (kō′jənt), *adj.* compelling belief; appealing forcibly to reason; convincing. —**co′gen·cy,** *n.*

cog·i·tate (koj′itāt), *v.* to meditate intently; reflect; ponder. —**cog·i·ta′ tion,** *n.* —**cog′i·ta·tive,** *adj.*

co·gi·to, er·go sum (kō′gitō er′gō sŏŏm′), *Latin.* I think therefore I am (a fundamental principle of Cartesian philosophy).

cog·nate (kog′nāt), *n.* **1.** a kinsman whose relationship is traceable through both males and females. —*adj.* **2.** related through a common source, as the words *shirt* and *skirt.* See also **agnate.** —**cog·na′tion,** *n.*

cog·ni·tion (kognish′ən), *n.* the faculty of perception or knowing; the product of such a faculty.

cog·no·men (kognō′mən), *n.,* *pl.* **cog·no·mens, cog·nom·i·na** (kognom′ənə). **1.** a family name or surname. **2.** a distinguishing name, as a nickname.

co·gno·scen·ti (konyəsHen′tē), *n. pl.,* *sing.* **co·gno·scen·te** (konyəsHen′tē). those who are well informed or have superior knowledge in a particular subject, esp. fine arts or literature.

cog·nos·ci·ble (kognos′əbəl), *adj.* capable of being known.

cog·nos·ci·tive (kognos′itiv), *adj.* having the capacity or ability to know.

coherent radiation, radiation with definite phase relationships at different positions in a cross section of the energy beam.

cois·trel (koi′strəl), *n.* a rascal or scoundrel.

col·a·co·bi·o·sis (kol′əkōbīō′sis), *n.,* *pl.* **col·a·co·bi·o·ses** (kol′əkōbīō′sēz). a mode of communal living among insects in which one species exists parasitically upon another.

coliform bacillus (kol′əfôrm), any of several varieties of bacillus found in the large intestine of man and animals.

co·li·tis (kəlī′tis), *n.* inflammation of the colon.

col·lage (kəläzH′), *n.* an artistic composition produced by pasting various materials as newspaper cuttings, old photographs, pieces of advertisements, etc., onto a surface.

col·la·gen (kol′əjən), *n.* a protein found in connective tissue and bones which produces gelatin and glue after prolonged boiling in water.

col·la·tion (kolā′sHən), *n.* a snack; light meal.

col·lec·ta·ne·a (kolektā′nēə), *n. pl.* collected writings; a miscellany or anthology.

col·lec·tiv·ism (kəlek′təvizm), *n.* the theory of collective control over a country's means of production and distribution.

col·let (kol′it), *n.* a metal band or collar; a flange in which a gem is set.

col·li·gate (kol′əgāt), *v.* to bind or fasten together.

col·li·mate (kol′əmāt), *v.* to bring into alignment; make parallel.

col·lo·cate (kol′əkāt), *v.* to arrange in proper order; set side by side.

col·lo·ca·tion (koləkā′sHən), *n.* proper arrangement, esp. of words in a sentence.

col·lo·qui·al (kəlō′kwēəl), *adj.* characteristic of everyday speech or familiar conversation.

col·lo·qui·um (kəlō′kwēəm), *n.,* *pl.* **col·lo·qui·ums, co·lo·qui·a** (kəlō′- kwēə), a conference, esp. an informal one.

col·lo·quy (kol′əkwē), *n.* a dialogue or conversation.

col·lo·type (kol′ətīp), *n.* a photomechanical process of making prints from a gelatin-coated plate.

col·lude (kəlŏŏd′), *v.* to cooperate together as a result of a secret agreement, esp. for a dishonest purpose. —**col·lu·sion** (kəlŏŏ′zHən), *n.* —**col· lu·sive** (kəlŏŏ′siv), *adj.*

col·lu·to·ry (kol′ətôrē), *n.* a mouthwash. Also **col·lu·to·ri·um** (koletôr'-ēəm).

col·lyr·i·um (kəlēr'ēəm), *n.* an eye lotion or eyewash.

co·lon (kō'lən), *n.* the lower part of the large intestine, extending from the cecum to the rectum.

col·o·nette (kolənet'), *n.* a small column.

co·lon·ic (kōlon'ik), *adj.* relating to the colon.

col·o·phon (kol'əfon), *n.* **1.** an inscription, usually inserted at the end of a book, giving details about the printer, author, publisher and place of publication. **2.** the identifying emblem of a publishing house.

col·or·im·e·ter (kulərim'itər), *n.* an instrument for analyzing colors and comparing their intensities. —**col·or·im'e·try,** *n.*

col·por·tage (kôl'pōr'tij), *n.* the business of a colporteur.

col·por·teur (kôl'pōrtər), *n.* **1.** one who peddles books. **2.** one who distributes cheap religious books.

col·u·brine (kol'əbrīn), *adj.* relating to or resembling a snake.

col·um·bar·i·um (koləmber'ēəm), *n.*, *pl.* **col·um·bar·i·a** (koləmber'ēə). a vault with recesses in the walls for holding funerary urns.

col·um·bar·y (kol'əmberē), *n.* a dovecote.

col·um·bine (kol'əmbīn), *adj.* resembling a dove.

co·lum·ni·a·tion (kəlum'nēā'sнən), *n.* **1.** the use of columns in a structure. **2.** the system of columns thus used.

co·ma[1] (kō'mə), *n.* a condition of deep unconsciousness due to injury, disease, etc.

co·ma[2] (kō'mə), *n.*, *pl.* **co·mae** (kō'-mē). the nebulous envelope that surrounds the nucleus of a comet.

co·mate (kō'māt), *adj.* covered with hair; shaggy; tufted.

com·a·tose (kom'ətōs), *adj.* relating to or affected by a coma; lethargic; drowsy.

com·e·do (kom'idō), *n.*, *pl.* **com·e·dos, com·e·do·nes** (komidō'nēz). a blackhead or pimple on the skin.

co·mes·ti·ble (kəmes'təbəl), *adj.* **1.** edible. —*n.* **2.** (*usually pl.*) food.

com·i·ty (kom'itē), *n.* civility; a courteous manner of behavior.

comme ci, comme ça (kômsē' kômsa'), *French.* indifferent; neither good nor bad; so-so.

comme il faut (kômēlfō'), *French.* in conformity with accepted standards; proper; suitable.

com·men·sal (kəmen'səl), *adj.* **1.** taking meals together. **2.** (of organisms, plants, etc.) living with or on another without damage to the other. **3.** (of an individual or group) occupying the same area as another individual or group having different standards, etc., but not competing with them.

com·men·su·ra·ble (kəmen'sərəbəl), *adj.* measurable by the same standard; proportionate; having a common measure.

com·men·su·rate (kəmen'sərit), *adj.* of equal extent; in accordance with; in proportion to.

com·mi·nate (kom'ənāt), *v.* to threaten with divine vengeance. —**com·mi·na'tion,** *n.*

com·mi·nute (kom'ənoot), *v.* to crush to a powder; pulverize.

com·mis·sure (kom'isноor), *n.* a juncture; seams; joint.

com·mon·al·ty (kom'ənəltē), *n.* the common people as distinguished from those in authority, the nobility, etc. Also **com·mon·al·i·ty** (komənal'itē).

common carrier, an individual or company which undertakes to transport people or goods in return for payment.

Common Market, an economic association of Western European countries created to abolish internal tariffs among its members and to set up a common external tariff.

com·move (kəmoov'), *v.* to agitate or move violently.

com·mune (kəmyoon'), *n.* a tightly organized community of people sharing common interests.

com·mun·ion (kəmyoon'yən), *n.* **1.**

the act of sharing in common. **2.** the celebration or receiving of the Eucharist.

com·mu·ni·qué (kəmyōō′nəkā′), *n.* an official report or bulletin.

com·mun·ism (kom′yənizm), *n.* a system of society in which all property is held in common, ownership being vested in the community as a whole or the state. —**com′mun·ist,** *n.*

com·mu·ta·tion (komyətā′sHən), *n.* the act of replacing one thing by another; substitution.

com·mu·ta·tive (kəmyōō′tətiv), *adj.* relating to or permitting exchange or substitution.

co·mose (kō′mōs), *adj.* covered in hairs; comate.

com·pa·ra·tor (kom′pərā′tər), *n.* an instrument for making comparisons of similar things, as lengths, shades of color, etc.

com·pa·ter·ni·ty (kom′pətur′nitē) *n.* the relationship between the godparents of a child or between the godparents and the parents.

com·pa·thy (kom′pəthē), *n.* the sharing of feelings with others.

com·peer (kəmpēr′), *n.* one having the same rank; an equal in position, ability, etc.

com·pel·la·tion (kompəlā′sHən), *n.* the action or manner of addressing somebody; designation.

com·pen·di·ous (kəmpen′dēəs), *adj.* expressing in brief form the substance of a subject; concise.

com·pen·di·um (kəmpen′dēəm), *n.,* *pl.* **com·pen·di·ums, com·pen·di·a** (kəmpen′dēə). a comprehensive summary of a subject; an abridgment. —**com·pen′di·ous,** *adj.*

com·pen·sa·to·ry damages (kəmpen′sətôrē), damages awarded to a plaintiff to provide compensation for injury suffered. See also **exemplary damages.**

com·pla·cent (kəmplā′sənt), *adj.* self-satisfied; showing undue regard for one's own merits or advantages. —**com·pla′cen·cy,** *n.*

com·plai·sant (kəmplā′sənt), *adj.*

obliging, agreeable; eager to please. —**com·plai′sance,** *n.*

com·pla·nate (kom′plənāt), *adj.* put into a level position.

com·plect·ed (kəmplek′tid), *adj.* complexioned.

com·pli·ca·cy (kom′pləkəsē), *n.* complicated state; complicatedness.

com·plot (kom′plot), *n.* **1.** a conspiracy. —*v.* **2.** to conspire together.

com·port (kəmpôrt′), *v.* to behave; conduct oneself.

com·pos·si·ble (kompos′əbəl), *adj.* consistent with; compatible.

com·po·ta·tion (kompətā′sHən), *n.* drinking together; convivial drinking.

com·pote (kom′pōt), *n.* **1.** fruit stewed in syrup. **2.** a dish or bowl of glass, china, metal, etc., having a base and stem, and used for serving fruit, nuts, etc.

compte ren·du (kôɴt räɴdy′), *pl.* **comptes rendus** (kôɴt räɴdy′), *French.* a record or account of a transaction, proceedings, etc.

com·pur·ga·tion (kompərgā′sHən), *n.* (formerly) a legal procedure whereby an accused man is cleared of a charge by the sworn oaths of a number of people.

com·pur·ga·tor (kom′pərgātər), *n.* one who under oath vouches for the innocence of another.

com·put·er (kəmpyōō′tər), *n.* an automatic electronic apparatus for performing complex mathematical calculations at high speeds. See also **analog computer, digital computer.**

co·na·tion (kōnā′sHən), *n.* mental activity concerned with striving, as desire and conscious volition. —**con′a·tive,** *adj.*

co·na·tus (kōnā′təs), *n., pl.* **co·na·tus.** an impulse or a striving.

con·cat·e·nate (konkat′ənāt), *v.* to link or join together; unite in a series. —**con·cat·e·na′tion,** *n.*

con·cel·e·brate (konsel′əbrāt), *v.* to take part in a concelebration.

con·cel·e·bra·tion (konsel′əbrā′-sHən), *n.* the performance of mass by more than one priest.

con·cen·ter (konsen′tər), *v.* to draw toward or converge upon a common center.

con·cen·tric (kənsen′trik), *adj.* having a common center or axis.

con·ces·sion (kənsesH′ən), *n.* the act of yielding or conceding; the admitting of a point in a dispute, etc.

con·ces·sive (kənses′iv), *adj.* denoting a concession; tending to concede.

con·chol·o·gy (konNGkol′əjē), *n.* the branch of study dealing with mollusks.

con·cil·i·ar (kənsil′ēər), *adj.* relating to a council, esp. an ecclesiastical one.

con·cil·i·ate (kənsil′ēāt), *v.* to placate; overcome the hostility of; reconcile. —**con·cil·i·a′tion**, *n.* —**con·cil′i·a·to·ry**, *adj.*

con·cin·nate (kon′sənāt), *v.* to fit together in a precise, appropriate, or harmonious fashion.

con·cin·nous (kənsin′əs), *adj.* elegant in style; harmonious; fitting.

con·ci·sion (kənsizH′ən), *n.* conciseness; brevity.

con·clave (kon′klāv), *n.* a private discussion; secret assembly.

con·com·i·tant (konkom′itnt), *adj.* accompanying; existing with something else; attendant.

con·cord·ant (konkôr′dnt), *adj.* harmonious; consistent; agreeing.

con·cor·dat (konkôr′dat), *n.* an official agreement; a compact or covenant.

con·cres·cence (konkres′əns), *n.* a growing together as of plants or cells.

con·cu·bi·nage (konkyoo′bənij), *n.* the cohabiting of a man and woman who are not legally married. —**con·cu·bi·nar·y** (konkyoo′bəner′ē), *adj.*

con·cu·bine (konG′kyəbīn), *n.* a woman who cohabits with a man to whom she is not married.

con·cu·pis·cence (konkyoo′pisəns), *n.* sexual desire; lust. —**con·cu·pis′cent,** *adj.*

con·dign (kəndīn′), *adj.* fitting; appropriate; well deserved.

con·dis·ci·ple (kon′disī′pəl), *n.* a fellow student.

con·do·lent (kəndō′lənt), *adj.* showing sympathy or sorrow. —**con·do′lence,** *n.*

con·do·min·i·um (kondəmin′ēəm), *n.* an apartment building whose apartments or dwelling units are under individual ownership. See also **cooperative.**

con·duce (kəndoos′), *v.* to lead or tend toward; tend to produce a particular result. —**con·du′cive,** *adj.*

con·fab·u·late (kənfab′yəlāt), *v.* 1. to engage in informal discussion; converse. 2. to take part in confabulation.

con·fab·u·la·tion (kənfab′yəlā′-sHən), *n.* 1. an informal conversation. 2. (in psychiatry) filling a blank in memory with a false memory which is accepted as being correct.

con·fect (kənfekt′), *v.* to prepare from ingredients; make up; put together.

con·fer·va (konfur′və), *n., pl.* **con·fer·vae** (konfur′vē), **con·fer·vas.** any of various filamentous green alga.

con·fig·u·ra·tion (kənfig′yərā′sHən), *n.* the relative arrangement of the elements or parts of something.

con·fi·ture (kon′fiCHŏŏr′), *n.* preserved fruit.

con·fla·grant (kənflā′grənt), *adj.* on fire; burning; ablaze.

con·fla·tion (kənflā′sHən), *n.* the combining of two texts into one; the resulting new text.

con·flu·ence (kon′flooəns), *n.* the flowing together of two or more rivers, etc.

con·flu·ent (kon′flooənt), *adj.* coming or flowing together; uniting into one.

con·gé (kon′zHā), *n.* 1. a formal leave-taking. 2. permission to take one's leave. Also **con·gee** (kon′jē).

con·ge·la·tion (konjəlā′sHən), *n.* 1. the process of freezing or congealing. 2. the result of this.

con·ge·ner (kon′jənər), *n.* a member of the same group, family, or class.

con·ge·ries (konjēr′ēz), *n.* a collection, assembly, heap, or pile.

con·glo·bate (konglō′bāt), *adj.* formed into a round mass or ball.

con·glu·ti·nate (kəngloot′ənāt), *v.* to

stick together as with glue; become glued together.

con·gru·ent (koNG′grōōənt), *adj.* in agreement; congruous. —**con′gru·ence,** *n.*

con·gru·i·ty (kəngrōō′itē), *n.* the state or quality of being congruous; accord or harmony.

con·gru·ous (koNG′grōōəs), *adj.* showing harmony in character, etc., suitable; appropriate; fitting.

co·ni·ol·o·gy (kō′nēol′əjē), *n.* See **koniology.**

con·joint (kənjoint′), *adj.* united; associated; combined.

con·ju·gal (kon′jəgəl), *adj.* relating to marriage or the married state.

con·junct (kənjuNGkt′), *adj.* joined closely together; united; joint.

con·junc·ti·va (kon′juNGktī′və), *n., pl.* **con·junc·ti·vas, con·junc·ti·vae** (kon′juNGtī′vē). the mucous membrane lining the inner surface of the eyelids.

con·junc·tive (kənjuNGk′tiv), *adj.* uniting; connective.

con·junc·ture (kənjuNGk′CHər), *n.* a combination of events or circumstances.

con·nate (kon′āt), *adj.* inborn or innate; associated in origin.

con·nat·u·ral (kənaCH′ərəl), *adj.* inborn; connected by nature.

con·no·ta·tion (konətā′sHən), *n.* an implied or associated meaning of a word apart from its explicit sense.

con·note (kənōt′), *v.* to imply or suggest.

co·noid (kō′noid), *adj.* having the shape of a cone.

con·san·guin·e·ous (kon′saNG- twin′ēəs), *adj.* descended from the same ancestor; related by blood.

con·san·guin·i·ty (kon′saNGgwin′- itē), *n.* relationship by blood; kinship.

con·script (*v.* kənskript′; *adj.* kon′- skript), *v.* **1.** to enroll compulsorily for military service. —*adj.* **2.** enrolled by conscription.

con·se·cu·tion (konsəkyōō′sHən), *n.* sequence; succession.

con·sen·su·al (kənsen′sHōōəl), *adj.* **1.** made by or resulting from mutual consent, without formal agreement. **2.** denoting an involuntary movement accompanying a voluntary movement.

con·sen·ta·ne·ous (kon′sentā′nēəs), *adj.* agreeing; in accord. —**con·sen·ta·ne′i·ty,** *n.*

con·sen·tient (kənsen′sHənt), *adj.* characterized by unanimous or harmonious agreement; accordant.

con·sis·to·ry (kənsis′tərē), *n.* a church tribunal or council.

con·so·ci·ate (kənsō′sHēit), *v.* to bring into association; associate.

con·so·nance (kon′sənəns), *n.* agreement; harmony; accord.

con·sor·ti·um (kənsôr′sHēəm), *n., pl.* **con·sor·ti·a** (kənsôr′sHēə). a combination of banking or business companies for the purpose of performing some operation involving large financial resources.

con·spe·cif·ic (kon′spisif′ik), *adj.* of the same species.

con·spec·tus (kənspek′təs), *n.* a synopsis or summary; survey; review.

con·stel·late (kon′stəlāt), *v.* to unite or cluster together, as stars to form a constellation.

con·ster·nate (kon′stərnāt), *v.* to dismay; terrify. —**con·ster·na′tion,** *n.*

con·sti·tu·tive (kon′stitōō′tiv), *adj.* **1.** essential; constituent. **2.** having the power to establish, enact, create, etc.

con·stringe (kənstrinj′), *v.* to compress; cause to shrink or contract. —**con·strin′gent,** *adj.*

con·sub·stan·tial (konsəbstan′sHəl), *adj.* having the same essence or substance.

con·sub·stan·ti·a·tion (konsəbstan′- sHēā′sHən), *n.* the doctrine that the body and blood of Christ are simultaneously present within the bread and wine of the Eucharist.

con·sue·tude (kon′switōōd), *n.* a custom, esp. one having the force of law; social usage. —**con·sue·tu·di·nar·y** (konswitōōd′ənerē), *adj.*

consumer price index, an index based on official statistics showing the change in the cost of goods and

services over a specified period. Also
price index.

con·tang·o (kəntaNG′gō), *n.*, *pl.* **con·
tan·gos, con·tan·goes.** (on the London Stock Exchange) an arrangement whereby a buyer of securities pays a fee to the seller in return for deferment of payment until the next settlement day. See also **backwardation.**

con·temn (kəntem′), *v.* to disdain, despise; treat with scorn.

con·ten·tious (kənten′sHəs), *adj.* causing strife; quarrelsome; controversial.

con·ter·mi·nous (kəntur′mənəs), *adj.* having a common boundary; adjacent; bordering.

con·tex·ture (kənteks′CHər), *n.* the arrangement of the parts of a whole; framework; structure.

con·tig·u·ous (kəntig′yo͞oəs), *adj.* in contact; adjoining; touching.

con·ti·nen·tal·i·ty (kontənəntal′itē), *n.* the degree to which the climate of a place is influenced by its land mass. See also **oceanity.**

con·tin·u·um (kəntin′yo͞oəm), *n.*, *pl.* **con·tin·u·a** (kəntin′yo͞oə). a continuous or uninterrupted sequence, series or extent.

con·trac·tile (kəntrak′tl), *adj.* having the power to contract; causing contraction.

con·tra·dic·tious (kontrədik′sHəs), *adj.* marked by contradiction; disputatious; inclined to contradict.

con·tra·dic·tive (kontrədik′tiv), *adj.* tending to contradict.

con·tra·dis·tin·guish (kon′trədis-stiNG′gwisH), *v.* to make distinction by contrast of qualities. —**con·tra·dis·tinc′tion,** *n.*

con·trail (kon′trāl), *n.* a trail of condensed water vapor caused by aircraft, rockets, etc.

con·tra·pose (kon′trəpōz), *v.* to place in contraposition.

con·tra·po·si·tion (kontrəpəzisH′ən), *n.* a setting in opposition; contrast; antithesis.

con·tra·ri·e·ty (kontrərī′itē), *n.* the state or quality of being contrary.

con·tra·vene (kontrəvēn′), *v.* to oppose; act contrary to; be in conflict with. —**con·tra·ven′tion,** *n.*

con·tre·temps (kon′trətäN), *n.*, *pl.*
con·tre·temps. an embarrassing situation; unfortunate occurrence.

con·trite (kəntrīt′), *adj.* full of remorse; truly repentant; penitent. —**con·tri·tion** (kəntrisH′ən), *n.*

con·tro·vert (kon′trəvurt), *v.* to dispute; contest; contradict.

con·tu·ma·cious (kon′to͞omā′sHəs), *adj.* strongly disobedient; rebellious; stubborn. —**con·tu·ma·cy** (kon′to͞o-məsē), *n.*

con·tu·me·ly (kon′to͞oməlē), *n.* insulting behavior in words or deeds; contemptuous treatment. —**con·tu·me′li·ous,** *adj.*

con·tuse (kənto͞oz′), *v.* to injure (tissue, etc.) without laceration of the skin; bruise.

con·ve·nance (kon′vənäns), *n.* propriety; suitability.

con·ven·tu·al (kənven′CHo͞oəl), *adj.* relating to or appropriate to a convent or monastic life.

con·vert·i·plane (kənvur′təplān), *n.* an airplane designed for vertical movement like a helicopter and also level forward flight.

con·vive (kon′vīv), *n.*, *pl.* **con·vives** (kon′vīvz). a dining companion; a fellow guest at a meal.

con·viv·ial (kənviv′ēəl), *adj.* relating to, indulging in, or suitable for feasting, eating and drinking, etc.

con·vo·ca·tor (kon′vəkātər), *n.* one who calls, arranges, or takes part in a meeting, etc.

con·vo·lut·ed (kon′vəlo͞otid), *adj.* tangled, twisted; intricate, complicated.

con·vo·lu·tion (konvəlo͞o′sHən), *n.* one of the ridges or folds on the brain's surface.

con·volve (kənvolv′), *v.* to roll together; twist round.

co·op·er·a·tive (kōop′ərətiv), *n.* an apartment house whose tenants each own shares of stock proportionate to the value his apartment bears to the total value of the building. See also **condominium.**

co·pa·cet·ic (kōpəset′ik), *adj.* entirely satisfactory; fine; excellent.

cop·ro·lag·ni·a (koprəlag′nēə), *n.* sexual excitement induced by fecal matter.

cop·ro·la·li·a (koprəlā′lēə), *n.* excessive swearing or use of obscene language.

cop·rol·o·gy (koprol′əjē), *n.* scatology.

cop·roph·a·gous (koprof′əgəs), *adj.* feeding on dung.

cop·ro·phil·i·a (koprəfil′ēə), *n.* a morbid interest in feces.

cop·ro·pho·bi·a (koprəfō′bēə), *n.* an obsessive fear of feces.

coq au vin (kôk ō vaɴ′), chicken cooked with red wine, onions, garlic, diced pork, etc.

co·quet (kōket′), *v.* (of a woman) to try to attract the amorous attentions of men; flirt.

co·quette (kōket′), *n.* a woman who tries to gain the attention of men by amorous flirtation.

co·quille (kōkil′), *n.* **1.** a dish, usually of meat or fish, cooked with a sauce, and served on a shell-shaped platter. **2.** the casserole or other utensil used for cooking such dishes.

cor·al·lif·er·ous (kôrəlif′ərəs), *adj.* bearing or producing coral.

cor·al·loid (kôr′əloid), *adj.* shaped like coral.

co·ram no·bis (kôr′am no′bis), a writ designed to rectify an injury caused by a mistake of a court of law.

cor·date (kôr′dāt), *adj.* shaped like a heart.

cor·delle (kôrdel′), *n.* a rope used for towing barges, etc.

cor·di·form (kôr′dəfôrm), *adj.* having the shape of a heart.

cor·dil·le·ra (kôr′dilyâr′ə), *n.* a system of mountain ranges; a mountain chain.

cor·don sa·ni·taire (kôr′dôɴ sanēter′), *pl.* **cor·dons sa·ni·taire** (kô′dôɴ sanēter′). a line marking off an area under quarantine.

co·re·spond·ent (kō′rispon′dənt), *n.* one charged with adultery together with the defendant in a divorce case.

co·ri·a·ceous (kôrēā′sнəs), *adj.* resembling leather.

cor·ne·ous (kôr′nēəs), *adj.* of a horny substance or texture.

cor·nic·u·late (kôrnik′yəlāt), *adj.* having horn-shaped parts; resembling a small horn.

cor·nu (kôr′nyoo͞), *n.* a horn or horn-shaped structure.

cor·nut·ed (kôrnoo͞′tid), *adj.* having horns, like a cuckold; horn-shaped.

co·ro·na (kərō′nə), *n., pl.* **co·ro·nas,** **co·ro·nae** (kərō′nē). a luminous circle of light surrounding the sun or moon.

corona discharge, a discharge occurring at the surface of a conductor, etc., and resulting in ionization of the surrounding atmosphere. Also **cor·po·sant** (kôr′pəzant).

co·ro·na·graph (kərō′nəgraf), *n.* an apparatus for observing the sun's corona.

cor·o·nar·y occlusion (kôr′əner′ē). obstruction of a coronary artery.

coronary thrombosis, the occlusion of a coronary artery caused by a blood clot.

cor·o·nate (kôr′ənāt), *adj.* having a crown or coronet.

cor·o·plast (kôr′əplast), *n.* one who sculpts figurines, esp. in terracotta.

cor·pu·lence (kôr′pyələns), *n.* stoutness of body; obesity; fatness. —**cor′pu·lent,** *adj.*

cor·pus·cle (kôr′pəsəl), *n.* a protoplasmic cell, esp. a blood cell.

cor·pus de·lic·ti (kôr′pəs dilik′tē), the fundamental facts about a crime.

cor·pus ju·ris (kôr′pəs joor′is), the body of laws of a country, state, etc.

cor·rade (kərād′), *v.* **1.** to wear away by abrasion or erosion. **2.** to disintegrate as a result of abrasion or erosion. —**cor·ra·sion** (kərā′zнən), *n.*

cor·ri·gen·dum (kôr′ijen′dəm), *n., pl.* **cor·ri·gen·da** (kôr′ijen′də), a note of an error to be corrected in a book.

cor·ri·gi·ble (kôr′ijəbəl), *adj.* capable of being corrected; submitting to correction.

cor·rob·o·rant (kərob′ərənt), *adj.* confirming; corroborating.

cor·tège (kôrtezH′), *n.* a ceremonial procession, esp. at a funeral.

cor·tex (kôr′teks), *n.*, *pl.* **cor·ti·ces** (kôr′tisēz). **1.** the bark of a tree. **2.** the protective matter that surrounds the brain.

cor·ti·co·ster·oid (kôr′tikōster′oid), *n*, any of a class of steroids produced by the adrenal cortex.

co·rus·cant (kərus′kənt), *adj.* flashing; gleaming; sparkling.

cor·us·cate (kôr′əskāt), *v.* to sparkle or gleam; glitter.

cor·us·ca·tion (kôrəskā′sHən), *n.* a sparkling or gleaming; a sudden flash of wit.

cor·vine (kôr′vīn), *adj.* relating to or resembling a crow or crow family.

cor·y·ban·tic (kôrəban′tik), *adj.* wild; unrestrained; frenzied.

cosh·er (kosH′ər), *v.* to spoil or pamper.

cos·me·tol·ogy (koz′mitol′əjē), *n.* the art or technique of using cosmetics.

cos·mog·o·ny (kozmog′ənē), *n.* a theory of the origin of the universe.

cos·mog·ra·phy (kozmog′rəfē), *n.* the science dealing with the constitution and description of the universe. —**cos·mog′ra·pher,** *n.*

cos·mo·line (koz′məlēn), *n.* a kind of grease used for protecting weapons against rust, etc., during storage or shipment.

cos·mo·naut (koz′mənôt), *n.* an astronaut. —**cos·mo·nau′tic,** *adj.*

cos·mop·o·lis (kozmop′əlis), *n.* a city composed of cosmopolitan elements.

cos·mop·o·lite (kozmop′əlīt), *n.* one having a cosmopolitan outlook.

cos·mol·o·gy (kozmol′əjē), *n.* metaphysics dealing with the origin and structure of the universe and the laws of space and time.

cos·mo·ra·ma (kozməram′ə), *n.* a display of pictures from various parts of the world.

cos·mos (koz′məs), *n.* the universe viewed as an ordered system. —**cos′mic,** *adj.*

Cos·sack (kos′ak), *n.* a member of one of several Slav tribes living in south-ern Russia and known for their horsemanship.

cos·set (kos′it), *v.* to spoil, pamper, or coddle.

cos·ta (kos′tə), *n.*, *pl.* **cos·tae** (kos′tē). a rib or something resembling a rib. —**cos′tal,** *adj.*

cos·tate (kos′tāt), *adj.* having ribs.

cos·ter·mon·ger (kos′tərmuNG′ger), *n.* one who hawks fruit and vegetables.

cos·tive (kos′tiv), *adj.* constipated.

cos·trel (kos′trəl), *n.* a container made of leather or earthenware and having ears by which it may be suspended.

co·te·rie (kō′tərē), *n.* a small, usually exclusive, group of people with shared tastes, a common viewpoint, etc.

co·thur·nus (kōthur′nəs), *n.* a grave, dignified style of drama or acting.

couch·ant (kou′cHənt), *adj.* lying down.

cou·lisse (kōōlēs′), *n.* a piece of timber with a groove to allow a panel to slide along it.

cou·loir (kōōlwär′), *n.* a gorge on a mountainside.

cou·lomb (kōō′lom), *n.* a unit of electricity equal to the quantity transferred by one ampere in one second.

coun·ter·in·sur·gen·cy (koun′-tərinsur′jənsē), *n.* the taking of measures against internal subversion or guerrilla warfare. —**coun·ter·in·sur′ gent,** *n.*

coun·ter·prod·uc·tive (koun′tər-prəduk′tiv), *adj.* having a result opposite to that intended.

coun·ter·vail (kountərvel′), *v.* **1.** to act against with equivalent power; exert equal force against. **2.** to compensate; provide an equivalent for.

coup de grace (kōōdəgräs′), *pl.* **coups de grace** (kōōzdəgräs′). *French.* a death blow, esp. one intended to end the agony of a mortally wounded person.

coup d'é·tat (kōō′dätä′), *pl.* **coups d'é·tat** (kōōz′ dätä′), a sudden change of government or regime, esp. by force.

coup de thé·a·tre (kōō də tāä′trə), *pl.*

61

credulity

coups de the·a·tre (kōō də tää'trə). *French.* a sudden change or startling development in a play.

coup d'oeil (kōō dōō'yə), *pl.* coups d'oeil (kōō dōō'yə). *French.* a brief survey or glance.

cour·te·san (kôr'tizən), *n.* a prostitute, esp. one with wealthy or highborn clientele.

cour·ti·er (kôr'tēər), *n.* an attendant upon a king at court.

cous·cous (kōōs'kōōs), *n.* a North African dish of semolina, meat, and vegetables.

cou·vade (kōōväd'), *n.* a custom among primitive peoples in which, at the time of a baby's birth, the father normally simulates pregnancy and performs other acts associated with the female role in society.

cov·e·nant (kuv'ənənt), *n.* 1. a formal agreement between two or more parties to perform some specified action. —*v.* 2. to enter into a covenant; promise; pledge.

cov·ert (kuv'ərt), *adj.* 1. sheltered; protected. 2. secret; disguised.

cov·er·ture (kuv'ərCHər), *n.* a shelter, cover, or covering; disguise or concealment.

cov·et (kuv'it), *v.* to desire avidly, esp. that which belongs to another. —cov'et·ous, *adj.*

cov·ey (kuv'ē), *n.* a flock of partridges or similar birds.

cox·al·gi·a (koksal'jēə), *n.* a pain in the hip.

cox·comb (koks'kōm), *n.* a conceited fop or dandy. —cox·comb·ry (koks'-kōmrē), *n.*

coze (kōz), *v.* to engage in friendly conversation.

coz·en (kuz'ən), *v.* to defraud, cheat or beguile.

coz·en·age (kuz'ənij), *n.* the practice of deceiving or cozening.

craal (kräl), *n.* See kraal.

crack·nel (krak'nl), *n.* a biscuit or cake having a hard and brittle texture.

cram·pon (kram'pən), *n.* 1. a spiked iron plate worn on shoes to prevent slipping on ice, etc. 2. a grappling iron used in raising weights.

cra·ni·al (krā'nēəl), *adj.* relating to the skull or cranium.

cra·ni·ate (krā'nēit), *adj.* having a cranium.

cra·ni·ol·o·gy (krā'nēol'əjē), *n.* the study of variations in the size and shape of human skulls.

cra·ni·om·e·try (krā'nēom'itrē), *n.* the science of cranial measurement.

cra·ni·o·phore (krā'nēəfôr'), *n.* an apparatus for holding a skull in position while it is being measured.

cra·ni·os·co·py (krā'nēos'kəpē), *n.* examination of the human skull.

cra·ni·ot·o·my (krā'nēot'əmē), *n.* the cutting open of the skull, usually for brain operations.

cra·ni·um (krā'nēəm), *n.* the skull, esp. that part which encloses the brain.

cran·kle (kraNG'kəl), *v.* to turn, wind or bend.

crap·au·dine door (krapədēn'), a door rotating on pivots.

crap·u·lent (krap'yōōlənt), *adj.* sick as a result of gross over-indulgence in food or drink.

crap·u·lous (krap'yōōləs), *adj.* 1. indulging in excessive eating and drinking. 2. suffering from the effects of excessive eating and drinking.

cra·que·lure (kraklōōr'), *n.* hairline cracks in the surfaces of very old paintings.

cra·sis (krā'sis), *n.* constitution; makeup.

crass (kras), *adj.* lacking delicacy or refinement; insensitive; boorish; stupid.

cras·si·tude (kras'itōōd), *n.* 1. stupidity or ignorance. 2. coarseness; grossness.

craunch (krônCH), *v.* to crunch.

cra·ven (krā'vən), *adj.* 1. cowardly. —*n.* 2. a cowardly person.

cre·den·dum (kriden'dəm), *n.*, *pl.* cre·den·da (kriden'də). that which must be believed; an article of faith.

cre·dent (krēd'nt), *adj.* trusting; believing.

cre·du·li·ty (krədōō'litē), *n.* excessive willingness to believe, esp. with only slight evidence.

cred·u·lous (krej′ələs), *adj.* ready to believe on insufficient evidence; gullible; naive.

creese (krēs), *n.* a Malay dagger with a wavy blade. Also **kris.**

crème de la crème (krem′ də la krem′), *French.* the very best part of something.

cre·morne bolt (krimôrn′), one of a pair of rods attached to full-length windows which slide into sockets at the top and bottom of the window to provide a secure fastening.

cre·nate (krē′nāt), *adj.* having the edge cut into scallop shapes, as certain leaves.

cre·na·tion (krinā′sнən), *n.* a crenate formation on the edge of a leaf. Also **cren′a·ture.**

cren·el, cre·nelle (kren′l), *n.* any of the recesses alternating with the merlons on a battlement.

cren·el·ate (kren′əlāt), *v.* to provide with crenels. —**cren·el·a′tion,** *n.*

cren·u·late (kren′yəlāt), *adj.* having tiny crenations.

cren·u·la·tion (krenyəlā′sнən), *n.* a minute crenation.

cre·o·lized (krē′əlīzd), *adj.* (of a language) having ceased to be pidgin and become a native language.

crep·i·tant (krep′itnt), *adj.* rustling; crackling.

crep·i·tate (krep′itāt), *v.* to make a rustling or crackling sound.

cre·pus·cule (kripus′kyōōl), *n.* twilight. —**cre·pus·cu·lar** (kripus′kyələr), *adj.*

cre·scen·do (krisнen′dō), *n., pl.* **cre·scen·dos, cre·scen·di** (krisнen′dē). a gradual increase in loudness, force, etc.

cres·cive (kres′iv), *adj.* growing; increasing.

cres·set (kres′it), *n.* an iron basket containing oil, pitch, etc., and suspended on high for use as a beacon or torch.

crest rail, the carved rail at the top of a settee or chair.

Cre·ta·ceous (kritā′sнəs), *adj.* relating to the last period of the Mesozoic era, characterized by the advent of insects and the extinction of the giant dinosaurs.

cre·tin (krēt′n), *n.* one suffering from cretinism.

cre·tin·ism (krēt′ənizm), *n.* a disease caused by extreme thyroid deficiency and marked by deformity and by the stunting of both mental and physical growth.

crew·el·work (krōō′əlwurk), *n.* embroidery done with worsted yarn.

crib·ble (krib′əl), *v.* to make a criblé surface.

cri·blé (krēblā′), *adj.* (of an engraving plate) having a pattern of dots designed to tone down the contrast between solid black areas and areas of type.

crib·ri·form (krib′rifôrm), *adj.* having holes like a sieve.

criminal conversation, adultery.

crim·i·nal·is·tics (krimənlis′tiks), *n.* the science of crime detection.

criminal syndicalism, the advocacy of terrorism as a means of achieving political and economic reforms.

crim·i·nate (krim′ənāt), *v.* 1. to accuse of a crime. 2. to incriminate. 3. to condemn. —**crim′i·na·tive,** *adj.*

crim·i·nol·o·gy (krimənol′əjē), *n.* the scientific study of crime and criminals.

crine (krīn), *n.* hair.

cri·no·gen·ic (krīnəjen′ik), *adj.* tending to produce secretions.

cri·nose (krī′nōs), *adj.* hairy.

cri·o·sphinx (krī′əsfiNGks), *n., pl.* **cri·o·sphinx·es, cri·o·sphin·ges** (krī′əsfin′jēz). a sphinx having a ram's head.

cris·pate (kris′pāt), *adj.* curled; wrinkled.

cris·pa·tion (krispā′sнən), *n.* the act or process of curling or of being curled.

cris·sum (kris′əm), *n.* the area around the cloacal vent, underneath the tail of a bird. —**cris′sal,** *adj.*

cris·tate (kris′tāt), *adj.* crested.

crit·ic·as·ter (krit′ikastər), *n.* a critic lacking in ability.

cri·tique (kritēk′), *n.* a critical estimate of some problem, etc.

croft (krôft), *n.* a small plot of land for tillage or pasture. —**croft'er,** *n.*

crois·sant (krwäsäN'), *n.,* *pl.* **crois· sants** (krwäsaN'), a crescent-shaped roll made of leavened dough or puff paste.

crom·lech (krom'lek), *n.* a circle of upright stones or of flat stones resting on upright ones. See also **dolmen.**

cro·quette (krōket'), *n.* a rissole of minced meat or fish, coated with egg, breadcrumbs, etc., and fried.

cro·sier (krō'zHər), *n.* the pastoral staff of a bishop.

cross·let (krôs'lit), *n.* a small cross, esp. one appearing in a heraldic bearing.

crotch·et (krocH'it), *n.* **1.** a hook or a device resembling a hook. **2.** a fanciful notion. —**crotch'et·y,** *adj.*

croûte (krōōt), *n.* a crust.

crou·ton (krōō'ton), *n.* a small cube of fried or toasted bread used in soups.

croze (krōz), *n.* a groove at the ends of the staves of a barrel into which the top and bottom parts fit.

cru·ci·ate (krōō'sHeit), *adj.* shaped like a cross.

cru·ci·fer (krōō'səfər), *n.* one who bears a cross in a religious procession, etc.

cru·cif·er·ous (krōōsif'ərəs), *adj.* having or bearing a cross.

cru·ci·form (krōōsəfôrm), *adj.* shaped like a cross.

cru·et (krōō'it), *n.* a container for vinegar, oil, etc.

cruis·er·weight (krōō'zərwāt), *n.* See **light heavyweight.**

cru·ral (krōōr'əl), *adj.* relating to the thigh or leg.

cruse (krōōz), *n.* a small jar or pot for holding liquids.

crus·ta·cean (krustā'sHən), *n.* any of a class of mainly aquatic arthropods including lobsters, shrimps, crabs, etc.

cry·o·gen (krī'əjən), *n.* an agent or substance for producing low temperatures; refrigerant.

cry·ol·o·gy (krīol'əjē), *n.* the scientific study of snow and ice.

cry·om·e·ter (krīom'itər), *n.* a thermometer for use at low temperatures.

cry·os·co·py (krīos'kəpē), *n.* the determination of the freezing points of liquids or of the lowering of freezing points produced in liquids by dissolved substances.

cry·o·stat (krī'əstat), *n.* an apparatus for maintaining low temperatures.

cry·o·ther·a·py (krī'ōther'əpē), *n.* medical treatment by the inducing of low bodily temperatures. Also **cry· mo·ther'a·py.**

crypt·a·nal·y·sis (kriptan'əlīz), *n.* the science of interpreting or translating codes, secret writings, cryptograms, etc. Also **cryp·to·a·nal'y·sis.**

cryp·to·clas·tic (kriptəklas'tik), *adj.* composed of minute fragments.

cryp·to·gram (krip'təgram), *n.* a message in code.

cryp·to·graph (krip'təgraf), *n.* **1.** a cryptogram. **2.** a method or system of secret writing.

cryp·tog·ra·phy (kriptog'rəfē), *n.* the study of secret codes. See also **plain text.**

cryp·tol·o·gy (kriptol'əjē), *n.* the science of cryptanalysis and cryptography.

cryp·tom·e·ter (kriptom'itər), *n.* a device for examining the surface underneath a coat of paint.

cryp·to·nym (krip'tənim), *n.* a secret name.

cryp·ton·y·mous (kripton'əməs), *adj.* anonymous.

cryp·to·phyte (krip'təfīt), *n.* a plant whose reproductive organs are formed underground.

cryp·to·por·ti·cus (kriptəpôr'təkəs), *n.* an enclosed passage with lights on one side.

crys·tal·log·ra·phy (kristəlog'rəfē), *n.* the science dealing with the structure and forms of crystals. —**crys· tal·lo·graph'ic,** *adj.*

cte·noid (tē'noid), *adj.* having a rough edge; pectinate.

cua·dril·la (kwädrē'yə), *n.* a group of five assistants to a bullfighter.

cub·age (kyōō'bij), *n.* cubic content.

cu·ba·ture (kyōō'bəcHər), *n.* determination of the cubic contents of a solid.

cu·bic·u·lum (kyōōbik′yələm), *n., pl.* **cu·bic·u·la** (kyōōbik′yələ). a tomb or burial chamber.

cu·bi·form (kyōō′bəfôrm), *adj.* having the shape of a cube.

Cub·ism (kyōō′bizm), *n.* an abstract style of painting characterized by attempts to reduce natural forms to their basic geometric shapes.

cu·bit (kyōō′bit), *n.* an ancient measure of length based on the length of the forearm.

cu·boid (kyōō′boid), *adj.* having a shape resembling a cube.

cuck·old (kuk′əld), *n.* **1.** a man whose wife is unfaithful. —*v.* **2.** to make (a man) a cuckold.

cu·cul·ate (kyōō′kəlāt), *adj.* shaped like a hood; hooded.

cu·cu·mi·form (kyōōkyōō′məfôrm), *adj.* having the shape of a cucumber; cylindrical.

cud·dy (kud′ē), *n.* a small cabin on a ship.

cuir·bouil·li (kwērbōōye′), *n. French.* leather which is hardened by soaking in hot water.

culch (kulCH), *n.* the mass of material, as stones, shells, etc., forming an oyster bed.

cul-de-sac (kul′dəsak′), *n., pl.* **culs-de-sac** (kulz′dəsak′), **1.** a body cavity or tube, resembling a sac and open only at one end. **2.** a road or passage shut at one end; blind alley; dead-end street.

cu·li·nar·y (kyōō′lənerē), *adj.* relating to cookery or the kitchen.

cul·let (kul′it), *n.* broken glass which can be remelted and used again.

culm (kulm), *n.* **1.** refuse coal; coal dust. **2.** a cheap variety of anthracite.

cul·pa (kul′pə), *n., pl.* **cul·pae** (kul′-pē), neglect; sin; guilt.

cul·pa·ble (kul′pəbəl), *adj.* meriting condemnation or censure; blameworthy.

cul·ti·gen (kul′tijən), *n.* a cultivated species of plant whose wild origin is not known.

cul·ti·var (kul′təvär), *n.* a plant which has been originated by cultivation.

cul·trate (kul′trāt), *adj.* having a sharp edge and point, as a leaf.

cultural anthropology, the study of the origins and evolution of human culture.

cultural lag, the relatively slow development of one section of a culture compared with another.

cum·brance (kum′brəns), *n.* a source of trouble; a burden or liability; encumbrance.

cum·brous (kum′brəs), *adj.* burdensome; cumbersome.

cum dividend, including a previously declared dividend. See also **ex dividend.**

cum gra·no sa·lis (kōōm grä′nō sä′-lis), *Latin.* with a grain of salt.

cum lau·de (kōōm lô′də), with honor; with (academic) distinction. See also **magna cum laude, summa cum laude.**

cu·mu·li·form (kyōō′myələfôrm), *adj.* resembling cumulus clouds.

cu·mu·lo·cir·rus (kyōō′myələsir′-əs), *n., pl.* **cu·mu·lo·cir·rus.** See **cirrocumulus.**

cu·mu·lo·nim·bus (kyōō′myələnim′bəs), *n., pl.* **cu·mu·lo·nim·bus.** a cumulus cloud of great depth with a tower—or mountain-shaped summit.

cu·mu·lo·stra·tus (kyōō′myələstrā′-təs), *n., pl.* **cu·mu·lo·stra·tus.** See **stratocumulus.**

cu·mu·lous (kyōō′myələs), *adj.* resembling a cumulus cloud.

cunc·ta·tion (kuNGktā′sHən), *n.* delay.

cunc·ta·tor (kuNGktā′tər), *n.* one who delays or procrastinates.

cu·ne·al (kyōō′nēəl), *adj.* wedge-shaped.

cu·ne·ate (kyōō′nēit), *adj.* wedge-shaped.

cu·ne·at·ic (kyōō′nēat′ik), *adj.* cuneiform.

cu·nic·u·lus (kyōōnik′yələs), *n., pl.* **cu·nic·u·li** (kyōōnik′yəlī). a small underground passage.

cu·pel (kyōō′pəl), *n.* a shallow porous

cup used for separating precious metals from lead.

cu·pid·i·ty (kyŏopid'itē), *n.* a strong or inordinate desire; avarice.

cu·pric (kyŏō'prik), *adj.* containing copper.

cu·prif·er·ous (kyŏōprif'ərəs), *adj.* yielding or bearing copper.

cu·pu·late (kyŏō'pyəlāt), *adj.* having the shape of a cupule.

cu·pule (kyŏō'pyŏōl), *n.* a cup-shaped process, as in the acorn.

cu·ra·trix (kyŏōrā'triks), *n.*, *pl.* **cu·ra·tri·ces** (kyŏōrətrī'sez). a woman curator.

cu·ret·tage (kyŏōret'ij), *n.* the operation of curetting.

cu·rette (kyŏōret'), *n.* **1.** a small spoon or scooplike instrument for scraping or cleaning body cavities. —*v.* **2.** to scrape with a curette.

curf (kurf), *n.* See **kerf.**

cu·rie (kyŏōr'ē), *n.* the unit of measurement of activity of a radioactive substance.

cu·ri·o·sa (kyŏōr'ēō'sə), *n.* books dealing with pornographic subjects; erotic literature.

cur·ric·u·lum vi·tae (kərik'yələm vī'tē), *pl.* **cur·ric·u·la vi·tae** (kərik'yələ vī'tē), a brief account of one's professional or business career.

cur·rish (kur'isн), *adj.* resembling a cur; quarrelsome or contemptible.

curtain shutter. See **focal-plane shutter.**

cur·tate (kur'tāt), *adj.* shortened; curtailed.

cu·rule (kyŏōr'ŏōl), *adj.* of the highest rank or position.

cur·vet (kərvet'), *v.* to prance, frisk or caper.

cus·pi·dal (kus'pidl), *adj.* resembling or having a cusp; cuspidate.

cus·pi·date (kus'pidāt), *adj.* having cusps.

cus·tom·ar·y (kus'təmer'ē), *n.* a book or code of legal customs. Also **cus·tu·mal** (kus'сноōməl), *n.*

cus·tom-made (kus'təm mād'), *adj.* made specially to order.

cu·ta·ne·ous (kyŏōtā'nēəs), *adj.* relating to or affecting the skin.

cu·tin (kut'in), *n.* a waxy substance forming a layer on the outer epidermal surface of plants.

cu·tin·ize (kyŏōt'ənīz), *v.* to make into cutin.

cu·tis (kyŏō'tis), *n.* the dermis or true skin.

cut·tage (kut'ij), *n.* the propagation of plants from vegetative means.

cu·vée (kŏōvā'), *n.* wine obtained by blending different vintages.

cy·an·e·ous (sīan'ēəs), *adj.* of a deep blue color.

cy·an·ic (sīan'ik), *adj.* of a bluish color.

cy·a·nom·e·ter (sīənom'itər), *n.* an instrument for measuring the intensity of blue in a sky, etc.

cy·a·no·sis (sīənō'sis), *n.* a bluish discoloration of the skin caused by insufficient oxygenation of the blood.

cy·ber·net·ics (sī'bərnet'iks), *n.* the comparative study of communication and control systems in machines, esp. computers, and similar functions in the human nervous system and brain.

cy·cle (sī'kəl), *n.* a series of regularly recurrent changes in an electric current.

cy·clo·gen·e·sis (sīkləjen'isis), *n.* the appearance and development of a cyclone.

cy·cloid (sī'kloid), *adj.* like a circle; circular.

cy·clol·y·sis (sīklol'isis), *n.* the diminution and disappearance of a cyclone.

cy·clom·e·ter (sīklom'itər), *n.* **1.** an instrument for measuring circular arcs. **2.** an instrument for recording the revolutions of a wheel; often used for registering the distance traveled by a wheeled vehicle.

cy·clone (sī'klōn), *n.* a region of low atmospheric pressure surrounded by circular wind motion. See also **anti-cyclone.**

cyclone furnace, a furnace which burns liquid fuel in a revolving column of air.

Cy·clo·pe·an (sīkləpē'ən), *adj.* relating to a method of building using large, irregular, or undressed stones.

cy·clo·ram·a (sīkləram′ə), *n.* **1.** a panoramic pictorial representation of a landscape, etc., that encircles the spectator as he sits in the center of a hall, etc. **2.** a curved backcloth, etc., in a theater designed to give an impression of great distance.

cy·clo·sis (sīklō′sis), *n.*, *pl.* **cy·clo·ses** (sīklō′sēz). the movement of protoplasm inside a cell.

cy·clo·stom·a·tous (sīkləstōm′ətəs), *adj.* having a circular mouth.

cy·clo·thy·mi·a (sīkləthī′mēə), *n.* a psychosis marked by alternating moods of depression and elation. —**cy·clo·thy′mi·ac,** *n.*

cy·clo·tron (sī′klətron), *n.* a device for causing electrified particles to move at very high speeds in spiral paths in a strong magnetic field.

cy·e·sis (sīē′sis), *n.*, *pl.* **cy·e·ses** (sīē′-sēz). pregnancy.

cyg·net (sig′nit), *n.* a young swan.

cyl·in·droid (sil′indroid), *n.* **1.** a solid shaped like a cylinder. —*adj.* **2.** resembling a cylinder.

cy·maise (sēmez′), *n.* a pewter container for wine with a spout and handle.

cym·bi·form (sim′bəfôrm), *adj.* shaped like a boat.

cy·mo·graph (sī′məgraf), *n.* See **kymograph.**

cy·mot·ri·chous (sīmo′trəkəs), *adj.* having curly or wavy hair.

Cym·ric (kim′rik), *n.* the Welsh language.

cy·no·sure (sī′nəshŏŏr), *n.* a center of attention; something which strongly attracts; something which guides or directs.

Cy·ril·lic (siril′ik), *adj.* relating to the alphabet used for writing Old Church Slavonic and now for Russian and various other languages.

cyr·to·sis (sərtō′sis), *n.* curvature of the spine.

cyst (sist), *n.* **1.** a sac in animal tissues. **2.** a sporelike cell in plants enclosing reproductive bodies.

cystic fibrosis (sis′tik fībrō′sis), a hereditary disease affecting the pancreas and lungs, and characterized by an inability to digest and difficulty in breathing.

cyst·oid (sis′toid), *adj.* resembling a cyst.

cys·to·scope (sis′təskōp), *n.* an instrument for examining the bladder.

cys·tos·co·py (sistos′kəpē), *n.* examination of the bladder by using a cystoscope.

cy·to·ar·chi·tec·ture (sī′tōär′kitek′-CHər), *n.* the structure of cells in a tissue.

cy·to·chem·is·try (sītəkem′istrē), *n.* the chemistry of living cells. —**cy·to·chem′i·cal,** *adj.*

cy·toc·la·sis (sītok′ləsis), *n.* the destruction of cells. **cy·to·clas·tic** (sītəklas′tik), *adj.*

cy·to·gen·e·sis (sītəjen′isis), *n.* the genesis and development of cells.

cy·to·ge·net·ics (sī′tōjənet′iks), *n.* the branch of biology dealing with the study of heredity using the methods of both cytology and genetics.

cy·toid (sī′toid), *adj.* resembling a cell.

cy·to·ki·ne·sis (sī′tōkinē′sis), *n.* cytoplasmic changes during mitosis, meiosis, and fertilization.

cy·tol·o·gist (sītol′əjist), *n.* one who specializes in cytology.

cy·tol·o·gy (sītol′əjē), *n.* the study of living cells.

cy·tol·y·sis (sītol′isis), *n.* the destruction or dissolution of living cells.

cy·ton (sīt′n), *n.* the body of a nerve cell.

cy·to·path·o·gen·ic (sī′tōpath′əjen′-ik), *adj.* destructive to cells.

cy·to·pa·thol·o·gy (sī′tōpəthol′əjē), *n.* the study of the diseases of cells.

cy·toph·a·gy (sītof′əjē), *n.* the engulfing of cells by other cells.

cy·to·plast (sī′təplast), *n.* the cytoplasmic contents of a cell.

cy·to·plasm (sī′təplazm), *n.* the protoplasm of a cell surrounding the nucleus.

cy·to·some (sī′təsōm), *n.* the cytoplasm of a cell.

cy·to·tax·is (sītətak′sis), *n.* the mutual attraction and repulsion of cells.

cy·to·tox·in (sītətok′sin), *n.* a substance in the blood which is harmful to certain cells.

cy·to·trop·ic (sītətrop′ik), *adj.* attracted toward or moving away from cells. —**cy·tot·ro·pism** (sīto′trəpizm), *n.*

cy·to·zo·on (sītəzō′ən), *n., pl.* **cy·to·zo·a** (sītəzō′ə). a parasite living inside a cell.

czar·e·vitch, tsar·e·vitch (zär′-əviCH), *n.* the son of a czar.

cza·rev·na, tsa·rev·na (zärev′nə), *n.* the daughter of a czar.

cza·ri·na, tsa·ri·na (zärē′nə), *n.* the wife of a czar.

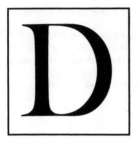

da·cha, dat·cha (dä′CHə), *n*. (in Russia) a country house.

da·coit, da·koit (dəkoit′), *n*. (in India and Burma) one of a group of robbers that plunder in bands.

da·coit·y, da·koit·y (dəkoi′tē), *n*. organized robbery by bands.

dac·ry·a·gogue (dak′rēəgôg), *adj*. causing the secretion of tears.

dac·tyl (dak′tl), *n*. a digit, as a finger or toe. —**dac·tyl′ic**, *adj*.

dac·tyl·o·gram (daktil′əgram), *n*. a fingerprint.

dac·ty·log·ra·phy (daktəlog′rəfē), *n*. study of fingerprints for identification.

dac·ty·lol·o·gy (daktəlol′əjē), *n*. method of communicating by hand and finger signs.

dac·ty·lo·meg·a·ly (dak′təlōmeg′əlē), *n*. enlargement of a finger or fingers.

Da·da (dä′dä), *n*. (sometimes *l.c.*) a movement in art and literature of the early 20th century to discredit all previous art by making use of inappropriate materials and unrelated techniques.

dae·dal (dē′dl), *adj*. 1. skillful; cleverly inventive. 2. intricate; diversified; maze-like.

dae·mon, dai·mon (dē′mən), *n*. 1. a lesser god, as the protector of a place or a man's attendant spirit. 2. an evil spirit.

dakh·ma (däk′mə), *n*. a stone platform, about 30 feet high, on which the Parsees leave their dead.

da·koit (dəkoit′), *n*. See **dacoit**.

da·koit·y (dəkoi′tē), *n*. See **dacoity**.

dalles (dalz), *n. pl.* the rapids of a river running down a canyon or gorge. Also **dells**.

dal·li·ance (dal′ēəns), *n*. amorous behavior; flirtatious trifling.

dam·a·scene (dam′əsēn), *v*. 1. to ornament steel with wavy lines. —*n*. 2. steel so ornamented.

D and C, dilation (or dilatation) and curettage; the surgical removal by scraping of tissue from the lining of the uterus.

danse ma·ca·bre (däns maka′brə). 1. a symbolic dance leading the dead to the grave. 2. an artist's representation of this. Also **dance of death**.

dap (dap), *v*. to dip into water.

dar·by (där′bē), *n*. a plasterer's float with two handles.

dark lan·tern (därk lan′tern), a lantern whose light can be concealed by a shutter.

dark·le (där′kəl), *v*. to be or become dark, gloomy, or indistinct.

dark·some (därk′səm), *adj*. dark.

dar·tle (där′tl), *v*. to dart back and forth rapidly.

da·sein (dä′zīn), *n*. awareness of the circumstances of one's own existence.

dash·pot (dasH′pot), *n*. a pneumatic

or hydraulic piston-like device for absorbing shocks or reversing the direction of a machine part.

das·tard (das′tərd), *n.* a contemptible coward. —**das·tard·ly,** *adj.*

da·sym·e·ter (dasim′itər), *n.* an instrument for measuring gas density.

das·y·phyl·lous (dasəfil′əs), *adj.* having hairy leaves.

dat·cha (dä′chə), *n.* See **dacha.**

daube (dōb), *n.* a meat and vegetable stew.

dau·er·schlaf (dou′ərsнläf), *n.* psychiatric treatment by drug-induced sleep.

daughter of Eve, a girl or woman.

dau·phin (dô′fin), *n. pl.* **dauphines** (dô′finz), the title of the eldest son of a King of France.

dau·phin·ess (dô′finis), *n.* the wife of a dauphin. Also **dauphine.**

dav·it (dav′it), *n.* any device on a ship or large boat for raising or lowering a small boat.

DDT, a white powder effective as an insecticide.

dead·fall (ded′fôl), *n.* a large trap for game in which the prey is struck or crushed by a heavy weight.

dead·ly sins, the sins of pride, covetousness, lust, anger, gluttony, envy, and sloth. Also **seven deadly sins.**

dead man's control, a device that must be held down by the driver of a train or other vehicle to control and maintain its motion.

dead man's hand, (in poker) a hand containing two aces and two eights.

dead reckoning, a method for calculating position using distance and directions run from last known position.

de·an·thro·po·mor·phism (dēan′-thrəpəmôr′fizm), *n.* the removal of anthromorphic beliefs from philosophy and religion.

dear text. See **plain text.**

dearth (dur*th*), *n.* scarcity or scanty supply; lack.

death instinct, inclination to suicide.

death rate, the number of deaths per thousand of population.

death rattle, a sound often produced

in the throat immediately before death, caused by the air forced through mucus.

de·ba·cle (dābä′kəl), *n.* **1.** a sudden, often ignominious collapse. **2.** the disintegration of ice in a river. See also **embacle.**

de·bauch (dibôcн′), *v.* to corrupt by excessive sexual pleasures; seduce. —**de·bauch′er·y,** *n.*

deb·au·chee (debôcнē′), *n.* one who indulges in excessive sensuality.

de·bil·i·tate (dibil′itāt), *v.* to weaken.

de·bil·i·ty (dibil′itē), *n.* state of being physically weak.

deb·o·nair, deb·o·naire, deb·on·naire (debəner′), *adj.* having pleasant manners; gracious, gay.

de·bouch (diboōsн), *v.* (of a river) to emerge from a narrow valley into a larger one.

de·bouch·ment (diboōsн′mənt), *n.* a mouth or outlet, as of a river or pass. Also **de·bou·chure** (dəboō′sнoŏr).

de·bride·ment (dibrēd′mənt), *n.* removal of dead tissue from a wound by surgery.

de·brief (dēbrēf′), *v.* to question closely on return from a mission to assess its conduct and results.

de·bug (dēbug′), *v.* to detect and eliminate errors, esp. from a computer program.

dec·a·gon (dek′əgon), *n.* a 10-sided plane figure.

dec·a·gram, dek·a·gram (dek′-əgram), *n.* a metric unit of 10 grams, equivalent to 0.3527 ounce avoirdupois.

dec·a·he·dron (dekəhē′drən), *n.* a solid with 10 faces.

de·cal·ci·fy (dēkal′səfī), *v.* to remove calcareous matter, as from a bone.

de·cal·co·ma·ni·a (dikal′kəmā′nēə), *n.* a paper bearing a picture, lettering, or design that may be transferred, usually by wetting it, onto another surface. Also **de·cal** (dē′kal).

de·ca·les·cence (dēkəles′əns), *n.* the more rapid absorption of heat in a piece of iron as it passes a certain temperature. —**de·ca·les′cent,** *adj.*

dec·a·li·ter, dek·a·li·ter (dek′əlēter),

n. a metric unit of 10 liters, equivalent to 9.08 quarts U.S. dry measure or 2.64 gallons U.S. liquid measure.

dec·a·logue, dec·a·log (dek′əlôg), *n.* the Ten Commandments. Ex. 20: 2–17.

de·cam·er·ous (dikam′ərəs), *adj.* having 10 parts.

dec·a·me·ter, dek·a·me·ter (dek′-əmētər), *n.* a linear measure of 10 meters.

de·camp (dikamp′), *v.* to depart hastily; run away.

dec·an (dek′ən), *n.* one division of 10° in a sign of the zodiac.

dec·a·nal (dek′ənl), *adj.* pertaining to a dean.

dec·a·pod (dek′əpod), *n.* **1.** a 10-legged crustacean, as a crab or lobster. **2.** a 10-armed cephalopod, as a cuttlefish.

de·cas·u·al·ize (dēkazH′ōōəlīz), *v.* to cease or curtail the hiring of temporary personnel.

dec·a·syl·la·ble (dek′əsil′əbəl), *n.* a word or verse containing 10 syllables. —**dec·a·syl·lab·ic** (dek ′əsilab′ik), *adj.*

de·cath·lon (dika*th*′lon), *n.* an athletic contest involving 10 different events with the same participants competing in all.

dec·at·ing (dek′ətiNG), *n.* an antishrinking process for textiles that provides a lustrous finish. Also **dec′a·tiz·ing.**

de·cay (dikā′), *v.* the disintegration of a radioactive substance in which a nucleus undergoes transformation into one or more different nuclei and simultaneously emits radiation, loses electrons, or undergoes fission. Also called **radioactive decay.**

de·ce·dent (disēd′nt), *n.* (in law) a deceased person.

de·cel·er·ate (dēsel′ərāt), *v.* to reduce in speed.

de·cel·er·on (dēsel′əron), *n.* (in aeronautics) an aileron acting as a brake.

de·cen·nial (disen′ēəl), *adj.* **1.** of or for 10 years; occurring every 10 years. **2.** an anniversary celebrating this.

de·cen·ni·um (disen′ēəm), *n.* a period of 10 years. Also **de·cen·na·ry.** (disen′ərē).

dec·i·bel (des′əbel), *n.* a unit in which the intensity of a sound wave is measured.

de·cid·u·ous (disij′ōōəs), *adj.* (of trees, teeth, etc.) dropping off or out after a period of growth.

dec·i·gram (des′əgram), *n.* a metric unit of weight of 1/10th gram, equivalent to 1.543 grains.

dec·ile (des′il), *n.* a value of a variable that divides its distribution into 10 equal sets.

dec·i·li·ter (des′əlētər), *n.* a metric unit of capacity of 1/10th liter, equivalent to 6.102 cu. in. or 3.381 U.S. fl. oz.

de·cil·lion (disil′yən), *n.* a number represented by a digit followed by 33 zeros.

dec·i·mate (des′əmāt), *v.* **1.** to destroy a large percentage of. **2.** to reduce by 1/10th.

dec·i·meter (des′əmētər), *n.* a metric unit of length equal to 1/10th of a meter.

deck·le edge (dek′əl ej), the irregular edge of handmade paper. Also **deckle.**

de·claim (diklām′), *v.* to make a speech, esp. in a dramatic manner. —**dec·la·ma·tion** (dekləmā′sHən), *n.* —**de·clama·tory** (diklam′ətôrē), *adj.*

de·clar·ant (dikler′ənt), *n.* one who makes a declaration.

de·clar·a·to·ry judgment (diklar′-ətôr′ē), a legal decision limited to declaring the rights of the parties.

de·clas·sé (dākləsā′), *adj.* (*fem.* **declassée**) of a lowered social class or status.

dec·li·nate (dek′lənāt), *adj.* curving downward. —**de·clin·a·to·ry** (diklī′-nətôr′ē), *adj.*

de·clin·a·ture (diklī′nəcHər), *n.* act of refusal.

dec·li·nom·e·ter (deklənom′itər), *n.* an instrument that measures the downward variation of a magnetic needle from true north or the angular distance of a star or planet from the celestial equator.

de·cliv·ity (dikliv′itē), *n.* a downward slope (from the observer's point of view). See also **acclivity.** —**de·cli·vous** (diklī′vəs), *adj.* —**de·cliv·i·tous** (dikliv′itəs), *adj.*

de·coct (dikokt′), *v.* to concentrate by boiling down. —**de·coc·tion** (dikok′sHən), *n.*

de·col·late (dikol′āt), *v.* to behead.

dé·colle·tage (dā′koltäzH′), *n.* the neck of a low-cut dress.

dé·colle·té (dā′koltā′), *adj.* (of a dress) cut low at the neck.

de·com·mis·sion (dēkəmisH′ən), *v.* to remove (equipment) from active service.

de·com·pen·sa·tion (de′kompənsā′-sHən), *n.* the inability of a defective heart to make up for its defect.

de·com·pres·sion sickness (dēkəm-presH′ən), a condition caused by the formation of nitrogen bubbles in the blood coming in coming from an atmosphere of high pressure to air of ordinary pressure. Also **bends, caisson disease, nitrogen narcosis.**

de·con·gest (dēkənjest′), *v.* to reduce the congestion of.

de·con·ges·tant (dēkənjes′tənt), *n.* a medicine that relieves congestion.

de·con·ges·tive (dēkənjes′tiv), *adj.* relieving congestion.

de·con·se·crate (dēkon′səkrāt), *v.* to secularize.

de·cor·ti·cate (dēkôr′təkāt), *v.* to peel; remove the husk or bark from. —**de·cor·ti·ca′tion,** *n.*

de·co·rum (dikôr′əm), *n.* dignified and appropriate demeanor, appearance, etc.

de·cou·page (dā′koōpäzH′), *n.* decoration with paper cutouts.

de·cree ni·si (dikrē′ nī′sī), a legal decree, usually of a divorce, rendering it effective at a future date.

dec·re·ment (dek′rəmənt), *n.* a gradual diminution or the amount so lost.

de·crep·i·tate (dikrep′itāt), *v.* to crackle.

de·crep·i·tude (dikrep′itoōd), *n.* a state of weakness; decrepit condition, esp. from old age.

de·cre·scen·do (dēkrisHen′dō), *n.* a gradual decrease in volume.

de·cres·cent (dikres′ənt), *adj.* decreasing; lessening.

de·cre·tal (dikrēt′l), *adj.* pertaining to or embodying a decree.

de·cre·tive (dikrē′tiv), *adj.* of or with the force of a decree.

dec·re·to·ry (dek′ritôrē), *adj.* of or in keeping with a decree.

de·crypt (dēkript′), *v.* to decode.

de·cub·i·tus (dikyoō′bitəs), *n. pl.* **de·cub·i·ti** (dikyoō′bitē). (in medicine) the position a patient assumes in bed.

dec·u·man (dek′yoōmən), *adj.* of great magnitude, as a wave.

de·cum·bent (dikum′bənt), *adj.* prone; recumbent.

dec·u·ple (dek′yoōpəl), *adj.* tenfold.

de·curved (dēkurvd′), *adj.* curving downward.

de·cus·sate (dikus′āt), *adj.* crossed; intersected.

deem·ster (dēm′stər), *n.* (on the Isle of Man) a judge.

deer·stalk·er (dēr′stôkər), *n.* a cloth cap with peaks front and back and flaps that can cover the ears.

de·es·ca·late (dēes′kəlāt), *v.* to lower and decrease the intensity of, as a war. —**de·es·ca·la′tion,** *n.*

de·e·sis (dēē′sis), *n. pl.* **de·e·ses** (dēē′-sēz). (in Byzantine art) a representation of Christ on a throne attended by St. John and the Virgin Mary.

de fac·to (dē fak′tō), *Latin.* **1.** actually existing, though not by legal right. **2.** in reality. See also **de jure.**

de·fal·cate (difal′kāt), *v.* to misappropriate money.

de·fal·ca·tion (dē′falkā′sHən), *n.* the misappropriation of money by a trusted official.

de·fea·sance (difē′zəns), *n.* (in law) the process of rendering something null and void.

de·fea·si·ble (difē′zəbəl), *adj.* able to be ended or annulled.

de·fend·ant (difen′dnt), *n.* a person against whom a legal suit or charge is being brought in a court of law. See also **plaintiff.**

de·fen·es·tra·tion (dēfen′istrā′-

defervesce

sʜən), *n.* the throwing of somebody
or something out of a window.

de·fer·vesce (dēfərves′), *v.* to have
a fever reduced.

de·fer·ves·cence (dēfərves′əns), *n.*
the lessening of fever.

de·fi·bril·late (dēfī′brəlāt), *v.* to stop
the formation of thread-like fibres in
the heart muscles.

de·fi·bril·la·tor (dēfī′brəlātər), *n.* a
device for defibribillating.

def·i·cit financ·ing (def′isit), a system of governmental finance that allows expenditures to exceed reve-
nues, usually through borrowing.

def·i·cit spend·ing (def′isit spend′-
diNG), a system of governmental finance that allows expenditures in excess of income.

def·i·lade (defəlād′), *n.* protection
afforded by any obstacle, as a hill,
from enemy fire.

de·fin·i·en·dum (difin′ēen′dəm), *n.
pl.* **de·fin·i·en·da** (difin′ēen′də).
something to be defined, as a dictionary headword.

de·fin·i·ens (difin′ēənz), *n. pl.* **de·fin·i·en·tia** (difin′ēen′sʜə). something
that defines, as a dictionary defini-
tion.

de·fin·i·tude (difin′ito͞od), *n.* precision; exactness.

def·la·grate (def′ləgrāt), *v.* to burn,
esp. with near-explosive force. —**def·la·gra′tion,** *n.*

de·floc·cu·lant (dēflok′yələnt), *n.* a
chemical for diluting ceramic slip.

de·floc·cu·late (dēflok′yəlāt), *v.* to
disperse compound masses of particles.

def·lo·ra·tion (deflərā′sʜən), *n.* act
of depriving a woman of virginity.

de·flow·er (diflou′ər), *v.* to ravish a
woman.

de·flux·ion (difluk′sʜən), *n.* a fluid
discharge, as catarrh.

de·fo·li·ant (dēfō′lēənt), *n.* a chemical
that strips the leaves of plants.

de·fo·li·ate (dēfō′lēāt), *v.* to strip the
leaves from (a plant or tree). —**de·fo·li·a′tion,** *n.*

de·funct (difuNGkt′), *adj.* **1.** no longer
functioning; dead.

de·func·tive (difuNGk′tiv), *adj.* pertaining to dead people.

de·fu·sion (dēfyo͞o′zʜən), *n.* (in psychoanalysis) the distinguishing between the instinct to live and the
death instinct.

dé·ga·gé (dāgazʜā′), *adj.* (*fem.* **dé·ga·gée**), *French.* free and easy in
manner; not emotionally involved.

de·gauss (dēgous′), *v.* to demagnetize
(equipment).

de·gla·ci·a·tion (dēglā′sēā′sʜən), *n.*
the melting of a glacier.

de·glu·ti·tion (dē′glo͞otisʜ′ən), *n.* act
of swallowing.

de·gres·sion (digresʜ′ən), *n.* **1.** a descent. **2.** a decrease in the rate of
taxation on incomes below a certain
amount. —**de·gres′sive,** *adj.*

de·gust (digust′), *v.* to taste. Also **de·gus′tate.**

de gus·ti·bus non est dis·pu·tan·dum (dego͞os′tibo͞os nōnest dis′-po͞otän′do͞om), *Latin.* there is no dis-
puting tastes.

de·hisce (dihis′), *v.* to burst open, as
a seed pod.

de·his·cence (dihis′əns), *n.* the
bursting open of seed pods and discharging of their seeds. —**de·his′cent,** *adj.*

de·i·cide (dē′isīd), *n.* **1.** the killing of
a god. **2.** one who kills a god. —**de·i·cid′al,** *adj.*

deic·tic (dīk′tik), *adj.* **1.** (in logic)
serving to prove directly. **2.** (in grammar) demonstrating.

de·if·ic (dēif′ik), *adj.* deifying.

de·i·form (dē′əfôrm), *adj.* like a god.

de·i·fy (dē′əfī), *v.* to exalt; make a god
of; adore and respect as a god. —**de·if·i·ca′tion,** *n.*

deign (dān), *v.* to condescend.

deip·nos·o·phist (dīpnos′əfist), *n.* a
good conversationalist.

dé·jà vu (dāzʜavY′), one's impression that he has already experienced
something when actually it is being
encountered for the first time.

de·jec·ta (dijek′tə), *n. pl.* human excrement.

de ju·re (dē jo͞or′ē), according to the
law; rightfully. See also **de facto.**

dek·a·gram (dek′əgram), *n.* See **decagram.**

dek·a·li·ter (dek′əlētər), *n.* See **decaliter.**

dek·a·me·ter (dek′əmētər), *n.* See **decameter.**

de·lam·i·nate (dēlam′ənāt), *v.* to divide into thin leaves or layers. —**de·lam·i·na′tion,** *n.*

de·le (dē′lē), *v.* (in printing) to delete.

del·e·te·ri·ous (del′itēr′ēəs), *adj.* harmful; noxious.

delft (delft), *n.* a white and blue earthenware.

del·i (del′ē), *n. pl.* **del·is** (del′ēz), a delicatessen.

de·lict (dilikt′), *n.* (in law) an offense.

de·lim·it (dilim′it), *v.* to fix the boundaries of. Also **de·lim·i·tate** (dilim′itāt).

de·lin·e·ate (dilin′ēāt), *v.* to describe precisely; portray in words. —**de·lin′e·a·tor,** *n.*

del·i·quesce (deləkwes′), *v.* to melt; become liquid. —**del·i·ques′cence,** *n.*

de·lir·i·um tre·mens (dilēr′ēəm trē′-mənz), delirium caused by chronic alcoholism. *Abbrev.:* **d.t.**

del·i·tes·cent (delites′ənt), *adj.* concealed; hidden away.

dells (delz), *n.* dalles.

del·phic (del′fik), *adj.* obscure; ambiguous.

de·lus·ter·ant (dēlus′tərənt), *n.* a chemical that reduces the luster on yarn.

dem·a·gogue (dem′əgôg), *n.* a politician who gains and holds power by playing on the passions and prejudices of the people. —**dem·a·gog·ic** (deməgoj′ik), *adj.*

dem·a·gog·u·er·y (dem′əgô′gərē), *n.* the techniques practised by a demagogue. Also **dem′a·gog·u·ism.**

dem·a·go·gy (dem′əgō′jē), *n.* a group of demagogues.

de·mar·cate (dimär′kāt), *v.* to mark out; limit; clearly separate. —**de·mar·ca′tion,** *n.*

de·mean (dimēn′), *v.* **1.** to degrade or debase. **2.** to behave (oneself). —**de·mean′ing·ly,** *adv.*

de·mean·or (dimē′nər), *n.* bearing; conduct; behavior.

de·men·ti·a (dimen′sнə), *n.* madness; severe loss of intellectual capacity combined with disintegration of personality.

dem·en·ti·a prae·cox (dimen′sнə prē′koks). a mental disease characterized by bizarre behavior and emotional deterioration; schizophrenia.

de·mesne (dimān′), *n.* the land round an estate, occupied and kept for the owner's sole use.

dem·i·john (dem′ijon), *n.* a large, narrow-necked bottle with wickerwork woven round it. See also **carboy.**

de·mil·i·ta·rize (dēmil′itərīz), *v.* to put under civil control.

dem·i·lune (dem′iloon), *n.* a crescent shape.

dem·i·mon·daine (dem′ēmondān′), *n.* a woman who has lost her reputation by indiscreet behavior.

dem·i·monde (dem′ēmond), *n.* a class of woman of dubious social standing.

dem·i·rep (dem′ērep), *n.* a woman with a reputation that has been compromised.

de·mis·sion (dimisн′ən), *n.* resignation; abdication.

dem·i·urge (dem′ēurj), *n.* **1.** the Platonic name for the maker of the world. **2.** a superhuman being in subordination to the supreme being.

de·moc·ra·cy (dimok′rəsē), *n.* government by the people; government by the majority.

de·mod·ed (dēmō′did), *adj.* old-fashioned; out of date.

de·mog·ra·phy (dimog′rəfē), *n.* the study of population statistics. —**de·mog′ra·pher,** *n.*

dem·oi·selle (demwäzel′), *n.* an unmarried girl.

de·mon·og·ra·phy (dēmənog′rəfē), *n.* a study or work about demons.

de·mon·ol·a·ter (dēmənol′ətər), *n.* a worshiper of demons.

de·mon·ol·a·try (dēmənol′ətrē), *n.* the worship of demons.

de·mon·ol·ogy (demənol′əjē), *n.* the

study of the beliefs held about demons.

de·mos (dē′mos), *n.* the population viewed as a political unit.

de·mot·ic (dimot′ik), *adj.* **1.** of the people; common. **2.** pertaining to the simplified form of ancient Egyptian writing. —*n.* **3. Demotic**, the common dialect of Modern Greek. See also **Katharevusa.**

de·mul·cent (dimul′sənt), *adj.* (of a medical substance) soothing.

de·mul·si·fy (dēmul′səfī), *v.* to separate (an emulsion) into components that cannot recombine to form the same emulsion.

de·mur (dimur′), *v.* to make difficulties; object; take exception.

de·mur·rage (dimur′ij), *n.* undue delaying of a ship, as in loading or unloading.

de·mur·rer (dimur′ər), *n.* an objection.

den·a·ry (den′ərē), *adj.* containing ten; having ten as the basic of reckoning; decimal.

de·na·tion·al·ize (dēnasн′ənəlīz), *v.* to remove (an industry) from the control of the government and place it in private hands.

de·nat·ure (dēnā′CHər), *v.* **1.** to destroy the natural character of. **2.** to add substance to (alcohol) to make it unfit for consumption.

den·drite (den′drīt), *n.* a tree-like pattern on a stone or mineral.

den·drit·ic (dendrit′ik), *adj.* marked like a dendrite; arborescent. Also **den·drit′i·cal.**

den·dro·chro·nol·o·gy (den′drōkrənol′əjē), *n.* the study of the annular rings of trees and their dating.

den·droid (den′droid), *adj.* branching, as a tree. Also **den·droi′dal.**

den·drol·o·gy (dendrol′əjē), *n.* the study of trees.

den·droph·a·gous (dendrof′əgəs), *adj.* feeding on trees.

den·droph·i·lous (dendrof′ələs), *adj.* living in trees.

den·e·ga·tion (denəgā′sнən), *n.* a denial.

den·gue (deNG′gā), *n.* an infectious tropical disease characterized by severe pains in the joints and muscles. Also **breakbone fever.**

de·ni·er (dənēr′), *n.* a unit of weight indicating the fineness of silk and synthetic yarns.

den·i·grate (den′əgrāt), *v.* to speak of in a derogatory manner; sneer; criticize.

de·nom·i·nate (dinom′ənāt), *v.* to name; designate. —**de·nom·i·na′ tion,** *n.* —**de·nom′i·na·tive,** *adj.*

de·no·ta·tion (dē′nōtā′sнən), *n.* the association of ideas that a word conjures up for most people. —**de′no·ta·tive,** *adj.*

de·note (dinōt′), *v.* to indicate; represent by a symbol.

de·noue·ment (dā′noōōmäN′), *n.* the climax and unraveling of a dramatic or literary plot.

de no·vo (denō′wō), *Latin.* again; afresh.

den·sim·e·ter (densim′itər), *n.* an instrument that measures density.

den·tate (den′tāt), *adj.* notched; with tooth-like projections.

den·ta·tion (dentā′sнən), *n.* a toothed form.

den·telle (dentel′), *n.* a tooled pattern used to decorate book covers.

den·ti·cle (den′tikəl), *n.* a small tooth; part shaped like a tooth.

den·tic·u·late (dentik′yəlit), *adj.* having many fine teeth, as the edge of a leaf.

den·tic·u·la·tion (dentik′yəlā′sнən), *n.* a group of denticles.

den·ti·form (den′təfôrm), *adj.* in the shape of a tooth.

den·til (den′tl), *n.* one of a continous pattern of small, square, tooth-like projections used in architecture on cornices and mouldings.

den·ti·tion (dentisн′ən), *n.* **1.** the number, arrangement, and kind of teeth. **2.** teething.

den·toid (den′toid), *adj.* like a tooth.

de·nu·mer·a·ble (dinoōō′mərəbəl), *adj.* countable.

de·on·tol·o·gy (dēonto′əjē), *n.* the study of duty and ethics. —**de·on·tol′o·gist,** *n.*

De·o vo·len·te (dā'ō vōlen'tā), *Latin.* God willing.

de·oxy·ri·bo·nu·cle·ase (dēok'siri'-bōnōō'klēās'), *n.* an enzyme found in the pancreas. Also **desoxyribonuclease.**

de·ox·y·ri·bo·nu·cle·ic ac·id (de-ok'siri'bōnōōklē'ik). See **DNA.**

de·paup·er·ate (dipô'pərit), *adj.* poorly developed.

dep·e·ter (dep'itər), *n.* a finish for exterior walls, consisting of mortar into which pebbles are pressed. Also **pebble dash.**

dep·i·late (dep'əlāt), *v.* to remove hair from. —**de·pil'a·to·ry,** *adj., n.*

de·pone (dipōn'), *v.* to declare under oath.

dep·re·date (dep'ridāt), *v.* to plunder; pillage; ravage. —**dep·re·da'tion,** *n.*

depressed area, a region characterized by much unemployment and low standards of living.

de·pres·sion (dipresH'ən), *n.* (in meteorology) an area of low atmospheric pressure.

de pro·fun·dis (dā prōfōōn'dis), *Latin.* out of the depths.

dep·u·rate (dep'yərāt), *v.* to purify; cleanse. —**dep'u·ra·tive,** *adj.*

de·pute (dəpyōot'), *v.* to appoint as a representative or agent.

de·rac·in·ate (diras'ənāt), *v.* to uproot; eradicate.

de·re·ism (dērē'izm), *n.* (in psychology) the tendency to regard life through daydreams and fantasies, with little regard to reality.

de·ride (dirīd'), *v.* to scoff; mock; ridicule.

de·ris·i·ble (diriz'əbəl), *adj.* worthy of being mocked.

de·ri·sion (dirizH'ən), *n.* act of deriding; state of being derided.

de·ri·sive (dirī'siv), *adj.* expressing ridicule; mocking.

der·ma (dur'mə), *n.* skin lying below the epidermis.

der·ma·bra·sion (durməbrā'zHən), *n.* the surgical removal of scars, etc., by abrasion.

der·ma·therm (dur'məthurm), *n.* an instrument for measuring the temperature of the skin.

der·ma·ti·tis (durmətī'tis), *n.* any mild inflammation of the skin.

der·mat·o·glyph·ics (dərmat'əglif'-iks), *n. pl.* the patterns and ridges on the skin of the hands and feet.

der·mat·o·graph·i·a (dərmat'əgraf'-ēə), *n.* a skin condition in which scratching causes red welts.

der·ma·toid (dur'mətoid), *adj.* skinlike. Also **dermoid.**

der·ma·tol·o·gy (durmətol'əjē), *n.* the study of the skin and its diseases. —**der·ma·tol'o·gist,** *n.*

der·ma·to·sis (durmətō'sis), *n. pl.* **der·ma·to·ses** (durmətō'sēz). a skin disease.

der·o·gate (der'əgāt), *v.* to detract or lessen as from estimation. —**der·o·ga'tion,** *n.*

de·rog·a·tive (dirog'ətiv), *adj.* belittling; lessening.

de·scend·er (disen'dər), *n.* (in lowercase letters) the part below the body or line. See also **ascender.**

de·scen·sion (disen'sHən), *n.* the part of the zodiac where a planet's influence is weakest.

de·seam (dēsēm'), *v.* to remove defects, as from ingots.

des·er·tic·o·lous (dezərtik'ələs), *adj.* growing or living in the desert.

des·ha·bille (dezəbēl'), *n.* See **dishabille.**

des·ic·cant (des'əkənt), *adj.* having an absorbing or drying effect.

des·ic·cate (des'əkāt), *v.* to dry; dehydrate. —**des'ic·ca·tor,** *n.*

de·sid·er·ate (disid'ərāt), *v.* to wish for; want.

de·sid·er·a·tive (disid'ərā'tiv), *adj.* wanting; desiring.

de·sid·er·a·tum (disid'ərā'təm), *n. pl.* **de·sid·er·a·ta** (disid'ərā'tə). something lacking and required.

des·i·nence (des'ənəns), *n.* termination, as the last syllable of a word.

des·mi·tis (desmī'tis), *n.* inflammation of a ligament.

des·moid (des'moid), *adj.* like a ligament.

des·ox·y·ri·bo·nu·cle·ase (desok'-

sirī′bŏnoo′klēas′), *n.* See **deoxyribonuclease.**

des·ox·y·ri·bo·nu·cle·ic ac·id (desok′sīrī′bŏnooklē′ik a′sid). See **DNA.**

des·pit·e·ous (dispit′ēəs), *adj.* spiteful, malicious, or contemptuous.

de·spoil (dispoil′), *v.* to plunder; rob; strip of possessions.

de·spo·li·a·tion (dispō′lēā′sHən), *n.* act of plunder or despoiling.

de·spond (dispond′), *v.* to lose heart; become dejected.

des·qua·mate (des′kwəmāt), *v.* (of skin) to peel off as scales, as in certain diseases.

de·ster·i·lize (dēster′əlīz), *v.* to use money or a commodity previously unused.

de·struct (distrukt′), *adj.* constructed so as to destroy itself.

des·ue·tude (des′witood), *n.* state of disuse. —**des·ue·tu′di·nous,** *adj.*

des·ul·to·ry (des′əltôre), *adj.* disconnected; casual; unmethodical.

de·su·per·heat·er (dēsoo′pərhē′tər), *n.* an apparatus, as in a boiler, for controlling and lowering the temperature of superheated steam.

de·tec·ta·phone (ditek′təfōn), *n.* a hidden device for listening in on telephone conversations.

de·tent (ditent′), *n.* a device for keeping one part of a machine in a certain position.

de·terge (diturj′), *v.* to clean, as a wound.

de·ter·gen·cy (ditur′jənsē), *n.* cleansing power.

de·ter·gent (ditur′jənt), *n.* a synthetic cleansing agent with strong emulsifying and cleansing powers.

de·ter·sive (ditur′siv), *adj.* **1.** cleansing. —*n.* **2.** a cleansing agent or medicine.

de·tox·i·cate (dētok′səkāt), *v.* to rid of poison. —**de·tox·i·ca′tion,** *n.*

de·tox·i·fy (dētok′səfī), *v.* to free from poison. —**de·tox·i·fi·ca′tion,** *n.*

de·tri·tal (ditrīt′l), *adj.* consisting of debris or detritus.

de·tri·tion (ditrisH′ən), *n.* a wearing away by abrasion.

det·ri·tiv·or·ous (de′tritiv′ərəs), *adj.* feeding on organic debris, as some insects.

de·tri·tus (ditrī′təs), *n.* any debris or disintegrated material.

de trop (dətrō′), *French.* too many; unwanted.

de·trude (ditrood′), *v.* to force or thrust down or away. —**de·tru·sion** (ditroo′zHən), *n.*

de·trun·cate (ditrunG′kāt), *v.* to cut down.

de·tu·mes·cence (dētoomes′əns), *n.* reduction of a swelling.

de·us ex ma·chi·na (de′ooseks mä′kinä), *Latin.* (orig. in classical Greek drama) a god who intervenes and sorts out the entanglements.

De·us vo·bis·cum (dā′oos vōbis′kum), *Latin.* God be with you.

deu·ter·a·nom·a·ly (doo′təranom′əlē), *n.* a vision defect in which there is a diminished response to green.

deu·ter·an·ope (doo′tərənōp), *n.* one with deuteranopia.

deu·ter·a·no·pi·a (doo′tərənō′pēə), *n.* a vision defect in which there is a lack of response to green.

deu·ter·og·a·my (dootərog′əmē), *n.* second marriage; digamy. See also **monogamy.**

dev·il·kin (dev′əlkin), *n.* an imp.

dev·il's tat·too (dev′əlz tatoo′), a nervous tapping with the hands or feet.

de·voir (dəvwär′), *n.* **1.** a formal act of respect. **2.** a duty or obligation.

dev·o·lu·tion (devəloo′sHən), *n.* **1.** the act of passing on from one stage to the next; bequeathal. **2.** biological degeneration.

de·volve (divolv′), *v.* to delegate or transfer (duties, etc.)

de·vote·ment (divōt′mənt), *n.* dedication.

dew·lap (doo′lap), *n.* a loose fold of skin under the throat of cattle.

dew·point (doo′point), *n.* the temperature at which dew forms, varying in relation to atmospheric pressure and humidity.

dew·point spread, the number of degrees between the dew point and the temperature of the air.

dex·ter (dek′stər), *adj.* on the right-hand side.

dex·tral (dek′strəl), *adj.* 1. on the right side. 2. right-handed.

dex·tro·car·di·a (dekstrōkär′dēə), *n.* a condition in which the heart is on the right side of the chest.

dex·troc·u·lar (dekstrok′yələr), *adj.* favoring the right eye rather than the left. See also **sinistrocular**.

dex·tro·ro·ta·to·ry (dekstrōrō′-tətôrē), *adj.* rotating to the right as the plane of polarization of light by certain crystals. —**dex·tro·ro·ta′tion,** *n.*

dex·trorse (dek′strôrs), *adj.* (of plants) twisting to the right. See also **sinistrorse**.

dex·tro·sin·is·tral (dekstrōsin′-istrəl), *adj.* 1. extending from right to left. 2. left-handed, but able to write right-handed.

dhar·ma (där′mə), *n.* (in Buddhism) natural law or essential quality of the world or of one's own nature.

dhar·na (där′nə), *n.* (in India) fasting at the doorstep of an offender to exact justice.

di·a·ble·rie (dēä′blərē), *n.* 1. sorcery; witchcraft. 2. those things or actions controlled by devils. 3. demonology; devil-lore. 4. reckless mischief or daring.

di·ac·o·nal (dīak′ənl), *adj.* pertaining to a deacon.

di·ac·o·nate (dīak′ənit), *n.* office of deacon.

di·a·crit·ic (dīəkrit′ik), *n.* a mark or sign used to distinguish sounds or values of the same letter, as a cedilla, etc. Also **diacritical mark**.

di·a·crit·i·cal (dīəkrit′ikəl), *adj.* distinguishing; distinctive. —**di·a·crit′i·cal·ly,** *adj.*

di·ad·o·cho·ki·ne·sia (dīad′əkōki-nē′zнə), *n.* (in medicine) the ability to perform normally alternating movements of muscles.

di·ad·ro·mous (dīad′rəməs), *adj.* (of certain fish) traveling between salt and fresh water. See also **anadromous, catadromous**.

di·a·graph (dī′əgraf), *n.* an instrument for reproducing scale drawings mechanically.

di·a·lec·tal (dīəlek′tl), *adj.* of or characteristic of a dialect. Also **di·a·lec′ti·cal**.

di·a·lec·tic (dīəlek′tik), *adj.* 1. pertaining to logical argumentation. —*n.* 2. the bases of dialectical materialism, as the superiority of mind over matter. Also **di·a·lec′tics**.

dialectical materialism, materialism as developed by Karl Marx.

di·a·lec·tol·o·gy (dīəlektol′əjē), *n.* the study of dialects.

di·a·log·ic (dīəloj′ik), *adj.* pertaining to or characteristic of dialogue.

di·al·o·gism (dīal′əjizm), *n.* (in an imaginary dialogue) the discussion of a subject. —**di·al′o·gist,** *n.*

di·a·mag·net·ic (dīəmagnet′ik), *adj.* pertaining to a substance, as copper, whose conducting power in a magnetic circuit is less than that of a vacuum and whose induced magnetism is opposite to that of iron. See also **ferromagnetic, paramagnetic**.

di·a·man·tif·er·ous (dī′əmantif′-ərəs), *adj.* diamond-bearing; diamond-producing.

di·a·mor·phine (dīəmôr′fēn), *n.* See **heroin**.

di·a·net·ics (dīənet′iks), *n.* the theory that personality behavior can be explained in terms of an individual's experiences before birth.

di·a·no·et·ic (dī′ənōet′ik), *adj.* pertaining to discursive reasonings.

di·a·noi·a (dīənoi′ə), *n.* the faculty used in discursive reasoning.

di·a·pa·son (dīəpā′zən), *n.* a tune or melody.

di·a·pause (dī′əpôz), *n.* a period of non-growth during the growth of insects.

di·a·pe·de·sis (dī′əpidē′sis), *n.* the normal passage of blood cells into the tissues through capillary walls.

di·a·phane (dī′əfān), *n.* a rigid material used to fix tissue for microscopic examination.

di·a·pha·ne·i·ty (diaf′ənē′itē), *n.* the property of being transparent.

di·aph·a·nom·e·ter (dīaf′ənom′-

itər), *n.* an instrument for measuring transparency.

di·a·phone (dī'əfōn), *n.* a foghorn with a low-pitched, penetrating tone.

di·a·pho·re·sis (dī'əfərē'sis), *n.* sweat.

di·a·pho·ret·ic (dī'əfəret'ik), *adj.* producing sweat.

di·aph·y·sis (dīaf'isis), *n. pl.* **di·aph·y·ses** (dīaf'isēz), the shaft of a bone.

di·ap·la·sis (dīap'ləsis), *n. pl.* **di·ap·la·ses** (dīap'ləsēz), the setting of bone which has been fractured or dislocated.

di·ar·chy (dī'ärkē), *n.* government by two rulers. Also **dinarchy, duarchy. dyarchy.**

di·ar·thro·sis (dīärthrō'sis), *n. pl.* **di·ar·thro·ses** (dīärthrō'sēz), articulation of the joints of the body that allow the greatest movement.

di·as·chi·sis (dīas'kisis), *n.* dysfunction of one part of the brain owing to injury in another part.

di·as·po·ra (dīas'pərə), *n.* (in the Old Testament) the dispersion of the Jews after the Babylonian captivity.

di·as·ta·sis (dīas'təsis), *n.* 1. the parting of bones normally jointed, as in a dislocation. 2. the period after the dilation of the heart and before the contraction. —**di·a·stat·ic** (dīəstat'ik), *adj.*

di·as·to·le (dīas'təlē), *n.* the dilation phase of the heart action. See also **systole.** —**di·as·tol·ic** (dīəstol'ik), *adj.*

di·as·tro·phism (dīas'trəfizm), *n.* the actions that change the earth's crust to produce mountains, etc.

di·ath·e·sis (dīath'isis), *n. pl.* **di·ath·e·sis** (dīath'isis). susceptibility to a certain disease.

di·ceph·a·lous (dīsef'ələs), *adj.* having two heads.

di·chot·o·mize (dikot'əmīz), *v.* to divide or become divided into two parts.

di·chot·o·my (dīkot'əmē), *n.* a split into two parts. —**di·chot'o·mous,** *adj.*

dick·er (dik'ər), *n.* a group of ten, especially ten hides.

dick·ey (dik'ē), *n., pl.* **dick·eys** (dik'-ēz). a woman's vest-like garment, without sides or sleeves but having a front and collar, for wear under a dress or suit.

Dick test, (in medicine) a test to determine a person's susceptibility or immunity to scarlet fever.

dic·ta·tor·ship (diktā'tərsHip), *n.* a country governed by a dictator; government by a dictator.

dic·tum (dik'təm), *n., pl.* **dic·ta** (dik'-tə), **dic·tums.** an expressed opinion of a judge that has no legal force; a maxim.

di·dac·tic (dīdak'tik), *adj.* 1. intended to instruct. 2. inclined to give unwanted instruction. 3. teaching a moral lesson. Also **di·dac'ti·cal.** —**di·dac'ti·cal·ly,** *adv.*

did·di·kai (did'əkī), *n.* a person who is part gipsy.

did·dle (did'l), *v.* to cheat or swindle.

di·do (dī'dō), *n., pl.* **di·dos, di·does.** a trick or prank.

did·y·mous (did'əməs), *adj.* paired; twin.

di·e·lec·tric (dīilek'trik), *n.* an electrical insulator; a non-conductor.

di·en·ceph·a·lon (dīensef'əlon), *n., pl.* **di·en·ceph·a·lons, di·en·ceph·a·la** (dīensef'ələ). the rear part of the forebrain.

di·er·e·sis (dīer'isis), *n., pl.* **di·er·e·ses** (dīer'isēz). a symbol consisting of two dots (¨) which, when placed over the second of two vowels, indicates they are to be pronounced separately, as in *coöperate*.

Dieu et mon droit (dyŏŏ' ā môN drwa'), *French.* God and my right.

dif·fer·en·ti·a (difərən'sHēə), *n., pl.* **dif·fer·en·ti·ae** (difərən'sHēē). the elementary attributes that distinguish one thing from another, as one species from another of the same genus.

dif·fer·en·tial (difərən'sHəl), *n.* an arrangement of gear wheels permitting two or more shafts to rotate at different speeds. Also **differential gear.**

differential calculus, the branch of

mathematics dealing with the calculation of the value of the rate of change of a function with respect to constants and variables.

dif·fi·cile (dif′isēl′), *adj.* difficult; hard to please.

dif·fi·dence (dif′idəns), *n.* a lack of self-confidence; self-effacement; timidity. —**dif′fi·dent,** *adj.*

dif·flu·ence (dif′lōōəns), *n.* a flowing away. —**dif′flu·ent,** *adj.*

dif·fract (difrakt′), *v.* **1.** to bend waves, esp. sound waves, around obstacles. **2.** to break up light waves by passing them through an aperture to form patterns of light and dark bands near the edges of the beam. —**dif·frac′tion,** *n.* —**dif·frac′tive,** *adj.*

diffraction grating, a device used for diffracting light to produce its spectrum.

dig·a·my (dig′əmē), *n.* a second marriage; deuterogamy. See also **monogamy.**

di·ges·tif (dēzHestēf′), *n. French.* a drink taken after a meal to aid digestion, as brandy.

dig·i·tal·is (dijital′is), *n.* a heart stimulant made from the dried leaves of the common foxglove.

digital computer, a computer that uses numerical representations to solve mathematical problems. See also **analog computer, hybrid computer.**

dig·i·tate (dij′itāt), *adj.* (of an animal) having fingers or finger-like parts. —**dig·i·ta′tion,** *n.*

dig·i·ti·form (dij′itəfôrm), *adj.* finger-like.

dig·i·ti·grade (dij′itəgrād), *adj.* walking on toes, as most four-footed animals. See also **plantigrade.**

dig·i·tize (dij′itīz), *v.* to convert material into a form suitable for processing by a digital computer.

di·glot (dī′glot), *adj.* fluent in two languages; bilingual.

di·graph (dī′graf), *n.* two letters, grouped together, and representing a single sound as *ie* in *sieve, sh* in *shoot,* etc.

di·he·dral (dīhē′drəl), *adj.* (in mathematics) forming or having two plane faces.

di·lac·er·ate (dilas′ərāt), *v.* to tear into two parts or into pieces. —**di·lac·er·a′tion,** *n.*

dil·a·ta·tion (dilətā′sHən), *n.* the act of expanding; condition of being widened, swollen or expanded. Also **di·la·tion** (dīlā′sHən).

dil·a·to·ry (dil′ətôr′ē), *adj.* tending to slowness; causing delay; slow.

dil·et·tan·te (dilitan′tē), *n., pl.* **dil·et·tan·tes, dil·et·tan·ti** (dilitan′tē). one who has a superficial and casual interest in a subject; amateur dabbler.

dil·i·gence (dil′ijəns), *n.* perseverence; earnest persistence in completing what is undertaken. —**dil′i·gent,** *adj.*

dil·u·ent (dil′yōōənt), *n.* a substance used to dilute or thin.

di·lu·vi·al (dilōō′vēəl), *adj.* pertaining to a flood, esp. the Flood in the Bible. Also **di·lu′vi·an.**

dim·er·ous (dim′ərəs), *adj.* in two parts.

di·mid·i·ate (dimid′ēāt), *adj.* divided into halves.

dim·i·nu·tion (dimənōō′sHən), *n.* the act of diminishing; condition of being diminished; a lessening. —**di·min′u·tive,** *adj.*

dim·is·so·ry (dim′isôrē), *adj.* giving leave to depart; dismissing.

dim·i·ty (dim′itē), *n.* a light cotton fabric with a heavier stripe or check woven in it.

di·mor·phism (dīmôr′fizm), *n.* the occurrence of two different distinct forms in animals of the same species. —**di·mor′phous,** *adj.*

din·ar·chy (din′ärkē), *n.* See **diarchy.**

ding·bat (diNG′bat), *n.* a piece of decorative type, as for printing ornamental borders.

din·gle (diNG′gəl), *n.* a narrow wooded valley; a deep dell.

di·no·saur (dī′nəsôr), *n.* a reptile, now extinct, in the Mesozoic era.

di·o·cese (dī′əsēs), *n.* an ecclesiastical area under a bishop's jurisdiction. —**di·oc·e·san** (dīos′isən), *adj.*

di·ode (dī′ōd), *n.* a thermionic valve with an anode and cathode designed with unequal characteristics.

di·oe·cious (dīē′sHəs), *adj.* having male and female parts on separate plants.

di·oes·trum (dīes′trəm), *n.* the intervals between the times when female animals are in heat.

Di·on·y·sian (dīənisH′ən), *adj.* pertaining to the Greek wine god, Dionysus, or to his worship; unrestrained; orgiastic. —**Di·o·nys·i·ac** (dīənis′ēak), *adj.*

di·op·ter (dīop′tər), *n.* a unit of measure of the refractive power of a lens.

di·op·tom·e·ter (dī′optom′iter), *n.* an instrument for measuring the refraction of the eye.

di·op·trics (dīop′triks), *n.* the branch of optics which deals with the refraction of light. —**di·op′tric,** *adj.*

di·o·ram·a (dīəram′ə), *n.* a scene painted on a back cloth, given a three-dimensional effect by placing figures, etc., in front.

di·os·mose (dīos′mōs), *v.* to make a fluid pass through a semipermeable membrane and thus equalize the concentration on both sides.

di·o·tic (dīō′tik), *adj.* involving both ears.

diph·the·ri·a (dif*th*ēr′ēə), *n.* an infectious disease characterized by a false membrane forming in the throat. —**diph·the·rit′ic,** *adj.* —**diph′the·roid,** *adj.*

diph·thong (dif′*th*ôNG), *n.* a speech sound combining two vowels in one syllable.

diph·thong·ize (dif′*th*ôNGīz), *v.* to pronounce as a diphthong; to become a diphthong.

dip·la·cu·sis (dipləkyōō′sis), *n., pl.* **dip·la·cu·ses** (dipləkyōō′sēz). a condition in which the ears hear with different acuity.

di·ple·gia (dīplē′jə), *n.* paralysis of the same parts on both sides of the body.

dip·loid (dip′loid), *adj.* double.

dip·lo·pho·ni·a (dipləfō′nēə), *n.* a condition in which two sounds of different pitch are produced simul-

taneously by the voice. Also **dip·ho·ni·a** (difō′nēə).

di·plo·pi·a (diplō′pēə), *n.* a vision disorder in which a single object appears as two. See also **haplopia.**

dip·so·ma·ni·a (dipsəmā′nēə), *n.* an insatiable craving for drink. —**dip·so·ma′ni·ac,** *n.*

dip·tych (dip′tik), *n.* **1.** a tablet with two hinged leaves used for writing in ancient times. **2.** a wood or metal tablet, similar to this, containing the names of those for whom prayers and Masses are said, with the living on one leaf and the dead on the other.

dire (dīr), *adj.* terrible; dreadful; calamitous.

Di·rec·toire (dērektwär′), *n.* a style of French furnishings of the late 18th century, characterized by Greco-Roman shapes and Egyptian motifs.

dirge (dûrj), *n.* a funeral tune or lament for the dead.

di·rhin·ous (dīrī′nəs), *adj.* with paired nostrils.

dirn·dl (dûrn′dl), *n.* a woman's dress with a full skirt and close-fitted top.

dis·a·buse (disəbyōōz′), *v.* to undeceive; reveal the truth to.

dis·ad·van·taged (disədvan′tijd), *adj.* lacking the normal advantages, as of a good home and family.

dis·af·fect (disəfekt′), *v.* to raise discontent in; alienate the affection of. —**dis·af·fec′tion,** *n.*

dis·af·fil·i·ate (disəfil′ēāt), *v.* to sever connections with; dissociate. —**dis·af·fil·i·a′tion,** *n.*

dis·af·for·est (disəfôr′ist), *v.* to clear forests; strip.

dis·ap·pro·ba·tion (dis′aprəbā′-sHən), *n.* disapproval.

dis·ar·tic·u·late (disärtik′yəlāt), *v.* to dislocate, as bones.

dis·a·vow (disəvou′), *v.* to refuse to acknowledge; disclaim; repudiate. —**dis·a·vow′al,** *n.*

dis·burse (disbûrs′), *v.* to pay out (money); expend; scatter. —**dis·burse′ment,** *n.*

dis·calced (diskalst′), *adj.* barefoot.

dis·car·nate (diskär′nit), *adj.* with no physical body or manifestation.

dis·cept (disept′), *v.* to debate; dispute.

dis·cerp (disurp′), *v.* to tear apart; divide. —**dis·cerp·ti·ble** (disurp′tə-bəl), *adj.*

dis·cla·ma·tion (diskləmā′sнən), *n.* the act of disclaiming; repudiation; renunciation.

dis·cog·ra·phy (diskog′rəfē), *n.* a complete list of the musical recordings of a composer, performer, or group of performers.

dis·coid (dis′koid), *adj.* in the shape of a discus or disk.

dis·com·bob·u·late (diskəmbob′-yəlāt), *v.* to disrupt; upset; confuse.

dis·com·fit (diskum′fit), *v.* **1.** to throw into disorder and confusion. **2.** to defeat completely; rout. **3.** to thwart; foil. —**dis·com′fi·ture**, *n.*

dis·com·mend (diskəmend′), *v.* to disapprove of; deprecate.

dis·com·mode (diskəmōd′), *v.* to inconvenience; trouble; disturb.

dis·co·phile (dis′kəfīl), *n.* a collector of phonograph records, especially of rare records.

dis·co·theque (dis′kōtek), *n.* a club where patrons dance to music played on records.

dis·cre·ate (diskrēāt′), *v.* to destroy; turn to nothing.

dis·jec·ta mem·bra (disjek′tä mem′brä), *Latin.* disjointed members or parts.

dis·junct (disjuнGkt′), *adj.* separated; disjoined. —**dis·junc′tion**, *n.* —**dis·junc′ture**, *n.*

dis·na·ture (disnā′cнər), *v.* to make unnatural; deprive (something) of its true nature.

disorderly house, a brothel.

dis·par·age (dispar′ij), *v.* to speak slightingly of; depreciate.

dis·pa·rate (dis′pərit), *adj.* unlike; dissimilar; essentially different.

dis·par·i·ty (dispar′itē), *n.* inequality; unlikeness; difference.

dis·part (dispärt′), *v.* to separate; divide.

dis·pas·sion·ate (dispasн′ənit), *adj.* without bias; calm; free from passion.

dis·peo·ple (dispē′pəl), *v.* to depopulate; deprive of people.

dis·perse (dispurs′), *v.* to scatter; spread widely; distribute. —**dis·per·sion** (dispur′zнən), *n.* —**dis·per′sive**, *adj.*

dis·plume (displōōm′), *v.* to strip of honors.

dis·port (dispôrt′), *v.* to play; divert or amuse oneself.

dis·praise (disprāz′), *v.* to disparage; blame; censure.

dis·pu·ta·tious (dispyōōtā′sнəs), *adj.* quarrelsome; argumentative; contentious.

dis·qui·et (diskwī′it), *n.* **1.** uneasiness; anxiety; restlessness. —*v.* **2.** to disturb; make uneasy or anxious.

dis·qui·e·tude (diskwī′itōōd), *n.* anxiety; uneasiness.

dis·qui·si·tion (diskwizisн′ən), *n.* a treatise examining and discussing a subject.

dis·sem·blance[1] (disem′bləns), *n.* unlikeness.

dis·sem·blance[2] (disem′bləns), *n.* a pretense; a feigning.

dis·sem·ble (disem′bəl), *v.* to conceal under a false appearance; speak or act hypocritically.

dis·sem·i·nate (disem′ənāt), *v.* to scatter; disperse; spread abroad.

dis·sen·sion (disen′sнən), *n.* disagreement; lack of unity; discord.

dis·sent (disent′), *v.* to disagree; withhold consent.

dis·sen·tient (disen′sнənt), *adj.* disagreeing with the opinion of the majority.

dis·sen·tious (disen′sнəs), *adj.* quarrelsome; argumentative.

dis·sep·i·ment (disep′əmənt), *n.* a dividing wall or membrane in a plant or animal.

dis·ser·tate (dis′ərtāt), *v.* to discuss learnedly.

dis·ser·ta·tion (disərtā′sнən), *n.* a treatise on a particular subject, esp. one written as a requirement for a degree.

dis·si·dence (dis′idns), *n.* disagreement; difference of opinion. —**dis′si·dent**, *adj.*

dis·sil·i·ent (disil'ēənt), *adj.* breaking or bursting open.

dis·sim·i·la·tion (disim'əlā'sнən), *n.* the making or becoming unlike. See also **assimilate.**

dis·si·mil·i·tude (dissimil'itōod), *n.* unlikeness; difference.

dis·sim·u·late (disim'yəlāt), *v.* to disguise or conceal the true nature of; dissemble. —**dis·sim·u·la'tion,** *n.*

dis·si·pate (dis'əpāt), *v.* 1. to scatter wastefully. 2. to engage in loose and intemperate pleasures. —**dis·si·pa'tion,** *n.*

dis·so·ci·a·ble (disō'sēā'sнən), *adj.* 1. separable. 2. not sociable. 3. irreconcilable.

dis·so·cial (disō'sнəl), *adj.* not sociable.

dis·so·ci·ate (disō'sнēāt), *v.* to cut association with; separate. —**dis·so·ci·a'tion,** *n.*

dis·so·lute (dis'əlōot), *adj.* given to dissipation; debauched; profligate.

dis·so·lu·tion (disəlōō'sнən), *n.* the dissolving or breaking up of a union, organization, or assembly.

dis·so·nance (dis'ənəns), *n.* a discord or harsh sound. —**dis'so·nant,** *adj.*

dis·suade (diswād'), *v.* to persuade against. —**dis·sua·sion** (diswā'-zнən), *n.* **dis·sua'sive,** *adj.*

dis·syl·la·bic (disilab'ik), *adj.* disyllabic.

dis·syl·la·ble (disil'əbəl), *n.* disyllable.

di·stad (dis'tad), *adv.* toward or at the opposite end from the point of attachment.

dis·tal (dis'tl), *adj.* away from the point of attachment as of a limb or appendage.

dis·tel·fink (dis'tlfiɴgk), *n.* a bird motif found in Pennsylvania-Dutch art.

dis·tem·per (distem'pər), *n.* a technique in art using glue to bind and achieve a mat surface.

dis·tend (distend'), *v.* to inflate; swell; expand. —**dis·ten'si·ble,** *adj.* —**dis·ten'sile,** *adj.* —**dis·ten'tion,** *n.*

dis·tin·gué (distaɴggā'), *adj.* distinguished in appearance and manner.

dis·trait (distrā'), *adj.* absent-minded because of worries, etc.

dis·traught (distrôt'), *adj.* agitated and distracted.

distressed area, an area devastated by a natural disaster, like a flood, and needing outside help in the form of food, medicine, clothing, shelter, and money.

distress flag, any flag or signal flown by a ship showing it to be in distress.

distress frequency, a radio frequency reserved for distress calls, as from ships and aircraft.

distress merchandise, goods sold at a lower than usual price in order to raise money rapidly.

dis·un·ion (disyōon'yən), *n.* severance of union; lack of unity. —**dis·un'ion·ist,** *n.*

di·syl·lab·ic (dīsilab'ik), *adj.* having two syllables. Also **dissyllabic.**

di·syl·la·ble (dī'siləbəl), *n.* a two-syllable word. Also **dissyllable.**

di·the·ism (dī'thēizm), *n.* 1. belief in two gods. 2. belief in two conflicting principles, one good, one evil.

dith·er (dith'ər), *n.* 1. a quivering or trembling. —*v.* 2. to hesitate nervously; vacillate.

dit·tog·ra·phy (ditog'rəfē), *n.* repetition in writing or printing, usually in error, of the same word or letter. See also **haplography.**

di·u·re·sis (dīyōoōrē'sis), *n.* excessive discharge of urine.

di·u·ret·ic (dīyōoōret'ik), *adj.* 1. promoting the increase of discharge of urine as by medicine. —*n.* 2. a medicine so acting.

di·ur·nal (dīur'nl), *adj.* 1. daily; happening daily. 2. belonging to the day.

di·va (dē'vä), *n., pl.* **di·vas, di·ve** (dē've). a leading female singer; prima donna.

di·va·gate (dī'vəgāt), *v.* to stray or wander, esp. in speech. —**di·va·ga'tion,** *n.*

di·var·i·cate (dīvar'əkāt), *v.* 1. to branch apart. —*adj.* 2. divergent; spread wide apart.

di·vers (dī′vərz), *adj*. various; several; sundry.

di·verse (divurs′), *adj*. **1.** dissimilar; unlike; different. **2.** varied; multiform.

di·ver·si·form (divur′səfôrm), *adj*. of various shapes; differing in form.

di·ver·tisse·ment (divur′tismənt), *n*. an entertainment.

di·ver·tive (divur′tiv), *adj*. entertaining; amusing.

di·vest (divest′), *v*. to strip, dispossess, or rid of something.

di·vest·i·ture (dives′ticHər), *n*. the act of divesting; state of being divested.

di·vi·sive (divī′siv), *adj*. causing or showing division; creating discord. —**di·vi′sive·ness,** *n*.

di·vul·gate (divul′gāt), *v*. to publish; make common property.

di·vulse (dīvuls′), *v*. (in surgery) to tear apart, as oppose to cutting. —**di·vul·sion** (dīvul′sHən), *n*.

dix·it (dik′sit), *n*. an utterance, esp. an official promulgation. [*Latin*: he has said]

di·zy·got·ic (dīzīgot′ik), *adj*. formed from two ova, as fraternal twins.

djin, djinn (jin), *n*., *pl*. **djins**. See **jinn.**

D layer, the lowest region of the ionosphere; from 40–50 to 60–75 miles in altitude.

DMSO, a colorless liquid, dimethyl sulfoxide, used as an antifreeze and for treating headaches, burns, and bruises.

DNA, any of a class of nucleic acids that transfers genetic characteristics.

D.O.A., dead on arrival.

do·cent (dō′sənt), *n*. a university lecturer.

doc·tri·naire (doktrəner′), *adj*. dogmatic or fanatical about another's acceptance of one's theories or teaching.

do·dec·a·gon (dōdek′əgon), *n*. a plane figure with 12 sides.

do·dec·a·he·dron (dōdek′əhē′drən), *n*. a solid figure with 12 faces.

doge (dōj), *n*. the former chief magistrate of Venice or Genoa.

dog·ger·el (dô′gərəl), *adj*. **1.** (of verse) irregular in meter and comic in content. —*n*. **2.** a comic verse; bad verse.

dog·go (dô′gō), *adv*. in hiding; out of sight.

dog·leg (dôg′leg), *n*. a sharp bend in a route or road.

dog·ma (dôg′mə), *n*. a doctrine laid down by an authority, as the church. —**dog·mat·ic** (dôgmat′ik), *adj*. —**dog′mat·ism,** *n*. —**dog′ma·tist,** *n*.

dog·watch (dôg′wocH), *n*. **1.** one of two two-hour watches on board ship, either from 4 pm to 6 pm or from 6 pm to 8 pm. **2.** the time staff stay after a newspaper has gone to press to await any further news developments.

dol·ce far nien·te (dôl′cHə fär nyen′te), *Italian*. pleasantly doing nothing; pleasing inactivity.

dol·ce vi·ta (dôl′cHe vē′tä), *Italian*. the good life; life devoted to the pursuit of pleasure.

dol·drums (dōl′drəmz), *n. pl*. a state of listlessness; inactivity; stagnation.

dole (dōl), *n*. money, food, etc., given by or as by a charity.

dollar gap, the difference in dollars between what a country earns from the U.S. and what it pays to the U.S.

dol·lop (dol′əp), *n*. a lump or small unmeasured quantity of something.

doll·y (dol′ē), *adj*. (of a girl) pretty; trendy; modern.

dol·man sleeve (dōl′mən), a sleeve tapering from a wide armhole to a narrow cuff.

dol·men (dōl′men), *n*. a prehistoric stone construction consisting of upright stones supporting a horizontal one. See also **cromlech.**

do·lor (dōlər), *n*. sorrow; grief. —**dol′or·ous,** *adj*.

do·lo·rim·e·try (dōlərim′itrē), *n*. (in medicine) a technique for measuring sensitivity to pain. —**do·lo·rim′e·ter,** *n*.

do·lo·ro·so (dōlərō′sō), *adj*. (used in musical direction) melancholy; plaintive.

do·min·i·cal (dəmin′ikəl), *adj*. **1.** pertaining to Jesus Christ. **2.** pertaining to Sunday.

do·min·i·ca·le (dəmin′əkä′lē), *n.* (formerly) a woman's veil worn at church.

don·a·tive (don′ətiv), *n.* something given; a gift or donation.

don·jon (dun′jən), *n.* the stronghold of a castle.

don·nish (don′isн), *adj.* pompously academic.

dope sheet, *n.* a list giving the names and other information on entries in various horse races.

Dop·pel·gäng·er (dop′əlgaNGər), *n.* a ghostly double of a person not yet dead.

Dopp·ler effect (dop′lər), the change in the frequency of a wave because of the change in the distance between the source and the receiver.

dor·mant (dôr′mənt), *adj.* asleep, or as if asleep; completely inactive; torpid. —**dor′man·cy,** *n.*

dor·mer (dôr′mər), *n.* a vertical window built out from a sloping roof, usually having a roof of its own. Also **dormer window.**

dor·mi·ent (dôr′mēənt), *adj.* sleeping.

dor·sad (dôr′sad), *adv.* toward the back, as of a body, or toward the outer surface, as of an organ.

dor·sal (dôr′səl), *adj.* pertaining to, near, or on the back, as of an organ or part.

dorse (dôrs), *n.* the back of a document or a book.

do·sim·e·ter (dōsim′itər), *n.* an instrument that measures the dosage of x-rays or other radiation. —**do·sim′e·try,** *n.*

dos·sal (dos′əl), *n.* a drape hanging behind an altar or around the chancel. Also **dor′sal.**

dos·ser (dos′ər), *n.* **1.** a pannier or basket carried on the back. **2.** a covering for the back of a throne.

dos·si·er (dosēā′), *n.* a set of documents concerned with some person or matter.

dot·age (dō′tij), *n.* weakness of mind due to old age.

do·tard (dō′tərd), *n.* a feeble-minded old person.

dot·tle, dot·tel (dot′l), *n.* the plug of partly burnt tobacco remaining in a pipe after smoking.

do·ta·tion (dōtā′sнən), *n.* an endowment or act of endowing.

double di·ode (dī′ōd). See **duodiode.**

double en·ten·dre (äntän′drə), *pl.* **double en·ten·dres** (äntän′drəz). a word or expression with two ambiguous meanings, one of which is usually slightly risqué.

double in·dem·ni·ty (indem′nətē), a life insurance policy paying double the face value in the event of accidental death.

double jeop·ar·dy (jep′ərdē), the trying of a person twice for the same offense.

double standard, a code of principles which bear more heavily on one group of people than on another.

double·think (dub′əlthiNGk), *v.* to believe in two conflicting versions, ideas, etc., at the same time.

dou·ceur (dōōsur′), *n.* a tip or gratuity.

dough·ty (dou′tē), *adj.* bravely formidable; steadfast; courageous.

dou·ter (dou′tər), *n.* a candle-snuffer.

dow·a·ger (dou′əjər), *n.* **1.** a title a widow of a titled man assumes to distinguish her from the wife of the heir to his title. **2.** a stately, wealthy, elderly widow.

dow·dy (dou′dē), *adj.* shabby; unfashionable.

Dow-Jones average, any of several indexes reflecting the price levels of various groups of stocks and bonds.

down·stage (doun′stāj′), *adv.* **1.** toward the front of a theatrical stage. —*adj.* **2.** of or pertaining to the front of a stage. See also **upstage.**

down-wind (doun′wind′), *adv.* in the same direction as the wind is blowing; with the wind.

dox·ol·ogy (doksol′əjē), *n.* a hymn of praise to God especially the one starting "Praise God from whom all blessings flow."

dox·y (dok′sē), *n.* opinion or view.

doy·en (doien′), *n.* the senior member of a group, society, profession,

drypoint

etc. —**doy·enne** (doien′), *n. fem.*

drab·ble (drab′əl), *v.* to make wet or dirty.

dra·con·ic (drākon′ik), *adj.* dragon-like.

dra·co·ni·an (drākō′nēən), *adj.* harsh; severe; inhuman.

dra·gée (drazHā′), *n.* **1.** a chocolate coated candy with a liquid center. **2.** a small, spherical, silver-colored, edible cake decoration.

drag·o·man (drag′əmən), *n.*, *pl.* **drag·o·mans. drag·o·men** (drag′əmən). a guide-interpreter in the East.

dra·goon (drəgoon′), *v.* to force by harsh measures; coerce.

drag race, an automobile race from a standing start, the winner being the one that accelerates the fastest.

drag·ster (drag′stər), *n.* an automobile prepared for drag races.

drag·strip (drag′strip), an area, as a straight section of road or aircraft runway, on which drag races are held.

drake (drāk), *n.* a male duck.

dram·a·turge (dram′əturj), *n.* a playwright. Also **dram′a·tur·gist.**

dram·a·tur·gy (dram′əturjē), *n.* the art of writing plays.

drawing account, a bank account used for cash withdrawals.

drawn butter, seasoned melted butter, served on vegetables.

draw runner. See loper.

draw slip. See loper.

drei·kan·ter (drī′käntər), *n.*, *pl.* **drei·kan·ters, drei·kan·ter,** a three-sided stone or boulder whose faces are formed by wind-blown sand.

dres·sage (drəsäzH′), *n.* the training of a horse in obedience, movement, and bearing.

drift bolt (drift′bōlt), a bolt or spike for securing heavy timbers together. Also **drift pin.**

drill (dril), *n.* a strong twilled linen or cotton material.

drilling mud, a mud-like substance pumped into an oil well to cool the drilling bit and to flush out the loose cuttings.

drogue (drōg), *n.* a sea anchor consisting of a canvas bag or bucket.

droit (droit), *n.* moral and legal right.

droll (drōl), *adj.* quaintly amusing; whimsical; comic. —**droll·er·y** (drō′lərē), *n.*

drom·os (drom′əs), *n.* **1.** the passage to an ancient subterranean tomb. **2.** (in ancient Greece) a race track.

drone (drōn), *n.* the male honeybee.

drop·out (drop′out), *n.* a student who never completes his course of studies.

drop shipment, a shipment of goods which, though billed through the wholesaler, goes directly from the manufacturer to the retailer.

drop·sy (drop′sē), *n.* an excessive accumulation of fluid in the cavities or tissues of the body. —**drop′si·cal,** *adj.*

drosh·ky (drosH′kē), *n.* a light, open, four-wheeled carriage used in Russia.

dross (drôs), *n.* waste matter or refuse, as from the melting of metals. —**dross′y,** *adj.*

drub (drub), *v.* to beat violently; abuse; flog.

drug·get (drug′it), *n.* a coarse rug made from hair woven with cotton or jute.

drum·beat·er (drum′bētər), *n* one who proclaims the virtues of a movie, product, etc.; publicist.

drum·fire (drum′fīr), *n.* heavy gunfire that sounds like the beating of drums.

drupe (droop), *n.* a fruit, as a cherry or plum, consisting of fleshy pulp surrounding a hard shell which encloses a kernel. —**dru·pa·ceous** (droopā′sHəs), *adj.*

dry cell, a type of electric battery or cell with no free fluid.

dry farming, a method of farming without irrigation in areas of low rainfall, by reducing evaporation and making the ground more retentive of moisture.

dry-gulch (drī′gulcH), *v.* to ambush or betray by a change of attitude.

dry·point (drī′point), *n.* a copper engraving made with a needle stylus that produces a print with soft, velvety-black lines.

dry rot (drī rot), timber decay caused by fungi, resulting in dry, crumbling wood.

dry sail (drī′ sāl), v. to cruise in or possess only a motor-driven boat. —**dry sailor.**

dry well, a large concrete cylinder sunk into the earth and surrounded by loose stones, used for the drainage and leaching of biological wastes.

du·ad (dōō′ad), n. a pair.

du·al·ism (dōō′əlizm), n. (in philosophy) the theory that there are two principal substances, mind and body. —**du·al·is′tic,** adj.

du·al·i·ty (dōōal′itē), n. the state of being dual.

dual personality, a mental disorder in which a person's behavior exhibits the presence of two different personalities.

du·ar·chy (dōō′ärkē), n. See **diarchy.**

du·bi·e·ty (dōōbī′itē), n. doubt; hesitation; doubtfulness.

du·bi·ta·tion (dōōbitā′sHən), n. doubt.

du·bi·ta·tive (dōō′bitātiv), adj. doubting.

duc·tile (duk′tl), adj. capable of being worked into wire or thin sheets, as certain metals; malleable.

dudg·eon (duj′ən), n. a feeling of being offended; angry resentment.

Du·e·cen·to (dōōəcHen′tō), n. the 13th century, esp. Italian art and literature of that period. Also **du·gen·to** (dōōjen′tō).

duff (duf), n. rotting vegetable matter on a forest floor.

du jour (dəzHōōr′), French. of the day; that being served on this particular day.

dul·cet (dul′sit), adj. pleasant; melodious; agreeable; soothing to the ear or eye.

dul·ci·fy (dul′sifī), v. to appease; mollify; make agreeable.

du·li·a (dōōlī′ə), n. (in Roman Catholicism) the veneration given to saints in their role as God's servants. See also **hyperdulia, latria.**

du·loc·ra·cy (dōōlok′rəsē), n. government by former slaves.

du·lo·sis (dōōlō′sis), n. the enslaving of members of any one colony by ants of a different species.

dum·dum (dum′dum), n. a soft-nosed bullet that expands on impact.

dump·ish (dum′pisH), adj. dejected; low-spirited; depressed.

dun[1] (dun), v. to demand payment of a debt repeatedly.

dun[2] (dun), adj. dull grayish-brown.

dun·nage (dun′ij), n. **1.** personal baggage. **2.** poor material stowed round a ship's or railroad's cargo to protect it from injury.

du·o·de·cil·lion (dōō′ōdisil′yən), n. a number represented by a digit followed by 39 zeros.

du·o·dec·i·mal (dōōədes′əməl), adj. of the number 12 or of twelfths.

du·o·de·num (dōōədē′nəm), n., pl. **du·o·de·na** (dōōədē′nə), **du·o·de·nas.** the first portion of the small intestine nearest the stomach. —**du·o·de′nal,** adj.

du·o·di·ode (dōōədī′ōd), n. a radio tube containing two diodes. Also **double diode.**

du·o·logue (dōō′əlôg), n. a conversation between two people; a dramatic dialogue. See also **monologue.**

du·op·o·ly (dōōop′əlē), n. a condition in the market in which there are two sellers only. See also **monopoly, oligopoly.**

du·op·so·ny (dōōop′sənē), n. a condition in the market in which there are two buyers only. See also **monopsony, oligopsony.**

du·o·tone (dōō′ətōn), n. **1.** a picture in two colors. **2.** a printing method enabling a monochrome illustration to be produced in two shades of the same color from duotypes.

du·o·type (dōō′ətīp), n. two plates made from the same original, but etched at different angles to produce two intensities when superimposed in printing.

dupe (dōōp), n. **1.** a person easily fooled. —v. **2.** to deceive, fool, or trick.

dup·er·y (dōō′pərē), n. an act or instance of trickery or fooling.

du·pla·tion (dōōplā′sнən), *n.* a doubling.

du·ple (dōō′pəl), *adj.* double; twofold.

du·pli·ca·ture (dōō′pləkā′tər), *n.* a doubling over of something, as a membrane.

du·plic·i·ty (dōōplis′itē), *n.* deceit; hypocrisy; double-dealing.

dur·ance (dōōr′əns), *n.* a long imprisonment.

dur·bar (dur′bär), *n.* a state reception of an Indian prince or British governor or viceroy.

Dutch (ducн), *adj.* referring to a style of painting in 17th-century Holland, characterized by muted tones and naturalistic colors and depicting landscapes or subjects drawn from contemporary life.

Dutch courage, courage inspired by alcohol.

Dutch oven, a heavy-bottomed utensil used for stews, etc.

du·um·vi·rate (dōōum′vərit), *n.* an alliance of two men holding together the same office.

du·ve·tine, du·ve·tyne, du·ve·tyn (dōō′vitēn), *n.* a fabric with a nap, made in a twilled or plain weave of cotton, silk, or wool.

dy·ad (dī′ad), *n.* a couple; pair. —**dy·ad′ic,** *adj.*

dy·ar·chy (dī′ärkē), *n.* See **diarchy.**

dy·na·mism (dī′nəmizm), *n.* a philosophical theory which explains all phenomena by the action of force. See also **mechanism, vitalism.**

dy·nast (dī′nast), *n.* a hereditary ruler.

dys·a·cou·sia, dys·a·cu·sia (dys′-əkōō′zнə), *n.* (in medicine) a condition in which the ear hurts when exposed to noise. Also **dys·a·cous·ma** (disəkōōz′mə).

dys·ad·ap·ta·tion (disad′əptā′sнən), *n.* an inability of the iris and retina of an eye to adapt correctly to light. Also **dys·ap·ta′tion.**

dys·an·ag·no·sia (disan′əgnō′zнə), *n.* the inability to understand some words; word-blindness.

dys·ar·thri·a (disär′thrēə), *n.* speech defects as stammering caused by

faults in the nerve. —**dys·ar′thric,** *adj.*

dys·bar·ism (dis′bärizm), *n.* a condition caused by two different pressures, the atmospheric pressure outside the body and the pressure of gases within the body.

dys·cra·sia (diskrā′zнə), *n.* a malfunction or unspecified disease of the blood. —**dys·cra′sic, dys·crat·ic** (diskrat′ik), *adj.*

dys·cri·nism (diskrī′nizm), *n.* a condition caused by defective glandular secretion.

dys·en·ter·y (dis′ənter′ē), *n.* an infectious disease which leads to an inflammation of the lower part of the bowels, resulting in diarrhea.

dys·er·gia (disur′jə), *n.* faulty muscular control due to bad conduction of the nerve.

dys·es·the·sia (disisthē′zнə), *n.* **1.** a faulty sense of touch. **2.** a condition in which any contact with the skin is painful.

dys·func·tion (disfuNGk′sнən), *n.* abnormal or impaired functioning, as of a bodily organ.

dys·gen·ic (disjen′ik), *adj.* causing degeneration in offspring. Also **cacogenic.** See also **eugenic.**

dys·gno·sia (disnō′zнə), *n.* (in psychiatry) an impairment in intellect.

dys·graph·ia (disgraf′ēə), *n.* the inability to write caused by damage to the brain.

dys·ki·ne·sia (diskinē′zнə), *n.* impairment of the ability to perform muscular movements.

dys·la·li·a (dislā′lēə), *n.* an inability to speak caused by a fault in the speech organs.

dys·lex·i·a (dislek′sēə), *n.* inability to read due to brain damage.

dys·lo·gia (dislō′jə), *n.* the inability to express ideas due to a mental disorder.

dys·lo·gis·tic (disləjis′tik), *adj.* not eulogistic or complimentary.

dys·men·or·rhe·a, dys·men·or·rhoe·a (dis′menərē′ə), *n.* painful menstruation.

dys·met·ri·a (disme′trēə), *n.* the inability to get muscles to produce the desired effect because of a defect in the judgment of distances.

dys·mne·sia (disnē′zнə), *n.* a defective or faulty memory.

dys·pa·reu·ni·a (dispəro͞o′nēə), *n.* coitus causing pain. See also **vaginismus.**

dys·pep·sia (dispep′sнə), *n.* chronic indigestion. —**dys·pep′tic, dys·pep′ti·cal,** *adj.*

dys·pha·gia (disfā′jə), *n.* trouble in swallowing.

dys·pha·sia (disfā′zнə), *n.* inability to speak because of brain damage.

dys·phe·mi·a (disfē′mēə), *n.* a speech disorder caused by neurosis.

dys·pho·ni·a (disfō′nēə), *n.* a speech disturbance. —**dys·phon·ic** (disfon′ik), *adj.*

dys·pho·ri·a (disfôr′ēə), *n.* a state of unease, anxiety, or dissatisfaction. —**dys·phor′ic,** *adj.*

dys·pla·sia (displā′zнə), *n.* an abnormal growth in tissue. —**dys·plas·tic** (displas′tik), *adj.*

dysp·ne·a, dysp·noe·a (dispnē′ə), *n.* labored breathing.

dys·prax·ia (disprak′sēə), *n.* the inability to coordinate movement.

dys·rhyth·mi·a (disriтн′mēə), *n.* a disorder in rhythm, as of speech, of brain wave recordings, etc.

dys·tel·e·ol·o·gy (dis′telēol′əjē), *n.* a philosophical doctrine that denies a final cause of existence.

dys·thy·mi·a (disthī′mēə), *n.* dejection; despondency.

dys·to·ni·a (distō′nēə), *n.* an abnormal state of tension or firmness of an organ or tissue in the body.

dys·tro·phy (dis′trəfē), *n.* any of several conditions characterized by muscular weakening and degeneration. Also **dys·tro·phi·a** (distrō′fēə). —**dys·troph·ic** (distrof′ik), *adj.*

dys·u·ri·a (disyo͝or′ēə), *n.* urination that causes pain.

ea·gle (ē′gəl), *n.* (in golf) two strokes under par on a hole. See also **birdie, bogey.**

ea·gre, ea·ger (ē′gər, ā′gər), *n.* tidal flood.

Early Christian, a style of early religious architecture, characterized by buildings with plain exteriors and lavishly decorated interiors.

Early Renaissance, a style of art in the 15th century using perspective and geometrically based compositions.

ear-mind·ed (ēr′mīn′did), *adj.* being more aware of or responsive to sound than sight, smell, etc. —**ear′mind·ed·ness,** *n.*

earth science, any science dealing with the earth.

earth·shine (urth′shīn′), *n.* reflected light from the earth illuminating the moon.

earth·y (urth′ē), *adj.* 1. made of earth or soil. 2. unsophisticated; direct.

ease·ment (ēz′mənt), *n.* (in Law) the right held by someone to use the territory of another for a specific purpose, as right of way.

east·er·ling (ē′stərling), *n.* someone living in a land to the east of another land.

Eastern Church, Byzantine Church. See also **Orthodox Church.**

Eastern Hemisphere, the eastern half of the world, including Asia east of the Ural Mountains, Australia and Oceania.

eau de vie (ōdəvē′), *French.* coarse unpurified brandy.

é·bauche (ābōsн′), *n.* a basic watch movement made without jewels, case, etc.

é·bé·niste (ābānēst′), *n., pl.* **é·bé·nistes** (ābānēst′), *French.* 1. one who works with veneers, inlay, etc. 2. one who works with ebony.

é·bé·nis·te·rie (ābānēstərē′), *n., French.* work done by an ébeniste.

e·bul·lient (ibul′yənt), *adj.* full of enthusiasm. —**e·bul′lience,** *n.* —**ebul·li·tion** (eb′əlisн′ən), *n.*

e·bur·na·tion (ē′bərnā′sнən), *n.* an abnormal bone condition causing bones to become hard and dense.

e·cau·date (ēkô′dāt), *adj.* without a tail; excaudate.

ec·ce ho·mo (ecн′ā hō′mō), *Latin.* behold the man; words of Pilate when presenting Christ to his accusers.

ec·cen·tric (iksen′trik), *adj.* 1. with the axis not at the center, as a wheel. 2. an instrument for changing circular motion into reciprocating motion.

ec·chy·mo·sis (ek′əmō′sis), *n., pl.* **ec·chy·mo·ses** (ek′əmō′sēz). discoloration caused by blood, as in a bruise; black-and-blue mark.

ec·cle·si·as·tic (iklē′zēas′tik), *n.* 1. a priest; vicar. —*adj.* 2. ecclesiastical.

ec·cle·si·as·ti·cal (iklē'zēas'tikəl), *adj.* of the church.

ec·cle·si·ol·a·try (iklēzēol'ətrē), *n.* excessive regard for tradition in religion.

ec·cri·nol·o·gy (ek'rənol'əjē), *n.* a branch of science concerned with the secretory glands.

ec·dem·ic (ekdem'ik), *adj.* (of a disease) originating elsewhere than where it is found, but neither epidemic nor endemic.

ec·dys·i·ast (ekdiz'ēast), *n.* an animal, insect, etc., that sheds its skin or covering, as a snake, caterpillar, etc.

ec·dy·sis (ek'disis), *n.*, *pl.* **ec·dy·ses** (ek'disēz). the shedding of a skin, etc., as a snake.

e·ce·sis (isē'sis), *n.* the establishment of a plant in a new region.

ech·i·nate (ek'ənāt), *adj.* having bristles; prickly.

e·chi·noid (ikī'noid), *adj.* like a sea urchin.

ech·o·graph (ek'ōgraf), *n.* an instrument that measures the depth of the ocean by means of sound. —**ech·o·gram** (ek'ōgram), *n.*

ech·o·la·li·a (ek'ōlā'lēə), *n.* the involuntary repetition of someone else's words immediately after they have been spoken.

ech·o·lo·ca·tion (ek'ōlōkā'sHən), *n.* the location of objects by radar or sonar by bats, etc.

ech·o·prax·i·a (ek'ōprak'sēə), *n.* the abnormal copying of another person's actions.

echt (eкнt), *adj. German.* genuine, real, true.

é·clair·cisse·ment (āklersēsmäN'), *n.*, *pl.* **é·clair·cisse·ments** (āklersēsmäN'). *French.* clarification, explanation.

é·clat (āklä'), *n.* a brilliant reputation, etc.

ec·lec·tic (iklek'tik), *adj.* choosing from many possibilities. —**ec·lec'ti·cism,** *n.*

e·clip·tic (iklip'tik), *n.* the apparent course of the sun through the sky once a year.

ec·logue (ek'lôg), *n.* an idyllic poem, often in dialogue.

e·clo·sion (iklō'zHən), *n.* the hatching of a larva from its egg or the emerging of an insect from its pupa.

e·col·o·gy (ikol'əjē), *n.* the study of the relations between organisms and their surroundings. Also **bionomics, bionomy.**

e·con·o·met·rics (ikon'əmet'riks), *n.* the application of statistical mathematics to actual problems as well as to the proof of theories.

economic determinism, the doctrine that all social phenomena are caused by economic factors.

economic geography, the study of the relationship between economic conditions, etc., and the utilization of raw materials.

economic geology, the study of the industrial uses of raw materials from the earth.

ec·o·spe·cies (e'kōspē'sHēz), *n.* a taxon containing one or several interbreeding ecotypes.

ec·o·sphere (e'kōsfēr'), *n.* a layer of the atmosphere where it is possible to breathe normally.

ec·o·sys·tem (ek'ōsis'təm), *n.* organisms and their surroundings considered together as a system.

ec·o·tone (ek'ətōn), *n.* a region of transition from one type of plant community to another, as from savanna to woodland.

ec·o·type (ek'ətīp), *n.* a race particularly adapted to a certain environment.

é·cra·sé (ākräzā'), *adj.* (of leather) crushed so as to appear grained.

ec·ru (ek'rōō, ā'krōō), *adj.* beige in color.

ec·tad (ek'tad), *adv.* outward; out from the inside.

ec·tal (ek'təl), *adj.* outside; exterior.

ec·tog·e·nous (ektoj'ənəs), *adj.* growing externally, as a parasite, etc. Also **ec·to·gen'ic.**

ec·to·mor·phic (ektəmôr'fik), *adj.* having a thin body. See also **endomorphic, mesomorphic.** —**ec'to·morph,** *n.*

ec·to·par·a·site (ek′tōpar′əsīt), *n.* an external parasite. See also **endoparasite.**

ec·to·phyte (ek′təfīt), *n.* an externally parasitic plant. See also **endophyte.**

ec·to·pi·a (ektō′pēə), *n.* a congenital displacement of an organ. See also **entopic.** —**ec·top·ic** (ektop′ik), *adj.*

ec·to·plasm (ek′təplazm), *n.* 1. the outer layer of the cytoplasm of a cell. 2. (in spiritualism) a substance that allegedly emanates from a medium.

ec·tro·dac·tyl·ism (ek′trōdak′-təlizm), *n.* the congenital absence of part or all of one or more fingers or toes from birth.

ec·type (ek′tīp), *n.* a copy, as opposed to an original. See also **prototype.**

ec·u·men·i·cal (ek′yōomen′ikəl), *adj.* 1. world-wide; universal. 2. favoring Christian unity. Also **ecumenic, oecumenic, oecumenical.** —**ec·u·men′i·cal·ism, ec·u·men′i·cism,** *n.* —**ec·u·men′i·cist,** *n.*

ec·u·me·nism (ek′yōomənizm), *n.* ecumenical doctrines.

ec·ze·ma (ek′səmə), *n.* a skin disease causing inflammation and itching. —**ec·zem·a·tous** (igzem′ətəs), *adj.*

ec·ze·ma·toid (igzē′mətoid), *adj.* like eczema.

e·da·cious (idā′shəs), *adj.* devouring; consuming.

e·dac·i·ty (idas′itē), *n.* voraciousness; appetite.

e·daph·ic (idaf′ik), *adj.* caused by soil conditions produced by drainage, etc., and not by climate.

ed·a·phon (ed′əfon), *n.* all organisms living in the soil.

ed·dy (ed′ē), *n.* a small whirlpool, or similar condition of air, fog, etc.

e·de·ma, oe·de·ma (idē′mə), *n., pl.* **e·de·ma·ta** (idē′mətə). the presence of serous fluid in body cavities or tissue spaces.

e·den·tate (ēden′tāt), *adj.* without teeth; toothless.

e·dict (ē′dikt), *n.* a governmental or authoritative decree.

ed·i·fy (ed′əfī), *v.* to instruct; uplift morally. —**ed·i·fi·ca′tion,** *n.* —**e·dif·i·ca′to·ry,** *adj.*

ed·u·ca·ble (ej′ōōkəbəl), *adj.* able to be educated; capable of learning.

ed·u·ca·tion·ist (ej′ōōkā′shənist), *n.* a specialist in education.

e·duce (idōōs′), *v.* to bring out, develop.

e·duct (ē′dukt), *n.* the act of bringing out, as something potential; something educed. —**e·duc′tion,** *n.* —**e·duc′tive,** *adj.* —**e·duc′tor,** *n.*

e·dul·co·rate (idul′kərāt), *v.* to purify; remove impurities from.

ef·fa·ble (ef′əbəl), *adj.* able to be expressed.

ef·face (ifās′), *v.* to rub out; destroy.

ef·fec·tor (ifek′tər), *n.* an organ or cell activated by a nerve impulse.

ef·fec·tu·al (ifek′chōōəl), *adj.* producing a desired effect.

ef·fec·tu·ate (ifek′chōōāt), *v.* to bring about; make happen; cause.

ef·fer·ent (ef′ərənt), *adj.* (in physiology) carrying from or away from, as a nerve carrying an impulse. See also **afferent.**

ef·fete (ifēt′), *adj.* 1. exhausted, depleted. 2. decadent, lax. 3. sterile, barren.

ef·fi·ca·cious (ef′əkā′shəs), *adj.* having the desired effect. —**ef′fi·ca·cy,** *n.*

ef·fig·i·ate (ifij′ēāt), *v.* to make a statue of.

ef·fleu·rage (efləräzh′), *n.* a gentle stroking used in massage.

ef·flo·resce (efləres′), *v.* to blossom forth. —**ef·flo·res′cence,** *n.* —**ef·flo·res′cent,** *adj.* —**ef·flo·res′cent·ly,** *adv.*

ef·flu·ence (ef′lōōəns), *n.* a flowing out. —**ef′flu·ent,** *adj.*

ef·flu·vi·um (iflōō′vēəm), *n., pl.* **ef·flu·vi·a** (iflōō′vēə). a small exhalation of an unpleasant gas.

ef·flux (ef′luks), *n.* an outward flow.

ef·frac·tion (ifrak′shən), *n.* a breaking into by forcible means. —**ef·frac′tor,** *n.*

ef·fron·ter·y (ifrun′tərē), *n.* shameless audacity.

ef·fulge (ifulj′), *v.* to shine brightly. —**ef·ful′gent,** *adj.* —**ef·ful′gence,** *n.*

ef·fuse (ifyōōz′), *v.* to pour out, flow

forth. —**ef·fu·sion** (ifyo͞o′zHən), *n.* —**ef·fu′sive,** *adj.*

e·gal·i·tar·i·an (egal′iter′ēən), *adj.* characterized by a belief in human equality.

e·gest (ējest′), *v.* to empty; discharge, as from the body. —**e·ges′tion,** *n.*

e·ges·ta (ējes′tə), *n. pl.* excrement.

egg roll, (in Chinese cooking) a casing of egg dough filled with roast pork, onions, etc., and fried.

eggs Benedict, a dish consisting of toast covered with cooked ham, poached eggs, and hollandaise sauce.

é·glo·mi·sé (ā′gləmizā′), *adj.* pertaining to the method of painting the back of glass so that the decorative pattern is visible from the front. Also **e·glo·mi·se′.**

e·go (ē′gō), *n., pl.* **e·gos.** the self; individual essence of a being.

e·go·cen·tric (ē′gōsen′trik), *adj.* seeing the self as the center of the universe.

e·go·ism (ē′gōizm), *n.* utter selfishness. —**e′go·ist,** *n.* —**e·go·is′tic,** *adj.*

e·go·ma·ni·a (ē′gōmā′nēə), *n.* abnormal egoism.

e·go·tism (ē′gətizm), *n.* unpleasant self-conceit; boastfulness. —**e′go·tist,** *n.* —**e·go·tis′tic,** *adj.*

e·gre·gious (igrē′jəs), *adj.* outstandingly bad.

e·gress (ē′gres), *n.* **1.** an act of leaving a place. **2.** the exit. —**e·gres·sion** (igresн′ən), *n.*

Egyptian cotton, cotton with long, silk-like fibers.

ei·det·ic (īdet′ik), *adj.* of or pertaining to complete visual memory.

ei·do·lon (īdō′lən), *n., pl.* **ei·do·la, ei·do·lons.** an apparition; a phantom.

ei·dos (ī′dos, ā′dos), *n., pl.* **ei·de** (ī′dē, ā′dē). the essence of a culture.

ein·kan·tor (īn′käntər), *n.* a stone shaped by wind and sand.

eis·e·ge·sis (ī′sijē′sis), *n., pl.* **eis·e·ge·ses** (ī′sijē′sēz). a biased interpretation, especially of Scripture.

eis·tedd·fod (āsteтн′vod), *n., pl.* **eis·tedd·fods, eis·tedd·fod·au** (asteтн′vodī). a gathering of Welsh poets and minstrels.

e·jac·u·late (ijak′yəlāt), *v.* **1.** to eject semen. **2.** speak swiftly and briefly. —**e·jac·u·la′tion,** *n.* —**e·jac′u·la·tor,** *n.* —**e·jac′u·la·to·ry,** *adj.*

e·jec·ta (ijek′tə), *n. pl.* matter thrown out, as from a volcano.

é·lan (ālän′), *n.* panache, dash.

é·lan vi·tal (ālän vētal′), (in Henri Bergson's philosophy) a force capable of producing growth or change in an organism.

e·las·to·mer (ilas′təmər), *n.* an elastic substance occurring naturally as rubber.

e·late (ilāt′), *v.* to make happy.

E layer, a layer of maximum electron density at a height of between 100 and 120 kilometers from the surface of the earth.

el·dritch, el·drich (el′dricн), *adj.* weird, uncanny. Also **elritch.**

electoral college, the chosen electors in each state who elect the President and Vice-President of the United States.

e·lec·tro·a·cous·tics (ilek′trōəko͞o′stiks), *n.* the conversion of acoustical energy into electricity and vice versa. —**e·lec·tro·a·cous′tic,** *adj.*

e·lec·tro·bal·lis·tics (ilek′trōbəlis′tiks), *n.* the measurement of the speed of projectiles with electronic equipment.

e·lec·tro·bi·ol·o·gy (ilek′trōbīol′əjē), *n.* the study of electric phenomena in plants and animals.

e·lec·tro·car·di·o·gram (ilek′trōkär′dēəgram), *n.* a graph made by an electrocardiograph.

e·lec·tro·car·di·o·graph (ilek′trōkär′dēəgraf), *n.* a device for recording heart action.

e·lec·tro·chem·is·try (ilek′trōkem′istrē), *n.* the study of chemical changes caused by electricity and vice versa.

e·lec·tro·co·ag·u·la·tion (ilek′trōkōag′yəlā′sнən), *n.* the hardening of diseased tissue by diathermy.

e·lec·trode (ilek′trōd), *n.* a conductor for leading electricity to or from a nonmetallic conductor, as a vacuum tube.

e·lec·tro·dy·nam·ics (ilek ′trō-dīnam′iks), *n.* the study of interactions between magnetic, electric, and mechanical phenomena. —**e·lec·tro·dy·nam′ic,** *adj.*

e·lec·tro·en·ceph·a·lo·gram (ilek ′-trōensef′ələgram), *n.* a graph made by an electroencephalograph.

e·lec·tro·en·ceph·a·lo·graph (ilek′-trōensef′ələgraf), *n.* an instrument for recording electric activity in the brain.

e·lec·tro·form (ilek′trəfôrm), *v.* to make something by electrically depositing metal on a mold.

e·lec·tro·ki·net·ics (ilek ′trōkinet′-iks), *n.* the study of electricity in motion. —**e·lec·tro·ki·net′ic,** *adj.*

e·lec·tro·lier (ilek ′trəlēr′), *n.* a chandelier lit by electricity.

e·lec·tro·lu·mi·nes·cence (ilek ′-trōlo͞o′mənes′əns), *n.* luminescence due to the activation of a dielectric phosphor.

e·lec·trol·y·sis (ilektrol′isis), *n.* **1.** the process of passing an electric current through an electrolyte to cause a change in its physical constitution. **2.** the burning out of hair follicles, tumors, etc., by an electric current.

e·lec·tro·lyte (ilek′trəlīt), *n.* an electric conductor in which an electric current induces a movement of matter in the form of ions. Also **electrolytic conductor.** —**e·lec·tro·lyt·ic** (ilek ′trəlit′ik), *adj.*

e·lec·tro·mo·tive (ilek ′trəmō′tiv), *adj.* tending to cause an electrical flow.

electromotive force, the difference in potential between the terminals of an electrical source, as a battery. *Abbrev.:* **emf.**

e·lec·tro·my·o·gram (ilek′trəmī′-əgram), *n.* a graph showing electric currents due to muscular action.

e·lec·tro·my·og·ra·phy (ilek ′trō-mīog′rəfē), *n.* the making of electromyograms. —**e·lec·tro·my·og′ra·pher,** *n.*

e·lec·tron (ilek′tron), *n.* an elementary particle found in all matter. Also **negatron.**

e·lec·tro·nar·co·sis (ilek′trōnärkō′-sis), *n.* electroshock therapy.

electronic music, sounds produced electronically and then combined by the composer. See also **musique concrète.**

e·lec·tron·ics (ilektron′iks), *n.* the science concerned with devices involving the flow of electrons in a vacuum, etc.

electron microscope, an extremely powerful microscope, using beams of electrons to produce a highly enlarged image.

e·lec·tro·phone (ilek′trəfōn ′), *n.* any musical instrument using oscillating electric current to produce sounds.

e·lec·tro·pho·re·sis (ilek ′trōfərē′-sis), *n.* the motion of colloidal particles in a fluid caused when electricity is passed through. Also **cataphoresis.**

e·lec·tro·shock (ilek′trəsHok ′), *n.* therapy involving the use of electric shocks.

e·lec·tro·stat·ics (ilek ′trəstat′iks), *n.* the study of electric phenomena not connected with electricity in motion. —**e·lec·tro·stat′ic,** *adj.*

e·lec·tro·sur·ger·y (ilek ′trōsur′-jərē), *n.* surgery in which an electric tool is used.

e·lec·tro·tech·nics (ilek ′trōtek′-niks), *n.* the study of practical applications of electricity.

e·lec·tro·ther·a·peu·tics (ilek ′trō-*ther*′əpyo͞o′tiks), *n.* therapy using electricity. Also **e·lec·tro·ther·a·py** (ilek ′trō*ther*′əpē).

e·lec·tro·ther·a·pist (ilek ′trō*ther*′-əpist), *n.* a specialist in electrotherapeutics.

e·lec·tro·ther·mal (ilek ′trəthur′-məl), *adj.* pertaining to electrically produced heat.

e·lec·tro·ther·mics (ilek ′trəthur′-miks), *n.* the science concerned with the interchange of heat and electric energy.

e·lec·trot·o·nus (ilektrot′ənəs), *n.* the change in a nerve while electricity is passed through it.

e·lec·tro·type (ilek′trətīp), *n.* a copy

of a block of type or engraving used in printing, made by electrolytic action in a mold.

el·ee·mos·y·nar·y (el′əmos′ənerē), *adj.* **1.** charitable. **2.** provided by charity. **3.** supported by charity.

el·e·gi·ac (el′əjī′ak), *adj.* suitable for use as a lamentation.

el·e·gy (el′ijē), *n.* mournful poetry or music, often for the dead.

elementary particle, any entity less complex than an atom. Also **fundamental particle.**

e·len·chus (ileNG′kəs), *n., pl.* **e·len·chi** (ileNG′kī). a logical refutation. **2.** a false refutation.

el·e·phan·ti·a·sis (el′əfəntī′əsis), *n.* a chronic lymphatic disease characterized by gross enlargement of the affected parts, usually the legs.

el·e·phan·tine (el′əfan′tin), *adj.* clumsy.

e·lic·it (ilis′it), *v.* to draw forth.

e·lide (ilīd′), *v.* **1.** to miss out (a sound or group of sounds) in pronunciation. **2.** to suppress; ignore.

e·li·sion (ilizH′ən), *n.* the missing out of a sound, etc., in speech.

e·lite (ilēt′), *n.* a select, aristocratic, or choice group of people.

e·lit·ism (ilē′tizm), *n.* the belief that only the elite of society should rule. **e·lit′ist,** *n., adj.*

el·lip·sis (ilip′sis), *n., pl.* **el·lip·ses** (ilip′sēz). the omission of a word or a phrase from a sentence that makes the construction incomplete.

elliptic geometry. See **iemannian geometry.**

el·lip·ti·cal (ilip′tikəl), *adj.* (of speech or writing) obscure because of its use of ellipsis.

el·o·cu·tion (el′əkyoō′sHən), *n.* **1.** the manner in which one speaks, esp. in public. **2.** the study of voice control.

e·loign, e·loin (iloin′), *v.* to move away; to keep at a distance.

el·o·quence (el′əkwəns), *n.* the art of speaking well and aptly. **el′o·quent,** *adj.*

el·ritch (el′riCH), *adj.* See **eldritch.**

el·u·ant (el′yoōənt), *n.* a liquid used for dissolving.

e·lu·ate (el′yoōit), *n.* a liquid solution resulting from dissolving matter.

e·lute (ēloōt′), *v.* to remove by dissolving.

e·lu·tri·ate (iloō′trēāt), *v.* to separate or purify by washing, straining, or suspending in a current of water or air.

e·lu·vi·ate (iloō′vēāt), *v.* (of materials) to move through the soil by the action of water. **—e·lu·vi·a′tion,** *n.*

e·lu·vi·um (iloō′vēəm), *n., pl.* **e·lu·vi·a.** the deposit of soil, etc., resulting from the decomposition of rock; residual soil. **—e·lu′vi·al,** *adj.*

el·ver (el′vər), *n.* a young eel.

el·y·troid (el′itroid), *adj.* like an elytron.

el·y·tron (el′itron), *n., pl.* **el·y·tra** (el′itrə). one of a pair of hardened forewings in insects used to protect the flight wings.

em (em), *n.* a square of any size of type, used as a unit of measurement for anything printed with that size of type.

em·a·nate (em′ənāt), *v.* to flow out, emit. **—em·a·na′tion,** *n.* **—em′a·na·tive,** *adj.*

e·man·ci·pate (iman′səpāt), *v.* **1.** to free from restraint. **2.** (in Roman and Civil Law) to end paternal control over someone. **—e·man·ci·pa′tion,** *n.* **—e·man′ci·pa·tor,** *n.*

e·mar·gi·nate (imär′jināt), *adj.* with notches along the edges.

e·mas·cu·late (imas′kyəlāt), *v.* to make weak or effeminate.

em·ba·cle (embä′kəl), *n.* an agglomeration of broken ice on a river. See also **debacle.**

em·bar·go (embär′gō), *n., pl.* **em·bar·goes.** a government order restricting the movement of merchant ships into or out of its harbors.

em·bay (embā′), *v.* to surround; make into a bay.

em·bo·lism (em′bəlizm), *n.* the blocking of a blood vessel by an embolus.

em·bo·lus (em′bələs), *n.* **em·bo·li** (em′bəlī). undissolved matter lodged in a blood vessel.

em·bon·point (äNbôNpwaN′), *n.*, *French.* obesity.

em·bosk (embosk′), *v.* to conceal with foliage.

em·bou·chure (äm′bōoshōor′), *n.*, *pl.* **em·bou·chures.** *French.* 1. a river mouth. 2. the place where a valley opens into a plain.

em·bow·er (embou′ər), *v.* to cover with or hide in foliage. Also **imbower.**

em·brac·er·y (embrā′sərē), *n.* (in Law) an attempt to sway a judge or jury by bribes or threats. Also **imbracery.** —**em·brace·or** (embrā′sər), *n.*

em·branch·ment (embranch′mənt), *n.* a branching out or ramification.

em·bran·gle (embraNG′gəl), *v.* to perplex, confuse. Also **imbrangle.**

em·bro·cate (em′brōkāt), *v.* to rub with an ointment or lotion. —**em·bro·ca′tion,** *n.*

em·brue (embrōo′), *v.* See **imbue.**

em·brute (embrōot′), *v.* See **imbrute.**

em·bry·ol·o·gy (em′brēol′əjē), *n.* the science concerned with embryos and the study of their growth and development. —**em·bry·ol′o·gist,** *n.* —**em·bry·o·log′i·cal,** *adj.*

em·bry·on·ic (em′brēon′ik), *adj.* like an embryo; undeveloped.

e·mend (imend′), *v.* to edit; remove mistakes. Also **amend.**

e·men·date (ē′məndāt), *v.* to correct, put right. —**e·men·da′tion,** *n.*

e·mer·i·tus (imer′itəs), *adj.* no longer actively employed, but honorably discharged and kept on the rolls (used esp. of academicians).

em·er·ize (em′ərīz), *v.* to give luster to a fabric by rubbing it with emery.

e·mer·sion (imur′zhən), *n.* the reappearance of one heavenly body after its eclipse by another.

e·met·ic (əmet′ik), *adj.* 1. producing vomiting. —*n.* 2. an emetic agent.

e·mic·tion (imik′shən), *n.* the passing of urine.

é·mi·gré (em′əgrā), *n.*, *pl.* **é·mi·grés** (em′əgrāz). *French.* an emigrant, esp. one who flees his native land because of political reasons.

é·min·cé (āmaNsā′), *n.*, *French.* a dish consisting of slices of left-over meat warmed in a sauce.

eminent domain, the power of a state to buy property by compulsory purchase.

em·me·tro·pi·a (em′itrō′pēə), *n.* the normal condition of the eye, when rays of light are correctly focused on the retina.

e·mol·lient (imol′yənt), *adj.* 1. able to soften tissue; soothing to the skin. —*n.* 2. an emollient medication.

e·mol·u·ment (imol′yəmənt), *n.* payment for a service, as salary.

em·pai·stic (empā′stik), *adj.* decorated with an inlaid, embossed, or stamped design. Also **empestic.**

em·pa·thize (em′pəthīz), *v.* to communicate; make contact with.

em·pa·thy (em′pəthē), *n.* identification with the feelings, etc., of someone else.

em·pen·nage (äNpənäzh′), *n.*, *pl.* **em·pen·nag·es** (äNpənäzh′). the tail assembly of an airplane.

em·per·y (em′pərē), *n.* 1. an empire. 2. the land belonging to an emperor.

em·pes·tic (empes′tik), *adj.* See **empaistic.**

em·phy·se·ma (em′fisē′mə), *n.* the abnormal enlargement of an organ due to air or gas.

em·pir·i·cal (empir′ikəl), *adj.* 1. discovered by experiment. 2. depending on observation without the application of theory. —**em·pir′ic,** *n.*

em·pir·i·cism (empir′isizm), *n.* 1. the empirical method. 2. (in philosophy) the theory that all knowledge comes from experience. 3. an over-reliance on personal experience to the exclusion of learning.

em·poi·son (empoi′zən), *v.* 1. to corrupt. 2. to make bitter.

em·py·e·ma (em′pēē′mə), *n.* pus in a body cavity, esp. in the thorax. Also **pyothorax.**

em·pyr·e·al (empir′ēəl), *adj.* belonging to the highest heaven in ancient cosmology.

em·py·re·an (empir′ēən), *n.* the most exalted of heavenly states.

em·u·lous (em′yələs), *adj.* wishing to equal.

e·mul·si·fy (imul′səfī), *v.* to make into an emulsion.

e·mul·sion (imul′sHən), *n.* the suspension of one liquid in another in which it is not soluble.

e·munc·to·ry (imuNG′tərē), *n.* **1.** an organ of the body that disposes of waste products. —*adj.* **2.** excretory.

en (en), *n.* (in printing) half an em in width.

en·ar·thro·sis (en′ärthrō′sis), *n.*, *pl.* **en·ar·thro·ses** (en′ärthrō′sēz). a ball-and-socket joint in the body.

e·nate (ē′nāt), *n.* a maternal relative. See also **agnate.**

en·cae·nia (ensēn′yə), *n.* a festival commemorating the founding of a city, etc.

en·car·pus (enkär′pəs), *n.*, *pl.* **en·car·pi** (enkär′pī). ornamentation in which draperies, weapons, etc., are arranged as a festoon.

en·caus·tic (enkô′stik), *adj.* painted by burning in the colors.

en·ceph·a·lal·gi·a (ensef′əlal′jēə), *n.* headache.

en·ceph·a·las·the·ni·a (ensef′-əlasthē′nēə), *n.* mental tiredness owing to emotional stress.

en·ceph·a·li·tis (ensef′əlī′tis), *n.* inflammation of the brain, esp. resulting from a viral disease.

en·ceph·a·lo·gram (ensef′ələgram), *n.* an X-ray of the brain. Also **encephalograph.**

en·ceph·a·lo·graph (ensef′ələgraf), *n.* **1.** an electroencephalograph. **2.** an encephalogram.

en·ceph·a·log·ra·phy (ensef′əlog′-rəfē), *n.* the making of encephalograms.

en·ceph·a·lo·ma (ensef′əlō′mə), *n.*, *pl.* **en·ceph·a·lo·ma·ta** (ensef′əlō′-mətə). a tumor of the brain.

en·ceph·a·lo·my·e·li·tis (ensef′-əlōmī′əlī′tis), *n.* a disease characterized by inflammation of the spinal cord and the brain. —**en·ceph·a·lo·my·e·lit′ic,** *adj.*

en·ceph·a·lon (ensef′əlon), *n.*, *pl.* **en·ceph·a·la.** the brain.

en·ceph·a·lop·a·thy (ensef′əlop′-əthē), *n.* a mental disease of the brain.

en·ceph·a·lo·sis (ensef′əlō′sis), *n.* an organic disease affecting the brain.

en·chase (enCHās′), *v.* **1.** to put jewels in a setting. **2.** to decorate with gems or designs in inlay or embossing.

en·chi·la·da (en′CHəlä′də), *n.* a Mexican dish consisting of a tortilla filled with highly seasoned meat mixture and covered with a chili sauce.

en·chi·rid·i·on (en′krīrid′ēən), *n.*, *pl.* **en·chi·rid·i·ons, en·chi·rid·i·a.** a handbook.

en·cinc·ture (ensiNGk′CHər), *v.* to encompass with a belt.

en·clave (en′klāv), *n.* outlying district of one country almost totally surrounded by the territory of another nation. See also **exclave.**

en·co·mi·ast (enkō′mēast), *n.* a eulogist; a giver of formal praise. —**en·co·mi·as′tic,** *adj.*

en·co·mi·um (enkō′mēəm), *n.*, *pl.* **en·co·mi·ums, en·co·mi·a.** a eulogy; ceremonious praise.

en·co·pre·sis (en′kōprē′sis), *n.* unintentional defecation.

en·crypt (enkript′), *v.* to put in code.

en·cul·tu·rate (enkul′CHərāt), *v.* to adapt to a culture. —**en·cul·tu·ra′tion,** *n.*

en·cyc·li·cal (ensik′likəl), *n.* a letter from the pope to all his bishops.

en·dem·ic (endem′ik), *adj.* native; indigenous. See also **enzootic, epidemic.**

end·er·gon·ic (en′dərgon′ik), *adj.* noting a biochemical process that needs energy to react. See also **exergonic.**

en·der·mic (endur′mik), *adj.* taking effect by absorption through the skin.

en·do·car·di·al (en′dōkär′dēəl), *adj.* in the heart.

en·do·car·di·tis (en′dōkärdī′tis), *n.* inflammation of the endocardium.

en·do·car·di·um (en′dōkär′dēəm), *n.*, *pl.* **en·do·car·di·a.** the membrane lining the heart.

en·do·cen·tric (en′dōsen′trik), *adj.*

with the same syntactic function as one of its constituents, such as "cold water," which functions as would "water." See also **exocentric**.

en·do·crine (en'dəkrin), *adj.* **1.** secreting internally, as an endocrine gland. —*n.* **2.** an internal secretion. See also **exocrine**.

endocrine gland, any gland secreting substances into the blood.

en·do·cri·nol·o·gy (en'dōkrənol'-əjē), *n.* the science of endocrine glands.

en·do·cri·nop·a·thy (en'dōkrənop'-əthē), *n.* a disease caused by the improper function of an endocrine gland.

en·do·crin·o·ther·a·py (en'dōkrin'-ōther'əpē), *n.* the treating of disease with hormones from endocrine glands.

en·do·don·tics (en'dōdon'tiks), *n.* a branch of dentistry concerned with diseases of the dental pulp. —**en·do·don'tist**, *n.*

en·do·er·gic (en'dōur'jik), *adj.* pertaining to a chemical reaction involving the absorption of energy. See also **exoergic**.

en·dog·a·my (endog'əmē), *n.* marriage within a social group. See also **exogamy**.

en·do·lith·ic (en'dōlith'ik), *adj.* living embedded in rock surfaces.

en·do·lymph (en'dəlimf), *n.* a fluid in the labyrinth of the ear.

en·do·morph·ic (en'dəmôr'fik), *adj.* having a relatively heavily built body. See also **ectomorphic, mesomorphic**. —**en'do·morph**, *n.*

en·do·par·a·site (en'dōpar'əsīt), *n.* an internal parasite. See also **ectoparasite**.

en·do·pha·sia (en'dōfā'ZHə), *n.* internalized, inaudible speech. See also **exophasia**.

en·do·phyte (en'dəfīt), *n.* an internally parasitic plant. See also **ectophyte**.

end organ, one of several specialized structures found at the ends of nerve fibers, etc.

en·do·scope (en'dəskōp), *n.* a small,

cylindrical instrument used for examining the interior of a bodily organ.

en·do·skel·e·ton (en'dōskel'itn), *n.* the internal skeleton. See also **exoskeleton**.

en·dos·mo·sis (en'dosmō'sis), *n.* the movement of a substance from an area of lesser concentration to an area of greater concentration. See also **exosmosis**.

en·do·ther·mic (en'dōthur'mik), *adj.* pertaining to a chemical change involving the absorption of heat. See also **exothermic**.

en·e·ma (en'əmə), *n.* the injection of fluid into the rectum.

en·er·gu·men (enərgyōō'mən), *n.* **1.** someone possessed by an evil spirit. **2.** a fanatic.

en·er·vate (en'ərvāt), *v.* to make weak.

en fa·mille (äN famē'), *French.* in the family.

en·fant per·du (äNfäN perdY'), *pl.* **en·fants per·du** (äNfäN perdY'), *French.* a suicide squad.

en·fant ter·ri·ble (äNfäN terē'bl), *pl.* **en·fants ter·ri·bles** (äNfäN terē'bl). *French.* a child who causes embarrassment because of his behavior.

en·fleu·rage (äNflo͞oräzH'), *n.* a method of making perfume by exposing oil to the scent of flowers.

en·ga·gé (äNgazHā'), *adj. French.* committed; involved. See also **dégagé**.

en·gen·der (enjen'dər), *v.* to cause; bring about.

en·glut (englut'), *v.* to gulp down; swallow.

en·gorge (engôrj'), *v.* **1.** to swallow at great speed. **2.** to fill or distend with blood.

en·grail (engrāl'), *v.* to decorate the edge with curved indentations.

en·gross (engrōs'), *v.* **1.** to take all the attention of. **2.** to copy clearly and in a formal manner, as a public record.

e·nig·ma (ənig'mə), *n., pl.* **e·nig·mas, e·nig·ma·ta** (ənig'mətə). something that cannot be explained. —**en·ig·mat·ic** (enigmat'ik), *adj.*

en·join (enjoin′), *v.* **1.** to give an
order; command. **2.** to proscribe.

en masse (än mas′), *French.* all together.

en·ne·ad (en′ēad), *n.* a group of nine.

en·ne·a·gon (en′ēəgon), *n.* nonagon.

en·ne·a·he·dron (en′ēəhē′dron), *n.*,
pl. **en·ne·a·he·dra** (en′ēəhē′drə). a
solid shape with nine surfaces.

en·nui (änwē′), *n.* weariness; indifference, boredom.

e·nol·o·gy (ēnol′əjē), *n.* See **oenology**.

e·nor·mi·ty (inôr′mitē), *n.* awful-
ness; horribleness.

e·no·sis (e′nôsēs), *n. Greek.* political
union, esp. that of Greece and
Cyprus.

e·nounce (inouns′), *v.* **1.** to declare.
2. to enunciate.

en rap·port (äN rapôr′), *French.* in
close relation with; in agreement
with.

en·san·guine (ensaNG′gwin), *v.* to
stain with blood.

en·sconce (enskons′), *v.* to make
snug and safe.

en·si·form (en′səfôrm), *adj.* sword-
shaped.

en·si·lage (en′səlij), *n.* fodder stored
in a silo.

en·sor·cell (ensôr′səl), *v.* to put a
spell on.

en suite (äN swēt′), *French.* in a series.

en·tab·la·ture (entab′ləchər), *n.* the
part of a classical temple between the
columns and the eaves, or an imitation of it.

en·ta·ble·ment (entā′bəlmənt), *n.* a
platform over the dado of a pedestal.

en·ta·sis (en′təsis), *n.* a convex outline given to a column, etc., to make
it appear straight.

en·tel·e·chy (entel′əkē), *n.* an actu-
alization or manifestation as contrasted with a possibility or potentiality.
—**en·te·lech′i·al**, *adj.*

en·tente (äntänt′), *n.*, *pl.* **en·tentes**
(äntänt′). an agreement between
nations on a common international
policy.

en·tente cor·diale (äntänt′ kôr-
dyäl′), *French.* amicable understanding, as between two nations.

en·ter·al·gia (en′təral′jə), *n.* intestinal pain.

en·ter·ic (enter′ik), *adj.* of or pertaining to the digestive tract; intestinal.
Also **en′ter·al.**

enteric fever, typhoid.

en·ter·i·tis (entərī′tis), *n.* intestinal
inflammation.

en·ter·ol·o·gy (entərol′əjē), *n.* a
branch of medicine concerned with
the intestines.

en·ter·on (en′təron), *n.*, *pl.* **en·ter·a**
(en′tərə). the alimentary canal.

en·ter·or·rhex·is (en′tərərek′sis), *n.*
an intestinal rupture.

en·thet·ic (enthet′ik), *adj.* brought
in from outside, as a disease introduced by inoculation.

en·to·mog·e·nous (en′təmoj′ənəs),
adj. (of a fungus) living parasitically
in or on insects.

en·to·mol·o·gy (en′təmol′əjē), *n.* the
study of insects.

en·to·moph·a·gous (en′təmof′əgəs),
adj. insect-eating; insectivorous.

en·to·moph·i·lous (en′təmof′ələs),
adj. pollinated by insects, as a plant.

en·top·ic (entop′ik), *adj.* (of a bodily
organ) in the normal place. See also
ectopic.

en·tou·rage (än′tŏŏräzh), *n.* servants,
attendants.

en·to·zo·a (entəzō′ə), *n. pl.*, *sing.* **en·
to·zo·on** (entəzō′on). animals living
parasitically inside another animal.
—**en·to·zo′ic**, *adj.*

en·tre·côte (äNtrəkōt′), *n.*, *pl.* **en·tre·
côtes** (äNtrəkōt′). a cut of steak from
between the ribs.

en·trée (äntrā′), *n.* **1.** the act of entering. **2.** means of entrance or access.
3. any food, esp. any food except a
roast served as the main course of a
meal.

en·tre·mets (än′trəmā), *n.*, *pl.* **en·tre·
mets.** **1.** a side dish between principal
courses. **2.** a dessert course.

en·tre nous (äntrə nŏŏ′), *French.*
secretly; just between the two of us.

en·tre·pre·neur (äntrəprənûr′), *n.* an
organizer of an enterprise, esp. one
that has some financial risk attached.
—**en·tre·pre·neur′ship**, *n.*

en·tre·sol (en′tərsol), *n.* the mezzanine floor.

en·tro·py (en′trəpē), *n.* **1.** the probability of the frequency of occurrence of an event. **2.** similarity; lack of differentiation.

e·nu·cle·ate (inoo′klēāt), *v.* **1.** to take away the nucleus of. **2.** to remove the outer covering of (a kernel, tumor, etc.). —*adj.* **3.** without a nucleus.

e·nun·ciate (inun′sēāt), *v.* to say clearly; proclaim. —**e·nun·ci·a′tion,** *n.*

en·u·re·sis (enyərē′sis), *n.* unintentional urination; incontinence.

en·zo·ot·ic (en′zōot′ik), *adj.* (of diseases) peculiar to animals in a particular area or region. See also **endemic, epidemic.**

en·zyme (en′zīm), *n.* any organic substance capable of changing other organic substances by acting as a catalyst. —**en·zy·mat′ic,** *adj.*

en·zy·mol·o·gy (en′zīmol′əjē), *n.* the science of enzymes.

E·o·cene (ē′əsēn), *adj.* noting an epoch occurring from 40,000,000 to 60,000,000 years ago, characterized by early forms of all modern animals, including man.

e·o·hip·pus (ē′ōhip′əs), *n.* a horse of the Eocene period.

e·o·lith (ē′əlith), *n.* a flint shaped by natural forces and probably used as a tool by early man. —**e·o·lith′ic,** *adj.*

e·on, ae·on (ē′on), *n.* a period of time comprising at least two geologic eras.

e·on·ism (ē′ənizm), *n.* the wearing of female clothes and adoption of feminine attitudes by a man.

e·pact (ē′pakt), *n.* the difference in length between a lunar year and a solar year.

e·pan·o·dos (ipan′ədos), *n.* the repetition of words or ideas in reverse order.

e·pei·ric (ipī′rik), *adj.* reaching inland, as part of the sea.

ep·ei·rog·e·ny (ep′īroj′ənē), *n.* the vertical tilting of the earth's crust.

e·pergne (ipurn′), *n.* an often elaborate centerpiece for a dinner table.

e·phem·er·a (ifem′ərə), *n.*, *pl.* **e·phem·er·as, e·phem·er·ae** (ifem′-ərē). something lasting only a short time. —**e·phem′er·al,** *adj.* —**e·phem·er·al′i·ty,** *n.*

e·phem·er·is (ifem′əris), *n.*, *pl.* **e·phe·mer·i·des** (ef′əmer′idēz). a table showing the position of a heavenly body on regular, recurring dates.

e·phem·er·on (ifem′əron), *n.*, *pl.* **e·phem·er·a** (ifem′ərə), **e·phem·er·ons.** something that lives only a short time.

ep·i·cene (ep′isēn), *adj.* **1.** reflecting both male and female characteristics. **2.** weak, feeble. **3.** effeminate. —**ep·i·cen′ism,** *n.*

ep·i·cen·ter (ep′isen′tər), *n.* the point directly above the center of an earthquake.

ep·i·con·ti·nen·tal (epi′ikon′tənen′-tl), *adj.* in or on a continent.

e·pic·ri·sis[1] (ipik′risis), *n.* a critical study.

ep·i·cri·sis[2] (ep′ikrī′sis), *n.* a minor crisis following a major crisis.

ep·i·crit·ic (epəkrit′ik), *adj.* pertaining to the ability to respond to small variations in temperature or pain. See also **protopathic.**

ep·i·cure (ep′əkyŏor), *n.* a person of fastidious tastes, esp. in eating and drinking.

e·pi·cu·re·an (ep′əkyŏorē′ən), *adj.* **1.** of luxurious habits, esp. in connection with food and drink. **2.** befitting an epicure.

Ep·i·cu·re·an·ism (ep′əkyŏorē′-ənizm), *n.* the hedonistic philosophy expounded by Epicurus, in which pleasure is the highest goal attainable.

ep·i·dem·ic (ep′idem′ik), *adj.* affecting many people at the same time, as a disease carried from person to person in an area where it is not usually found. See also **endemic, enzootic.**

ep·i·de·mi·ol·o·gy (ep′idē′mēol′-əjē), *n.* the study of epidemic diseases. —**ep·i·demi·ol′o·gist,** *n.*

ep·i·der·mis (ep′idur′mis), *n.* the outer layer of skin. —**ep·i·der′moid,** *adj.*

ep·i·di·a·scope (ep′idī′əskōp), *n.* an

instrument for projecting the enlarged image of an opaque object.

ep·i·gam·ic (epəgam′ik), adj. attractive to the opposite sex during the mating season, as plumage of certain birds.

ep·i·gas·tric (epəgas′trik), adj. pertaining to the epigastrium.

ep·i·gas·tri·um (epəgas′trēəm), n., pl. **ep·i·gas·tri·a** (epəgas′trēə). that part of the abdomen situated above the stomach.

ep·i·ge·al (ep′ijē′əl), adj. (of insects) living near the ground, as on low plants.

ep·i·gene (ep′əjēn), adj. (in geology) originating on the surface of the earth. See also **hypogene.**

ep·i·gen·e·sis (epəjen′isis), n. the theory that embryonic development depends on an undifferentiated structure becoming successively more differentiated. See also **preformation.**

e·pig·e·nous (ipij′inəs), adj. (of fungi) growing on the surface, as of leaves.

ep·i·ge·ous (epəjē′əs), adj. (of plants) growing near the ground.

ep·i·gone (ep′əgōn), n. a disciple of a famous writer, etc., not famous in his own right. Also **ep·i·gon** (ep′əgon).

ep·i·gram (ep′əgram), n. a cryptic, witty, or pointed remark. —**ep·i·gram·mat′ic,** adj. —**ep·i·gram′ma·tist,** n.

ep·i·graph (ep′əgraf), n. 1. an inscription on a monument, etc. 2. a quotation at the beginning of a work. —**ep·i·graph′ic,** adj.

e·pig·ra·phy (ipig′rəfē), n. 1. the study of inscriptions. 2. inscriptions in general; graffiti. —**e·pig′ra·phist, e·pig′ra·pher,** n.

ep·i·late (ep′əlāt), v. to remove hair from.

ep·i·lep·sy (ep′əlepsē), n. a nervous illness characterized by convulsions and ending in loss of consciousness. See also **grand mal, petit mal.** —**ep·i·lep′tic,** n., adj.

ep·i·lim·ni·on (epəlim′nēon), n., pl. **ep·i·lim·ni·a** (epəlim′nēə). a layer of

water above the thermocline in some lakes. See also **hypolimnion.**

ep·i·lith·ic (epəlith′ik), adj. (of plants) growing on stones.

ep·i·logue, ep·i·log (ep′əlôg), n. a conclusion added to a novel, play, etc.

ep·i·mor·pho·sis (epəmôr′fəsis), n. (in segmented animals) the development of segmentation before hatching.

ep·i·nas·ty (ep′ənastē), n. excessive growth on the top surface of a plant causing it to bend downward.

ep·i·neph·rine (epənef′rin), n. an adrenal hormone that causes a rise in blood pressure.

ep·i·neu·ri·um (epənŏŏr′ēəm), n., pl. **ep·i·neu·ri·a** (epənŏŏrēə). the sheath of tissue protecting the trunk of a nerve.

ep·i·o·nych·i·um (ep′ēōnik′ēəm), n. See **eponychium.**

ep·i·pas·tic (epəpas′tik), adj. suitable as a dusting powder.

E·piph·a·ny (ipif′ənē), n. 1. a Christian feast, on January 6, to commemorate the appearance of Christ to the Magi. 2. (e-) (in literature) the sudden realization of the essential meaning of something. 3. (e-) (in literature) the symbolic representation of such a realization.

ep·i·phe·nom·e·nal·ism (ep′ēfənom′inəlizm), n. the belief that consciousness is a secondary phenomenon and cannot affect physiological processes.

ep·i·phe·nom·e·non (ep′ēfənom′ənon), n. a secondary complication during the course of an illness.

ep·i·phloe·dal (epəflē′dl), adj. growing on the bark of a tree. Also **ep·i·phloe′dic.**

ep·i·pho·ne·ma (epəfōnē′mə), n., pl. **ep·i·pho·ne·mas, ep·i·phon·ne·mae** (epəfōnē′mē). a summary of what has been said before.

e·piph·o·ra (ipif′ərə), n. an overflow of tears due to a blockage or to excessive secretion.

ep·i·phragm (ep′əfram), n. a secretion which a snail in dry weather uses to seal its shell and thus prevent drying out.

ep·i·phy·lax·is (epəfīlak'sis), *n*. the boosting of bodily defenses against disease.

ep·i·phyte (ep'əfīt), *n*. a plant growing on another but not feeding parasitically on it.

ep·i·phy·tot·ic (epəfītot'ik), *adj*. (of a disease) destroying many plants in a given area at one time.

e·pis·co·pa·cy (ipis'kəpəsē), *n*. **1.** the government of the church by bishops. **2.** the office of a bishop.

e·pis·co·pal (ipis'kəpəl), *adj*. **1.** of a bishop or bishops. **2.** indicating all or part of the Anglican Church.

e·pis·co·pal·ism (ipis'kəpəlizm), *n*. the vesting of ecclesiastical authority in the episcopal order as a whole and not in any individual.

e·pis·co·pize (ipis'kəpīz), *v*. to create a bishop of.

e·pis·co·tist·er, e·pis·ko·tist·er (ipis'kətistər), *n*. a solid disk with a segment missing, thus allowing the passage of flashes of light when rotated in front of a light source.

ep·i·spas·tic (epəspas'tik), *adj*. causing a blister.

e·pis·ta·sis (ipis'təsis), *n.*, *pl.* **e·pis·ta·ses** (ipis'təsēz). **1.** (in genetics) the interaction between nonallelic genes. **2.** (in medicine) blockage of a discharge.

ep·i·stax·is (ep'istak'sis), *n*. a nosebleed.

ep·i·ste·mic (ep'istē'mik), *adj*. pertaining to knowledge.

e·pis·te·mol·o·gy (ipis'təmol'əjē), *n*. a branch of philosophy concerned with human knowledge and its limitations.

e·pis·to·lar·y (ipis'tələr'ē), *adj*. carried on in letters, as *epistolary orders*.

e·pis·to·lize (ipis'təlīz), *v*. to write a letter to (someone).

e·pis·to·log·ra·phy (ipis'təlog'rəfē), *n*. the art of letter writing.

e·pit·a·sis (ipit'əsis), *n*. (in ancient drama) the portion in which the main action develops. See also **catastasis, catastrophe, protasis.**

ep·i·tha·la·mi·on (epəthəlā'mēən), *n.*, *pl.* **ep·i·tha·la·mi·a** (epəthəlā'mēə). a poem or song to celebrate a marriage. Also **ep·i·tha·la'mi·um.**

ep·i·the·li·o·ma (epəthē'lēō'mə), *n.*, *pl.* **ep·i·the·li·o·ma·ta** (epəthē'lēō'mətə), **ep·i·the·li·o·mas.** a cancer of the cells that line blood vessels, etc.

ep·i·the·li·um (epəthē'lēəm), *n.*, *pl.* **ep·i·the·li·ums, ep·i·the·li·a.** any protective tissue, as the epidermis. —**ep·i·the'li·al,** *adj*. —**ep·i·the'li·oid,** *adj*.

ep·i·the·li·za·tion (epəthē'ləzā'sHən), *n*. the forming of epithelium.

ep·i·thet (ep'əthet), *n*. a word or phrase ascribing an attribute to someone or something, as *Ivan the Terrible*.

e·pit·o·me (ipit'əmē), *n*. a summary.

e·pit·o·mize (ipit'əmīz), *v*. to be typical of; typify.

ep·i·zo·on (ep'izō'ən), *n.*, *pl.* **ep·i·zo·a** (ep'izō'ə). an external parasite. —**ep·i·zo'ic,** *adj*.

ep·i·zo·ot·ic (ep'izōot'ik), *adj*. (of a disease) prevalent amongst animals for a short time.

ep·i·zo·o·ty (ep'izō'ətē), *n*. an epizootic disease.

e plu·ri·bus unum (ē' plŏŏr'əbəs yōō'nəm), *Latin*. one out of the many: the motto of the U.S.

ep·och (ep'ək), *n*. any of several divisions of a geological period.

ep·o·nych·i·um (epənik'ēəm), *n*. a layer of skin that covers the nails of a fetus and that becomes the cuticle after birth. Also **epionychium.**

ep·o·nym (ep'ənim), *n*. a real or fictitious person whose name is adopted by a tribe or nation. —**ep·on·y·mous** (epon'əməs), *adj*.

ep·on·y·my (epon'əmē), *n*. the making of names from eponyms.

ep·ox·y (epok'sē), *n*. any substance, esp. a powerful cement, made by polymerization from certain chemicals. Also **epoxy resin.**

ep·u·ra·tion (epyərā'sHən), *n*. a purge, as of officials suspected of treachery.

eq·ua·ble (ek'wəbəl), *adj*. uniform; unvarying.

e·qual·i·tar·i·an (ikwol'əter'ēən),

adj. pertaining to the doctrine that all men are equal.

e·qua·nim·i·ty (ēkwənim′itē), *n.* calmness; composure; serenity. —**e·quan′i·mous** (ikwan′əməs), *adj.*

eq·uer·ry (ek′wərē), *n.* an officer in charge of the horses of a royal household.

e·qui·dis·tant (ēkwədis′tint), *adj.* at equal distances from.

e·qui·form (ē′kwəfôrm), *adj.* with the same shape or serving the same purpose. Also **e·qui·form′al.**

e·qui·lat·er·al (ē′kwəlat′ərəl), *adj.* with all sides of equal length.

e·quil·i·brant (ikwil′əbrənt), *n.* a force or forces that counterbalance.

e·qui·li·brate (ikwil′əbrāt), *v.* to balance; to cause to balance equally.

e·quil·i·brist (ikwil′əbrist), *n.* someone skilled at balancing, as a tightrope performer.

e·qui·noc·tial (ēkwənok′SHəl), *adj.* pertaining to the equal length of day and night.

e·qui·nox (ē′kwənoks), *n.* the time when night and day are of equal length everywhere, occurring about March 21 and September 22.

eq·ui·page (ek′wəpij), *n.* **1.** a horse-drawn carriage. **2.** all of the equipment or furnishings, as of a home or military unit, considered together.

e·qui·poise (ē′kwəpoiz), *n.* an equality of force or weight; balance.

e·qui·pol·lent (ēkwəpol′ənt), *adj.* equally effective in force or meaning; equivalent.

e·qui·pon·der·ance (ēkwəpon′dərəns), *n.* equality of weight.

e·qui·pon·der·ate (ēkwəpon′dərāt), *v.* to counterbalance; equal in importance.

e·qui·po·tent (ēkwəpō′tnt), *adj.* equally powerful.

e·qui·prob·a·ble (ēkwəprob′əbəl), *adj.* equally probable.

e·qui·ro·tal (ēkwərō′tl), *adj.* with wheels of equal size.

eq·ui·ta·ble (ek′witəbəl), *adj.* fair, just.

eq·ui·ta·tion (ek′witā′SHən), *n.* the art or act of horseback riding.

e·quiv·o·cal (ikwiv′əkəl), *adj.* ambiguous; with various meanings, as *an equivocal reply.*

e·quiv·o·cate (ikwiv′əkāt), *v.* to speak in a deliberately vague manner. —**e·quiv·o·ca′tion,** *n.*

eq·ui·voque, eq·ui·voke (ek′wəvōk), *n.* an ambiguous phrase or amusing play on words.

e·ra·di·ate (irā′dēāt), *v.* to radiate. —**e·ra·di·a′tion,** *n.*

er·e·mite (er′əmīt), *n.* a hermit.

er·e·moph·i·lous (erəmof′ələs), *adj.* inhabiting a desert.

er·e·mo·phyte (er′əmōfīt), *n.* a desert plant.

er·e·thism (er′əthizm), *n.* an excessive stimulation of any organ or tissue.

erg (urg), *n.* a unit for measuring energy or work.

erg (erg), *n.* any large expanse of sand, as a desert.

er·gate (ur′gāt), *n.* a worker ant.

er·go·graph (ur′gəgraf), *n.* a device for recording the amount of work done when a muscle contracts.

er·go·nom·ics (urgənom′iks), *n.* the science of making the job fit the worker; study of men at work; biotechnology.

er·gos·ter·ol (urgos′tərōl), *n.* a substance, found in yeast, that is converted into vitamin D when subjected to ultraviolet light.

er·i·ce·tic·o·lous (erəsətik′ələs), *adj.* living in or on a heath.

er·is·tic (eris′tik), *adj.* controversial. Also **er·is′ti·cal.**

erl·king (url′kiNG), *n.* a mischievous spirit.

erne, ern (urn), *n.* a sea eagle.

e·rod·ent (irō′dnt), *adj.* erosive; causing erosion.

e·rog·e·nous (iroj′ənəs), *adj.* sensitive to sexual stimulation.

e·rose (irōs′), *adj.* uneven, as from the effects of erosion.

e·ro·to·gen·e·sis (irō′təjen′isis), *n.* the stimulation of erotic impulses. —**e·ro·to·gen′ic,** *adj.*

e·ro·to·ma·ni·a (irō′təmā′nēə), *n.* an abnormally powerful sexual desire.

er·rat·ic (irat′ik), *adj.* **1.** eccentric, unusual. **2.** without aim; with no fixed course.

er·rhine (er′īn), *adj.* **1.** made to be sniffed into the nose. **2.** causing discharges from the nose.

er·satz (er′zäts), *adj.* artificial; used as a substitute for a superior, usually natural, product.

er·u·bes·cent (er′ŏŏbes′ənt), *adj.* becoming red.

e·ru·ci·form (irŏŏ′səfôrm), *adj.* like a caterpillar.

e·ruct (irukt′), *v.* to belch. Also **e·ruc·tate** (iruk′tāt).

e·rum·pent (irum′pənt), *adj.* bursting out or from.

er·y·sip·e·las (er′isip′ələs), *n.* an infectious disease causing inflammation of the skin.

er·y·the·ma (erəthē′mə), *n.* a condition in which the skin is abnormally red.

e·ryth·rism (irith′rizm), *n.* an unusual redness, as of hair.

e·ryth·ro·cyte (irith′rəsīt), *n.* a red blood cell, carrying oxygen to tissue and taking carbon dioxide away.

e·ryth·ro·cy·tom·e·ter (irith′rōsītom′itər), *n.* an instrument for counting red blood cells.

e·ryth·ro·my·cin (irith′rōmī′sin), *n.* an antibiotic.

e·ryth·ro·pho·bi·a (irith′rəfō′bēə), *n.* an abnormal fear of anything red, or of blushing.

e·ryth·ro·poi·e·sis (irith′rōpoiē′sis), *n.* the production of erythrocytes.

e·ryth·ro·poi·e·tin (irith′rōpoiē′tin), *n.* a substance that stimulates production of red blood cells in bone marrow.

es·ca·lade (eskəlād′), *n.* the climbing up by means of ladders.

es·ca·late (es′kəlāt), *v.* **1.** to intensify, as a war. **2.** to rise or descend, as on an escalator. —**es·ca·la′tion,** *n.*

es·carp (eskärp′), *n.* the inner slope of a ditch; any steep slope.

es·carp·ment (eskärp′mənt), *n.* a ridge of high land like a cliff.

es·char (es′kär), *n.* a scab, esp. one formed from a burn.

es·cha·rot·ic (eskərot′ik), *adj.* causing an eschar; caustic.

es·cha·tol·o·gy (eskətol′əjē), *n.* any doctrine dealing with future or final matters, such as death. —**es·cha·tol′o·gist,** *n.*

es·cheat (esCHēt′), *n.* the reversion of property to the state or crown when no legal heir or inheritor exists.

es·chew (esCHŏŏ′), *v.* to avoid; shun.

es·cri·toire (es′kritwär′), *n.* a writing desk.

es·crow (es′krō), *n.* a written agreement lodged with a third person and handed over when certain conditions have been fulfilled.

es·cu·lent (es′kyələnt), *adj.* edible.

es·cutch·eon (eskuCH′ən), *n.* a shield that bears a coat of arms.

es·ne (ez′nē), *n.* (in Anglo-Saxon England) a laborer.

e·soph·a·ge·al, oe·soph·a·ge·al (isof′əjē′əl), *adj.* of or pertaining to the esophagus.

esophageal speech, a method of producing sounds without using the larynx.

e·soph·a·gi·tis (isof′əjī′tis), *n.* inflammation of the esophagus.

e·soph·a·gus, oe·soph·a·gus (isof′-əgəs), *n., pl.* **e·soph·a·gi, oe·soph·a·gi** (isof′əjī). the tubular connection between the mouth and the stomach.

es·o·ter·ic (esəter′ik), *adj.* intended for or intelligible to only the initiated few.

es·o·ter·i·ca (esəter′ikə), *n. pl.* things meant only for the initiated few.

es·pal·ier (espal′yər), *n.* **1.** a flat trellis on which plants, esp. fruit trees, are grown. —*v.* **2.** to train on an espalier.

es·per·ance (es′pərəns), *n.* hope.

es·pi·al (espī′əl), *n.* the act of spying; an observing.

es·pla·nade (esplənād′), *n.* any public spaces, esp. one for the public to walk or drive on.

es·pous·al (espou′zəl), *n.* the taking up of a cause.

es·pres·so (espres′ō), *n.* coffee made by forcing boiling water through ground coffee beans under pressure.

es·prit (esprē′), *n.* sharp intelligence or spirit.

es·prit de corps (esprē′ də kôr′), a

feeling of common interest uniting a group of people.

e·squa·mate (ēskwā′māt), *adj.* without scales.

Es·tab·lish·ment (estab′lisHmənt), *n.* the existing authority in an institution or state.

es·ta·fette (estəfet′), *n.* a courier on horseback.

es·ta·mi·net (estamēne′), *n.*, *pl.* **es·ta·mi·nets** (estamēne′), *French.* a small café.

es·the·sia, aes·the·sia (esthē′zHə), *n.* sensitivity; ability to feel.

es·the·si·om·e·ter (esthē′zēom′itər), *n.* a device to measure the degree of tactile sensitivity.

es·the·si·om·e·try (esthē′zēom′itrē), *n.* the process of using an esthesiometer.

es·the·sis, aes·the·sis (esthē′sis), *n.* feeling; sensation.

es·thete (es′thēt), *n.* See **aesthete.**

es·thet·ic (esthet′ik), *adj.* See **aesthetic.**

es·ti·ma·ble (es′təməbəl), *adj.* worthy of respect.

es·ti·val, aes·ti·val (es′təvəl), *adj.* of the summer.

es·ti·vate, aes·ti·vate (es′təvāt), *v.* to pass the summer, as in a certain place. —**es·ti·va′tion, aes·ti·va′tion**, *n.*

es·to·ca·da (estəkä′də), *n.* a sword thrust intended to kill the bull in bullfighting.

es·trade (esträd′), *n.* a low platform.

es·tray (estrā′), *n.* something which has gone astray.

es·treat (estrēt′), *n.* a copy of all or of part of a written record.

es·tro·gen, oes·tro·gen (es′trəjən), *n.* any female hormone causing an estrus in immature animals. —**es·tro·gen′ic**, *adj.*

es·trus, oes·trus (es′trəs), *n.* a period of female sexual heat. —**es·trous, oes·trous** (es′trəs), *adj.*

es·tu·a·rine (es′cHŌŌərīn), *adj.* formed in, found in, or pertaining to estuaries.

es·tu·ar·y (es′cHŌŌerē), *n.* an area at a rivermouth where the current of the river meets the tide of the sea.

e·su·ri·ent (isŌŌr′ēənt), *adj.* greedy; voracious.

é·ta·gère (ātazHer′), *n.*, *pl.* **é·ta·gères** (ātazHer′). *French.* open shelves used for storing bric-a-brac.

et·a·mine (et′əmēn), *n.* light, loosely woven cloth of cotton or similar fabric.

et·a·oin shrd·lu (et′ēoin sHurd′lŌŌ), letters produced from the first two vertical rows of keys on the left of a Linotype machine and used as a temporary marker.

e·the·re·al, ae·the·re·al (ithēr′ēəl), *adj.* **1.** delicate; tenuous. **2.** celestial; spiritual.

eth·ic (eth′ik), *n.* moral values characterizing a culture or tribe.

eth·i·cal (eth′ikəl), *adj.* (of drugs) sold only when prescribed.

eth·narch (eth′närk), *n.* a ruler, as of a tribe or nation.

eth·nar·chy (eth′närkē), *n.* the government or rule of an ethnarch.

eth·nic (eth′nik), *adj.* characteristic of a group, esp. a racial group.

eth·no·cen·trism (eth′nōsen′trizm), *n.* a feeling that one's own group is superior to any other.

eth·noc·ra·cy (ethnok′rəsē), *n.* rule by a certain ethnic group.

eth·nog·e·ny (ethnoj′ənē), *n.* the study of the origin of distinctive groups or tribes.

eth·nog·ra·phy (ethnog′rəfē), *n.* a study of characteristics of races of men and their cultures.

eth·no·lin·guis·tics (eth′nōliNGgwis′tiks), *n.* the study of language within a culture, and the effect on the culture.

eth·nol·o·gy (ethnol′əjē), *n.* the study of the origins, development, etc., of the races of mankind.

eth·no·mu·si·col·o·gy (eth′nōmyŌŌ′zikol′əjē), *n.* the study of primitive music and its cultural background.

e·thol·o·gy (ethnol′əjē), *n.* the study of animal behavior in relation to habitat.

e·thos (ē′thos), *n.* the basic characteristics of a culture.

e·ti·o·late (ē'tēəlāt), *v.* to make (plants) white by denying light.

e·ti·ol·o·gy, ae·ti·ol·ogy (ē'tēol'əjē), *n.* any study of causes, esp. of causes of disease.

et·y·mol·o·gize (etəmol'əjīz), *v.* to trace (a word) historically.

et·y·mol·o·gy (etəmol'əjē), *n.* the study of the derivation and history of a word.

et·y·mon (et'əmon), *n., pl.* **et·y·mons, et·y·ma** (et'əmə). a linguistic form giving rise to another form historically, as Latin *luna*, "moon" is the etymon of English *lunar*.

Eu·clid·e·an geometry (yŏōklid'-ēən), geometry based on Euclid's theory, esp. the postulate that only one line may be drawn through a given point parallel to a given line. See also **hyperbolic geometry, Riemannian geometry.**

eu·de·mon, eu·dae·mon (yŏōdē'-mən), *n.* a beneficial demon.

eu·de·mo·ni·a, eu·dae·mo·ni·a (yŏō'dēmō'nēə), *n.* happiness. —**eu·de·mon·ic, eu·dae·mon·ic** (yŏō'dimon'ik), *adj.*

eu·de·mon·ics, eu·dae·mon·ics (yŏō'dimon'iks), *n.* the art of being happy.

eu·de·mon·ism, eu·dae·mon·ism (yŏōdē'mənizm), *n.* the theory that correct actions produce happiness. —**eu·de'mon·ist, eu·dae'mon·ist,** *n.*

eu·gen·ic (yŏōjen'ik), *adj.* connected with improving the type of offspring produced. See also **dysgenic.**

eu·gen·ics (yŏōjen'iks), *n.* the science of improving the human race by careful choice of parents. —**eu·gen'ic,** *adj.* —**eu·gen'i·cist,** *n.*

eu·gon·ic (yŏōgon'ik), *adj.* (of bacteria) living on artificial foodstuffs.

eu·he·mer·ism (yŏōhē'mərizm), *n.* the theory that the mythologies of various gods came from the stories of dead heroes.

eu·lo·gize (yŏō'ləjīz), *v.* to praise highly; extol.

eu·lo·gy (yŏō'ləjē), *n., pl.* **eu·lo·gies.** a speech or writing showing high praise for someone or something.

Also **eu·lo·gi·um** (yŏōlō'jēəm). —**eu·lo·gis'tic,** *adj.* —**eu'lo·gist,** *n.*

eu·no·my (yŏō'nəmē), *n.* good order due to just government and just laws.

eu·pep·sia (yŏōpep'sнə), *n.* normal, good, digestion. Also **eu'pep·sy.** See also **dyspepsia.**

eu·phe·mism (yŏō'fəmizm), *n.* a mild expression to replace an ugly or hurtful one, as *gone to rest* for *to die.* —**eu·phe·mist'ic,** *adj.*

eu·pho·nize (yŏō'fənīz), *v.* to render pleasing to the ear.

eu·pho·ny (yŏō'fənē), *n.* pleasant to hear; smooth pleasant enunciation of sounds. See also **cacophony.** —**eu·phon'ic,** *adj.* —**eu·pho·ni·ous** (yŏōfō'nēəs), *adj.*

eu·pho·ri·a (yŏōfôr'ēə), *n.* an abnormal, unreal state of happiness.

eu·phu·ism (yŏō'fyŏōizm), *n.* an ornate style of language or writing.

eu·plas·tic (yŏōplas'tik), *adj.* able to be made into organized tissue.

eup·ne·a, eup·noe·a (yŏōpnē'ə), *n.* normal breathing. See also **dyspnea.**

eu·po·tam·ic (yŏōpətam'ik), *adj.* inhabiting fresh water.

eu·rhyth·mics, eu·ryth·mics (yŏō-riтн'miks), *n.* an interpretation of musical rhythms by body movements. —**eu·rhyth'mic, eu·ryth'mic,** *adj.*

eu·rhyth·my, eu·ryth·my (yŏōriтн'-mē), *n.* a rhythmical motion.

eu·ri·pus (yŏōrī'pəs), *n., pl.* **eu·ri·pi** (yŏōrī'pī). a strait, esp. with a strong current.

eu·ri·ther·mo·phil·ic (yŏōr'əthur'-məfil'ik), *adj.* (of bacteria) multiplying up to temperatures of 60°C.

Eu·ro·dol·lars (yŏōr'ədol'ərz), *n. pl.* U.S. dollars used as international money in European banks.

European plan, a hotel plan in which the fixed daily charge covers only lodging and service. See also **American plan.**

eu·ry·ha·line (yŏōrəhā'līn), *adj.* capable of existing in an environment where the salinity varies greatly. See also **stenohaline.**

eu·ry·ther·mal (yŏōrəthur'məl), *adj.*

capable of withstanding great temperature variations. See also **stenothermal.**

eu·ry·top·ic (yo͞orətop′ik), *adj.* capable of withstanding wide variations in climate, humidity, etc. See also **stenotopic.**

eu·sta·cy (yo͞o′stəsē), *n.* a change of sea level throughout the world.

eu·tha·na·sia (yo͞othənā′zнə), *n.* the killing of an incurably ill person. Also **mercy killing.**

eu·then·ics (yo͞othen′iks), *n.* a science concerned with improving human conditions by improving their surroundings.

eu·ther·mic (yo͞othur′mik), *adj.* producing heat.

eu·to·ci·a (yo͞otō′sнēə), *n.* normal childbirth.

eu·troph·ic (yo͞otrof′ik), *adj.* **1.** being in a condition of healthy development. **2.** (of lakes) supporting many nutrients inducing dense plant growth. —**eu′tro·phy,** *n.*

e·vag·i·nate (ivaj′ənāt), *v.* (of a tubular organ) to turn inside out.

ev·a·nesce (evənes′), *v.* to fade slowly. —**ev·a·nes′cent,** *adj.*

e·van·gel·i·cal (ē′vanjel′ikəl), *adj.* being ardently enthusiastic about a cause. Also **e·van·gel′ic.** —**e·van·gel′i·cal·ly,** *adv.*

e·van·ge·lism (ivan′jəlizm), *n.* the dissemination of the gospel; activity of a missionary. —**e·van′ge·list,** *n.*

é·va·sé (āväzā′), *adj.* wider at the top, as a vase.

e·vec·tion (ivek′sнən), *n.* a recurring irregularity in the motion of the moon owing to the attraction of the sun.

ever-normal granary, surplus farm produce bought by the state, both to stabilize prices and to guard against shortages.

e·ver·si·ble (ivur′səbəl), *adj.* able to be everted, or turned inside out.

e·vert (ivurt′), *v.* to turn to the outside, or inside out. —**e·ver′sion,** *n.*

e·ver·tor (ivur′tər), *n.* a muscle by which a part or parts are turned toward the outside.

ev·i·ta·ble (ev′itəbəl), *adj.* that can be avoided or missed.

ev·o·ca·ble (ev′əkəbəl), *adj.* that can be evoked or drawn forth.

ev·o·ca·tion (evəkā′sнən), *n.* the process of summoning forth; calling forth; bringing to mind. —**e·voc·a·tive** (ivok′ətiv), *adj.*

e·volve (ivolv′), *v.* **1.** to develop slowly as by evolution; come slowly into being. **2.** to give off, as a vapor.

e·vul·sion (ivul′sнən), *n.* the act of pulling out; extracting; ripping out by force.

ev·zone (ev′zōn), *n.* an infantryman of a crack corps in the Greek army.

ex·ac·er·bate (igzas′ərbāt), *v.* to intensify the irritation or virulence of.

ex·ac·tion (igzak′sнən), *n.* extortion.

ex·an·i·mate (igzan′əmit), *adj.* **1.** lifeless; dead. **2.** disheartened.

ex·a·rate (ek′sərāt), *adj.* (of a pupa) with free wings, antennae, and legs. See also **obtect.**

ex·cau·date (ekskô′dāt), *adj.* without a tail; ecaudate.

ex·cerp·ta (iksurp′tə), *n. pl.* extracts from or summaries of a longer work.

excess-profits tax, a tax on profits made beyond the average return on capital.

ex·cide (iksīd′), *v.* to cut out.

ex·cip·i·ent (iksip′ēənt), *n.* an inactive, adhesive substance used to bind together the constituents of pills, etc.

ex·cise (iksīz′), *v.* to cut out.

ex·ci·to·mo·tor (iksī′təmō′tər), *adj.* causing increased motor activity. Also **ex·ci·to·mo·tor·y** (iksī′təmō′tərē).

ex·ci·tor (iksī′tər), *n.* a nerve that, when stimulated, causes greater action.

ex·clave (eks′klāv), *n.* a part of a country totally surrounded by the territory of another nation. See also **enclave.**

ex·clo·sure (iksklō′zнər), *n.* an area defended by fences, etc., against all intruders.

ex·cog·i·tate (ekskoj′itāt), *v.* to think out; study carefully to understand completely.

ex·com·mu·ni·cate (ekskəmyoo′-nəkāt), v. to deny (someone) the sacraments of the church. —**ex·com·mu·ni·ca′tion,** n.

ex·co·ri·ate (ikskôr′ēāt), v. to take the skin from; peel. —**ex·co·ri·a′tion,** n.

ex·cor·ti·cate (ekskôr′təkāt), v. to husk; peel the bark from.

ex·cul·pate (ek′skulpāt), v. to free from blame.

ex·cur·sive (ikskur′siv), adj. digressive in speech.

ex·cur·sus (ekskur′səs), n., pl. **ex·cur·sus·es, ex·cur·sus.** 1. a detailed discussion of something in a book. 2. a written digression.

ex·curved (eks′kurvd), adj. curving outward; convex. Also **ex′cur·vate.**

ex dividend, not including the recently declared dividend. See also **cum dividend.**

ex·e·cra·ble (ek′səkrəbəl), adj. horrible; detestable; accursed.

ex·e·crate (ek′səkrāt), v. 1. to hate; detest; loathe. 2. to damn; curse. —**ex·e·cra′tion,** n.

ex·e·ge·sis (ek′sijē′sis), n., pl. **ex·e·ge·ses** (ek′sijē′sēz). a critical explanation, esp. of the Scriptures. —**ex·e·get′ic,** adj.

exemplary damages, damages awarded in excess of fair compensation to punish a plaintiff for reckless behavior. See also **compensatory damages.**

ex·em·plum (igzem′pləm), n., pl. **ex·em·pla** (igzem′plə). a story illustrating a moral point.

ex·en·ter·ate (eksen′tərāt), v. to disembowel.

ex·e·qua·tur (eksəkwā′tər), n. written permission given to a consul by the state where he is resident authorizing him to carry on his functions.

ex·e·quy (ek′səkwē), n. obsequy; funeral ceremony.

ex·er·gon·ic (eksərgon′ik), adj. noting a biochemical process that frees energy during reaction. See also **endergonic.**

ex fa·ci·e (eks fā′sHēē) (of a document in law) presumably; apparently; on the face of it.

ex fac·to (eks fäk′tō), Latin. according to fact.

ex·hort (igzôrt′), v. to urge; admonish. —**ex·hor·ta′tion,** n. —**ex·hor′ta·tive,** adj.

ex·hume (igzoom′), v. to dig up, esp. a body, from the earth.

ex·i·gent, ex·i·geant (ek′sijənt), adj. urgent; pressing.

ex·i·gen·cy (ek′sijənsē), n. 1. a state of emergency; urgency or strong necessity. 2. (usually pl.) the needs or demands arising as a result of a particular circumstance, as exigencies of travel.

ex·i·gi·ble (ek′sijəbəl), adj. demandable; capable of being exacted.

ex·i·gu·ous (igzig′yooəs), adj. small; scanty; slender.

ex·im·i·ous (egzim′ēəs), adj. outstanding; eminent.

ex·is·ten·tial·ism (eg′zisten′sHə-lizm), n. the theory that man forms his essence from his deeds. —**ex·is·ten′tial·ist,** n., adj.

existential psychology, a psychology based only on existent data.

ex·o·cen·tric (ek′sōsen′trik), adj. with a different syntactic function than any of its constituents, as "in the house" which has a different function from the noun "house." See also **endocentric.**

ex·o·crine (ek′səkrin), adj. secreting externally. See also **endocrine.**

exocrine gland, any gland secreting externally.

ex·o·don·tics (eksədon′tiks), n. a branch of dentistry concerned with the extraction of teeth. —**ex·o·don′tist,** n.

ex·o·dus (ek′sədəs), n. 1. a leaving; migration. 2. The Exodus. the migration of the Israelites from Egypt, led by Moses.

ex·o·er·gic (ek′sōur′jik), adj. (in chemistry) denoting a reaction in which energy is liberated. See also **endoergic.**

ex of·fi·ci·o (eks əfisH′ēō). in the capacity of one holding an official position.

ex·og·a·my (eksog′əmē), n. marriage

outside a specified group. See also
endogamy.

ex·og·e·nous (eksoj'ənəs), *adj.* with
an external origin.

ex·o·path·ic (eksəpa*th*'ik), *adj.* (of a
disease) externally caused.

ex·o·pha·sia (ek'sōfā'zHə), *n.* normal,
voiced speech. See also **endophasia.**

ex·o·ra·ble (ek'sərəbəl), *adj.* able to
be persuaded.

ex·or·cise (ek'sôrsīz), *v.* to attempt to
expel an evil presence by religious
ceremonies. —**ex'or·cism,** *n.* —**ex'
or·cist,** *n.*

ex·or·di·um (igzôr'dēəm), *n., pl.* **ex·
or·di·ums, ex·or·di·a** (igzôr'dēə). a
beginning.

ex·o·skel·e·ton (ek'sōskel'itn), *n.* a
hard, external covering, as that of an
insect, turtle, etc. See also **endo-
skeleton.**

ex·os·mo·sis (ek'sosmō'sis), *n.* 1. osmosis from the inside to the outside.
2. (in osmosis) movement from an
area of high density to one of low
density. Also **ex·os·mose'.** See also
endosmosis.

ex·o·sphere (ek'sōsfēr'), *n.* the top-
most layer of the atmosphere.

ex·o·ter·ic (eksəter'ik), *adj.* appropriate for general dissemination.

ex·o·ter·i·ca (eksəter'əkə), *n.* exoteric
ideas, etc.

ex·o·ther·mic (ek'sō*th*ir'mik), *adj.*
pertaining to a chemical change involving the giving off of heat. See also
endothermic.

ex par·te (eks pär'tē), from one side
only, as in a dispute.

ex·pa·ti·ate (ekspā'trēāt), *v.* to enlarge upon.

ex·pec·to·rant (ikspek'tərənt), *adj.*
inducing fluid, as saliva or mucus, to
flow from the respiratory tract.

ex·pec·to·rate (ikspek'tərāt), *v.* to
spit; to cough up from the lungs.
—**ex·pec·to·ra'tion,** *n.*

ex·pe·di·ent (ikspē'dēənt), *adj.* **1.**
suitable; advantageous. —*n.* **2.** the
means to an end; a necessary action.
—**ex·pe·di·en·tial** (ikspē'dēen'sHəl),
adj. —**ex·pe'di·en·cy,** *n.*

ex·ped·i·tate (eksped'itāt), *v.* to re-

move the claws or pads of (a hound)
to discourage its deer chasing. —**ex·
ped·i·ta'tion,** *n.*

ex·pe·di·tious (ekspədisH'əs), *adj.*
quick; fast; speedy.

ex·pe·ri·en·tial (ikspēr'ēen'sHəl),
adj. acquired through experience.

ex·per·tise (ekspərtēz'), *n.* skill; expert knowledge.

ex·pi·ate (ek'spēāt), *v.* to make
amends for. —**ex·pi·a'tion,** *n.*

ex·pla·nate (eks'plənāt), *adj.* flattened out; spread.

ex·plant (eksplant'), *v.* to put living
tissue into a culture medium.

ex·ple·tive (eks'plətiv), *adj.* **1.** (of
words) without real meaning but for
emphasis; serving to fill up a sentence. —*n.* **2.** a profane word or oath.

ex·pli·can·dum (ekspləkan'dəm), *n.,
pl.* **ex·pli·can·da** (ekspləkan'də).
something to be explained, as a philosophical term.

ex·pli·cans (eks'pləkanz), *n., pl.* **ex·
pli·can·ti·a** (eks'pləkan'cHēə). the
meaning of a term, as in philosophy.

ex·pli·cate (eks'pləkāt), *v.* to make
clear. —**ex·pli·ca'tion,** *n.*

ex·pli·ca·tion de texte (eksplēkäsyôn də tekst'), *pl.* **ex·pli·ca·tions de
texte** (eksplēkäsyôn də tekst'),
French. literary criticism involving
analysis with emphasis on language,
style, and content to explain the
meaning and symbolism of the integrated whole.

ex·plic·it (iksplis'it), *adj.* completely
expressed; plainly stated. See also
implicit.

ex·pos·i·tor (ikspoz'itər), *n.* someone
who provides an explanation.

ex post fac·to (eks' pōst fak'tō), from
or by subsequent action; subsequently.

ex·pos·tu·late (ikspos'cHəlāt), *v.* to
protest, remonstrate. —**ex·pos·tu·la'
tion,** *n.*

ex·pro·pri·ate (eksprō'prēāt), *v.* to
take over esp. by the state for
the public benefit. —**ex·pro·pri·a'
tion,** *n.*

ex·pugn·a·ble (ekspyoo̅'nəbəl), *adj.*
defeatable, conquerable.

109

exude

ex·punc·tion (ikspuNGk′sHən), *n.* an
erasion; an act of expunging.
ex·pur·gate (eks′pərgāt), *v.* to remove
offensive parts from (a book).
ex·san·gui·nate (ekssaNG′gwənāt), *v.*
to take the blood from.
ex·san·guine (ekssaNG′gwin), *adj.*
anemic.
ex·san·guin·ous (ekssaNG′gwənəs),
adj. bloodless; anemic.
ex·scind (eksind′), *v.* to cut out;
destroy.
ex·sect (eksekt′), *v.* to cut out.
ex·sert (eksurt′), *v.* to thrust out;
project.
ex·sic·cate (ek′səkāt), *v.* to dry; dehydrate.
ex·tant (ek′stənt), *adj.* remaining; still
in existence.
ex·ten·sile (iksten′səl), *adj.* able to
be extended.
ex·ten·sion (iksten′sHən), *n.* (in logic)
a class of things that can be covered
by one term, as *Hamlet* and *Death of
a Salesman* can be classed as "tragedy." Also **extent.** See also **inten-
sion.**
ex·ten·som·e·ter (eks′tensom′itər),
n. a device for measuring extremely
small amounts of expansion.
ex·ten·sor (iksten′sər), *n.* a muscle
which stretches or straightens part of
the body.
ex·ten·u·ate (iksten′yōōāt), *v.* to
show an offense, etc., to be less serious. —**ex·ten·u·a′tion,** *n.*
ex·tern (eks′turn), *n.* someone connected with an institution but not
living in it. See also **intern.**
ex·ter·o·cep·tor (ekstərəsep′tər), *n.*
a receptor responsive to outside stimuli. —**ex·ter·o·cep′tive,** *adj.*
ex·tir·pate (ek′stərpāt), *v.* to uproot;
destroy totally. —**ex·tir·pa′tion,** *n.*
ex·tor·tion (ikstôr′sHən), *n.* to exact
from someone illegally, as by threat,
violence, illegal use of authority of an
office, etc.
ex·tor·tion·ate (ikstôr′sHənit), *adj.*
excessive; exorbitant; amounting to
extortion.
ex·trac·tive (ekstrak′tiv), *adj.* serving to extract; able to be extracted.

ex·tra·dite (eks′trədīt), *v.* to hand
over (a criminal, etc.) to another nation. —**ex′tra·dit·a·ble,** *adj.* —**ex·
tra·di·tion** (ekstrədisH′ən), *n.*
ex·tra·ga·lac·tic (ek′strəgəlak′tik),
adj. beyond the Milky Way.
ex·tra·mar·i·tal (ek′strəmar′itl), *adj.*
pertaining to sexual relations with a
person other than one's wife or husband.
ex·tra·mun·dane (ek′strəmun′dān),
adj. outside the world or the known
universe.
ex·tra·mu·ral (ek′strəmyōōr′əl), *adj.*
involving members of several schools.
See also **intramural.**
ex·tra·phys·i·cal (ek′strəfiz′ikəl),
adj. not subject to physical laws.
ex·trap·o·late (ikstrap′əlāt), *v.* to de-
duce (something unknown) from
something known.
ex·tra·pu·ni·tive (ek′strəpyōō′nitiv),
adj. (in ridding oneself of frustra-
tions) behaving hostilely toward
other people or objects. See also **im-
punitive.**
ex·tra·sen·so·ry (ek′strəsen′sərē),
adj. beyond normal perception.
ex·tra·sys·to·le (ek′strəsis′təlē), *n.* a
premature contraction of the heart
interrupting the normal heartbeat.
See also **systole.**
ex·tra·ter·res·tri·al (ek′strətəres′-
trēəl), *adj.* from a place other than the
earth.
ex·trav·a·sate (ikstrav′əsāt), *v.* to
force out or pour out, as blood or
lava. —**ex·trav·a·sa′tion,** *n.*
ex·tra·vert (ek′strəvərt), *n.* a person
concerned with his environment.
Also **ex·tro·vert** (ek′strəvərt). See
also **introvert.**
ex·trin·sic (ikstrin′sik), *adj.* external;
coming from outside.
ex·tro·spec·tion (ek′strəspek′sHən),
n. the observation of externals.
ex·tru·sile (ikstrōō′sil), *adj.* able to be
extruded.
ex·u·date (eks′yōōdāt), *n.* something
exuded.
ex·ude (igzōōd′), *v.* to seep out slowly
in small quantities, as sweat. —**ex·u·
da′tion,** *n.*

ex·urb (ek′sərb), *n.* a relatively small community outside a city's suburbs.

ex·ur·bi·a (eksur′bēə), *n.* all communities constituting the totality of all exurbs.

ex·u·vi·ae (igzōō′vēē), *n. pl.* any shells or coverings of animals that have been shed.

ex·u·vi·ate (igzōō′vēāt), *v.* to shed, as exuviae.

eyre (er), *n.* a journey in a circuit, as that traveled by circuit justices.

Fa·ber·gé (fabərjā´, fabərzHā´), *n.* fine gold and enamel ware made in Russia before the Russian revolution.

Fabian Society, a society dedicated to the peaceful spread of socialism.

fab·ri·cant (fab´rəkənt), *n.* a manufacturer.

fab·u·list (fab´yəlist), *n.* a liar.

fa·çade (fəsäd´, fasäd´), *n.* the front of an impressive building.

fa·ce·ti·ae (fəsē´sHēē), *n. pl.* humorous or clever sayings.

fa·ce·tious (fəsē´sHəs), *adj.* witty; amusing; frivolous, as *a facetious remark.*

fa·ci·es (fā´sHēēz), *n., pl.* **fa·ci·es. 1.** appearance, aspect, or nature of anything. **2.** (in medicine) a facial expression symptomatic of a certain disease or condition.

fac·ile (fas´il), *adj.* dexterous; fluent, moving or acting with ease.

fa·cil·i·tate (fəsil´iteit), *v.* to make easy or easier; to further. —**fa·cil·i·ta´tion,** *n.*

fa·cin·o·rous (fəsin´ərəs), *adj.* excessively wicked.

fac·tion (fak´sHən), *n.* a united body of persons, esp. a group within a larger group. —**fac´tion·al,** *adj.* **fac·tious** (fak´sHəs), *adj.*

fac·ti·tious (faktisH´əs), *adj.* artificial; conventional, affected.

fac·tor (fak´tər), *n.* (in commerce) a commercial organization engaged in financing wholesale or retail sales, through the purchase of accounts receivable.

fac·ture (fak´CHər), *n.* the act of making or constructing something.

fac·ul·ta·tive (fak´əltā´tiv), *adj.* granting a privilege, permission, or faculty.

faille (fīl, fāl), *n.* a soft, ribbed fabric of rayon or silk.

fail-safe (fāl´sāf´), *adj.* involving or designating a built-in mechanism or device designed to prevent malfunction or unintentional operation, as in a nuclear-armed aircraft or warning system.

fai·naigue (fənāg´), *v.* to deceive; to finagle or cheat someone.

fai·né·ant (fā´nēənt), *adj.* idle; lazy; indolent.

fair-trade agreement, an agreement under which a retailer undertakes to sell a product at no less than a minimum price set by the manufacturer.

fait ac·com·pli (fetakônplē´), *pl.* **faits ac·com·pli** (fezakônplē´). a thing already done; an accomplished fact, so that argument or discussion are useless.

Fa·lange (fā´lanj), *n.* a fascist organization that became the official political party of Spain after the Spanish civil war of 1936–39. —**Fa´lan·gist,** *n.*

111

fa·cate (fal′kāt), *adj.* curved; sickle-shaped; hooked.

fal·ci·form (fal′səfôrm), *adj.* shaped like a sickle; falcate.

fal·la·cy (fal′əsē), *n.* a deceptive or false notion, quality or belief. —**fal·la′cious**, *adj.*

fal·lal, fal-lal (fallal′), *n.* a frivolous piece of finery; a useless article of dress.

fal·li·ble (fal′əbəl), *adj.* **1.** (of persons) likely to be mistaken or to err. **2.** likely to be false or inaccurate.

fa·ma·cide (fā′məsīd), *n.* (in law) a person who defames the reputation of another; a slanderer.

fam·u·lus (fam′yələs), *n.*, *pl.* **fam·u·li** (fam′yəlī). an assistant, esp. of a medieval sorcerer or scholar.

fan·fa·ron (fan′fəron), *n.* a boaster or braggart.

fan·fa·ron·ade (fan′fərənād′), *n.* boasting talk; bravado; bluster.

Fanny May, nickname for the Federal National Mortgage Association. [from the initials FNMA.]

fan·tasm (fan′tazm), *n.* phantasm.

fan·tast, phan·tast (fan′tast), *n.* a fanciful dreamer; visionary.

far·ad (far′əd), *n.* an electrical unit of capacitance equivalent to one coulomb per volt.

far·ceur (farsoor′), *n. French.* **1.** a writer of farces. **2.** an actor in farces. **3.** a practical joker.

far·ci (färsē′), *adj.* (in cookery) stuffed.

far·i·na·ceous (far′ənā′sнəs), *adj.* containing or made from flour or meal.

far·i·nose (far′ənōs), *adj.* resembling farina; mealy.

far·rag·i·nous (fəraj′ənəs), *adj.* mixed; heterogenous.

far·ra·go (fərä′gō, fərā′gō), *n.*, *pl.* **far·ra·goes.** a jumbled mixture; hodge-podge; confusion.

far·ri·er (far′ēər), *n.* a man who shoes horses; a blacksmith. —**far′ri·er·y**, *n.*

far·thin·gale (fär′тнinggāl′), *n.* a hoop or openwork frame worn under a woman's skirt in the 16th and 17th centuries to make it bell out.

fas·ces (fas′ēz), *n.* a bundle of rods bound around an ax with projecting blade, carried before Roman magistrates as a symbol of authority.

fas·ci·a (fasн′ēə), *n.*, *pl.* **fas·ci·ae** (fasн′ēē). any long, flat, vertical surface.

fas·ci·ate (fasн′ēāt), *adj.* bound with a band, strip or bandage. Also **fas′ci·at·ed.** —**fas·ci·a′tion,** *n.*

fas·ci·cle (fas′ikəl), *n.* **1.** a close cluster or tight bundle. **2.** one part of a book being published in installments. —**fas·cic′u·lar,** *adj.* —**fas·cic′u·late,** *adj.* —**fas·cic·u·la′tion,** *n.*

fas·ci·cule (fas′əkyool), *n.* a fascicle, esp. of a book. Also **fas·cic·u·lus** (fəsik′yələs).

fas·cism (fasн′izm), *n.* (sometimes F-) an authoritarian and aggressively nationalistic dictatorship that forcibly suppresses opposition, completely controls industry and commerce, etc. —**fas′cist,** *n.*

fas·tid·i·ous (fastid′ēəs), *adj.* particular; hard to please; excessively critical.

fas·tig·i·ate (fastij′ēit, fastij′ēāt), *adj.* tapering to a point. Also **fas·tig′i·at·ed.**

fas·tu·ous (fas′сноoəs), *adj.* **1.** haughty; overbearing. **2.** ostentatious; pretentious.

fat cat, *U.S. Slang.* an important, wealthy or influential person.

fath·o·gram (fatн′əgram), *n.* a visual representation of sound waves recorded by a sonic depth finder.

fa·tid·ic (fātid′ik), *adj.* pertaining to divination or prophecy; prophetic. Also **fa·tid′i·cal.**

fa·tu·i·tous (fətoo′itəs), *adj.* foolish; imbecile.

fa·tu·i·ty (fətoo′itē), *n.* **1.** stupidity; foolishness. **2.** something silly or inane.

fat·u·ous (facн′ooəs), *adj.* complacently foolish or stupid; silly, as *a fatuous remark.*

fau·cal (fô′kəl), *adj.* **1.** concerning or involving the fauces or opening of the throat. **2.** guttural.

faute de mieux (fōt də myoo′),

French. for want of anything better.

faux pas (fōpä′), *pl.* **faux pas.** a blunder, esp. in manners or etiquette; an indiscretion.

fa·ve·o·late (fəvē′əlāt), *adj.* honeycombed; containing cells.

Fa·vrile Glass (fəvrēl′), *Trademark.* a blown glass introduced by Tiffany c. 1890 and used for vases, etc. Also **Tiffany glass.**

fa·vus (fā′vəs), *n.*, *pl.* **fa·vi** (fā′vī). a hexagonal tile or stone for paving.

faze (fāz), *v.* to cause to feel disturbed, embarrassed, or disconcerted.

fe·al·ty (fē′əltē), *n.* loyalty; fidelity.

feather tract. See **pteryla.**

featherweight, *n.* a boxer between bantamweight and lightweight, weighing 126 lb. or less.

feat·ly (fēt′lē), *adv.* **1.** suitably; aptly. **2.** nimbly, adroitly. **3.** neatly, gracefully.

fe·bric·i·ty (fibris′itē), *n.* the state of being feverish.

fe·bric·u·la (fibrik′yələ), *n.* a slight and brief fever.

feb·ri·fa·cient (feb′rəkā′shənt), *adj.* producing fever.

fe·brif·er·ous (fibrif′ərəs), *adj.* producing fever.

fe·brif·ic (fibrif′ik), *adj.* having or producing fever.

feb·ri·fuge (feb′rəfyo͞oj), *adj.* **1.** reducing fever, as a medicine. —*n.* **2.** a fever-reducing agent. **3.** a cooling drink. —**fe·brif′u·gal,** *adj.*

fe·brile (fē′brəl, feb′rəl), *adj.* of or characterized by a fever; feverish.

fe·cit (fā′kit), *v.* *Latin.* he (or she) made (it); at one time used on works of art after the name of the artist. Abbrev.: **fe., fec.**

feck·less (fek′lis), *adj.* reckless; inefficient; incompetent; without worth or spirit; indifferent.

fec·u·la (fek′yələ), *n.*, *pl.* **fec·u·lae** (fek′yəlē). fecal matter esp. of insects; dregs; filth; foul matter. —**fec′u·lent,** *adj.*

fe·cund (fē′kənd, fek′ənd), *adj.* fertile; prolific; fruitful. —**fe·cun′di·ty,** *n.*

fe·cun·date (fē′kəndāt, fek′əndāt), *v.*

1. to make fruitful. **2.** to fertilize; impregnate; pollinate.

feign (fān), *v.* to pretend; to make a false show of, as *to feign sleep.*

feist·y (fī′stē), *adj.* quarrelsome; belligerent.

fe·li·cif·ic (fē′lisif′ik), *adj.* producing or tending to produce happiness.

fe·lic·i·tous (filis′itəs), *adj.* suitable to the occasion; apt; appropriate.

fe·lic·i·ty (filis′itē), *n.* bliss; happiness.

fel·lah (fel′ə), *n.*, *pl.* **fel·lahs, fel·la·heen** (fel′əhēn′). Egyptian peasant or laborer.

fell·mon·ger (fel′mung′gər, fel′mong′gər), *n.* a dealer in sheepskins or other animal skins.

fel·loe (fel′ō), *n.* the rim, or portion of the rim, of a spoked wheel. Also **fel′ly.**

fe·lo-de-se (fē′lōdisē′), *n.*, *pl.* **fe·lo·nes-de-se** (fē′lōnez′dise′). one who commits suicide.

feme (fem), *n.* (in law) a woman or wife.

feme co·vert (kuv′ərt), (in law) a married woman.

feme sole (sōl), (in law) an unmarried woman; spinster, widow, or divorcée; a married woman financially independent of her husband.

fem·i·cide (fem′isīd), *n.* the act of killing a woman.

fem·i·nie (fem′ənē), *n.* women collectively; womankind.

femme fa·tale (famfatal′), *pl.* **femmes fa·tales** (famfatalz′). *French.* an alluring woman, esp. one who leads men to their downfall.

fem·o·ral (fem′ərəl), *adj.* relating to the thigh or thigh-bone.

fe·mur (fē′mər), *n.* the thigh-bone.

fe·nes·tra (fines′trə), *n.*, *pl.* **fe·nes·trae** (fines′trē). a small opening, as in a bone or membrane.

fen·es·tra·tion (fen′istrā′shən), *n.* the arrangement of windows and doors in a building.

fe·ra·cious (fərā′shəs), *adj.* fruitful; producing abundantly.

fe·ral (fēr′əl, fer′əl), *adj.* wild; undomesticated; uncivilized.

fe·ral (fēr′əl), *adj.* fatal; funereal; gloomy.

fe·ri·al (fēr′ēəl), *adj.* pertaining to a holiday.

fe·rine (fēr′īn, fēr′in), *adj.* wild; untamed; feral.

fer·i·ty (fer′itē), *n.* the state of being wild or savage; ferocity.

fer·re·ous (fer′ēəs), *adj.* like, of, or containing iron.

fer·ro·mag·net·ic (fer′ōmagnet′ik), *adj.* pertaining to a material, such as iron, that below a certain temperature can possess magnetization in the absence of any external magnetic field. See also **antiferromagnetic, diamagnetic, paramagnetic.**

fer·ru·gi·nous (fəroo′jənəs), *adj.* containing iron or iron rust; rust-colored.

fer·u·la·ceous (fer′ool ā′ sHəs), *adj.* like or pertaining to canes or reeds.

fer·vent (fur′vənt), *adj.* having or showing great warmth of feeling; passionate; ardent.

fer·vid (fur′vid), *adj.* passionate; intense; fervent.

fer·vor (fur′vər), *n.* intense feeling, zeal; ardor.

fes·tal (fes′tl), *adj.* of or suitable to a joyous occasion or festival.

fes·ti·na len·te (festē′nä len′te), *Latin.* make haste slowly.

Fest·schrift (fest′sHrift′), *n., pl.* **Fest·schrift·en** (fest′sHrift′ən), **Fest·schrifts.** a collection of articles contributed by the colleagues of a writer or scholar and published in his honor.

fe·tial (fēsHəl), *adj.* relating to declarations of war and peace treaties.

fet·id, foet·id (fet′id, fē′tid), *adj.* stinking; putrid.

fe·tip·a·rous, foe·tip·a·rous (fētip′-ərəs), *adj.* bearing young that are not fully developed, as marsupials.

fe·tor, foe·tor (fē′tər), *n.* a strong, disagreeable smell; stench.

fet·tle (fet′l), *n.* condition, state; health.

feuil·le·ton (foi′litn), *n.* a part of a newspaper containing serialized fiction, light or popular pieces of writing, etc.

fi·a·cre (fēä′kər, fēäk′), *n., pl.* **fi·a·cres.** a four-wheeled carriage for hire.

fi·as·co (fēas′kō), *n., pl.* **fi·as·cos, fi·as·coes.** an utter failure.

fi·at (fī′ət, fī′at), *n.* order; decree; sanction.

fi·ber·glass (fī′bərglas′), *n.* molten glass processed into fine filaments, often used in wooly masses as insulating material or pressed and molded into construction material.

fiber optics, the study of the longitudinal transmission of images through a flexible bundle of optical glass fibers.

fi·bri·form (fī′brəfôrm, fib′rəfôrm), *adj.* like a fiber.

fi·bril (fī′brəl, fib′rəl), *n.* a small, thread-like fiber or filament. —**fi·bril·lar** (fī′brələr, fib′rələr), **fi·bril′li·form,** *adj.*

fi·bril·la·tion (fī′brəlā′sHən, fib′rə-lā′sHən), *n.* uncontrolled contractions of muscular fibrils, as in a tic.

fi·bril·lose (fī′brəlōs, fib′rəlōs), *adj.* composed of or containing fibrils.

fi·brin (fī′brin), *n.* an elastic, fibrous, insoluble protein found in coagulated blood. —**fi′brin·ous,** *adj.*

fi·broid (fī′broid), *adj.* like, or consisting of fibers or fibrous tissue.

fi·bro·ma (fībrō′mə), *n., pl.* **fi·bro·ma·ta** (fībrō′mətə), **fi·bro·mas.** a tumor composed largely of fibrous tissue.

fi·bro·pla·sia (fī′brəplā′zHə), *n.* the formation of fibrous tissue. —**fi·bro·plas′tic,** *adj.*

fi·bro·sis (fībrō′sis), *n.* abnormal growth of excess fibroid tissue in an organ. —**fi·brot′ic** (fībrot′ik), *adj.*

fic·tile (fik′tl), *adj.* that can be molded; plastic.

fic·tive (fik′tiv), *adj.* invented; fictitious.

FIFO., Abbrev. for **first in, first out.**

Fifth Amendment, an amendment to the U.S. Constitution guaranteeing chiefly that no person be required to testify against himself or be tried twice for the same offense.

fifth column, persons within a country who are in secret sympathy with and prepared to help an enemy. —**fifth-col′umn,** *adj.*

fig·ment (fig'mənt), *n.* something made up or imagined; a fantasy.

fi·lar (fī'lər), *adj.* of, relating to, or having threads.

fi·lasse (filas'), *n.* any of several vegetable fibers, excluding cotton, processed for yarn manufacture.

fi·late (fī'lāt), *adj.* threadlike.

fil·a·ture (fil'əCHər), *n.* a device for the reeling of silk from cocoons.

fil·i·cide (fil'isīd), *n.* the killing of a son or daughter.

fil·i·form (fil'əfôrm, fī'ləfôrm), *adj.* having the form of a thread; threadlike.

fi·lose (fī'lōs), *adj.* threadlike.

fim·bri·ate (fim'brēit, fim'brēāt), *adj.* having a border of hairs; fringed. Also **fim'bri·at·ed.** —**fim·bri·a'tion,** *n.*

fim·bril·late (fimbril'it), *adj.* having a small fringe or fringelike border.

fi·na·gle (finā'gəl), *v.* to obtain or maneuver by trickery; to cheat.

fi·nal·ism (fī'nəlizm), *n.* the belief that events are determined by final causes.

fin de siè·cle (faN də sye'kl), *French.* the end of the century.

fi·nesse (fines'), *n.* **1.** subtlety and skill in performance. —*v.* **2.** to manage by finesse.

fi·nes·tra (fines'trə), *n.* an opening, esp. for ventilation in the wall of a tomb.

fin·ger·ling (fiNG'gərliNG), *n.* a small or young fish less than a year old.

fin·i·al (fin'ēəl, fī'nēəl), *n.* an ornamental feature terminating the top of a piece of furniture, as a lamp.

fin·i·cal (fin'ikəl), *adj.* fussy; finicky.

fin·nan had·die (fin'ən had'ē), smoked haddock. Also **fin'nan had'dock.**

fire·damp (fīr'damp'), *n.* a combustible gas, largely methane, formed in coal mines, that is highly explosive when mixed with a certain proportion of air.

fir·kin (fur'kin), *n.* a small wooden tub for butter, lard, etc.

fir·ma·ment (fur'məmənt), *n.* the sky.

firn (firn), *n.* See **névé.**

firn·i·fi·ca·tion (fir'nəfəkā'sHən), *n.* the process by which snow changes into névé.

First Amendment, an amendment to the U.S. Constitution guaranteeing freedom from laws respecting establishment of a religion and freedom of worship, of speech, of the press, of assembly, and of the right to petition the government for a redress of grievances.

first-in, first-out, a bookkeeping device that assumes items purchased first will be sold first. Abbrev.: **FIFO.** See also **last-in, first-out.**

fisc (fisk), *n.* a royal or state treasury.

fishskin disease. See **ichyosis.**

fis·sile (fis'əl), *adj.* able to be split; fissionable.

fis·sion (fizH'ən), *n.* **1.** a splitting apart; a breaking up into parts. **2.** Also **nuclear fission.** the splitting of heavy atoms into lighter atoms producing atomic energy: the principle of the atom bomb. See also **fusion.**

fis·sip·a·rous (fisip'ərəs), *adj.* reproducing young by fission.

fis·tu·la (fis'CHŌŌlə), *n.* a narrow tube or duct. —**fis'tu·lous,** *adj.*

fitch·er (fiCH'ər), *v.* (in drilling) to clog from accumulation of the substance being drilled.

fix·ate (fik'sāt), *v.* to make or become fixed. —**fix·a'tion,** *n.*

fix·a·tive (fik'sətiv), *n.* a liquid sprayed on something to preserve it by preventing contact with the air.

fla·bel·late (fləbel'it), *adj.* fanshaped. Also **fla·bel'li·form.**

fla·bel·lum (fləbel'əm), *n., pl.* **fla·bel·la** (fləbel'ə), a large fan used in religious ceremonies.

flac·cid (flak'sid), *adj.* flabby; limp.

flac·on (flak'ən), *n.* a small flask with a stopper. See also **flagon.**

flag (flag), *n.* See **masthead.**

flag·el·lant (flaj'ələnt, fləjel'ənt), *n.* one who whips himself for religious discipline or sexual stimulation.

flag·el·late (flaj'əlit), *adj.* producing runners, as the strawberry.

fla·gel·li·form (fləjel'əfôrm'), *adj.*

long, slender, and tapering; whip-like.

fla·gi·tious (fləjisн′əs), *adj.* shamefully wicked; vile; heinous.

fla·gon (flag′ən), *n.* a large vessel for liquids; a large wine bottle. See also **flacon.**

fla·grant (flā′grənt), *adj.* glaringly bad; notorious; outrageous. —**fla′grant·ly,** *adv.*

fla·gran·te de·lic·to (fləgran′tē dilik′tō), (in law) in the act of committing the crime.

flail (flāl), *n.* **1.** a wooden instrument for threshing grain by hand. —*v.* **2.** to strike or beat as with a flail.

flail·ing (flā′liNG), *adj.* (of arms) threshing wildly; waving; swinging.

flam·bé (flämbā′), *adj.* served in a sauce containing liquor set afire to flame. Also **flam·béed.**

flam·beau (flambō′), *n.* a lighted torch.

flame-out, flame·out (flām′out′), *n.* the stopping of combustion in a jet engine. Also **blowout.**

flan (flan, flän), *n.* **1.** an open tart, filled with fruit, custard, cheese, etc. **2.** a sweetened egg custard made in Spain.

flâ·ne·rie (flänrē′), *n. French.* idle strolling; dawdling.

flâ·neur (fläno͞or′), *n. French.* idler; loafer; lounger.

flan·nel (flan′l), *n.* a soft, loosely woven woolen material with a slightly napped surface.

flan·nel·board (flan′lbôrd′), *n.* a flannel-covered surface to which flannel cut-outs, such as letters and numbers, adhere, used in schools as a teaching aid.

flan·nel·et, flan·nel·ette (flan′əlet′), *n.* a soft cotton cloth resembling flannel.

flat sour, fermentation that occurs in canned food after sealing.

flat·u·lent (flacн′ələnt), *adj.* producing gas in the stomach or intestines.

fla·tus (flā′təs), *n.*, *pl.* **fla·tus·es.** an accumulation of gas in the stomach or intestines.

flaunt (flônt), *v.* to display oneself conspicuously; to show off ostentatiously.

F layer, the highest layer of the ionosphere where high-frequency radio waves are reflected back to earth.

flense (flens), *v.* to cut blubber or skin from a whale, seal, etc.

flesh·ly (flesн′lē), *adj.* of the body; carnal; sensual.

flesh·pot (flesн′pot′), *n.* a place providing luxurious bodily comforts and pleasures.

fletch·er (flecн′ər), *n.* a person who makes arrows.

fleu·rette (fluret′), *n.* an ornament formed like a small flower.

fleu·ron (flur′on), *n.* a floral motif used in decoration.

flews (flooz), *n. pl.* the loose, hanging parts of the upper lip of certain dogs, as bloodhounds.

flex·ile (flek′sil), *adj.* flexible, pliant.

flex·or (flek′sər), *n.* a muscle that bends a limb or other part of the body.

flex·u·ous (flek′shoo͞əs), *adj.* winding; full of bends. Also **flex′u·ose.** —**flex·u·os′i·ty,** *n.*

flex·ure (flek′shər), *n.* act of bending; state of being flexed or bent.

flim·flam (flim′flam), *n.* nonsense; rubbish; humbug.

flin·ders (flin′dərs), *n. pl.* splinters or fragments.

flip·pant (flip′ənt), *adj.* disrespectful; frivolous; lacking in seriousness. —**flip′pan·cy,** *n.*

flitch (flicн), *n.* a side of bacon, salted and cured.

floc, flock (flok), *n.* a fine, fluffy mass of particles, as in a precipitate.

floc·cil·la·tion (flok′səlā′sнən), *n.* delirious picking of the bedclothes by a patient. Also **carphology.**

floc·cu·late (flok′yəlāt), *v.* to form flocculent masses, as clouds, precipitates, etc.

floc·cule (flok′yoo͞l), *n.* something resembling a tuft of wool.

floc·cu·lent (flok′yələnt), *adj.* like or consisting of small tufts of wool; flaky; fluffy.

floc·cus (flok′əs), *n.*, *pl.* **floc·ci** (flok′sī). a wooly or hairy tuft.

flo·res·cence (flôres′əns), *n.* period of flowering; blossoming. —**flo·res′ cent,** *adj.*

flo·ret (flôr′it), *n.* a small flower.

flo·ri·at·ed (flô′rēātid), *adj.* decorated with floral ornament.

flo·ri·cul·ture (flō′rəkul′CHər), *n.* cultivation of flowering plants, esp. under glass.

flor·id (flôr′id), *adj.* **1.** ruddy; rosy. **2.** flowery; elaborately ornamented.

flo·rif·er·ous (flôrif′ərəs), *adj.* bearing flowers; flowering abundantly.

flo·ris·tic (flôris′tik), *adj.* of or having to do with flowers.

flout (flout), *v.* to mock; scorn; to show disdain or contempt for.

flow chart, a diagram showing the progress of work in a manufacturing process, a sequence of operations in a computer program, etc.

flow diagram, (in computer technology) a chart showing the general flow of information for solving a problem by a computer.

flow·er·et (flou′ərit), *n.* a small flower; floret.

fluc·tu·ant (fluk′CHŌŌənt), *adj.* varying; unstable.

flume (flōōm), *n.* a narrow ravine with a stream running through it.

flum·mer·y (flum′ərē), *n.* **1.** any of several dessert dishes made of flour, milk, sugar, and eggs. **2.** meaningless flattery; nonsense.

flu·o·resce (flōō′əres′), *v.* to produce or show fluorescence. —**flu·o·res′ cent,** *adj.*

flu·o·res·cence (flōō′əres′əns), *n.* the emission of light by a substance while it is being acted upon by radiant energy, as light or x-rays. See also **phosphorescence.**

fluor·i·date (flŌŌr′idāt), *v.* to add fluorides to (a water supply), esp. to strengthen teeth. —**fluor·i·da′tion,** *n.*

fluor·o·scope (flŌŌr′əskōp), *n.* an instrument for examining internal structures by shadows cast by x-rays on a fluorescent screen. —**fluor·o· scop′ic,** *adj.*

flu·vi·al (flōō′vēəl), *adj.* of or having to do with a river.

flu·vi·a·tile (flōō′vēətil), *adj.* of or peculiar to rivers; found in rivers.

flu·vi·o·ma·rine (flōō′vēəmərēn′), *adj.* formed by the combined action of river and sea.

flux (fluks), *n.* **1.** a state of insecurity; continuous change; lack of direction. **2.** a substance used in metal refining that combines with impurities causing them to float off or coagulate. **3.** abnormal discharge of fluid from the bowels.

flux·ion (fluk′SHən), *n.* **1.** the act of flowing. **2.** a flux.

fly·weight (flī′wāt′), *n.* a boxer of the lightest class, weighing 112 lb. or less.

focal length, the distance from the optical center of a lens to the point where the light rays converge. Also **focal distance.**

focal-plane shutter, (in photography) a camera shutter placed directly in front of the film. See also **curtain shutter.**

fo·com·e·ter (fōkom′itər), *n.* an instrument for measuring the focal length of a lens.

foet·id. See **fetid.**

foe·tip·a·rous. See **fetiparous.**

foe·tor. See **fetor.**

fog·bow (fog′bō′), *n.* a phenomenon like a white rainbow, sometimes seen in a fog. Also **mistbow, seadog, white rainbow.**

fog·dog (fog′dôg′), *n.* a bright spot sometimes seen in a fog.

fo·gram (fō′grəm), *n.* an old-fashioned or stuffy person. Also **fogrum.**

foi·ble (foi′bəl), *n.* a slight weakness or frailty in character.

foie gras (fwä grä′), the liver of specially fattened geese considered a table delicacy, esp. in paste form (**pâté de foie gras**).

foi·son (foi′zən), *n.* abundance; plenty.

foist (foist), *v.* to palm off; pass fraudulently.

fo·li·a·ture (fō′lēəCHər), *n.* mass of leaves; foliage.

fo·li·ic·o·lous (fō′lēik′ələs), *adj.* parasitic on the leaves of plants.

fo·li·if·er·ous (fō ′lēif′ərəs), *adj.* leaf-bearing.

fo·li·o·late (fō′lēəlāt), *adj.* having or relating to leaflets.

fo·li·ose (fō′lēōs), *adj.* covered with leaves; leafy.

fo·li·um (fō′lēəm), *n., pl.* **fo·li·a** (fō′-lēə). a thin layer or stratum.

folk etymology, popular but incorrect notion of the origin of a word, as *Welsh rarebit* from *Welsh rabbit.*

fol·li·cle (fol′ikəl), *n.* a small sac or gland. —**fol·lic′u·lar,** *adj.*

fo·ment (fōment′), *v.* to instigate; incite; stir up (trouble). —**fo·men·ta′ tion,** *n.*

fo·mes (fō′mēz), *n., pl.* **fom·i·tes** (fō′-mitēz). any agent, as clothing or bedding, capable of absorbing and transmitting germs.

fon·dant (fon′dənt), *n.* a soft, creamy sugar paste.

fon·du (fondoo′), *n.* (in ballet) a gradual bending of the supporting leg.

fon·due (fondoo′, fon′doo), *n.* a Swiss dish of melted cheese, seasoning, and wine, flavored with Kirsch, served as a dip for cubes of bread.

font (font), *n.* (in printing) a complete set of type of one particular face and size.

font·al (fon′tl), *adj.* of or coming from a fountain or spring.

foot·le (foot′l), *v.* to talk or act in a foolish or trivial way.

foo·zle (foo′zəl), *v.* to spoil by clumsiness; bungle.

fop (fop), *n.* a dandy; a man who is foolishly vain about his clothes, manners, etc. —**fop′per·y,** *n.* —**fop′pish,** *adj.*

for·age (fôr′ij), *n.* **1.** horse or cattle food; fodder. —*v.* **2.** to search for provisions; hunt; rummage.

fo·ra·men (fôrā′mən), *n., pl.* **fo·ram· i·na** (fôram′inə). a small perforation, esp. in a bone or plant ovule.

fo·ram·i·nate (fôram′ənit), *adj.* having many holes or foramina. Also **fo·ram′i·nous.**

force ma·jeure (fôrs mazHoor′), *pl.* **forces ma·jeures** (fôrs mazHoor′). (in law) an unavoidable event, as an act of God, that may serve as an excuse to abrogate a contract.

for·ci·pate (fôr′səpāt), *adj.* like or having the shape of a forceps.

for·el, for·rel (fôr′əl), *n.* a slipcase for a book.

fo·ren·sic (fəren′sik), *adj.* pertaining to law courts; suited to argumentation, rhetorical.

forensic chemistry, the use of chemical facts in answering questions of law.

forensic medicine, the use of medical facts in answering questions of law; medical jurisprudence.

for·est·ry (fôr′istrē), *n.* the science of planting and taking care of forests.

for·fend (fôrfend′), *v.* to defend or protect.

for·fi·cate (fôr′fəkit), *adj.* deeply notched or forked, as the tails of some birds.

for·mic (fôr′mik), *adj.* pertaining to ants.

for·mi·car·y (fôr′məker′ē), *n.* an anthill or ants' nest. Also **for·mi·car′ i·um.**

for·nic·i·form (fôrnis′əfôrm), *adj.* in the form of an arched or vaulted structure.

forte (fôrt), *n.* something at which one is exceptionally good.

for·ti·tu·di·nous (fôr ′titoo′dənəs), *adj.* having patient courage; marked by strength of mind.

for·tu·i·tous (fôrtoo′itəs), *adj.* happening by chance; accidental.

for·tu·i·ty (fôrtoo′itē), *n.* the condition of being fortuitous; an accident or chance.

fos·sa (fos′ə), *n., pl.* **fos·sae** (fos′ē), cavity or pit, as in a bone.

fos·sette (foset′), *n.* a small hollow; a dimple.

fos·sil·if·er·ous (fos ′əlif′ərəs), *adj.* containing fossils.

fos·so·ri·al (fosôr′ēəl), *adj.* burrowing or digging.

fou·droy·ant (foodroi′ənt), *adj.* dazzling or stunning.

fou·lard (foolärd′), *n.* a thin material of silk or rayon with printed design.

Four Horsemen of the Apocalypse,

riders on white, red, black, and pale horses symbolizing pestilence, war, famine, and death.

four·ra·gère (foor'əzHer), *n.* an ornamental cord worn on the shoulder of a military uniform.

fourth dimension, time, considered as an added dimension to three spatial dimensions.

fourth estate, journalism or journalists; the press.

fo·ve·a (fō'vēə), *n., pl.* **fo·ve·ae** (fō'vēē). a small pit or depression in a bone or other structure. —**fo'·ve·ate,** *adj.*

fo·ve·o·la (fōvē'ələ), *n., pl.* **fo·ve·o·lae** (fōvē'əlē). a small fovea or pit. —**fo'·ve·o·late,** *adj.*

foxed (fokst), *adj.* 1. tricked or deceived. 2. (of book pages) stained reddish-brown or yellowish.

frac·tious (frak'sHəs), *adj.* irritable, cross; rebellious; unruly.

fram·be·sia, fram·boe·sia (frambē'-zHə), *n.* yaws.

fran·gi·ble (fran'jəbəl), *adj.* breakable; fragile.

frat·ri·cide (frat'risīd), *n.* the killing of one's own brother.

fraught (frôt), *adj.* filled or involved (with).

free association, (in psychoanalysis) the uninhibited expression of whatever ideas, memories, etc., come to mind, used to uncover and clarify the unconscious processes.

frem·i·tus (frem'itəs), *n., pl.* **frem·i·tus.** a vibration felt in palpation of the chest.

fre·nate (frē'nāt), *adj.* having a frenum or frenulum.

fre·ne·tic (frənet'ik), *adj.* frenzied; frantic.

fren·u·lum (fren'yələm), *n., pl.* **fren·u·la** (fren'yələ). a small frenum.

fre·num (frē'nəm), *n., pl.* **fre·na** (frē'-nə). the fold of skin or membrane that checks the movement of an organ or part, as the fold under the tongue.

fres·co (fres'kō), *n., pl.* **fres·coes, fres·cos.** the technique of painting with water colors on wet plaster. See also **fresco secco.**

fre·sco sec·co (sek'ō), the technique of painting with water colors on a dry plaster surface. See also **fresco.**

Fres·nel lens (frānel'), a large lens composed of many small lenses producing a short focal length, used in spotlights, etc.

fress (fres), *v.* to eat often and in large amounts; gourmandize. —**fress'er,** *n.*

fret·work (fret'wurk), *adj.* decorative carving of interlacing parts; openwork.

friars' lantern. See **ignis fatuus.**

frib·ble (frib'əl), *v.* to act frivolously; trifle; waste time.

frieze (frēz), *n.* an ornamental band on a building façade, often decorated with sculpture.

frig·i·do·re·cep·tor (frij'idōrēsep'-tər), *n.* an end organ of a sensory neuron stimulated by cold.

frig·o·rif·ic (frij'ərif'ik), *adj.* making or producing cold.

frip·per·y (frip'ərē), *n.* gaudy or tawdry finery; ostentatious display.

fri·sé (frizā'), *n.* a piled fabric with cut or uncut loops.

fri·sette, fri·zette (frizet'), *n.* a fringe of tightly curled hair, often artificial.

fris·ket (fris'kit), *n.* a thin paper mask used when retouching artwork with an airbrush.

fron·des·cence (frondes'əns), *n.* the process or period of coming into leaf. —**fron·des'cent,** *adj.*

front bench, one of two benches near the Speaker where the leaders of the major parties sit in the British House of Commons. See also **back bench.**

front money, money advanced to a financier in return for a promise to procure funds for a company.

frot·tage (frôtäzH'), *n.* a technique of producing images by rubbing chalk, colored wax, etc., over paper laid on a surface with a raised design. See also **rubbing.**

frot·teur (frôtoo̅r'), *n.* one who does frottage.

fruc·tif·er·ous (fruktif'ərəs), *adj.* yielding fruit.

fruc·ti·fi·ca·tion (fruk'təfəkā'sHən),

n. the act of bearing fruit; the fruit of a plant.

fruc·ti·fi·ca·tive (fruk′təfəkā′tiv), *adj.* able to yield fruit.

fruc·ti·fy (fruk′təfī), *v.* to become or make fruitful. —**fruc′ti·fi·er,** *n.*

fruc·tose (fruk′tōs), *n.* a fruit sugar found in sweet, ripe fruits, nectar, and honey.

fruc·tu·ous (fruk′chōōəs), *adj.* fruitful; productive; profitable.

fru·giv·o·rous (frōōjiv′ərəs), *adj.* fruit-eating.

fru·i·tion (frōōish′ən), *n.* full realization; fulfillment.

fru·men·ta·ceous (frōō′məntā′-shəs), *adj.* like or having the nature of wheat or other grain.

fru·tes·cent (frōōtes′ənt), *adj.* shrubby or becoming like a shrub.

fru·ti·cose (frōō′təkōs), *adj.* of or like a shrub.

fu·ga·cious (fyōōgā′shəs), *adj.* fleeting; passing quickly away; ephemeral.

fu·gu (fōō′gōō), *n.* a puffer fish, eaten as a delicacy in Japan after the removal of the skin and certain deadly poisonous organs.

ful·crum (fōōl′krəm), *n., pl.* **ful·crums, ful·cra** (fōōl′krə). the stationary support or pivot on which a lever turns in raising or moving something.

ful·gent (ful′jənt), *adj.* very bright; dazzling; radiant.

ful·gid (ful′jid), *adj.* shining; glittering; flashing.

ful·gu·rant (ful′gyərənt), *adj.* flashing like lightning.

ful·gu·rate (ful′gyərāt), *v.* to dart like lightning.

ful·gu·rous (ful′gyərəs), *adj.* like or full of lightning.

ful·ham, ful·lam, ful·lom (fōōl′əm), *n.* one of a pair of loaded dice.

fu·lig·i·nous (fyōōlij′ənəs), *adj.* full of smoke or soot.

full-fashioned (fōōl′fash′ənd), *adj.* knitted to conform to the contours of the body, as sweaters and hosiery.

ful·mi·nant (ful′mənənt), *adj.* exploding or occurring suddenly.

ful·mi·nate (ful′mənāt), *v.* to explode or cause to explode. —**ful·mi·na′ tion,** *n.*

ful·min·ic (fulmin′ik), *adj.* highly unstable or explosive.

ful·mi·nous (ful′mənəs), *adj.* of or like thunder and lightning.

ful·vous (ful′vəs), *adj.* tawny; yellowish-brown.

fu·ma·role (fyōō′mərōl), *n.* a hole emitting smoke and gases in a volcanic area.

fu·mu·lus (fyōō′myələs), *n., pl.* **fu·mu·lus.** a thin layer of clouds or haze.

fu·nam·bu·list (fyōōnam′byəlist), *n.* a tightrope walker.

func·tion·ar·y (fungk′shənerē), *n.* one who performs a certain function; an official.

func·tor (fung′tər), *n.* something that performs a particular function.

fun·da·ment (fun′dəmənt), *n.* **1.** the characteristics of a region, as climate, land forms, soils, etc. **2.** the buttocks.

fundamental particle. See **elementary particle.**

fun·dus (fun′dəs), *n., pl.* **fun·di** (fun′-dī). the base of an organ, or the part farthest from its opening.

fu·nest (fyōōnest′), *adj.* portending evil; fatal; sinister.

fun·gi·cide (fun′jisīd), *n.* a substance for killing fungi.

fun·gi·form (fun′jifôrm), *adj.* like a fungus in form.

fun·gi·stat (fun′jistat), *n.* a fungistatic preparation.

fun·gi·stat·ic (fun′jistat′ik), *adj.* of a preparation that stops the growth of a fungus.

fun·gi·tox·ic (fun′jitok′sik), *adj.* poisonous to fungi.

fun·giv·or·ous (funjiv′ərəs), *adj.* fungus-eating.

fun·goid (fung′goid), *adj.* like or characteristic of a fungus.

fun·gos·i·ty (funggos′itē), *n.* the condition of being fungous.

fun·gous (fung′gəs), *adj.* of or caused by fungi; resembling a fungus.

fu·nic·u·lar (fyōōnik′yələr), *adj.* of, worked by or hanging from a rope or cable.

fu·nic·u·lus (fyōōnik′yələs), *n.*, *pl.* **fu·nic·u·li** (fyōōnik′yəlī). a conducting cord, as an umbilical cord.

fur·be·low (fur′bəlō), *n.* a flounce; showy trimmings or finery.

fur·bish (fur′bisH), *v.* to brighten up; restore; smarten.

fur·cate (fur′kāt), *adj.* forked; branched.

fur·cu·la (fur′kyələ), *n.*, *pl.* **fur·cu·lae** (fur′kyəlē). the wishbone.

fur·fur (fur′fər), *n.*, *pl.* **fur·fur·es** (fur′fyərēz). dandruff; scurf.

fur·fu·ra·ceous (fur′fyərā′sHəs), *adj.* of or like bran; covered with dandruff or scurf.

fu·ri·bund (fyōōr′əbund), *adj.* furious; frenzied.

fu·run·cle (fyōōr′uNGkəl), *n.* a boil.

fu·run·cu·lo·sis (fyōōruNG′kyəlō′sis), *n.* a disorder of which furuncles are symptomatic.

fu·sa·role (fyōō′zərōl), *n.* a molding resembling a string of beads.

fus·cous (fus′kəs), *adj.* dusky; brownish-gray.

fu·see (fyōōzē′), *n.* a friction match with a large head.

fu·si·form (fyōō′zəfôrm), *adj.* spindle-shaped.

fu·sil (fyōō′zəl), *n.* made by casting; founded.

fu·sion (fyōō′zHən), *n.* a thermonuclear reaction in which lightweight atomic nuclei join to form nuclei of heavier atoms, with a resultant release of energy: the principle of the hydrogen bomb. Also **nuclear fusion.** See also **fission.**

fus·tian (fus′cHən), *n.* **1.** a thick cotton cloth with a short nap. **2.** bombastic language.

fus·ti·gate (fus′təgāt), *v.* to beat with a stick; cudgel.

fus·ty (fus′tē), *adj.* moldy; musty; stale-smelling.

fu·su·ma (fyōō′səmä), *n.* a sliding door or partition in a Japanese house.

future shock, the inability to adapt psychologically to rapid and novel advances and changes, esp. cultural, technological, moral, and social innovations.

fu·tu·ri·ty race (fyōōtōōr′itē), a horse race in which the contestants are selected long beforehand.

ga·belle (gəbel′), *n.* a tax; an excise.
ga·bi·on (gā′bēən), *n.* a wicker cylinder filled with earth or stones used in military fortifications; a similar cylinder used in building dams.
ga·bi·on·ade (gā′bēənād′), *n.* a construction made of or with gabions.
ga·droon (gədrōōn′), *n.* a series of flutings used esp. as an ornamental border on silver dishes.
gaffe (gaf), *n.* a blunder; a tactless remark or action.
gait·er (gā′tər), *n.* a cloth or leather covering for the ankle, instep, and the lower leg; a spat or spatterdash.
gal (gal), *n.* a unit of acceleration equal to one centimeter per second per second. [after Galileo]
ga·lac·ta·gogue (gəlak′təgog), *adj.* increasing the yield of milk.
ga·lac·tic (gəlak′tik), *adj.* 1. pertaining to a galaxy. 2. pertaining to milk.
ga·lac·toid (gəlak′toid), *adj.* milk-like.
ga·lac·to·phore (gəlak′təfôr), *n.* a milk-bearing duct.
gal·ac·toph·or·ous (galəktof′ərəs), *adj.* secreting milk.
ga·lac·to·poi·et·ic (gəlak′təpoiet′ik), *adj.* increasing milk secretion.
gal·an·tine (gal′əntēn), *n.* a cold dish of boned fish or meat served in savory jelly. Also **gal′a·tine.**
gal·ax·y (gal′əksē), *n.* a vast number of stars held together in one system.

ga·le·a (gā′lēə), *n., pl.* **ga·le·ae** (gā′lēē). a part, as of a flower, shaped like a helmet.
ga·le·ate (gā′lēāt), *adj.* having a galea.
ga·le·i·form (gəlē′əfôrm), *adj.* helmet-shaped.
ga·len·i·cal (gālen′ikəl), *n.* 1. a drug made from herbs or vegetable matter rather than from minerals or chemicals. 2. an unrefined, crude drug.
gal·i·ma·ti·as (galəmā′shēəs), *n.* unintelligible talk; nonsense.
gal·li·gas·kins (galəgas′kins), *n. pl.* leather breeches or leggings.
gal·li·mau·fry (galəmô′frē), *n.* a jumble or confused medley.
gal·li·na·ceous (galənā′shəs), *adj.* like or of the family of birds which includes the domestic fowl.
gal·li·pot (gal′əpot), *n.* a small ceramic pot for ointments, medicines, etc.
gal·li·vant (gal′əvant), *v.* to gad gaily about.
gall·stone (gôl′stōn′), *n.* a stone-like concretion in the gall bladder.
gal·lus (gal′əs), *n., pl.* **gal·lus·es.** suspenders for a pair of trousers.
gal·van·ic (galvan′ik), *adj.* 1. pertaining to, caused by, or produced by an electric current. 2. startling; convulsive; shocking.
gal·van·ize (gal′vənīz), *v.* 1. to stir into sudden activity; rouse. 2. to cover with a zinc coating, esp. to prevent rust.

gal·va·nom·e·ter (galvənom′itər), *n.* an instrument for detecting, comparing, and measuring small electric currents.

gal·va·no·tax·is (gal′vənōtak′sis), *n.* movement of an organism in response to an electric current.

gal·va·not·ro·pism (galvənot′rəpizm), *n.* tendency of an organism to grow toward or away from an electric current.

gam (gam), *n.* a school of whales.

gam·ba·do (gambā′dō), *n.*, *pl.* **gam·ba·dos, gam·ba·does.** one of a pair of boots or gaiters attached to the saddle instead of stirrups.

gam·bit (gam′bit), *n.* any initial move, esp. in chess, seeking an advantage; a cunning strategy.

gam·boge (gambōj′), *n.* a yellow or yellow-orange pigment.

gam·brel roof (gam′brəl), a gable roof made up of two surfaces at each side that slope to the ridge at different angles.

gam·e·lan (gam′əlan), *n.* an orchestra consisting of bowed, stringed, and percussion instruments, and flutes, characteristic of southeast Asia.

games·man·ship (gāmz′mənsHip), *n.* the art of winning games by disconcerting one's opponent.

game·some (gām′səm), *adj.* gay or playful.

gam·ete (gam′ēt), *n.* a reproductive cell which, uniting with another, produces a new organism.

ga·me·to·cyte (gəmē′təsīt), *n.* a cell producing gametes.

gam·e·to·gen·e·sis (gam′itōjen′isis), *n.* development of gametes.

ga·me·to·phore (gəmē′təfôr), *n.* a gamete-producing part.

ga·me·to·phyte (gəmē′təfīt), *n.* a plant that reproduces sexually. See also **sporophyte.**

gam·ma·di·on (gəmā′dēən), *n.*, *pl.* **gam·ma·di·a** (gəmā′dēə). a figure used in ornamentation formed from the Greek capital letter gamma, as a swastika.

gam·ma glob·u·lin (gam′ə glob′yəlin), a protein in blood plasma containing antibodies effective against measles and poliomyelitis.

gamma ray, rays produced by radioactive material.

gam·mon (gam′ən), *n.* a ham that has been smoked or cured.

gam·o·gen·e·sis (gaməjen′isis), *n.* reproduction by the union of two gametes.

ga·nef (gä′nef), *n.* (slang) a thief.

gan·gli·a (gaNG′glēə), *n. pl.* of **ganglion.**

gan·gli·ate (gaNG′glēāt), *adj.* possessing ganglia. Also **gan′gli·on·ate.**

gan·gli·form (gaNG′gləfôrm), *adj.* with the form of a ganglion.

gan·gli·oid (gaNG′glēoid), *adj.* like a ganglion.

gan·gli·on (gaNG′glēən), *n.*, *pl.* **gan·gli·a** (gaNG′glēə), **gan·gli·ons. 1.** a small mass of nerve tissue outside the brain and spinal cord. **2.** a tumor in the sheath of a tendon, as at the wrist. **3.** a center of activities. —**gan·gli·on′ic,** *adj.*

gangue (gaNG), *n.* valueless minerals occurring in a vein or deposit of ore.

gan·is·ter (gan′istər), *n.* a hard, siliceous rock used to line furnaces.

gan·o·in (gan′ōin), *n.* a hard, shiny surface on the outer layer of the scales of some fishes.

gan·try (gan′trē), *n.* a framework of scaffolding for erecting vertically launched missiles.

gar·ban·zo (gärban′zō), *n.* a leguminous plant with edible pea-like seeds; chickpea.

garde·robe (gärd′rōb′), *n.* a wardrobe, or the clothes kept in one; clothespress.

gar·goyl·ism (gär′goilizəm), *n.* a congenital abnormality characterized by grotesque deformities to parts of the body.

gar·ner (gär′nər), *v.* to gather, hoard, and store up.

gar·net (gär′nit), *n.* a dark red color.

gar·nish·ee (gär′nisHē′), *v.* to place (property or money) under garnishment.

gar·nish·ment (gär′nisHmənt), *n.* a notice to withhold a defendant's money or property subject to a court's direction.

gar·ni·ture (gär'niCHər), *n.* that which decorates; ornamentation.

gar·rote (gərōt', gərot'), *n.* **1.** an iron collar, wire, or cord used to execute by throttling. **2.** this method of capital punishment. —*v.* **3.** to throttle or strangle. Also **ga·rote', ga·rotte', gar·rotte'.**

gar·ru·li·ty (gərōō'litē), *n.* the quality of being talkative.

gar·ru·lous (gar'ələs), *adj.* excessively loquacious; talkative about trivial matters; wordy.

garth (gär*th*), *n.* an enclosed yard or courtyard.

gas·ser (gas'ər), *n.* (slang) anything that is extremely funny or pleasing, as *That hat is a gasser*.

gas·tral·gi·a (gastral'jēə), *n.* a violent stomach pain.

gas·tric (gas'trik), *adj.* of or in the stomach.

gas·tri·tis (gastrī'tis), *n.* inflammation of the stomach.

gas·tro·en·ter·i·tis (gas'trōen'tərī-tis), *n.* inflammation of the intestines and stomach.

gas·tro·en·ter·ol·ogy (gas'trōen'-tərol'əjē), *n.* study of the digestive organs.

gas·tro·he·pat·ic (gas'trōhipat'ik), *adj.* affecting the liver and stomach.

gas·tro·in·tes·ti·nal (gas'trōintes'-tinl), *adj.* affecting the stomach and intestines.

gas·tro·lith (gas'trəli*th*), *n.* a stone or concretion in the stomach.

gas·trol·o·gy (gastrol'əjē), *n.* study of the stomach.

gas·tro·nome (gas'trənōm), *n.* a lover and judge of good food. Also **gas·tron'o·mist.**

gas·tron·o·my (gastron'əmē), *n.* art and science of good eating.

gas·tro·scope (gas'trəskōp), *n.* an instrument for inspecting the interior of the stomach. —**gas·tros'copy,** *n.*

gat (gat), *n.* a channel extending inland through shoals, etc.

ga·teau (gätō'), *n., pl.* **ga·teaux** (gä-tōz'). a decorated cake.

gate·fold (gāt'fōld'), *n.* a page larger than the book or periodical it is bound in and folded so as not to extend beyond the edges.

gate·leg (gāt'leg'), *n.* a table having an extra leg which can be swung round to support a drop leaf.

Gat·ling gun (gat'liNG), an early type of machine gun.

gauche (gōsh), *adj.* clumsy; lacking in social graces; tactless.

gau·che·rie (gōsHərē'), *n.* a lack of social grace; an act that is awkward or tactless.

gaud (gôd), *n.* a cheap ornament or bit of finery; showy display. —**gau'der·y,** *adj.*

ga·ze·bo (gəzē'bō), *n.* a building such as an ornamental summerhouse.

gaz·o·gene (gaz'əjēn), *n.* an apparatus used to impregnate a liquid with a gas, as in making soda water.

gaz·pa·cho (gəzpä'CHō), *n.* a Spanish vegetable soup served cold.

Ge·brauchs·mu·sik (gəbrouKHs'-mōōzēk'), *n.* music written in a simple manner for performance by amateurs.

ge·füll·te fish (gəfil'tə), boned fish shaped into balls and served cold. Also **ge·fil'te fish.**

ge·gen·schein (gā'gənsHīn), *n.* a pale patch of light in the night sky, which is a reflection of sunlight on particles in space.

Gei·ger counter (gī'gər), an instrument used chiefly to measure radioactivity.

ge·la·tion (jelā'sHən), *n.* the act or process of freezing; making solidly cold.

gel·id (jel'id), *adj.* icy cold; frozen.

ge·mein·schaft (gəmīn'sHäft), *n., pl.* **ge·mein·schaf·ten** (gəmīn'sHäf-tən). **1.** a fellowship of people having similar tastes. **2.** a group with a strong sense of common identity.

gem·el bottle (jem'əl), a pair of cruets coupled together, with the necks curving in opposite directions, used as for oil and vinegar.

gem·eled (jem'əld), *adj.* coupled, as two architectural members.

gem·i·nate (jem′ənāt), *v*. to mate or become paired or doubled. —**gem·i·na′tion**, *n*.

gem·i·ni·flo·rous (jem′ənēflô′rəs), *adj*. with flowers arranged in pairs.

gem·ma·ceous (jemā′sHəs), *adj*. of, or resembling buds.

gem·mate (jem′āt), *adj*. reproducing by budding.

gem·ma·tion (jemā′sHən), *n*. reproduction by buds. Also **gem·mu·la′tion.**

gem·mif·er·ous (jemif′ərəs), *adj*. having buds.

gem·mi·form (jem′əfôrm), *adj*. having a bud-like shape.

gem·mip·a·rous (jemip′ərəs), *adj*. producing or reproducing by buds.

gem·ol·o·gy, gem·mol·o·gy (jemol′əjē), *n*. the science or study of gemstones.

ge·müt·lich (gəmyt′likH), *adj*. agreeable. Also **ge·muet′lich.**

Ge·müt·lich·keit (gəmyt′likHkīt′), *n*. agreeableness. Also **Ge·muet′lich·keit.**

ge·nappe (jənap′), *v*. to singe (yarn) to remove loose threads.

gen·e·arch (jen′ēärk), *n*. the head of a family or tribe.

general semantics, a discipline involving the interrelationships between symbols and human behavior. See also **semantics.**

ge·ner·ic (jəner′ik), *adj*. referring to all members of a genus or class.

ge·neth·li·ac (jineth′lēak), *adj*. referring to the position of the stars at one's birth.

ge·neth·li·al·o·gy (jəneth′lēol′əjē), *n*. science of calculating the position of the stars, as on a birthday.

ge·net·ics (jənet′iks), *n*. science of heredity.

ge·nic·u·late (jənik′yəlit), *adj*. **1.** having joints. **2.** bent as the knee at the knee joint. —**ge·nic·u·la′tion**, *n*.

gen·i·to·u·ri·nar·y (jen′itōyo͝or′-ənerē), *adj*. of or pertaining to the urinary and genital organs.

gen·o·cide (jen′əsīd), *n*. the systematic mass murder of a race or of a religious group.

gen·o·type (jen′ətīp), *n*. **1.** the genetic constitution of an organism. **2.** a group sharing a common genetic constitution.

gens (jenz), *n*., *pl*. **gen·tes** (jen′tēz). a group with a common male ancestor.

ge·nu (jē′noō), *n*., *pl*. **ge·nu·a** (jen′-oōə). the knee; a knee-like part.

gen·u·flect (jen′yoōflekt), *v*. to bend the knee as an expression of reverence. —**gen·u·flec′tion**, *n*.

gen·u·pec·tor·al (jen′yoōpek′tərəl), *adj*. pertaining to the knee and chest.

ge·o·cen·tric (jen′əsen′trik), *adj*. reckoned from the center of the earth; having the earth as center.

ge·o·chem·is·try (jē′ōkem′istrē), *n*. the science of the chemistry of the earth.

ge·o·chro·nol·o·gy (jē′ōkrənol′əjē), *n*. the dating of the earth on the basis of geological information.

ge·o·des·ic (jēədes′ik, jēədē′sik), *adj*. pertaining to the geometry of curved surfaces. Also **ge·o·des′i·cal.**

geodesic dome, a dome-like structure created by R. Buckminster Fuller.

ge·od·e·sy (jēod′isē), *n*. the science of calculating the measurement of large tracts of land, and the dimensions of the earth. Also **ge′o·det′ics.** —**ge′o·det′ic**, *adj*.

ge·o·dy·nam·ics (jē′ōdīnam′iks), *n*. the science of the dynamics within the earth.

ge·og·no·sy (jēog′nəsē), *n*. geology dealing with the earth's water, air, and crust.

ge·oid (jē′oid), *n*. an imaginary ellipsoid, flattened at the poles, that coincides with sea level.

ge·o·mag·net·ic (jē′ōmagnet′ik), *adj*. of or pertaining to the earth's magnetism.

ge·o·man·cy (jē′əmansē), *n*. divination by means of a handful of earth thrown at random or by means of figures or lines. —**ge′o·man·cer,** *n*.

ge·o·med·i·cine (jē′ōmed′isən), *n*. medicine dealing with the effect of geography on disease.

ge·o·met·ric progression (jēəmet′-

rik). a mathematical sequence in which each term is obtained by multiplying the preceding by a constant factor. See also **arithmetic progression, harmonic progression.**

ge·o·mor·phic (jēəmôr′fik), *adj*. of or pertaining to the form of the surface of the earth.

ge·o·mor·phol·o·gy (jē′əmôrfol′əjē), *n*. the study of the origins and development of land forms.

ge·o·nav·i·ga·tion (jē′ōnavəgā′-sHən), *n*. navigation by terrestrial objects.

ge·oph·a·gy (jēof′əjē), *n*. the eating of earth or of earthy matter, as clay.

ge·oph·i·lous (jēof′ələs), *adj*. earthbound, as certain snails.

ge·o·phys·ics (jē′ōfiz′iks), *n*. the science of the physics of the earth.

ge·o·phyte (jē′əfīt), *n*. a plant that buds underground.

ge·o·pon·ics (jēəpon′iks), *n*. (*construed as sing.*) the science of agriculture. —**ge·o·pon′ic,** *adj*.

Geor·gian (jôr′jən), *adj*. of a style of architecture, art, and design predominant in England for a hundred years from about 1714, during the reigns of George I through George III, typified in buildings and dwellings by a basic construction of brick, with white wooden window and door frames, and neo-classical porticos.

geor·gic (jôr′jik), *adj*. agricultural.

ge·o·stat·ic (jēəstat′ik), *adj*. of or pertaining to the pressure of earth, as in a mine.

ge·o·stroph·ic (jēəstrō′fik), *adj*. of or pertaining to the pressure in the atmosphere in relation to the Coriolis force.

ge·o·syn·cline (jē′ōsin′klīn), *n*. a part of the earth's crust subject to downward movement.

ge·o·tax·is (jē′ōtak′sis), *n*. movement of an organism in response to gravitational force.

ge·o·tec·ton·ic (jē′ōtekton′ik), *adj*. of or pertaining to the structure of the earth's crust.

ge·o·ther·mal (jē′ōthur′məl), *adj*. of or pertaining to the internal heat of the earth. Also **ge·o·ther′mic.**

ge·o·trop·ic (jē′ōtrop′ik), *adj*. of or pertaining to movement with respect to the force of gravity. —**ge·o′tro·pism,** *n*.

ger·a·tol·o·gy (jerətol′əjē), *n*. the study of old age.

ge·rent (jēr′ənt), *n*. a manager.

ger·i·at·rics (jer′ēat′riks), *n*. (*construed as sing.*) **1.** the science dealing with the diseases and care of old people. **2.** the study of aging.

ger·mane (jərmān′), *adj*. relevant; pertinent; appropriate.

ger·mi·cide (jur′misīd), *n*. a germ-killing substance.

ger·mi·nal (jur′mənl), *adj*. **1.** of or like a germ or germ cell. **2.** being in an early stage of development; embryonic.

ger·mi·nant (jur′mənənt), *adj*. germinating; growing.

ger·mi·nate (jur′mənāt), *v*. to begin to develop; start to grow. —**ger′mi·na·tive,** *adj*.

ger·o·don·tics (jerədon′tiks), *n*. (*construed as sing.*) dentistry dealing with aging people. Also **ger·o·don·tia** (jerədon′sHə).

ger·on·toc·ra·cy (jerəntok′rəsē), *n*. government by elders.

ge·ron·to·ge·ous (jəron′təjē′əs), *n*. belonging to Europe, Asia, or Africa.

ger·on·tol·o·gy (jerəntol′əjē), *n*. the scientific study of aging and of old age.

ger·ry·man·der (jer′ēman′dər), *v*. **1.** to manipulate with a gerrymander. —*n.* **2.** reorganization of the election districts of a state, etc., to give one political party an advantage.

ge·sell·schaft (gəzel′sHäft), *n., pl.* **ge·sell·schaf·ten** (gəzel′sHäftən). **1.** an association of people with a common intellectual, cultural, or business goal. **2.** a formal organization usually non-traditional and not sentimental. See also **gemeinschaft.**

ges·so (jes′ō), *n*. any preparation like plaster used to prepare a surface before painting.

gest (jest), *n*. **1.** bearing; conduct. **2.** gesture.

ge·stalt (gəsHtält′), *n., pl.* **ge·stalts,**

ges·tal·ten (gəsʜtäl′tən). (in psychology) a unified whole that cannot be derived from the sum of its parts.

Gestalt psychology, the theory in psychology that phenomena do not happen through reflexes or sensations.

ges·tate (jes′tāt), *v.* to be pregnant. —**ges·ta′tion,** *n.*

ges·tic·u·late (jestik′yəlāt), *v.* to use gestures to emphasize or communicate; to express with gestures. —**ges·tic′u·lar,** *adj.* —**ges·tic·u·la′tion,** *n.*

gew·gaw (gyoō′gô), *n.* a gaudy or useless trinket or trifle.

gib·be·rel·lic acid (jibərel′ik), an acid that stimulates plant growth.

gib·bet (jib′it), *n.* a gallows.

gib·bos·i·ty (gibos′itē), *n.* the condition of being gibbous.

gib·bous (gib′əs), *adj.* **1.** humpbacked. **2.** (of the moon) between half and full; convex at both edges. Also **gib·bose** (gib′ōs).

gi·ga·cy·cle (jī′gəsīkəl), *n.* a billion cycles.

gi·ga·hertz (jī′gəhurts), *n.* a billion hertz.

gi·gan·tism (jīgan′tizm), *n.* an abnormal growth in size of the whole body or of parts of the body. Also **gi·′ant·ism.**

gi·ga·sec·ond (jī′gəsekənt), *n.* a billion seconds.

gig·ot (jig′ət), *n.* **1.** a leg of mutton. **2.** a sleeve puffed out only above the elbows; leg-of-mutton sleeve.

gim·bals (jim′bəlz), *n.* (*construed as sing.*) a device for mounting nautical instruments or equipment on a vessel so as to allow them to remain in a horizontal position regardless of the angle of the vessel. Also **gim′bal ring.**

gim·let (gim′lit), *n.* **1.** a tool with a sharp screw end for boring holes. **2.** a cocktail of gin and lime juice.

gin·ger·bread (jin′jərbred′), *n.* elaborate ornamentation.

gin·gi·val (jinjī′vəl), *adj.* of the gums.

gir·a·sol (jir′əsôl), *n.* **1.** an opal with a luminous glow. —*adj.* **2.** (of a stone) bluish-white with red reflections. Also **gir′a·sole.**

gla·brate (glā′brāt), *adj.* glabrous or becoming glabrous.

gla·bres·cent (glābres′ənt), *adj.* becoming glabrous.

gla·brous (glā′brəs), *adj.* bald; hairless; smooth.

gla·cé (glasā′), *adj.* frozen; frosted, as a cake; candied.

gla·cial·ist (glā′sʜəlist), *n.* a specialist in the geological phenomena caused by glacial activity.

gla·ci·ate (glā′sʜēāt), *v.* to make or become frozen or covered with ice.

gla·ci·ol·o·gy (glā′sʜeol′əjē), *n.* study of glaciers.

gla·cis (glā′sis), *n.* a gentle slope.

glad·i·ate (glad′ēit), *adj.* swordshaped; ensiform; xiphoid.

glair (gler), *n.* **1.** raw white of egg. **2.** a glaze made of egg white. **3.** any similar viscous substance. —**glair′y,** *adj.*

glau·co·ma (glôkō′mə), *n.* a disease of the eye leading to loss of vision. —**glau·co′ma·tous,** *adj.*

glau·cous (glô′kəs), *adj.* greenishblue.

gle·noid (glē′noid), *adj.* shallow or slightly cupped, as a bone cavity.

glis·sade (glisäd′), *n.* a skillful descending glide over snow, as on skis.

glo·bate (glō′bāt), *adj.* globe-shaped.

glo·big·er·i·na ooze (glōbij′ərī′nə), a deposit on the ocean floor consisting mainly of shells.

glo·boid (glō′boid), *adj.* globular.

glo·bose (glō′bōs), *adj.* globe-like.

glob·u·lar (glob′yələr), *adj.* spherical. Also **glob′u·lous.**

glob·ule (glob′yoōl), *n.* a small round body.

glob·u·lif·er·ous (globyəlif′ərəs), *adj.* yielding or having globules.

glo·chid·i·ate (glōkid′ēāt), *adj.* barbed at the apex.

glo·chid·i·um (glōkid′ēəm), *n., pl.* **glo·chid·i·a** (glōkid′ēə). a hair with a barbed tip.

glo·chis (glō′kis), *n., pl.* **glo·chi·nes** (glōkī′nēz). a barbed hair.

glom·er·ate (glom′ərit), *adj.* gathered into a compact mass.

glom·er·a·tion (glomərā′sʜən), *n.* a glomerate mass; conglomeration.

gloss (glos), *n.* **1.** an explication of a term or expression in a text, usually in the form of a note. —*v.* **2.** to interpret by means of a gloss.

glos·sa (glos′ə), *n.* the tongue. —**glos′sal,** *adj.*

glos·se·mat·ics (glosəmat′iks), *n.* (*used as singular*) the linguistic study of glossemes.

glos·seme (glos′ēm), *n.* the smallest meaningful signal in language, made up of a morpheme and a tagmeme. —**glos·se′mic,** *adj.*

glos·si·tis (glosī′tis), *n.* inflammation of the tongue.

glot·tal (glot′l), *adj.* of or produced in the glottis.

glot·tic (glot′ik), *adj.* glottal.

glot·tis (glot′is), *n.* the opening between the vocal cords.

gloze (glōz), *v.* to extenuate; explain away.

glu·cose (gloo′kōs), *n.* a sugar occurring in many fruits, about one half as sweet as ordinary sugar.

glu·tam·ic acid (glootam′ik). an amino acid found in meteorites. Also **glu·ta·min′ic acid.**

glu·ten (gloo′tn), *n.* substance remaining when wheat flour is washed to remove the starch. —**glu′te·nous,** *adj.*

glu·ti·nous (gloo′tənəs), *adj.* like glue; sticky.

gly·cine (glī′sēn), *n.* a simple, common amino acid, traces of which have been found in meteorites.

glyph (glif), *n.* a relief carving; hieroglyph.

glyp·tic (glip′tik), *adj.* pertaining to engraving on gems, ivory, etc.

glyp·tics (glip′tiks), *n.* art of engraving on gems, etc.

glyp·to·graph (glip′təgraf), *n.* an engraved design as on a gem.

glyp·tog·ra·phy (gliptog′rəfē), *n.* study of engraved gems.

gnath·ic (nath′ik), *adj.* pertaining to the jaw. Also **gnath′al.**

gna·thon·ic (nathon′ik), *adj.* obsequious; toadying.

gnome (nōm), *n.* an aphorism; maxim; pithy saying. —**gno′mic,** *adj.*

gno·mist (nō′mist), *n.* a writer of maxims.

gno·mol·o·gy (nōmol′əjē), *n.* a collection of aphorisms; gnomic writing.

gno·mon (nō′mon), *n.* the part of a sundial that casts the shadow indicating the time.

gnos·tic (nos′tik), *adj.* possessing mystical knowledge; pertaining to knowledge. Also **gnos′ti·cal.**

gno·to·bi·o·sis (nō′tōbīō′sis), *n.* a condition in which germfree animals have been inoculated with microorganisms of a given type. —**gno·to·bi·ot·ic** (nō′tōbīot′ik), *adj.*

gno·to·bi·ote (nō′tōbī′ōt), *n.* a gnotobiotic animal.

GNP, gross national product.

gob·bet (gob′it), *n.* a morsel; lump or mass.

go·det (gōdet′), *n.* a triangular piece of fabric added to a garment to give fullness.

goi·ter (goi′tər), *n.* an enlargement of the thyroid gland in the neck. —**goi·trous** (goi′trəs), *adj.*

go·nad (gō′nad), *n.* the organ producing gametes; reproductive gland.

go·nad·o·trope (gōnad′ətrōp), *n.* a gonadotropic substance.

go·nad·o·trop·ic (gōnad′ətrop′ik), *adj.* pertaining to certain substances that affect the ovary or testis.

gon·fa·lon (gon′fələn), *n.* a banner, with streamers, hanging from a crossbar.

go·ni·om·e·ter (gō′nēom′itər), *n.* an instrument for measuring angles.

gon·o·coc·cus (gonəkok′əs), *n.*, *pl.* **gon·o·coc·ci** (gonəkok′sī). bacteria causing gonorrhea.

gon·o·cyte (gon′əsīt), *n.* a germ cell when it is maturing.

gon·or·rhe·a (gonərē′ə), *n.* a contagious inflammation of the urethra or the vagina.

goof-ball (goof′bôl′), *n. Slang.* a barbiturate pill.

goo·gol (goo′gol), *n.* the number 1 followed by 100 zeros.

gore (gôr), *n.* a triangular piece of material added to a garment or sail for extra width.

gor·gon·ize (gôr′gənīz), v. to hypnotize; turn as to stone.

Gor·gon·zo·la (gôgənzō′lə), n. a very strongly flavored blue-veined Italian cheese.

gos·port (gos′pôrt), n. a speaking tube allowing communication between parts of an aircraft.

Goth·ic (goth′ik), adj. **1.** pertaining to a medieval style of art, music, and architecture, characterized in the last by the use of pointed arches, ribbed vaults, delicate tracery in stonework, and flying buttresses, gargoyles, and grotesquery. **2.** pertaining to a later style of writing characterized by violent events and a decaying atmosphere.

gouache (gwäsh), n. a method of painting in water colors mixed with gum.

gour·mand·ize (goor′məndīz), v. to eat well; eat excessively or gluttonously.

gout (gout), n. a disease characterized by swellings in the joints, esp. in the great toe, and caused by excess uric acid in the blood.

goût (goo), n. French. style or preference; taste.

gov·ern·ance (guv′ərnəns), n. control; act of governing.

gra·ben (grä′bən), n. a part of the earth that has been pushed downward. See also **horst.**

gra·di·ent (grā′dēənt), n. the angle of ascent or descent of a highway, railroad, etc.

grad·u·al·ism (graj′ōōəlizm), n. the method of achieving a goal by gradual steps rather than drastic action.

grad·u·al·ist (graj′ōōəlist), n. one who advocates a gradual enforcement of desegregation laws (esp. in the Southern states).

graf·fi·ti (grəfē′tē), n. pl. writings or drawings, often of an obscene nature, found on the walls of public buildings such as restrooms.

graft·age (graf′tij), n. the inserting of a part of one plant into another to produce a new combined variety.

gral·la·to·ri·al (gralətôr′ēəl), adj. pertaining to birds that wade, as the herons, cranes, etc.

gram (gram), n. a metric unit of mass which equals 15.432 grains.

gram·a·ry (gram′ərē), n. the lore of sorcery.

gram·i·niv·o·rous (graməniv′ərəs), adj. feeding on seeds.

gram·ma·logue (gram′əlôg), n. a word shown as a sign or letter, as " &, " which signifies "and."

Gram-neg·a·tive (gram′neg′ətiv), adj. (of bacteria) not remaining violet when dyed by Gram's method.

Gram-pos·i·tive (gram′poz′ətiv), adj. (of bacteria) remaining violet when dyed by Gram's method.

Gram's method, a method of staining bacteria treated with a solution of iodine, potassium iodide, and water.

Grand Gui·gnol (gräN gēnyôl′), drama with strong overtones of horror.

gran·dil·o·quence (grandil′əkwəns), n. a pompous and lofty style of speech. —**gran·dil′o·quent,** adj.

gran·di·ose (gran′dēōs), adj. grand; imposing; impressive.

grand mal (gran′ mal′). epilepsy characterized by loss of consciousness, frothing at the mouth, etc. See also **epilepsy, petit mal.**

gran·drelle (grandrel′), n. yarn made by twisting two strands of contrasting colors.

grang·er·ize (grān′jərīz), v. **1.** to add illustrations to a book by inserting additional prints, drawings, etc. **2.** to mutilate (books) to get illustrations.

gra·nif·er·ous (grənif′ərəs), adj. bearing grain.

gra·niv·o·rous (graniv′ərəs), adj. feeding on grain.

gran·u·lo·ma (granyəlō′mə), n., pl. **gran·u·lo·mas, gran·u·lo·ma·ta** (granyəlō′mətə). a tumor composed of proud flesh.

gran·u·lo·ma·to·sis (gran′yəlōmətō′sis), n. a condition characterized by many granulomas.

graph·ol·o·gy (grafol′əjē), n. the analysis of handwriting to determine the writer's personality.

graph·o·mo·tor (grafəmō′tər), adj.

pertaining to muscular control in writing.

gra·phon·o·my (grafon'əmē), *n.* the study of different systems of writing.

grap·pa (gräp'pä), *n.* brandy that has not been aged.

grat·i·cule (grat'əkyōōl), *n.* a grid of lines on a map or chart.

grat·i·nate (grat'ənāt), *v.* to cook food with a topping of browned crumbs and butter or grated cheese.

gra·ti·né (gratēnā'), *adj.* gratinated.

grat·u·lant (graCH'ələnt), *adj.* expressing joy and congratulations.

Grau·stark·i·an (groustärk'ēən), *adj.* typically romantic and melodramatic, as the adventures of military and court figures in certain literature.

gra·va·men (grəvā'mən), *n., pl.* **gra·vam·i·na** (grəvam'ənə). the most important part of a legal accusation.

gra·vim·e·ter (grəvim'itər), *n.* 1. an instrument for measuring specific gravity. 2. an instrument to measure differences in the earth's gravitational field. Also **gravity meter.**

gra·vim·e·try (grəvim'itrē), *n.* the measurement of weight. —**grav·i·met'ric,** *adj.*

gra·vure (grəvyōōr'), *n.* a method of printing from engraved plates.

gray eminence, a person who holds power but wields it through another; power behind the throne. [from French *éminence grise*]

great circle, 1. a circle obtained by cutting a sphere by a plane passing through its center. See also **small circle.** 2. line of shortest distance between two points on the earth's surface.

greater omentum, an omentum joined to the stomach and extending over the small intestine. See also **lesser omentum.**

greenhouse effect, the effect of screening the earth's surface by raising its temperature by short-wave radiant heat without allowing the escape of long-wave radiant heat, produced by gases in the atmosphere, as carbon dioxide.

gre·gar·i·ous (griger'ēəs), *adj.* living in groups, or flocks; loving company.

Gre·go·ri·an calendar (grigôr'ēən), the calendar (still in use) introduced by Pope Gregory XIII in the 16th century, calculating a year as having 365 days, and a leap year, which consists of 366 days, as occurring every fourth year excepting those divisible by 400.

gren·a·dine[1] (grenədēn'), *n.* a type of light, loosely woven cloth.

gren·a·dine[2] (grenədēn'), *n.* a sweet syrup made from pomegranates.

gres·so·ri·al (gresôr'ēəl), *adj.* adapted for walking.

gride (grīd), *v.* 1. to grate or scrape. 2. to cut.

gri·gri (grē'grē), *n.* a charm or amulet of African origin.

gril·lade (griläd'), *n.* a dish of broiled or grilled meat.

gri·mal·kin (grimal'kin), *n.* a cat, esp. an old female cat.

gri·saille (grizī'), *n.* a painting entirely executed in shades of gray.

gross national product, the monetary value of all goods and services of one country in one year. *Abbrev.:* **GNP.**

gris·e·ous (gris'ēəs), *adj.* gray.

groin (groin), *n.* 1. the meeting point of the belly and thigh. 2. the curved line formed by the intersection of two vaults.

ground layer. See **surface boundary layer.**

ground·speed (ground'spēd'), *n.* the speed of an aircraft in relation to the ground, which is considered as stationary. See also **airspeed.**

group therapy, psychiatric treatment in which a group of patients discuss their problems together with a therapist.

grout (grout), *n.* mortar used to fill joints in masonry.

grum (grum), *adj.* appearing grim, glum, or surly.

grume (grōōm), *n.* clotting blood.

Gru·yère (grōōyer'), *n.* a firm, lightly flavored, Swiss cheese having small holes.

gu·ber·na·to·ri·al (gōo'bərnətôr'-ēəl), *adj.* of or pertaining to a governor.

gudg·eon (guj'ən), *n.* **1.** someone easily duped. **2.** a bait.

guer·don (gur'dn), *n.* **1.** a reward. —*v.* **2.** to recompense.

gué·rite (gārēt'), *n.* a wicker chair with a hood over the seat.

guile (gīl), *n.* underhand cunning; deceitfulness; duplicity. —**guile'ful**, *adj.* —**guile'less**, *adj.*

guimpe (gimp), *n.* **1.** a yoke as of lace or embroidered linen worn to fill the neck of a low-cut dress. **2.** stiffly starched cloth that covers the neck and shoulders of habits of certain nuns.

gui·pure (gipyōor'), *n.* any of various heavy, large-patterned laces.

gu·la (gyōo'lə), *n.* the upper part of the throat.

gulch (gulcH), *n.* a ravine, usually deep and narrow, marking the course of a stream.

gul·gul (gul'gul), *n.* a concoction of powdered seashells in oil, used as a protective coat for wooden ships.

gull (gul), *v.* **1.** to dupe; fool; trick. —*n.* **2.** one who is easily tricked or deceived.

gu·los·i·ty (gyōolos'itē), *n.* greed; gluttony.

gunk·hole (guNGk'hōl'), *v.* to sail gently along the coast stopping in quiet anchorages.

gurge (gurj), *n.* a whirlpool.

gur·gi·ta·tion (gur'jitā'sHən), *n.* a surging and eddying as of water.

gu·ru (gōo'rōo), *n.* a Hindu teacher of religion, giving personal religious instruction.

gus·set (gus'it), *n.* a triangular piece of material inserted for strengthening or enlarging the original.

gus·ta·tion (gustā'sHən), *n.* act or faculty of tasting.

gus·ta·to·ry (gustətôr'ē), *adj.* pertaining to the sense of taste or tasting.

gut·buck·et (gut'bukit), *n.* jazz played in early traditional barrelhouse style.

gut·ta (gut'ə), *n., pl.* **gut·tae** (gut'ē). a drop or something like one.

gut·ta·per·cha (gut'əpurcH'ə), *n.* a substance obtained from the sap of certain Malayan trees and used for insulating electric wires and dental fillings.

gut·tate (gut'āt), *adj.* resembling or in the form of a drop.

gut·ti·form (gut'əfôrm), *adj.* shaped like a drop.

gut·tle (gut'l), *v.* to guzzle; eat greedily.

guy·ot (gēō), *n.* a flat undersea mountain in the Pacific Ocean.

gym·kha·na (jimkä'nə), *n.* a meeting held for horsemen to display equitation.

gym·nog·e·nous (jimnoj'ənəs), *adj.* featherless at birth, as certain birds.

gym·no·rhi·nal (jimnərī'nl), *adj.* (of a bird) having the nostrils not covered with feathers.

gym·no·sperm (jim'nəspurm), *n.* a plant with its seeds not enclosed in an ovary. —**gym·no·sper'mous**, *adj.*

gym·no·spore (jim'nəspōr), *n.* a spore with no protective envelope.

gy·nan·dro·morph (jinan'drəmôrf), *n.* an organism of mixed sex; hermaphrodite; a monoecious individual.

gy·nan·dry (jinan'drē), *n.* the condition of having both male and female organs in one individual; hermaphroditism. Also **gy·nan'drism**.

gy·nar·chy (jin'ärkē), *n.* government by a woman or women. Also **gyn·e·coc·ra·cy, gyn·ae·coc·ra·cy** (jinəkok'rəsē).

gy·ne·cic, gy·nae·cic (jinē'sik), *adj.* of or pertaining to women.

gyn·e·coid, gyn·ae·coid (jin'əkoid), *adj.* of or like a woman.

gy·ne·col·o·gy, gy·nae·col·ogy (gīnəkol'əjē), *n.* the study of the functions and diseases of the reproductive organs of women. —**gy·ne·col'o·gist, gy·nae·col'o·gist**, *n.*

gyn·e·co·mor·phous, gyn·ae·co·mor·phous (jin'əkōmôr'fəs), *adj.* having the appearance of a female.

gyn·e·cop·a·thy, gyn·ae·cop·a·thy (jinəkop'əthē), *n.* a disease peculiar to women.

gyn·e·pho·bi·a, gyn·ae·pho·bi·a (jinəfō′bēə), *n.* a fear of women.

gyn·i·at·rics (jin′ēat′riks), *n.* treatment of diseases peculiar to females. Also **gyn·i·a′try.**

gy·ro·com·pass (jī′rōkumpəs), *n.* a nonmagnetic navigational compass making use of a gyroscope to indicate true north.

gy·noe·ci·um, gy·ne·ci·um (jinē′-sēəm), *n.* the innermost part of a flower, lying within the ring of stamens and comprising one or more carpels. Also **pistil.**

gy·rose (jī′rōs), *adj.* having wavy striations.

gy·ro·vague (jī′rōvāg), *n.* an itinerant monk who traveled between monasteries.

gyve (jīv), *n.* **1.** (*usually pl.*) a shackle for the leg; fetter. —*v.* **2.** to shackle or fetter by the leg.

ha·bil·i·ments (həbil′əmənts), *n. pl.* furniture; decorations; equipment.

hab·i·tude (hab′itōod), *n.* usual condition or state of mind; usual way of acting.

ha·chure (hasHŏor′), *n.* one of the fine parallel lines of shading drawn on a map to indicate the steepness of a slope.

hack·a·more (hak′əmôr), *n.* a horsehair or rawhide bridle with a nosepiece, used mainly for breaking colts.

hadj (haj), *n., pl.* **hadj·es.** See **hajj.**

had·ji (haj′ē), *n., pl.* **hadj·is.** See **hajji.**

haec·ce·i·ty (heksē′itē), *n.* the quality that gives something its individuality. See also **quiddity.**

haema- For words beginning with this prefix, see **hema-.**

hag·gis (hag′is), *n.* a Scottish dish made of sheep's or calf's heart, lungs, and liver, chopped with suet and oatmeal, and boiled in the animal's stomach.

hag·i·oc·ra·cy (hag′ēok′rəsē), *n.* government by saints, priests, or others deemed holy.

hag·i·og·ra·pher (hag′ēog′rəfər), *n.* a writer of the lives of saints. Also **hag·i·og′ra·phist.**

hag·i·og·ra·phy (hag′ēog′rəfē), *n.* the writing and study of the lives of saints.

hag·i·ol·a·try (hag′ēol′ətrē), *n.* the worship or veneration of saints.

hag·i·ol·o·gy (hag′ēol′əjē), *n.* a single work or branch of literature describing the lives and legends of saints.

hag·rid·den (hag′ridn), *adj.* worried or tormented, as by a hag or witch.

Hague Tribunal, a court of arbitration set up at The Hague, Holland, in 1899 for the peaceful settlement of international disputes.

ha-ha (hä′hä), *n.* a boundary to a garden or park, usually a fence sunk in a ditch.

haik, haick (hīk, hāk), *n.* an outer garment worn by Arabs, made from a rectangular piece of cloth.

hai·kai (hī′kī), *n.* a form of Japanese verse, originated in 17th-century Japan.

hai·ku (hī′kōo), *n.* a Japanese poem consisting of 17 syllables.

hajj (haj), *n., pl.* **hajj·es.** a pilgrimage to Mecca made at least once by pious Muslims. Also **hadj.**

haj·ji (haj′ē), *n., pl.* **haj·jis. 1.** a Muslim who has made the pilgrimage to Mecca. **2.** an Eastern Christian who has visited the Holy Sepulcher in Jerusalem. Also **hadji, haji.**

ha·la·tion (hālā′sHən), *n.* a bright, halo-like patch or blur on a developed photograph, caused by light reflected through the surface emulsion from the surface of the backing.

ha·la·vah (häləvä′), *n.* See **halvah.**

hal·cy·on (hal′sēən), *n.* **1.** a mythical bird said to breed at the winter solstice in a nest floating on the sea and to calm the waves; identified with the kingfisher. —*adj.* **2.** calm; peaceful; happy; prosperous.

half·life (haf′līf), *n.*, *pl.* **half-lives.** (in physics) the time in which one half the atoms in a quantity of radioactive substance disintegrate. Also **half-life period.**

half title, a page in a book bearing the title only, usually placed before the title page. Also **bastard title.**

half·tone (haf′tōn′), *n.* **1.** a process of photoengraving in which tone gradations are reproduced in the form of minute dots by means of a screen placed before the film. **2.** the metal plate thus prepared for letterpress reproduction. **3.** the print obtained from the plate.

half·track (haf′trak′), *n.* a motor vehicle, particularly for military use, equipped with caterpillar treads on the rear driving wheels.

hal·i·dom (hal′idəm), *n.* a holy place or sanctuary, as a chapel or church. Also **hal′i·dome.**

hal·i·to·sis (halitō′sis), *n.* foul, offensive breath.

hal·lu·cin·o·gen (həloo′sənəjen), *n.* a substance, as a drug, that causes hallucinations or fantasies.

hal·lu·ci·no·sis (həloosənō′sis), *n.* mental illness, accompanied by and caused by hallucinations.

hal·lux (hal′əks), *n.*, *pl.* **hal·lu·ces** (hal′yəsēz). the great toe or the innermost digit of the hind foot of a mammal.

hal·o·phile (hal′əfīl), *n.* a plant or animal favoring an alkaline or salty environment.

hal·o·phyte (hal′əfīt), *n.* a plant favoring alkaline or salty soil.

hal·vah (hälvä′), *n.* a sweet, sticky, gelatinous form of candy made of ground sesame seed, honey, and flavoring. Also **halava, halva.**

ha·mate (hā′māt), *adj.* **1.** equipped with hooks; hook-like. —*n.* **2.** Also **unciform.** the anatomical name for a bone of the carpus with a hook-like process.

ham·mer·toe (ham′ərtō), *n.* a toe permanently deformed by being bent downward.

ham·u·lus (ham′yələs), *n.*, *pl.* **ham·u·li** (ham′yəlī). a small hook-like projection as on a bone, bristle, or feather.

han·a·per (han′əpər), *n.* a wicker case or basket formerly used to carry documents.

hand·sel (han′səl), *n.* **1.** a gift or present, bringing good luck, as at the beginning of a new year or a new enterprise. —*v.* **2.** to give a handsel to. Also **han′sel.**

hanging valley, a valley, the lower end of which opens high above a beach or stretch of coast, usually as a result of erosion.

Han·sard (han′sərd), *n.* the published reports of the debates and proceedings of the two Houses of the British Parliament at Westminster.

Han·sen's disease (han′sənz), leprosy, so named after the Norwegian physician who discovered the causative bacterium.

ha·pax le·go·me·non (hap′aks ligom′ənon), *pl.* **hap·ax le·go·me·na** (hap′aks ligom′ənə), *Greek.* a word or group of words of which there is only one recorded use.

hap·less (hap′lis), *adj.* unfortunate; unlucky.

hap·log·ra·phy (haplog′rəfē), *n.* a copying or printing error by which a letter or group of letters which should be repeated are omitted, as *dention* for *dentition.*

hap·loid (hap′loid), *adj.* (in biology) single.

hap·lol·o·gy (haplol′əjē), *n.* the contraction of a word by elimination of a syllable, as *symbology* for *symbolology.*

hap·lo·pi·a (haplō′pēə), *n.* normal vision. See also **diplopia.**

hap·tics (hap′tiks), *n.* a branch of psychology dealing with the sense of touch.

hap·tom·e·ter (haptom′itər), *n.* a machine that measures the sense of touch.

ha·ra·ki·ri (här′əkēr′ē), *n.* a form of suicide, by slitting open the abdomen, practised in Japan, usually after signal disgrace; seppuku. Also **har′i-kar′i**.

hard·fist·ed (härd′fis′tid), *adj.* stingy; miserly; ruthless.

hard goods, non-perishable merchandise, as furniture, automobiles, and household appliances. See also **soft goods.**

hard-hat (härd′hat′), *n.* a worker in a hazardous location who wears a protective helmet.

hard·pan (härd′pan), *n.* hard subsoil, as of clay, gravel, or sand; any firm unbroken ground.

hard sauce, a creamlike blend of butter and sugar, often flavored, esp. with brandy, whiskey, etc., used for pies and puddings.

hard sell, a direct, high-pressure method of advertising or selling. See also **soft sell.**

hard·tack (härd′tak), *n.* a hard biscuit, once a part of navy or army rations. Also **ship biscuit.**

harl (härl), *n.* a fiber of flax or hemp.

har·le·quin (här′ləkwin), *n.* the leading male actor in old Italian comedy, traditionally masked and wearing parti-colored tights, carrying a magic wand, and given to playing comic tricks.

har·le·quin·ade (här′ləkwinād′), *n.* a play or pantomime in which harlequin plays the lead; horseplay.

har·le·quin·esque (här′ləkwinesk′), *adj.* in the guise or manner of a harlequin.

har·mon·ic pro·gres·sion, a series of numbers whose reciprocals are in arithmetic progression as $1, \frac{1}{2}, \frac{1}{3}, \frac{1}{4}, \frac{1}{5}$. See also **arithmetic progression, geometric progression.**

har·mo·ni·um (härmō′nēəm), *n.* a small keyboard instrument, similar to an organ, the sounds of which are produced by metal reeds set into vibration by air from a foot-operated bellows.

har·ri·dan (har′idn), *n.* a bad-tempered, disreputable old woman; a hag.

har·ri·er (har′ēər), *n.* one of a breed of hound, smaller than a foxhound, used for hunting, esp. hares.

ha·sen·pfef·fer, has·sen·pfef·fer (hä′sənfefər), *n.* a stew of pickled rabbit meat, usually served with sour cream.

hash·ish (hasн′ēsн), *n.* a narcotic or intoxicant, prepared from cannabis, and drunk, smoked, or chewed. Also **hash′eesh.**

Ha·sid (hä′sid), *n., pl.* **Ha·sid·im** (häsid′im), a member of an orthodox Jewish sect, originating in 18th-century Poland, characterized by its blend of mysticism and prayer with joyful singing and dancing. Also **Chasid. —Has′i·dism,** *n.*

has·let (has′lit), *n.* the edible entrails, heart, liver, etc., of an animal, esp. the pig, formerly roasted on a spit.

has·lock (has′lok), *n.* a coarse type of wool.

has·tate (has′tāt), *adj.* shaped like a spearhead.

hate·mon·ger (hāt′muNGgər), *n.* someone who stirs up hatred or prejudice.

haus·tel·late (hôstel′it), *adj.* adapted for sucking, as the mouth parts of certain crustaceans and insects.

haus·tel·lum (hôstel′əm), *n., pl.* **haus·tel·la** (hôstel′ə). the sucking organ or proboscis of some crustaceans and insects.

haute cou·ture (ōt kootyr′), *French.* high fashion, applied particularly to fashionable dressmaking and to the establishments engaged in it.

haute cui·sine (ōt kwēzēn′), *French.* the art of fine cooking and food preparation.

hau·teur (hōtur′), *n.* a lofty or haughty manner and bearing.

haut monde (ō mônd′), *French.* high society. See also **beau monde.**

have·lock (hav′lok), *n.* a cloth covering for a cap, with a flap to protect the back of the neck from the sun.

heart·burn (härt′burn), *n.* an uncomfortable burning sensation in the stomach caused by excess acidity. Also **cardialgia.**

heart murmur. See **murmur.**

heat exchanger, an engineering device for cooling and heating fluids simultaneously, or for transferring the heat of one substance to another, as in reclaiming exhaust gases.

heavy water, water in which deuterium has replaced hydrogen atoms, chiefly used to control nuclear reaction in the furnaces of atomic power plants.

heav·y·weight (hev′ēwāt′), *n.* a boxer of any weight fighting in the heaviest class.

heb·do·mad (heb′dəmad), *n.* **1.** the number seven, or group of seven. **2.** a week.

heb·dom·a·dal (hebdom′ədl), *adj.* occurring, meeting, or being published every week.

he·be·phre·nia (hēbəfrē′nēə), *n.* a form of split-personality disorder, allied to puberty, marked by hallucinations and severe emotional disturbance. —**he·be·phren·ic** (hēbəfren′-ik), *adj.*

heb·e·tate (heb′itāt), *v.* **1.** to make or become dull or inert. —*adj.* **2.** (of a plant part) having a blunt or soft point.

he·be·tic (hibet′ik), *adj.* characteristic of or pertaining to puberty.

heb·e·tude (heb′itood), *n.* state of being dull, inert, and listless.

hec·a·tomb (hek′ətōm), *n.* a mass slaughter or sacrifice.

hec·to·li·ter, hek·to·li·ter (hek′təlē′-tər), *n.* a metric measure of capacity, equivalent to 100 liters or 26.418 U.S. gallons.

hec·to·me·ter, hek·to·me·ter (hek′-təmē′tər), *n.* a metric measurement of length, equaling 100 meters or 328.089 feet.

hec·to·stere, hek·to·stere (hek′tə-stēr), *n.* a metric measurement of capacity, equal to 100 steres.

he·don·ics (hēdon′iks), *n.* (in psychology) the study of pleasurable and nonpleasurable states of mind. —**he·don′ic,** *adj.*

he·don·ism (hē′dənizəm), *n.* **1.** ethical theory or doctrine that the pursuit of pleasure is the highest good. **2.** devotion to pleasure or happiness as a way of life. —**he′don·ist,** *n.*

he·gem·o·ny (hijem′ənē, heg′əmō-nē), *n.* political or economic leadership or dominance by one state over others in a confederacy.

he·gi·ra, he·ji·ra (hijī′rə), *n.* a flight or escape from one situation or place to a better one, esp. (**H-**) the flight of Mohammed from Mecca to Medina in A.D. 622, regarded as the beginning of the Mohammedan era. Also **hijra.**

Hei·li·gen·schein (hī′ligənsHīn), *n.,* *pl.* **Hei·li·gen·scheine** (hī′ligənsHī-nə), *German.* a halo; specifically, the circle of light around the shadow cast on wet grass in sunlight by someone's head.

hei·nous (hā′nəs), *adj.* wicked; atrocious; abominable.

heir apparent, *pl.* **heirs apparent.** one who is in line to succeed to a property or title and whose rights are unassailable.

heir presumptive, *pl.* **heirs presumptive.** one who is in line to succeed to a property or title, unless a closer direct heir is subsequently born.

hek·to·li·ter (hek′təlē′tər), *n.* See **hectoliter.**

hek·to·me·ter (hek′təmē′tər), *n.* See **hectometer.**

hek·to·stere (hek′təstēr), *n.* See **hectostere.**

he·li·a·cal (hilī′əkəl), *adj.* near or pertaining to the sun, esp. applied to the appearance of a visible star before sunrise or its disappearance after sunset. Also **he′li·ac.**

hel·i·cal (hel′ikəl), *adj.* of or in the form of a helix.

he·liced (hē′list), *adj.* adorned or decorated with spirals.

hel·i·cline (hel′əklīn), *n.* a curving ramp.

hel·i·co·graph (hel′əkōgraf), *n.* an instrument for drawing spirals.

hel·i·coid (hel′əkoid), *adj.* coiled or shaped like a spiral.

he·li·o·cen·tric (hē′lēōsen′trik), *adj.* **1.** having or depicting the sun as central. **2.** seen or measured as from the center of the sun.

he·li·o·gram (hē′lēəgram), *n.* a message signaled by a heliograph.

he·li·o·graph (hē′lēəgraf), *n.* **1.** an instrument for signaling messages by reflecting sunlight intermittently through a mirror by means of a shutter. **2.** an apparatus for photographing the sun. **3.** an instrument for measuring the intensity of the sun's rays. —*v.* **4.** to signal by heliograph. —**he·li·og′ra·phy,** *n.*

he·li·ol·a·try (hē′lēol′ətrē), *n.* sun worship.

he·li·o·scope (hē′lēəskōp), *n.* a telescope for observing the sun, with a device to protect the eyes.

he·li·o·stat (hē′lēəstat), *n.* an apparatus comprising a mirror turned by clockwork, for reflecting the light of the sun in a certain direction.

he·li·o·tax·is (hē′lēōtak′sis), *n.* movement of an organism in relation to the light of the sun.

he·li·o·ther·a·py (hē′lēōther′əpē), *n.* treatment of sickness by sunlight.

he·li·o·trope (hē′lēətrōp), *n.* **1.** any plant whose flowers turn to face the sun. **2.** pale reddish lavender. **3.** a surveyor's construction consisting of mirrors that focus sunlight from a distance to a single point for observation and measurement.

he·li·o·trop·ic (hē′lēətrop′ik), *adj.* (of a plant) growing toward the sun or light. —**he·li·ot′ro·pism,** *n.*

he·lix (hē′liks), *n.*, *pl.* **hel·i·ces** (hel′isēz), **he·lix·es.** a spiral.

hel·minth (hel′minth), *n.* a worm, esp. a parasitic one.

hel·min·thi·a·sis (hel′minthī′əsis), *n.* a disease caused by the presence of worms in the body.

hel·min·thic (helmin′thik), *adj.* pertaining to, or caused by, parasitic intestinal worms.

hel·min·thoid (helmin′thoid), *adj.* resembling a helminth; wormlike.

hel·min·thol·o·gy (hel′minthol′əjē), *n.* the medical or scientific study of worms, esp. helminths.

hel·ot (hel′ət), *n.* a serf or slave.

hel·ot·ism (hel′ətizəm), *n.* condition or system of being a helot or serf.

hel·ot·ry (hel′ətrē), *n.* state of serfdom or slavery.

helve (helv), *n.* the handle of an ax, chisel, hammer, or similar tool.

he·ma·chrome, hae·ma·chrome (hē′məkrōm), *n.* the blood's red coloring matter.

he·mag·glu·ti·nate, hae·mag·glu·ti·nate (hēməgloo′tənāt), *v.* (in immunology) to gather in clumps. —**he·mag·glu·ti·na′tion, hae·mag·glu·ti·na′tion,** *n.*

he·ma·gogue (hē′məgog), *adj.* encouraging a flow of blood. Also **he·ma·gog·ic** (hēməgoj′ik).

he·mal, hae·mal (hē′məl), *adj.* belonging or pertaining to the blood or blood system. Also **hem′a·tal.**

he·ma·nal·y·sis (hēmənal′isis), *n.* analysis of the blood, particularly its chemical constituents.

hem·a·ther·mal (heməthur′məl), *adj.* warm-blooded.

he·mat·ic, hae·mat·ic (həmat′ik), *adj.* of or containing blood.

hem·a·to·blast, haem·a·to·blast (hem′ətōblast′), *n.* an immature cell, smaller than the corpuscles, found in the blood.

hem·a·to·cele, haem·a·to·cele (hem′ətōsēl′), *n.* a tumor or hemorrhage containing blood.

hem·a·to·crit (hem′ətōkrit), *n.* a machine separating blood cells from plasma by centrifugal force.

hem·a·toc·ry·al, haem·a·toc·ry·al (hemətok′rēəl), *adj.* cold-blooded. See also **hemathermal, homoiothermal.**

hem·a·to·cyst, haem·a·to·cyst (hem′ətōsist′), *n.* a cyst containing blood.

hem·a·to·cyte, haem·a·to·cyte (hem′ətōsīt′), *n.* See **hemocyte.**

hem·a·to·gen·e·sis, haem·a·to·gen·e·sis (hem′ətōjen′isis), *n.* the formation of blood.

hem·a·tog·e·nous, haem·a·tog·e·nous (hemətoj′ənəs), *adj.* producing blood, originating in the blood, or borne by the blood.

hem·a·tol·ogy, haem·a·tol·o·gy (hemətol′əjē), *n.* the branch of biology or medicine dealing with the blood and its organs.

hem·a·to·ma, haem·a·to·ma (hemətō′mə), *n.* a tumor or swelling filled with blood.

hem·a·to·phyte, haem·a·to·phyte (hem′ətōfīt′), *n.* a plant parasite that lives in the blood. See also **hematocoon.**

hem·a·to·poi·e·sis, haem·a·to·poi·e·sis (hem′ətōpoiē′sis), *n.* the production of blood.

hem·a·to·sis, haem·a·to·sis (hemətō′sis), *n.* 1. the production of blood. 2. the oxygenation of blood in the lungs.

hem·a·to·thermal, haem·a·to·ther·mal (hem′ətōthur′məl), *adj.* warm-blooded. Also **hemathermal.**

hem·a·to·zo·on, haem·a·to·zo·on (hemətəzō′ən), *n., pl.* **hem·a·to·zo·a** (hemətəzō′ə). an animal parasite living in the blood. See also **hematophyte.**

he·ma·tu·ri·a, hae·ma·tu·ri·a (hēmətōŏr′ēə), *n.* the presence of blood in the urine.

hem·er·a·lo·pi·a (hemərəlō′pēə), *n.* an eye condition in which sight is poor or absent in daylight, but adequate or normal at night or by artificial light; day blindness. See also **nyctalopia.**

hem·i·al·gi·a (hem′ēal′jēə), *n.* severe pain confined to only one side of the head or body.

hem·i·a·nop·si·a (hem′ēanop′sēə), *n.* a condition of half or partial blindness, affecting one or both eyes.

hem·i·cra·ni·a (hemikrā′nēə), *n.* pain confined to one side of the head; migraine.

hem·i·dem·i·sem·i·qua·ver (hem′ēdem′esem′ēkwā′vər), *n.* a musical note having one-eighth the length of a quaver; the sixty-fourth part of a semibreve.

hem·i·me·tab·o·lous (hem′ēmitab′ələs), *adj.* (of an insect) incompletely metamorphosing.

hem·i·pa·re·sis (hem′ēpərē′sis), *n.* mild paralysis on one side of the body.

hem·i·ple·gi·a (hemiplē′jēə), *n.* paralysis on one side of the face or body.

he·mo·cyte, hae·mo·cyte (hē′məsīt), *n.* a blood cell. Also **hematocyte.**

he·mo·cy·tom·e·ter (hē′mōsītom′itər), *n.* an instrument for counting the number of blood cells in a sample.

he·mo·di·a (himō′dēə), *n.* extreme sensitivity of the teeth.

he·mo·dy·nam·ics, hae·mo·dy·nam·ics (hē′mədīnam′iks), *n.* the branch of science studying the dynamics of blood circulation.

he·mo·flag·el·late (hēməflaj′əlāt), *n.* a parasitic flagellate in the blood.

he·mo·glo·bin, hae·mo·glo·bin (hē′məglō′bin), *n.* the coloring substance of the red blood corpuscles, carrying oxygen to the tissues, present also in reduced form in the blood of the veins, and mixed with oxygen, in that of the arteries.

he·moid, hae·moid (hē′moid), *adj.* blood-like.

he·mol·y·sis, hae·mol·y·sis (himol′isis), *n.* the dissolution of red blood cells by the release of hemoglobin. —**he·mo·ly·tic** (hēməlit′ik), *adj.*

he·mo·phile (hē′məfīl), *n.* a hemophiliac.

he·mo·phil·i·a, hae·mo·phil·i·a (hēməfil′ēə), *n.* an abnormal blood condition marked by severe bleeding and hemorrhaging from slight wounds and contusions due to improper clotting, and inherited by males only through the mother.

he·mo·phil·i·ac, hae·mo·phil·i·ac (hēməfil′ēak), *n.* a sufferer from hemophilia.

he·mo·phil·ic, hae·mo·phil·ic (hēməfil′ik), *adj.* 1. affected by or pertaining to hemophilia. 2. (of bacteria) developed in blood or in a blood culture.

he·mo·pho·bi·a, hae·mo·pho·bi·a (hēməfō′bēə), *n.* an abnormal dread of blood.

he·mop·ty·sis, hae·mop·ty·sis (himop′tisis), *n.* the spitting out of blood or of blood-flecked mucus.

he·mos·ta·sis, hae·mos·ta·sis (himos′təsis), *n.* 1. the arrest of bleeding or hemorrhage. **2.** the cutting off of circulation of the blood in a part.

he·mo·stat, hae·mo·stat (hē′məstat), *n.* an instrument to stop bleeding in order to arrest hemorrhage.

he·mo·stat·ic, hae·mo·stat·ic (hēməstat′ik), *adj.* arresting bleeding; styptic.

he·mo·ther·a·py, hae·mo·ther·a·py (hēmə*ther*′əpē), *n.* treatment of disease by means of blood or plasma transfusion.

he·mo·tho·rax, hae·mo·tho·rax (hēmə*thô*r′aks), *n.* a condition characterized by presence of blood in the pleural cavity.

hen·dec·a·he·dron (hendek′əhē′drən), *n.,* *pl.* **hen·dec·a·he·drons, hen·dec·a·he·dra** (hendek′əhē′drə). a three-dimensional solid figure with eleven faces.

hen·dec·a·syl·lab·ic (hendek′əsilab′ik), *adj.* (of a line of verse) having eleven syllables.

hen·e·quen (hen′əkin), *n.* the sisal fiber of a species of agave, used for making hemp.

hen·o·the·ism (hen′ə*th*ēizm), *n.* a system of religion in which any one of several gods is worshiped.

hen·ry (hen′rē), *n.,* *pl.* **hen·ries, hen·rys.** the unit of inductance in which the electromotive force of one volt is produced by a current varying at one ampere per second.

he·or·tol·o·gy (hē′ôrtol′əjē), *n.* a branch of study related to religious festivals.

hep·a·rin (hep′ərin), *n.* an anticoagulant used in the treatment of thrombosis, occurring naturally in human tissues and made commercially from the lungs and liver of domestic food animals.

hep·a·rin·ize (hep′ərənīz), *v.* to use heparin to prevent blood clotting.

hep·a·ta·tro·phi·a (hepətətrō′fēə), *n.* a wasting away of the liver.

he·pat·ic (hipat′ik), *adj.* **1.** relating to, or acting upon, the liver. **2.** liver-colored, dark brownish-red.

hep·a·ti·tis (hepətī′tis), *n.* inflammation of the liver.

hep·a·tos·co·py (hepətos′kəpē), *n.* divination by examining the livers of slaughtered animals.

hep·tam·er·ous (heptam′ərəs), *adj.* consisting of seven parts.

hep·tar·chy (hep′tärkē), *n.* **1.** government by seven rulers. **2.** seven kingdoms, each with a separate ruler.

hep·ta·syl·la·ble (hep′təsil′əbəl), *n.* a line of verse, or a word, containing seven syllables.

her·ba·ceous (hurbā′sHəs), *adj.* **1.** herb-like. **2.** (of a plant) with a soft stem.

her·bage (ur′bij), *n.* herbaceous vegetation, as grass.

her·ba·list (hur′bəlist), *n.* a collector of or dealer in herbs, formerly botanical, now chiefly medicinal.

her·bar·i·um (hurber′ēəm), *n.,* *pl.* **her·bar·i·ums, her·bar·i·a** (hurber′ēə). a systematically arranged collection of dried plants.

herb·i·cide (urb′isīd), *n.* a chemical preparation for killing plants, particularly weeds.

her·biv·ore (hur′bəvōr), *n.* a grass- or plant-eating mammal, esp. a hoofed mammal. —**her·biv·o·rous** (hurbiv′ərəs), *adj.*

he·re·si·arch (hərē′zēärk), *n.* a founder or leader of a heretical group.

he·re·si·mach (hərē′zəmak), *n.* one engaged in combating heresy.

he·re·si·og·ra·phy (hərē′zēog′rəfē), *n.* a written work on heresy.

he·re·si·ol·o·gist (hərē′zēol′əjist), *n.* one who studies or writes about heresy.

he·re·si·ol·o·gy (hərē′zēol′əjē), *n.* the study of heresy.

her·e·sy (her′isē), *n.* a religious doctrine or belief opposed to that of the orthodox system. —**her·e·tic** (her′itik), *n.* —**he·ret·i·cal** (həret′ikəl), *adj.*

her·i·tage (her′itij), *n.* anything to which a person succeeds by right of birth.

herl (hurl), *n.* a barb or fiber of a feather, esp. as used in fly-fishing.

her·maph·ro·dite (hurmaf′rədīt), *n.* a human being or animal with both

hermaphroditism

male and female sex organs; gynandromorph.

her·maph·ro·dit·ism (hurmaf′rədī-tizm), *n.* the condition of being a hermaphrodite; gynandry. Also **her·maph′ro·dism.**

her·me·neu·tic (hurmənoo′tik), *adj.* pertaining to explanation or interpretation. Also **her·me·neu′ti·cal.**

her·me·neu·tics (hurmənoo′tiks), *n.* the science of interpretation, esp. of the Bible.

her·ni·o·plas·ty (hur′nēəplas′tē), *n.* an operation to treat a hernia.

her·ni·or·rha·phy (hur′nēôr′əfē), *n.* the treatment of a hernia by suturing.

her·ni·ot·o·my (hur′nēot′əmē), *n.* the treatment of a hernia by incision. Also **celotomy, kelotomy.**

her·pes fa·ci·a·lis (hur′pēz fā′sнēā′-lis). a skin inflammation of the face, often affecting the lips. Also **her′pes la·bi·a′lis** (lā′bēā′lis).

herpes sim·plex (sim′pleks), a skin infection marked by the appearance of clusters of vesicles.

herpes zos·ter (zos′tər), an infection affecting the posterior roots of the nerves, commonly called shingles.

her·pe·tol·o·gy (hur′pitol′əjē), *n.* a branch of science dealing with reptiles.

Hes·pe·ri·an (hespēr′ēən), *adj.* western; pertaining to the west.

hes·per·id·i·um (hespərid′ēəm), *n.*, *pl.* **hes·per·id·i·a** (hespərid′ēə). the fruit of a citrus plant, as an orange or lemon.

Hes·per·us (hes′pəris), *n.* the evening star; Venus. Also **Hes′per.**

he·tae·ra, he·tai·ra (hitēr′ə), *n.*, *pl.* **he·tae·rae, he·tai·rai** (hitēr′ē). a courtesan; a woman who uses her beauty and charm to further her social ambitions.

he·tae·rism, he·tai·rism (hətēr′-izm), *n.* a social system in which women are regarded as communal property.

het·er·o·cer·cal (hetərəsur′kəl), *adj.* (of fish) having an unevenly divided tail. See also **homocercal.**

het·er·o·chro·mat·ic (het′ərəkrō-mat′ik), *adj.* having more than one color. See also **homochromatic.**

het·er·o·chro·mous (hetərəkrō′-məs), *adj.* consisting of different colors.

het·er·och·tho·nous (hetərok′thə-nəs), *adj.* not native; foreign. See also **autochthonous.**

het·er·o·clite (het′ərəklīt), *adj.* irregular; abnormal.

het·er·o·dox (het′ərədoks), *adj.* with opinions or doctrines, chiefly religious, not in accordance with established, orthodox belief. —**het′er·o·dox·y,** *n.*

het·er·o·ge·ne·ous (hetərəjē′nēəs), *adj.* different in kind; made up of different kinds or parts. See also **homogeneous.**

het·er·og·ra·phy (hetərog′əfē), *n.* **1.** different spelling from that in common use. **2.** the use of a letter or group of letters to represent different sounds, as the *c* in *comb* and *city.*

het·er·og·y·nous (hetəroj′ənəs), *adj.* having two different forms of female, one sexual, the other asexual.

het·er·o·ki·ne·sia (het′ərōkinē′zнə), *n.* (in medicine) the performance of movements opposite to those instructed.

het·er·ol·o·gy (hetərol′əjē), *n.* **1.** abnormality, structural departure from the normal. **2.** the failure of apparently similar organs to correspond, owing to different origins of constituent parts.

het·er·om·er·ous (hetərom′ərəs), *adj.* having parts which differ in quality or quantity.

het·er·o·mor·phic (hetərəmôr′fik), *adj.* **1.** of dissimilar shape or form; existing in different forms. **2.** undergoing incomplete metamorphosis, as in certain insects.

het·er·on·o·mous (hetəron′əməs), *adj.* **1.** subject to different laws. **2.** (in biology) having different laws of growth.

het·er·on·o·my (hetəron′əmē), *n.* the state of subjection to another's rule or domination.

het·er·o·nym (het′ərənim), *n.* a word

spelled like another, but with an alternative sound and meaning, as *lead* (to guide) and *lead* (a metal). See also **homograph, homonym, homophone.**

het·er·on·y·mous (hetəron′əməs), *adj.* **1.** pertaining to, or having the nature of, a heteronym. **2.** correlated, but having different names, as *husband* and *wife.*

het·er·o·pho·ri·a (hetərəfôr′ēə), *n.* latent strabismus of either or both eyes.

het·er·op·tics (hetərop′tiks), *n.* incorrect or distorted vision.

het·er·o·sex·u·al (hetərəsek′shōōəl), *adj.* **1.** relating to the opposite sex or both sexes. **2.** pertaining to, or displaying heterosexuality. —*n.* **3.** a heterosexual individual.

het·er·o·sex·u·al·i·ty (het′ərəsek-shōōal′itē), *n.* sexual attraction toward the opposite sex.

het·er·o·sis (hetərō′sis), *n.* (in biology) the tendency of hybrids to surpass their parents in size, growth, or yield.

het·er·o·tax·is (hetərətak′sis), *n.* an abnormal arrangement of parts or organs. —**het·er·o·tac′tic,** *adj.*

het·er·o·to·pi·a (hetərətō′pēə), *n.* misplacement of an organ, as the formation of tissue where not normally present. Also **het·er·ot′o·py.**

het·er·o·troph (het′ərətrof), *n.* a microorganism whose energy is derived from a complex organic compound, such as glucose. —**het·er·o·troph·ic** (hetərətrō′fik). See also **autotrophe.**

het·er·o·zy·go·sis (het′ərəzīgō′sis), *n.* the condition of being a heterozygote.

het·er·o·zy·gote (hetərəzī′gōt), *n.* a zygote with dissimilar pairs of genes for an inherited character. See also **homozygote.** —**het·er·o·zy′gous,** *adj.*

het·man (het′mən), *n., pl.* **het·mans.** a Cossack leader or commander.

het·man·ate (het′mənāt), *n.* the domain or authority of a hetman. Also **het′man·ship.**

heu·ris·tic (hyōōris′tik), *adj.* **1.** serving to find out. **2.** stimulating a pupil to find out things for himself.

hex·ad (hek′sad), *n.* **1.** six. **2.** a group of six.

hex·a·em·er·on (heksəem′əron), *n.* **1.** the six days of the Creation. **2.** a written work on this subject. Also **hex·a·hem·er·on** (heksəhem′əron), **hex·am′er·on.**

hex·a·gram (hek′səgram), *n.* a six-pointed figure, made up of two overlapping equilateral triangles arranged so that the sides of each are mutually parallel to those of the other.

hex·a·he·dron (heksəhē′dron), *n., pl.* **hex·a·he·drons, hex·a·he·dra.** a six-faced three-dimensional figure.

hex·am·er·ous (heksam′ərəs), *adj.* having six parts.

hex·an·gu·lar (heksaNG′gyələr), *adj.* having six angles.

hex·a·par·tite (heksəpär′tīt), *adj.* divided into six parts.

hex·a·pod (hek′səpod), *n.* **1.** a member of the class *Insecta*; an insect. —*adj.* **2.** having six feet.

hex·ar·chy (hek′särkē), *n.* a group of six states, each with its own ruler.

hex·a·syl·la·ble (hek′səsil′əbəl), *n.* a line of verse or word containing six syllables. —**hex·a·syl·lab·ic** (hek′səsilab′ik), *adj.*

Hex·a·teuch (hek′sətōōk), *n.* the first six books of the Old Testament.

hi·a·tus (hīā′təs), *n., pl.* **hi·a·tus·es, hi·a·tus.** a break or gap in a written work, series, or course of action.

hi·ber·nac·u·lum (hībərnak′jələm), *n., pl.* **hi·ber·nac·u·la** (hībərnak′jələ). **1.** a protective cover for winter. **2.** Also **hi·ber·na·cle** (hī′bərnakəl). winter quarters, esp. of a hibernating animal.

hi·ber·nal (hībur′nl), *adj.* pertaining to or appearing in winter.

hid·ro·poi·e·sis (hid′rōpoiē′sis), *n.* the production of perspiration.

hi·dro·sis (hidrō′sis), *n.* a condition in which excessive perspiration is secreted, as in sickness.

hi·e·mal (hī′əməl), *adj.* pertaining to winter; wintry.

hi·er·at·ic (hīərət'ik), *adj.* **1.** pertaining to priests or sacred things. **2.** pertaining to an ancient Egyptian form of writing abbreviated hieroglyphics, used by priests.

hi·er·oc·ra·cy (hīərok'rəsē), *n.* government or rule by priests.

hi·er·o·gram (hī'ərəgram), *n.* a sacred emblem or symbol.

hi·er·o·gram·mat (hīərəgram'it), *n.* a writer of sacred symbols. Also **hi·er·o·gram'mate.**

hi·er·ol·a·try (hīərol'ətrē), *n.* worship of saints or sacred things.

hi·er·ol·o·gy (hīərol'əjē), *n.* literature or study of sacred things.

hi·er·o·phant (hī'ərəfant), *n.* an interpreter of religious mysteries.

hi·er·ur·gy (hī'ərurjē), *n.* a holy act or religious observance.

hig·gler (hig'lər), *n.* a traveling dealer; peddler; huckster.

high·bind·er (hī'bīndər), *n.* a confidence trickster; swindler.

hij·ra (hij'rə), *n.* See **hegira.**

Hi·na·ya·na (hēnəyä'nə), *n.* one of the two main schools of Buddhism, in which the believer is expected to work out his own salvation. Also **Theravada.** See also **Mahaijana, Bodhisattva.**

hin·ny (hin'ē), *n.* the offspring of a female ass or donkey and a stallion.

hip·pi·at·rics (hip'ēat'riks), *n.* a branch of veterinary medicine specializing in horses.

hip·pie (hip'ē), *n.* a person who affects informal, unconventional attire and an individual hairstyle, and either uses or pretends to use psychedelic drugs or marijuana as an expression of nonconformist attitude toward the Establishment.

hip·po·cam·pus (hipəkam'pəs), *n.,* *pl.* **hip·po·cam·pi** (hipəkam'pī). **1.** a mythical sea monster having a tail of a dolphin and two forefeet. **2.** a fold, in cross-section resembling the profile of a sea horse, that forms part of the cerebral cortex and extends into a fissure of a cerebral hemisphere.

hip·pol·o·gy (hipol'əjē), *n.* the study of horses.

hip·poph·a·gist (hipof'əjist), *n.* an eater of horseflesh.

hip·po·phile (hip'əfīl), *n.* a lover of horses.

hir·cine (hur'sīn), *adj.* **1.** goat-like. **2.** lecherous; lustful.

hir·sute (hur'sōot), *adj.* shaggy; hairy.

hir·sut·ism (hur'sōotizm), *n.* extreme hairiness, esp. in women.

hir·tel·lous (hurtel'əs), *adj.* minutely hairy.

hi·ru·di·noid (hirōō'dənoid), *adj.* resembling or pertaining to a leech.

hi·run·dine (hirun'din), *adj.* resembling, or pertaining to, a swallow.

His·pa·nism (his'pənizm), *n.* a Latin American movement dedicated to the spread of Spanish culture and traditions.

his·pid (his'pid), *adj.* rough with stiff bristles or hairs.

his·pid·u·lous (hispij'ələs), *adj.* covered with tiny, stiff hairs.

his·ta·mine (his'təmēn), *n.* a substance found in all animal and plant cells, thought to be responsible for symptoms of certain allergic reactions as asthma, hay fever, hives, etc., causing capillary dilatation, reduction of blood pressure, and contraction of the uterus. Used in pharmacology for diagnosing gastric and circulatory functions. Also **his·ta·min** (his'təmin). See also **antihistamine.**

his·ti·o·cyte (his'tēəsīt), *n.* a large blood cell in connective tissue. Also **macrophage.**

his·to·gen·e·sis (histəjen'isis), *n.* the production and development of tissues.

his·toid (his'toid), *adj.* resembling tissue, esp. as of a tumor. Also **his·ti·oid** (his'tēoid).

his·tol·o·gy (histol'əjē), *n.* the scientific study of organic tissue. —**his·tol'o·gist,** *n.*

his·to·mor·phol·o·gy (his'tōmôrfol'-əjē), *n.* histology.

his·to·pa·thol·o·gy (his'tōpəthol'-əjē), *n.* the study and treatment of abnormal or diseased tissue.

his·to·phys·i·ol·o·gy (his'tōfiz'ēol'-

əjē), *n.* the physiological study of organic tissues.

his·to·ri·at·ed (histôr′ēātid), *adj.* decorated with figures of men or animals, as in an illuminated capital or border of a medieval manuscript.

his·tor·i·cism (histôr′isizm), *n.* the theory that all historical events are predetermined, and unaffected by human thought and action.

his·to·ric·i·ty (histəris′itē), *n.* authenticity substantiated by history.

his·to·ri·og·ra·phy (histôr′ēog′-rəfē), *n.* 1. written history considered as a body of material. 2. the techniques and procedures of historical scholarship. —**his·to·ri·og′ra·pher,** *n.*

his·to·tome (his′tətōm), *n.* an instrument for cutting very small sections of organic tissue for microscopic examination.

his·tot·o·my (histot′əmē), *n.* the cutting into minute sections of pieces of tissue for microscopic examination.

his·tri·on·ics (his′trēon′iks), *n.* 1. a stage representation. 2. exaggerated, insincere speech or behavior. —**his·tri·on′ic,** *adj.* —**his′tri·o·nism,** *n.*

hitch·y (hicH′ē), *adj.* moving in starts or jerks.

hives (hīvz), *n.* any of various forms of skin eruptions, as urticaria.

hoar·y (hôr′ē), *adj.* gray- or white-haired with age.

Hob·bism (hob′izm), *n.* the theories of the philosopher and political thinker Thomas Hobbes, esp. the belief in obedience to an absolute sovereign.

hob·ble·de·hoy (hob′əldēhoi′), *n.* an awkward, overgrown boy.

Hob·son-Job·son (hob′sənjob′sən), *n.* the modification of originally foreign words which are assimilated into already familiar sounds.

Hob·son's choice (hob′sənz), a course of action that offers no alternative. [after Thomas Hobson, 16th-17th century stable owner of Cambridge, who insisted on a client's taking the horse nearest to the door]

Ho Chi Minh Trail (hō′ CHē′ min′), a jungle supply route, passing through Laos and Cambodia, used by the North Vietnamese in support of the Vietcong during the Vietnam war.

hock (hok), *n.* any white Rhine wine.

Hodg·kin's disease (hoj′kinz), a disease marked by inflammation of the lymph glands and spleen.

ho·dom·e·ter (hōdom′itər), *n.* See **odometer.**

hoe·down (hō′doun′), *n.* a gathering where folk and square dances are performed to the accompaniment of hillbilly music.

ho·gan (hō′gôn), *n.* a Navaho Indian hut, made of earth, mud, and branches.

hog·back (hôg′bak′), *n.* a steeply sloped hill-ridge, somewhat in the shape of a hog's back, that resists erosion.

hogs·head (hôgz′hed′), *n.* 1. a large cask for liquids. 2. a liquid measure equivalent to 63 wine gallons.

hoi pol·loi (hoi′ pəloi′), the majority; the common people.

Hol·arc·tic (holärk′tik), *adj.* belonging or pertaining to the Nearctic and Palearctic regions.

hole-and-corner (hōl′ənkôr′nər), *adj.* 1. secret; underhand; furtive. 2. trivial; undistinguished. Also **hole′-in-cor′ner.**

ho·lism (hō′lizm), *n.* a philosophical theory that holds that natural phenomena are entities, more than a sum of different parts.

hol·lan·daise sauce (hol′əndāz), a sauce, esp. used with fish and vegetables made of egg yolks, butter, and seasoning.

Hol·ler·ith code (hol′ərith), a system in computer technology for coding data into punch cards, in which letters, numbers, etc., are expressed in code form in a pattern of horizontal lines and vertical columns.

hol·lus·chick (hol′əscHik′), *n., pl.* **hol·lus·chick·ie** (hol′əscHik′ē). a young male fur seal.

hol·o·caust (hol′əkôst), *n.* an immense or complete slaughter or destruction, esp. by fire.

hol·o·crine (hol′əkrin), *adj.* (of a

gland) producing secretion as a result of disintegrating cells.

ho·lo·gram (hol'əgram), *n.* a three-dimensional photographic image, obtained without a camera or lens, by using coherent radiation, as from a laser beam.

hol·o·graph (hol'əgraf), *n.* a document hand-written by the person in whose name it appears. —**hol·o·graph'ic, hol·o·graph'i·cal,** *adj.*

holographic will, a will entirely handwritten by the testator. See also **nuncupative will.**

hol·o·lith (hol'əlith), *n.* a piece of jewelry fashioned from a single stone.

hol·o·me·tab·o·lous (hol'əmitab'-ələs), *adj.* (of insects) undergoing incomplete metabolism.

hol·o·phrase (hol'əfrāz'), *n.* a phrase expressed in a single word, as an imperative command.

ho·loph·ra·sis (həlof'rəsis), *n., pl.* **ho·loph·ra·ses** (həlof'rəsēz). the use of a single word to express the ideas contained in a sentence or phrase. —**hol·o·phras·tic** (hol'əfras'tik), *adj.*

hol·o·phyt·ic (holəfit'ik), *adj.* (of plants) feeding by means of synthesis of inorganic substances.

hol·o·ser·i·ceous (holəsərisн'əs), *adj.* covered with small, silky hairs.

hol·o·type (hol'ətīp), *n.* the original type specimen used in defining a species.

hol·o·zo·ic (holəzō'ik), *adj.* feeding on solid food, as most animals.

ho·ly·stone (hō'lēstōn'), *n.* a soft sandstone for scouring decks of ships.

ho·ma·lo·graph·ic (hom'əlōgraf'ik), *adj.* See **homolographic.**

home economics, the art and study of homemaking, including cookery, child care, furnishing, and other domestic crafts.

ho·me·op·a·thy, ho·moe·op·a·thy (hō'mēop'əthē), *n.* the treatment of disease by administering minute doses of drugs normally producing symptoms like those of the disease itself. See also **allopathy.** —**ho·me·o·path'ic, ho·moe·o·path'ic,** *adj.* —**ho·me·op'a·thist,** *n.*

ho·me·o·pla·sia (hō'mēəplā'zнə), *n.* the formation of new, healthy tissue, similar to existing tissue.

ho·me·o·sta·sis (hō'mēəstā'sis), *n.* the tendency, esp. in higher animals, to maintain its physiological balance despite stimuli tending to disrupt it.

ho·me·o·ther·a·py (hō'mēəther'-əpē), *n.* the treatment of a disease by use of an agent similar to that causing the disease.

ho·me·o·therm (hō'mēəthurm'), *n.* See **homoiotherm.**

ho·me·o·therm·al (hō'mēəthur'-məl), *adj.* See **homoiothermal.**

hom·i·let·ic (homəlet'ik), *adj.* pertaining to sermons or homilies.

hom·i·let·ics (homəlet'iks), *n.* the art of preaching.

hom·i·ly (hom'əlē), *n.* a sermon or moral lecture.

hom·i·nid (hom'ənid), *n.* a member of the human family; man and his ancestors.

hom·i·nine (hom'ənīn), *adj.* resembling a man; human.

hom·i·noid (hom'ənoid), *n.* a member of the superfamily that includes the large apes and humans.

ho·mo·bront (hō'məbront), *n.* a line on a weather map linking points where simultaneous thunderstorm activity is recorded. Also **isobront.**

ho·mo·cen·tric (hōməsen'trik), *adj.* having the same center; diverging from or converging on a central point.

ho·mo·cer·cal (hōməsur'kəl), *adj.* (of fish) having a symmetrical, evenly divided tail. See also **heterocercal.**

ho·mo·chro·mat·ic (hō'məkrōmat'-ik), *adj.* of, or relating to one color. See also **heterochromatic.**

ho·mo·chrome (hō'məkrōm), *adj.* See **homochromatic.**

ho·moch·ro·mous (hōmok'rənəs), *adj.* being of one color, as a flower head.

ho·moe·op·a·thy (hō'mēop'əthē), *n.* See **homeopathy.**

ho·mo·ge·ne·i·ty (hōməjənē'itē), *n.* the state of being homogeneous; made up of like parts. Also **ho·mo·ge'ne·ous·ness.**

ho·mo·ge·ne·ous (hōməjē′nēəs), *adj.* similar, of the same kind or nature; composed of identical parts. See also **heterogeneous.**

ho·mo·gen·e·sis (hōməjen′isis), *n.* of reproduction in which the offspring is like the parent and develops in the same way. —**ho·mo·ge·net′ic,** *adj.*

ho·mog·e·nize (həmoj′ənīz), *v.* to make homogeneous; to form by mixing or blending unlike elements.

ho·mog·e·nous (həmoj′ənəs), *adj.* having the same structure, owing to a common descent or origin.

ho·mog·e·ny (həmoj′ənē), *n.* analogy in structure, because of a common descent or origin.

hom·o·graph (hom′əgraf), *n.* a word spelt but not necessarily sounded in the same way as another, and with a different meaning, as *tear* "to rip," and *tear* "to fill with tears; cry." See also **heteronym, homonym, homophone.**

ho·moi·o·therm (hōmoi′əthurm), *n.* a warm-blooded animal, with a relatively constant body temperature. Also **homeotherm, homotherm.**

ho·moi·o·ther·mal (hōmoi′əthur′məl), *adj.* warm-blooded; possessing a more or less constant body temperature regardless of environment. Also **homeothermal, homothermal.**

ho·mol·o·gate (həmol′əgāt), *v.* to condone; assent.

ho·mo·log·i·cal (hōməloj′ikəl), *adj.* having the same relative structure or condition; homologous.

ho·mol·o·gize (həmol′əjīz), *v.* to correspond; make homologous.

ho·mol·o·gous (həmol′əgəs), *adj.* corresponding as the several parts of a reptile and those of a bird; with a similar relationship, form, or position.

ho·mol·o·graph·ic (həmol′əgraf′ik), *adj.* showing parts with similar proportions. Also **homalographic.**

hom·o·logue (hom′əlôg), *n.* anything that is homologous.

ho·mol·o·gy (həmol′əjē), *n.* condition of being homologous; identity of relation.

ho·mo·mor·phism (hō′məmôr′fizm), *n.* the state of being correspondent or analogous in outward form but not in structure. —**ho·mo·mor′phic,** *adj.*

hom·o·nym (hom′ənim), *n.* a word sounding and spelt like another, but with a different meaning, as *bear* "carry," and *bear* "animal." See also **heteronym, homograph, homophone.** —**ho·mon·y·mous** (həmon′əməs), *adj.* —**ho·mon·y·my** (həmon′əmē), *n.*

hom·o·phone (hom′əfōn), *n.* a word that sounds, but is not necessarily spelt the same as another, and that has a different meaning, as *pair* and *pear.* See also **heteronym, homograph, homonym.**

hom·o·phon·ic (homəfon′ik), *adj.* having the same sound. Also **ho·moph·o·nous** (həmof′ənəs). —**ho·moph′o·ny,** *n.*

ho·mop·la·sy (həmop′ləsē), *n.* analogy of form or structure, because of a similar environment.

ho·mo·tax·is (hōmətak′sis), *n.* similarity of relative position, but not necessarily contemporaneous, as geological strata.

ho·mo·therm (hō′məthurm), *n.* See **homoiotherm.**

ho·mo·ther·mal (hōməthur′məl), *adj.* See **homoiothermal.**

ho·mo·thet·ic (hōməthet′ik), *adj.* similarly positioned.

ho·mo·type (hō′mətīp), *n.* a part or organ with a similar structure to that of another; homologue. —**ho·mo·typ·ic** (hōmətip′ik), **ho·mo·typ·i·cal** (hōmətip′ikəl), *adj.*

ho·mo·zy·gote (hōməzī′gōt), *n.* a zygote with the same pairs of genes for an inherited character. See also **heterozygote.** —**ho·mo·zy·go′sis,** *n.* —**ho·mo·zy′gous,** *adj.*

ho·mun·cu·lus (hōmuNG′kyələs), *n., pl.* **ho·mun·cu·li** (hōmuNG′kyəlī). a diminutive man; midget.

ho·ni soi qui mal y pense (ônē swa′ kē mal ē päNs′), *French.* may he be shamed who thinks evil of it; motto of the English Order of the Garter.

hon·or·and (on'ərand), *n*. the receiver of an honorary degree.

hon·or·if·ic (onərif'ik), *adj*. **1.** doing or conferring honor. —*n*. **2.** a grammatical form in a language used to convey respect.

hoo·doo (hoo'doo), *n*. **1.** bad luck. —*v*. **2.** to bring bad luck to.

hook·ah (hook'ə), *n*. a pipe, of oriental origin, with a long tube which draws the smoke through scented water. Also **hook'a.**

hoot·en·an·ny (hoo'tənan'ē), *n*. an informal gathering at which folk singing and, sometimes, dancing take place.

ho·ra (hôr'ə), *n*. a traditional round dance, performed in Rumania and Israel.

ho·ral (hôr'əl), *adj*. pertaining to an hour or hours; hourly.

hor·me (hôr'mē), *n*. an impulsive effort, directed toward a fixed goal. —**hor'mic,** *adj*.

hormic theory, a theory that all action and behavior, conscious or unconscious, have a purpose or a specific goal.

hor·mone (hôr'mōn), *n*. a substance secreted by the endocrine glands that stimulates the functions of certain vital organs and tissues.

horn·book (hôrn'book'), *n*. a primer; a book of the alphabet or early reader.

hor·ni·to (hôrnē'tō), *n*. a low volcanic mound that gives out smoke and vapor.

hor·o·lo·gi·um (hôrəlō'jēəm), *n*., *pl*. **hor·o·lo·gi·a** (hôrəlō'jēə). a clock tower.

ho·rol·o·gy (hôrol'əjē), *n*. the science of measuring time or of making clocks and watches. —**hor·o·log'ic,** *adj*. —**ho·rol'o·gist,** *n*.

hor·o·scope (hor'əskōp), *n*. a chart showing the position of the planets in relation to the signs of the zodiac, used to predict fortunes and future events. —**hor·o·scop·ic** (horəskop'-ik), *adj*. —**hor·os·co·py** (həros'-kəpē), *n*.

hor·o·tel·ic (hôrətel'ik), *adj*. noting a rate of evolution normal for certain plants and animals. See also **bradytelic, tachytelic.**

hor·rent (hôrənt), *adj*. standing up like bristles; bristly.

hor·rip·i·late (hôrip'əlāt), *v*. to produce goose flesh; strike cold with fear. —**hor·rip·i·la'tion,** *n*.

hors d'oeu·vre (ôr durv'), *pl*. **hors d'oeu·vre, hors d'oeu·vres** (ôr durv'). a light savory dish served as an appetizer; small appetizing delicacies served on toast, etc., with alcoholic drinks.

horse latitudes, the zones of high barometric pressure, with calms and light winds, lying about 30°N and 30°S and forming the edges of the trade-wind belt.

horst (hôrst), *n*. a part of the earth's surface that has been forced upward in relation to adjoining portions. See also **graben.**

hor·ta·tive (hôr'tətiv), *adj*. encouraging; exhorting; giving advice; hortatory; urging.

hor·ta·to·ry (hôr'tətôr'ē), *adj*. urging; hortative.

hor·ti·cul·ture (hôr'təkul'chər), *n*. the cultivation of gardens; the growing of flowers, fruits, and vegetables.

hor·tus sic·cus (hôr'təs sik'əs), a collection of dried, preserved plants; herbarium.

hos·pice (hos'pis), *n*. a house of rest for travelers or pilgrims.

hos·tler (hos'lər, os'lər), *n*. a groom or stableman at an inn.

hotch·potch (hoch'poch), *n*. **1.** hodgepodge. **2.** a stew or soup with several kinds of vegetables and meat.

hot line, a direct telephone link between heads of state, esp. between those at Washington and Moscow, for use in case of international emergency.

hot·spur (hot'spur), *n*. a rash, impetuous person.

Hov·er·craft (huv'ərkraft'), *n*. trademark for a vehicle capable of traveling across land or water by hovering a few feet above the surface, suspended on a cushion of air provided by large downward-blowing fans.

hoy·den (hoi′dn), *n.* a rude, boisterous girl or woman; a tomboy.

hua·ra·che (wərä′cнē), *n.* a Mexican sandal with the upper of strips of leather.

hub·bly (hub′lē), *adj.* rough; uneven.

hu·bris (hyoo′bris), *n.* excessive or insolent pride; arrogance.

Hu·di·bras·tic (hyoodəbras′tik), *adj.* mock-heroic.

hug·ger·mug·ger (hug′ərmug′ər), *n.* **1.** muddle; confusion. **2.** secrecy.

hu·man·ics (hyooman′iks), *n.* the study of the affairs of mankind.

hu·man·ism (hyoo′mənizm), *n.* a system of thought or action concentrating particularly on human interests. —**hu′man·ist,** *n.*

hu·ma·num est er·ra·re (ōomä′noom est errä′re), *Latin.* to err is human.

humble pie, enforced humiliation.

hu·mec·tant (hyoomek′tənt), *n.* a substance that helps keep another substance moist.

hu·mer·al (hyoo′mərəl), *adj.* pertaining to the humerus or to the shoulder.

hu·mer·us (hyoo′mərəs), *n., pl.* **hu·mer·i** (hyoo′mərī). the bone in the arm that runs from the elbow to the shoulder.

hu·mid·i·stat (hyoomid′istat), *n.* a device for measuring and controlling humidity. Also **hygrostat.**

hu·mor (hyoo′mər), *n.* a fluid or juice of an animal or plant, either natural or morbid.

hu·mor·al (hyoo′mərəl), *adj.* pertaining to a bodily fluid.

hun·dred·weight (hun′dridwāt′), *n.* a unit of avoirdupois weight, equivalent to 100 lbs. in U.S., 112 lbs. in England. *Abbrev.:* **cwt.**

hunks (huNGks), *n.* **1.** a mean, disagreeable old person. **2.** a miser.

hurst (hurst), *n.* a hillock, wood, or copse.

hus·band (huz′bənd), *v.* to save; conserve.

hus·band·man (huz′bəndmən), *n., pl.* **hus·band·men.** a farmer; one who tends animals or crops.

hus·band·ry (huz′bəndrē), *n.* farming, agriculture; cultivation of edible crops or food animals.

hy·a·line (hī′əlin), *adj.* glassy; crystalline; transparent.

hy·a·lo·graph (hī′əlōgraf′), *n.* a device used in hyalography.

hy·a·log·ra·phy (hīəlog′rəfē), *n.* the process of writing or engraving on glass.

hy·a·loid (hī′əloid), *n.* glasslike; hyaline.

hy·brid (hī′brid), *n.* **1.** the offspring of two plants or animals of different species. —*adj.* **2.** bred from two different species. —**hy′brid·ism,** *n.*

hybrid computer, a computer using numerical representations or properties of known physical processes to solve appropriate parts of mathematical problems. See also **analog computer, digital computer.**

hy·dra·gogue (hī′drəgôg), *adj.* tending to expel or causing the expulsion of watery fluid from the body, as from the bowels.

hy·drau·lics (hīdrô′liks), *n.* the science dealing with the motive power of water and other liquids. —**hy·drau′lic,** *adj.*

hy·dre·mi·a, hy·drae·mi·a (hīdrē′mēə), *n.* a condition in which there is an excessive amount of water in the blood.

hy·dric[1] (hī′drik), *adj.* pertaining to or containing hydrogen. [from *hydr-* (*ogen*) + *-ic*, adj. suffix]

hy·dric[2] (hī′drik), *adj.* pertaining to, or adapted to wet, moist surroundings. [from *hydr-*, stem of Greek for water, + *-ic*, adj. suffix]

hy·dro·ceph·a·lus (hīdrəsef′ələs), *n.* a brain disease often occurring in infancy, in which fluid accumulates in the cranium, causing enlargement of the head and mental deterioration. Also **hy·dro·ceph′a·ly.** —**hy·dro·ce·phal·ic** (hī′drōsəfal′ik), *adj.* —**hy·dro·ceph′a·loid,** *adj.*

hy·dro·cor·ti·sone (hīdrəkôr′tisōn′), *n.* a natural steroid hormone of the adrenal cortex or a synthetic imitation of it used in the treatment of arthritis and some skin complaints.

hy·dro·dy·nam·ics (hī'drōdīnam'iks), *n*. the branch of physics, including hydrostatics and hydrokinetics, dealing with the forces or dynamics of liquids. Also **hydromechanics.** —**hy·dro·dy·nam'ic,** *adj*.

hy·dro·e·lec·tric (hī'drōilek'trik), *adj*. pertaining to the production of electric energy by means of the motive power of water.

hy·dro·foil (hī'drəfoil'), *n*. a vessel with submerged wings that lift the hull clear of the water when a certain speed has been attained, thus reducing friction and, hence, the motive power normally needed, enabling it to fly at surface level.

hy·dro·ge·ol·o·gy (hī'drōjēol'əjē), *n*. the science dealing with the occurrence and nature of water beneath the earth's surface.

hy·dro·graph (hī'drəgraf), *n*. a chart, in graph form, showing rises and falls or seasonal changes in water level.

hy·drog·ra·phy (hīdrog'rəfē), *n*. the science describing and charting the waters of the earth's surface, including tides and currents and particularly their application to navigation.

hy·dro·kin·e·ter (hīdrəkin'itər), *n*. a device, using jets of water or steam, for circulating water.

hy·dro·ki·net·ics (hī'drōkinet'iks), *n*. the branch of hydrodynamics dealing with liquids in motion. —**hy·dro·ki·net'ic,** *adj*.

hy·drol·o·gy (hīdrol'əjē), *n*. the science treating of the occurrence, movement, and distribution of water over the earth's surface.

hy·dro·mag·net·ics (hī'drōmagnet'iks), *n*. See **magnetohydrodynamics.**

hy·dro·man·cy (hī'drəmansē), *n*. divination by means of water.

hy·dro·me·chan·ics (hī'drōməkan'iks), *n*. hydrodynamics. —**hy·dro·me·chan'i·cal,** *adj*.

hy·dro·mel (hī'drəmel), *n*. a drink containing honey and water, which, when fermented, is called mead.

hy·drom·e·ter (hīdrom'itər), *n*. an instrument for measuring the specific gravity of liquids, and sometimes of solids.

hy·drop·a·thy (hīdrop'əthē), *n*. treatment of disease by the internal and external application of water.

hy·dro·phil·ic (hī'drəfil'ik), *adj*. having a strong liking for water.

hy·droph·i·lous (hīdrof'ələs), *adj*. pollinated through the medium of water.

hy·dro·phobe (hī'drəfōb), *n*. an animal or person suffering from hydrophobia.

hy·dro·pho·bi·a (hīdrəfō'bēə), *n*. **1.** an abnormal fear of water. **2.** rabies. —**hy·dro·pho'bic,** *adj*.

hy·dro·phone (hī'drəfōn), *n*. an instrument for detecting and pinpointing sources of sounds under water.

hy·dro·phyte (hī'drəfīt), *n*. an aquatic plant. —**hy·dro·phyt'ic** (hīdrəfit'ik), *adj*.

hy·dro·plane (hī'drəplān'), *n*. an airplane with floats enabling it to land on or lift off from water.

hy·dro·pon·ics (hīdrəpon'iks), *n*. the cultivation of plants without the use of soil, by placing roots in water or liquid solutions.

hy·dro·scope (hī'drəskōp'), *n*. an optical instrument for seeing objects under water.

hy·dro·sphere (hī'drəsfēr'), *n*. the waters of the earth, both in the oceans and the atmosphere.

hy·dro·stat·ics (hīdrəstat'iks), *n*. the branch of hydrodynamics dealing with the pressure and equilibrium of liquids at rest. —**hy·dro·stat'ic,** *adj*.

hy·dro·tax·is (hīdrətak'sis), *n*. the movement in the direction of, or away from water. —**hy·dro·tac'tic,** *adj*.

hy·dro·ther·a·peu·tics (hī'drōther'əpyōō'tiks), *n*. the treatment of disease by use of water.

hy·dro·ther·a·py (hīdrəther'əpē), *n*. the treatment of disease by the external application of water.

hy·dro·ther·mal (hīdrəthur'məl), *adj*. relating to the action of gases on or below the earth's surface.

hy·dro·tho·rax (hīdrəthôr'aks), *n*. a disease marked by the presence of serous fluid in one or both pleural cavities.

hy·dro·trop·ic (hīdrətrop′ik), *adj.* (of a plant) turning toward or away from water.

hy·drot·ro·pism (hīdrot′rəpizm), *n.* (of a plant) the tendency to grow or bend under the influence of water.

hy·drous (hī′drəs), *adj.* containing water.

hy·e·tal (hī′itl), *adj.* relating to rainfall; rainy.

hy·et·o·graph (hīet′əgraf), *n.* a chart showing average rainfall.

hy·e·tog·ra·phy (hī′itog′rəfē), *n.* the study of the distribution and volume of rainfall.

hy·giene (hī′jēn), *n.* the system or rules relating to the preservation of health. —**hy·gi·en·ic** (hī′jēen′ik), *adj.*

hy·gro·gram (hī′grəgram), *n.* the record kept by a hygrograph.

hy·gro·graph (hī′grəgraf), *n.* an instrument for measuring atmospheric humidity automatically.

hy·grom·e·ter (hīgrom′itər), *n.* an instrument for measuring atmospheric humidity.

hy·gro·met·ric (hīgrəmet′rik), *adj.* pertaining to hygrometry.

hy·grom·et·ry (hīgrom′itrē), *n.* the branch of physics studying atmospheric humidity.

hy·gro·phyte (hī′grəfīt), *n.* a plant flourishing in wet ground.

hy·gro·scope (hī′grəskōp′), *n.* an instrument indicating, though not precisely measuring, the degree of atmospheric humidity. —**hy·gro·scop·ic** (hīgrəskop′ik), *adj.*

hy·gro·stat (hī′grəstat), *n.* See **humidistat.**

hy·gro·ther·mo·graph (hīgrəthur′-məgraf), *n.* a meteorological device for recording temperature and humidity.

hy·lo·mor·phic (hīləmôr′fik), *adj.* made up of corporeal and spiritual matter.

hy·lo·mor·phism (hīləmôr′fizm), *n.* the theory that only matter and material forms have real existence.

hy·loph·a·gous (hīlof′əgəs), *adj.* feeding on wood, as certain larvae; xylophagus.

hy·lo·the·ism (hīlə*th*ē′izm), *n.* a philosophical theory relating gods to matter.

hy·lo·trop·ic (hīlətrop′ik), *adj.* (of a substance) capable of changing form as in sublimation, evaporation, etc., without changing the proportions of the original constituents.

hy·me·ne·al (hīmənē′əl), *adj.* pertaining to marriage.

hy·men·o·tome (hīmen′ətōm), *n.* an instrument for cutting a membrane.

hym·nol·o·gy (himnol′əjē), *n.* the study of hymns.

hy·oid (hī′oid), *adj.* pertaining to the U-shaped bone at the base of the tongue.

hyp·aes·the·sia (hip′is*th*ē′zhə), *n.* See **hypesthesia.**

hyp·al·ge·si·a (hip′aljē′zēə), *n.* diminished sensitivity to pain. See also **hyperalgesia.**

hy·per·a·cid·i·ty (hī′pərəsid′itē), *n.* excessive amount of acid, as in the gastric juice.

hy·per·ac·tive (hīpərak′tiv), *adj.* excessively or abnormally active.

hy·per·a·cu·sis (hī′pərəkyōō′sis), *n.* unusually acute hearing.

hy·per·a·dre·nal·e·mi·a (hīpərə-drē′nəlē′mēə), *n.* excessively large amount of adrenalin in the blood. Also **hyperepinephrinemia.**

hy·per·a·dre·nal·ism (hī′pərədrē′-nəlizm), *n.* a metabolic and urine disorder caused by increased secretory activity of the adrenal gland.

hy·per·aes·the·sia (hī′pəris*th*ē′zhə), *n.* See **hyperesthesia.**

hy·per·al·ge·si·a (hī′pəraljē′zēə), *n.* heightened feeling of, or reaction to pain. See also **hypalgesia.**

hy·per·an·a·ki·ne·si·a hī′pəran′ə-kənē′zēə), *n.* abnormal automatic movement, as of internal organs.

hy·per·a·phi·a hīpərā′fēə), *n.* abnormal sensitivity to touch.

hy·per·bar·ic (hīpərbar′ik), *adj.* (applied to anesthetics), having a specific gravity greater than that of the fluid of the brain and spinal cord. See also **hypobaric**.

hy·per·bo·le (hīpur′bəlē), *n.* a deliberately inflated, exaggerated statement, not to be taken literally. —**hy·per·bol·ic** (hīpərbol′ik), *adj.*

hyperbolic geometry, non-Euclidean geometry with the postulate that two distinct lines may be drawn parallel to a given line through a point not on the line. See also **Riemannian geometry**.

hy·per·bo·lize (hīpur′bəlīz), *v.* to exaggerate or use hyperbole.

hy·per·bo·re·an (hīpərbôr′ēən), *adj.* pertaining to the extreme north; frigid.

hy·per·cal·ce·mi·a, hy·per·cal·cae·mi·a (hī′pərkalsē′mēə), *n.* an excessive amount of calcium in the blood.

hy·per·cal·ci·u·ri·a (hī′pərkal′si-yŏŏr′ēə), *n.* an excessive amount of blood in the urine.

hy·per·cap·ni·a (hīpərkap′nēə), *n.* an excessive amount of carbon dioxide in the blood.

hy·per·chlo·re·mi·a, hy·per·chlo·rae·mi·a (hī′pərklôrē′mēə), *n.* an excessive amount of chloride in the blood.

hy·per·chlor·hy·dri·a (hī′pərklôr-hī′drēə), *n.* an excessive amount of hydrochloric acid in the stomach.

hy·per·cho·les·ter·ol·e·mi·a (hī′-pərkəles′tərôlē′mēə), *n.* an excessive quantity of cholesterol in the blood. See also **hypocholesteremia**.

hy·per·cho·les·ter·o·li·a (hī′pərkə-les′tərō′lēə), *n.* an excessive amount of cholesterol in the bile.

hy·per·cho·li·a (hīpərkō′lēə), *n.* an abnormally large secretion of bile.

hy·per·con·scious (hīpərkon′sHəs), *adj.* unusually alert or aware.

hy·per·crin·ism (hīpərkrin′izm), *n.* a disorder caused by excessive secretion of an endocrine gland.

hy·per·cry·al·ge·si·a (hī′pərkrī′-aljē′zēə), *n.* unusual sensitivity to cold.

hy·per·cy·the·mi·a (hī′pərsīthē′-mēə), *n.* an excessive number of red corpuscles in the blood.

hy·per·cy·to·sis (hī′pərsītō′sis), *n.* an excessive number of cells, especially white, in the blood. Also **hyperleucocytosis**.

hy·per·dac·tyl·i·a (hī′pərdaktil′ēə), *n.* the presence of extra fingers or toes.

hy·per·du·li·a (hī′pərdŏŏlē′ə), *n.* the veneration, above all others, of the Virgin Mary, by Roman Catholics. See also **dulia, latria**.

hy·per·e·mi·a, hy·per·ae·mi·a (hī-pərē′mēə), *n.* an excessive amount of blood in any portion of the body.

hy·per·en·do·crin·ism (hīpəren′-dōkrinizm), *n.* an abnormally increased activity in internally secreting organs.

hy·per·ep·i·neph·ri·ne·mi·a (hī′-pərep′inef′rənē′mēə), *n.* See **hyperadrenalemia**.

hy·per·ep·i·neph·ry (hī′pərep′ənef′-rē), *n.* an abnormal increase in adrenal secretion.

hy·per·es·the·sia, hy·per·aes·the·si·a (hī′pəristhē′zHə), *n.* an unusually acute reaction or sensitivity to pain, heat, cold, etc.

hy·per·gly·ce·mi·a, hy·per·gly·cae·mi·a (hī′pərglīsē′mēə), *n.* an excessive amount of glucose in the blood. See also **hypoglycemia**.

hy·per·gly·cis·ti·a (hī′pərglīsis′tēə), *n.* an excessive amount of sugar in the tissues.

hy·per·gol·ic (hīpərgô′lik), *adj.* igniting upon contact with a complementary substance, as the constituents of rocket propellants.

hy·per·he·pat·i·a (hī′pərhipat′ēə), *n.* an excessive functioning of the liver.

hy·per·hi·dro·sis (hī′pərhidrō′sis), *n.* excessive perspiration.

hy·per·ka·le·mi·a (hī′pərkəlē′mēə), *n.* an excessive amount of potassium in the blood.

hy·per·ker·a·to·sis (hī′pərker′ətō′-sis), *n.* a thickening of the horny layer of the skin.

hy·per·ki·ne·si·a (hī′pərkinē′zHə), *n.* an excessive involuntary muscular activity; spasm.

hy·per·leu·co·cy·to·sis (hī′pərlŏŏ′-kōsītō′sis), *n.* See **hypercytosis**.

hy·per·li·pe·mi·a (hī′pərlipē′mēə), *n.* excessive quantities of fatty substances in the blood.

hy·per·meg·a·so·ma (hī′pərmēg′-əsō′mə), *n.* abnormal, excessive growth; gigantism.

hy·per·met·a·mor·pho·sis (hī′pərmet′əmôr′fəsis), *n., pl.* **hy·per·met·a·mor·pho·ses** (hī′pərmet′əmôr′fə-sēz). an unusual form of metamorphosis in some insects in which two or more successive larval stages occur.

hy·per·met·rope (hīpərmet′rōp), *n.* a person who suffers from hypermetropia. Also **hy′per·ope.**

hy·per·me·tro·pi·a (hī′pərmitrō′pēə), *n.* far-sightedness in which the focal point of parallel rays is behind instead of on the retina. Also **hy·per·o·pi·a** (hīpərō′pēə). See also **myopia, presbyopia. —hy·per·me·trop·ic** (hī′pərmitrop′ik), *adj.*

hy·per·mo·til·i·ty (hī′pərmōtil′itē), *n.* excessive movement capacity of the stomach or intestines.

hy·per·na·tre·mi·a (hī′pərnətrē′-mēə), *n.* an excessive amount of sodium in the blood.

hy·per·os·mi·a (hīpəroz′mēə), *n.* an unusually acute sense of smell. **—hy·per·os′mic,** *adj.*

hy·per·os·te·og·e·ny (hī′pəros′tēog′-ənē), *n.* exaggerated bone development.

hy·per·os·to·sis (hī′pərostō′sis), *n.* an abnormal increase of bone tissue.

hy·per·o·var·i·a (hī′pərōver′ēə), *n.* unusually early and advanced sexual development in girls, owing to excessive secretion in the ovaries.

hy·per·ox·e·mi·a (hī′pəroksē′mēə), *n.* excessive acidity of the blood.

hy·per·par·a·site (hīpərpar′əsīt), *n.* a parasite that feeds on or in another parasite.

hy·per·par·a·thy·roid·ism (hī′pərpar′əthī′roidizm), *n.* an abnormal bone and muscular condition, caused by excessive activity of the parathyroid gland.

hy·per·pha·gi·a (hīpərfā′jēə), *n.* excessive hunger; bulimia.

hy·per·phos·phe·re·mi·a (hī′pər-fos′fərē′mēə), *n.* an excessive quantity of inorganic phosphorous compounds in the blood.

hy·per·phys·i·cal (hīpərfiz′ikəl), *adj.* above or beyond the physical; supernatural.

hy·per·pi·et·ic (hī′pərpīet′ik), *adj.* pertaining to hypertension.

hy·per·pi·tu·i·ta·rism (hī′pərpətoo′-itərizm), *n.* gigantism caused by overactivity of the pituitary gland.

hy·per·pla·sia (hīpərplā′zHə), *n.* abnormal cell multiplication, causing organic enlargement.

hy·perp·ne·a, hy·perp·noe·a (hī′-pərpnē′ə), *n.* excessively rapid or labored breathing.

hy·per·pot·as·se·mi·a (hī′pərpot′-əsē′mēə), *n.* an excessive amount of potassium in the blood; hyperkalemia.

hy·per·pro·sex·i·a (hī′pərprōsek′-sēə), *n.* an obsessive attention to a relatively unimportant stimulus. See also **hypoprosexia.**

hy·per·py·rex·i·a (hī′pərpīrek′sēə), *n.* an abnormally severe fever.

hy·per·se·cre·tion (hī′pərsikrē′-sHən), *n.* excessive secretion. See also **hyposecretion.**

hy·per·som·ni·a (hīpərsom′nēə), *n.* abnormally prolonged sleep. **—hy·per·som′ni·ac,** *adj.*

hy·per·son·ic (hīpərson′ik), *adj.* pertaining to speeds at least five times that of sound.

hy·per·space (hī′pərspās′), *n.* Euclidean space of more than three dimensions.

hy·per·tel·y (hīpur′təlē), *n.* (in the coloring and structure of plants and animals) excessive imitation without discernible purpose.

hy·per·ten·sion (hīpərten′sHən), *n.* high blood pressure and the arterial disease caused by it.

hy·per·ten·sive (hīpərten′siv), *adj.* pertaining to or caused by high blood pressure.

hy·per·ther·mi·a (hipərthur′mēə), *n.* **1.** exceptionally high fever. **2.** treatment of disease by inducing fever, as by heat or injection.

hy·per·throm·bin·e·mi·a (hī′pər-*throm*′binē′mēə), *n.* an excessive amount of thrombin in the blood.

hy·per·thy·mi·a (hīpərthī′mēə), *n.* (in psychiatry) a condition characterized by overactivity.

hy·per·thy·roid (hīpərthī′roid), *adj.* 1. concerning or suffering from hyperthyroidism. 2. of an unrestrained, highly emotional nature.

hy·per·thy·roid·ism (hīpərthī′roidizm), *n.* hyperactivity of the thyroid gland leading to an increased metabolic rate and protruding eyeballs.

hy·per·ton·ic (hīpərton′ik), *adj.* (of tissue) having a greater than normal tone.

hy·per·tro·phy (hīpur′trəfē), *n.* abnormal growth or enlargement of a part or organ.

hy·per·ven·ti·la·tion (hī′pərven′təlā′sʜən), *n.* abnormally rapid and heavy breathing.

hyp·es·the·sia, hyp·aes·the·sia (hip′isthē′zʜə), *n.* a poor sense of pain.

hy·pe·thral (hipē′thrəl), *adj.* wholly or partially open to the sky, as a building. See also **clithral.**

hyp·no·a·nal·y·sis (hip′nōənal′isis), *n.* a method of psychoanalysis in which the patient is examined while under hypnosis.

hyp·no·gen·e·sis (hip′nōjen′isis), *n.* the process of inducing hypnosis.

hyp·no·graph (hip′nəgraf), *n.* a device for measuring bodily activities during sleep.

hyp·noi·dal (hipnoi′dl), *adj.* (of a state) resembling hypnosis, but not brought about by it.

hyp·nol·o·gy (hipnol′əjē), *n.* the study of the nature and characteristics of sleep.

hyp·no·ther·a·py (hip′nōther′əpē), *n.* the treatment of disease by hypnotic means.

hyp·not·ic (hipnot′ik), *adj.* 1. sleep-inducing. —*n.* 2. a sedative; a substance inducing sleep.

hy·po·a·cid·i·ty (hī′pōəsid′itē), *n.* reduced or subnormal acidity, as of gastric juice.

hy·po·a·cu·sis (hī′pōəkyoō′sis), *n.* a hearing deficiency.

hy·po·a·de·ni·a (hī′pōədē′nēə), *n.* subnormal glandular activity.

hy·po·al·i·men·ta·tion (hī′pōal′-əmentā′sʜən), *n.* insufficient nourishment.

hy·po·al·o·ne·mi·a (hī′pōal′ənē′-mēə), *n.* an excessively low quantity of salts in the blood.

hy·po·az·o·tu·ri·a (hī′pōaz′ətoōr′-ēə), *n.* an abnormally small quantity of nitrogenous matter in the urine.

hy·po·bar·ic (hīpəbar′ik), *adj.* (of an anesthetic) having a specific gravity lower than that of the fluid of the brain and spinal cord. See also **hyperbaric.**

hy·po·ba·rop·a·thy (hī′pōbərop′-əthē), *n.* mountain sickness, caused by lowered air pressure and reduced intake of oxygen.

hy·po·cal·ce·mi·a (hī′pōkalsē′mēə), *n.* a subnormal quantity of calcium in the blood.

hy·po·chlo·re·mi·a (hī′pōklôrē′-mēə), *n.* an abnormally small quantity of chloride in the blood.

hy·po·chlor·hy·dri·a (hī′pōklôrhī′-drēə), *n.* an abnormally low quantity of hydrochloric acid in the gastric secretions.

hy·po·cho·les·ter·e·mi·a (hī′pō-kəles′tərē′mēə), *n.* a reduction in the amount of cholesterol in the blood. See also **hypercholesterolemia.**

hy·po·chon·dri·a (hīpəkon′drēə), *n.* a depressed mental and emotional condition owing to an unfounded belief that some serious bodily disease is present. Also **hy·po·chon·dri·a·sis** (hī′pōkəndrī′əsis).

hy·po·chon·dri·ac (hīpəkon′drēak), *n.* 1. a person subject to hypochondria, or excessively worried and obsessed by his state of health. —*adj.* 2. of or pertaining to hypochrondria.

hy·po·chon·dri·um (hīpəkon′drēəm), *n., pl.* **hy·po·chon·dri·a** (hīpəkon′drēə). each of the two regions of the abdomen referred to as right and left.

hy·poc·o·rism (hīpok′ərizm), *n.* a pet

name, or adult imitation of baby talk. —**hy·po·co·ris·tic** (hī′pəkôris′tik), *adj.*

hy·po·cri·nism (hīpəkrī′nizm), *n.* a condition caused by an abnormally small glandular secretion.

hy·poc·ri·sy (hipok′rəsē), *n.* the pretence, with a view to popular approval, of possessing virtues and holding principles quite alien to one's true nature.

hyp·o·crite (hip′əkrit), *n.* a person affecting ethical or religious principles and ideals which he does not truly possess. —**hyp·o·crit′i·cal,** *adj.*

hy·po·cy·to·sis (hi′pōsitō′sis), *n.* a deficient number of blood cells; cytopenia. See also **hypercytosis.**

hy·po·dy·nam·i·a (hī′pōdīnam′ēə), *n.* reduced energy or strength.

hy·po·en·doc·rin·ism (hī′pōendok′-rənizm), *n.* subnormal activity of the internally secreting organs. See also **hyperendocrinism.**

hy·po·gas·tri·um (hīpəgas′trēəm), *n.,* *pl.* **hy·po·gas·tri·a** (hīpəgas′trēə). the lower part of the abdomen. —**hy·po·gas′tric,** *adj.*

hy·po·ge·al (hīpəjē′əl), *adj.* below ground; subterranean.

hy·po·gene (hī′pəjēn), *adj.* **1.** formed below the surface, as rocks. **2.** formed by rising water, as mineral deposits. See also **epigene, supergene.**

hy·po·ge·ous (hīpəjē′əs), *adj.* hypogeal; underground.

hy·po·ge·um (hīpəjē′əm), *n.* a subterranean vault or chamber.

hy·po·geu·si·a (hīpəjoō′sēə), *n.* a reduction in sensitivity to taste.

hy·po·glo·bu·li·a (hī′pōglobyoō′lēə), *n.* subnormal quantity of red cells in the blood.

hy·po·glos·sal (hīpəglos′əl), *adj.* situated beneath the tongue.

hy·po·glot·tis (hīpəglot′is), *n.* the underside of the tongue.

hy·po·gly·ce·mi·a, hy·po·gly·cae·mi·a (hī′pōglīsē′mēə), *n.* an insufficient quantity of glucose in the blood.

hy·pog·na·thous (hīpog′nəthəs), *adj.* having a long, protruding lower jaw.

hy·po·gon·ad·ism (hī′pōgō′nadizm),

n. a reduced internal secretion of the gonads.

hy·po·he·pat·i·a (hī′pōhipat′ēə), *n.* subnormal liver function.

hy·po·hi·dro·sis (hī′pōhīdrō′sis), *n.* inability to produce sufficient perspiration.

hy·po·hy·poph·y·sism (hī′pōhīpof′-isizm), *n.* abnormally reduced activity of the pituitary gland. Also **hypopituitarism.**

hy·poid (hī′poid), *adj.* (of a gear) designed to mesh with another gear with the axes overlapping approximately at right angles rather than intersecting.

hy·po·in·o·se·mi·a (hī′pōin′əsē′-mēə), *n.* abnormally reduced formation of fibrin in the blood, causing difficulty in coagulation.

hy·po·ka·le·mi·a (hī′pōkālē′mēə), *n.* excessively low quantity of potassium in the blood.

hy·po·ki·ne·si·a (hī′pōkinē′zHə), *n.* subnormal motor activity or mobility.

hy·po·lim·ni·on (hīpəlim′nēon), *n.,* *pl.* **hy·po·lim·ni·a** (hīpəlim′nēə). a layer of water below the thermocline in some lakes. See also **epilimnion.**

hy·po·ma·ni·a (hīpəmā′nēə), *n.* (in psychiatry) a mania of not too severe a nature.

hy·pom·ne·sia (hīpəmnē′zHə), *n.* impaired memory.

hy·po·mo·til·i·ty (hī′pəmōtil′itē), *n.* subnormal motility of the stomach and intestines.

hy·po·my·o·to·ni·a (hī′pəmī′ətō′-nēə), *n.* abnormally reduced muscular tone.

hy·po·nas·ty (hī′pənas′tē), *n.* the tendency of certain plants to grow more rapidly on the lower rather than the upper side, causing upward bending.

hy·po·na·tre·mi·a (hī′pōnətrē′-mēə), *n.* an excessively low quantity of sodium in the blood.

hy·po·noi·a (hīpənoi′ə), *n.* dulled or reduced mental activity; hypopsychosis.

hy·po·pha·lan·gism (hī′pōfəlan′-jizm), *n.* fewer than the normal number of bones in a finger or toe.

hypophonesis

hy·po·pho·ne·sis (hī'pōfənē'sis), *n.* a sound of less than normal intensity.

hy·po·pho·nia (hīpəfō'nēə), *n.* an abnormally weak voice due to a deficiency in the vocal cords.

hy·poph·y·ge (hīpof'ijē), *n.* the section of a column joined to the base or capital. Also **apophyge.**

hy·poph·y·sis (hīpof'isis), *n., pl.* **hypoph·y·ses** (hīpof'isēz). the pituitary gland.

hy·poph·y·si·tis (hīpof'isī'tis), *n.* inflammation or irritation of the pituitary gland.

hy·po·pi·e·sis (hī'pōpīē'sis), *n.* unusually low arterial blood pressure.

hy·po·pi·tu·i·ta·rism (hī'pōpitoo'itərizm), *n.* subnormal activity of the pituitary gland. Also **hypohypophysism.**

hy·po·pla·sia (hīpəplā'zhə), *n.* a serious deficiency of cells or structural constituents.

hy·pop·ne·a (hīpop'nēə), *n.* unusually shallow breathing.

hy·po·po·tas·se·mi·a (hī'pōpətasē'mēə), *n.* a subnormal quantity of potassium in the blood; hypokalemia.

hy·po·prax·i·a (hīpəprak'sēə), *n.* diminished activity; listlessness.

hy·po·pro·sex·i·a (hī'pōprəsek'sēə), *n.* inability to concentrate for more than short periods. See also **hyperprosexia.**

hy·po·pro·tein·e·mi·a (hī'pəprō'tēnē'mēə), *n.* a subnormal amount of protein in the blood.

hy·po·pro·tein·o·sis (hī'pəprō'tēnō'sis), *n.* a protein deficiency.

hy·pop·sel·a·phe·si·a (hī'popsel'əfē'zēə), *n.* a deficiency in the sense of touch.

hy·po·psy·cho·sis (hī'pōsīkō'sis), *n.* dulled or diminished mental activity; hyponoia.

hy·pop·ty·al·ism (hīpətī'əlizm), *n.* insufficient salivary secretion.

hy·po·sal·e·mi·a (hī'pōsalē'mēə), *n.* an abnormally low salt content in the blood.

hy·po·se·cre·tion (hī'pōsikrē'shən), *n.* a subnormal secretion. See also **hypersecretion.**

hy·po·sen·si·tize (hīpəsen'sitīz), *v.* to reduce a person's sensitivity; desensitize.

hy·pos·mi·a (hīpoz'mēə), *n.* a deficient sense of smell.

hy·pos·ta·sis (hīpos'təsis), *n., pl.* **hypos·ta·ses** (hīpos'təsēz). (in metaphysics) something that supports or underlines.

hy·pos·ta·size (hīpos'təsīz), *v.* to regard as substance or reality.

hy·po·stat·ic (hīpəstat'ik), *adj.* pertaining to essence or substance; fundamental.

hy·pos·ta·tize (hīpos'tətīz), *v.* to treat as substance or reality; hypostasize.

hy·pos·the·ni·a (hī'posthē'nēə), *n.* serious lack of strength; weakness.

hy·po·ten·sion (hīpəten'shən), *n.* diminished or low blood pressure. See also **hypertension.**

hy·po·ten·sive (hī'pōten'siv), *adj.* pertaining to or causing low blood pressure.

hy·pot·e·nuse (hīpot'ənoos), *n.* the side of a right-angled triangle opposite the right angle.

hy·po·thal·a·mus (hīpəthal'əməs), *n., pl.* **hy·po·thal·a·mi** (hipəthal'əmī). the forebrain that coordinates the control over temperature, rage, etc.

hy·poth·e·cate (hīpoth'ikāt), *v.* to give or pledge as security, without parting with possession or title.

hy·poth·e·nar (hīpoth'inär), *n.* the fleshy portion of the hand at the base of the little finger.

hy·po·ther·mal (hīpəthur'məl), *adj.* having abnormally low body temperature.

hy·po·ther·mi·a (hīpəthur'mēə), *n.* subnormal body temperature.

hy·po·thy·roid·ism (hīpəthī'roidizm), *n.* a disorder, such as goiter, caused by deficient activity of the thyroid gland. See also **hyperthyroidism.** —**hy·po·thy'roid,** *adj.*

hy·po·ton·ic (hīpəton'ik), *adj.* (of tissue) having subnormal tone.

hy·po·ty·po·sis (hī'pətīpō'sis), *n.* a vivid, lifelike description of a scene or event.

hy·pox·e·mi·a (hī'poksē'mēə), *n.* a

condition brought about by insufficient oxygen in the blood.

hy·pox·i·a (hīpok′sēə), *n.* an insufficient amount of oxygen reaching the body tissues.

hyp·si·ceph·a·ly (hip′sisef′əlē), *n.* a malformation of the head; acrocephaly.

hyp·sog·ra·phy (hipsog′rəfē), *n.* geographic study relating to surveying and mapping the parts of the earth above sea level.

hyp·som·e·ter (hipsom′itər), *n.* an instrument for measuring heights above sea level.

hyp·som·e·try (hipsom′itrē), *n.* the measuring of altitudes.

hys·ter·ec·to·my (histərek′təmē), *n.* excision of the womb.

hys·ter·e·sis (histərē′sis), *n.* the time lag in the effect of a magnetic force in relation to the force causing it.

hys·ter·o·cat·a·lep·sy (his′tərəkat′-əlepsē), *n.* hysteria with symptoms of cataleptic seizure or trance. —**hys·ter·o·cat·a·lep′tic,** *adj.*

hys·ter·o·gen·ic (his′tərəjen′ik), *adj.* producing hysteria.

hys·ter·oid (his′təroid), *adj.* resembling hysteria.

hy·ther·graph (hī′thərgraf), *n.* a weather or climate graph indicating the relationship between temperature and humidity.

i·amb (ī′am, ī′amb), *n.* (in poetry) a metric foot consisting of one unstressed followed by one stressed syllable. —**i·am·bic** (īam′bik), *adj.*

iar·o·vize (yär′əvīz), *v.* See **jarovize.**

i·a·tric (īa′trik), *adj.* relating to a doctor or to medicine.

i·at·ro·chem·is·try (īat′rəkem′istrē), *n.* the study and application of chemistry in relation to diseases.

i·at·ro·gen·ic (īat′rəjen′ik), *adj.* (of a disorder) resulting from the diagnosis or treatment of a doctor.

ib·i·dem (ib′idəm), *adv. Latin.* in the same place, on the same page, etc. (used to avoid repetition). *Abbrev.:* **ibid.**

ice·blink (īs′bliNGk′), *n.* a luminous appearance near the horizon caused by the reflection of light from an icefield. See also **snowblink.**

ice·fall (īs′fôl′), *n.* a wall of ice overhanging a precipice.

ice foot, a belt or ledge of ice in polar regions attached to the shore.

ice front, the edge of an ice shelf nearest the sea.

ich·nite (ik′nīt), *n.* a fossilized footprint.

ich·nog·ra·phy (iknog′rəfē), *n.* the art of drawing horizontal sections or ground plans.

ich·nol·o·gy (iknol′əjē), *n.* the branch of science dealing with fossil footprints.

i·chor (ī′kôr), *n.* a colorless, watery discharge from a wound or sore.

ich·thy·ic (ik′*th*ēik), *adj.* pertaining to fishes.

ich·thy·og·ra·phy (ik′*th*ēog′rəfē), *n.* a written work on fishes.

ich·thy·oid (ik′*th*ēoid), *adj.* fish-like. Also **ich·thy·oi′dal.**

ich·thy·o·lite (ik′*th*ēəlīt), *n.* a fish in fossil form.

ich·thy·ol·o·gy (ik′*th*ēol′əjē), *n.* the branch of zoology relating to fishes.

ich·thy·oph·a·gy (ik′*th*ēof′əjē), *n.* the practice of eating fish. —**ich·thy·oph′a·gist,** *n.*

ich·thy·o·sis (ik′*th*ēō′sis), *n.* a congenital skin disease characterized by flaking skin. Also **fish skin disease.**

i·con·o·clasm (īkon′əklazm), *n.* the act of destroying or breaking images.

i·con·o·clast (īkon′əklast), *n.* a breaker of images, or attacker of traditional doctrines and institutions.

i·con·o·dule (īkon′ədōōl), *n.* one who worships icons.

i·con·o·du·ly (īkon′ədōōlē), *n.* the worship of icons.

i·con·og·ra·phy (īkənog′rəfē), *n.* a pictorial or symbolic representation. —**i·con·o·graph′ic,** *adj.*

i·co·nol·a·try (īkənol′ətrē), *n.* the worship of images.

i·co·nol·o·gy (īkənol′əjē), *n.* the study and analysis of symbols and icons.

i·co·nos·ta·sis (īkənos′təsis), *n., pl.*

156

i·co·nos·ta·ses (īkənos′təsēz). a screen in a Byzantine church, separating the sanctuary from the main body of the building, on which icons are placed. Also **i′con·o·stas.**

i·co·sa·he·dron (īkō′səhē′drən), *n.*, *pl.* **i·co·sa·he·drons, i·co·sa·he·dra** (īkō′səhē′drə). a solid figure with twenty faces.

i·co·si·tet·ra·he·dron (īkō′site′trəhē′drən), *n.*, *pl.* **i·co·si·tet·ra·he·drons, i·co·si·tet·ra·he·dra** (īkō′site′trəhē′drə). a solid figure with twenty-four faces.

ic·ter·us (ik′tərəs), *n.* jaundice. —**ic·ter′ic**, *adj.*

ic·tus (ik′təs), *n.*, *pl.* **ic·tus·es, ic·tus.** (in medicine) a fit, a stroke, as sunstroke.

id (id), *n.* a term in psychoanalysis for the unconscious part of the mind, the source of primal, instinctive urges.

i·de·a·is·tic (īdē′əis′tik), *adj.* pertaining to ideas.

i·de·al·ism (īdē′əlizm), *n.* (in art or literature) the theory and practice of treating a subject in an imaginative rather than realistic manner, by emphasizing certain aspects or features approximating to a standard of absolute perfection. See also **naturalism, realism.**

i·de·ate (ī′dēāt), *v.* to form ideas; to think; to imagine. —**i·de·a′tion**, *n.* —**i·de·a′tion·al**, *adj.*

i·dem (ī′dem, id′em), *pron.*, *adj. Latin.* the same as previously given or stated.

id·e·o·gram (id′ēəgram), *n.* a written symbol directly representing an object or an idea, rather than a phonetic description of it.

id·e·o·graph (id′ēəgraf), *n.* an ideogram.

id·e·og·ra·phy (id′ēog′rəfē), *n.* the use of ideograms or ideographs.

i·de·o·mo·tor (ī′dēəmō′tər), *adj.* relating to motor activity arising from an idea.

id·i·o·blast (id′ēəblast), *n.* a cell differently constituted to those surrounding it.

id·i·oc·ra·sy (id′ēok′rəsē), *n.* a peculiar, individual mannerism; idiosyncrasy.

id·i·o·dy·nam·ics (id′ēōdīnam′iks), *n.* (in psychology) a belief in the individual's importance in choosing and responding to stimuli. —**id·i·o·dy·nam′ic**, *adj.*

id·i·o·glos·si·a (id′ēəglos′ēə), *n.* an invented form of speech for private communication by children who are closely related or associated, as twins.

id·i·o·graph (id′ēəgraf), *n.* a private mark or signature; a trademark. See also **logotype.**

id·i·o·graph·ic (id′ēəgraf′ik), *adj.* (in psychology) pertaining to the separate study of cases or happenings. See also **nomothetic.**

id·i·o·mor·phic (id′ēəmôr′fik), *adj.* having its own proper characteristic form.

id·i·op·a·thy (id′ēop′əthē), *n.* a disease not preceded or caused by any other. —**id·i·o·path′ic**, *adj.*

id·i·o·syn·cra·sy (id′ēəsiNG′krəsē), *n.* a habit, mannerism or temperament peculiar to an individual.

id·i·o·trop·ic (id′ēətrop′ik), *adj.* introspective, inward-looking.

id·i·ot sa·vant (id′ēət savänt′), *pl.* **id·i·ot sa·vants, id·i·ots sa·vants.** a mentally backward person with one special talent, such as art, music, mathematical calculation, etc.

i·dol·a·ter (īdol′ətər), *n.* one who worships idols. Also **i′dol·ist.** —**i·dol′a·trous**, *adj.*

i·dol·a·try (īdol′ətrē), *n.* the worship of idols and images.

idols of the cave, errors arising from personal bias or prejudice.

idols of the market place, popular fallacies arising from factors such as language or custom, and exploited for commercial reasons.

idols of the theater, errors caused by perpetuation of traditional beliefs.

idols of the tribe, fallacies related to man's nature and social organization.

i·do·ne·ous (īdō′nēəs), *adj.* apt; fit; suitable.

i·dyl·lic (īdil′ik), *adj.* simple and peaceful; charming and poetic.

ig·ne·ous (ig′nēəs), *adj.* produced by the action of fire or intense heat, as volcanic rock.

ig·nes·cent (ignes′ənt), *adj.* giving off sparks of fire.

ig·nis fat·u·us (ig′nis facH′ōōəs), *n.*, *pl.* **ig·nes fat·u·i** (ig′nēz facH′ōōī). a phosphorescent light that hovers or flickers at night over marshy ground, believed to be due to spontaneous combustion of gas from decayed organic matter. Also **friars' lantern, will-o'-the-wisp.**

ig·no·ble (ignō′bəl), *adj.* of low character; mean; contemptible. —**ig·no·bil′i·ty,** *n.*

ig·no·min·y (ig′nəmine), *n.* disgrace, infamy, dishonor. —**ig·no·min′i·ous,** *adj.*

il·e·i·tis (il′ēī′tis), *n.* inflammation of the ileum.

il·e·o·ce·cal (il′ēōsē′kəl), *adj.* pertaining to the ileum and cecum.

il·e·o·co·li·tis (il′ēōkəlī′tis), *n.* inflammation of the mucous membrane of the ileum and colon.

il·e·um (il′ēəm), *n.* the lower portion of the small intestine, from the jejunum to the cecum.

il·e·us (il′ēəs), *n.* painful intestinal obstruction.

il·i·ac (il′ēak), *adj.* pertaining to the ilium.

il·i·um (il′ēəm), *n.*, *pl.* **il·i·a** (il′ēə). one of the upper bones of the pelvis, part of the hip-bone.

il·la·tion (ilā′sHən), *n.* a deduction; inference; conclusion. —**il′la·tive,** *adj.*

il·lu·mi·na·ti (ilōō′mənā′tī), *n. pl.* persons claiming special perception or enlightenment.

il·lu·vi·ate (ilōō′vēāt), *v.* to undergo or cause illuviation.

il·lu·vi·a·tion (ilōō′vēā′sHən), *n.* the accumulation in a soil layer of materials that have percolated from another layer.

il·lu·vi·um (ilōō′vēəm), *n.*, *pl.* **il·lu·vi·ums, il·lu·vi·a** (ilōō′vēə). material built up through illuviation. —**il·lu′vi·al,** *adj.*

im·age·ry (im′ijrē), *n.* the creation of mental figures or representations; images collectively.

im·ag·ism (im′əjizm), *n.* the theory and work of early 20th century poets reacting against romanticism and advocating the use of precise images, new rhythms and language of everyday speech.

i·ma·go (imā′gō), *n.*, *pl.* **i·ma·goes, i·ma·gi·nes** (imaj′ənēz). **1.** a fully developed insect. **2.** an idealized image of someone, formed in infancy and maintained unaltered as an adult.

im·bibe (imbīb′), *v.* to absorb liquid; to drink. —**im·bi·bi′ti·on,** *n.*

im·bow·er (imbou′ər), *v.* to embower.

im·brac·er·y (imbrā′sərē), *n.* See **embracery.**

im·bran·gle (imbraNG′gəl), *v.* to perplex; entangle; embrangle.

im·bri·cate (im′brəkit), *adj.* methodical overlapping, as of roof tiles. —**im·bri·ca′tion,** *n.*

im·bro·glio (imbrōl′yō), *n.*, *pl.* **im·bro·glios.** a state of confusion; a perplexing situation.

im·brue (imbrōō′), *v.* to dye or stain, as with blood. Also **embrue.**

im·brute (imbrōōt′), *v.* to degrade, become brutish.

im·bue (imbyōō′), *v.* to inspire, as with feelings, opinions, etc., or impregnate with moisture, color, etc.

im·ma·nent (im′ənənt), *adj.* inherent; remaining within.

im·med·i·ca·ble (imed′əkəbəl), *adj.* unable to be healed; incurable.

im·men·su·ra·ble (imen′sHŏŏrəbəl), *adj.* immeasurable; incapable of being measured.

im·merge (imurj′), *v.* **1.** to plunge or dip in a liquid. **2.** (in astronomy) to disappear, as the sun below the horizon, the moon or sun in an eclipse, etc.

im·mer·sion (imur′zHən), *n.* (in astronomy) the disappearance of a celestial body behind or in the shadow of another, as in an eclipse. See also **emersion.**

im·mis·ci·ble (imis′əbəl), *adj.* incapable of being mixed.

im·mix (imiks'), *v.* to mix in; mix up; mingle. —**im·mix'ture,** *n.*

im·mo·late (im'əlāt), *v.* to kill as a sacrifice, esp. by fire. —**im·mo·la' tion,** *n.*

im·mo·tile (imō'tl), *adj.* incapable of movement.

im·mu·no·ge·net·ics (im'yənō-jənet'iks), *n.* the branch of immunology relating to immunity as affected by genetic makeup.

im·mu·nol·o·gy (imyənol'əjē), *n.* the branch of medicine studying animal and human immunity to infection and disease, and the ways of producing such immunity.

im·mure (imyŏŏr'), *v.t.* to wall in, enclose within or as within walls.

im·mu·ta·ble (imyŏŏ'təbəl), *adj.* not subject to change, unalterable.

im·pa·na·tion (impənā'sHən), *n.* the doctrine that the material body of Christ is present in the bread after consecration.

im·passe (im'pas), *n.* a situation from which there is no way out; deadlock.

im·pas·to (impas'tō), *n.* (in painting) color laid on in a thick manner.

im·pec·cant (impek'ənt), *adj.* faultless, without sin.

im·pe·di·ent (impē'dēənt), *adj.* obstructive; hindering.

im·ped·i·men·ta (imped'əmen'tə), *n. pl.* objects which hinder progress, esp. army supplies.

im·ped·i·tive (imped'itiv), *adj.* causing hindrance or obstruction.

im·pe·ra·tor (impərā'tər), *n.* an absolute ruler or commander.

im·per·cip·i·ent (impərsip'ēənt), *adj.* not perceiving; lacking perception.

im·pe·ri·ous (impēr'ēəs), *adj.* domineering; dictatorial.

im·pe·ri·um (impēr'ēəm), *n., pl.* **im·pe·ri·a** (impēr'ēə). command; absolute or supreme power.

im·pe·ti·go (im'piti'gō), *n.* a skin disease characterized by clusters of pustules.

im·pe·trate (im'pitrāt), *v.* to obtain by request or entreaty.

im·pig·no·rate (impig'nərāt), *v.* to pawn; pledge; mortgage.

im·plac·a·ble (implak'əbəl), *adj.* not to be appeased; irreconcilable; inexorable.

im·plic·it (implis'it), *adj.* **1.** unquestioning, absolute. **2.** implied, rather than plainly stated. See also **explicit.**

im·plode (implōd'), *v.* to burst inward. —**im·plo'sion,** *n.* —**im·plo' sive,** *adj.*

im·pol·i·tic (impol'itik), *adj.* unwise; inexpedient.

im·por·tune (im'pôrtōōn'), *v.* to demand urgently and persistently. —**im·por'tu·na·cy,** *n.* —**im·por'tu·nate,** *adj.* —**im·por·tu'ni·ty,** *n.*

im·pre·cate (im'prəkāt), *v.* to curse; invoke evil on a person. —**im·pre·ca' tion,** *n.*

Im·pres·sion·ism (impresH'ənizm), *n.* a 19th-century art movement endeavoring to capture the immediate sensuous impressions, obtained by the use of bold color and short brush strokes to convey light and shade effects.

im·pri·ma·tur (im'primä'tər), *n.* a licence or mark of approval from an authority.

im·pro·bi·ty (imprō'bitē), *n.* lack of principle; wickedness.

im·pu·dic·i·ty (im'pyŏŏdis'itē), *n.* lack of shame; immodesty.

im·pugn (impyŏŏn'), *v.* to assail by argument; call in question or oppose as false.

im·pu·is·sant (impyŏŏ'isənt), *adj.* feeble; powerless.

im·pu·ni·tive (impyŏŏ'nitiv), *adj.* (in a situation) not condemning anyone, but accompanied by feelings of shame. See also **extrapunitive.**

im·pu·ni·ty (impyŏŏ'nitē), *n.* exemption from penalty or punishment.

im·pu·tres·ci·ble (im'pyŏŏtres'-əbəl), *adj.* not subject to decomposition; incorruptible.

in ab·sen·tia (in absen'sHə), *Latin.* in absence.

in·ad·vert·ent (inədvur'tnt), *adj.* unthinking; unintentional. —**in·ad· vert'ence, in·ad·vert'en·cy,** *n.*

in·ap·pe·tence (inap'itəns), *n.* lack of appetite. Also **in·ap'pe·ten·cy.**

in·ca·les·cent (inkəles′ənt), *adj.* increasing in warmth or heat.

in·can·des·cence (inkəndes′əns), *n.* the state of glowing at high temperatures.

in·cept (insept′), *v.* to take in, as of an organism.

in·cho·ate (inkō′it), *adj.* just begun; incomplete; imperfect. —**in·cho·a′ tion,** *n.*

in·cip·i·ent (insip′ēənt), *adj.* beginning; in an early or initial stage.

in·con·dite (inkon′dit), *adj.* ill-composed; unpolished.

in·con·nu (inkənoo′, aNkônY′), *n., pl.* **in·con·nus.** an unknown person; novice; stranger.

in·con·ti·nent (inkon′tənənt), *adj.* unable to control natural evacuations. —**in·con′ti·nence,** *n.*

in·cras·sate (inkras′āt), *v.* to thicken a liquid by adding another substance or by evaporation.

in·cu·bus (in′kyəbəs), *n., pl.* **in·cu·bi** (in′kyəbī), **in·cu·bus·es.** an evil spirit said to annoy people while asleep, esp. one seeking sexual intercourse with women. See also **succubus.**

in·cul·cate (inkul′kāt), *v.* to impress on the mind by constant repetition; to teach forcibly.

in·cul·pate (inkul′pāt), *v.* to accuse; blame. —**in·cul′pa·to·ry,** *adj.*

in·cur·sion (inkur′zHən), *n.* an invasion; a raid; a harmful inroad.

in·cuse (inkyooz′), *adj.* hammered or stamped in, as an impression on a coin.

in·de·fea·si·ble (in′difē′zəbəl), *adj.* not to be forfeited or annulled.

in·de·fect·i·ble (in′difekt′əbəl), *adj.* unfailing; faultless.

in·de·his·cent (in′dihis′ənt), *adj.* (of plants) not opening when mature.

in·dem·ni·ty (indem′nitē), *n.* protection or insurance against loss; compensation for loss.

in·di·ci·a (indisH′ēə), *n., pl.* **in·di·ci·a, in·di·ci·as.** a marking on an envelope in place of a stamp. —**in·di′cial,** *adj.*

in·dict (indīt′), *v.* to charge or accuse of a crime. —**in·dict′ment,** *n.*

in·di·gene (in′dijēn), *n.* a native.

in·dig·e·nous (indij′ənəs), *adj.* originating in or characteristic of a particular country or region.

in·di·gent (in′dijent), *adj.* poor; needy; lacking the necessities of life.

indirect discourse, a written version of a statement, not exactly quoted but altered grammatically so as to be included in a longer sentence. See also **direct discourse.**

in·dite (indīt′), *v.* to compose; put into words; write.

in·dul·gent (indul′jənt), *adj.* showing lenience or tolerance.

in·du·men·tum (in′doomen′təm), *n., pl.* **in·du·men·ta** (in′doomen′tə), **in·du·men·tums.** a thick, hairy covering.

in·du·rate (in′doorāt), *v.* to harden; to make stubborn. —**in·du·ra′tion,** *n.*

in·ef·fa·ble (inef′əbəl), *adj.* indescribable; unutterable.

in·e·nar·ra·ble (in′inar′əbəl), *adj.* unspeakable; incapable of being told or described.

in·er·rant (iner′ənt), *adj.* unerring; free from error.

inertial guidance (inur′sHəl), a system of automatic guidance in a missile, by internal instruments regulated by the direction and magnitude of acceleration of the missile in flight.

in·ex·o·ra·ble (inek′sərəbəl), *adj.* incapable of persuasion by entreaty; unyielding; relentless.

in·ex·pug·na·ble (in′ikspug′nəbəl), *adj.* incapable of being taken by force; invincible.

in ex·tre·mis (in ekstre′mēs), *Latin.* near death.

in·fan·tile par·al·y·sis. See **poliomyelitis.**

in·farct (infärkt′), *n.* a portion of dying or dead tissue, caused by curtailed blood supply. —**in·farc′tion,** *n.*

infectious mononucleosis, glandular fever; a virus disease affecting the white blood cells, not severe but often prolonged.

in fla·gran·te de·lic·to (in flägrän′te delik′tō), *Latin.* the very act of committing an offense, specifically a sexual one.

in·flo·res·cence (in′flôres′əns), *n.* the process or condition of blossoming; flowering.

in·flu·ent (in′flo͞oənt), *adj.* **1.** flowing in, as a tributary into a larger river. —*n.* **2.** a tributary.

in·fra (in′frə), *adv.* below, as in a textual reference. See also **supra.**

in·fra·cos·tal (infrəkos′tl), *adj.* situated under the ribs.

in·fract (infrakt′), *v.* to break; infringe.

in·fra dig (in′frə dig′), beneath one's dignity; undignified. [Abbrev. for *infra dignitatem*]

in·fun·dib·u·lum (in′fundib′yələm), *n., pl.* **in·fun·dib·u·la** (in′fundib′-yələ). a funnel-shaped part or structure.

in·gem·i·nate (injem′ənāt), *v.* to reiterate; repeat.

in·gest (injest′), *v.* to take into the body, esp. food.

in·ges·ta (injes′tə), *n. pl.* substances taken in as nourishment.

in·gle·nook (ing′gəlno͝ok), *n.* a chimney corner.

in·grate (in′grāt), *n.* an ungrateful person.

in·gra·ves·cent (ingrəves′ənt), *adj.* increasing in severity or gravity, as an illness.

in·gress (in′gres), *n.* the act, right, or means of entering.

in·gui·nal (ing′gwənl), *adj.* situated in, or pertaining to the groin.

in·gur·gi·tate (ingur′jitāt), *v.* to swallow up greedily.

in·here (inhēr′), *v.* to remain fixed, to belong or exist permanently. —**in·her′ence,** *n.* —**in·her′ent,** *n.*

in·he·sion (inhē′zʜən), *n.* the fact or condition of inhering.

in·hume (inhyo͞om′), *v.* to bury.

in·im·i·cal (inim′ikəl), *adj.* hostile; unfriendly.

in·iq·ui·ty (inik′witē), *n.* unfairness; injustice; wickedness. —**in·iq′ui·tous,** *adj.*

in·lo·co·pa·ren·tis (inlō′kō pərən′tis), *Latin.* in place of a parent.

inn·age (in′ij), *n.* the quantity of goods left in a container when re-

ceived after dispatch. See also **out·age.**

in·ner·vate (inur′vāt, in′ərvāt), *v.* to furnish with nervous energy, stimulate. —**in·ner·va′tion,** *n.*

in·nerve (inurv′), *v.* to supply with nervous energy; innervate.

in·noc·u·ous (inok′yo͞oəs), *adj.* harmless; not injurious.

in·nom·i·nate (inom′init), *adj.* anonymous; without a name.

innominate bone, the hipbone, as made up of three bones: ilium, ischium, and pubis.

in·os·cu·late (inos′kyəlāt), *v.* to join so as to become continuous.

in·qui·e·tude (inkwī′ito͞od), *n.* restlessness; disturbance; uneasiness.

in·sa·lu·bri·ous (insəlo͞o′brēəs), *adj.* detrimental to health; unhealthy.

in·sa·tia·ble (insā′sʜəbəl), *adj.* incapable of being satisfied.

in·sec·ti·cide (insek′tisīd), *n.* a preparation used for destroying insects.

in·sec·ti·fuge (insek′təfyo͞oj), *n.* a preparation used for repelling insects.

in·sec·ti·vore (insek′təvôr), *n.* a plant or animal that feeds on insects. —**in·sec·tiv′o·rous,** *adj.*

in·sec·tol·o·gy (in′sektol′əjē), *n.* the scientific study of insects; entomology.

in·sen·ti·ent (insen′sʜēənt), *adj.* without feeling or sensation.

in·sid·i·ous (insid′ēəs), *adj.* treacherous; cunning; designed to entrap or deceive.

in si·tu (in sit′o͞o), *Latin.* in its original place; in position.

in·so·late (in′sōlāt), *v.* to expose to the rays of the sun. —**in·so·la′tion,** *n.*

in·sou·ci·ance (inso͞o′sēəns), *n.* indifference, lack of concern. —**in·sou′ci·ant,** *adj.*

in·spis·sate (inspis′āt), *v.* to make dense or thick.

in·stan·ter (instan′tər), *adv.* instantly; urgently.

in·suf·flate (insuf′lāt), *v.* to blow or breathe in.

in·su·lin (in′səlin), *n.* a hormone secreted in cells of the pancreas, used for the treatment of diabetes.

insulin shock, a collapsed condition arising from a decrease in blood sugar as a result of excessive doses of insulin. Also **insulin reaction.**

in·sur·gen·cy (insur′jənsē), *n.* an insurrection or rebellion.

in·sur·rec·tion (insərek′sHən), *n.* an act of revolt or rebellion against an established authority.

in·tagl·io (intal′yō), *n.*, *pl.* **in·tagl·ios.** a design incised or engraved on a hard surface. See also **cavo-relievo.**

in·tar·si·a (intär′sēə), *n.* the art of decorating a surface with inlaid patterns. Also **tarsia.** —**in·tar′sist,** *n.*

in·teg·u·ment (integ′yəmənt), *n.* a skin; covering; coating. —**in·teg·u·men′ta·ry,** *adj.*

in·tel·lec·tion (intəlek′sHən), *n.* the action or process of understanding.

in·tel·li·gent·si·a (intel′ijent′sēə), *n. pl.* intellectuals, considered as an educated, influential class, esp. as an élite.

in·ten·sion (inten′sHən), *n.* comprehension; connotation. See also **extension.**

in·ter a·li·a (in′tər ā′lēə), *Latin.* among other things.

in·ter a·li·os (in′tər ā′lēōs), *Latin.* among other persons.

in·ter·ca·lar·y (intur′kəlerē), *adj.* interposed; intervening.

in·ter·ca·late (intur′kəlāt), *v.* to interpose; interpolate. —**in·ter·ca·la′tion,** *n.*

in·ter·cen·sal (intərsen′səl), *adj.* of or pertaining to the period between two censuses; happening between two censuses.

in·ter·cos·tal (intərkos′tl), *adj.* relating to muscles or parts situated between the ribs. —**in·ter·cos′tal·ly,** *adv.*

in·ter·dict (intədikt′), *v.* to forbid; prohibit. —**in·ter·dic′tion,** *n.* —**in·ter·dic′tor·y,** *adj.*

in·ter·dig·i·tate (intərdij′itāt), *v.* to interlock, like the fingers of both hands when clasped.

in·ter·fer·om·e·ter (in′tərfərom′-itər), *n.* an instrument for measuring lengths, distances, etc., by means of

the interference properties of two rays of light.

in·ter·ja·cent (intərjā′sənt), *adj.* lying in between; intervening.

in·ter·loc·u·to·ry (intərlok′yətôrē), *adj.* intermediate; not finally decisive.

International Monetary Fund, an organization set up to stabilize world currencies and to help member nations to overcome financial crises.

International Style, a form of architecture, originating in the 1920's, emphasizing geometric shapes and large surfaces, and making much use of glass, steel, and reinforced concrete.

in·ter·ne·cine (intərnē′sēn), *adj.* mutually destructive; relating to feuds and struggles within a group.

in·ter·o·cep·tor (in′tərōsep′tər), *n.* a receptor which responds to stimuli that originate inside the body.

in·ter·os·cu·late (intəros′kyəlāt), *v.* to form a connecting link.

in·ter·pel·la·tion (in′tərpəlā′sHən), *n.* (in some legislative bodies) the process of demanding statements or explanations from ministers, often leading to a debate and vote of confidence in the government.

in·ter·reg·num (intəreg′nəm), *n., pl.* **in·ter·reg·nums, in·ter·reg·na** (intəreg′nə). a period between the end of a reign and the beginning of a new one.

in·ter·stice (intur′stis), *n.* a small or narrow opening between things or parts. —**in·ter·sti′tial,** *adj.*

in·tes·tines (intes′tinz), *n. pl.* the lower part of the alimentary canal between the stomach and the anus. —**in·tes′ti·nal,** *adj.*

in·ti·ma (in′təmə), *n., pl.* **in·ti·mae** (in′təmē). the innermost lining of a bodily part or organ, as a vein, etc.

in·time (aNtēm′), *adj. French.* cozy; intimate.

in·tim·i·date (intim′idāt), *v.* to make timid; cow; overawe. —**in·tim·i·da′tion,** *n.*

in·ti·mism (in′təmizm), *n.* a style of painting emphasizing an impressionistic portrayal of domestic scenes. —**in′ti·mist,** *adj.*

in·tort (intôrt′), *v.* to twist about a fixed point; curl. —**in·tor′sion**, *n.*

in·tra·mu·ral (intrəmyŏŏr′əl), *adj.* involving only the members of one school.

in·tran·si·gent (intran′sijənt), *adj.* unyielding; stubborn; uncompromising.

in·tra·u·ter·ine device (intrəyŏŏ′-tərin), a device, as a loop, placed in the uterus to stop conception. *Abbrev.:* **I.U.D.**

in·trav·a·sa·tion (intrav′əsā′sHən), *n.* the introduction of foreign matter into a blood vessel.

in·tro·mit (intrəmit′), *v.* to put or let in; admit; introduce.

in·tro·vert (in′trəvərt), *n.* a person primarily concerned with his own feelings, thoughts, and actions. See also **extrovert.**

in·tu·mesce (in′tŏŏmes′), *v.* to swell; inflate. —**in·tu·mes′cence**, *n.*

in·tus·sus·cept (in′tusəsept′), *v.* to take in; invaginate. —**in·tus·sus·cep′tion**, *n.*

in·unc·tion (inuNGk′sHən), *n.* the action of anointing.

in·u·tile (inyŏŏ′tl), *adj.* useless; of no service. —**in·u·til′i·ty**, *n.*

in va·cu·o (in vak′yŏŏō), *Latin.* in a vacuum; isolated; separate.

in·vag·i·nate (invaj′ənāt), *v.* to insert, as into a sheath; to draw back within itself. —**in·vag·i·na′tion**, *n.*

in·vec·tive (invek′tiv), *n.* violent and abusive denunciation or censure.

in·veigh (invā′), *v.* to attack verbally; denounce; rail.

in·vid·i·ous (invid′ēəs), *adj.* causing dislike or resentment; giving offense; hateful or harmful.

in·vig·i·late (invij′ilāt), *v.* to supervise students at an examination.

in·vin·ci·ble (invin′səbəl), *adj.* undefeatable; that cannot be conquered or surmounted.

in vi·tro (in vē′trō), *Latin.* within an artificial environment, as a laboratory; literally, in glass.

in vi·vo (in vē′vō), *Latin.* (in biology) within a live organism.

in·vo·lu·cre (in′vəlŏŏkər), *n.* a case or covering, esp. a membranous envelope.

in·vo·lut·ed (in′vəlŏŏtid), *adj.* involved; complex; complicated.

i·on·o·pause (īon′əpôz), *n.* the zone between the ionosphere and mesosphere.

i·on·o·sphere (īon′əsfēr), *n.* **1.** the portion of the earth's atmosphere between the stratosphere and exosphere. **2.** E layer.

i·on propulsion (ī′ən, ī′on), a projected form of propulsion for craft in outer space, the motive force being supplied by exhaust consisting of positive ions and negative electrons repelled by electrostatic forces.

ip·se dix·it (ip′sē dik′sit), *Latin.* **1.** he himself said it. **2.** an unproved, dogmatic statement.

ip·so fac·to (ip′sō fak′tō), *Latin.* literally; by the fact itself; by that very fact.

i·ra·cund (ī′rəkund), *adj.* angry, passionate.

i·ras·ci·ble (iras′əbəl), *adj.* easily angered; irritable. —**i·ras·ci·bil′i·ty**, *n.*

i·ren·ic (īren′ik), *adj.* pacific; promoting peace.

ir·re·cu·sa·ble (ir′ikyŏŏ′zəbəl), *adj.* not to be refused or rejected.

ir·re·den·ta (ir′iden′tə), *n.* a region linked historically, ethnically, or culturally with one nation, but governed by another.

ir·re·den·tist (ir′iden′tist), *n.* a member of a regional or national party advocating acquisition of foreign territory by reason of close historic, ethnic, or cultural ties.

ir·ref·ra·ga·ble (iref′rəgəbəl), *adj.* not to be refuted or disproved; undeniable.

ir·re·fran·gi·ble (ir′ifranj′əbəl), *adj.* not to be broken; inviolable.

ir·rem·e·a·ble (irem′ēəbəl), *adj.* permitting no return; irreversible.

ir·re·plev·i·sa·ble (ir′iplev′isəbəl), *adj.* (in law) not capable of being replevied or delivered on sureties.

ir·ro·rate (ir′ərāt), *adj.* marked with minute dots; speckled. Also **ir′ro·rat·ed.**

ir·rupt (irupt′), *v.* to burst or break in violently; to display emotion or activity. —**ir·rup′tion,** *n.* —**ir·rup′tive,** *adj.*

is·a·go·ge (ī′səgōjē), *n.* an introduction, as to a work of research. —**is·a·gog′ic** (īsəgoj′ik), *adj.*

is·al·lo·bar (īsal′əbär), *n.* (in meteorology) a line on a weather map linking points with equal pressure changes.

is·al·lo·therm (īsal′əthurm), *n.* (in meteorology) a line on a weather chart linking points with equal temperature variations over a given period.

is·a·nom·al (īsənom′əl), *n.* (in meteorology) a line on a map connecting points with equal anomaly or irregularity of a meteorological quantity.

i·sa·rithm (ī′səriTHəm), *n.* See **isopleth.**

is·aux·e·sis (ī′sôgzē′sis), *n.* (in biology) the growth rate of a part equal to that of the complete organism. See also **bradyauxesis, tachyauxesis.**

is·chi·um (is′kēəm), *n.*, *pl.* **is·chi·a.** **1.** the lowest of the three parts of the innominate bone. **2.** either of the bones on which the body rests when seated. —**is·chi·at′ic,** *adj.*

Ish·i·ha·ra test (isH′ēhä′rə), a color blindness test, developed in Japan, using cards which reveal different patterns to eyes with normal sight and eyes that are color blind.

islet of Lang·er·hans (laNG′gərhänz), one of several masses of cells in the pancreas secreting insulin.

i·so·bar (ī′səbär), *n.* (in meteorology) a line on a weather map connecting points with the same barometric pressure at a given time. —**i·so·bar′ic,** *adj.*

i·so·bath (ī′səbath), *n.* a line drawn on a map to connect points of equal depth below the water surface. —**i·so·bath′ic,** *adj.*

i·so·bath·y·therm (īsəbath′əthurm), *n.* a line on a sea chart, linking depths with the same temperature.

i·so·bront (ī′səbront), *n.* See **homobront.**

i·so·ce·phal·ic (ī′sōsəfal′ik), *adj.* (in a painting) having the representa-

tion of heads on the same level. Also **i·so·ceph·a·lous** (ī′sōsef′ələs).

i·so·ce·rau·nic (ī′sōsərô′nik), *adj.* (in meteorology) having the same frequency or intensity or simultaneous activity of thunderstorms. Also **isokeraunic.**

i·so·chasm (ī′səkazm), *n.* a line on a map linking points where auroras occur with equal frequency.

i·so·chro·mat·ic (ī′səkrōmat′ik), *adj.* having the same color.

i·soch·ro·nal (īsok′rənl), *adj.* occupying or happening in an equal amount of time. Also **i·soch′ro·nous.**

i·so·chrone (ī′səkrōm), *n.* a line on a map or chart made up of all points displaying some common and simultaneous property. —**i·soch′ro·nism,** *n.*

i·soch·ro·ny (īsok′rənē), *n.* the state or condition of occurring simultaneously.

i·soch·ro·ous (īsok′rōəs), *adj.* having the same color.

i·soc·ra·cy (īsok′rəsē), *n.* a form of government in which all people have equal power.

i·so·dose (ī′sədōs), *adj.* relating to all points having an equal intensity of radiation in a contaminated area.

i·so·dros·o·therm (īsədros′əthurm), *n.* (in meteorology) a line on a weather chart joining places with an equal dew point.

i·so·dy·nam·ic (ī′sōdīnam′ik), *adj.* **1.** marked by equal force or intensity. **2.** relating to an imaginary line linking points of equal horizontal intensity in the earth's magnetic field.

i·so·ge·o·therm (īsəjē′əthurm), *n.* an imaginary line connecting all points on the earth's surface with the same mean temperature.

i·sog·o·nal (īsog′ənl), *adj.* having equal angles, isogonic.

isogonal line, a line on a map linking points where the magnetic declination is the same. Also **i′so·gone.**

i·so·gon·ic (īsəgon′ik), *adj.* **1.** with equal angles. **2.** pertaining to an isogone.

i·so·gra·dient (īsəgrā′dēənt), *n.* (in

meteorology) a line on a weather map joining points with equal horizontal gradients, such as pressure or temperature.

i·so·gram (ī′sōgram), *n.* a line on a map or chart linking points with some common meteorological factor.

i·so·ha·line (īsəhā′lēn), *n.* a line on an ocean chart or map linking all points of equal salinity. Also **i·so·hal′sine.**

i·so·hel (ī′səhel), *n.* (in meteorology) a line on a weather chart linking points receiving equal amounts of sunshine.

i·so·hume (ī′səhyōōm), *n.* (in meteorology) a line on a weather chart joining points of equal relative humidity.

i·so·hy·et (īsəhī′ət), *n.* a line on a map connecting points having equal amounts of rainfall over a given period.

i·so·ke·rau·nic (ī′sōkirô′nik), *adj.* See **isoceraunic.**

i·so·mag·net·ic (ī′sōmagnet′ik), *adj.* pertaining to a line on a map connecting points with equal magnetic elements.

i·so·me·tro·pi·a (ī′sōmətrō′pēə), *n.* a condition in which the refraction is the same in either eye.

i·som·e·try (īsom′itrē), *n.* equality of measure.

i·so·morph (ī′səmôrf), *n.* an organism which has the same shape and appearance as another, but a different ancestry.

i·so·mor·phic (īsəmôr′fik), *adj.* having the same form or appearance, but different ancestry.

i·so·mor·phism (īsəmôr′fizm), *n.* the state of being isomorphic.

i·so·neph (ī′sənef), *n.* (in meteorology) a line on a weather map connecting points with equal amounts of cloudiness.

i·son·o·my (īson′əmē), *n.* equality of laws or political rights.

i·so·pach (ī′səpak), *n.* a line on a map connecting all points of equal geological thickness.

i·so·pach·ous (īsəpak′əs), *adj.* having equal thickness.

i·so·pag (ī′səpag), *n.* a line on a map

linking all points where winter ice exists at approximately the same time.

i·so·pec·tic (īsəpek′tik), *n.* a line on a map joining all points where winter ice begins to form at approximately the same time.

i·so·pi·es·tic (ī′sōpīes′tik), *adj.* of equal pressure.

i·so·pleth (ī′səpleth), *n.* a line on a map joining all points with equal numerical values. Also **isarithm.**

i·so·pod (ī′səpod), *n.* a crustacean with a flattened body and seven pairs of legs.

i·so·pol·i·ty (īsəpol′itē), *n.* equal civic and political rights.

i·so·por (ī′səpôr), *n.* an imaginary line on a map of the earth, joining points with equal annual variations in magnetic phenomena.

i·so·pyc·nic (īsəpik′nik), *n.* a line on a map linking points having equal water density.

i·sos·ce·les (īsos′əlēz), *adj.* (of a triangle) having two equal sides.

i·sos·ta·sy (īsos′təsē), *n.* the equilibrium of the earth's crust. —**i·so·stat′ic,** *adj.*

i·so·stere (ī′səstēr), *n.* (in meteorology) a line on a chart or map linking points of equal atmospheric density.

i·so·tac (ī′sətak), *n.* a line on a map connecting points where ice begins to melt during spring at approximately the same time.

i·so·tach (ī′sətak), *n.* (in meteorology) a line on a weather chart connecting points where the same wind velocities exist.

i·so·ten·i·scope (īsəten′iskōp), *n.* an instrument for measuring vapor pressure.

i·so·there (ī′səthēr), *n.* (in meteorology) a line on a weather map joining points with the same mean summer temperature.

i·so·therm (ī′səthurm), *n.* (in meteorology) a line on a weather map linking points with the same temperature.

i·so·ther·mal (īsəthur′məl), *adj.* taking place at a constant temperature.

i·so·ther·mo·bath (īsəthur′məbath),

n. a line on a vertical section of the sea linking all points having equal temperature.

i·so·tim·ic (īsətim′ik), *adj.* possessing an equal quantitative value at a given time.

i·so·tope (ī′sətōp), *n.* a chemical element having the same character as another but with a different radioactive property or atomic weight. —**i·sot·o·py** (īsot′əpē), *n.*

i·so·type (ī′sətīp), *n.* a symbol or drawing representing a certain general fact or quantity about the object depicted. —**i·so·typ′ic,** *adj.*

i·tai·i·tai (ē′tīē′tī), *n.* a bone-weakening disease caused by the presence of cadmium in the system. [from Japanese "Ouch! Ouch!"]

it·er (it′er), *n.* (in anatomy) a canal or passage.

it·er·ant (it′ərənt), *adj.* repeating; recurrent.

it·er·ate (it′ərāt), *v.* to utter or do repeatedly.

it·er·a·tive (it′ərətiv), *adj.* repeating; repetitious.

ith·y·phal·lic (ithəfal′ik), *adj.* indecent; obscene.

i·tin·er·ate (ītin′ərāt), *v.* to travel from place to place. —**i·tin′er·ant,** *adj., n.*

I.U.D., abbrev. for **intrauterine device.**

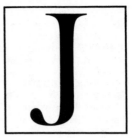

ja·bot (zHabō′), *n.* a ruffle or arrangement of lace worn at the neck or waist.

jack·leg (jak′leg′), *adj.* **1.** unskilled for one's job. **2.** dishonest in dealings.

jac·o·net (jak′ənet), *n.* a lightweight cotton material, used for clothing and bandages.

jac·ta·tion (jaktā′sHən), *n.* boasting; showing-off.

jac·u·late (jak′yəlāt), *v.* to throw (a javelin or spear).

jac·u·lif·er·ous (jak′yəlif′ərəs), *adj.* possessing spines like darts.

ja·pan (jəpan′), *n.* a hard, long-lasting black varnish, of Japanese origin, used on wood or other similar materials.

jape (jāp), *v.* **1.** to joke or make fun of. —*n.* **2.** a practical joke or wisecrack.

jar·di·niere (järdənēr′), *n.* an ornamental container for plants and flowers.

jar·o·vize (yär′əvīz), *v.* to hasten the development of seeds, etc., by some process. Also **iarovize, yarovize.**

jas·pé (jaspā′), *adj.* made to look veined, like jasper.

ja·to (jā′tō), *n.* a takeoff assisted by jet propulsion, esp. one assisted by rockets which are then jettisoned. [from *j(et)-a(ssisted) t(ake)-o(ff)*]

jaun·dice (jôn′dis), *n.* an illness caused by increased bile pigments in the blood, characterized by yellowness of skin. Also **icterus.**

jaun·diced (jôn′dist), *adj.* showing prejudice, often as the result of a personal experience.

jaw·bon·ing (jô′bōniNG), *adj.* using the power and prestige of the Government to persuade business and labor to moderate their demands in the national interest.

je·june (jijōōn′), *adj.* **1.** (of food) low in nutritive value. **2.** dull; uninteresting. **3.** lacking wisdom; immature.

je·ju·num (jijōō′nəm), *n.* part of the small intestine between the duodenum and the ileum.

je ne sais quoi (zHənsākwa′), *French.* a pleasing and undefinable quality of personality.

jeop·ard·y (jep′ərdē), *n., pl.* **jeop·ard·ies.** risk of exposure to harm or death.

jer·e·mi·ad (jer′əmī′ad), *n.* a lamentation or mourning.

jet·a·va·tor (jet′əvātər), *n.* an extended exhaust nozzle on a rocket, used to control the direction of the exhaust.

jet engine, an engine which imparts motion to a vehicle, esp. a plane, by thrusting backward a stream of liquid or air and gases.

jet·ton (jet′n), *n.* a stamped counter, used in card-playing, etc.

jeu d'es·prit (zHōōdesprē′), *pl.* **jeux d'es·prit** (zHōōdesprē′). *French.* **1.** a joke. **2.** a piece of sharply witty literature.

167

jig·ger (jig′ər), *n.* See **chigoe.**

jig·ger·y-pok·er·y (jig′ərēpō′kərē), *n.* falseness, deception, or trickery.

ji·had (jihäd′), *n.* a holy war waged by Muslims as a duty, or any such undertaking for a certain principle or concept. Also **je·had** (jēhäd′).

jin·go (jiNG′gō), *n.*, *pl.* **jin·goes.** someone who is patriotic to excess and wishes always to be prepared for war.

jin·go·ism (jiNG′gōizm), *n.* the policy of being prepared for war; aggressive patriotism.

jinn (jin), *n.* (in Islamic mythology) a type of spirit, lower than an angel, which can take human or animal form and influence man. Also **djin, djinn.**

jo·cose (jōkōs′), *adj.* given to humor or joking. —**jo·cos′i·ty,** *n.*

joc·u·lar (jok′yələr), *adj.* characterized by joking. —**joc·u·lar′i·ty,** *n.*

joc·und (jok′ənd, jō′kənd), *adj.* cheerful; happy. —**jo·cun′di·ty,** *n.*

joie de vi·vre (ZHwadəvēvr′), *French.* pleasure at being alive, esp. carefree enjoyment of life.

joule (jōōl, joul), *n.* the unit of work or energy equal to work achieved by one newton when it moves one meter in the direction of the force.

ju·bate (jōō′bāt), *adj.* hairy, as if covered by a mane.

ju·gal (jōō′gəl), *adj.* belonging to the cheek or cheekbone.

ju·gu·late (jōō′gyəlāt), *v.* **1.** to check a disease by drastic measures. **2.** to cut the throat of.

Jukes (jōōks), *n.* pseudonym for an actual family that over several generations exhibited a history of poverty, crime, illness, and social degeneracy. See also **Kallikak.**

ju·ras·sic (jōōras′ik), *adj.* a part of the Mesozoic epoch, 135,000,000 to 180,000,000 years ago, when dinosaurs and conifers were prevalent.

ju·rat (jōōr′at), *n.* a sworn public officer such as a magistrate.

ju·ra·tion (jōōrā′sHən), *n.* the taking or administering of an oath.

ju·ra·to·ry (jōōr′ətôrē), *adj.* constituting, expressed in, or pertaining to an oath.

ju·ris·dic·tion (jōōr′isdik′sHən), *n.* **1.** the authority to administer law. **2.** the extent, range, or territory where such authority is valid and can be exercised.

ju·ris·pru·dence (jōōr′isprōō′dns), *n.* the science and philosophy of law; a legal system.

juste-mi·lieu (ZHYstmēlyōō′), *n.*, *pl.* **juste-mi·lieux** (ZHY stmēlyōō′). *French.* the midpoint between two extremes.

ju·ve·nes·cent (jōō′vənes′ənt), *adj.* young or becoming young.

ju·ve·nil·ia (jōō′vənil′ēə), *n. pl.* works, esp. literature, produced for or by young people.

jux·ta·pose (juk′stəpōz), *v.* to put next to each other, esp. for comparison. —**jux·ta·po·si·tion** (juk′stəpəzisH′ən), *n.*

j'y suis, j'y reste (ZHēswē′ ZHērest′), *French.* here I am, and here I stay.

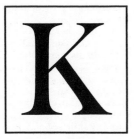

kaf·tan (käf′tn, käftän′), *n.* See **caftan.**

kak·is·toc·ra·cy (kak′istok′rəsē), *n.* government by the worst people in the state.

ka·lif, ka·liph (kā′lif, kal′if), *n.* See **caliph.**

kal·if·ate (kal′əfāt), *n.* See **caliphate.**

Kal·li·kak (kal′əkak), *n.* pseudonym for an actual family that over several generations exhibited a history of poverty, crime, illness and social degeneracy. See also **Jukes.**

ka·o·lin, ka·o·line (kā′əlin), *n.* a fine china clay used in making porcelain.

kar·ma (kär′mə), *n.* fate; destiny.

kar·y·og·a·my (kar′ēog′əmē), *n.* the fusion of cell nuclei, as in fertilization.

kar·y·o·ki·ne·sis (kar′ēōkinē′sis), *n.* the series of changes which take place in a cell nucleus in the process of dividing.

kar·y·o·plasm (kar′ēəplazm), *n.* the substance of a cell nucleus.

kar·y·o·type (kar′ēətīp′), *n.* the sum total of the characteristics of a set of somatic chromosomes.

ka·sha (kä′sнə), *n.* groats, especially of buckwheat when mulled and crushed. [from Russian]

ka·tab·a·sis (kətab′əsis), *n., pl.* **ka·tab·a·ses** (kətab′əsēz). a military retreat. See also **anabasis.**

kat·a·bat·ic (kat′əbat′ik), *adj.* (of a wind) moving downward or down a slope or valley. See also **anabatic.**

kat·a·mor·phism (kat′əmôr′fizm), *n.* metamorphism which changes complex minerals to simple minerals. See also **anamorphism.**

kat·a·pla·sia (kat′əplā′zнə), *n.* See **cataplasia.**

kat·a·to·ni·a (kat′ətō′nēə), *n.* See **catatonia.**

Ka·thar·e·vu·sa (kəthar′əvoo′sə), *n.* the literary form of modern Greek. See also **Demotic.**

ka·thar·sis (kəthär′sis), *n.* See **catharsis.**

keck (kek), *v.* to retch or heave; be nauseated.

kef (kāf), *n.* **1.** a drowsy, dreamy condition produced by narcotics, esp. marijuana. **2.** a hemp preparation smoked to produce such a condition. Also spelled **keef** (kēf), **kif.**

keg·ler (keg′lər), *n.* a person who bowls; a bowler.

ke·loid, che·loid (kē′loid), an excessive growth of scar tissue on the skin surface.

ke·lot·o·my, ce·lot·o·my (kəlot′-əmē), *n.* See **herniotomy.**

ken (ken), *n.* mental perception or recognition; range of knowledge.

ker·a·tal·gia (ker′ətal′jə), *n.* pain in the cornea.

ker·a·tin (ker′ətin), *n.* a substance found in horn, hair, nails, etc. Also **ceratin.** —**ker·at′i·nous,** *adj.*

ker·a·tog·e·nous (ker′ətoj′ənəs), *adj.*

169

causing the growth of horn or horny tissue.

ker·a·toid (ker′ətoid), *adj.* horn-like; horny. Also **ceratoid.**

ker·a·to·sis (ker′ətō′sis), *n., pl.* **ker·a·to·ses** (ker′ətō′sēz). any disease characterized by horny growth; any horny growth.

kerf, curf (kurf), *n.* the cut or channel made by a saw.

ker·sey (kur′zē), *n.* a heavy fabric of wool, similar to beaver, used for overcoats.

key punch, a machine with a simplified typewriter keyboard, used for punching holes in cards. Also **card punch.**

khan (kän), *n.* a public inn; caravansary.

kib·ble (kib′əl), *v.* to grind or divide into coarse particles or bits, as prepared dry dog food.

kib·butz (kibōōts′), *n., pl.* **kib·but·zim** (kibōōtsēm′). an Israeli collective settlement, esp. agricultural.

kib·itz·er (kib′itsər), *n.* a giver of unwanted advice; a meddler or busybody.

kick·shaw (kik′shô), *n.* **1.** a tidbit or delicacy. **2.** a trinket or gewgaw.

kid·ney (kid′nē), *n.* disposition or temperament; kind, class, or sort.

kiel·ba·sa (kilbä′sə), *n., pl.* **kiel·ba·sas, kiel·ba·sy** (kilbä′sē). a spicy smoked sausage of beef and pork, originated in Poland. Also **kiel·ba·sy** (kilbä′sē).

kif (kif), *n.* See **kef.**

kil·o·cy·cle (kil′əsī′kəl), *n.* former word for kilohertz.

kil·o·gauss (kil′əgous), *n.* a unit equal to 1000 gauss.

kil·o·gram (kil′əgram), *n.* a unit of mass and weight equal to 1000 grams (2.2046 lbs.).

kil·o·hertz (kil′əhurts), *n.* a unit of frequency equal to 1000 cycles per second.

kil·o·li·ter (kil′əlē′tər), *n.* 1000 liters; a cubic meter.

kil·o·me·ter (kil′əmē′tər), *n.* the common measure of distances of 1000 meters (0.621 mile).

kil·o·volt (kil′əvōlt), *n.* a unit of force equal to 1000 volts.

kil·o·watt (kil′əwot), *n.* a unit of power equal to 1000 watts.

kil·o·watt·hour (kil′əwotour′), *n.* a unit rate of consumption of electrical power equal to one kilowatt in one hour.

kin (kin), *n.* relatives; family; kinfolk.

kin·e·mat·ics (kin′əmat′iks), *n.* the branch of mechanics that deals with motion in the abstract, without reference to the masses or forces involved in it.

ki·ne·sics (kinē′siks), *n.* the study of bodily and facial movements as related to and accompanying communication or speech.

ki·ne·si·ol·o·gy (kinē′sēol′əjē), *n.* the study of human muscular movements and their relationship to human anatomy and physiology.

kin·es·the·sia, kin·aes·the·sia (kin′-isthē′zhə), *n.* the sensation of movement or position of limbs felt through nerves in the muscles, tendons, or joints. Also **kin·es·the′sis.**

kin·et·ic (kinet′ik), *adj.* of, resulting from, or characterized by motion.

ki·net·ics (kinet′iks), *n.* the branch of mechanics dealing with the relation between the motions of bodies and the forces acting upon them.

kin·e·to·sis (kin′itō′sis), *n.* illness caused by travel, usually in a vehicle; motion sickness.

kip (kip), *n.* the untanned hide of a young or small animal.

kirsch (kērsh), *n.* a colorless, unaged brandy made from cherries.

kish·ke (kish′kə), *n.* in Jewish cookery, a beef intestine stuffed with seasoned flour, breadcrumbs, etc., and roasted. Also **stuffed derma.**

kis·met (kiz′mit), *n.* fate; destiny. Also **kis·mat.**

kith (kith), *n.* friends, acquaintances, or neighbors.

kitsch (kich), *n.* art or writing of popular but shallow appeal; pretentious nonsense.

klep·to·ma·ni·a, clep·to·ma·ni·a (klep′təmā′nēə), *n.* an abnormal, persistent impulse to steal. —**klep·to· ma′ni·ac,** *n.*

klis·ter (klis′tər), *n.* a wax applied to skis when the snow is particularly wet.

knag·gy (nag′ē), *adj.* knotty; rough.

knar (när), *n.* a knot in wood.

knell (nel), *n.* the sound of a bell tolling, as for a funeral.

knish (knisH), *n.* in Jewish cookery, a thin piece of dough folded over a filling usually of potato or meat and baked or fried.

knoll (nōl), *n.* a small elevation; hillock or mound.

knop (nop), *n.* a knob or knob-like decoration.

knosp (nosp), *n.* an ornament in the shape of a bud.

knout (nout), *n.* a Russian whip with leather thongs.

knur (nur), *n.* a hard nob or knot on a tree.

knurl, nurl (nurl), *n.* any of a series of small beads or ridges, as along the edge of a coin.

ko·bold (kō′bold), *n.* (in German folklore) a house-haunting, often mischievous goblin.

ko·la (kō′lə), *n.* an extract of the kola nut.

kola nut, a brownish seed, produced by a tropical African and West Indian tree, formerly used as a stimulant in some soft drinks.

ko·nim·e·ter (kōnim′itər), *n.* a device for measuring the amount of dust in the air.

ko·ni·ol·o·gy, co·ni·ol·o·gy (kō′nē-ol′əjē), *n.* the study of impurities in the air, such as pollen, dust, etc.

ko·sher (kō′sHər), *adj.* (in Judaism) clean or fit to eat according to the dietary laws.

kour·bash (koŏr′basH). See **kurbash.**

kraal, craal (kräl), *n.* a South African native fenced village, often surrounding a cattle enclosure.

kra·ken (krä′kən), *n.* a legendary sea monster of northern seas.

krep·lach, krep·lech (krep′ləKH), *n.* small casings of dough, usually filled with chopped meat, etc., boiled and served in soup.

krieg·spiel (krēg′spēl), *n.* **1.** a game in which pieces representing military units are maneuvered on maps. **2.** a form of chess in which each player sees only his own pieces, his opponent's moves being told to him by a referee.

kris (krēs), *n.* See **creese.**

krumm·holz (kroŏm′hōlts), *n., pl.* **krumm·holz.** a forest of stunted trees near the timber line.

ku·chen (koō′KHən), *n.* a coffee cake made of yeast dough and often including raisings, nuts, etc.

ku·dos (koō′dōz), *n.* credit; praise; glory.

ku·gel (koō′gəl), *n.* (in Jewish cookery) a baked pudding-like casserole.

Kul·tur·kreis (koŏltoŏr′krīs), *n., pl.* **Kul·tur·krei·se** (koŏltoŏr′krīzə). (in anthropology) culture traits regarded as the nuclei of subsequent cultures. [German]

Kunst·lied (koŏnst′lēt), *n., pl.* **Kunst· lie·der** (koŏnst′lēdər). *German.* art song.

kur·bash, kour·bash (koŏr′basH), *n.* a leather whip.

kwash·i·or·kor (kwasH′ēôr′kôr), *n.* a nutritional disease of infants and children, occurring chiefly in Africa.

ky·mo·graph (kī′məgraf), *n.* **1.** an instrument that measures and records on a graph variations as of a human pulse. **2.** Also, **cymograph.** a device for measuring the oscillations of an aircraft in flight.

ky·pho·sis (kīfō′sis), *n.* a hunched back caused by curvature of the spine.

lab·a·rum (lab′ərəm), *n.*, *pl.* **lab·a·ra** (lab′ərə). a banner or standard bearing Christian symbols.

lab·e·fac·tion (lab′əfak′sHən), *n.* a weakening or downfall.

la·bi·al (lā′bēəl), *adj.* pertaining to a lip or lip-like part.

la·bi·a ma·jo·ra (lā′bēə məjôr′ə), *pl.*, *sing.* **la·bi·um ma·jus** (lā′bēəm mā′jəs). lip-like outer folds of the female external genital organs.

la·bi·a mi·no·ra (lā′bēə minôr′ə), *pl.*, *sing.* **la·bi·um mi·nus** (lā′bēəm mī′nəs). lip-like inner folds of the female external genital organs.

la·bile (lā′bil), *adj.* unstable; liable to change, esp. chemical change.

la·bi·um (lā′bēəm), *n.*, *pl.* **la·bi·a** (lā′bēə). a lip or lip-like part.

la·bret (lā′bret), *n.* an ornament inserted in a hole made through the lip.

la·brum (lā′brəm), *n.*, *pl.* **la·bra** (lā′brə). a lip or part resembling a lip.

lab·y·rin·thi·tis (lab′ərinthī′tis), *n.* inflammation of the inner ear. Also **otitis interna.**

lac·co·lith (lak′əlith), *n.* a domed mass of igneous rock formed by lava which, upon rising, forced up overlying strata without rupturing them. Also **lac·co·lite** (lak′əlīt).

lac·er·til·i·an (lasərtil′ēən), *adj.* **1.** pertaining to the suborder comprising the lizards; lizard-like. —*n.* **2.** a lizard. Also **la·cer·tian** (ləsur′sHən).

lach·ry·mal (lak′rəməl), *adj.* pertaining to tears.

lach·ry·mose (lak′rəmōs), *adj.* given to weeping; tearful.

la·cin·i·ate (ləsin′ēāt), *adj.* deeply lobed, with jagged edges; (of leaves) fringed.

la·con·ic (ləkon′ik), *adj.* brief or concise in speech. Also **la·con′i·cal.**

lac·o·nism (lak′ənizm), *n.* brevity of speech. Also **la·con·i·cism** (lakon′isizm).

lac·tal·bu·min (laktəlbyōō′min), *n.* the water-soluble protein contained in milk; in industry it is obtained by evaporating whey and is used in some prepared foods, in adhesives, and in varnishes.

lac·ta·ry (lak′tərē), *adj.* relating to or resembling milk.

lac·tate (lak′tāt), *v.* to produce or secrete milk naturally. —**lac·ta′tion,** *n.*

lac·tes·cent (laktes′ənt), *adj.* milky; secreting a milky juice.

lac·tif·er·ous (laktif′ərəs), *adj.* secreting or bearing milk or milky juice.

lac·to·scope (lak′təskōp), *n.* an optical instrument for measuring the cream content of milk.

la·cu·na (lakyōō′nə), *n.*, *pl.* **la·cu·nae** (ləkyōō′nē), **la·cu·nas.** a missing portion; gap. —**la·cu′nal, la′cu·nar·y,** *adj.*

la·cus·trine (ləkus′trin), *adj.* relating to a lake.

la·gen·i·form (ləjen′əfôrm), *adj.* flask-shaped.

la·ic (lā′ik), *adj.* non-clerical; lay; secular. Also **la′i·cal.**

la·i·cism (lā′isizm), *n.* secular control of a society; government by non-clerics.

la·i·cize (lā′isīz), *v.* to secularize; put under the control of non-clerics.

lais·sez faire (les′ā fer′), *French.* non-interference in the conduct of others.

la·i·ty (lā′itē), *n.* laymen; those not belonging to a particular profession and thus without first-hand knowledge of it.

lal·la·tion (lalā′sнən), *n.* substitution of the sound "*l*" for "*r*" or mispronunciation of the sound "*l*".

la·lop·a·thy (lalop′əthē), *n.* any speech defect.

lal·o·pho·bi·a (laləfō′bēə), *n.* morbid dread of speaking.

lal·o·ple·gi·a (laləplē′jēə), *n.* paralysis of the organs of speech except for the tongue.

La·maze technique (ləmäz′). See **psychoprophylaxis.**

lamb·da·cism (lam′dəsizm), *n.* (in phonetics) overuse of the sound "*l*" or its substitution for the sound "*r*".

lam·bent (lam′bənt), *adj.* **1.** running lightly over or playing on a surface. **2.** softly radiant. **3.** dealing gently and brilliantly with a topic. —**lam′ben·cy,** *n.*

lam·bert (lam′bərt), *n.* a unit used in measuring brightness, equal to the brightness of a perfectly diffusing surface radiating or reflecting one lumen per square centimeter.

lam·bre·quin (lam′brəkin), *n.* **1.** a short curtain covering the top of a door or window or hung from a shelf. **2.** a protective covering of cloth for a helmet.

lame duck, a disabled or ineffective person or thing, esp. an elected official completing a term of office after failing to win election for the following term.

la·mel·la (ləmel′ə), *n., pl.* **la·mel·lae** (ləmel′ē), **la·mel·las.** a thin plate, scale, or membrane, esp. of bone or

tissue. —**la·mel′lar, la·mel′late,** *adj.*

la·mel·li·form (ləmel′əfôrm), *adj.* like a lamella in shape; scale-like.

la·mel·lose (ləmel′ōs), *adj.* having or composed of lamellae. —**lam·el·los′i·ty,** *n.*

lam·i·na (lam′ənə), *n., pl.* **lam·i·nae** (lam′ənē), **lam·i·nas.** a thin layer or plate. —**lam′i·nar,** *adj.*

lam·i·nose (lam′ənōs), *adj.* composed of laminae; laminar. Also **lam′i·nous.**

lam·poon (lampōōn′), *v.* **1.** to satirize or ridicule. —*n.* **2.** a satire.

lam·proph·o·ny (lamprof′ənē), *n.* strength and clearness of voice. Also **lam·pro·pho′ni·a.**

la·nate (lā′nāt), *adj.* covered with wool or a woolly substance. Also **la·nose.**

lan·ce·o·late (lan′sēəlāt), *adj.* shaped like a spearhead; narrow and tapering to the apex.

lan·cet (lan′sit), *n.* a small, sharply pointed, double-edged, surgical knife.

lan·ci·form (lan′səfôrm), *adj.* lance-shaped.

lan·ci·nate (lan′sənāt), *v.* to pierce; stab.

land·lop·er (land′lōpər), *n.* a wanderer; adventurer. Also **land′loup·er.**

lang·lauf (läNG′louf), *n.* a ski race over undulating open country. —**lang′lau·fer,** *n.*

lan·guet (laNG′gwet), *n.* a small tongue-shaped part.

lan·guid (laNG′gwid), *adj.* sluggish; lacking in energy or spirit.

lan·guish (laNG′gwish), *v.* **1.** to be or become languid. **2.** to suffer weakening conditions, as in prison or sickbed. **3.** to long for or pretend to long for.

lan·guor (laNG′gər), *n.* **1.** weakness; lack of energy or spirit. **2.** mood of tenderness. **3.** stillness. —**lan′guor·ous,** *adj.*

la·ni·ar·y (lā′nēer′ē), *adj.* (of teeth) shaped for tearing.

la·nif·er·ous (lənif′ərəs), *adj.* wool-bearing. Also **la·nig′er·ous.**

lan·o·lin (lan′əlin), *n.* fatty matter extracted from sheep's wool, used in ointments and toiletries. Also **lan′o·line.**

la·nose (lā′nōs), *adj.* See **lanate.**

la·nu·gi·nose (lənōō′jənōs), *adj.* covered with lanugo; downy. Also **la·nu′gi·nous.**

la·nu·go (lənōō′gō), *n.* a covering of soft, downy hairs, esp. that of a newborn baby.

la·pac·tic (ləpak′tik), *adj.* aperient; effecting a purge.

lap·a·rot·o·my (lapərot′əmē), *n.* a surgical procedure of cutting the abdominal wall to gain access to the abdominal cavity.

lap·i·dar·y (lap′ədere), *n.* **1.** Also **lap′i·dist.** one who cuts, polishes, and engraves stones. **2.** the art of cutting, polishing, and engraving stones. —*adj.* **3.** relating to stones and their cutting, polishing, and engraving. **4.** distinguished by the sharpness and accuracy belonging to gem cutting.

lap·i·date (lap′idāt), *v.* to stone to death.

la·pil·lus (ləpil′əs), *n.*, *pl.* **la·pil·li** (ləpil′ī). a small pebble thrown out by a volcano.

lap·pet (lap′it), *n.* **1.** a small flap or loosely hanging piece (of a garment). **2.** a lobe of flesh.

lap·sus lin·guae (lap′səs liNG′gwē), *Latin.* a slip of the tongue.

lap·sus me·mo·ri·ae (lap′səs memôr′ēē), *Latin.* a lapse of memory.

lar·ce·ner (lär′sənər), *n.* one who has committed larceny. Also **lar′ce·nist.**

lar·da·ceous (lärdā′sHəs), *adj.* lardlike.

large-scale (lärj′skāl′), *adj.* large in relation to the original, as of a model, drawing, or other representation. See also **small-scale.**

lar·gess (lärjes′), *n.* **1.** the free and ample giving of money or gifts. **2.** the money or gifts thus given. Also **lar·gesse′.**

lar·ine (lar′in), *adj.* gull-like.

la·rith·mics (ləriTH′miks), *n.* the study of the relative numbers comprising different groups within a total population.

lar·va (lär′və), *n.*, *pl.* **lar·vae** (lär′vē). an insect between the time it leaves the egg and its metamorphosis into a pupa. —**lar′val,** *adj.*

lar·vi·cide (lär′visīd), *n.* a preparation for killing larvae.

lar·vip·a·rous (lärvip′ərəs), *adj.* of or pertaining to a larva-producing creature, as some insects and mollusks.

lar·viv·o·rous (lärviv′ərəs), *adj.* of or pertaining to a creature that eats larvae.

la·ryn·ge·al (lərin′jēəl), *adj.* **1.** relating to or in the larynx. **2.** of a sound formed in the larynx. —*n.* **3.** a sound formed in the larynx. Also **la·ryn·gal** (ləriNG′gəl).

lar·yn·gec·to·my (lərənjek′təmē), *n.* the surgical removal of all or part of the larynx.

lar·yn·gi·tis (lərənjī′tis), *n.* inflammation of the lining of the larynx.

lar·yn·gol·o·gy (lar′iNGgol′əjē), *n.* the field of medicine concerned with diseases of the throat.

la·ryn·go·pha·ryn·ge·al (ləriNG′-gōfərin′jēəl), *adj.* relating to or employing the larynx and pharynx.

la·ryn·go·phar·ynx (ləriNG′gōfar′-iNGks), *n.*, *pl.* **la·ryn·go·phar·yn·ges** (ləriNG′gōfərin′jēz), **la·ryn·go·phar·ynx·es.** the lower part of the pharynx, where it passes behind the larynx.

la·ryn·go·scope (ləriNG′gəskōp), *n.* a medical instrument for inspecting the larynx by means of a mirror.

lar·yn·gos·co·py (lar′iNGgos′kəpē), *n.* medical examination with a laryngoscope.

la·ryn·go·tra·che·al (ləriNG′gōtrā′-kēəl), *adj.* relating to the larynx and trachea.

lar·ynx (lar′iNGks), *n.*, *pl.* **la·ryn·ges** (lərin′jēz), **lar·ynx·es.** the cavity, at the top of the windpipe where it joins the pharynx, that contains the vocal cords.

la·sa·gna (ləzän′yə), *n.* a dish of broad ribbons of pasta cooked with meat and tomatoes and topped with cheese.

las·civ·i·ous (ləsiv′ēəs), *adj.* lustful; wanton.

la·ser (lā′zər), *n.* an optical maser; a

maser that amplifies radiation within or near the range of visible light.

lash·ings (lasH'iNGz), n. pl. (Colloquial) plenty; an abundance.

las·si·tude (las'itoōd), n. weariness; languor; indolence.

last-in, first-out (lastin' furstout'), a book-keeping device of entering materials constituting manufacturing costs at their current market price. *Abbrev.*: **LIFO.** See also **first-in, first-out.**

la·tah (lä'tə), n. a neurotic compulsion to imitate others in speech and action, occurring mainly among Malays. Also, **la'ta.**

la·ten·cy (lā'tənsē), n. the condition of being latent.

la·tent (lā'tnt), adj. existing but not manifest; potential; hidden.

lat·er·al (lat'ərəl), adj. of, at, from, or toward a side or sides.

lat·e·ral·i·ty (latəral'itē), n. the preference for using one hand rather than the other.

lat·er·i·tious (latərisH'əs), adj. of a brick-red colour. Also **lat·er·i'ceous.**

la·tex (lā'teks), n., pl. **lat·i·ces** (lat'isēz), **la·tex·es.** a milky fluid contained by various plants and exuded when they are cut, esp. that of some plants used in industry to make rubber.

lat·i·cif·er·ous (lat'isif'ərəs), adj. latex-bearing.

lat·i·tu·di·nar·i·an (lat'itoō'dəner'ēən), adj. tolerating widely differing opinions, esp. in matters of religion.

lat·i·tu·di·nous (lat'itoō'dənəs), adj. having latitude; having a liberal breadth of mind.

la·tri·a (lətrī'ə), n. (in the Roman Catholic Church) supreme worship to be offered only to God. See also **dulia, hyperdulia.**

lat·ten (lat'n), n. a brass-like alloy of copper, zinc, lead, and tin, formerly used for church utensils.

lat·ti·ci·nio (lat'iCHē'nyō), n., pl. **lat·ti·ci·ni** (lat'iCHē'nē). opaque white glass first made in Renaissance Venice, frequently used to decorate clear glass with thin white lines.

laud (lôd), v. to praise; honor by celebrating. —**laud'a·ble, laud'a·to·ry,** adj. —**lau·da'tion,** n.

lau·re·ate (lôr'ēit), adj. **1.** wreathed with laurel as a token of honor. **2.** worthy of honor; distinguished, as *the laureate artist.*

lau·rence (lôr'əns), n. mirage-like shimmering seen over a hot surface, caused by the refraction (bending) of light rays in the lower density of air at the hot surface.

lav·age (ləvāzH'), n. a washing.

lav·a·liere (lavəlēr'), n. an ornament worn on a chain round the neck.

lave (lāv), v. (in poetic use) to wash; to bathe. —**la·va'tion,** n.

la·ver (lā'vər), n. a basin or font.

lawn (lôn), n. fine, plain-woven material usually of cotton, formerly of linen.

lax·a·tion (laksā'sHən), n. a relaxing or loosening.

lay analyst, a psychoanalyst without medical qualification.

laz·ar (laz'ər), n. a diseased person, esp. a leper.

laz·a·ret·to (lazəret'ō), n. a hospital for indigent people suffering from contagious diseases, esp. from leprosy.

leach (lēCH), v. **1.** to percolate a liquid through some material. **2.** to be subjected to the action of percolating liquid, as soil.

Le·bens·raum (lā'bənzroum), n. extra scope, either territorial or in the way of freedom, claimed by a person or a nation so as to be able to achieve full development.

lech·er (leCH'ər), n. a man who excessively indulges his sexual desires. —**lech'er·ous,** adj. —**lech'er·y,** n.

lec·i·thal (les'əthəl), adj. having a yolk. Also **lec'i·thic.**

lec·tion (lek'sHən), n. one of variant readings of the same passage in a copy or edition of a written work.

lec·tor (lek'tər), n. a lecturer in a university or college.

lee (lē), n. the sheltered side of something; side away from the wind.

lee·ward (lē'wərd), adj. relating to,

leg·end·ist (lej′əndist), *n.* a writer or compiler of legends.

leg·end·ize (lej′əndīz), *v.* to make a legend of, as *his admirers legendized his exploits.*

leg·er·de·main (lej′ərdəmān′), *n.* dexterity in using the hands to perform conjuring tricks, juggling, and similar feats; any trickery, deception.

le·ger·i·ty (ləjer′itē), *n.* agility of mind or of limb.

leg·man (leg′man), *n.* one who does the work requiring travel outside the office, usually for another whose duties prevent his leaving the office.

leg-of-mutton sleeve. See gigot.

lei·o·my·o·ma (lī′ōmīō′mə), *n., pl.* **lei·o·my·o·mas, lei·o·my·o·ma·ta** (lī′ōmīō′mətə). an abnormal swelling composed of nonstriated muscle tissue.

leish·man·i·a·sis (lēsHmənī′əsis), *n.* infection by a certain flagellate protozoan.

leis·ter (lē′stər), *n.* a spear with three or more prongs, used to catch fish.

leit·mo·tif (līt′mōtēf), *n.* theme associated throughout a musical drama with a particular character, situation, or sentiment.

lem·ma (lem′ə), *n., pl.* **lem·mas, lem·ma·ta** (lem′ətə). an argument or subject in a literary composition.

len·i·ty (len′itē), *n.* gentleness; the quality of being soothing. —**len′i·tive,** *adj.*

len·tic (len′tik), *adj.* relating to or dwelling in still water. Also **le·nit′ic.**

len·ti·cle (len′tikəl), *n.* a window in a clock case allowing the movement of the pendulum weight to be seen.

len·tic·u·lar (lentik′jələr), *adj.* **1.** relating to a lens. **2.** lens-shaped, either with two convex surfaces or with one plane and one convex surface.

len·ti·go (lentī′gō), *n., pl.* **len·tig·i·nes** (lentij′ənēz). a freckle. —**len·tig′i·nous, len·tig′i·nose,** *adj.*

len·toid (len′toid), *adj.* lens-shaped.

le·o·nine (lē′ənīn), *adj.* of lions; lion-like.

lep·i·dop·ter·ol·o·gy (lep′idop′-tərol′əjē), *n.* the study of butterflies and moths. Also **lep·i·dop′te·ry.** —**lep·i·dop·te·rol′o·gist, lep·i·dop′ter·ist,** *n.*

lep·i·dop·ter·ous (lep′idop′tərəs), *adj.* belonging to or relating to the order of insects comprising butterflies and moths.

lep·o·rid (lep′ərid), *adj.* of or relating to the family comprising rabbits and hares.

lep·o·rine (lep′ərīn), *adj.* relating to or resembling a rabbit or hare.

lep·rol·o·gy (leprol′əjē), *n.* the medical field of study dealing with leprosy and its treatment.

lep·ro·sar·i·um (leprəser′ēəm), *n., pl.* **lep·ro·sar·i·a** (leprəser′ēə). a hospital where lepers are treated.

lep·rose (lep′rōs), *adj.* leprous.

lep·ro·sy (lep′rəsē), *n.* a mildly infectious bacterial disease giving rise to thickening and ulceration of the skin, excessive or deficient pigmentation, loss of sensation in certain nerve regions, and, in severe cases, deformity and blindness.

lep·rot·ic (leprot′ik), *adj.* of leprosy; leprous.

lep·rous (lep′rəs), *adj.* having, of, or like leprosy.

lep·to·dac·ty·lous (leptədak′tələs), *adj.* slender-toed; having slender toes.

lep·to·phyl·lous (lep′tōfil′əs), *adj.* slender-leaved.

lep·to·pro·so·pic (lep′tōprəsō′pik), *adj.* having a narrow face.

lep·tor·rhine (lep′tərīn), *adj.* having a narrow, prominent nose.

lep·to·some (lep′təsōm), *n.* a person of long narrow build.

les·bi·an·ism (lez′bēənizm), *n.* homosexuality in women. —**les′bi·an,** *n., adj.*

lese majesty (lēz), attack or outrage upon any institution or custom venerated or held in great affection by a large number of people.

le·sion (lē′zHən), *n.* wound; injury; damage.

lesser omentum, an omentum joined

to the stomach, and supporting the vessels of the liver. See also **omentum, greater omentum.**

les·to·bi·o·sis (les′tōbīō′sis), *n.*, *pl.* **les·to·bi·o·ses** (les′tōbīō′sēz). a form of living distinguished by furtive stealing; as one of the ways that ants order their society, in which two species live side by side and one lives by furtively stealing the food collected by the other. —**les·to·bi·ot·ic** (les′tōbīot′ik), *adj.*

le·thar·gic (ləthär′jik), *adj.* relating to or suffering from lethargy.

leth·ar·gy (leth′ərjē), *n.* drowsiness; apathy; torpor.

leu·ke·mia, leu·kae·mi·a (lookē′-mēə), *n.* an incurable blood disease characterized by excessive production of white cells; cancer of the blood. Also **leu·ce·mi·a** (loosē′mēə).

leu·ko·cyte, leu·co·cyte (loo′kəsīt), *n.* a white blood cell. —**leu·ko·cyt′ic**, *adj.*

leu·ko·ma, leu·co·ma (lookō′mə), *n.* a disorder in which the cornea is white and opaque.

leu·ko·pe·ni·a, leu·co·pe·ni·a (lookəpē′nēə), *n.* a decrease in the number of white cells in the blood.

leu·ko·poi·e·sis, leu·co·poi·e·sis (loo′kōpoiē′sis), *n.* the development of white blood cells.

le·va·tor (livā′tər), *n.*, *pl.* **lev·a·to·res** (levətôr′ēz). any muscle used to raise a part of the body.

lev·ee[1] (lev′ē), *n.* an artificial embankment built to prevent flooding.

lev·ee[2] (lev′ē, levē′), *n.* a reception; assembly of visitors.

lev·er·et (lev′ərit), *n.* a young hare.

lev·i·gate (lev′əgāt), *v.* to reduce to a fine powder or smooth paste. —**lev·i·ga′tion**, *n.*

lev·i·rate (lev′ərit), *n.* the custom by which a dead man's brother or next of kin had to marry his widow, practised formerly in parts of America and Asia, and in Biblical Jewry under certain conditions.

lev·i·ty (lev′itē), *n.* frivolity; lack of serious thought; making light of a serious matter.

le·vo·gy·rate, lae·vo·gy·rate (lēvə-jī′rāt), *adj.* levorotatory.

le·vo·ro·ta·tion, lae·vo·ro·ta·tion (lē′vōrōtā′sнən), *n.* a turning to the left of the plane of polarization of a ray of polarized light, caused by various chemical substances and solutions.

le·vo·ro·ta·to·ry, lae·vo·ro·ta·to·ry (lēvərō′tətôrē), *adj.* having the property of levorotation.

lev·u·lose (lev′yəlōs), *n.* a levorotatory form of glucose; fructose; fruit sugar.

lex·i·cal (lek′sikəl), *adj.* pertaining to the vocabulary of a language.

lex·i·cog·ra·pher (lek′sikog′rəfər), *n.* a maker or compiler of a dictionary.

lex·i·cog·ra·phy (lek′sikog′rəfē), *n.* the making or compiling of dictionaries.

lex·i·col·o·gy (lek′sikol′əjē), *n.* **1.** the study of words and their meanings and idiomatic usage. **2.** the study of the theory of lexicography and of lexicon. —**lex·i·col′o·gist**, *n.*

lex·i·con (lek′səkon), *n.*, *pl.* **lex·i·ca** (lek′səkə), **lex·i·cons.** the vocabulary of a language, individual, or particular group of people.

lex·i·phan·ic (leksəfan′ik), *adj.* bombastic or pretentious.

lex ta·li·o·nis (leks tal′ēō′nis), *Latin.* the law of retaliation, as an eye for an eye, a tooth for a tooth. Also **talion.**

li·ba·tion (lībā′sнən), *n.* the pouring of a drink, esp. of wine, as an offering to a god.

lib·er·tar·i·an (libərter′ēən), *n.* an advocate of liberty of thought and action.

lib·er·tine (lib′ərtēn), *n.* a dissolute, licentious man; one who gives free rein to his sexual or immoral wishes. —**lib′er·tin·age, lib′er·tin·ism**, *n.*

li·bid·i·nous (libid′inəs), *adj.* lustful; relating to the libido.

li·bi·do (libē′dō), *n.* the sexual drive; the instinctive desire that prompts all human activities.

li·brate (lī′brāt), *v.* to oscillate; swing from side to side. —**li·bra′tion**, *n.*

li·cen·ti·ate (līsen′sнēit), *n.* holder of

a certificate of competence awarded by some academic or professional examination board.

li·cen·tious (līsen′sḤəs), *adj.* lustful; uncontrolled in sexual indulgence.

li·chen (lī′kən), *n.* a dual plant organism of fungus and alga in symbiosis, forming a gray, yellow, green, or brown crust-like covering where it grows on trees, stones, etc. —**li′chen·oid, li′chen·ous,** *adj.*

lic·it (lis′it), *adj.* lawful; permitted.

lick·er·ish (lik′ərisḤ), *adj.* lustful; lecherous. Also **liqu′or·ish.**

lick·spit·tle (lik′spitl), *n.* toady; sycophant. Also **lick′spit.**

lieb·frau·milch (lēb′froumilk′), *n.* a white wine from West Germany, produced mainly in the province of Hesse.

Lie·der·kranz (lē′dərkränts), *n.* trademark of a strong-flavored, soft-ripening cheese made up in small blocks.

lief (lēf), *adv.* willingly; gladly.

lien[1] (lēn), *n.* the legal right to keep possession of another's property until a debt due on it is paid.

li·en[2] (lī′ən), *n.* the spleen.

li·en·ec·to·my (līənek′təmē), *n.* the surgical removal of the spleen; splenectomy.

li·en·i·tis (līənī′tis), *n.* inflammation of the spleen.

life style, the integrated way a person's individual taste and style is expressed through the clothes he wears, the furniture and decor of his home, and the social life he leads. Also **life-style.**

LIFO (lī′fō). See **last-in, first-out.**

lig·a·ment (lig′əmənt), *n.* a short band of strong, flexible fibrous tissue holding two bones together at a joint and preventing dislocation. —**lig·a·men′tous,** *adj.*

li·gate (lī′gāt), *v.* to bind with a ligature.

lig·a·ture (lig′əcḤər), *n.* **1.** a binding up. **2.** a thing used for binding up, esp. a cord or bandage. **3.** a character or type combining two or more letters, as "fi".

light·er (lī′tər), *n.* a boat, often flat-bottomed, used for loading and unloading ships standing off a wharf and for carrying goods into the harbor or for other short distances.

light·er·age (lī′tərij), *n.* the use of lighters to load and unload ships.

light heavyweight, a boxer of the class intermediate between middle-weight and heavyweight, weighing 178 lb. or less if an amateur, 175 lb. or less if a professional. Also **cruiser-weight.**

light middleweight, an amateur boxer of the class intermediate between welterweight and middle-weight and weighing 156 lb. or less.

light·some (līt′səm), *adj.* **1.** light in movement or spirits. **2.** giving out light; brightly illuminated.

light·weight (līt′wāt), *n.* a boxer of the class intermediate between feather-weight and welterweight and weighing 133 lb. or less if an amateur, 135 lb. or less if a professional.

light welterweight, an amateur boxer of the class between lightweight and welterweight, weighing 140 lb. or less.

light-year (līt′yēr), *n.* the distance traveled by light in one solar year; used as a unit in measuring stellar distances. See also **parsec.**

lig·ne·ous (lig′nēəs), *adj.* woody.

lig·nic·o·lous (lignik′ələs), *adj.* growing on or in wood.

lig·ni·form (lig′nəfôrm), *adj.* wood-like in form.

lig·ni·fy (lig′nəfī), *v.* to become or cause to become wood or woody.

lig·nin (lig′nin), *n.* a compound chemical substance formed in the walls of certain plant cells and giving them strength and rigidity; it forms up to 50 per cent of the wood in trees.

lig·nite (lig′nīt), *n.* a brown woody coal.

lig·niv·or·ous (ligniv′ərəs), *adj.* wood-eating; feeding on or boring into wood.

lig·u·la (lig′yələ), *n., pl.* **lig·u·lae** (lig′yəlē), **lig·u·las.** a strap-shaped part, esp. a thin membrane at the base of a leaf-blade in grasses. —**lig′u·late,** *adj.*

li·la·ceous (līlā′sнəs), *adj.* of lilac color.

lil·i·a·ceous (lil′ēā′sнəs), *adj.* **1.** relating to the lily; lily-like. **2.** belonging to the family of lilies.

lim·a·cine (lim′əsīn)˘ *adj.* relating to or resembling a slug.

lim·bate (lim′bāt), *adj.* having a different-colored border, esp. of flowers.

lim·bo (lim′bō), *n.* a supposed place in which forgotten and unwanted things are regarded as being.

li·men (lī′mən), *n.*, *pl.* **li·mens, lim·in·a** (lim′ənə). threshold; limit below which a given stimulus ceases to be perceptible.

li·mes (lī′mēs), *n.*, *pl.* **lim·i·tes** (lim′itēz). a boundary, esp. a fortified boundary of a country.

li·mic·o·line (līmik′əlīn) *adj.* dwelling on the shore.

li·mic·o·lous (limik′ələs), *adj.* living in mud or in a muddy place.

lim·i·nal (lim′ənl), *adj.* at or relating to the limen.

lim·ner (lim′nər), *n.* a painter, esp. of portraits.

lim·net·ic (limnet′ik), *adj.* of or relating to creatures and plants that live in fresh waters.

lim·nol·o·gy (limnol′əjē), *n.* the study of fresh waters and the plants and creatures that live in them. —**lim·no·log′i·cal,** *adj.*

lim·pid (lim′pid), *adj.* clear and transparent, as water, air, eyes, etc.

lim·u·lus (lim′yələs), *n.*, *pl.* **lim·u·li** (lim′yəlī). a horseshoe crab. —**lim′u·loid,** *adj.*

lin·e·a·ments (lin′ēəmənts), *n.* (sometimes used in singular) distinctive features or characteristics, esp. of the face.

lin·e·ar accelerator (lin′ēər), a device to propel charged particles in straight lines by alternating electric voltages arranged to give increasing gains of energy to the particles.

lin·e·ate (lin′ēit), *adj.* lined; striped.

lin·e·a·tion (lin′ēā′sнən), *n.* the drawing, tracing, or arrangement of lines.

lin·e·o·late (lin′ēəlāt), *adj.* marked with fine lines.

lin·gua (liNG′gwə), *n.*, *pl.* **lin·guae** (liNG′gwē). the tongue. —**lin′gual,** *adj.*

lin·gua fran·ca (liNG′gwə fraNG′kə), *n.*, *pl.* **lin·gua fran·cas, lin·guae fran·cae** (liNG′gwē fran′sē). any language used by various different peoples who have different native languages.

lin·gui·form (liNG′gwəfôrm), *adj.* tongue-shaped.

lin·gui·ni (liNGgwē′nē), *n.* long, flat strips of pasta.

lin·guis·tics (liNGgwis′tiks), *n.* the scientific study of language, including its sounds, word forms, grammar, orthography, and historical development.

lin·gu·late (liNG′gyəlāt), *adj.* tongue-shaped.

lin·sey-wool·sey (lin′zēwо̄о̄l′zē), *n.* a fabric with coarse woolen weft and linen or cotton warp. Also **lin′sey.**

lin·tel (lin′tl), *n.* a horizontal support of timber, stone, or concrete across the top of a window- or door-opening.

li·on·ize (lī′ənīz), *v.* to treat a person as a celebrity.

li·pase (lī′pās), *n.* one of a class of enzymes that break down the fat produced by the liver or pancreas.

li·pec·to·my (lipek′təmē), *n.* the surgical removal of a superficial layer of fat.

li·pe·mi·a, li·pae·mi·a (lipē′mēə), *n.* the presence of excessive fat or fatty substance in the blood. —**li·pe′mic,** *adj.*

lip·o·gram (lip′əgram), *n.* a written work using only words that do not contain a certain letter or letters of the alphabet. —**lip·o·gram·mat′ic,** *adj.*

li·pog·ra·phy (lipog′rəfē), *n.* the accidental elimination of some letter, syllable, etc., in writing.

lip·oid (lip′oid), *adj.* fat-like. Also **lip·oi′dal.**

li·po·ma (lipō′mə), *n.*, *pl.* **li·po·mas, li·po·ma·ta** (lipō′mətə). a benign tumor composed of fatty tissue.

lip·o·pex·i·a (lipəpek′sēə), *n.* the storage of fat in the body. Also **adipo-pexia, adipopexis.**

li·quate (lī′kwāt), *v.* to separate or purify metals by heating sufficiently to melt out the various constituents.

liq·ue·fa·cient (likwəfā′sHənt), *n.* that which causes liquefaction.

liq·ue·fac·tion (likwəfak′sHən), *n.* the act of becoming or making liquid.

li·ques·cent (likwes′ənt), *adj.* becoming liquid. —**li·ques′cence,** *n.*

liqu·or·ish (lik′ərisH), *adj.* See **lickerish.**

lis·some, lis·som (lis′əm), *adj.* lithe; supple; agile; active.

lis·sot·ri·chous (liso′trikəs), *adj.* straight-haired.

lit·a·ny (lit′ənē), *n.* a lengthy, monotonous narration, as *a litany of complaints.*

li·ter (lē′tər), *n.* a metric unit of measurement equal to 1.0567 U.S. liquid quarts.

lit·e·ra·ti (litərä′tē), *n. pl.* men of letters; intellectuals.

lit·e·ra·tion (litərā′sHən), *adv.* letter for letter; with exact correspondence to an original text.

lithe (līTH), *adj.* flexible; supple. Also **lithe′some.**

li·the·mi·a (lithē′mēə), *n.* an excess of uric acid in the blood. Also called **uricacidemia.**

li·thi·a·sis (lithī′əsis), *n.* the presence or development in the body of stony solids usually consisting of layers of mineral salts.

lith·ic (lith′ik), *adj.* composed of or relating to stone, esp. the stony solids formed in the body.

li·thog·ra·phy (lithog′rəfē), *n.* a method of printing using a flat plate of metal, formerly stone, on which specially greased or treated portions take up ink and transfer it to paper while the other parts make no impression. —**lith′o·graph,** *n.* —**li·thog′ra·pher,** *n.*

lith·oid (lith′oid), *adj.* stone-like.

li·thol·a·pax·y (lithol′əpak′sē), *n.* a surgical operation in which stones are crushed within the organ where they formed and are washed out.

li·thol·o·gy (lithol′əjē), *n.* **1.** the study of the nature and composition of stones and rocks. **2.** the field of medicine that deals with the stony substance known as calculus which forms in the human body.

lith·o·me·te·or (lithəmē′tēər), *n.* a mass of solid particles suspended in the air, as dust.

lith·o·phile (lith′əfīl), *adj.* having a tendency to react to rocks in the earth's crust, as a chemical element.

lith·o·sphere (lith′əsfēr), *n.* the earth's outer crust.

li·thot·ri·ty (lithot′ritē), *n.* a surgical procedure in which a stone that has formed in the bladder is crushed into particles small enough to pass out when the bladder is emptied.

li·thu·ri·a (lithyŏŏr′ēə), *n.* a condition in which the urine contains an excess of uric acid.

lit·to·ral (lit′tərəl), *adj.* **1.** of, on, or near the shore. —*n.* **2.** an area lying along the shore.

lit·ur·gy (lit′ərjē), *n.* **1.** a set form or ritual for public worship. **2.** a collection or arrangement of services for public worship. —**li·tur′gi·cal,** *adj.*

liv·er·ish (liv′ərisH), *adj.* having a personality that is bilious; unpleasant and disagreeable.

liv·id (liv′id), *adj.* having a leaden, blue-gray discoloration of the flesh, as from bruising or strangulation.

load·stone, lode·stone (lōd′stōn′), *n.* a magnetic oxide of iron (magnetite) that acts as a natural magnet in attracting iron.

loath (lōth, lōTH), *adj.* disinclined; reluctant; unwilling.

loathe (lōTH), *v.* to regard with disgust; to detest. —**loath′some,** *adj.*

lo·bar (lō′bər), *adj.* relating to a lobe.

lo·bate (lō′bāt), *adj.* having or being a lobe.

lo·be·line (lō′bəlēn), *n.* a chemical substance extracted from lobelia, used as a nicotine substitute in discouraging tobacco smoking because it produces similar physiological reactions.

lo·bot·o·my (lōbot′əmē), *n.* a surgical

incision made in a lobe of the brain to change the behavior of a person, usually one suffering severe mental illness.

lobster thermidor, cooked lobster flesh in a cream sauce sprinkled with grated cheese and browned on top, usually served in the lobster shell.

lob·u·late (lob′yəlit), *adj.* composed of or having small lobes.

lob·ule (lob′yōōl), *n.* a small lobe.

lob·u·lus (lob′yələs), *n., pl.* **lob·u·li** (lob′yəlī). (in anatomy) a lobule.

lo·bus (lō′bəs), *n., pl.* **lo·bi** (lō′bī). (in anatomy) a lobe.

lock·jaw (lok′jô), *n.* a form of blood poisoning in which the victim is unable to open his jaws. See also **tetanus.**

loc·u·lar (lok′yələr), *adj.* relating to or having one or more small cavities or compartments.

loc·u·late (lok′yəlāt), *adj.* having one or more small cavities or compartments.

loc·u·lus (lok′yələs), *n., pl.* **loc·u·li** (lok′yəlī). a small cavity or compartment.

lo·cus (lō′kəs), *n., pl.* **lo·ci** (lō′sī). the exact place; locality.

lo·cu·tion (lōkyōō′sнən), *n.* a particular idiom or turn of phrase.

lode·stone (lōd′stōn′), *n.* See **loadstone.**

log·gia (loj′ə), *n. Italian.* an arcade or gallery open on one or both sides.

logical positivism, a contemporary philosophical doctrine based on empiricist traditions, characterized by its attempt to show all philosophical problems to be linguistic in nature and to avoid all metaphysical statements, and aiming to provide a comprehensive philosophy of science founded on linguistic analysis.

lo·gi·on (lō′gēon), *n., pl.* **lo·gi·a** (lō′-gēə), **lo·gi·ons.** a traditional saying; adage; proverb.

lo·gis·tics (lōjis′tiks), *n. (used as sing. or pl.)* the military science and practice of moving, accommodating, and providing supplies for troops. —**lo·gis′tic, lo·gis′tic·al,** *adj.*

log·o·gram (lô′gəgram), *n.* a short-

hand sign for a word or phrase. Also **log′o·graph.** —**log·o·graph′ic,** *adj.*

lo·gog·ra·phy (lōgog′rəfē), *n.* a method of recording in longhand in which several people in turn write down a few words.

log·o·griph (lô′gəgrif), *n.* an anagram or anagrammatic word-puzzle, sometimes involving clues in verse.

lo·gom·a·chy (lōgom′əkē), *n.* **1.** a dispute about words; a controversy turning on a verbal point. **2.** a card game in which words are formed with letters shown singly on cards.

log·o·pe·dics (lôgəpē′diks), *n.* the study and treatment of speech defects. Also **log·o·pe′di·a.**

log·or·rhe·a (lôgərē′ə), *n.* **1.** a medical condition in which speech is incoherent. **2.** (Informal) excessive talking; prattle.

lo·gos (lō′gos), *n.* **1.** the word of God incarnate; Christ. **2.** (in philosophy) the principles that govern the universe.

log·o·type (lô′gətīp), *n.* the trademark or emblem of a company. See also **ideograph.**

log·roll (lôg′rōl), *v.* to bring about the passing of legislation by logrolling.

log·roll·ing (lôg′rōliNG), *n.* (in U.S. politics) the mutual patronage or support among politicians to achieve their (sometimes unprincipled) purposes.

lon·ga·nim·i·ty (loNGgənim′itē), *n.* long-suffering; endurance of hardship.

longe (lunj), *n.* a long rope for leading and directing a horse during training or exercise.

lon·ge·vous (lonjē′vəs), *adj.* long-lived.

long·hair (lôNG′her), *n.* an intellectual or person involved with the arts. —**long′haired,** *adj.*

lon·gi·corn (lon′jikôrn), *adj.* with long antennae.

long pig, pidgin for human flesh as a food for cannibals.

long·some (lôNG′səm), *adj.* tedious; so long as to cause boredom.

lon·gueur (lôNGgur′), *n.* a tedious

long wave

long wave 182

stretch, as of time or of a passage in a musical or literary work.

long wave. 1. a radio wave more than 60 meters long. See also **short wave. 2.** See **L wave.**

loo·by (lо̄о̄′bē), *n.* a silly, stupid fellow.

loo·fa, loo·fah (lо̄о̄′fə), *n.* See **luffa.**

loo·kum (lо̄о̄′kəm), *n.* a shelter or roof for some equipment.

lop·er (lō′pər), *n.* one of two supports which comes forward to support a hinged leaf of a desk or table in horizontal position. Also called **draw runner, draw slip.**

loph·o·dont (lof′ədont), *adj.* having transverse ridges on the crown of the molar teeth.

lo·quac·i·ty (lōkwas′itē), *n.* talkativeness. —**lo·qua·cious** (lōkwā′sHəs), *adj.*

lord·ling (lôrd′liNG), *n.* a young or unimportant lord; insignificant person behaving in a lordly manner.

lor·gnette (lôrnyet′), *n.* a pair of spectacles or opera glasses in a rigid frame with a handle.

lor·gnon (lôrnyôN′), *n.* a pair of glasses or spectacles, esp. in the form of a pince-nez.

lo·ri·ca (lōrī′kə), *n., pl.* **lo·ri·cae** (lōrī′sē). **1.** the defensive covering of hard scales, plates, bone, etc., found on some species of animals. **2.** body armor consisting of a breastplate and backplate made of leather or metal; cuirass. —**lor′i·cate,** *adj.*

lor·i·mer (lôr′əmər), *n.* a maker of metal parts for harnesses and riding equipment.

loss leader, an item sold in a store at a loss to attract custom.

lost-wax process, a technique for metal casting of sculpture in which a core of clay is covered with wax which in turn is enclosed by the mold made from the artist's work; molten metal is then poured into a hole at the top and replaces the wax, which melts and runs out at the bottom. Also **cire perdue.**

Lo·thar·i·o (lōther′ēō), *n.* a man who charms and deceives women; rake.

lo·toph·a·gi (lətof′əjī), *n. pl.* lotuseaters.

lo·tus-eat·er (lō′təsē′tər), *n.* **1.** one of the Lotophagi, in ancient Greek legend a people found by Odysseus living in luxurious indolence and dreaminess because of eating the fruit of the lotus plant. **2.** one who leads a life of dreamy indolence.

Louis XIII, designating a style in furniture and architecture prevalent in early 17th-century France, characterized by the beginning of a return to classicism from Renaissance freedom and inventiveness. Also **Louis Treize** (trez).

Louis XIV, designating a style in furniture and architecture prevalent in late 17th-century France, characterized by its classical features. Also **Louis Qua·torze** (kətôrz′).

Louis XV, designating a style in furniture and architecture prevalent in early- and mid-18th century France, characterized by Rococo features. Also **Louis Quinze** (kanz).

Louis XVI, designating a style in furniture and architecture prevalent in late 18th-century France, characterized by classical models with Rococo embellishment. Also **Louis Seize** (sez).

loupe (lо̄о̄p), *n.* a magnifying instrument made to fit in the eye socket, used by jewelers and watchmakers.

loup-ga·rou (lо̄о̄garо̄о̄′), *n., pl.* **loups-ga·rous** (lо̄о̄garо̄о̄′), *French.* a werewolf; lycanthrope.

low·er (lou′ər), *v.* to frown; to look sullen; (of the sky, etc.) be dark and threatening. Also **lour.** —**low′er·y,** *adj.*

lox[1] (loks), *n.* smoked salmon.

lox[2] (loks), *n.* liquid oxygen.

lox·o·dont (lok′sədont), *adj.* with only shallow depressions between the ridges of the molar teeth.

lox·o·drome (lok′sədrōm), *n.* (in map projection) a line that cuts all the meridians at a constant angle. Also called **rhumb line.** —**lox·o·drom′ic,** *adj.*

lox·o·drom·ics (loksədrom′iks), *n.*

navigational technique of following or being guided by loxodromes.

LSD, lysergic acid diethylamide, a drug that produces temporary hallucinations. Also **LSD-25.**

lu·au (lōō′ou), *n.* a Hawaiian feast, usually with Hawaiian entertainment.

lu·bri·cous (lōō′brəkəs), *adj.* **1.** (of a surface) slippery; smooth; oily. **2.** lecherous; wanton. Also **lu·bri·cious.** (lōōbrisн′əs).

lu·bric·i·ty (lōōbris′itē), *n.* **1.** slipperiness; smoothness, as of a surface. **2.** lecherousness; salaciousness.

lu·cent (lōō′sənt), *adj.* luminous; translucent.

lu·cid (lōō′sid), *adj.* **1.** clear; shining. **2.** clearly expressed and therefore easily understood. —**lu·cid′i·ty,** *n.*

lu·cif·er·ase (lōōsif′ərās), *n.* an enzyme in the luminous organs of fireflies that causes the pigment in them to give off light.

lu·cif·er·in (lōōsif′ərin), *n.* a pigment in the luminous organs of fireflies that gives off light when acted upon by luciferase.

lu·cra·tive (lōō′krətiv), *adj.* yielding profit; money-making.

lucre (lōō′kər), *n.* gain; money.

lu·cu·brate (lōō′kyōōbrāt), *v.* to work or study at night.

lu·cu·bra·tion (lōō′kyōōbrā′sнən), *n.* **1.** nocturnal study. **2.** (*usually pl.*) literary work of a pedantic character.

lu·cu·lent (lōō′kyōōlənt), *adj.* clear; lucid; convincing.

lu·es (lōō′ēz), *n.* syphilis. —**lu·et·ic** (lōōet′ik), *adj.*

luf·fa (luf′ə), *n.* the fibrous contents of the dried pod of a gourd-like plant, used as a hard sponge. Also **loofa, loofah, vegetable sponge.**

lu·gu·bri·ous (lōōgōō′brēəs), *adj.* doleful; gloomy in manner, tone, etc., esp. in an exaggerated way.

lum·ba·go (lumbā′gō), *n.* pain in the small of the back, often chronic, caused by muscle inflammation.

lum·bar (lum′bər), *adj.* in or having to do with the loins, the area round the lumbar joints of the lower spine.

lum·bo·sa·cral (lum′bōsā′krəl), *adj.* of or relating to the lower joints of the spine; of the lumbar and sacral area.

lum·bri·cal (lum′brikəl), *n.* any of the muscles of the hand and foot that flex the fingers and toes. Also **lum·bri·ca·lis** (lumbrəkā′lis).

lum·bri·coid (lum′brəkoid), *adj.* of or like an earthworm.

lu·men (lōō′mən), *n.* the measurement of the rate of transmission of light energy, equivalent to the light energy radiated per second per unit solid angle by a point source of one-candle intensity. *Abbrev.*: **lm.**

lu·men-hour (lōō′mənour′), *n.* a measurement of light energy equal to that radiated in one hour by a source of one lumen power.

lu·mi·nes·cence (lōōmənes′əns), *n.* **1.** cold emission of light; light stimulated by any means other than heating by incandescence. **2.** light so emitted. —**lu·mi·nes′cent,** *adj.*

lu·mi·nif·er·ous (lōōmənif′ərəs), *adj.* producing or transmitting light.

lu·mi·no·phore, lu·mi·no·phor (lōō′mənəfôr), *n.* a molecule or molecular group that radiates light when illuminated.

lum·pen (lum′pən), *adj.* relating to people deprived of their rights and homes or degraded in status.

lu·nate (lōō′nāt), *adj.* crescent-shaped. Also **lu′nat·ed.**

lu·na·tion (lōōnā′sнən), *n.* the time between one new moon and the next.

lune (lōōn), *n.* anything crescent-shaped or half-moon-shaped.

lunes (lōōnz), *n. pl.* attacks of lunacy.

lu·nette (lōōnet′), *n.* a crescent-shaped or semicircular object.

lun·gi, lun·gee, lun·gyi (lōōng′gē), *n.* (in India) a length of cloth used as a loincloth, turban, or scarf.

lu·ni·so·lar (lōō′nisō′lər), *adj.* concerning the mutual relations or joint action of the moon and sun.

lu·ni·tid·al (lōō′nitī′dl), *adj.* relating to tidal movement governed by the moon.

lu·nu·la (lōō′nyələ), *n., pl.* **lu·nu·lae** (lōō′nyəlē). a narrow crescent-shaped area, object, etc., as the white area at the bottom of a fingernail. Also **lu'nule.** —**lu'nu·lar,** *adj.*

lu·pine (lōō'pīn), *adj.* relating to or resembling a wolf; savage; predatory.

lus·trate (lus'trāt), *v.* to purify by performing some ritual to make amends for a wrong, as a sacrifice or ceremonial washing. —**lus·tra'tion,** *n.*

lus·trum (lus'trəm), *n.* **1.** a period of five years. **2.** (in ancient Rome) a purification ceremony, held every five years. —**lus'tral,** *adj.*

lu·sus na·tu·rae (lōō'səs nətōōr'ē), a freak of nature, as a deformed creature or object.

lu·tan·ist (lōō'tənist), *n.* one who plays the lute.

lu·te·ous (lōō'tēəs), *adj.* of a greenish yellow color.

Lu·tine bell (lōō'tēn), the bell salvaged from *H.M.S. Lutine,* a wrecked British warship, now hanging in Lloyd's insurance office in London, England, and rung at announcements of ships missing or sunk.

lu·ting (lōō'tiNG), *n.* a general term for several malleable substances used for joining, sealing, or waterproofing objects.

lux (luks), *n., pl.* **lu·ces** (lōō'sēz). a unit for measuring the degree of illumination, equal to the illumination produced on one square meter by one lumen at a perpendicular distance of one meter.

lux·ate (luk'sāt), *v.* (of a joint) to dislocate.

lux·u·ri·ant (lugzHōōr'ēənt), *adj.* profuse; abundant; as of plant growth. —**lux·u'ri·ance,** *n.*

lux·u·ri·ate (lugzHōōr'ēāt), *v.* to take one's ease in luxury; to abandon oneself to enjoyment.

lux·u·ri·ous (lugzHōōr'ēəs), *adj.* contributing to or full of luxury.

L wave, a shock wave radiating from an earthquake, usually the third major wave. Also **long wave.** See also **P wave, S wave.**

ly·can·thrope (lī'kənthrōp), *n.* **1.** a person suffering from the form of insanity known as lycanthropy. **2.** a

werewolf; a person in folklore who changes into a wolf.

ly·can·thro·py (līkan'thrəpē), *n.* **1.** a form of insanity in which a person imagines himself to be and behaves like a wolf or some other wild beast. **2.** (in folklore) the taking on by a man of the form and nature of a wolf.

ly·cée (lēsā'), *n.* a state secondary school in France.

Lyd·i·an (lid'ēən), *adj.* (of music) softly and voluptuously sweet.

lymph (limf), *n.* a colorless fluid drained from the intercellular spaces in body tissue by lymphatic vessels that return it to the blood.

lym·phad·e·ni·tis (limfad'ənī'tis), *n.* inflammation of lymph glands, owing to an infection spreading along the lymphatics from the body tissue. —**lym·phad·e·nit'ic,** *adj.*

lym·phad·e·no·ma (limfad'ənō'mə), *n., pl.* **lym·phad·e·no·mas, lym·phad·e·no·ma·ta** (limfad'ənō'mətə). a swollen lymph gland.

lym·phan·gi·o·ma (limfan'jēō'mə), *n., pl.* **lym·phan·gi·o·mas, lym·phan·gi·o·ma·ta** (limfan'jēō'mətə). benign growth of new and enlarged lymphatic vessels.

lym·phan·gi·tis (lim'fanjī'tis), *n., pl.* **lym·phan·git·i·des** (lim'fanjit'idēz). inflammation of a lymphatic vessel.

lym·phat·ic (limfat'ik), *adj.* **1.** of, secreting, or carrying lymph. **2.** pale; flabby; sluggish; formerly used of persons thought to have an excess of lymph.

lymph gland, one of the many small masses of tissue in the lymphatic vessels which filter out from the lymph substances and produce lymphocytes. Also **lymphatic gland, lymph node.**

lym·pho·blast (lim'fəblast), *n.* an immature white blood cell.

lym·pho·cyte (lim'fəsīt), *n.* a kind of white blood cell formed in the lymph glands.

lym·pho·cy·to·sis (lim'fəsītō'sis), *n.* a condition in which the blood contains an abnormally large number of lymphocytes.

lym·pho·gran·u·lo·ma(lim′fəgran′- yəlō′mə), *n., pl.* **lym·pho·gran·u·lo· mas, lym·pho·gran·u·lo·ma·ta** (lim′fəgran′yəlō′mətə). one of several disorders distinguished by the formation on the lymph glands of grain-like prominences that develop into broken tissue and ulceration.

lym·phoid (lim′foid), *adj.* resembling lymph.

lym·pho·ma (limfō′mə), *n.* a tumor arising from a cell in a lymph gland.

lym·pho·pe·ni·a (lim′fōpē′nēə), *n.* a condition in which the blood contains an abnormally low number of lymphocytes.

lyn·ce·an (linsē′ən), *adj.* lynx-like, esp. lynx-eyed, keen-sighted.

ly·on·naise (līənāz′), *adj.* (of any dish, esp. potatoes) cooked with pieces of onion.

ly·rate (lī′rāt), *adj.* lyre-shaped.

lyse (līs), *v.* to undergo or carry out lysis; to treat with lysins.

ly·ser·gic ac·id di·eth·yl·am·ide (lisur′jik as′id dīeth′ələmīd). See **LSD.**

ly·sin (lī′sin), *n.* an antibody causing the disintegration of bacterial or other cells.

ly·sis (lī′sis), *n.* **1.** disintegration of bacterial or other cells as a result of the presence of the antibody lysin. **2.** the gradual decline of a fever or other illness.

ly·so·zyme (lī′səzīm), *n.* an enzyme that destroys bacteria and thus serves as an antiseptic, occurring in tears, mucus, white blood cells, egg white, and some plants.

lys·so·pho·bi·a (lisəfō′bēə), *n.* a morbid dread of going insane.

mac·a·ron·ic (makərŏn′ik), *adj.* (of comic verse) written in Latin mixed with vernacular words given Latin endings.

mac·é·doine (masidwän′), *n.* mixed fruit or vegetables, often diced.

mac·er·ate (mas′ərāt), *v.* to make or become soft by soaking.

ma·chic·o·late (məchik′əlāt), *v.* (in a castle or stronghold) to furnish openings in the floor of a gallery or chamber over an entry or passage so that stones or boiling liquid could be dropped on attackers. —**ma·chic′o·lat·ed,** *adj.* —**ma·chic·o·la′tion,** *n.*

mach·i·nate (mak′ənāt), *v.* to contrive artfully; to plot; to intrigue. —**mach·i·na′tion,** *n.*

Mach number (mäk), a number indicating the ratio of the velocity of a body to the local speed of sound, thus where a speed of sound is 750 m.p.h. and an aircraft travels at 1500 m.p.h. the aircraft's Mach number is 2. Also **Mach.**

mack·le (mak′əl), *n.* a blur in printing. Also **mac′ule.**

mac·ra·mé (mak′rəmā), *n.* a cotton fringe knotted to form patterns and used as a trimming.

mac·ro·car·pous (mak′rōkär′pəs), *adj.* producing large fruit.

mac·ro·cli·mate (mak′rəklī′mit), *n.* the climate of a large area, as of a country. See also **microclimate.**

mac·ro·cli·ma·tol·o·gy (mak′rōklī′-mətol′əjē), *n.* the study of the climate of a large area. See also **microclimatology.**

mac·ro·cosm (mak′rəkozm), *n.* the whole world; the universe regarded as a whole. See also **microcosm.**

mac·ro·cyst (mak′rəsist), *n.* a large cyst.

mac·ro·cyte (mak′rəsīt), *n.* a red blood cell of abnormal size. See also **microcyte.**

mac·ro·dont (mak′rədont), *adj.* with teeth of abnormal largeness or length. See also **microdont.**

mac·ro·don·tia (makrədon′shə), *n.* a condition in which the teeth are of abnormal largeness or length. Also **megadontia.** See also **microdontia.**

mac·ro·graph (mak′rəgraf), *n.* a representation of an object, as a photograph or drawing, that is life size or larger. See also **micrograph.**

ma·crog·ra·phy (məkrog′rəfē), *n.* examination or study of an object with the naked eye. See also **micrography.**

ma·cro·nu·cle·us (makrənoo′klēəs), *n.* See **micronucleus.**

ma·cro·phage (mak′rəfāj), *n.* See **histiocyte.**

mac·ro·phyl·lous (makrōfil′əs), *adj.* large-leaved.

mac·ro·phys·ics (makrəfiz′iks), *n.* the science of the physical properties of objects sufficiently large to be observed and dealt with directly.

ma·crop·si·a (makrop'sēə), *n.* a condition of the eye which causes objects to be seen larger than life size. Also **megalopsia.** —**mac·rop'tic,** *adj.*

mac·rop·ter·ous (makrop'tərəs), *adj.* having large wings or fins. —**mac·rop'ter·y,** *n.*

mac·ro·scop·ic (makrəskop'ik), *adj.* visible to the naked eye.

mac·ro·sto·mi·a (makrəstō'mēə), *n.* the condition of having an abnormal extension of one or both corners of the mouth.

mac·ro·struc·ture (mak'rōstruk'-chər), *n.* the general arrangement or pattern of crystals in a metal or alloy as visible in low magnification or to the naked eye after deep etching of the metal.

ma·cru·ran (məkrŏŏr'ən), *adj.* of or relating to the suborder comprising lobsters, crayfishes, shrimps, and prawns.

ma·cru·rous (məkrŏŏr'əs), *adj.* long-tailed.

mac·u·la (mak'yələ), *n.,* *pl.* **mac·u·lae** (mak'yəlē). a spot or blemish, as on the sun, moon, skin, etc.

mac·u·late (mak'yəlāt), *v.* **1.** to mark with spots; to sully. —*adj.* **2.** spotted; stained; sullied. —**mac·u·la'tion,** *n.*

mac·ule (mak'yōōl), *n.* **1.** See **mackle. 2.** a macula.

mad·ri·lène (mad'rəlen), *n.* tomato-flavored consommé, served jellied and chilled, or hot and liquid.

mael·strom (māl'strəm), *n.* a large whirlpool.

mae·nad, me·nad (mē'nad), *n.* a frenzied or shrewish woman.

Ma·gi (mā'jī), *n.* *pl.,* *sing.* **Ma·gus** (mā'gəs). the three wise men who came bearing gifts for the baby Jesus. Matt. 2: 1–12.

mag·is·te·ri·al (majistēr'ēəl), *adj.* of or like a master; imperious.

mag·is·tral (maj'istrəl), *adj.* (of a medical preparation) specially made up. See also **officinal.**

mag·ma (mag'mə), *n.,* *pl.* **mag·mas, mag·ma·ta** (mag'mətə). a soft, paste-like mixture of mineral or organic dust.

mag·na cum lau·de (mäg'nə kŏŏm lou'də), *Latin.* with great praise; the next-to-highest of three special grades of honor for above average results in a diploma examination. See also **cum laude, summa cum laude.**

mag·nan·i·mous (magnan'əməs), *adj.* generous or forgiving in spirit; above petty spite. —**mag·na·nim·i·ty** (magnənim'itē), *n.*

mag·ne·to (magnē'tō), *n.* a small electric generator using permanent magnets.

mag·ne·to·chem·is·try (magnē'tōkem'istrē), *n.* the branch of science dealing with the relation to each other of magnetic and chemical phenomena.

mag·ne·to·e·lec·tric·i·ty (magnē'tōilektris'itē), *n.* electricity generated by means of permanent magnets and electric conductors. —**mag·ne·to·e·lec'tric,** *adj.*

mag·ne·to·hy·dro·dy·nam·ic (magnē'tōhī'drōdīnam'ik), *adj.* relating to the phenomena occurring when a fluid electric conductor passes through a magnetic field.

mag·ne·to·hy·dro·dy·nam·ics (magnē'tōhī'drōdīnam'iks), *n.* the branch of physics concerned with magnetohydrodynamic phenomena. Also **hydromagnetics.**

mag·ne·tom·e·ter (mag'nitom'itər), *n.* instrument for measuring magnetic force, esp. the earth's magnetism.

mag·ne·to·mo·tive (magnē'tōmō'tiv), *adj.* producing magnetism.

mag·ne·to·op·tics (magnē'toop'tiks), *n.* the study of the effect of magnetism on light. —**mag·ne·to·op'tic,** *adj.*

mag·ne·to·ther·mo·e·lec·tric·i·ty (magnē'tōthur'mōilektris'itē), *n.* the production of or effect made on thermoelectricity by a magnetic field.

mag·nil·o·quent (magnil'əkwənt), *adj.* grandiose in speech; boastful.

mag·num (mag'nəm), *n.* a large bottle of wine, etc., containing about 50 ounces.

mag·num o·pus (mag'nəm ō'pəs), *n.* a great work; the greatest work of a writer, composer, or artist.

ma·hat·ma (məhät'mə), *n.* (among the Buddhists of India and Tibet) one of a class of persons of extraordinary wisdom and virtue.

Ma·ha·ya·na (mähəyä'nə), *n.* one of the two divergent schools of Buddhism; Northern Buddhism, the form practised in China, Tibet, Korea and Japan, which stresses the hope of personal salvation, the duty to save others, and the power of prayer. See also **Bodhisattva, Hinayana.**

mahl·stick (mäl'stik), *n.* a long thin stick with a padded ball at one end held in one hand by a painter as a support for the hand with the brush. Also **maulstick.**

ma·hout (məhout'), *n.* an elephant-driver.

mai·gre (mā'gər), *adj.* without any meat or meat juices in it, as food allowed on days of religious abstinence in Roman Catholic church.

mail·lot (mäyō'), *n.* 1. a one-piece bathing suit. 2. a close-fitting shirt of knitted fabric.

main·line (mān'līn), *v.* (in slang usage) to inject a narcotic drug directly into a vein.

mai·son·ette (māzənet'), *n.* part of a house let or used separately, with rooms on more than one floor.

ma·jol·i·ca (məjol'əkə), *n.* Italian earthenware with a white enamel glaze decorated with metallic colors.

ma·jus·cule (məjus'kyool), *adj.* (of alphabetic letters) capital, large, or uncial. See also **minuscule.**

ma·la·ceous (məlā'shəs), *adj.* of or relating to the family of plants including the apple, pear, hawthorn, medlar, quince, etc.

mal·a·chite (mal'əkīt), *n.* a dense, bright-green mineral which is brought to a high polish and used in decorative articles.

ma·la·cia (məlā'shə), *n.* 1. softening of an organ or tissue. 2. abnormal craving for spiced food. —**ma'la·coid, mal·a·cot'ic,** *adj.*

mal·a·col·o·gy (maləkol'əjē), *n.* the scientific study of mollusks.

mal·a·coph·i·lous (maləkof'ələs), *adj.* (of a flower) pollinated by snails.

mal·a·cos·tra·can (maləkos'trəkən), *adj.* of or relating to the subclass that includes lobsters, shrimps, crabs, etc.

mal·a·droit (malədroit'), *adj.* clumsy; awkward; tactless.

ma·laise (malāz'), *n.* a general feeling of physical discomfort or uneasiness.

mal·a·prop·ism (mal'əpropizm), *n.* an instance or the habit of confusing similar-sounding words with ludicrous results, as *illiterate him from your memory.*

mal·ap·ro·pos (mal'aprəpō'), *adj.* inappropriate; untimely.

ma·lar (mā'lər), *adj.* relating to the cheek bone.

mal·a·thi·on (maləthī'on), *n.* an insecticide used as a substitute for DDT. See also **rotenone.**

mal·e·dict (mal'idikt), *adj.* accursed. —**mal·e·dic'tion,** *n.*

mal·e·fac·tion (maləfak'shən), *n.* an instance of evil-doing; a crime.

mal·e·fac·tor (mal'əfaktər), *n.* a criminal; an evil-doer. Also (of a woman) **mal'e·fac·tress.**

ma·lef·ic (məlef'ik), *adj.* of evil effect; malign, as *a malefic spirit possessed him.*

ma·lef·i·cence (məlef'isəns), *n.* the doing of evil; harmful character.

ma·lef·i·cent (məlef'isənt), *adj.* harmful; evil.

ma·lev·o·lence (məlev'ələns), *n.* the wishing of ill to others; malice. —**ma·lev'o·lent,** *adj.*

mal·fea·sance (malfē'zəns), *n.* official misconduct; breach of law or public trust by a public official in the course of his duties. See also **misfeasance, nonfeasance.**

mal·ic (mal'ik), *adj.* of or from apples.

ma·lign (məlīn'), *v.* 1. to speak ill of; to slander. —*adj.* 2. causing evil; malignant.

ma·lig·nant (məlig'nənt), *adj.* 1. feeling or showing intense ill-will; dangerous in effect. 2. deadly; of a form which tends to cause death, esp. of an illness or a tumor. —**ma·lig·ni·ty** (məlig′nitē), *n.*

ma·lin·ger (məliNG′gər), *v.* to pretend to be ill so as to escape duty or work.

mal·le·a·ble (mal′ēəbəl), *adj.* that can be hammered or rolled into another shape without breaking, esp. metal.

mal·le·ate (mal′ēāt), *v.* to hammer into shape, as in metalworking.

mal·le·o·lus (məlē′ələs), *n., pl.* **mal·le·o·li** (məlē′əlī). the hammer-head shaped bone of the ankle. —**mal·le′o·lar,** *adj.*

malm·sey (mäm′zē), *n.* a strong sweet wine formerly made in Greece but now also in Spain, Madeira, and the Azores.

mal·oc·clu·sion (maləklōō′zHən), *n.* imperfect meeting of opposing teeth in upper and lower jaws.

mal·prac·tice (malprak′tis), *n.* improper, corrupt, illegal, or incompetent performance of duty by a professional person.

mal·ver·sa·tion (malversā′sHən), *n.* corruption in handling public funds or in performing public office.

mam·mec·to·my (məmek′təmē), *n.* See **mastectomy.**

man·a·kin (man′əkin), *n.* **1.** any one of the small, songless, brightly-colored passerine birds native to Central and S. America. **2.** manikin.

man·ci·ple (man′səpəl), *n.* official who purchases provisions for a college, monastery, etc.

man·date (man′dāt), *n.* **1.** an order or command, esp. one given by an electorate exhorting a representative to act on a certain issue. —*v.* **2.** to give an order or command.

man·di·ble (man′dəbəl), *n.* the lower jawbone. —**man·dib·u·lar** (mandib′yələr), *adj.* —**man·dib·u·late** (mandib′yəlit), *adj.*

ma·nège (manezH′), *n.* **1.** the art of training horses; horsemanship. **2.** the movement of a trained horse.

ma·nes (mā′nēz), *n.* the ghost or spirit of a dead person.

ma·net (mä′net), *v., pl.* **ma·nent.** he or she remains (a stage direction indicating that the character named should remain on stage while others leave).

man·ic-de·pres·sive (man′ikdipres′iv), *adj.* suffering from a psychosis in which periods of great excitement, perhaps with violence and delusions, alternate with periods of acute depression.

ma·ni·cot·ti (manəkot′ē), *n.* an Italian dish of short tubes of pasta stuffed with cheese and cooked in a tomato sauce.

man·i·fest (man′əfest), *adj.* **1.** clearly apparent to the eye or the mind. —*v.* **2.** to show plainly. —*n.* **3.** a list of cargo carried, by land, on ship, or by plane, to be shown to customs officials or other authority at destination.

man·i·form (man′əfôrm), *adj.* hand-shaped.

man·i·kin, man·ni·kin (man′əkin), *n.* **1.** a dwarf; small person. **2.** a mannequin. **3.** a model of the human body used in the teaching of various branches of medicine. Also **manakin.**

ma·nism (mā′nizm), *n.* ancestor-worship; attempted communication with the spirits of ancestors.

man·ne·quin (man′əkin), *n.* **1.** a person who wears clothes to display them to potential buyers. **2.** a model of a man or woman for displaying clothing, as in shop windows. **3.** a wooden or stuffed model, often adjustable in size, of the human trunk used by dressmakers and tailors for fitting clothes.

man·ni·kin (man′əkin), *n.* **1.** manikin. **2.** any of several finches native to Asia, Australia, and the Pacific islands but often kept as pets elsewhere.

ma·nom·e·ter (mənom′itər), *n.* an instrument for measuring the pressure of gases and vapors; a U-shaped tube containing liquid and with one arm a vacuum or open to the air, so that a gas or vapor in the other arm forces the liquid to move up this arm giving a pressure reading on a scale marked on the glass.

man·qué (mäNkā′), *adj. French.* that

might have been; failed; unfulfilled.

man·sard (man'särd), *n.* a roof in which each side has two slopes, the lower much steeper than the upper and usually with projecting windows in it.

manse (mans), *n.* the residence of a minister of religion.

man·sue·tude (man'switōōd), *n.* gentleness; meekness, as *to exhibit mansuetude to the aged*.

man·tic (man'tik), *adj.* relating to or with the power of foretelling the future by supernatural means.

ma·nu·bi·al column (mənōō'bēəl), a triumphal or memorial column, originally one displaying spoils taken from the enemy.

ma·nu·bri·um (mənōō'brēəm), *n.*, *pl.* **ma·nu·bri·a** (mənōō'brēə), **ma·nu·bri·ums.** an anatomical feature, as a bone, cell, segment, that resembles a handle.

man·u·mit (manyəmit'), *v.* to give freedom to; set free, of a slave. —**man·u·mis·sion** (manyəmisн'ən), *n.*

ma·quette (maket'), *n.* a small preliminary model or three-dimensional study for a sculpture or an architectural work.

ma·ras·mus (məraz'məs), *n.* a wasting away of the body from unknown cause, mainly in infants.

marc (märk), *n.* the residue after the juice has been pressed from grapes.

mar·ces·cent (märses'ənt), *adj.* in the process of withering, as a leaf.

march·pane (märcн'pān), *n.* marzipan.

ma·re (mär'ā), *n.*, *pl.* **ma·ri·a** (mär'ēə). any one of the large, comparatively flat areas on the moon, seen as dark patches from earth and formerly believed to be seas.

ma·re li·be·rum (mer'ē lib'ərəm), *Latin.* a sea open to all nations.

ma·rem·ma (mərem'ə), *n.*, *pl.* **ma·rem·me** (mərem'ē). **1.** a marshland near the coast, esp. in Italy. **2.** the foul gases given off by such land.

ma·re nos·trum (mä're nōs'trōōm), *Latin.* our sea, esp. the Mediterran-

ean as referred to by the ancient Romans.

mare's-nest (merz'nest), *n.* **1.** something thought to be a discovery but actually a delusion or a hoax. **2.** an extreme muddle.

mar·ga·ri·ta·ceous (mär'gəritā'-sнəs), *adj.* like mother-of-pearl; pearly.

mar·i·gram (mar'əgram), *n.* a record made by a marigraph.

mar·i·graph (mar'əgraf), *n.* an automatic device for registering the rise and fall of the tide. Also **mar·e·o·graph** (mar'ēəgraf).

ma·ri·jua·na (marəwä'nə), *n.* Indian hemp; the dried leaves of Indian hemp smoked as a narcotic.

mar·i·nade (marənād'), *n.* a liquid, usually wine or vinegar, containing herbs, spices, and seasonings, in which meat or fish is soaked before being cooked.

ma·ri·na·ra (märənär'ə), *n.* **1.** a highly seasoned Italian tomato sauce. —*adj.* **2.** served with marinara.

mar·i·nate (mar'ənāt), *v.* to soak in a marinade.

marl (märl), *n.* a crumbly rock of mud and lime used in broken or powdered form as a soil conditioner on ground deficient in lime.

mar·mite (mär'mīt), *n.* a deep, lidded cooking pot of metal or earthenware, sometimes with legs.

mar·mo·re·al (märmôr'ēəl), *adj.* of or resembling marble.

ma·rou·flage (mär'əfläzн), *n.* a method of sticking canvas to a surface.

mar·plot (mär'plot), *n.* one who spoils a scheme or plan.

mar·que·try (mär'kitrē), *n.* decoration of a flat surface, esp. of furniture, by covering it with glued-on, thin, shaped pieces of colored woods, ivory, etc.

Mar·ra·no (mərä'nō), *n.*, *pl.* **Mar·ra·nos.** a Spanish or Portuguese Jew who, in the late Middle Ages, was or pretended to be converted to Christianity, esp. by threats.

mar·ron (mar'ən), *n.* a sweet chestnut, esp. in syrup.

mar·rons gla·cés (marôn′ glasā′), candied chestnuts.

marsh gas, an inflammable gas, mainly of methane, formed by decaying vegetable matter, as in marshes and coalmines.

mar·su·pi·al (märsoo′pēəl), *n.* any animal of the order comprised of mammals that are very immature at birth and are carried and suckled in the mother's marsupium or pouch until able to fend for themselves, as kangaroos, opossums, etc.

mar·su·pi·um (märsoo′pēəm), *n., pl.* **mar·su·pi·a** (märsoo′pēə). the pouch on the abdomen of a female marsupial.

mart (märt), *n.* marketplace; auction room; trade center.

mar·ti·net (märtənet′), *n.* a strict disciplinarian, esp. a military man.

Marx·ism (märk′sizm), *n.* the political philosophy of Karl Marx, set out in *Das Kapital*, that capitalism takes all the benefits of progress to itself, leaving the workers in increasing dependency and that it should be destroyed by a class war that would put all the property and the means of production in the hands of the community. —**Marx′ist,** *n., adj.*

ma·ser (mā′zər), *n.* abbrev. of **m**icrowave **a**mplification by **s**timulated **e**mission of **r**adiation; a device used to provide a high, selective amplification of a particular microwave frequency. See also **laser.**

mas·och·ism (mas′əkizm), *n.* a condition in which sexual or other gratification depends on suffering physical pain and humiliation. See also **sadism.** —**mas·o·chis′tic,** *adj.*

mas·sif (mas′if), *n.* **1.** a compact plateau-like mass of several mountains. **2.** a large upstanding block of old rock which has resisted erosion.

mast (mast), *n.* fruit of forest trees such as oak and beech, used as food for animals, esp. pigs.

mas·tec·to·my (mastek′təmē), *n.* a surgical operation to remove a breast. Also **mammectomy.**

mast·head (mast′hed), *n.* the name

of a publication, its owners, its address, and sometimes its staff, which appear in every issue of a newspaper, magazine, or periodical, usually on the editorial page. Also **flag.**

mas·ti·cate (mas′təkāt), *v.* to chew; to grind to a pulp. —**mas′ti·ca·to·ry,** *adj., n.*

mas·to·car·ci·no·ma (mas′tōkär′sənō′mə), *n., pl.* **mas·to·car·ci·no·mas, mas·to·car·ci·no·ma·ta** (mas′tōkär′sənō′mətə). cancer of the breast.

mas·to·don (mas′tədon), *n.* **1.** an extinct genus of large elephant-like mammals with nipple-shaped projections on the crowns of molar teeth, living in the Oligocene and Pliocene epochs. **2.** a person of great size, stature, influence, etc.

mas·toid (mas′toid), *adj.* **1.** breast-shaped or nipple-shaped. **2.** relating to the nipple-like prominence of the temporal bone behind the ear, which contains air spaces connecting with the ear.

mas·toid·ec·to·my (mastoidek′təmē), *n.* surgical removal of part of a mastoid, as to drain an infection in one of its air spaces.

mas·toid·i·tis (mastoidī′tis), *n.* inflammation of the mastoid.

ma·ta·dor (mat′ədôr), *n.* the bullfighter of the final stage of a bullfight, who kills the bull.

mat·e·las·sé (mät′əläsā), *n.* a heavy embossed fabric.

ma·té·ri·el (mətēr′ēel′), *n.* the stock of materials and equipment used in an undertaking, as arms, ammunition, etc., in a military operation.

ma·tri·arch (mā′trēärk), *n.* a woman head of a family or tribe. See also **patriarch.** —**ma·tri·ar′chal, ma·tri·ar′chic,** *adj.*

ma·tri·ar·chate (mā′trēär′kit), *n.* a matriarchal society.

ma·tri·ar·chy (mā′trēär′kē), *n.* a form of social order in which the mother is head of the family and descent and relationship are through the female line.

mat·ri·cide (ma′trisīd), *n.* the killing of one's own mother.

ma·tric·u·late (mətrik′yəlāt), *v.* to admit to membership and privileges of a college, university, etc., by enrolling. —**ma·tric′u·lant**, *n.* —**ma·tric·u·la′tion**, *n.*

mat·ri·lat·er·al (matrəlat′ərəl), *adj.* of a relative on the mother's side of a family. See also **patrilateral.**

mat·ri·lin·e·age (matrəlin′ēij), *n.* descent through the female line.

mat·ri·lin·e·al (matrəlin′ēəl), *adj.* of descent, relationship, or inheritance through the female line.

mat·ri·lin·y (ma′trəlin′ē), *n.* the tracing of descent through the female line.

mat·ri·lo·cal (ma′trəlōkəl), *adj.* of or relating to living with the wife's family or tribe. See also **patrilocal.**

mat·ri·po·tes·tal (ma′trēpōtes′tl), *adj.* of or relating to authority wielded by a mother or a mother's side of a family.

ma·trix (mā′triks), *n.*, *pl.* **ma·tri·ces** (mā′trisēz). the cavity, die, or mould in which anything is cast, formed, or developed.

mat·tock (mat′ək), *n.* a farming tool consisting of a long handle with a metal head having a pick on one side and a hoe-like blade on the other.

ma·tu·ti·nal (mətoo′tnl), *adj.* of or in the morning, esp. early morning.

maul·stick (môl′stik), *n.* mahlstick.

maun·der (môn′dər), *v.* to talk or walk in a rambling, confused manner.

maun·dy (môn′dē), *n.* **1.** the ceremony of washing the feet of the poor by an eminent person on the Thursday before Easter, in commemoration of Jesus' washing of his disciples' feet, frequently followed by almsgiving. **2.** Also **maundy money,** the alms given at a maundy ceremony.

mawk·ish (mô′kisн), *adj.* of sickly flavor or sentimentality.

max·il·la (maksil′ə), *n.*, *pl.* **max·il·lae** (maksil′ē). the upper jawbone of vertebrates. —**max′il·la·ry**, *adj.*

max·im (mak′sim), *n.* a general truth, esp. neatly phrased; a rule of conduct.

max·i·min (mak′səmin), *n.* a strategy used in games to increase to the ut-

most a player's possible gain. See also **minimax.**

maz·a·rine (mazərēn′), *n.* a silver strainer fitting over a plate, used to strain liquid or juices from meats and fish.

ma·zel tov, ma·zal tov (mä′zel tôv), a Hebrew expression of good wishes.

me·a cul·pa (me′ä kool′pä), *Latin.* by my own fault; my fault.

mead (mēd), *n.* an alcoholic liquor made from fermented honey and water.

mech·an·ism (mek′ənizm), *n.* (in philosophy and biology) a process of nature explained or regarded as being explicable as a product of mechanical forces. See also **dynamism, vitalism.** —**mech·a·nis·tic** (mekənis′tik), *adj.*

me·cism (mē′sizm), *n.* the abnormal length of a part or parts of the body.

me·com·e·ter (məkom′itər), *n.* an instrument for measuring length, esp. a graduated instrument similar to a caliper, for measuring the length of newborn infants.

me·co·ni·um (məkō′nēəm), *n.* the contents of the intestine of a newborn mammal evacuated as the first excrement, composed mainly of bile, mucus, and swallowed amniotic fluid.

mé·dail·lon (mādayôn′), *n. French.* a portion of food, esp. meat, served as a small round thick slice.

me·dic·a·ment (mədik′əmənt), *n.* a substance used to heal or to alleviate discomfort; a medicine.

med·i·co·chi·rur·gi·cal (med′-əkōkīrur′jikəl), *adj.* of or relating to medicine and surgery jointly.

me·di·us (mē′dēəs), *n.*, *pl.* **me·di·i** (mē′dēī). the middle finger.

me·du·sa (mədoo′sə), *n.*, *pl.* **me·du·sas, me·du·sae** (mədoo′sē), a jellyfish. —**me·du′san,** *adj.*

meet (mēt), *adj.* appropriate; fitting; suitable. —**meet′ly,** *adv.*

meg·a·cit·y (meg′əsitē), *n.* a city with a population of 1,000,000 or more.

meg·a·cy·cle (meg′əsīkəl), *n.* former name for **megahertz.** *Abbrev.*: **mc, MC.**

meg·a·don·tia (megədon**′**sHə), *n*. See **macrodontia**.

meg·a·hertz (meg**′**əhurts), *n*. a unit equal to 1,000,000 cycles per second, used in measuring the frequency of electromagnetic waves. *Abbrev.* :**Mh.** Also, formerly, **megacycle**.

meg·a·joule (meg**′**əjoul), *n*. a unit equal to 1,000,000 joules, used in measuring work or energy. *Abbrev.* : **MJ.**

meg·a·lith (meg**′**əli*th*), *n*. a very large stone used in buildings or as a monument in prehistoric or ancient periods.

meg·a·lo·car·di·a (meg**′**əlōkär**′**dēə), *n*. abnormal enlargement of the heart due to the addition of new tissue.

meg·a·lo·ma·ni·a (meg**′**əlōmā**′**nēə), *n*. a mental illness characterized by delusions of grandeur. —**meg·a·lo·ma′ni·ac,** *n*.

meg·a·lop·o·lis (megəlop**′**əlis), *n*. a very large city or several cities which merge together to form an extensive urban area. —**meg·a·lo·pol′i·tan,** *adj., n*.

meg·a·lop·si·a (megəlop**′**sēə), *n*. See **macropsia**.

meg·a·me·ter (meg**′**əmētər), *n*. a metric unit of measurement equal to 1,000,000 meters. *Abbrev.* : **Mm.**

meg·a·pod (meg**′**əpod), *adj*. with large feet.

meg·a·therm (meg**′**ə*th*urm), *n*. a plant which needs a high temperature and plenty of moisture constantly to make growth.

meg·a·ton (meg**′**ətun), *n*. a measurement of explosive force equal to that of 1,000,000 tons of TNT. *Abbrev.* : **MT.**

meg·a·volt (meg**′**əvōlt), *n*. a unit for measuring electromotive force, equal to 1,000,000 volts. *Abbrev.* :**MV, Mv.**

meg·a·volt-am·pere (meg**′**əvōltam**′**pēr), *n*. a unit of measurement of electric current equal to 1,000,000 volt-amperes. *Abbrev.* : **MVA, Mva.**

meg·a·watt (meg**′**əwot), *n*. a unit of measurement of electric power equal to 1,000,000 watts. *Abbrev.* : **Mw.**

meg·a·watt-hour (meg**′**əwotour**′**), *n*. a unit used to expressed the rate of expenditure of electric power in terms of megawatts used in one hour. *Abbrev.* : **MWh, Mwhr.**

me·gil·lah (məgil**′**ə), *n*. (slang) a long, detailed relating of events.

meg·ohm (meg**′**ōm), *n*. a unit for measuring electrical resistance, equal to 1,000,000 ohms. *Abbrev.* : **meg,** **MΩ.**

meg·ohm·me·ter (meg**′**ōmmētər), *n*. an instrument for measuring large electrical resistance.

me·grims (mē**′**grimz), *n. pl*. low spirits, depression.

mei·o·sis (mīō**′**sis), *n*. the maturation of gametes when two cell divisions starting in a diploid cell result in the diploid chromosome number becoming reduced to the haploid.

me·lae·na (milē**′**nə), *n*. melena.

mé·lange (mālä*nzh***′**), *n. French*. a mixture.

me·lan·ic (məlan**′**ik), *adj*. relating to melanism; melanotic.

mel·a·nif·er·ous (melənif**′**ərəs), *adj*. containing melanin.

mel·a·nin (mel**′**ənin), *n*. a dark brown pigment present in many animals, including man, which in varying concentrations gives the yellow, brown, and black coloring to skin, hair, feathers, etc.

mel·a·nism (mel**′**ənizm), *n*. darkness of color due to the presence of a large amount of melanin.

mel·a·noch·ro·i (melənok**′**rōī), *n. pl*. a class of humans characterized by dark smooth hair and pale skin.

mel·a·no·cyte (mel**′**ənəsīt), *n*. a cell that contains and produces melanin.

melanocyte-stimulating hormone, a hormone that produces general darkening of the skin by causing dispersal of the melanin in melanocytes.

mel·an·o·derm (mel**′**ənədurm), *n*. a person whose skin is darkly pigmented.

mel·a·noid (mel**′**ənoid), *adj*. melanin-like; with dark pigmentation.

mel·a·no·ma (melənō**′**mə), *n., pl*. **mel·a·no·mas, mel·a·no·ma·ta**

melanosis

(melənō′mətə). a tumor of cells containing melanin and thus of dark color, most frequent on the skin or eye.

mel·a·no·sis (melənō′sis), *n.* an abnormal deposit or development of melanin in the tissues. —**mel·a·not·ic** (melənot′ik), *adj.*

me·le·na, me·lae·na (məlē′nə), *n.* the presence of blood, blackened through partial digestion, in the feces owing to a hemorrhage in the stomach or small intestine.

mel·ic (mel′ik), *adj.* **1.** for singing, as *melic verse.* **2.** relating to the more elaborate strophic species of Greek lyric poetry, as distinct from iambic and elegaic poetry.

mel·io·rate (mēl′yərāt), *v.* to improve. —**mel·io·ra′tion,** *n.*

mel·io·rism (mēl′yərizm), *n.* the doctrine that the world is or can be improved by human effort.

mel·ior·i·ty (mēlyôr′itē), *n.* the quality or condition of being better; superiority.

mel·lif·er·ous (məlif′ərəs), *adj.* making or yielding honey.

mel·lif·lu·ous (məlif′lōōəs), *adj.* **1.** sweet- and smooth-sounding. **2.** flowing with honey; sweetened with or sweet as honey. Also **mel·lif′lu·ent.**

me·mo·ri·ter (məmôr′itər), *adv. Latin.* from memory; by heart.

men·ac·me (mənak′mē), *n.* that period of years in a female life during which menstruation takes place.

me·nad (mē′nad), *n.* maenad.

mé·nage (mānäzH′), *n.* household; management of a household.

mé·nage à trois (mānäzH′ a trwä′), *French.* a household consisting of a married couple and the lover of one of them.

men·ar·che (mənär′kē), *n.* the age at which menstruation begins; the first menstruation.

men·da·cious (mendā′sHəs), *adj.* untrue; untruthful.

men·dac·i·ty (mendas′itē), *n.* the tendency to tell lies; an instance of telling a lie.

men·di·cant (men′dəkənt), **1.** *adj.* living by begging. **2.** *n.* a beggar.

men·dic·i·ty (mendis′itē), *n.* the practice of begging; the condition of being a beggar.

men·hir (men′hir), *n.* an upright monumental stone of prehistoric date.

me·ni·al (mē′nēəl), *adj.* relating to or proper to domestic servants; servile; degrading.

me·nin·ges (minin′jēz), *n. pl., sing.* **me·ninx** (mē′niNGks). the three membranes (dura mater, arachnoid, pia mater) enveloping the brain and spinal cord.

men·in·gi·tis (meninjī′tis), *n.* inflammation of the meninges.

me·nin·go·coc·cus (məniNG′gōkok′əs), *n., pl.* **me·nin·go·coc·ci.** a bacterium that causes meningitis.

me·nis·cus (minis′kəs), *n., pl.* **me·nis·ci** (minis′ī), **me·nis·cus·es.** a crescent-shaped body.

me·nol·o·gy (minol′əjē), *n.* a calendar of the months.

men·o·pause (men′əpôz), *n.* the period of female life, usually between the ages of 45 and 50, when menstruation stops.

men·o·pha·ni·a (men′ōfā′nēə), *n.* the first appearance of menstrual discharge during puberty.

men·or·rha·gi·a (menərā′jēə), *n.* excessive discharge at menstruation.

me·nos·che·sis (mənos′kisis), *n.* temporary suppression of menstruation.

men·o·stax·is (menəstak′sis), *n.* an abnormally long menstrual period.

men·sal[1] (men′səl), *adj.* monthly.

men·sal[2] (men′səl), *adj.* relating to or used at the table.

men·ses (men′sēz), *n., pl.* **men·ses.** the blood and tissue debris discharged from the uterus of female higher primates usually at monthly intervals.

mens sa·na in cor·po·re sa·no (mens sä′nä in kōr′pōre sä′nō), *Latin.* a sound mind in a healthy body.

men·stru·al (men′strōōəl), *adj.* **1.** relating to menstruation or the menses. **2.** monthly.

195

men·stru·ate (men'strōoāt), *v.* to shed the lining of the womb each month (except during pregnancy) during the fertile period of life in a female higher primate. —**men·stru·a′tion**, *n.* —**men′stru·ous**, *adj.*

men·stru·um (men'strōoəm), *n., pl.* **men·stru·ums**, **men·stru·a** (men'-strōoə). a solvent.

men·sur·a·ble (men'sHərəbəl), *adj.* measurable.

men·su·ral (men'sHərəl), *adj.* of or relating to measure.

men·su·ra·tion (mensHərā'sHən), *n.* the branch of mathematics concerned with measuring lengths, areas, and volumes. —**men′su·ra·tive**, *adj.*

men·tal·ism (men'təlizm), *n.* the philosophical doctrine that, in the last analysis, mind or consciousness is the ultimate reality and matter or objects of knowledge only a mode or form of mind and thus without existence except within the mind of the perceiver.

men·ti·cide (men'tisīd), *n.* an organized attempt, as by interrogation, beating, etc., to remove a person's previous opinions and replace them by radically different ones; brainwashing.

me·phit·ic (məfit'ik), *adj.* offensive to the smell; noisome.

me·phi·tis (məfī'tis), *n.* any noxious stench.

me·pro·ba·mate (məprō'bəmāt), *n.* a pharmacological preparation used as a tranquilizer.

mer·cer·ize (mur'sərīz), *v.* to treat (cotton) with a solution of caustic alkali to give greater strength, a silky luster, and an increased affinity for dye.

mer·cu·ri·al (mərkyŏŏr'ēəl), *adj.* lively; volatile; changeable.

mercy killing. See **euthanasia.**

mer·div·or·ous (mərdiv'ərəs), *adj.* dung-eating; coprophagous.

mer·e·tri·cious (meritrisH'əs), *adj.* showily attractive; flashy; founded on deception.

me·rid·i·o·nal (mərid'ēənl), *adj.* southern.

mer·i·sis (mer'isis), *n.* biological growth, esp. growth by cell division. See also **auxesis.**

merle (murl), *adj.* bluish-gray marked with black.

mer·lon (mur'lən), *n.* the part between two crenels in a battlement.

me·rog·o·ny (mərog'ənē), *n.* the production of an embryo from a fragment of an egg not containing a nucleus.

me·ro·pi·a (mərō'pēə), *n.* dullness or obscuration of sight; partial blindness.

me·sa (mā'sə), *n.* high, rocky tableland with precipitous sides, commonly found in desert regions of SW United States and Mexico.

mé·sal·li·ance (māzəlī'əns), *n.* marriage with a social inferior; a bad or improper association.

mes·cal (meskal'), *n.* a strong intoxicant distilled from the fermented juice of some species of agave.

mescal buttons, the button-like tops of a genus of cacti, dried and used as an intoxicant; peyote.

mes·ca·line (mes'kəlēn), *n.* an alkaloid obtained from mescal buttons, capable of producing hallucinations and occasionally used in medicine; peyote.

mes·en·ter·i·tis (mes'əntərī'tis), *n.* inflammation of the mesentery.

mes·en·ter·y (mes'ənterē), *n.* a fold of the peritoneum that attaches the intestinal canal to the posterior wall of the abdomen and supplies it with blood, lymph, and nerves.

me·shu·ga (məsHŏŏg'ə), *adj.* (in slang usage) crazy.

me·sic (mez'ik), *adj.* of or adapted to an environment with a balanced moisture-supply.

mes·mer·ism (mez'mərizm), *n.* hypnotism.

mes·mer·ize (mez'mərīz), *v.* to hypnotize.

mes·o·dont (mez'ədont), *adj.* with teeth of medium size.

mes·o·dont·ism (mezədon'tizm), *n.* the condition of having teeth of medium size. Also **mes′o·don·ty.**

mes·o·lith·ic (mezəli*th*'ik), *adj.* pertaining to the period between the Stone Age and Neolithic Age.

mes·o·me·te·or·ol·o·gy (mez′ōmē′-tēərol′əjē), *n.* the study of relatively small atmospheric disturbances, such as thunderstorms, and of details of larger disturbances.

mes·o·morph (mez′əmôrf), *n.* a mesomorphic type of person.

mes·o·mor·phic (mezəmôr′fik), *adj.* **1.** relating to or being in an intermediate state. **2.** with or relating to a muscular, sturdy body build in which the structures developed from the middle germ-layer of the embryo (muscle, blood, connective tissue, etc.) are prominent. See also **ectomorphic, endomorphic.**

mes·o·phil·ic (mezəfil′ik), *adj.* (in bacteriology) thriving in temperatures in the moderate range between 25°C and 40°C. —**mes′o·phile,** *adj., n.*

mes·o·phyte (mez′əfīt), *n.* one of the class of plants, including most trees for example, that grow under average conditions of water supply.

mes·o·sphere (mez′əsfēr), *n.* **1.** the part of the earth's atmosphere between the ionosphere and the exosphere, distinguished from them by its chemical properties, and extending from about 250–650 miles above the earth's surface. **2.** the part of the earth's atmosphere between the stratosphere and the thermosphere, distinguished by decreasing temperature with increasing height, and extending from about 20–50 miles above the earth's surface.

mes·o·tho·rax (mezəthôr′aks), *n., pl.* **mes·o·thor·ax·es, mes·o·thor·a·ces** (mezəthôr′əsēz). the middle segment of the three segments of an insect's thorax, bearing the second pair of walking legs and, in winged insects, the first pair of wings.

Mes·o·zo·ic (mezəzō′ik), *adj.* denoting or belonging to the geological era when the rocks above the paleozoic rocks were formed, occurring between 220,000,000 and 70,000,000 years ago, comprising the Triassic,

Jurassic, and Cretaceous periods, and characterized by the appearance of flowering plants and the evolution and extinction of dinosaurs.

mes·ti·zo (mestē′zō), *n., pl.* **mes·ti·zos, mes·ti·zoes.** a person of mixed ancestry.

met·a·bi·o·sis (met′əbīō′sis), *n.* a biological association of different organisms in which one depends on another to prepare the environment in which it can live.

me·tab·o·lism (mətab′əlizm), *n.* all the chemical processes which govern a living organism including the building up of nutritive matter into living matter, the breaking down of food materials to release energy, and the maintenance and renewal of all parts of the organism. —**met·a·bol′ic,** *adj.* — **me·tab′o·lize,** *v.*

met·a·car·pus (metəkär′pəs), *n., pl.* **met·a·car·pi** (metəkär′pī). the bones of the hand between the wrist and the fingers or of the corresponding part of the front foot in four-legged creatures.

met·a·chro·ma·tism (metəkrō′mətizm), *n.* a change of color, esp. that caused by a change in temperature of a body.

me·tach·ro·nal (mətak′rənl), *adj.* of or relating to a rhythmic wave, esp. of muscular contraction which passes along ciliated tissue of multi-limbed creatures causing the cilia or limbs to beat, giving the appearance of wave motion and bringing about locomotion.

met·a·gal·ax·y (metəgal′əksē), *n.* the entire galactic system; the Milky Way and all the surrounding galaxies.

met·a·in·fec·tive (met′əinfek′tiv), *adj.* of a medical disorder arising after an infection.

met·a·lan·guage (met′əlaNG′gwij), *n.* a language or set of symbols used for describing or analyzing another language or set of symbols.

met·a·lin·guis·tics (met′əliNGgwis′-tiks), *n.* the study of the interrelationship of languages and the cultures they refer to.

met·al·log·ra·phy (metəlog**′**rəfē), *n.* the minute study and description of the structure and properties of metals and alloys.

me·tal·lo·ther·a·py (mətal**′**ōther**′**əpē), *n.* medical treatment making use of metals or their salts.

met·al·lur·gy (met**′**əlurjē), *n.* the science of extracting, working, compounding, and establishing the properties of metals and their alloys.

met·a·mor·pho·sis (metəmôr**′**fəsis), *n., pl.* **met·a·mor·pho·ses** (metəmôr**′**fəsēz). **1.** any complete change in structure, substance, appearance, or character, or the form resulting from such a change. **2.** a zoological process of rapid change or successive changes from an immature to a mature state. —**met·a·mor′phic, met·a·mor′phous,** *adj.*

met·a·phor (met**′**əfôr), *n.* a figure of speech in which a word or phrase is applied to a concept to which it is not literally applicable so as to imply a comparison with the word or phrase applied, as *he swallowed his pride.*

met·a·phrase (met**′**əfrāz), *n.* **1.** a word for word translation. —*v.* **2.** to translate word for word. —**met·a·phrast** (met**′**əfrast), *n.*

met·a·phys·i·cal (metəfiz**′**ikəl), *adj.* **1.** (in philosophy) dealing with abstract subjects or first principles. **2.** abstruse. **3.** designating a group of 17th-century English poets, including Donne, Cowley, Herbert, whose style is intellectual and makes use of ingenious imagery and turns of wit.

met·a·phys·ics (metəfiz**′**iks), *n.* the branch of philosophy dealing with first principles, as being, substance, space, time, identity, etc.

me·tas·ta·sis (mətas**′**təsis), *n., pl.* **me·tas·ta·ses** (mətas**′**təsēz). the transference of disease from a primary focus to one in another part of the body by blood, lymph, or membranes.

me·tas·ta·size (mətas**′**təsīz), *v.* (of disease) to achieve metastasis.

met·a·tar·sus (metətär**′**səs), *n., pl.* **met·a·tar·si** (metətär**′**sī). the bones of the foot or hind limb between the ankle bone and the toes. —**met·a·tar′sal,** *adj.*

me·tath·e·sis (mətath**′**isis), *n., pl.* **me·tath·e·ses** (mətath**′**isēz). the transposition of letters or sounds in a word. —**me·tath′e·size,** *v.*

met·a·tho·rax (metəthôr**′**aks), *n., pl.* **met·a·thor·ax·es, met·a·thor·a·ces** (metəthôr**′**əsēz). the hindmost of the three segments of an insect's thorax bearing the third pair of walking legs and, in many winged insects, the second pair of wings.

met·a·troph·ic (metətrof**′**ik), *adj.* living on decayed organic matter; saprophytic.

met·em·pir·ics (metempir**′**iks), *n.* the branch of philosophy dealing with things outside experience. —**met·em·pir′i·cal,** *adj.*

me·tem·psy·cho·sis (mətem**′**səkō**′**sis), *n., pl.* **me·tem·psy·cho·ses** (mətem**′**səkō**′**sēz). the supposed migration of the soul at death to another body, human, or animal.

me·te·or·o·gram (mē**′**tēôr**′**əgram), *n.* a record made by a meteorograph.

me·te·or·o·graph (me**′**tēôr**′**əgraf), *n.* an instrument for making simultaneous records of several meteorological conditions.

me·te·or·ol·o·gy (mē**′**tēərol**′**əjē), *n.* the science and study of atmospheric phenomena, esp. for weather-forecasting.

me·te·or·o·path·o·log·ic (mē**′**tēərəpath**′**əloj**′**ik), *adj.* relating to the harmful effect of climate on health.

me·ter (me**′**tər), *n.* the basic metric unit of length equal to 39.37 inches.

me·ter-kil·o·gram-sec·ond (mē**′**tərkil**′**əgramsek**′**ənd), *adj.* relating to the system of units in which the meter, kilogram, and second are the principle units of measurement. *Abbrev. :* **mks, m.k.s., MKS.**

meth·a·done (meth**′**ədōn), *n.* a synthetic narcotic used as a long-lasting drug to curb an addict's craving for heroin.

meth·ane (meth**′**ān), *n.* a flammable, colorless, odorless gas, formed by the decay of organic matter, which, together with water vapor, ammonia, and hydrogen, was part of the early atmosphere on earth.

meth·yl·tri·ni·tro·ben·zene (meth'-əltrīnī'trōben'zēn), *n.* See **TNT.**

mé·tier (mā'tyā), *n.* **1.** trade or profession. **2.** occupation or activity in which a person has special ability; forte.

mé·tis (mātēs'), *n., sing.* and *pl.* a person of mixed blood, esp. a Canadian of French and Indian blood.

met·o·nym (met'ənim), *n.* an instance of metonymy.

me·ton·y·my (miton'əmē), *n.* a rhetorical device in which an attribute or related concept is substituted for the name of the thing meant, as *the bottle* for *drink.* —**met·o·nym'i·cal,** *adj.*

me·top·ic (mətop'ik), *adj.* of or relating to the forehead.

me·trol·o·gy (mitrol'əjē), *n.* the science or system of weights and measures.

me·tro·nym·ic (mētrənim'ik), *adj.* derived from the name of the mother or of a female ancestor.

met·tle (met'l), *n.* natural vigor; spirit. —**met'tle·some,** *adj.*

meu·nière (mənyer'), *adj.* (of food) shallow-fried in butter and served with the butter mixed with lemon juice and chopped parsley to make a sauce.

mez·za·nine (mez'ənēn), *n.* an intermediate floor in a building esp. a low story between two other stories.

mez·zo-re·lie·vo (met'sōrilē'vō), *n.* medium relief; carving in which the projection of the design from the plane is intermediate between high- and low-relief. Also **mez'zo-ri·lie'vo.**

mez·zo·tint (met'sōtint), *n.* a method of engraving on copper or steel by roughening the plate uniformly and then scraping away the roughness to different degrees according to whether shadow, half-light, or light is required.

mho (mō), *n., pl.* **mhos.** a unit of measurement of electrical conductance equal to the conductance of a conductor in which a one-volt potential difference maintains a current of one ampere.

mi·as·ma (mīaz'mə), *n., pl.* **mi·as·ma·ta** (mīaz'mətə), **mi·as·mas.** the foul-smelling gases given off by marshes, putrid matter, etc.

mi·cro·aer·o·phil·ic (mī'krōer'əfil'ik), *adj.* (of organisms) needing only a minute amount of free oxygen to live. —**mi·cro·aer'o·phile,** *n.*

mi·cro·am·me·ter (mīkrōam'mētər), *n.* instrument for measuring very small electric currents in microamperes.

mi·cro·am·pere (mīkrōam'pēr), *n.* a unit of measurement of electric current, equal to one millionth of an ampere. *Abbrev.* : μA.

mi·cro·a·nal·y·sis (mī'krōənal'isis), *n., pl.* **mi·cro·a·nal·y·ses** (mī'krōənal'isēz). the chemical analysis of minute amounts of substances.

mi·cro·bal·ance (mī'krəbal'əns), *n.* a device for weighing extremely small amounts of chemical substances.

mi·cro·bar (mī'krəbär), *n.* a unit of atmospheric pressure equal to one millionth of a bar. *Abbrev.* : μb. Also **barye.**

mi·cro·bar·o·gram (mīkrəbär'əgram), *n.* a record made by a microbarograph.

mi·cro·bar·o·graph (mīkrəbär'əgraf), *n.* a device used in meteorology for making a continuous graph of minute fluctuations in atmospheric pressure.

mi·crobe (mī'krōb), *n.* a minute organism, esp. one causing disease.

mi·cro·bi·cide (mīkrō'bisīd), *n.* a substance which kills microbes.

mi·cro·bi·ol·o·gy (mī'krōbīol'əjē), *n.* the scientific study of microscopically small organisms.

mi·crob·ism (mī'krōbizm), *n.* infection with disease-producing microbes.

mi·cro·cli·mate (mī'krəklīmit), *n.* the climate of a small locality, as a cave, a wood, a garden, a hillside, a built-up area. See also **macrocli-mate.**

mi·cro·cli·ma·tol·o·gy (mī′krōklī′-mətol′əjē), *n.* the study of microclimates. See also **macroclimatology.**

mi·cro·con·stit·u·ent (mī′krōkən-stiCH′ōōənt), *n.* a constituent of a metal or alloy that is present in a microscopically small amount.

mi·cro·cop·y (mīkrəkop′ē), *n.* a very small copy, usually made by photographic reduction, of a printed page or a similar item.

mi·cro·cosm (mī′krəkozm), *n.* a world in miniature; anything regarded as an epitome of the world. See also **macrocosm.**

mi·cro·cou·lomb (mī′krəkōō′lom), *n.* a unit of measurement of electric charge equal to one millionth of a coulomb. *Abbrev.: μC.*

mi·cro·cu·rie (mī′krəkyŏŏr′ē), *n.* a unit of measurement of radioactivity equal to one millionth of a curie. *Abbrev.: μCi, μc.*

mi·cro·cyte (mī′krəsīt), *n.* a minute, or abnormally small, blood cell or corpuscle. See also **macrocyte.**

mi·cro·de·tec·tor (mī′krōditek′tər), *n.* **1.** an instrument for measuring minute quantities or changes. **2.** a sensitive device for measuring or detecting minute quantities of electric current.

mi·cro·dis·sec·tion (mī′krōdisek′-sHən), *n.* the dissection of material under a microscope.

mi·cro·dis·til·la·tion (mī′krōdis′-təlā′sHən), *n.* the distillation of extremely small quantities of chemical substances.

mi·cro·dont (mī′krədont), *adj.* with teeth of abnormally small size. See also **macrodont.**

mi·cro·don·tia (mīkrədon′sHə), *n.* the condition of being microdont or an instance of the condition. Also **mi′cro·dont·ism, mi′cro·don·ty.** See also **macrodontia.**

mi·cro·dyne (mī′krədīn), *n.* a unit of measurement of force, equal to one millionth of a dyne. *Abbrev.: μ dyn.*

mi·cro·e·co·nom·ics (mī′krōē′kə-nom′iks), *n.* economics as applied to specific aspects of an economy, as the investment-profit relationship in a company.

mi·cro·e·lec·tron·ics (mī′krōilek-tron′iks), *n.* the science and technology of using microminiaturized components such as solid-state devices in electronic systems.

mi·cro·e·lec·tro·pho·re·sis (mī′-krōilek′trōfərē′sis), *n.* a technique used in chemistry for examining under a microscope the migration of minute surface particles under the influence of an electric field.

mi·cro·en·vi·ron·ment (mī′krōen-vī′ərnmənt), *n.* the conditions prevailing in a small area or surrounding one organism in a community.

mi·cro·far·ad (mī′krəfar′əd), *n.* a unit of measurement of electrical capacity, equal to one millionth of a farad. *Abbrev.: μF, μf.*

mi·cro·fiche (mī′krəfēsH), *n.* microfilms grouped in a sheet for filing.

mi·cro·film (mī′krəfilm), *n.* very small film bearing miniature photographic reproduction of documents, etc., and projected on a screen for reading.

mi·cro·fos·sil (mī′krōfos′il), *n.* a fossil too small to be studied without a microscope.

mi·cro·gram (mī′krəgram), *n.* a unit of measurement of mass equal to one millionth of a gram. *Abbrev.: μg.*

mi·cro·graph (mī′krəgraf), *n.* **1.** an instrument for writing or engraving minutely. **2.** a photograph or drawing of an item as seen under a microscope. See also **macrograph.**

mi·crog·ra·phy (mīkrog′rəfē), *n.* **1.** the verbal or graphic representation of extremely small objects. **2.** examination or study of an object under a microscope. See also **macrography.**

mi·cro·groove (mī′krəgrōōv), *n.* an extremely narrow needle groove on a phonograph record, used to enable the record to carry much more material.

mi·cro·hard·ness (mī′krōhärd′nis),

n. a measurement of the hardness of a metal denoting that it was indented by a slight pressure on one small area of it.

mi·cro·hen·ry (mī′krəhen′rē), *n., pl.* **mi·cro·hen·ries, mi·cro·hen·rys.** a unit of measurement of electrical inductance equal to one millionth of a henry. *Abbrev.* : **μH, μh.**

mi·crohm (mī′krōm), *n.* a unit of measurement of electrical resistance equal to one millionth of an ohm. *Abbrev.* : **μΩ.**

mi·cro·im·age (mī′krōim′ij), *n.* a photographic reproduction of such small scale that it cannot be seen clearly without a microscope.

mi·cro·inch (mī′krōincH), *n.* a unit used in measuring length, equal to one millionth of an inch. *Abbrev.* : **μin.**

mi·cro·in·jec·tion (mī′krōinjek′-sHən), *n.* an injection made under a microscope.

mi·cro·lam·bert (mī′krəlam′bərt), *n.* a unit used in measuring brightness, equal to one millionth of a lambert. *Abbrev.* : **μL.**

mi·cro·li·ter (mī′krəlē′tər), *n.* a metric unit used in measuring capacity, equal to one millionth of a liter. *Abbrev.* : **μl.**

mi·cro·lith (mī′krəli*th*), *n.* a small flint usually worked to triangular shape for mounting on a handle or haft and using as a cutting tool or barbed weapon, common in mesolithic and early neolithic times. —**mi·cro·lith′ic,** *adj.*

mi·crol·o·gy (mīkrol′əjē), *n.* excessive consideration of minute matters.

mi·cro·lux (mī′krəluks), *n.* a unit used in measuring illumination, equal to one millionth of a lux. *Abbrev.* : **μlx.**

mi·cro·me·te·or·ite (mī′krōəmē′tē-ərīt), *n.* a minute meteorite, usually less than a millimeter in diameter.

mi·cro·me·te·or·o·gram (mī′krō-mē′tēôr′əgram), *n.* a record made by a micrometeorograph.

mi·cro·me·te·or·o·graph (mī′krō-mē′tēôr′əgraf), *n.* a small instrument for use in aircraft for making a simultaneous record of various atmospheric conditions, adapted form of the meteorograph.

mi·cro·me·te·or·ol·o·gy (mī′krō-mē′tēərol′əjē), *n.* the study of small atmospheric phenomena and usually only those that occur in a shallow layer of air immediately above the ground.

mi·crom·e·ter (mīkrom′itər), *n.* any of several precision instruments used to measure minute distances and angles.

mi·crom·e·try (mīkrom′itrē), *n.* the taking of measurements with a micrometer.

mi·cro·mho (mī′krəmō), *n.* a unit of measurement of electrical conductance, equal to one millionth of a mho. *Abbrev.* : **μmho.**

mi·cro·mi·cro·cu·rie (mī′krōmī′-krōkyŏŏr′ē), *n.* a unit used in measuring radioactivity, equal to one millionth of a microcurie. *Abbrev.* : **μμCi, μμc.**

mi·cro·mi·cro·far·ad (mī′krōmī′-krōfar′əd), *n.* a unit used in measuring electrical capacity, equal to one millionth of a microfarad. *Abbrev.* : **μμf.**

mi·cro·mi·cron (mī′krōmī′kron), *n., pl.* **mi·cro·mi·crons, mi·cro·mi·cra** (mī′krōmī′krə). a metric unit used in measuring length, equal to one millionth of a micron. *Abbrev.* : **μμ, mu mu.**

mi·cro·mil·li·me·ter (mī′krōmil′ə-mē′tər), *n.* a metric unit used in measuring length, equal to one millionth of a millimeter. *Abbrev.* : **μmm.**

mi·cro·min·i·a·ture (mī′krōmin′ēə-cHər), *adj.* of extremely minute size, esp. of small electronic devices using solid-state components.

mi·cro·min·i·a·tur·i·za·tion (mī′-krōmin′ēəcHərizā′sHən), *n.* extreme size reduction, esp. the making small of electronic devices by using solid-state components instead of vacuum tubes. —**mi·cro·min′i·a·tur·ize,** *v.*

mi·cron, mi·kron (mī′kron), *n.*, *pl.* **mi·crons, mi·krons, mi·cra, mi·kra** (mī′krə). **1.** a metric unit used in measuring length, equal to one millionth of a meter. *Abbrev.*: **μ, mu. 2.** a colloidal particle with a diameter between .2 and 10 millionths of a meter.

mi·cro·ne·mous (mīkrənē′məs), *adj.* with short filaments.

mi·cro·nu·cle·us (mī′krōnōō′klēəs), *n.*, *pl.* **mi·cro·nu·cle·i** (mīkrōnōō′-klēī). the smaller of the two kinds of nuclear material present in ciliated organisms, the other kind being the macronucleus. —**mi·cro·nu′cle·ate,** *adj.*

mi·cro·or·gan·ism (mī′krōôr′gə-nizm), *n.* any of the organisms too small to be seen by the naked eye, as bacteria, viruses, etc.

mi·cro·pa·le·on·tol·o·gy (mī′krō-pā′lēəntol′əjē), *n.* the scientific study of microfossils.

mi·cro·par·a·site (mī′krōpar′əsīt), *n.* a microorganism which lives in or on another organism from which it gets its food.

mi·cro·pa·thol·o·gy (mī′krōpəthol′-əjē), *n.* the scientific study of the microscopic effects of disease on cells and tissue.

mi·cro·phage (mī′krəfāj), *n.* a minute cell that engulfs particles in its surroundings, present particularly in the white cells of blood or lymph where it is part of the defence mechanism against bacteria. See also **macrophage.**

mi·cro·phon·ism (mīkrəfō′nizm), *n.* a fault in an electronic device whereby the signal being transmitted is interfered with by noise produced by a vibrating component. —**mi·cro·phon′ic,** *adj.* —**mi·cro·phon′ics,** *n.*

mi·cro·pho·to·graph (mīkrəfō′tə-graf), *n.* **1.** microfilm. **2.** a photograph so small that it cannot be seen clearly without being enlarged. **3.** a photomicrograph.

mi·cro·pho·tom·e·ter (mī′krōfō-tom′itər), *n.* an instrument for measuring light intensity given out, trans-

mitted, or reflected by minute objects.

mi·cro·phyl·lous (mīkrəfil′əs), *adj.* with very small leaves. See also **macrophyllous.**

mi·cro·phys·ics (mīkrəfiz′iks), *n.* the science of the physical properties of objects too small to be dealt with directly, as atoms, molecules, etc. See also **macrophysics.**

mi·cro·phyte (mī′krəfīt), *n.* a plant too small to be seen clearly without a microscope.

mi·cro·po·rous (mīkrəpôr′əs), *adj.* consisting of or having microscopic pores.

mi·cro·print (mī′krəprint), *n.* a print of a microphotograph for reading or viewing under a magnifying glass.

mi·crop·si·a (mīkrop′sēə), *n.* a condition of the eye which causes objects to be seen smaller than life size. See also **macropsia.**

mi·cro·py·rom·e·ter (mī′krōpī-rom′itər), *n.* an adaptation of an optical pyrometer to deal with minute objects, by means of which temperatures above 550°C are measured according to their degree of incandescence.

mi·cro·read·er (mī′krōrē′dər), *n.* a device for projecting microfilm or microphotographic images onto a screen to give sufficient enlargement for them to be seen clearly.

mi·cro·re·pro·duc·tion (mī′krōrē′-prəduk′sHən), *n.* a photographic image too small to be seen clearly without being magnified.

mi·cro·sec·ond (mī′krəsek′ənd), *n.* a unit of measurement of time, equal to one millionth of a second. *Abbrev.*: **μsec.**

mi·cro·seism (mī′krəsīzm), *n.* a small tremor in the earth's crust recorded by a seismograph and supposed to be caused by an earthquake or a storm at sea.

mi·cro·sie·mens (mī′krəsē′mənz), *n.* a unit of measurement of electrical conductance, equal to one millionth of a siemens. *Abbrev.*: **μs.**

mi·cro·spec·tro·pho·tom·e·ter

(mī'krŏspek'trəfōtom'itər), *n.* an instrument for examining the light given out, transmitted, or reflected by minute objects.

mi·cro·stat (mī'krəstat), *n.* a photographic copy of a negative of a microphotograph.

mi·cro·steth·o·scope (mīkrəste*th*'ə-skōp), *n.* a stethoscope adapted to pick up and greatly amplify minute sounds.

mi·cro·stom·a·tous (mīkrəstom'-ətəs), *adj.* with an extremely small mouth or opening.

mi·cro·struc·ture (mī'krōstruk'-CHər), *n.* the size, shape, and detailed arrangement of crystals in a metal or alloy as seen under a powerful microscope after etching and polishing. See also **macrostructure.**

mi·cro·switch (mī'krəswiCH), *n.* an extremely sensitive switch used in automatically controlled machines.

mi·cro·therm (mī'krə*th*urm), *n.* a plant which grows in conditions of minimum heat.

mi·cro·tome (mī'krətōm), *n.* a machine for cutting extremely thin slices of tissue, usually frozen or embedded in paraffin wax, for easy examination under a microscope. —**mi·crot'o·my,** *n.*

mi·cro·volt (mī'krəvōlt), *n.* a unit used in measuring electromotive force, equal to one millionth of a volt. *Abbre .: µV, µv.*

mi·cro·watt (mī'krōwot), *n.* a unit used in measuring electric power, equal to one millionth of a watt. *Abbrev.: µW, µw.*

mi·cro·wave (mī'krōwāv), *n.* a very high frequency electromagnetic (radio) wave, usually one with a wavelength less than 20 cm.

mic·tu·rate (mik'CHərāt), *v.* to urinate, esp. to urinate with uncontrollable frequency. —**mic·tu·ri'tion,** *n.*

Middle Ages, the period in European history between ancient and modern times, generally applied to the time between the fall of the western Roman Empire in A.D. 476 and the general establishment of the Renaissance about 1450, but sometimes referring to only the part of this period after 1100.

mid·dle·weight (mid'lwāt), *n.* a boxer of the class intermediate between lightmiddleweight and lightheavyweight in amateur boxing, welterweight and lightheavyweight in professional boxing, and weighing 167 lb. or less if an amateur, 160 lb. or less if a professional.

midge (mij), *v.* any one of many minute kinds of two-winged biting insects.

mid·i·nette (midənet'), *n.* a Parisian shop-girl or seamstress.

mi·gnon (minyon'), *adj.* small and delicately formed. Also (of a woman) **mi·gnonne'.**

mi·graine (mī'grān), *n.* recurrent paroxysmal headache in one side of the head, following nausea and vomiting and sometimes accompanied by visual disturbances.

mi·kron (mī'kron), *n.*, *pl.* **mi·krons, mi·kra** (mī'krə). micron.

mil (mil), *n.* a unit of measurement of length equal to a thousandth of an inch, used in measuring the thickness of wires.

mil·a·naise (mil'ənāz), *adj.* (of meat) served with pasta, esp. macaroni, that has been topped with a tomato sauce flavored with finely chopped meat, mushrooms, and grated cheese.

milch (milCH), *adj.* giving milk; kept for milking.

mil·i·ar·i·a (mil'ēer'ēə), *n.* a skin disease characterized by small red pustules resembling millet seeds erupting around the sweat glands; prickly heat; miliary fever.

mi·lieu (milyōō'), *n.* environment, surrounding conditions.

mil·i·tate (mil'itāt), *v.* (of facts, evidence, attitudes, etc.) to exert force; influence; as *their disapproval militated against a speedy settlement.*

milk·sop (milk'sop), *n.* an effeminate man or one lacking in spirit.

milk-toast (milk'tōst), *adj.* (of a man) easily dominated; completely lacking in assertiveness.

Milky Way, the band of faint diffuse light, visible at night in the sky, composed of many stars too distant to be seen clearly with the naked eye.

mill (mil), *n.* a unit of money equal to a thousandth of a U.S. dollar, used in accounting, esp. in calculating taxes on real estate.

mill·dam (mil′dam), *n.* a dam across a stream to build up a force of water to operate a mill wheel.

mille-feuille (mēlfoi′), *n.* a sweet dessert of custard or whipped cream filling in a flat, rectangular base and top of flaky puff pastry with fondant and usually flavored with fruit; Napoleon.

mil·le·fi·o·ri (mil′əfēôr′ē), *n.* decorative glass made by fusing bundles of different-colored glass rods together and slicing them into disks to give flower-like pieces which are grouped in clear glass for blowing to a desired form.

mille-fleur (mēlflur′), *adj.* with a flowered background.

mil·le·nar·i·an (miləner′ēən), *adj.* of or relating to the millennium.

mil·le·nar·y (mil′ənerē), *adj.* **1.** consisting of or relating to a thousand, esp. a thousand years. **2.** relating to the millennium.

mil·len·ni·al (milen′ēəl), *adj.* of or relating to a millennium.

mil·len·ni·um (milen′ēəm), *n., pl.* **mil·len·ni·ums, mil·len·ni·a** (milen′ēə). **1.** a period of a thousand years. **2.** the period of a thousand years when Christ will reign on earth, as prophesied in the Book of Revelations. **3.** a supposedly coming period of general happiness, prosperity, and justice.

mil·les·i·mal (miles′əməl), *adj.* thousandth.

mil·li·am·me·ter (milēam′mētər), *n.* an instrument for measuring small electric currents in milliamperes.

mil·li·am·pere (mileam′pēr), *n.* a unit used in measuring electric current, equal to one thousandth of an ampere. *Abbrev.* : **mA.**

mil·li·ang·strom (milēaNG′strəm), *n.*

a unit used to express light wavelengths, equal to one thousandth of an angstrom. *Abbrev.* : **mA, mA.U.**

mil·li·ard (mil′yərd), *n.* (in Britain) one thousand millions; a billion.

mil·li·are (mil′ēer), *n.* a unit used in measuring area, equal to one thousandth of an are.

mil·li·ar·y (mil′ēer′ē), *adj.* indicating a mile.

mil·li·bar (mil′əbär), *n.* a unit used in measuring atmospheric pressure, equal to one thousandth of a bar. *Abbrev.* : **mb.**

mil·li·barn (mil′əbärn), *n.* a unit used in measuring a nuclear cross-section, equal to one thousandth of a barn. *Abbrev.* : **mb.**

mil·li·cou·lomb (mil′əkoo′lom), *n.* a unit of measurement of electrical charge, equal to one thousandth of a coulomb. *Abbrev.* : **mC.**

mil·li·cur·ie (mil′əkyoor′ē), *n.* a unit of measurement of radioactivity equal to one thousandth of a curie. *Abbrev.* : **mCi, mc.**

mil·lier (mēlyā′), *n.* a unit of measurement of weight, equal to one thousand kilograms. Also **tonneau.**

mil·li·far·ad (mil′əfarəd), *n.* a unit of measurement of electrical capacity, equal to one thousandth of a farad. *Abbrev.* : **mF, mf.**

mil·li·gal (mil′əgal), *n.* a unit used in measuring acceleration, equal to one thousandth of a gal. *Abbrev.* : **mGal.**

mil·li·gram (mil′əgram), *n.* a unit used in measuring weight, equal to one thousandth of a gram. *Abbrev.* : **mg.**

mil·li·gram-hour (mil′əgram′our), *n.* a unit used in measuring doses of radium received by a person undergoing radiotherapy, equal to the amount of radiation received by exposure for one hour to one milligram of radium.

mil·li·hen·ry (mil′əhen′rē), *n.* a unit used in measuring electrical inductance, equal to one thousandth of a henry. *Abbrev.* : **mH, mh.**

mil·li·lam·bert (mil′əlambərt), *n.* a unit used in measuring brightness, equal to one thousandth of a lambert. *Abbrev.* : **mL.**

mil·li·li·ter (mil′əlētər), *n.* a unit used in measuring capacity, equal to one thousandth of a liter. *Abbrev.* : **ml.**

mil·li·lux (mil′əluks), *n.* a unit of measurement of illumination, equal to one thousandth of a lux. *Abbrev.* : **mlx.**

mil·li·me·ter (mil′əmētər), *n.* a unit of measurement of length, equal to one thousandth of a meter. *Abbrev.* : **mm.**

mil·li·mho (mil′əmō), *n.* a unit used in measuring electrical conductance, equal to one thousandth of a mho. *Abbrev.* : **mmho.**

mil·li·mi·cron (mil′əmī′kron), *n.*, *pl.* **mil·li·mi·crons, mil·li·mi·cra** (mil′əmī′krə). a unit used in measuring length, equal to one thousandth of a micron. *Abbrev.* : **mμ, m, mu.**

mil·li·mole (mil′əmōl), *n.* a unit used to express the molecular weight of a chemical substance in terms of grams, equal to one thousandth of a mole or gram molecule. *Abbrev.* : **mM.**

mil·line (mil′līn), *n.* an advertisement consisting of one line of agate-size type across one column appearing in one million copies of a newspaper or magazine.

mil·li·ohm (mil′ēōm), *n.* a unit used in measuring electrical resistance, equal to one thousandth of an ohm. *Abbrev.* : **mΩ.**

mil·li·poise (mil′əpoiz), *n.* a unit used in the measurement of viscosity, equal to one thousandth of a poise. *Abbrev.* : **mP.**

mil·li·rem (mil′ərem), *n.* a unit used in measuring dosage of radioactivity, equal to one thousandth of a rem. *Abbrev.* : **mrem.**

mil·li·roent·gen (mil′ərentgən), *n.* a unit of measurement of x-ray dosage, equal to one thousandth of a roentgen. *Abbrev.* : **mR, mr.**

mil·li·sec·ond (mil′isek′ənd), *n.* a unit of measurement of time equal to one thousandth of a second. *Abbrev.* : **msec.**

mil·li·sie·mens (mil′əsēmənz), *n.* a unit used in measuring electrical conductance, equal to one thousandth of a siemens. *Abbrev.* : **mS.**

mil·li·volt (mil′əvolt), *n.* a unit used in measuring electromotive force, equal to one thousandth of a volt. *Abbrev.* : **mV, mv.**

mil·li·watt (mil′əwot), *n.* a unit used in measuring electric power, equal to one thousandth of a watt. *Abbrev.* : **mW, mw.**

milque·toast (milk′tōst), *n.* a timid person, esp. a weak-willed man.

milt (milt), *n.* the roe or reproductive gland of male fish.

milt·er (mil′tər), *n.* a male fish during the breeding season.

Mil·town (mil′toun), *n.* tradename of a preparation of the tranquilizing drug meprobanate.

mi·me·sis (mimē′sis), *n.* mimicry in which one species of animal develops for its protection against predators a similar coloring or marking to another species which is protected from predators, by being poisonous for example. —**mi·met·ic** (mimet′ik), *adj.*

mi·na·cious (minā′sHəs), *adj.* threatening.

min·a·to·ry (min′ətôrē), *adj.* threatening.

min·er·al·o·gy (minərol′əjē), *n.* the scientific study of minerals. —**min·er·al′o·gist**, *n.*

min·e·stro·ne (ministrō′nē), *n.* a thick Italian soup made with many vegetables, herbs, and pieces of pasta in meat stock, usually served with finely grated Parmesan cheese.

Ming (miNG), *n.* the porcelain produced in China during the Ming dynasty (1368–1644), esp. before 1620 by the imperial factory, characterized by fine porcelain bodies decorated with brilliantly colored underglaze or enamel.

min·gy (min′jē), *adj.* mean; niggardly.

min·i·a·tur·ize (min′ēəcHərīz), *v.* to make a small version, to reduce in size.

min·i·fy (min′əfī), *v.* to make smaller; minimize.

min·i·kin (min′əkin), *n.* a delicate or diminutive person or object.

min·im (min′əm), *n.* the smallest unit of fluid measure, equal to one sixtieth of a fluid dram. *Abbrev.:* **M, min.**

min·i·max (min′əmaks), *n.* a strategy used in games to reduce to the utmost a player's possible loss. See also **maximin.**

min·i·mus (min′əməs), *n.* **1.** the smallest or least important person or item in a classification. **2.** the little finger or toe.

min·ion (min′yən), *n.* a servile follower or a favorite of a person in power; a minor official.

min·ne·sing·er (min′isiNG′ər), *n.,* *sing.* and *pl.* German lyric poets and songwriters of the 12th to 14th centuries.

mi·nus·cule (min′əskyōōl), *adj.* **1.** very small. **2.** of a cursive script developed in the 7th century using small, non-capital letters. See also **majuscule.**

mi·nu·ti·a (minōō′SHēə), *n.,* usually in *pl.* **mi·nu·ti·ae** (minōō′SHēē). small details; trivial points.

minx (miNGks), *n.* a pert or flirtatious girl.

Mi·o·cene (mī′əsēn), *adj.* of or relating to the geological epoch (and the rock systems formed during it) that occurred between the Oligocene and Pliocene epochs that lasted from about 25 million to 10 million years ago, and was characterized by the presence of grazing mammals.

mi·o·sis, my·o·sis (mīō′sis), *n., pl.* **mi·o·ses** (mīō′sēz). a medical condition in which the pupil of the eye is abnormally constricted, as by drugs, etc. —**mi·ot·ic** (mīot′ik), *adj.*

mi·ra·bi·le dic·tu (mērä′bile dik′-tōō), *Latin.* wonderful to relate; strange to tell.

mire·poix (mirpwä′), *n.* a garnish of diced vegetables, herbs, seasonings, and chopped ham cooked in butter or with the meat or fish with which it is to be served.

mis·al·li·ance (misəlī′əns), *n.* **1.** an unsuitable association, esp. marriage. **2.** mésalliance.

mis·al·ly (misəlī′), *v.* to make a misalliance.

mis·an·thrope (mis′ənthrōp), *n.* one who hates mankind or shuns company.

mis·an·thro·py (misan′thrəpē), *n.* hatred, dislike, or avoidance of mankind. —**mis·an·thro′pic,** *adj.*

mis·be·got·ten (misbigot′n), *adj.* illegitimate; ill-conceived.

mis·ce·ge·na·tion (mis′ijənā′SHən), *n.* marriage or cohabitation between couples of different race.

mis·cel·la·ne·a (misəlā′nēə), *n. pl.* a miscellany of writings or objects; a random collection.

mis·ci·ble (mis′əbəl), *adj.* capable of being mixed.

mis·cre·ance (mis′krēəns), *n.* a false belief or religious faith.

mis·cre·ant (mis′krēənt), *adj.* **1.** depraved, villainous. **2.** holding a false belief or religious faith. —**mis′cre·an·cy,** *n.*

mis·de·mean·ant (misdimē′nənt), *n.* one who has performed a misdeed or misbehaved.

mise en scène (mēzäNsen′), *French.* the producer's arrangement of all matters relating to the staging of a play, including the acting, sets, costumes, lighting, etc.

mis·fea·sance (misfē′zəns), *n.* the wrongful exercise of lawful authority. See also **malfeasance.** —**mis·fea′sor,** *n.*

mis·no·mer (misnō′mər), *n.* a name wrongly applied.

mis·o·cai·ne·a (misōkī′nēə), *n.* an abnormally strong dislike of all things new.

mi·sog·a·my (misog′əmē), *n.* hatred of marriage. —**mi·sog′a·mist,** *n.*

mi·sog·y·ny (misoj′ənē), *n.* hatred of women. —**mi·sog′y·nist,** *n.*

mi·sol·o·gy (misol′əjē), *n.* strong aversion to reason or reasoning.

mis·o·ne·ism (misōnē′izm), *n.* hatred of newness or change.

mis·o·pe·di·a, mis·o·pae·di·a (misopē′dēə), *n.* hatred of children, esp. of one's own children.

mis·pri·sion[1] (misprizH′ən), *n.* a wrongful act, esp. by a public official.

mis·pri·sion[2] (misprizH′ən), *n.* contempt; disdain.

mis·prize (misprīz′), *v.* to despise, to fail to appreciate rightly.

mist·bow (mist′bō), *n.* See **fog bow.**

mith·ri·da·tism (mith′ridā′tizm), *n.* the making proof against a poison by dosing with gradually increasing amounts of it.

mith·ri·da·tize (mith′ridā′tīz), *v.* to make a person proof against a poison by dosing with gradually increasing amounts of it.

mit·i·cide (mit′isīd), *n.* a chemical for killing mites.

mit·i·gate (mit′əgāt), *v.* to make or become less intense or severe.

mi·to·sis (mītō′sis), *n.* the usual process of cell division, in which the nucleus splits into two, each chromosome duplicates, and one of each pair of chromosomes groups with one or other nucleus so that two identical cells result.

mi·tral valve (mī′trəl), a valve consisting of two triangular flaps of membrane and located between the atrium and ventricle of the left side of the heart to prevent blood from flowing back into the atrium when the ventricle contracts. Also **bicuspid valve.**

mix·ol·o·gy (miksol′əjē), *n.* (in colloquial humor) the art of preparing cocktails. —**mix·ol′o·gist,** *n.*

mne·me (nē′mē), *n.* that feature of the mind or of an organism which accounts for memory.

mne·mon·ics (nēmon′iks), *n.* the art of aiding or improving the memory. —**mne·mon′ic,** *adj.*

Mö·bi·us strip (mā′bēəs), a continuous one-sided surface formed from a rectangular strip by twisting one end through a complete turn about the longitudinal axis and joining it to the other end.

mob·oc·ra·cy (mobok′rəsē), *n.* government by a mob.

mock-he·ro·ic (mok′hirō′ik), *adj.* burlesquely imitating heroic style, as in manner, action, literary form.

mo·derne (mōdern′), *adj.* noting a style of the 1920's and 1930's characterized by linear geometric motifs executed in solid-colored materials with much use of plastics and enamelware; Art Deco.

mo·diste (mōdēst′), *n.* a maker or seller of women's fashions, esp. dresses and millinery.

mod·ule (moj′ool), *n.* a measurement that may range from a few inches to several feet selected as the basis in planning or standardizing a building, building components, a range of furniture, etc. —**mod′u·lar,** *adj.*

mo·dus o·pe·ran·di (mō′doos ōperän′dē), *Latin.* way of working, system of operation.

mo·dus vi·ven·di (mō′doos wēwen′-dē), way or mode of living.

mo·fette (mōfet′), *n.* an unpleasantly smelling emanation of carbon dioxide, with some oxygen and nitrogen, from a nearly extinct volcano through a small fissure in the earth's crust.

mog·i·la·li·a (mojəlā′lēə), *n.* any defect in speech.

mo·go·te (məgō′tē), *n.* a hillock of cavity-riddled limestone left standing between flat valleys.

Mo·hole (mō′hōl), *n.* a hole drilled through the earth's crust, through the Mohorovičič discontinuity, and into the mantle beneath, for geological research into the mantle.

Mo·ho·ri·vi·čič discontinuity (mō′-hōrō′vəcHicH), the boundary between the earth's crust and the mantle below it, distinguished from them in its physical properties, and occurring on average at 22 miles below the continents and 6 miles below the ocean bed.

moi·e·ty (moi′itē), *n.* half.

moil (moil), *v.* **1.** to toil; drudge. —*n.* **2.** hard work; drudgery. **3.** turmoil; confusion.

moi·ré (mwärā′), *adj.* (of fabrics) watered; with a marking that suggests rippling water.

moit (moit), *n.* a foreign body in wool, as a seed, splinter, etc.

mold·board (mōld′bôrd), *n.* a large metal plate at the front of a bulldozer to push ahead loose earth.

mole[1] (mōl), *n.* a very large structure, usually of stone, built in water to act as a pier or breakwater.

mole[2] (mōl), *n.* a gram molecule; the weight of a molecule of a chemical element or compound expressed in grams. Also **mol.**

molecular film, a layer or film of the thickness of one molecule. Also **monolayer.**

mol·e·cule (mol′əkyōōl), *n.* the smallest particle of a substance that can exist in a free state without losing its chemical identity, consisting of a minute group of atoms, one or more like atoms in the case of chemical elements and two or more different atoms in the case of chemical compounds. —**mo·lec′u·lar,** *adj.*

mol·les·cent (məles′ənt), *adj.* softening; tending to become soft.

mol·li·fy (mol′əfī), *v.* to appease; to calm down.

Mo·lo·tov cocktail (mol′ətov), a homemade grenade consisting of a bottle filled with flammable liquid and fitted with a wick which is ignited just before the grenade is thrown so that the liquid bursts into flame and explodes the bottle.

mom·ism (mom′izm), *n.* excessive dependence on a mother figure with resulting inhibition of maturity.

mon·a·chal (mon′əkəl), *adj.* monastic.

mon·ad (mon′ad), *n.* any one-celled organism.

mo·nan·dry (mənan′drē), *n.* the custom or state of having only one husband at a time. See also **polyandry.** —**mo·nan′drous,** *adj.*

mon·arch (mon′ərk), *n.* 1. a hereditary sovereign, as a king, emperor, etc. 2. a supreme ruler. 3. a large orange butterfly with black and white markings.

mon·ar·chy (mon′ərkē), *n.* a government or state in which the actual or titular ruler is a monarch. —**mo·nar′chal, mo·nar′chi·cal,** *adj.*

mon·au·ral (monôr′əl), *adj.* See **monophonic.**

mon·go (moNG′gō), *n.* See **mungo.**

Mon·gol·ism (moNG′gəlizm), *n.* a congenital defect in which the subject has a broad, flat skull, high cheekbones, flattened nose, and slanting eyes and is usually mentally subnormal.

mon·grel·ize (muNG′grəlīz), *v.* to mix, esp. to interbreed, different races, breeds, kinds.

mon·ism (mon′izm), *n.* a metaphysical theory that there is only one basis of all reality and that mind and matter are not distinct entities. See also **dualism, pluralism.**

mo·ni·tion (mōnisH′ən), *n.* a warning; a caution.

mon·o·car·pic (monəkär′pik), *adj.* (in plants) bearing fruit only once and then dying.

mon·o·chro·mat·ic (mon′əkrōmat′-ik), *adj.* of one color.

mon·o·chro·ma·tism (monəkrō′-mətizm), *n.* a defect of the eye, in which no differences of color are perceived.

mon·o·chrome (mon′əkrōm), *n.* a painting or drawing executed in different shades of one color.

mon·o·coque (mon′əkōk), *n.* a type of construction of aircraft, boats, cars, etc., in which the fuselage, outer casing, or skin bears all or most of the structural loads.

mo·noc·ra·cy (mōnok′rəsē), *n.* autocracy; government by one person.

mon·o·crat (mon′əkrat), *n.* a believer in monocracy.

mo·noc·u·lar (mənok′yələr), *adj.* 1. one-eyed. 2. of, relating to, or adapted for one eye, as a telescope.

mon·o·cul·ture (mon′əkulcHər), *n.* the cultivation of only one kind of crop.

mon·o·dac·ty·lous (monədak′tələs), *adj.* with only one finger, toe, or claw.

mo·nod·o·mous (mənod′əməs), *adj.* living in a single nest, as ants and wasps. See also **polydomous.**

mon·o·dra·ma (mon'ədrämə), *n.* a dramatic work for performance by a single person.

mon·o·dy (mon'ədē), *n.* a threnody in which one person laments the death of another.

mo·noe·cious (mənē'sнəs), *adj.* hermaphroditic; gynandromorphic.

mon·o·fil·a·ment (monəfil'əmənt), *n.* a single, comparatively large filament of a synthetic fiber, as used in a fishing line.

mo·nog·a·my (mənog'əmē), *n.* the practice or condition of being married to only one person at a time. See also **polygamy.** —**mon·o·gam'ic, mo·nog'a·mous,** *adj.* —**mo·nog'a·mist,** *n.*

mon·o·gen·e·sis (monəjen'isis), *n.* the supposed descent of all mankind from one couple. Also **mo·nog'e·ny.** —**mo·nog'e·nous, mon·o·ge·net'ic,** *adj.*

mon·o·gen·ic (monəjen'ik), *adj.* bearing only male offspring or only female offspring.

mo·nog·e·nism (mənoj'ənizm), *n.* the theory that all mankind descended from one couple or from one type of ancestor.

mon·o·graph (mon'əgraf), *n.* a treatise on a single subject or single class of subjects, as on an author or the works of an author.

mo·nog·y·ny (mənoj'ənē), *n.* the custom or state of having only one wife at a time. See also **polygyny.** —**mo·nog'y·nist,** *n.*

mon·o·ki·ni (monəkē'nē), *n.* a topless bathing suit for women.

mo·nol·a·try (mənol'ətrē), *n.* the worship of one only god out of a number accepted as existing.

mon·o·lay·er (monəlā'ər), *n.* See **molecular film.**

mon·o·lith (mon'əlith), *n.* 1. a single large piece of stone or similar material. 2. a large political or social structure giving an impression of unbreakable unity. —**mon·o·lith'ic,** *adj.*

mon·o·logue (mon'əlôg), *n.* a long uninterrupted speech or dramatic presentation by one person speaking alone. See also **duologue.**

mo·nol·o·gy (mənol'əjē), *n.* the practice or act of a person speaking to himself, discoursing at length, or performing a work or part of a work which is written for a single person speaking alone.

mon·o·ma·ni·a (monəmā'nēə), *n.* an obsessive enthusiasm for a single idea, interest, pursuit, etc.

mo·nom·er·ous (mənom'ərəs), *adj.* consisting of a single part.

mon·o·mor·phic (monəmôr'fik), *adj.* 1. (of an animal or plant) existing in only one form. 2. of identical or basically like structure.

mon·o·nu·cle·o·sis (mon'ənoo'-klēo'sis), *n.* 1. a disease in which the blood contains an abnormally large number of white blood cells with a single nucleus or of the large white blood cells which ingest dead or foreign material in the blood. 2. See **infectious mononucleosis.**

mon·o·pet·al·ous (monəpet'ələs), *adj.* with only one petal.

mon·o·pha·gia (monəfā'jə), *n.* the practice of eating or craving only one kind of food, normal in some animals but considered a disorder in humans.

mo·noph·a·gous (mənof'əgəs), *adj.* feeding on one variety of food only. See also **oligophagous.**

mon·o·pho·bi·a (monəfō'bēə), *n.* an abnormal dread of being alone. —**mon·o·pho'bic,** *adj.*

mon·o·phon·ic (monəfon'ik), *adj.* relating to a system of sound reproduction in which a single signal is put out whether one or more signals are put in. Also **monaural.** See also **stereophonic.**

mon·o·phy·let·ic (mon'ōfīlet'ik), *adj.* of a biological class whose members are descended from the same ancestral type.

mon·o·phyl·lous (monəfil'əs), *adj.* with a single leaf.

mon·o·ple·gi·a (monəplē'jēə), *n.* paralysis of one part of the body, as of one extremity, muscle, or group of muscles.

mon·o·pode (mon′əpōd), *adj.* one-footed.

mo·nop·o·ly (mənop′əlē), *n.* the exclusive possession of a trading right which makes possible the manipulation of prices. See also **duopoly, oligopoly.**

mon·o·pol·y·logue (mənəpol′ilôg), *n.* a theatrical piece in which one player takes several parts.

mo·nop·so·ny (mənop′sənē), *n.* a condition in which there is only one buyer in a particular market. See also **duopsony, oligopsony.**

mon·o·rail (mon′ərāl), *n.* a railroad in which the track consists of a single rail on which the cars balance or from which they hang.

mon·o·rhi·nous (monərī′nəs), *adj.* having only one nostril, as lampreys, etc.

mon·o·rhyme (mon′ərīm), *n.* a poem or stanza with all the lines rhyming with each other.

mon·o·so·di·um glu·ta·mate (monəsō′dēəm glōō′təmāt), a white powder manufactured from salt and beet molasses and used to intensify the flavor of meat and vegetable dishes or products. Also **sodium glutamate.**

mon·o·sper·mous (monəspur′məs), *adj.* having only a single seed.

mon·o·sper·my (mon′əspurmē), *n.* the fertilizing of an ovum by a single spermatozoon.

mon·o·stom (mon′əstōm), *adj.* with one stoma or other mouth-like opening.

mon·o·the·ism (mon′əthēizm), *n.* the doctrine that there is only one God.

mon·o·tone (mon′ətōn), *n.* **1.** sounds or speech continuing or repeated in the same pitch. **2.** the lack of any variation in style, as in writing or music. —**mon·o·ton·ic** (monəton′-ik), *adj.*

mon·o·treme (mon′ətrēm), *n.* any mammal of a sub-class of primitive egg-layers found in Australasia and comprising only the duck-billed platypus and spiny anteater. —**mon·o·tre′ma·tous,** *adj.*

mon·soon (monsōōn′), *n.* the rainy season that accompanies the SW monsoon wind in southern Asia.

mon·tane (mon′tān), *adj.* of or relating to mountainous country.

mon·teith (montēth′), *n.* a punch bowl, usually of silver, with a notched rim on which punch cups can be hung.

Mon·tes·so·ri method (mon′tisôr′-ē), a system of training small children, devised by the Italian educator Maria Montessori (1870–1952), in which the main emphasis is on discovery through exercise of the senses.

mont·gol·fi·er (montgol′fēər), *n.* a balloon raised by heated air.

mon·ti·cule (mon′təkyōōl), *n.* a small mountain or hill; a mound; a subsidiary cone of a volcano.

moon·calf (mōōn′kaf), *n.* a congenital mentally defective person.

moot (mōōt), *adj.* debatable; on which opinions differ.

mo·quette (mōket′), *n.* a velvety fabric with a thick pile of wool on a cotton or jute base, used particularly for upholstery.

mo·raine (mərān′), *n.* a mass of rocks, sand, and clay carried along by a glacier.

Mo·ral Re-Ar·ma·ment (môr′əl rē-är′məmənt), a movement based on the theory that absolute morality in a person's private and public life leads to a better world. Also **Buchmanism.**

mor·a·to·ri·um (môrətôr′ēəm), *n.,* *pl.* **mor·a·tor·i·a** (môrətôr′ēə), **mor·a·tor·i·ums.** a temporary cessation of activity, esp. of hostilities.

mor·bid (môr′bid), *adj.* **1.** given to gloomy ideas; of unwholesome mind; suggesting a sick mind. **2.** gruesome; causing dread. —**mor·bid′i·ty,** *n.*

mor·bif·ic (môrbif′ik), *adj.* disease-producing. Also **mor·bif′i·cal.**

mor·da·cious (môrdā′sHəs), *adj.* given to biting.

mor·dant (môr′dnt), *adj.* (of wit, etc.) biting, sarcastic. —**mor′dan·cy,** *n.*

mo·res (môr′āz), *n. pl.* the generally accepted customs and ways of a society which has grown out of its fundamental beliefs.

mor·ga·nat·ic (môrgənat′ik), *adj.* of or pertaining to a marriage between a man of high rank and a woman of lower rank in which the wife and any children may not lay claim to the husband's rank or property.

mor·i·bund (môr′əbund), *adj.* in a dying state; at the point of death.

mo·rose (mərōs′), *adj.* of gloomy ill-temper; sullenly unsociable.

mor·pheme (môr′fēm), *n.* the smallest element in language to have semantic or grammatical meaning. —**mor·phe′mic**, *adj.*

mor·phe·mics (môrfē′miks), *n.* the study of morphemes.

mor·phol·o·gy (môrfol′əjē), *n.* the branch of any science, as biology, philology, etc., that deals with form and structure.

mor·ro (môr′ō), *n.* a rounded hill or headland.

mor·ta·del·la (môrtədel′ə), *n.* a cooked, smoked sausage of pork, beef, and pork fat with seasonings and garlic.

mor·tif·er·ous (môrtif′ərəs), *adj.* fatal; causing death.

mor·ti·fy (môr′təfī), *v.* 1. to humiliate; to wound a person's feelings. 2. to become gangrenous. —**mor·ti·fi·ca′tion**, *n.*

mos·chate (mos′kāt), *adj.* with a musky smell.

moss·back (môs′bak), *n.* (in colloquial usage) a person of old-fashioned ideas; a person of extremely conservative notions.

mot (mō), *n.* a witty saying or remark.

mote (mōt), *n.* a dust particle.

moth·er-of-pearl (muTH′ərəvpurl′), an iridescent hard lining of some shells, as that of the pearl oyster; nacre.

mo·tile (mōt′l), *adj.* capable of motion; in motion.

motion sickness, a feeling of sickness and nausea resulting from the motion on a ship, car, etc. See also **naupathia.**

mot juste (mōzHγst′), *French.* an expression or word that conveys precisely the right shade of meaning.

mou·jik (mōōzHik′), *n.* muzhik.

mou·lage (mōōläzH′), *n.* a plaster-of-Paris mold of objects or imprints, as of footprints for identification purposes.

mou·lin (mōōlaN′), *n.* a circular shaft in a glacier or the bedrock beneath it caused by water formed from ice or snow melting on its surface falling through a crevasse.

mountain sickness, a disorder occurring in the rarefied air at high altitude and characterized by difficulty in breathing, muscular weakness, mental lethargy, headache, and nausea.

mountain wave, steep wave-like air currents that occur when fast-flowing air meets an abruptly rising mountain range.

moun·te·bank (moun′təbaNgk), *n.* an itinerant seller of quack remedies who attracts buyers by patter and tricks performed on a platform in a public place; any trickster or charlatan.

mousse (mōōs), *n.* a cold dish based on frothy whipped cream or cream and egg-white with a sweet or a meaty flavoring set in a mold, sometimes by gelatin.

mousse·line (mōōslēn′), *n.* any dish made light and fluffy by the addition of beaten egg white or whipped cream. Also **chantilly.**

mousse·line de soie (mōōslēndəswä′), *French.* a fine, stiff fabric of silk or rayon.

mou·ton·née (mōōtənā′), *adj.* scattered with rounded rocks that have been smoothed and shaped by glacial action. Also **mou·ton·néed′.**

Mo·vie·o·la (mōō′vēo′lə), *n.* the trademark of a motion-picture viewing device for use by one person who can control its movement and speed; used in film editing.

mox·a (mok′sə), *n.* down from the dried leaves of certain plants or some similarly downy substance for forming into a cone or cylinder to be put on the skin and burned as a counter-irritant for gout, etc.

211

multipartite

mox·ie (mok′sē), *n.* (in colloquial use) verve; nerve; vigorous assertiveness.

moz·za·rel·la (motsərel′lə), *n.* a mild, soft, white cheese, originally made in Italy.

mu·ced·i·nous (myōōsed′ənəs), *adj.* of or like mold or mildew.

mu·cif·er·ous (myōōsif′ərəs), *adj.* secreting or containing mucus.

mu·cip·a·rous (myōōsip′ərəs), *adj.* muciferous.

mu·coid (myōō′koid), *adj.* mucuslike. Also **mu·coi′dal.**

mu·co·pu·ru·lent (myōōkəpyōōr′- yələnt), *adj.* consisting of or bearing mucus and pus.

mu·cor (myōō′kər), *n.* any fungus that forms a fur-like layer on food and dead or dying plants.

mu·co·sa (myōōkō′sə), *n., pl.* **mu·co·sae** (myōōkō′sē). mucous membrane.

mucous membrane, the moist, inner-surface lining of hollow organs of the body that provides them with lubrication.

mu·cro (myōō′krō), *n., pl.* **mu·cro·nes** (myōōkrō′nēz). a pointed projection on a botanical or zoological organ, as on a leaf or feather.

mu·cro·nate (myōō′krōnit), *adj.* having a mucro. Also **mu′cro·nat·ed.**

mu·cus (myōō′kəs), *n.* a slimy fluid secreted by mucous membrane. —**mu′cous,** *adj.*

mu·dra (mədrä′), *n.* any of the gestures of the hand in the classical dancing of India, each representing a particular feeling.

muen·ster (mōōn′stər), *n.* a mild, semi-hard, fermented whole milk cheese often flavored with caraway or anise seed.

muf·ti (muf′tē), *n.* civilian clothes worn by one who usually wears a uniform or distinguished from uniform.

mug·wump (mug′wump), *n.* **1.** one who acts independently of political parties or affects superiority in political or other issues. **2.** one who cannot decide his views or who takes a neutral view in political or other issues.

mu·jik (mōōzhik′), *n.* muzhik.

muk·luk (muk′luk), *n.* a soft boot worn by Eskimos, usually of seal or reindeer skin and fur-lined.

mulch (mulch), *n.* **1.** a layer of straw, leaves, compost, etc., spread on soil to enrich it, to conserve moisture, or to protect the roots of plants. —*v.* **2.** to apply a mulch.

mulct (mulkt), *v.* **1.** to exact money from a person by fraud, by fine, etc. —*n.* **2.** a fine, penalty, or other method used to exact money.

mu·le·ta (mōōlā′tə), *n.* a red cloth on a stick used in a bullfight by a matador to entice and divert the bull. See also **capa.**

mul·ey (myōō′lē), *adj.* (of cattle) hornless; polled.

mu·li·eb·ri·ty (myōō′lēeb′ritē), *n.* the characteristics and qualities of women.

mul·ler (mul′ər), *n.* a machine for grinding.

mul·li·ga·taw·ny (mul′əgətô′nē), *n.* a curry-flavored soup, originally of the E. Indies.

mul·tan·gu·lar (multang′gyələr), *adj.* with many angles.

mul·ti·cel·lu·lar (multisel′yələr), *adj.* consisting of more than one cell.

mul·ti·far·i·ous (multəfer′ēəs), *adj.* of many kinds, parts, forms, etc.

mul·ti·fid (mul′təfid), *adj.* divided into many parts or lobes.

mul·ti·flo·rous (multiflôr′əs), *adj.* bearing many flowers.

mul·ti·fo·li·ate (multəfō′lēit), *adj.* having many leaves or leaflets.

mul·ti·lat·er·al (multilat′ərəl), *adj.* having many sides.

mul·ti·loc·u·lar (multilok′yələr), *adj.* consisting of more than one cell or chamber.

mul·ti·nom·i·nal (multinom′ənl), *n.* having many names.

mul·ti·nu·cle·ar (multinōō′klēər), *adj.* having more than one nucleus.

mul·tip·a·ra (multip′ərə), *n., pl.* **mul·tip·a·rae** (multip′ərē). a woman pregnant for the second or further time; a woman who has borne more than one child.

mul·ti·par·tite (multipär′tīt), *adj.* divided into many parts.

mul·ti·ped (mul′təped), *adj.* having many feet. Also **mul′ti·pede.**

multiple sclerosis, a progressive disease of the nervous system in which small areas of the spinal cord and the brain lose their function with resultant speech disturbance and muscular incoordination.

mul·ti·plex (mul′təpleks), *adj.* **1.** manifold; having many elements. **2.** relating to radio, television, telephone, or telegraph equipment able to carry more than one signal at a time.

mul·ti·pli·cate (mul′təplikāt′), *adj.* manifold; having many and varied forms or elements.

mul·ti·plic·i·ty (multəplis′itē), *n.* a great number; a great and varied number.

mul·ti·ver·si·ty (multəvur′sitē), *n.* a university with several separate campuses.

mul·tiv·o·cal (multiv′əkəl), *adj.* having more than one meaning.

mul·tum in par·vo (mŏŏl′tŏŏm in pär′vō), *Latin.* a great deal in little space or compass.

mum·mer (mum′ər), *n.* a person wearing a mask or fancy dress at some festive gathering or masquerade. —**mum′mer·y,** *n.*

mun·dane (mundān′), *adj.* relating to the world or universe; worldly; earthly.

mun·di·fy (mun′dəfī), *v.* to free from noxious matter, as a wound, an ulcer, the blood, etc.

mun·go (muNG′gō), *n.* a cloth or yarn made from heavily felted woolen rags. Also **mongo.**

mu·nif·i·cent (myōōnif′isənt), *adj.* liberal in giving; splendidly generous.

mun·tin (mun′tn), *n.* a bar for holding window panes within the main framework.

mure (myŏŏr), *v.* to immure; to imprison; to shut up.

mu·rex (myŏŏr′eks), *n., pl.* **mu·ri·ces** (myŏŏr′isēz), **mu·rex·es.** the mollusk common to tropical seas and giving a reddish-purple dye that was used in the ancient world esp. for the garments of royalty or rulers.

mu·ri·cate (myŏŏr′əkāt), *adj.* having or covered with short, pointed projections. Also **mu′ri·cat·ed.**

mur·mur (mur′mər), *n.* an abnormal noise arising within the heart because of alteration of blood flow, esp. such as is caused by faulty valves, and audible through a stethoscope. Also **heart murmur.**

mur·rey (mur′ē), *n.* a deep reddish-purple color.

mu·sa·ceous (myōōzā′sHəs), *adj.* of or relating to the genus of plants that includes the plantain or banana.

musc·ae vo·li·tan·tes (mus′ē vol′i-tan′tēz), dark spots that seem to float before the eyes, due to an eye defect.

mus·ca·tel (muskətel′), *n.* a strong sweet white wine made from muscat grapes.

mus·cid (mus′id), *adj.* of or relating to the family of insects that includes the common housefly.

mus·cu·la·ture (mus′kyələcHər), *n.* the system or arrangement of muscles in an animal's body or part of a body.

mu·se·ol·o·gy (myōō′zēol′əjē), *n.* the study of the administration and functioning of a museum.

mu·si·col·o·gy (myōōzəkol′əjē), *n.* all aspects of the study of music except performance or composition, as musical theory, historical research, etc.

mu·sique con·crète (myzēk′kôN-kret′), *French.* music contrived from various sounds, made both by musical instruments and other objects, recorded and often distorted electronically. See also **electronic music.**

mus·keg (mus′keg), *n.* a waterlogged depression in the sub-arctic zone of Canada, commonly with a ground covering of sphagnum moss and sedge and with a scattering of lakes and stunted trees.

mus·lin (muz′lin), *n.* a fine cotton fabric usually of plain weave, varying in thickness according to its purpose, as for making into diapers, girls' and

lades' dresses, curtains, sheets, etc.

mus·si·ta·tion (musitā′sHən), *n.* silent imitation of the lip movements made in speech.

mus·te·line (mus′təlīn), *adj.* of or relating to the family that includes the weasels, badgers, otters, etc.

musth (must), *n.* a state of dangerous frenzy occurring periodically in male elephants and camels and accompanied by the secretion of an oily fluid from glands above the mouth. Also **must.**

mu·ta·gen (myōo′təjin), *n.* any substance that can give rise to a mutation.

mu·ta·gen·e·sis (myōotəjen′isis), *n.* the origin and process of mutation.

mu·ta·gen·ic (myōotəjen′ik), *n.* capable of giving rise to mutation.

mu·tant (myōot′nt), *adj.* **1.** in the process of mutating. —*n.* **2.** the product of a mutation, as a new type of gene, cell, or organism.

mu·tate (myōo′tāt), *v.* to change, as in form or character.

mu·ta·tion (myōotā′sHən), *n.* **1.** the process of changing; a change, as in form or character. **2.** a sudden biological change from the parent form due to the alteration of a chromosome.

mu·ta·tis mu·tan·dis (mōotä′tēs mōotän′dēs), *Latin.* after making the necessary changes.

mu·ti·cous (myōo′təkəs), *adj.* (in biology) having no pointed defensive projections, as thorns, spines, claws, etc.

mut·ism (myōo′tizm), *n.* a deliberate or unconscious refusal to reply when questioned, a feature of some mental illnesses.

mu·to·scope (myōo′təskōp), *n.* a machine in which a series of sequential pictures on cards is mounted radially on a drum which is rotated to cause the cards to spring up and become visible rapidly in turn through the eyepiece, thus giving the viewer the impression of seeing a motion picture.

muu·muu (mōo′mōo), *n.* a simple straight loose dress, often bright in

color or pattern, originally the garment worn by Hawaiian women.

mu·zhik, mou·jik, mu·jik (mōozHik′), *n.* a Russian peasant.

my·al·gi·a (mīal′jēə), *n.* pain in the muscles; muscular rheumatism. Also **myoneuralgia.**

my·as·the·ni·a (mīəsthē′nēə), *n.* an abnormal weakness in a muscle.

myasthenia gra·vis (grä′vis), a disease of the muscles, characterized by progressive loss of the power to contract, resulting in paralysis if not treated.

my·a·to·ni·a (mīətō′nēə), *n.* abnormally deficient muscle tone.

my·at·ro·phy (mīa′trəfē), *n.* See **myoatrophy.**

my·col·o·gy (mīkoĺ′əjē), *n.* the scientific study of fungi, lichens, etc. —**my·col′o·gist,** *n.*

my·co·sis (mīkō′sis), *n.* the presence in a body of any parasitic fungi, as ringworm.

my·co·stat (mī′kōstat), *n.* a substance that prevents or represses the growth of fungi on vegetable or animal matter.

my·dri·a·sis (midrī′əsis), *n.* an abnormal dilatation of the pupil of the eye, due to drugs, disease, etc. —**myd·ri·at′ic,** *adj.*

my·e·lin (mī′əlin), *n.* a soft, white, fatty substance forming a sheath around larger nerve fibers.

my·e·li·tis (mīəlī′tis), *n.* inflammation of the substance of the spinal cord or of the bone marrow.

my·e·lo·gram (mī′əlōgram′), *n.* an x-ray photograph of the spinal cord after introducing a radio-opaque substance into the spinal fluid.

my·e·log·ra·phy (mīəlog′rəfē), *n.* the taking and developing of myelograms.

my·e·loid (mī′əloid), *adj.* **1.** relating to the spinal cord. **2.** relating to marrow.

my·i·a·sis (mī′əsis), *n., pl.* **my·i·a·ses** (mī′əsēz). any disease caused by larvae of flies infesting body tissues or cavities.

my·lo·hy·oid (mī′lōhī′oid), *adj.* relating to or near the lower jaw and hyoid bone.

my·o·at·ro·phy (mīōa′trəfē), *n.* atrophy of muscle tissue. Also **myatrophy.**

my·o·car·di·al in·farc·tion (mīəkär′dēəl infärk′sнən), the destruction of part of the heart muscle due to interruption of its blood supply, as in a coronary thrombosis.

my·o·car·di·o·gram (mīəkär′dēəgram′), *n.* the record produced by a myocardiograph.

my·o·car·di·o·graph (mīəkär′dēəgraf′), *n.* an instrument for making a graphic record of the muscular activity of the heart.

my·o·car·di·tis (mī′ōkärdī′tis), *n.* inflammation of the heart muscle, as in rheumatic fever.

my·o·car·di·um (mīəkär′dēəm), *n.* the muscular substance of the heart.

my·o·clo·ni·a (mīəklō′nēə), *n.* a disease characterized by myoclonus.

my·o·clo·nus (mīok′lənəs), *n.* muscle spasm in which violent contractions and relaxations occur in rapid succession.

my·o·cyte (mī′əsīt), *n.* a contractile cell, present esp. in sphincters.

my·o·e·de·ma (mī′ōidē′mə), *n.* swelling of a muscle due to an increase in its fluid content, as in inflammation.

my·o·gen·ic (mīəjen′ik), *adj.* arising spontaneously in a muscle independently of nervous stimuli.

my·o·glo·bin (mīəglō′bin), *n.* a variety of hemoglobin occurring in muscle fibers and differing from blood hemoglobin in carrying more oxygen and less carbon monoxide and in having a smaller molecular weight. Also **my·o·he·mo·glo′bin.**

my·o·gram (mī′əgram), *n.* the record made by a myograph.

my·o·graph (mī′əgraf), *n.* an instrument for making a graphic record of muscular contractions and relaxations.

my·o·he·mo·glo·bi·nu·ri·a (mī′-əhē′məglō′bənŏŏr′ēə), *n.* a medical condition in which myoglobin is present in the urine. Also **my·o·glo·bi·nu′ri·a.**

my·o·kym·i·a (mīəkim′ēə), *n.* a twitch in a segment of a muscle.

my·ol·o·gy (mīol′əjē), *n.* the scientific study of muscles.

my·o·ma (mīō′mə), *n.*, *pl.* **my·o·mas, my·o·ma·ta** (mīoī′mətə). a tumor consisting of muscle tissue.

my·o·neu·ral (mīənŏŏr′əl), *adj.* of or relating to muscle and nerve.

my·o·neu·ral·gia (mī′ōnŏŏral′jə), *n.* See **myalgia.**

my·o·neu·ras·the·ni·a (mī′ənŏŏr′-əsthē′nēə), *n.* muscular weakness in conjunction with nervous debility.

my·op·a·thy (mīop′əthē), *n.* any disease or abnormality affecting the muscles.

my·o·pi·a (mīō′pēə), *n.* near-sightedness; a condition of the eye in which the rays from distant objects are brought to a focus before they reach the retina and so produce a blurred image. See also **hypermetropia.** —**my·op′ic,** *adj.*

my·o·psy·chop·a·thy (mī′ōsīkop′əthē), *n.* a muscle disease or abnormality in association with mental disorder.

my·o·scope (mī′əskōp), *n.* an instrument for observing the functioning of muscles.

my·o·sis (mīō′sis), *n.* miosis.

my·ot·o·my (mīot′əmē), *n.* surgical incision into a muscle.

my·o·to·ni·a (mīətō′nēə), *n.* a disorder characterized by difficulty in relaxation of muscles after voluntary effort; muscular rigidity.

myr·i·ad (mir′ēəd), *n.* a huge number; ten thousand.

myr·i·a·gram (mir′ēəgram′), *n.* a unit used in the measurement of weight, equal to 10,000 grams. *Abbrev.:* **myg.**

myr·i·a·li·ter (mir′ēəlē′tər), *n.* a unit used in the measurement of capacity, equal to 10,000 liters. *Abbrev.:* **myl.**

myr·i·a·me·ter (mir′ēəmē′tər), *n.* a unit used in measuring distance, equal to 10,000 meters. *Abbrev.:* **mym.**

myr·i·a·pod (mir′ēəpod), *n.* a many-legged arthropod of the class comprising centipedes and millipedes.

myr·i·are (mir′ēer′), *n.* a unit used in measuring area, equal to 10,000 ares.

myr·me·col·o·gy (murməkol′əjē), *n.* the scientific study of ants.

myr·me·coph·a·gous (murməkof′-əgəs), *adj.* ant-eating; adapted for feeding on ants or termites, as the long, extensile tongue of anteaters.

myr·me·co·phile (mur′məkōfīl′), *n.* an insect of another species living in an ant colony. —**myr·me·coph′i·lous,** *adj.*

myr·mi·don (mur′midon), *n.* one who follows and obeys his master or leader without question or scruple; a hired ruffian.

my·so·phil·i·a (mīsəfil′ēə), *n.* a mental abnormality characterized by an attraction to filth and dirt.

my·so·pho·bi·a (mīsəfō′bēə), *n.* a mental abnormality characterized by dread of filth or dirt.

mys·ta·gogue (mis′təgôg), *n.* an instructor in mystical doctrines; one who instructs persons before they take part in religious mysteries or sacraments.

mys·tique (mistēk′), *n.* an atmo-sphere of mystery or mysterious power surrounding a profession or pursuit, as *the mystique of medicine, the mystique of wine-drinking.*

myth·o·ma·ni·a (mithəmā′nēə), *n.* telling lies to an abnormal extent.

myth·o·poe·ia (mithəpē′ə), *n.* a mythopoeic act, trait, etc.

myth·o·poe·ic (mithəpē′ik), *adj.* causing a myth to arise.

myx·as·the·ni·a (miksəsthē′nēə), *n.* deficiency in mucus secretion.

myx·e·de·ma (miksidē′mə), *n.* a disease characterized by the slowing of mental processes and increased thickness of skin, associated with a deficiency of thyroid secretion.

myx·o·ma (miksō′mə), *n., pl.* **myx·o·mas, myx·o·ma·ta** (miksō′mətə). a tumor of mucoid tissue.

myx·o·ma·to·sis (mik′səmətō′sis), *n.* **1.** the presence of many myxomas. **2.** an infectious disease of rabbits, introduced into England and Australia to curb the number of rabbits.

myx·o·neu·ro·sis (mik′sōno͞orō′sis), *n., pl.* **myx·o·neu·ro·ses** (mik′sōno͞o-rō′sēz). a neurosis characterized by excessive secretions of the respiratory or intestinal mucous membranes.

N

Na·bi (nä′bē), *n.* a school of late nineteenth century French painters who used flat shapes and strong colors in their work. See also **Synthetism.**

na·bob (nā′bob), *n.* a man of great wealth, esp. one who has made his fortune in India or some other eastern country.

na·cre (nā′kər), *n.* mother-of-pearl.

na·cre·ous (nā′krēəs), *adj.* having the appearance of mother-of-pearl.

na·dir (nā′dər), *n.* a point in the celestial sphere immediately opposite the zenith and vertically downward from a given position.

nai·ad (nā′ad), *n., pl.* **nai·ads, nai·a·des** (nā′ədēz). a nymph of classical mythology associated with lakes, springs, and rivers.

nain·sook (nān′sŏŏk), *n.* a soft cotton fabric used for underwear and babies' clothes.

nais·sance (nā′səns), *n.* the origin or development of an organization, concept, movement, etc.

nal·ox·one (nal′oksōn), *n.* a short-term drug being researched as an antidote to heroin; made from thebaine.

na·ma·ste (num′əstā), *n.* a customary expression used by Hindus when greeting or saying good-bye.

na·nism (nā′nizm), *n.* abnormal smallness in build or size; the condition of being a dwarf.

na·no·cu·rie (nā′nəkyŏŏr′ē), *n.* a billionth of a curie.

na·no·far·ad (nā′nəfarəd), *n.* a billionth of a farad.

na·no·hen·ry (nā′nəhen′rē), *n.* a billionth of a henry.

na·noid (nā′noid), *adj.* abnormally small; dwarfish.

na·no·me·ter (nā′nəmētər), *n.* a millionth of a millimeter.

na·no·sec·ond (nā′nəsekənd), *n.* a billionth of a second.

na·no·watt (nā′nəwot), *n.* a billionth of a watt.

Nan·sen bottle (nan′sən), a self-closing receptacle for collecting samples of sea water at great depth.

na·os (nā′os), *n.* a temple.

na·palm (nā′päm), *n.* a jellified, highly inflammable fuel used in the manufacture of incendiary bombs, flamethrowers, etc.

na·pi·form (nā′pəfôrm), *adj.* having the shape of a turnip.

na·po·le·on (nəpō′lēən), *n.* a pastry made of paper-thin layers of puff paste filled with cream.

na·prap·a·thy (nəprap′əthē), *n.* treatment of disease by manipulation of the joints or massage based on the theory that illness results from disorders in connective tissue.

nar·cis·sism (när′sisizm), *n.* **1.** excessive admiration of oneself; self-love. **2.** love of one's own body; erotic stimulus derived from this. —**nar·cis·sis'tic**, *adj.*

nar·co·a·nal·y·sis (när'kōənal'isis), *n.* the psychological analysis of a patient under the influence of relaxing drugs.

nar·co·di·ag·no·sis (när'kōdī'əgnō'sis), *n.* diagnosis of psychiatric disorders with the use of drugs.

nar·co·lep·sy (när'kəlep'sē), *n.* a condition characterized by an overwhelming desire for brief periods of deep sleep.

nar·co·ma (närkō'mə), *n., pl.* **nar·co·mas, nar·co·ma·ta** (närkō'mətə). a state of partial unconsciousness resulting from the use of narcotics.

nar·co·ma·ni·a (närkəmā'nēə), *n.* **1.** an abnormal desire for drugs to relieve pain, etc. **2.** psychopathy caused by addiction to narcotics.

nar·cose (när'kōs), *adj.* in a state of partial unconsciousness or stupor.

nar·co·sis (närkō'sis), *n.* a state of unconsciousness or stupor, esp. one produced by drugs, extremes of temperature, etc.

nar·co·syn·the·sis (närkōsin'thisis), *n.* treatment of mental disorders by the use of drugs.

nar·co·ther·a·py (närkōther'əpē), *n.* treatment of mental illness by the injection of barbiturates into the veins.

nar·co·tism (när'kətizm), *n.* the habit of taking narcotics regularly; drug addiction.

nar·cot·ic (närkot'ik), *n.* any of a number of drugs which, when used in moderate quantities, induce unconsciousness, sleep, and insensibility to pain, but in large doses cause stupor or convulsions and may be habit forming.

nar·co·tize (när'kətīz), *v.* to stupefy or render insensible by means of a narcotic.

nard (närd), *n.* an aromatic ointment used in antiquity, supposedly extracted from the spikenard. Also **spikenard.**

nar·es (ner'ēz), *n. pl., sing.* **nar·is** (ner'is). the nostrils or nasal cavities. —**nar'i·al**, *adj.*

nar·ghi·le (när'gəlē), *n.* an Oriental pipe in which the smoke is passed through water to cool it before being inhaled; hookah.

nas·cent (nas'ənt), *adj.* coming into existence; about to develop.

na·so·fron·tal (nā'zōfrun'tl), *adj.* relating to the nose or the frontal bones of the forehead.

na·so·lac·ri·mal (nāzōlak'rəməl), *adj.* relating to the nose and the lacrimal ducts and glands.

na·sol·o·gy (nāzol'əjē), *n.* the study of the nose.

na·so·pal·a·tine (nāzōpal'ətīn), *adj.* relating to the nose and the palate.

na·so·phar·ynx (nā'zōfar'iNGks), *n., pl.* **na·so·pha·ryn·ges** (nā'zōfərin'jēz), **na·so·phar·ynx·es.** the upper part of the pharynx, behind the soft palate and continuous with the nasal passages. —**na·so·pha·ryn'geal**, *adj.*

na·so·scope (nā'zəskōp), *n.* a medical instrument for examining the nasal passages; rhinoscope.

na·tant (nāt'nt), *adj.* floating in water; swimming.

na·ta·tion (nātā'sHən), *n.* the action of swimming.

na·ta·tor (nā'tətər), *n.* one who swims.

na·ta·to·ri·al (nātətôr'ēəl), *adj.* relating to or adapted for swimming.

na·ta·to·ri·um (nātətôr'ēəm), *n., pl.* **na·ta·to·ri·ums, na·ta·to·ri·a** (nātətôr'ēə). an indoor swimming pool.

na·tes (nā'tēz), *n. pl.* the buttocks.

nat·u·ral·ism (naCH'ərəlizm), *n.* **1.** (in literature) a theory advocating a completely realistic and scientifically objective approach to the depiction of life. **2.** (in art) the treatment of forms and colors exactly as they are in nature.

na·tur·o·path (nā'CHərəpath), *n.* one who is a practitioner of naturopathy.

na·tur·op·a·thy (nāCHərop'əthē), *n.* the treatment of disease which lays stress on the assistance of the natural healing processes by the use of exercise, heat, etc.

nau·ma·chi·a (nômā'kēə), *n., pl.* **nau·ma·chi·ae** (nômā'kēē), **nau·ma·chi·as.** a spectacle presented by the ancient Romans depicting a mock naval battle.

nau·path·i·a (nôpa*th*′ēə), *n.* seasickness. See also **motion sickness.**

nautch (nôCH), *n.* an Oriental dance characterized by lithe, supple movements. Also **nautch dance.**

na·vette (navet′), *n.* a gem, as a diamond, cut in the shape of an oval with many faces.

na·vic·u·lar (nəvik′yələr), *adj.* shaped like a boat; scaphoid. Also **na·vi·cu·lar·e** (nəvik′yələr′ē).

N-bomb. See **neutron bomb.**

Ne·an·der·thal man (nēan′dərthôl), an extinct species of man inhabiting Europe and western Asia in the Paleolithic period. —**Ne·an·der·thal·oid** (nēan′dərthô′loid), *adj., n.*

neap (nēp), *adj.* relating to tides of minimum range.

neat[1] (nēt), *adj.* unmixed; straight, as whiskey.

neat[2] (nēt), *n., pl.* **neat.** a bovine mammal.

neb·u·la (neb′yəlā), *n., pl.* **neb·u·lae** (neb′yəlē), **neb·u·las. 1.** a luminous or dark shape in the sky consisting of gases and dust. **2.** a star surrounded by a gaseous envelope. **3.** a galaxy lying outside the Milky Way.

neb·u·lose (neb′yələs), *adj.* resembling a cloud in shape. —**neb·u·los′i·ty,** *n.*

neb·u·lous (neb′yələs), *adj.* indistinct; hazy; vague.

ne·ces·si·tous (nəses′itəs), *adj.* needy; in want; poor.

ne·cre·mi·a (nəkrē′mēə), *n.* a pathological condition characterized by the circulation in the blood stream of a large number of dead erythrocytes.

ne·cre·mi·a (nəkrē′mēə), *n.* a pathodeath of tissue or cells as a result of age or wear.

ne·crol·a·try (nəkrol′ətrē), *n.* the worship of the dead.

ne·crol·o·gy (nəkrol′əjē), *n.* an obituary notice.

nec·ro·man·cy (nek′rəman′sē), *n.* sorcery; witchcraft. —**nec′ro·man·cer,** *n.*

nec·ro·mi·me·sis (nek′rōmimē′sis),

n. a morbid mental state in which the sufferer believes himself to be dead.

ne·croph·a·gous (nəkrof′əgəs), *adj.* normally feeding on corpses or carrion.

nec·ro·phil·i·a (nekrəfil′ēə), *n.* a morbid sexual attraction for dead bodies. Also **ne·croph′i·lism.**

nec·ro·pho·bi·a (nekrəfō′bēə), *n.* a morbid horror of death or of the dead.

ne·crop·o·lis (nəkrop′əlis), *n.* a large cemetery.

nec·rop·sy (nek′ropsē), *n.* a postmortem examination. Also **ne·cros′co·py.**

ne·crose (nekrōs′), *v.* to cause or be affected with necrosis.

ne·cro·sis (nəkrō′sis), *n.* the localized death of a tissue or organ inside a living body.

nec·tar·ous (nek′tərəs), *adj.* sweet; pleasing to the taste.

ne·far·i·ous (nifer′ēəs), *adj.* very wicked; evil.

neg·a·tron (neg′ətron), *n.* See **electron.**

ne·gus (nē′gəs), *n.* a drink made of wine, hot water, lemon, sugar, and nutmeg.

nem·a·tode (nem′ətōd), *n.* an elongated roundworm, cylindrical in shape.

nem·a·tol·o·gy (nemətol′əjē), *n.* the scientific study of nematodes.

Nem·bu·tal (nem′byətôl), *n.* a trademark for pentobarbital.

ne·mer·te·an (nimur′tēən), *n.* any of a group of marine worms usually found in mud or sand on seashores.

ne·o·clas·sic (nē′ōklas′ik), *adj.* **1.** relating to the literature of the 17th century which revived and adapted the style of classical antiquity. **2.** relating to a style of art and sculpture, originating in the mid-18th century, which derived its discipline from the style of classical antiquity.

Ne·o·clas·si·cism (nē′ōklas′isizm), *n.* a style of architecture of the late 18th and early 19th centuries which was derived directly from the models of classical antiquity.

ne·o·for·ma·tion (nē′ōfôrmā′sHən),

n. a tumor or abnormal growth in a tissue.

Ne·o·gene (nē′əjēn), *adj.* **1.** relating to the latter half of the Tertiary period and including the Pliocene and Miocene. —*n.* **2.** the Neogene period. See also **Paleogene.**

ne·o·lith (nē′əlith), *n.* a stone tool of the Neolithic period.

Ne·o·lith·ic (nēəlith′ik), *adj.* relating to the latter part of the Stone Age characterized by the use of polished stone implements. See also **Mesolithic, Paleolithic.**

ne·ol·o·gism (nēol′əjizm), *n.* a new word, usage, or idiom in a language. Also **ne·ol′o·gy.**

ne·o·my·cin (nē′ōmī′sin), *n.* an antibiotic used against certain infections.

ne·o·nate (nē′ənāt), *n.* a newborn child. —**ne·o·na′tal,** *adj.*

ne·o·phyte (nē′əfīt), *n.* a novice or beginner.

ne·o·plasm (nē′əplazm), *n.* a new and abnormal growth of tissue.

ne·o·plas·ty (nē′əplas′tē), *n.* the repairing of damaged tissue, etc., by plastic surgery.

ne·o·prene (nē′əprēn), *n.* a synthetic rubber having a high resistance to oils, etc.

Ne·o-Ro·man·ti·cism (nē′ōrōman′- tisizm), *n.* any movement in literature, architecture, or the arts that is characterized by a return to a more romantic style.

ne·ot·e·ny (nēot′ənē), *n.* the achievement of sexual maturity during the larval stage.

ne·o·ter·ic (nēəter′ik), *adj.* modern; recent.

ne·ot·er·ism (nēot′ərizm), *n.* a new word or expression.

ne·o·type (nē′ətīp), *n.* a biological specimen that replaces a lost or destroyed holotype.

ne·pen·the (nipen′thē), *n.* anything which brings forgetfulness of sorrow or suffering. —**ne·pen′the·an,** *adj.*

neph·a·nal·y·sis (nefənal′isis), *n.* a chart showing cloud patterns, distribution, and precipitation.

neph·e·lom·e·ter (nefəlom′itər), *n.* an apparatus for determining the density of suspensions by the measurement of scattered light.

neph·o·gram (nef′əgram), *n.* a photograph of cloud formations.

neph·o·graph (nef′əgraf), *n.* an apparatus for photographing clouds.

ne·phol·o·gy (nefol′əjē), *n.* the scientific study of clouds.

ne·phom·e·ter (nefom′itər), *n.* an instrument that measures the proportion of sky covered by cloud.

neph·o·scope (nef′əskōp), *n.* an apparatus that measures the height, direction, and velocity of clouds.

ne·phral·gi·a (nəfral′jēə), *n.* pain in the kidneys.

ne·phrec·to·my (nəfrek′təmē), *n.* the removal of a kidney by surgery.

ne·phrid·i·um (nəfrid′ēəm), *n., pl.* **ne·phrid·i·a** (nəfrid′ēə). the tubular excretory organ characteristic of many invertebrates.

neph·rism (nef′rizm), *n.* ill health resulting from chronic kidney disease.

ne·phrit·ic (nəfrit′ik), *adj.* relating to or suffering from nephritis.

ne·phri·tis (nəfrī′tis), *n.* inflammation of the kidneys.

ne·phrog·e·nous (nəfroj′ənəs), *adj.* developing in or proceeding from the kidney. Also **neph·ro·gen·ic** (nefrəjen′ik).

neph·ro·lith (nef′rəlith), *n.* a stone in the kidney.

neph·ro·li·thot·o·my (nef′rōlithot′- əmē), *n.* the opening of a kidney to remove a stone.

ne·phrol·o·gy (nəfrol′əjē), *n.* the study of the kidney and its functions.

neph·ro·lyt·ic (nefrəlit′ik), *adj.* tending to destroy the kidney cells.

neph·ron (nef′ron), *n.* a functional part of the kidney of vertebrates.

ne·phrop·a·thy (nəfrop′əthē), *n.* a disease which affects the kidneys.

ne·phro·sis (nəfrō′sis), *n.* a degenerative kidney disease of the renal tubules.

ne·phrot·o·my (nəfrot′əmē), *n.* surgical incision into the kidneys, esp. for removing a stone.

neph·ro·tox·ic (nefrətok′sik), *adj*. having a toxic effect on the kidney cells.

ne plus ul·tra (ne plŏŏsŏŏl′trä), *Latin*. the highest degree; culminating point.

nep·o·tism (nep′ətizm), *n*. favoritism shown toward relatives, esp. by a person in a high position in business, politics, etc.

ne·rit·ic (nərit′ik), *adj*. relating to or forming the belt of shallow waters near land.

nerve gas, any of various gases that damage the nervous system.

ner·vule (nur′vyŏŏl), *n*. a small nerve found in the wing of insects.

ner·vu·ra·tion (nurvyərā′sʜən), *n*. the arrangement of veins on an insect's wing. Also **ner·vu·la′tion.**

ner·vure (nur′vyŏŏr), *n*. **1.** one of the veins that help to strengthen the wings of an insect. **2.** a rib, as in a Gothic vault, that resembles this part.

nes·cience (nesʜ′əns), *n*. ignorance; lack of knowledge. —**nes′cient,** *adj*.

ness (nes), *n*. a promontory or headland.

neth·er (netʜ′ər), *adj*. lying beneath, under or lower, as *the nether regions; nether lip.*

neth·er·most (netʜ′ərmōst), *adj*. lowest.

ne·tsu·ke (net′skē), *n*. a small, carved object of ivory, wood, etc., used by Japanese as an ornamental fastening for a sash, girdle, etc.

neu·ral (nŏŏr′əl), *adj*. relating to or concerned with a nerve or the nervous system.

neu·ral·gia (nŏŏral′jə), *n*. an acute pain that moves along a nerve.

neu·ral·gi·form (nŏŏral′jifôrm), *adj*. resembling neuralgia.

neu·ras·the·ni·a (nŏŏrəstʜē′nēə), *n*. a state of nervous exhaustion marked by minor physical complaints such as disturbances of the digestive system, headaches, etc. —**neu·ras· then′ic,** *adj*.

neu·rec·to·my (nŏŏrek′təmē), *n*. the removal by surgery of a nerve or part of a nerve.

neu·ri·lem·ma (nŏŏrəlem′ə), *n*. the outer sheath of a nerve fiber.

neu·rite (nŏŏr′īt), *n*. See **axon.**

neu·ri·tis (nŏŏrī′tis), *n*. constant pain in a nerve often accompanying paralysis or disturbances in the sense organs.

neu·ro·a·nat·o·my (nŏŏr′ōənat′- əmē), *n*. the anatomy of the nervous system. —**neu·ro·a·nat′o·mist,** *n*.

neu·ro·em·bry·ol·o·gy (nŏŏr′ōem′- brēol′əjē), *n*. the study of the origin and development of the nervous system.

neu·rog·li·a (nŏŏrog′lēə), *n*. the supporting tissue that binds together the nerve tissue in the brain, spinal cord, etc.

neu·rol·o·gy (nŏŏrol′əjē), *n*. the study of the nervous system and its diseases. —**neu·rol′o·gist,** *n*.

neu·rol·y·sis (nŏŏrol′isis), *n*. the disintegration of a nerve or nervous tissue.

neu·ro·ma (nŏŏrō′mə), *n., pl*. **neu· ro·mas, neu·ro·ma·ta** (nŏŏrō′mətə). a tumor growing from nerve tissue.

neu·ro·mus·cu·lar (nŏŏrəmus′kyə- lər), *adj*. relating to both nerves and muscles.

neu·ron (nŏŏr′on), *n*. the basic unit of nervous tissue; nerve cell. Also **neu·rone** (nŏŏr′ōn).

neu·ro·path (nŏŏr′əpatʰ), *n*. a person suffering from a nervous disorder.

neu·ro·pa·thol·o·gy (nŏŏr′ōpəthol′- əjē), *n*. the study of the diseases of the nervous system. —**neu·ro·pa·thol′o· gist,** *n*.

neu·rop·a·thy (nŏŏrop′əthē), *n*. a disease of the nervous system.

neu·ro·phys·i·ol·o·gy (nŏŏr′əfiz′- ēol′əjē), *n*. the study of the physiology of the nervous system. —**neu·ro· phys·i·ol′o·gist,** *n*.

neu·ro·plasm (nŏŏr′əplazm), *n*. protoplasm in a nerve cell.

neu·ro·psy·chi·a·try (nŏŏr′ōsīkī′- ətrē), *n*. the study and treatment of mental disorders and diseases of the nervous system. —**neu·ro·psy·chi′a· trist,** *n*.

neu·ro·psy·cho·sis (nŏŏr′ōsīkō′sis),

n. insanity associated with disease of the nervous system. —**neu·ro·psy·chot′ic**, *adj.*, *n.*

neu·ro·sis (nŏŏrō′sis), *n.*, *pl.* **neu·ro·ses** (nŏŏrō′sēz). a mental disturbance characterized by feelings of anxiety, obsessions, compulsive acts, and minor physical disorders without physical cause. See also **psychoneurosis.**

neu·ro·sur·ger·y (nŏŏrōsur′jərē), *n.* the surgery of the nervous system. —**neu′ro·sur′geon**, *n.*

neu·rot·ic (nŏŏrot′ik), *adj.* a person suffering from a neurosis.

neu·rot·o·my (nŏŏrot′əmē), *n.* the cutting of a nerve to relieve pain, as that caused by neuralgia.

neu·ro·tox·in (nŏŏr′ōtok′sin), *n.* a poison that attacks nervous tissue. —**neu·ro·tox′ic**, *adj.*

neu·rot·ro·phy (nŏŏrō′trəfē), *n.* the influence of the nervous system on the nourishment of body tissue. —**neu·ro·troph′ic**, *adj.*

neu·ro·trop·ic (nŏŏrətrop′ik), *adj.* displaying an affinity for nerve tissue. —**neu·rot·ro·pism** (nŏŏrot′rəpizm), **neu·rot′ro·py**, *n.*

neus·ton (nŏŏ′ston), *n.* the mass of minute organisms which float on the surface of a body of water.

neutral spirits, alcohol of 190 proof (95% pure) used for making gin, liqueurs, etc., and for blending with other alcoholic liquors.

neutron bomb, a nuclear bomb which releases neutrons but relatively little blast and causes only a small amount of contamination. Also **N-bomb.**

neu·tro·sphere (nŏŏ′trəsfēr), *n.* that part of the atmosphere, stretching from the surface of the earth to the ionosphere, which is generally electrically neutral.

né·vé (nāvā′), *n.* granular snow on high mountains that turns into glacial ice. Also **firn.**

ne·vus (nē′vəs), *n.*, *pl.* **ne·vi** (nē′vī). a congenital skin blemish, as a birthmark or mole.

new criticism, a method of literary criticism which confines itself to analysis of text excluding all other considerations as irrelevant. See also **explication de texte.**

New Left, a group of left-wing U.S. intellectuals characterized by strong support for disarmament, racial equality, and fundamental changes in the economic and political structure.

new·ton (nŏŏt′n), *n.* a unit of force that gives an acceleration of one meter per second to a mass of one kilogram.

new wave, a movement in literature, the arts, etc., that breaks away from traditional ideas and values. See also **nouvelle vague.**

New York cut, a porterhouse steak without the fillet or bone.

nex·us (nek′səs), *n.*, *pl.* **nex·us.** something that joins or connects; link; tie.

ni·a·cin (nī′əsin), *n.* See **nicotinic acid.**

nice·nel·ly·ism (nīs′nel′ēizm), *n.* the use of euphemistic expressions; prudery.

nic·o·tin·a·mide (nikətin′əmīd), *n.* a colorless crystalline solid forming part of the vitamin-B complex and used in medicine. Also called **ni·a·cin·a·mide** (nīəsin′əmīd), **nicotinic acid amide.**

nic·o·tine (nik′ətēn), *n.* a poisonous, oily alkaloid obtained from tobacco.

nicotinic acid, a crystalline acid forming part of the vitamin-B complex, found in fresh meat, etc., and used in the treatment of pellagra. Also **niacin.**

nic·o·tin·ism (nik′ətēnizm), *n.* a condition resulting from the excessive use of tobacco.

nic·ti·tate (nik′titāt), *v.* to wink. Also **nic′tate.**

ni·dic·o·lous (nīdik′ələs), *adj.* noting birds that are reared for a time in the nest after hatching.

nid·i·fi·cate (nid′əfəkāt), *v.* to build a nest. Also **nid′i·fy.**

ni·dif·u·gous (nīdif′yəgəs), *adj.* noting birds that leave the nest soon after hatching.

ni·el·lo (nēel′ō), *n.*, *pl.* **ni·el·li** (nēel′ī). a black metallic alloy of copper, lead, silver, and sulfur used to fill in patterns engraved on other metals.

Nier·stein·er (nēr′stīnər), *n.* a white wine from Nierstein in the central part of West Germany.

nig·gard (nig′ərd), *n.* a miserly or stingy person. —**nig′gard·ly,** *adj.*

nig·gle (nig′əl), *v.* to spend too much time over petty details; work ineffectively.

nig·gling (nig′liNG), *adj.* excessively fussy; finicky; petty-minded.

night blindness. See **nyctalopia.**

night·rid·er (nīt′rīdər), *n.* a member of a gang of men who perform acts of violence in order to intimidate or punish.

night·shade (nīt′sHād), *n.* any of various plants, as the deadly nightshade, yielding a variety of drugs.

ni·gres·cent (nīgres′ənt), *adj.* becoming a blackish color.

nig·ri·fy (nig′rəfī), *v.* to make black.

nig·ri·tude (nig′ritōōd), *n.* blackness; complete darkness.

ni·hil·ism (nī′əlizm), *n.* **1.** a form of complete skepticism that denies that there can be any objective basis of truth. **2.** the doctrine of a 19th century Russian revolutionary group advocating the overthrow of the existing social order.

ni·hil·i·ty (nīhil′itē), *n.* nothingness.

nim·bus (nim′bəs), *n.,* *pl.* **nim·bi** (nim′bī), **nim·bus·es.** a cloud or atmosphere about a person or thing; aura.

ni·mi·e·ty (nimī′itē), *n.* excess.

nim·i·ny-pim·i·ny (nim′ənēpim′-ənē), *adj.* effeminate; mincing; affected.

niph·a·blep·si·a (nifəblep′sēə), *n.* See **snow blindness.**

nir·va·na (nirvä′nə), *n.* the extinction of desire and suffering and release from the cycle of reincarnation sought by Buddhists.

ni·sus (nī′səs), *n.,* *pl.* **ni·sus.** an effort or impulse; striving.

nit[1] (nit), *n.* the egg of a louse or other parasitic insect, esp. one attached to human hair.

nit[2] (nit), *n.* a unit of brightness of light equaling one candela per square meter.

nit·id (nit′id), *adj.* bright; shining.

nitrogen narcosis. See **decompression sickness.**

ni·trog·e·nous (nītroj′ənəs), *adj.* containing nitrogen.

ni·tro·glyc·er·in (nītrəglis′ərin), *n.* a liquid high explosive used in making dynamite, in rocket propellants, and, medically, in the treatment of angina pectoris.

nit·ty-grit·ty (nit′ē grit′ē), *n.* the tedious, though essential, details.

ni·val (nī′vəl), *adj.* relating to or growing in snow.

niv·e·ous (niv′ēəs), *adj.* having the appearance of snow; snowy.

no·blesse o·blige (nōbles′ ōblēzн′), *French.* moral obligations entailed by high rank or wealth.

no·cent (nō′sənt), *adj.* hurtful; harmful.

noc·tam·bu·lism (noktam′byəlizm), *n.* sleepwalking. Also **noc·tam·bu·la′tion.**

noc·u·ous (nok′yōōəs), *adj.* harmful; causing damage.

no·dus (nō′dəs), *n.,* *pl.* **no·di** (nō′dī). a complicated situation; complication; difficulty.

no·e·gen·e·sis (nōējen′isis), *n.* fresh or firsthand knowledge acquired through the experience of the senses or the intellect.

no·e·sis (nōē′sis), *n.* the activity of the intellect in the process of cognition.

no·et·ic (nōet′ik), *adj.* relating to reason or the mind.

nog·gin (nog′ən), *n.* a small mug or cup.

noi·some (noi′səm), *adj.* disagreeable, as a smell.

nol·le pros·e·qui (nol′ē pros′əkwī), *Latin.* an entry in a court's record showing that proceedings in a case have been dropped.

no·lo con·ten·de·re (nō′lō kənten′-dərē), *Latin.* the pleading of a defendant not admitting guilt, but leaving the determining of guilt open in other proceedings.

no·ma (nō′mə), *n.* gangrene of the

lips and cheeks, found in debilitated people.

nom de guerre (nôɴdəger′), *pl.* **noms de guerre** (nôɴdəger′), *French.* a pseudonym.

nom de plume (nomdəploom′), *pl.* **noms de plume** (nomdəploom′). *French.* a pen name.

no·men·cla·ture (nō′mənklā′cHər), *n.* a system of names or terms used for purposes of classification.

nom·i·nal (nom′ənl), *adj.* 1. in name or form only. 2. small; insignificant; trifling.

no·mism (nō′mizm), *n.* religious conduct which follows certain laws.

nom·o·gram (nom′əgram), *n.* a kind of graph that enables the value of one dependent variable to be read off when the value of two independent variables are known.

no·mog·ra·phy (nōmog′rəfē), *n.* 1, the art of compiling laws. 2. the art of constructing nomograms to solve closely related problems.

no·mol·o·gy (nōmol′əjē), *n.* the science of law.

nom·o·thet·ic (noməthet′ik), *adj.* making laws; legislative.

non·age (non′ij), *n.* the period of being a minor in law.

non·a·gon (non′əgon), *n.* a polygon with nine angles and nine sides. Also **enneagon.**

no·na·ry (nō′nərē), *adj.* being nine in number.

non·bel·lig·er·en·cy (nonbəlij′ərən-sē), *n.* a policy of a country which supports one of the countries taking part in a war but without openly intervening. —**non·bel·lig′er·ent,** *n.*, *adj.*

nonce (nons), *n.* the immediate moment; the present occasion.

non·cha·lance (nonsHəläns′), *n.* casual unconcern; indifference. —**non·cha·lant′,** *adj.*

non com·pos men·tis (non kōm′pōs men′tis), *Latin.* of unsound mind.

none·such (nunsucH′), *n.* a person or thing that has no equal. See also **nonpareil.**

non·fea·sance (nonfē′zəns), *n.* the failure to perform some action which ought to have been done. See also **malfeasance, misfeasance.**

non·fer·rous (nonfer′əs), *adj.* 1. (of a metal) having no iron. 2. relating to metals other than iron or steel.

no·nil·lion (nōnil′yən), *n.* a number represented by the figure one followed by 30 zeros (but in the United Kingdom and Germany by the figure one followed by 54 zeros).

non ob·stan·te (nōn ōbstän′te), *Latin.* notwithstanding.

non·pa·reil (nonpərel′), *adj.* without equal.

non·par·ous (nonpar′əs), *adj.* not having given birth to any children.

non·plus (nonplus′), *v.* to confuse or disconcert; puzzle.

non se·qui·tur (nōn se′kwitoor), *Latin.* a conclusion which does not follow logically from a premise.

non-U (nonyoo′), *adj.* (of speech, behavior, etc.) not of the upper class.

no·ri·a (nôr′ēə), *n.* an apparatus for raising water, consisting of buckets attached to a wheel.

normal tax, an income tax levied at a fixed rate. See also **surtax.**

nor·ma·tive (nôr′mətiv), *adj.* relating to an accepted standard of behavior, dress, speech, etc.

nor·mo·cyte (nôr′məsīt), *n.* a red blood corpuscle of normal size.

nor·mo·ten·sive (nôr′mōten′siv), *adj.* having normal blood pressure.

nos·o·gen·e·sis (nosəjen′isis), *n.* the origination and development of a disease. Also **no·sog′e·ny.**

nos·o·ge·og·ra·phy (nos′ōjēog′rəfē), *n.* the study of diseases with reference to their geographical distribution and causes. Also **nos·och·tho·nog·ra·phy** (nos′okthənog′rəfē).

no·sog·ra·phy (nōsog′rəfē), *n.* the description of diseases.

no·sol·o·gy (nōsol′əjē), *n.* 1. the classification of diseases. 2. the information available on a disease.

nos·o·pho·bi·a (nosəfō′bēə), *n.* a morbid fear of disease.

nos·tol·o·gy (nostol′əjē), *n.* the branch of medicine dealing with the problems and diseases of old age; gerontology; geriatrics.

nos·to·ma·ni·a (nostəmā′nēə), *n.* profound homesickness.

nos·trum (nos′trəm), *n.* **1.** a patent medicine. **2.** a remedy, scheme, etc., intended to solve all problems; panacea.

no·tum (nō′təm), *n.*, *pl.* **no·ta** (nō′tə). a segmental plate on the back of an insect.

nou·me·non (noo′mənon), *n.*, *pl.* **nou·me·na** (noo′mənə). (in philosophy) a thing as its true nature determines it as contrasted with how it may appear to be.

nous (noos), *n.* the intellect; reason.

nou·veau riche (noovō rēsH′), *pl.* **nou·veaux riches** (noovō rēsH′). *French.* a person who has recently become rich.

nou·veau·té (noovōtā′), *n.*, *pl.* **nou·veau·tés** (noovōtā′). *French.* a novelty.

nou·velle vague (noovel vag′), *pl.* **nou·velles vagues** (noovel vag′). *French.* a new movement in an art form, esp. in the cinema. See also **new wave.**

no·va (nō′və), *n.*, *pl.* **no·vae** (nō′vē), **no·vas.** a star that suddenly becomes very bright for a short time and then grows faint again. See also **supernova.**

no·vel·la (nōvel′ə), *n.*, *pl.* **no·vel·las,** **no·vel·le** (nōvel′ə). a short novel.

no·vem·de·cil·lion (nō′vəmdisil′yən), *n.* a number represented by the figure one followed by 60 zeros (but in the United Kingdom and Germany by the figure one followed by 114 zeros).

no·ver·cal (nōvur′kəl), *adj.* relating to or appropriate to a stepmother.

no·vi·ti·ate (nōvisH′eit), *n.* the period or state of being a novice.

nox·ious (nok′sHəs), *adj.* harmful to health.

no·yade (nwäyäd′), *n.* execution by drowning.

nu·ance (noo′äns), *n.* a subtle distinction in color, meaning, expression, etc.

nub·bin (nub′in), *n.* a small piece or lump; stub.

nu·bi·a (noo′bēə), *n.* a kind of knitted head scarf for women.

nu·bile (noo′bil), *adj.* (of a woman) of marriageable age or condition.

nu·bi·lous (noo′bələs), *adj.* cloudy; vague; obscure.

nu·cha (noo′kə), *n.*, *pl.* **nu·chae** (noo′kē). the nape of the neck.

nu·ci·form (noo′səfôrm), *adj.* shaped like a nut.

nu·cle·ar (noo′klēər), *adj.* **1.** relating to or comprising a nucleus. **2.** relating to the use of atomic weapons.

nuclear fission. See **fission.**

nuclear fusion. See **fusion.**

nu·cle·ate (noo′klēit), *adj.* possessing a nucleus.

nu·cle·ic acid (nooklē′ik), any of various complex acids found in all living cells.

nu·cle·o·lat·ed (noo′klēəlā′tid), *adj.* having a nucleus. Also **nu′cle·o·late.**

nu·cle·o·lus (nooklē′ələs), *n.*, *pl.* **nu·cle·o·li** (nooklē′əlī). a body lying within the nucleus of a cell. Also **nu′cle·ole.**

nu·cle·on·ics (noo′klēon′iks), *n.* the branch of physical science concerned with the engineering applications of the properties of atomic nuclei.

nu·cle·us (noo′klēəs), *n.*, *pl.* **nu·cle·i** (noo′klēī), **nu·cle·us·es.** a central core or point.

nu·di·caul (noo′dəkôl), *adj.* (of plants) having stems without leaves.

nud·nik (nood′nik), *n.* an importunate or tiring person; a nuisance.

nu·ga·to·ry (noo′gətôrē), *adj.* worthless; ineffective; insignificant.

nul·li·fid·i·an (nuləfid′ēən), *n.* a person without religious belief.

nul·lip·a·ra (nulip′ərə), *n.*, *pl.* **nul·lip·a·rae** (nulip′ərē). a woman who has never given birth to a child.

nul·li·ty (nul′itē), *n.* the state of being nothing.

nu·men (noo′min), *n.*, *pl.* **nu·mi·na** (noo′mənə). a spirit or deity supposed to inhabit a particular object or place. —**nu′mi·nous,** *adj.*

nu·mer·ol·o·gy (noomərol′əjē), *n.*

the study of numbers as a means of predicting the future. —**nu·mer·ol′o·gist,** *n.*

nu·mis·mat·ics (nōō′mizmat′iks), *n.* the study of coins and medals. Also **nu·mis·ma·tol·o·gy** (numiz′mətol′-əjē). —**nu·mis′ma·tist, nu·mis·ma·tol′o·gist,** *n.*

num·ma·ry (num′ərē), *adj.* relating to coins or money.

num·mu·lar (num′yələr), *adj.* **1.** relating to coins or money. **2.** shaped like a coin.

nunc di·mit·tis (nuNGk′ dimit′is), *Latin.* permission to leave.

nun·ci·o (nun′shēō), *n., pl.* **nun·ci·os** (nun′shēōz). an envoy of the pope accredited to the government of a foreign country. See also **apostolic delegate.** —**nun·ci·a·ture** (nun′shē-əchər), *n.*

nun·cu·pa·tive (nuNG′kyəpā′tiv), *adj.* (of a will) not written; by word of mouth.

nuque (nōōk), *n.* the back of the neck.

nu·tant (nōōt′nt), *adj.* (of plants) drooping.

nu·ta·tion (nōōtā′shən), *n.* **1.** the action of nodding. **2.** a periodic oscillation in the axis of the earth.

nyc·ta·lo·pi·a (niktəlō′pēə), *n.* a condition of the eye in which vision is extremely poor in reduced light, as at night, but normal in daylight. Also **night blindness.**

nyc·ti·trop·ic (niktitrop′ik), *adj.* (of the leaves of plants) having a tendency to assume at night positions different from those held during the day.

nyc·to·pho·bi·a (niktəfō′bēə), *n.* a morbid fear of darkness.

nym·pha (nim′fə), *n., pl.* **nym·phae** (nim′fē). one of the inner lips of the vulva.

nym·phae·um (nimfē′əm), *n., pl.* **nym·phae·a** (nimfē′ə). a room, hall, etc., fitted with a fountain and decorated with statues, etc.

nymph·et (nimfet′), *n.* a sexually attractive young girl.

nym·pho·lep·sy (nim′fəlep′sē), *n.* violent emotional longings, esp. for something unattainable. —**nym·pho·lept** (nim′fəlept), *n.*

nym·pho·ma·ni·a (nimfəmā′nēə), *n.* abnormally strong sexual desire in women.

nys·tag·mus (nistag′məs), *n.* an involuntary spasmodic movement of the eyeball.

nys·ta·tin (nis′tətin), *n.* an antibiotic used especially for treating fungal diseases.

ob·con·i·cal (obkon′ikəl), *adj.* (of a leaf) conical with the pointed end forming the place of attachment. Also **ob·con′ic.**

ob·cor·date (obkôr′dāt), *adj.* (of a leaf) heart-shaped, with the pointed end forming the place of attachment.

ob·du·rate (ob′dŏŏrit), *adj.* hardened against tender feelings; unyielding.

o·bei·sance (ōbā′səns), *n.* a bodily movement expressing submission, homage, respect, etc.

ob·fus·cate (obfus′kāt), *v.* to render obscure; confuse.

ob·i·ter dic·tum (ō′bitər dik′təm), *pl.* **ob·i·ter dic·ta** (ō′bitər dik′tə), *Latin.* a comment made in passing; incidental remark.

o·bit·u·ar·y (ōbicH′ŏŏer′ē), *n.* a newspaper announcement of a person's death together with short biographical details. Also **o′bit.**

ob·jet d'art (ôbzнe dar′), *pl.* **ob·jets d'art** (ôbzнe dar′). *French.* an article or object of artistic merit.

ob·jur·gate (ob′jərgāt), *v.* to denounce, scold or upbraid vehemently.

ob·last (ob′last), *n.*, *pl.* **ob·lasts, ob·las·ti** (ob′lästē). a region or province; an autonomous administrative area.

ob·late[1] (ob′lāt), *adj.* (of a spheroid) flattened at the poles. See also **prolate.**

ob·late[2] (ob′lāt), *n.* one dedicated to monastic life, but not under monastic vows.

ob·la·tion (oblā′sнən), *n.* an offering made to a deity or for religious or charitable purposes.

ob·liq·ui·ty (əblik′witē), *n.* deviation from proper moral conduct; immorality; perversity.

ob·li·ves·cence (obləves′əns), *n.* forgetfulness.

ob·lo·quy (ob′ləkwē), *n.* **1.** disgrace resulting from public censure. **2.** blame; condemnatory language; abuse.

ob·o·vate (obō′vāt), *adj.* (of a leaf, etc.) ovate with the narrower end forming the base.

ob·o·void (obō′void), *adj.* (of certain fruits, etc.) ovoid with the narrower end forming the base.

ob·pyr·i·form (obpir′əfôrm), *adj.* shaped like a pear with the narrower end forming the base.

ob·scene (əbsēn′), *adj.* abhorrent to feelings of decency or modesty; designed to arouse sexual excitement.

ob·scu·rant·ism (əbskyŏŏr′əntizm), *n.* opposition to the spread of knowledge and enlightenment; intentional vagueness or obscurity. —**ob·scu′ rant,** *n.*, *adj.*

ob·se·crate (ob′səkrāt), *v.* to implore; beg; beseech.

ob·se·quence (ob′səkwəns), *n.* eagerness to please; willing compliance. Also **ob·se·que·ence** (əbsē′kwēəns). —**ob′se·quent,** *adj.*

226

ob·se·qui·ous (əbsē′kwēəs), *adj.* excessively deferential or humble; fawning; servile.

ob·se·quy (ob′səkwē), *n.*, *pl.* **ob·se·quies.** (*usually in the pl.*) a funeral ceremony or rite.

ob·so·lesce (obsəles′), *v.* to be or become obsolescent. —**ob·so·les′ cence,** *n.*

ob·so·les·cent (obsəles′ənt), *adj.* passing out of use; becoming outdated or obsolete.

ob·stet·rics (əbstet′riks), *n.* the branch of medicine concerned with childbirth. —**ob·stet′ric,** *adj.* —**ob· ste·tri·cian** (obstətrisн′ən), *n.*

ob·sti·pant (ob′stəpənt), *n.* something which causes prolonged constipation.

ob·sti·pa·tion (obstəpā′sнən), *n.* prolonged constipation.

ob·strep·er·ous (əbstrep′ərəs), *adj.* noisily unruly; clamorous; turbulent.

ob·stru·ent (ob′strōōənt), *adj.* causing an obstruction. See also **sonorant.**

ob·tect (obtekt′), *adj.* denoting a pupa in which the wings and legs are stuck to the body by a secretion. Also **ob· tect′ed.**

ob·test (obtest′), *v.* **1.** to call as witness. **2.** to implore or beseech.

ob·trude (əbtrōōd′), *v.* to thrust upon; compel to notice; bring forcibly to the attention of. —**ob·tru′sion,** *n.* —**ob·tru′sive,** *adj.*

ob·tund (obtund′), *v.* to make blunt; dull.

ob·tu·rate (ob′tərāt), *v.* to obstruct or stop up; close; block.

ob·tuse (əbtōōs′), *adj.* **1.** lacking sharpness in form; blunt. **2.** lacking alertness; mentally sluggish; stupid.

ob·um·brate (obum′brāt), *v.* to cloud over; darken; cast a shadow over. —**ob·um′brant,** *adj.*

ob·verse (ob′vurs), *n.* the main or chief surface of anything; front.

ob·vert (obvurt′), *v.* to turn so as to present a different view, side, or surface. —**ob·ver′sion,** *n.*

ob·vi·ate (ob′vēāt), *v.* to make unnecessary; avoid; prevent.

ob·vo·lute (ob′vəlōōt), *adj.* turned inward.

Oc·cam's razor, Ock·ham's razor (ok′əm), the principle that assumptions put forward to explain phenomena should be kept to a minimum.

oc·ci·put (ok′səput), *n.*, *pl.* **oc·ci·puts, oc·ci·pi·ta** (oksip′itə). the back part of the skull. —**oc·cip′i·tal,** *adj.*

oc·clude (əklōōd′), *v.* to stop up; block; shut off. —**oc·clu′sion,** *n.* —**oc·clu′sive,** *adj.*

oc·cul·ta·tion (ok′ultā′sнən), *n.* the state of having disappeared from view; disappearance.

o·ce·a·nic·i·ty (ō′sнēənis′itē), *n.* the effect of the sea upon the climate of a particular region. See also **continentality.**

o·ce·a·nog·ra·phy (ō′sнēənog′rəfē), *n.* the study of the ocean.

oc·el·lat·ed (os′əlātid), *adj.* (of a marking) resembling an eye; having an eye like spot, as a peacock. Also **oc·el·late** (os′əlāt). —**oc·el·la′ tion,** *n.*

o·cel·lus (ōsel′əs), *n.*, *pl.* **o·cel·li** (ōsel′ī). a simple kind of eye found in invertebrate animals. —**o·cel′lar,** *adj.*

och·le·sis (oklē′sis), *n.* an illness or disease caused by population congestion, overcrowded living space, etc. —**och·le·sit′ic, och·let′ik,** *adj.*

och·loc·ra·cy (oklok′rəsē), *n.* mob rule; government by the mob.

och·lo·pho·bi·a (okləfō′bēə), *n.* a morbid fear of crowds.

o·chroid (ō′kroid), *adj.* of the color of yellow ocher.

oc·re·a (ok′rēə), *n.*, *pl.* **oc·re·ae** (okrēē). something which forms a sheath. —**oc·re·ate** (ok′rēit), *adj.*

oc·tad (ok′tad), *n.* a set or series of eight.

oc·ta·he·dron (oktəhē′drən), *n.*, *pl.* **oc·ta·he·drons, oc·ta·he·dra** (oktəhē′drə). a three-dimensional figure with eight sides. —**oc·ta·he′dral,** *adj.*

oc·tam·er·ous (oktam′ərəs), *adj.* having or containing eight parts.

oc·tan (ok′tən), *adj.* (of a fever) recurring every eight days.

oc·tane (ok′tān), *n.* any of several saturated hydrocarbons, some of which are obtained in the refining of petroleum.

octane number, the measure of the antiknock characteristics of a fuel, esp. gasoline.

oc·tant (ok′tənt), *n.* an eighth part of a circle.

oc·tar·chy (ok′tärkē), *n.* rule or government by eight persons.

oc·til·lion (oktil′yən), *n.* a number represented by the figure one followed by 27 zeros (but in the United Kingdom and Germany by the figure one followed by 48 zeros).

oc·to·de·cil·lion (ok′tōdisil′yən), *n.* a number represented by the figure one followed by 57 zeros (but in the United Kingdom and Germany by the figure one followed by 108 zeros).

oc·to·ge·nar·i·an (ok′təjəner′ēən), *adj.* **1.** between the ages of 80 and 90. —*n.* **2.** a person of this age.

oc·to·nar·y (ok′tənerē), *adj.* relating to the number 8.

oc·to·pod (ok′təpod), *n.* any member of an order of eight-armed or -legged animals, which includes the octopuses.

oc·troi (ok′troi), *n.* a tax imposed on certain goods when brought into a city.

oc·tu·ple (ok′to͞opəl), *adj.* eight times as much or as great.

oc·tup·let (oktup′lit), *n.* a combination, set, or series of eight connected items.

oc·tu·pli·cate (okto͞o′pləkit), *adj.* consisting of eight identical parts or of one original and seven copies.

oc·u·lo·mo·tor (ok′yəlōmō′tər), *adj.* causing the eyeball to move.

oc·u·lus (ok′yələs), *n.*, *pl.* **oc·u·li** (ok′-yəlī). an eye.

o·da·lisque (ō′dəlisk), *n.* a female slave or concubine in a harem.

o·di·ous (ō′dēəs), *adj.* hateful; repugnant; offensive; disgusting.

o·di·um (ō′dēəm), *n.* extreme dislike marked by feelings of loathing or contempt; abhorrence.

o·dom·e·ter (ōdom′itər), *n.* a device for measuring the distance covered by a vehicle. Also **hodometer.**

o·don·tal·gia (ō′dontal′jə), *n.* toothache.

o·don·ti·a·sis (ō′dontī′əsis), *n.* teething; the cutting of teeth.

o·don·to·blast (ōdon′təblast), *n.* any of the outer cells lining the tooth cavity, which secrete dentin.

o·don·tog·e·ny (ō′dontoj′ənē), *n.* the growth and development of teeth. Also **o·don·to·gen′e·sis,** —**o·don·to·gen′ic,** *adj.*

o·don·toid (ōdon′toid), *adj.* having the form of a tooth; like a tooth.

o·don·tol·o·gy (ō′dontol′əjē), *n.* the care of teeth; dentistry.

oec·u·men·i·cal (ek′yo͞omen′ikəl), *adj.* See **ecumenical.** Also **oec·u·men′ic.**

oe·de·ma (idē′mə), *n.*, *pl.* **oe·de·ma·ta** (idē′mətə). See **edema.**

oeil·lade (oiyad′), *n.*, *pl.* **oeil·lades** (oiyad′). *French.* a coquettish glance; amorous look.

oe·nol·o·gy, e·nol·o·gy (ēnol′əjē), *n.* the science of wine and wine making. —**oe·nol′o·gist,** *n.*

oe·no·mel (ē′nəmel), *n.* **1.** a beverage made of wine and honey. **2.** something that blends strength with sweetness.

oer·sted (ur′sted), *n.* a unit of magnetic intensity that is equal to the intensity of a magnetic field in a vacuum when experiencing a force of one dyne.

oe·soph·a·ge·al (isof′əjē′əl), *adj.* See **esophageal.**

oe·soph·a·gus (isof′əgəs), *n.*, *pl.* **oe·soph·a·gi** (isof′əjī). See **esophagus.**

oes·tro·gen (es′trəjen), *n.* See **estrogen.**

oes·trus (es′trəs), *n.* See **estrus.**

oeu·vre (o͞o′vrə), *n.*, *pl.* **oeu·vres** (o͞o′vrə). *French.* the work of a writer, artist, etc., considered as a whole, or an individual work.

of·fic·i·nal (əfis′ənl), *adj.* (of a drug, etc.) available without need for any special preparation; kept in stock. See also **magistral.**

of·fi·cious (əfisн′əs), *adj.* interfering; meddling; offering unwanted advice or help.

off·print (ôf′print), *n.* a reprint by itself of an article originally published with other articles in a journal, magazine, etc.

og·do·ad (og′dōad), *n.* the number eight or any set, series, or group of eight.

ohm (ōm), *n.* a measure of resistance to electric current by the medium (as a wire) through which it passes, such that one volt acts to produce one ampere. See also **ampere, volt.** —**ohm′ic,** *adj.*

ohm·age (ō′mij), *n.* the resistance in a conductor measured in ohms.

ohm·me·ter (ōm′mētər), *n.* a device for measuring or indicating electric resistance in ohms.

o·le·ag·i·nous (ō′lēaj′ənəs), *adj.* oily or producing oil.

ol·fac·tion (olfak′sHən), *n.* **1.** the act or process of smelling. **2.** the sense of smell.

ol·fac·to·re·cep·tor (olfak′tōrisep′tər), *n.* a sense organ which is sensitive to smell.

ol·fac·to·ry (olfak′tərē), *adj.* relating to the sense of smell.

ol·i·garch (ol′əgärk), *n.* a ruler in an oligarchy.

ol·i·gar·chy (ol′əgärkē), *n.* **1.** a government in which a small group, such as a dominant class or faction, exercises effective control. **2.** a country or state ruled in this manner. —**ol·i·gar′chic,** *adj.*

ol·i·go·car·pous (ol′əgōkär′pəs), *adj.* bearing or producing only a few fruits; not fruitful.

Ol·i·go·cene (ol′əgōsēn), *adj.* relating to a division of the Tertiary epoch between the Eocene and the Miocene, about 25,000,000 to 40,000,000 years ago.

ol·i·go·cy·the·mi·a (ol′əgōsithē′mēə), *n.* an anemic condition characterized by loss of corpuscles in the blood.

ol·i·go·don·tia (ol′əgōdon′sHə), *n.* an abnormal condition which results in the growth of fewer than the normal number of teeth.

ol·i·goph·a·gous (oləgof′əgəs), *adj.* eating only a few particular kinds of food. See also **monophagous.**

ol·i·go·phre·ni·a (ol′əgōfrē′nēə), *n.* failure of normal mental growth; feeblemindedness.

ol·i·gop·o·ly (oləgop′əlē), *n.* a market situation in which there are only a few producers or sellers and many buyers. See also **duopoly, monopoly.**

ol·i·gop·so·ny (oləgop′sənē), *n.* a market situation in which there are only a few buyers and many sellers. See also **duopsony, monopsony.**

ol·i·gu·ri·a (oləgyŏŏr′ēə), *n.* lack of urine resulting from reduced secretion. Also **ol·i·gu·re·sis** (ol′əgyŏŏrē′sis).

o·li·o (ō′lēō), *n.* a mixture or combination of miscellaneous elements.

ol·i·va·ceous (ol′əvā′sHəs), *adj.* deep green in color; olive.

ol·i·va·ry (ol′əverē), *adj.* having the shape of an olive.

olivary body, either of two olive-shaped bodies in the brain, lying alongside the medulla oblongata.

ol·la-po·dri·da (ol′əpədrē′də), *n.* **1.** a highly seasoned Spanish stew of meat and vegetables. **2.** a miscellany or mixture of diverse elements.

o·lo·ro·so (ōlərō′sō), *n.* a variety of sweet, dark-colored sherry.

O·lym·pi·an (ōlim′pēən), *adj.* detached; lofty; imposing; greatly superior; regal.

o·ma·sum (ōmā′səm), *n., pl.* **o·ma·sa** (ōmā′sə). the third of the four stomachs of a ruminant. See also **rumen, reticulum, abomasum.**

om·buds·man (ôm′bŏŏdzman), *n., pl.* **om·buds·men** (ôm′bŏŏdzmen). an official empowered to investigate complaints made by private citizens about injustice or abuse on the part of the government or public service.

o·me·ga (ōmē′gə), *n.* the end; ending; the last of a series; final letter of classical Greek alphabet.

o·men·tum (ōmen′təm), *n., pl.* **o·men·ta** (ōmen′tə). a fold in the peritoneum connecting certain viscera. See also **greater omentum, lesser omentum.**

om·ni·far·i·ous (omnəfer′ēəs), *adj.* of all varieties or forms.
om·nif·ic (omnif′ik), *adj.* creating or producing everything.
om·nif·i·cent (omnif′isənt), *adj.* having unlimited creative power; creating all things.
om·nis·cience (omnisн′əns), *n.* the state of having infinite awareness or insight; unlimited knowledge. —**om·nis′cient,** *adj.*
om·ni·um-gath·er·um (om′nēəm-gaтн′ərəm), *n.* a variety or miscellaneous collection of people or things.
om·ni·vore (om′nəvôr), *n.* a person or animal that is omnivorous.
om·niv·or·ous (omniv′ərəs), *adj.* eating all kinds of food; unrestricted in diet.
om·pha·los (om′fələs), *n.* the navel.
om·pha·lo·skep·sis (om′fələskep′-sis), *n.* the study of one's navel as part of an exercise in mysticism.
o·nan·ism (ō′nənizm), *n.* (in sexual intercourse) the withdrawal of the penis from the vagina before the occurrence of orgasm.
on·co·sis (oɴɢkō′sis), *n.* any pathological condition resulting in the growth of tumors.
on·do·gram (on′dəgram), *n.* a record made on an ondograph.
on·do·graph (on′dəgraf), *n.* a device for measuring variations in oscillatory movements, as in an alternating current.
on·dom·e·ter (ondom′itər), *n.* a device for measuring the wavelengths of radio waves.
o·nei·ric (ōnī′rik), *adj.* relating to dreams.
o·nei·ro·crit·ic (ōnī′rəkrit′ik), *n.* one who specializes in the interpretation of dreams. —**o·nei·ro·crit′i·cism,** *n.*
o·nei·ro·man·cy (ōnī′rəmansē), *n.* divination by the interpretation of dreams.
on·er·ous (on′ərəs), *adj.* constituting a burden or hardship; irksome; troublesome.
o·ni·o·ma·ni·a (on′ēəmā′nēə), *n.* an irrepressible urge to buy things.
on·o·mas·tics (onəmas′tiks), *n.* the scientific study of the origins of proper names. Also **on·o·ma·tol·o·gy** (onəmətol′əjē). —**on·o·mas′tic,** *adj.*
on·o·mat·o·poe·ia (on′əmat′əpē′ə), *n.* the formation of a word by imitation of a sound associated with the thing to be designated.
on·tog·e·ny (ontoj′ənē), *n.* the growth or history of development of a particular organism. Also **on·to·gen′e·sis.** See also **phylogeny.**
ontological argument, a philosophical argument that claims to prove the existence of God by declaring that since existence is a state of perfection and God is the most perfect being conceivable, He must therefore exist, or else a still more perfect being would be possible. Also called **ontological proof.**
on·tol·o·gism (ontol′əjizm), *n.* the theological doctrine which asserts that the human mind immediately perceives God to be the appropriate object of its cognitions.
on·tol·o·gy (ontol′əjē), *n.* a branch of metaphysics concerned with the nature of being.
o·nus (ō′nəs), *n., pl.* **o·nus·es.** a responsibility, obligation, or burden.
o·nych·i·a (ōnik′ēə), *n.* inflammation of the tissue beneath the nail.
on·y·cho·pha·gia (on′əkōfā′jə), *n.* nail biting; esp. as a characteristic of an emotionally disturbed condition.
o·ol·o·gy, o·öl·o·gy (ōol′əjē), *n.* the study of birds' eggs.
o·o·pho·rec·to·my, o·ö·pho·rec·to·my (ō′əfərek′təmē), *n.* the removal of one or both ovaries; ovariectomy.
o·o·pho·ri·tis, o·ö·pho·ri·tis (ō′-əfərī′tis), *n.* inflammation of the ovaries; ovaritis.
o·o·sperm, o·ö·sperm (ō′əspurm), *n.* a fertilized egg.
o·o·the·ca, o·ö·the·ca (ōə*th*ē′kə), *n., pl.* **o·o·the·cae, o·ö·the·cae** (ōə*th*ē′-sē). a capsule-like container for the eggs of snails and of certain insects.
o·pac·i·fy (ōpas′əfī), *v.* to make impenetrable to light; render opaque.
o·pa·cim·e·ter (ōpəsim′itər), *n.* a

231

device for determining the opacity of something.

o·pal·esce (ōpəles′), *v.* to shine with various colors, as an opal. —**o·pal·es′cent**, *adj.*

op art (op), a form of modern abstract art that makes use of various patterns and materials to create special optical effects.

op cit. (op′ sit′), in the work already mentioned.

open shop, an organization in which union membership is not an essential condition of employment although a democratically elected union represents all the employees in negotiations with the management. See also **closed shop.**

o·pen·work (ō′pənwurk), *n.* work in any material, as stone, wood, lace, etc., that has openings in it as part of its decorative pattern.

op·er·ant (op′ərənt), *adj.* effective; functioning; in operation.

o·per·cu·lum (ōpur′kyələm), *n., pl.* **o·per·cu·la** (ōpur′kyələ), **o·per·cu·lums.** an organ of a plant or animal that acts as a lid or covering.

o·phid·i·an (ōfid′ēən), *adj.* relating to or belonging to snakes.

oph·i·ol·a·try (of′ēol′ətrē), *n.* snake worship.

oph·i·ol·o·gy (of′ēol′əjē), *n.* the study of snakes. See also **herpetology.**

oph·thal·mic (ofthal′mik), *adj.* relating to or connected with the eye.

oph·thal·mi·a (ofthal′mēə), *n.* inflammation of the eyeball or its mucous membranes. Also **oph·thal·mi·tis** (ofthalmī′tis).

oph·thal·mo·dy·na·mom·e·ter (ofthal′mōdīnəmom′itər), *n.* an instrument for determining the blood pressure in the blood vessels of the retina.

oph·thal·mol·o·gy (ofthəlmol′əjē), *n.* the branch of medicine concerned with the structure, function, and diseases of the eye. —**oph·thal·mol′o·gist**, *n.*

oph·thal·mom·e·ter (ofthəlmom′itər), *n.* a device for examining the eye, usually in order to ascertain the presence of astigmatism.

oph·thal·mo·ple·gi·a (ofthal′məplē′jə), *n.* paralysis of the muscles of the eye.

oph·thal·mo·scope (ofthal′məskōp), *n.* an instrument for examining the inner part of the eye.

oph·thal·mos·co·py (ofthəlmos′kəpə), *n.* the art of using an ophthalmoscope.

o·pis·the·nar (əpis′thənär), *n.* the back of the hand.

op·is·thog·na·thous (op′isthog′nəthəs), *adj.* having jaws that recede.

o·pi·um (ō′pēəm), *n.* the dried juice of the poppy, used in medicine to relieve pain, induce sleep, etc.; an addictive narcotic drug, poisonous in large quantities.

op·pi·late (op′əlāt), *v.* to block up; stop up; obstruct.

op·po·nens (əpō′nenz), *n., pl.* **op·po·nen·tes** (opənen′tēz). a muscle of the hand or foot which brings the fingers or toes together in such a way as to form a hollow in the palm or sole.

op·pro·bri·um (əprō′brēəm), *n.* disgrace caused by shameful behavior; dishonor. —**op·pro′bri·ous**, *adj.*

op·pugn (əpyōon′), *v.* to attack with argument or criticism; fight against. —**op·pug·nant** (əpug′nənt), *adj.*

op·ti·cist (op′tisist), *n.* one who is concerned with optics.

op·tics (op′tiks), *n.* the scientific study of the properties and phenomena of light and of vision.

op·tom·e·ter (optom′itər), *n.* a device for determining the extent of defective vision in an eye.

op·tom·e·try (optom′itrē), *n.* the measuring of defects in vision in order to prescribe suitable correctional lenses. —**op·tom′e·trist**, *n.*

o·pus (ō′pəs), *n., pl.* **o·pus·es, o·pe·ra** (op′ərə). a literary work or a musical composition.

o·pus·cule (ōpus′kyōol), *n.* a minor or short literary or musical work.

o·rac·u·lar (ôrak′yələr), *adj.* relating to or resembling an oracle; making decisions or passing judgments as if possessing special insight or knowledge.

Or·ange·man (ôr′injmən), *n.* a member of a secret society founded in the north of Ireland in 1795 with the aim of maintaining the political dominance of Protestantism.

or·bic·u·lar (ôrbik′yələr), *adj.* circular; spherical; rounded. Also **or·bic′u·late.**

or·bi·cu·lar·is (ôr′bikyəler′is), *n., pl.* **or·bi·cu·lar·es** (ôr′bikyəler′ēz). a muscle surrounding an opening in the body.

or·chi·dot·o·my (ôr′kidot′əmē), *n.* a surgical incision of the testis. Also **or·chot′o·my.**

or·chi·ec·to·my (ôr′kēek′təmē), *n.* the surgical excision of one or both testes; castration. Also **or·chec′to·my, or·chi·dec′to·my.**

or·chi·tis (ôrkī′tis), *n.* an inflamed condition of the testis.

or·di·nal (ôr′dənl), *adj.* relating to an order or subdivision of plants or animals.

Or·do·vi·cian (ôrdəvisH′ən), *adj.* relating to an early period of the Paleozoic era, between the Cambrian and the Silurian, occurring 440 to 500 million years ago.

o·rec·tic (ôrek′tik), *adj.* relating to desire.

o·rex·is (ôrek′sis), *n.* the aspect of mental activity concerned with emotion and desire rather than cognition.

or·gan·dy, or·gan·die (ôr′gəndē), *n.* a very fine cotton fabric used for blouses, dresses, etc.

or·ga·no·gen·e·sis (ôr′gənōjen′isis), *n.* the origin and development of organs, as those of the body. Also **or·ga·nog·e·ny** (ôrgənoj′ənē).

or·ga·nog·ra·phy (ôrgənog′rəfē), *n.* the scientific study of the organs of plants or animals.

or·ga·nol·o·gy (ôrgənol′əjē), *n.* the study of the form and functions of the organs of animals and plants.

or·ga·non (ôr′gənon), *n.* anything that serves as an instrument to facilitate the acquisition of knowledge, esp. a system of rules or body of principles of scientific investigation.

o·ga·no·ther·a·py (ôr′gənōther′əpē),

n. the treatment of illness by the use of preparations extracted from the organs of animals. Also **or·ga·no·ther·a·peu·tics** (ôr′gənōther′əpyōō′tiks).

or·gan·za (ôrgan′zə), *n.* a sheer fabric of silk or man-made fibers used as a dress material.

o·ri·el (ôr′ēəl), *n.* a bay window projecting out of a wall and supported by a bracket.

or·i·flamme (ôr′əflam), *n.* a standard or banner, esp. one which serves to rally troops in battle.

o·ri·ga·mi (ôrəgä′mē), *n.* the art of folding paper so as to achieve a variety of decorative patterns.

or·nis (ôr′nis), *n., pl.* **or·ni·thes** (ôrnī′thēz). the birds of a particular region or environment considered together.

or·nith·ic (ôrnith′ik), *adj.* relating to birds; bird-like.

or·ni·thoid (ôr′nəthoid), *adj.* like a bird.

or·ni·thol·o·gy (ôrnəthol′əjē), *n.* the scientific study of birds.

or·ni·thop·ter (ôrnəthop′tər), *n.* an airplane which is powered by flapping wings. Also **or·thop·ter** (ôrthop′tər).

o·rog·e·ny (ôroj′ənē), *n.* the process by which mountains are formed, esp. by folding of the earth's crust.

o·rog·ra·phy (ôrog′rəfē), *n.* the branch of geography concerned with mountains.

o·rol·o·gy (ôrol′əjē), *n.* the scientific study of mountains.

o·rom·e·ter (ôrom′itər), *n.* a type of barometer used for measuring the heights of mountains. —**or·o·met·ric** (ôrəmet′rik), *adj.*

o·rom·e·try (ôrom′itrē), *n.* the art or science of measuring the heights of mountains.

o·ro·phar·ynx (ôr′ōfar′inks), *n., pl.* **o·ro·pha·ryn·ges** (ôr′ōfərin′jēz), **o·ro·phar·ynx·es.** the pharynx proper as distinct from the nasopharynx and the laryngeal pharynx.

or·phrey (ôr′frē), *n.* elaborately decorated embroidery.

or·rer·y (ôr′ərē), *n.* an apparatus for

showing the movements of bodies in the solar system.

or·tho·don·tics (ôrthədon′tiks), *n.* the branch of dentistry concerned with the correction of irregularities of the teeth. —**or·tho·don′tist,** *n.*

Orthodox Church, that part of the Christian Church that combines under the patriarch of Constantinople, including national and local Eastern Churches.

or·tho·e·py, or·tho·ë·py (ôrthō′ipē), *n.* the study of the correct pronunciation of a language.

or·tho·gen·e·sis (ôrthəjen′isis), *n.* **1.** the evolution of a species along a predetermined path. **2.** the theory that social evolution in all cultures must pass through equivalent stages, despite differing environmental factors. —**or·tho·ge·net′ic,** *adj.*

or·tho·gen·ic (ôrthəjen′ik), *adj.* relating to the treatment of emotionally disturbed or mentally backward children.

or·thog·na·thous (ôrthog′nəthəs), *adj.* having straight jaws so that the face is approximately vertical when seen in profile. Also **or·thog·nath′ic.**

or·tho·o·nal (ôrthog′ənl), *adj.* relating to or containing right angles or perpendiculars.

or·thog·ra·phize (ôrthog′rəfīz), *v.* to spell correctly or in accordance with the rules of orthography.

or·thog·ra·phy (ôrthog′rəfē), *n.* the correct spelling of words according to established rules or usage. See also **cacography.** —**or·thog′ra·pher,** *n.* —**or·tho·graph′ic,** *adj.*

or·tho·pe·dics, or·tho·pae·dics (ôrthəpē′diks), *n.* the branch of surgery concerned with the correction of deformities of the bones, muscles, spinal system, etc. —**or·tho·pe′dic,** *adj.* —**or·tho·pe′dist,** *n.*

or·thop·ne·a, or·thop·noe·a (ôrthop′nēə), *n.* difficulty in breathing when lying down.

or·tho·prax·i·a (ôrthəprak′sēə), *n.* the correction of bodily deformities.

or·tho·prax·y (ôr′thəpraksē), *n.* correct or orthodox use or practice.

or·tho·psy·chi·a·try (ôr′thōsīkī′ətrē), *n.* the treatment of mental illness, esp. in young people.

or·thop·ter (ôrthop′tər), *n.* See **ornithopter.**

or·thop·ter·ous (ôrthop′tərəs), *adj.* relating to or belonging to an order of insects having hind wings that fold longitudinally down the back.

or·thop·tic (ôrthop′tik), *adj.* relating to or giving normal vision with both eyes.

or·tho·scope (ôr′thəskōp), *n.* an instrument for examining the inner part of the eye. —**or·tho·scop′ic,** *adj.*

or·tho·se·lec·tion (ôr′thōsilek′sHən), *n.* a kind of evolution which favors adaptation to environment.

or·tho·trop·ic (ôrthətrop′ik), *n.* (of plants, etc.) tending to grow more or less vertically. —**or·thot·ro·pism** (ôrthot′rəpizm), *n.*

os[1] (os), *n., pl.* **os·sa** (os′ə). a bone.

os[2] (os), *n., pl.* **o·ra** (ô′rə). an opening, orifice, or entrance.

os·cil·lo·gram (əsil′əgram), *n.* a recording made by an oscillograph or oscilloscope.

os·cil·lo·graph (əsil′əgraf), *n.* an instrument for recording electric oscillations, as the wave forms of alternating currents, etc.

os·cil·lom·e·ter (osəlom′itər), *n.* a device that records or measures changes in the arterial pulse.

os·cil·lo·scope (əsil′əskōp), *n.* an instrument which shows on the screen of a cathode ray tube electrical changes in a voltage, current, etc.

os·ci·tant (os′itənt), *adj.* lazy; drowsy; lacking attention; careless.

os·cu·lant (os′kyələnt), *adj.* sharing certain characteristics in common.

os·cu·lar (os′kyələr), *adj.* relating to an osculum or mouth.

os·cu·late (os′kyəlāt), *v.* **1.** to kiss or embrace. **2.** to make close contact with. —**os·cu·la′tion,** *n.*

os·cu·lum (os′kyələm), *n., pl.* **os·cu·la** (os′kyələ). a small opening or orifice having the shape of a mouth.

os·mics (oz′miks), *n.* the scientific study of the sense of smell.

os·mi·dro·sis (oz′midrō′sis), *n.* the secretion of sweat or bad odor.

os·mom·e·ter (ozmom′itər), *n.* a device used to measure osmotic pressure.

os·mom·e·try (ozmom′itrē), *n.* the measurement of osmotic pressure.

os·mose (oz′mōs), *v.* to subject to or to be subjected to osmosis. —**os·mot·ic** (ozmot′ik), *adj.*

os·mo·sis (ozmō′sis), *n.* the diffusion of a liquid through a semipermeable membrane until it is in equal concentrations on both sides of the membrane.

os·o·phone (os′əfōn), *n.* a telephone receiver that transmits vibrations directly to the bones of the head, used by the hard of hearing.

os·se·ous (os′ēəs), *adj.* consisting of bone; bony; bonelike.

Os·si·an·ic (os′ēan′ik), *adj.* given to pompous or pretentious utterances; bombastic.

os·si·cle (os′ikəl), *n.* a small bone.

os·sif·er·ous (osif′ərəs), *adj.* containing bones or fossilized deposits of bones.

os·si·fy (os′əfī), *v.* **1.** to make or become bone or bonelike; change into bone. **2.** to become rigid or fixed in outlook, attitudes, etc. —**os·si·fi·ca′tion,** *n.*

os·su·ar·y (osH′o͞oer′ē), *n.* a place where the bones of the dead are deposited. Also **os·su·ar·i·um** (osH′-o͞oer′ēəm).

os·tec·to·my (ostek′təmē), *n.* the surgical excision of a bone. Also **os·te·ec·to·my** (os′tēek′təmē).

os·te·i·tis (os′tēī′tis), *n.* inflammation of the bone or bone tissue.

os·ten·sive (osten′siv), *adj.* **1.** obviously or clearly showing. **2.** pretended, professed, or seeming.

os·te·o·ar·thri·tis (os′tēōärthrī′tis), *n.* a kind of chronic arthritis causing degeneration of the joints, found mainly in old people. Also **degenerative joint disease.**

os·te·o·blast (os′tēəblast), *n.* a cell that forms bone.

os·te·oc·la·sis (os′tēok′ləsis), *n.* the deliberate breaking of a bone in order to correct a deformity.

os·te·o·scope (os′tēəskōp), *n.* acute pain in the bones.

os·te·o·gen·e·sis (os′tēəjen′isis), *n.* the formation of bone.

os·te·oid (os′tēoid), *adj.* having the appearance of bone; bone-like.

os·te·ol·o·gy (os′tēol′əjē), *n.* the branch of anatomy dealing with bones.

os·te·o·ma (os′tēō′mə), *n., pl.* **os·te·o·mas, os·te·o·ma·ta** (os′tēō′mətə). a tumor consisting of bony tissue.

os·te·o·ma·la·cia (os′tēōməlā′sнə), *n.* a softening of the bones resulting from vitamin D, calcium, and phosphorus deficiencies and often leading to severe deformities.

os·te·om·e·try (os′tēom′itrē), *n.* the measurement of bones to enable the comparative study of the proportions of the human body.

os·te·o·my·e·li·tis (os′tēōmī′əlī′tis), *n.* an inflammatory disease of bone tissue.

os·te·o·path (os′tēəpath), *n.* one who practices osteopathy. Also **os·te·op·a·thist** (os′tēop′əthist).

os·te·op·a·thy (os′tēop′əthē), *n.* the treatment of disease by massage and manipulation of the bones.

os·te·o·plas·ty (os′tēəplas′tē), *n.* the surgical replacement of bones. —**os·te·o·plas′tic,** *adj.*

os·ti·ar·y (os′tēer′ē), *n.* one who guards a door; doorkeeper.

os·tra·con, os·tra·kon (os′trakon), *n., pl.* **os·tra·ca, os·tra·ka** (os′trakə). (in ancient Greece) a fragment of pottery esp. one used as a ballot.

o·tal·gi·a (ōtal′jēə), *n.* earache.

o·tic (ō′tik), *adj.* relating to the ear.

o·ti·ose (ō′sнēōs), *adj.* idle; useless; unnecessary.

o·ti·tis in·ter·na (ōtī′tis intur′nə). See **labyrinthitis.**

o·to·hem·i·neur·as·the·ni·a (ō′tōhem′ēno͞orəsthē′nēə), *n.* the state of being able to hear with only one ear.

o·to·rhi·no·lar·yn·gol·o·gy (ō′tōrī′nōlar′iNGgol′əjē), *n.* the branch of medicine dealing with the ear, nose, and throat. Also **o·to·lar·yn·gol′o·gy.**

o·to·lith (ō′təli*th*), *n.* a calcareous mass which forms in the inner ear of vertebrates.

o·tol·o·gy (ōtol′əjē), *n.* the study of the structure, function, and diseases of the ear.

o·to·neur·as·the·ni·a (ō′tōno͞or′-əsthē′nēə), *n.* a malfunction of the nervous system caused by disease of the ear.

o·to·plas·ty (ō′təplastē), *n.* plastic surgery of the ear.

o·to·scle·ro·sis (ō′təsklirō′sis), *n.* the growth of new bone around the innermost bones of the middle ear, causing deafness.

Ot·to·man Empire (ot′əmən), the former Turkish empire that existed from 1300 to the end of World War I and was replaced by the Republic of Turkey.

ou·bli·ette (o͞o′blēet′), *n.* a hidden dungeon that can be entered only from above.

out·age (ou′tij), *n.* a stopping in the functioning of a machine due to a lack of power.

out-Her·od (outher′əd), *v.* to surpass or exceed in evil, violence, extravagance, etc.

outing flannel, a lightweight cotton flannel having a short nap.

ou·trance (o͞oträNs′), *n. French.* the extreme limit; utmost extremity.

ou·tré (o͞otrā′), *n. French.* going beyond the limits of what is acceptable, proper, or decent.

ou·zo (o͞o′zō), *n.* a Greek liqueur flavored with anise.

o·va (ō′və), *n.* Plural of **ovum.**

o·var·i·an (ōver′ēən), *adj.* relating to or involving an ovary.

o·var·i·ec·to·mize (ōver′ēek′təmīz), *v.* to remove one or both ovaries.

o·var·i·ec·to·my (ōver′ēek′təmē), *n.* the removal of one or both ovaries by surgical operation; oophorectomy.

o·var·i·ot·o·my (ōver′ēot′əmē), *n.* the surgical incision or removal of an ovary.

o·va·ri·tis (ōvərī′tis), *n.* inflammation of the ovaries; oophoritis.

o·va·ry (ō′vərē), *n.* the female reproductive organ producing ova.

o·ver·kill (ō′vərkil), *n.* the capacity of a country to cause destruction by nuclear weapons in excess of the amount required for victory over an enemy.

o·vert (ōvurt′), *adj.* open; unconcealed; public. —**o·vert′ly,** *adv.*

o·ver·ture (ō′vərCHər), *n.* an introductory move; preliminary step.

o·ver·ween·ing (ō′vərwē′niNG), *adj.* presumptuous; conceited; arrogant; excessive.

o·vi·duct (ō′vidukt), *n.* either of the two tubes which carry ova from the ovary to the outside.

o·vif·er·ous (ōvif′ərəs), *adj.* bearing or producing eggs.

o·vi·form (ō′vəfôrm), *adj.* shaped like an egg.

o·vine (ō′vīn), *adj.* relating to or concerned with sleep.

o·vip·a·ra (ōvip′ərə), *n. pl.* animals that lay eggs.

o·vip·a·rous (ōvip′ərəs), *adj.* producing eggs that hatch outside the body of the mother, as birds, some fishes, etc.

o·vi·pos·it (ō′vipoz′it), *v.* to lay eggs by means of an ovipositor.

o·vi·pos·i·tor (ō′vipoz′itər), *n.* (in certain insects and fish) a specialized organ through which eggs are expelled.

o·vi·sac (ō′visak), *n.* a container or capsule for holding an ovum or ova.

o·void (ō′void), *adj.* having the shape of an egg.

o·vo·vi·vip·a·rous (ō′vōvīvip′ərəs), *adj.* producing eggs that hatch inside the body of the mother.

o·vu·lar (ō′vyələr), *adj.* relating to or having the nature of an ovule.

o·vu·late (ō′vyəlāt), *v.* to expel or release eggs from an ovule.

o·vule (ō′vyo͞ol), *n.* the sac containing the unfertilized female germ cell.

o·vum (ō′vəm), *n., pl.* **o·va** (ō′və). the female reproductive cell of animals or plants.

ox·im·e·ter (oksim′itər), *n.* a device to measure the extent of oxygen saturation of the hemoglobin in a sample quantity of blood.

ox·im·e·try (oksim'itrē), *n.* the measurement of oxygen saturation of the hemoglobin with an oximeter.

Ox·o·ni·an (oksō'nēən), *adj.* relating to or belonging to Oxford, England, or to Oxford University.

oys·tered (oi'stərd), *adj.* (of furniture) veneered with designs made up of concentric rings.

o·zo·no·sphere (ōzō'nəsfēr), *n.* an atmospheric layer, ranging from 8 to 30 miles above the surface of the earth, characterized by a high concentration of ozone.

pab·u·lum (pab′yələm), *n.* food; anything nourishing.

pach·y·derm (pak′idurm), *n.* any thick-skinned nonruminant hoofed quadruped, as the elephant, rhinoceros, etc. —**pach·y·der′ma·tous,** *adj.*

pach·y·lo·sis (pakəlō′sis), *n.* a medical disorder in which the skin, esp. on the legs, becomes scaly and thickens.

pac·tion (pak′sHən), *n.* **1.** a contract; an agreement; a bargain. **2.** the action of making a contract, etc.

pad·nag (pad′nag), *n.* an old, slow horse; a nag.

pa·dro·ne (pədrō′nē), *n., pl.* **pa·dro· nes.** an employer who controls almost totally the lives of his workers, providing them with accommodation and food as well as employment so as to exploit them to the full.

pad·u·a·soy (paj′ōōəsoi), *n.* a smooth, rich silk fabric. See also **peau de soie, poult-de-soie.**

pae·an, pe·an (pē′ən), *n.* a song of praise or triumph.

paed·er·ast (ped′ərast), *n.* pederast.

paed·er·as·ty (ped′ərastē), *n.* pederasty.

pae·di·at·rics (pē′dēat′riks), *n.* pediatrics.

pae·do·bap·tism (pē′dōbap′tizm), *n.* pedobaptism.

pae·do·gen·e·sis (pēdəjen′isis), *n.* re-production by animals in the larval or some other juvenile form, which persists into the adult stage of life, as in the axolotl.

pa·el·la (pää′lə), *n.* a Spanish dish consisting of chicken, rice, saffron, tomatoes, seasonings, stock, and often shellfish, all cooked slowly together until the moisture is absorbed.

pag·i·nate (paj′ənāt), *v.* to indicate the order of pages in a book, as by marking each with a number. —**pag· i·na′tion,** *n.*

pail·lette (palyet′), *n.* a small shining decoration, resembling a bead or sequin, sewn onto a dress; a spangle.

pail·lon (päyôN′), *n.* a thin sheet of metal foil used in enameling and gilding.

paint·er·ly (pān′tərlē), *adj.* of a style of painting relying on the use of light and shade, tonal relations, and multiple brush strokes to give a naturalistic impression of shape and outline without using firm outlines that can be observed at close quarters.

pais·ley (pāz′lē), *n.* **1.** a soft woolen fabric with a characteristic brightly colored and finely detailed pattern woven in, first made in Paisley, Scotland. **2.** Also called **paisley print.** a pattern resembling that of paisley fabric.

pal·a·din (pal′ədin), *n.* a knight errant; a chivalrous champion.

palaeobiology

pa·lae·o·bi·ol·o·gy (pā'lēōbīol'əjē), *n*. paleobiology.

pa·lae·o·bot·a·ny (pā'lēōbot'ənē), *n*. paleobotany.

Pa·lae·o·cene (pā'lēəsēn), *adj*. Paleocene.

pa·lae·o·cli·ma·tol·o·gy (pā'lēōklī'-mətol'əjē), *n*. paleoclimatology.

pa·lae·o·e·col·o·gy (pā'lēōikol'əjē), *n*. paleoecology.

pa·lae·o·en·to·mol·o·gy (pā'lēōen'-təmol'əjē), *n*. paleoentomology.

Pa·lae·o·gene (pā'lēəjēn), *adj*. Paleogene.

pa·lae·o·ge·og·ra·phy (pā'lēōjēog'-rəfē), *n*. paleogeography.

Pa·lae·o·lith·ic (pā'lēəlith'ik), *adj*. Paleolithic.

pa·lae·ol·o·gy (pā'lēol'əjē), *n*. paleology.

pa·lae·on·tog·ra·phy (pā'lēəntog'-rəfē), *n*. paleontography.

pa·lae·on·tol·o·gy (pā'lēəntol'əjē), *n*. paleontology.

pa·lae·o·pa·thol·o·gy (pā'lēōpəthol'-əjē), *n*. paleopathology.

pa·lae·o·pe·dol·o·gy (pā'lēōpidol'-əjē), *n*. paleopedology.

pa·lae·o·trop·i·cal (pā'lēōtrop'ikəl), *adj*. paleotropical.

Pa·lae·o·zo·ic (pā'lēəzō'ik), *adj*. Paleozoic.

pa·lae·o·zo·ol·o·gy (pā'lēōzōol'əjē), *n*. paleozoology.

pal·a·tine[1] (pal'ətīn), *adj*. relating to a palace.

pal·a·tine[2] (pal'ətīn), *adj*. relating to the palate.

pa·lav·er (pəlav'ər), *n*. **1**. a lengthy conference, esp. with primitive natives by traders or the like. **2**. idle chatter.

Pa·le·arc·tic, Pa·lae·arc·tic (pā'lēärk'tik), *adj*. of or relating to the geographical area made up of Europe, that part of Asia lying north of the Himalayas, the northern part of the Arabian peninsula, and that part of Africa lying north of the tropic of Cancer.

pa·le·eth·nol·o·gy (pā'lēethnol'əjē), *n*. the scientific study of the early or primitive human races.

pa·le·o·bi·ol·o·gy, pa·lae·o·bi·ol·o·gy (pā'lēōbīol'əjē), *n*. the scientific study of fossil plants and animals.

pa·le·o·bot·a·ny, pa·lae·o·bot·a·ny (pā'lēōbot'ənē), *n*. the scientific study of fossil plants.

Pa·le·o·cene, Pa·lae·o·cene (pā'lēəsēn), *adj*. relating to or denoting a geological epoch of the Tertiary period of the Cenozoic era, lasting from 70,000,000 years ago to 60,000,000 years ago and characterized by the development of birds and mammals. See also **Tertiary, Neocene.**

pa·le·o·cli·ma·tol·o·gy, pa·lae·o·cli·ma·tol·o·gy (pā'lēōklī'mətol'-əjē), *n*. the scientific study of the climates of past geological periods.

pa·le·o·e·col·o·gy, pa·lae·o·e·col·o·gy (pā'lēōikol'əjē), *n*. the branch of ecology dealing with past geological periods.

pa·le·o·en·to·mol·o·gy, pa·lae·o·en·to·mol·o·gy (pā'lēōen'təmol'-əjē), *n*. the scientific study of fossil insects.

Pa·le·o·gene, Pa·lae·o·gene (pā'lēəjēn), *adj*. relating to or denoting the earlier part of the Tertiary period of the Cenozoic era of geological time, divided into the Paleocene, Eocene, and Oligocene epochs, and lasting from 70,000,000 years ago to 25,000,000 years ago. See also **Neogene.**

pa·le·o·ge·og·ra·phy, pa·lae·o·ge·og·ra·phy (pā'lēōjēog'rəfē), *n*. the science of reconstructing or representing the geographic features of the earth as they existed in the various periods of geological time.

pa·le·o·ge·ol·o·gy (pā'lēōjēol'əjē), *n*. the scientific representation of the geological conditions prevailing in the various periods of geological time.

pa·le·og·ra·phy (pā'lēog'rəfē), *n*. the study of ancient writing and inscriptions.

pa·le·o·lith (pā'lēəlith), *n*. a chipped stone implement of the early Stone Age.

Pa·le·o·lith·ic, Pa·lae·o·lith·ic (pā'lēəlith'ik), *adj*. of or relating to the early Stone Age culture of the Pleistocene epoch, which lasted from *c.* 500,000 to 10,000 B.C. and was characterized by the use of tools and weapons chipped from stone or bone. See also **Neolithic.**

pa·le·ol·o·gy, pa·lae·ol·o·gy (pā′lē-ol′əjē), *n.* the study of ancient relics. —**pa·le·o·log′i·cal,** *adj.*

pa·le·on·tog·ra·phy, pa·lae·on·tog·ra·phy (pā′lēontog′rəfē), *n.* the scientific description of extinct animals and plants.

pa·le·on·tol·o·gy, pa·lae·on·tol·o·gy (pā′lēontol′əjē), *n.* the scientific study of the life existing in the various geological periods by means of fossil plants and animals. —**pa·le·on·tol′o·gist,** *n.*

pa·le·o·pa·thol·o·gy, pa·lae·o·pa·thol·o·gy (pā′lēopəthol′əjē), *n.* the study of disease and other features of medical interest found in fossils of animals and early man.

pa·le·o·pe·dol·o·gy, pa·lae·o·pe·dol·o·gy (pā′lēopidol′əjē), *n.* the scientific study of the soil conditions of past geological periods.

pa·le·o·psy·chol·o·gy (pā′lēōsīkol′əjē), *n.* the study of those psychological processes that are thought to have survived from a previous stage in evolution. —**pa·le·o·psy′chic,** *adj.*

pa·le·o·trop·i·cal, pa·lae·o·trop·i·cal (pā′lēōtrop′ikəl), *adj.* of or relating to the geographical area consisting of the Oriental and Ethiopian regions.

Pa·le·o·zo·ic, Pa·lae·o·zo·ic (pā′lēəzō′ik), *adj.* relating to or denoting the geological era that lasted from 600,000,000 years ago to 220,000,000 years ago and was characterized by the advent of fish, insects, and reptiles.

pa·le·o·zo·ol·o·gy, pa·lae·o·zo·ol·o·gy (pā′lēōzōōl′əjē), *n.* the scientific study of fossil animals.

pal·frey (pôl′frē), *n.* a horse for ordinary riding, as distinct from riding to war, and esp. for use by women.

pal·imp·sest (pal′impsest), *n.* a parchment or other early writing sheet used for the second time after erasure of the writing originally on it.

pal·in·drome (pal′indrōm), *n.* a word, phrase, line of verse, etc. that reads the same backward as forward, as *evil madam, live.*

pal·in·gen·e·sis (pal′injen′isis), *n.* **1.** rebirth; revival. **2.** the type of development in which individuals repeat the features of their ancestral race or group. See also **cenogenesis.**

pal·in·gen·e·sist (pal′injen′isist), *n.* one who believes in the transmigration of souls. Also **pal·in·gen′ist.**

pal·li·ate (pal′ēāt), *v.* to alleviate; to extenuate; to make excuses in attempted mitigation. —**pal·li·a·tive,** *adj., n.*

pal·lid (pal′id), *adj.* pale; colorless; lacking vitality.

pal·ma·ry (pal′mərē), *adj.* deserving of praise.

pal·mate (pal′māt), *adj.* shaped like an open and spread hand, as certain leaves. —**pal·ma′tion,** *n.*

palm·is·try (pä′mistrē), *n.* fortune-telling based on interpretation of the lines on the palm of the hand.

pal·pa·ble (pal′pəbəl), *adj.* capable of being readily perceived by the senses or the mind; evident.

pal·pate (pal′pāt), *v.* to carry out an examination, esp. medical, by touch. —**pal·pa′tion,** *n.*

pal·pe·bral (pal′pəbrəl), *adj.* relating to the eyelid.

pal·pe·brate (pal′pəbrāt), *adj.* with eyelids.

pal·ter (pôl′tər), *v.* to be insincere in speech or action; to equivocate; to haggle; to trifle.

pa·lu·dal (pəlōō′dl), *adj.* relating to or caused by marshes.

pal·u·dism (pal′yədizm), *n.* malaria.

pal·y·nol·o·gy (palənol′əjē), *n.* the scientific study of fossil and live microscopic plant structures, as spores, pollen grains, etc.

pam·ple·gia (pamplē′jə), *n.* See **pan·plegia.**

pan·a·ce·a (panəsē′ə), *n.* a cure for all diseases.

pa·nache (pənasн′), *n.* **1.** an ornament, as a plume or tassel, esp. on headgear. **2.** a stylish or swaggering manner.

pan·at·ro·phy (panat′rəfē), *n.* the wasting away or other degeneration of a whole structure or body.

pan·car·di·tis (pan′kärdī′tis), *n.* inflammation of all parts of the heart.

pan·chro·mat·ic (pan′krōmat′ik), *adj.* reacting to all colors of the spectrum, as a photographic color film.

pan·cre·as (pan′krēəs), *n.* a large gland near the stomach secreting digestive juices into the duodenum and insulin into the bloodstream.

pan·cre·a·tec·to·mize (pan′krēətek′təmīz), *v.* to perform a pancreatectomy.

pan·cre·a·tec·to·my (pan′krēətek′təmē), *n.* the surgical removal of all or a part of the pancreas.

pan·cre·at·ic juice (pan′krēat′ik), the digestive juice secreted by the pancreas, consisting of a colorless thick alkaline fluid capable of breaking down protein, fat, and starch by enzyme action.

pan·cre·a·tin (pan′krēətin), *n.* a substance containing the enzymes, found in pancreatic juice, amylase, lipase, and trypsin, used esp. as an aid to digestion.

pan·cre·a·ti·tis (pan′krēətī′tis), *n.* inflammation of the pancreas.

pan·cre·a·tot·o·my (pan′krēətot′əmē), *n.* surgical incision of the pancreas.

pan·dect (pan′dekt), *n.* a comprehensive summary; a digest, as of a code of laws.

pan·dem·ic (pandem′ik), *adj.* distributed or prevalent throughout the world or some large area of it, as a disease; universal.

pan·der (pan′dər), *n.* **1.** a go-between in secret love affairs; a procurer. **2.** one who provides the means for or profits from the vices of others. Also **pan′der·er.**

pan·dic·u·la·tion (pandik′yəlā′sнən), *n.* the process or act of stretching, esp. as used in medical treatment.

pan·dit (pun′dit), *n.* a highly respected scholar or wise man in India.

pan·dour (pan′dōōr), *n.* a ferocious, rapacious soldier.

pan·dow·dy (pandou′dē), *n.* an apple pie or pudding sweetened with molasses. Also **apple pandowdy.**

pan·du·rate (pan′dyərāt), *adj.* fiddle-shaped, as certain leaves. Also **pan·du′ri·form.**

pan·e·gyr·ic (pan′ijir′ik), *n.* a eulogy; a speech in praise of someone or something. —**pan·e·gyr′ist,** *n.*

pan·e·gy·rize (pan′ijərīz), *v.* to deliver or write a discourse in praise of a person or thing; to eulogize.

pan·et·to·ne (pan′itō′nē), *n.* an Italian leavened bread containing dried fruits, nuts, etc., eaten on holidays.

pa·niv·o·rous (paniv′ərəs), *adj.* bread-eating; living on bread.

pan·jan·drum (panjan′drəm), *n.* a pompous official; an official who supposes himself to be important.

pan·lo·gism (pan′ləjizm), *n.* the philosophical theory that only the logos, the rational principle, is truly real and the universe is but an act or realization of it.

pan·nic·u·lus (pənik′yələs), *n., pl.* **pan·nic·u·li** (pənik′yəlī). a layer of tissue, as the layer of fat beneath the skin.

pan·nier (pan′yər), *n.* **1.** a large basket, as for carrying provisions or small items for trade. **2.** a frame of oval shape for holding out the skirt of a woman's dress at the hips.

pan·nus (pan′əs), *n.* an abnormal condition of the eye, in which the cornea becomes thickened.

pan·o·ply (pan′əplē), *n.* a complete covering or array, either material or ideal and esp. splendid.

pan·op·tic (panop′tik), *adj.* allowing a view of or taking into consideration all parts or aspects.

pan·ple·gi·a (panplē′jēə), *n.* paralysis of all four limbs; quadriplegia. Also **pamplegia.**

pan·psy·chism (pansī′kizm), *n.* the philosophical theory that every object has a mind or a psyche. —**pan·psy′chist,** *n.*

pan·soph·ism (pan′səfizm), *n.* a claim

to have complete knowledge or wisdom.

pan·so·phy (pan'səfē), *n.* complete knowledge or wisdom.

pan·sper·mi·a (panspur'mēə), *n.* the theory that there are distributed throughout the universe germs or spores capable of developing into living things and that they do develop wherever the conditions are favorable. Also **pan·sper'ma·tism.**

pan·the·ism (pan'thēizm), *n.* the doctrine that all parts of the universe, esp. nature, are only manifestations of God who is the supreme reality; any doctrine or belief that God is the universe and the universe is God.

pan·to·fle, pan·tof·fle (pan'təfəl), *n.* an indoor shoe; a slipper.

pan·to·graph (pan'təgraf), *n.* **1.** an instrument for copying plans or the like in any given scale. **2.** a device for carrying electric current from an overhead cable to a vehicle such as a trolley car.

pan·tol·o·gy (pantol'əjē), *n.* a survey or systematic review of all fields of human knowledge.

pan·trop·ic (pantrop'ik), *adj.* affecting or drawn toward many kinds of body tissue.

pan·trop·i·cal (pantrop'ikəl), *adj.* (esp. of living things) distributed throughout the tropics.

pan·zer (pan'zər), *adj.* furnished with armor; armored, as a military unit with tanks or the like.

pap (pap), *n.* **1.** soft or semi-liquid food for babies or invalids. **2.** any written or spoken material that is weak in content and lacks substance.

pa·pav·er·a·ceous (pəpav'ərā'sHəs), *adj.* of any plant belonging to the poppy family.

pa·per (pā'pər), *n.* corporate and municipal (stocks and) bonds, treasury notes, negotiable notes, etc.

pap·e·terie (pap'itrē), *n.* a case or box of writing paper and other writing materials.

pap·il·lote (pap'əlōt), *n.* a fringed paper decoration wrapped round the end of a chop or cutlet bone.

pap·ule (pap'yōol), *n.* a small pointed inflamed prominence on the skin.

pap·y·ra·ceous (papərā'sHəs), *adj.* of a paper-like nature; papery.

par·a·bi·o·sis (par'əbīō'sis), *n.* a union of two individuals, often by surgery as an experiment, so that their blood circulations become one continuous process.

par·a·ble (par'əbəl), *n.* a short story conveying a moral or truth by allegory; any statement conveying its meaning indirectly, as by analogy.

par·a·cen·te·sis (par'əsentē'sis), *n.,* *pl.* **par·a·cen·te·ses** (par'əsentē'sēz). the surgical draining of fluid from a body cavity through a hole punctured in its wall. Also **tapping.**

pa·rach·ro·nism (parak'rənizm), *n.* an error in chronology whereby a date later than the correct one is given to an event or the like. See also **anachronism, prochronism.**

par·a·clete (par'əklēt), *n.* one called upon for help or to intercede.

par·a·cu·sis (parəkyōo'sis), *n.* partial deafness. Also **par·a·cu'sia.**

par·a·digm (par'ədim), *n.* an example; a model to use as a standard.

par·aes·the·sia (par'isthē'zHə), *n.* paresthesia.

par·a·geu·sia (parəgyōo'zHə), *n.* a psychiatric disorder in which the sense of taste is disordered and subject to hallucinations.

par·a·go·ge (parəgō'jē), *n.* the incorrect adding of a sound or sounds to the end of a word, as *coolth* for *cool.*

par·a·gon (par'əgon), *n.* an example or model of excellence in general or of a particular excellence.

par·a·graph·i·a (parəgraf'ēə), *n.* the mental disorder characterized by the inability to put thoughts into writing or the writing of words or letters different from those intended.

par·ai·son (pər'əzon), *n.* See **parison.**

par·a·lex·i·a (parəlek'sēə), *n.* a defect in the ability to read, characterized by the mental transposing of letters or words.

par·a·li·pom·e·na (par'əlipom'ənə), *n. pl.* things added as a supplement

parallelepiped

after being left out of or dealt with inadequately in the main text.

par·al·lel·e·pi·ped, par·al·lel·o·pi·ped (par′əlel′əpī′pid), *n.* a prism with six faces, each of which is a parallelogram. Also **par·al·lel·e·pip′e·don.**

pa·ral·o·gize (pəral′əjīz), *v.* to draw illogical conclusions from a set of facts or assumptions.

paralysis agitans. See **Parkinson's disease.**

par·a·mag·net·ic (par′əmagnet′ik), *adj.* relating to or denoting a substance that possesses magnetization in direct proportion to the strength of the magnetic field in which it is placed. See also **antiferromagnetic, diamagnetic, ferromagnetic.**

par·a·med·i·cal (parəmed′ikəl), *adj.* having a supplementary or secondary capacity in relation to the medical profession.

par·a·ment (par′əmənt), *n.*, *pl.* **par·a·ments, par·a·men·ta.** a decorative hanging or other ornament for a room.

pa·ram·e·ter (pəram′itər), *n.* something used as a standard against which other things are measured. —**par·a·met′ric,** *adj.*

par·a·mil·i·tar·y (parəmil′iterē), *adj.* relating to or denoting an organized force ancillary to or taking the place of a regular military force.

par·a·mour (par′əmŏŏr), *n.* a lover, esp. that of a married person.

par·a·na·sal (parənā′zəl), *adj.* near the nasal passages.

par·a·noi·a (parənoi′ə), *n.* a mental disorder in which the patient suffers delusions and imagines himself persecuted by others. —**par·a·noi′ac, par·a·noid,** *adj.*

par·a·nymph (par′ənimf), *n.* a groomsman or bridesmaid at a wedding ceremony.

par·a·pa·re·sis (par′əpərē′sis), *n.* partial paralysis, affecting in particular the legs.

par·aph (par′əf), *n.* an elaborate flourish following a signature, originally made to make forgery difficult.

par·a·phras·tic (parəfras′tik), *adj.* of the nature of a paraphrase; expressed in different words; reworded, as to make clearer. —**pa·raph′ra·sis, par′a·phrast,** *n.*

par·a·ple·gi·a (parəplē′jēə), *n.* paralysis of both legs.

par·a·psy·chol·o·gy (par′əsīkol′əjē), *n.* the scientific study of psychic phenomena, as telepathy, clairvoyance, etc.

par·a·sit·i·cide (parəsit′isīd), *adj.* **1.** that kills parasites of plants or animals. —*n.* **2.** a substance or preparation that kills parasites.

par·a·sit·ol·o·gy (par′əsītol′əjē), *n.* the scientific study of parasites and their effect.

par·a·si·to·sis (par′əsītō′sis), *n.* any abnormal condition caused by parasites.

par·a·sym·pa·thet·ic (par′əsim′pəthet′ik), *adj.* relating to one of the two types of nerve in the autonomic nerve system, consisting of nerve fibers and ganglia which leave the central nervous system at the cranial and sacral regions, and working in opposition to the sympathetic nerves, as in stimulating peristalsis in the gut which sympathetic nerves inhibit, and contracting the eye pupil which sympathetic nerves dilate.

par·a·tax·ic (parətak′sik), *adj.* relating to or characterized by emotional or personality conflicts.

par·a·thi·on (parəthī′on), *n.* a yellowish-brown insecticide related to nerve gas and extremely poisonous to mammals.

par·a·thy·roid (parəthī′roid), *adj.* close to the thyroid gland.

parathyroid gland, one of four small glands or gland-like masses adjacent to the thyroid gland, which produce secretions that control the calcium balance between blood and bones.

par·a·troph·ic (parətrof′ik), *adj.* living on live organic matter; parasitic.

par·a·ty·phoid (parətī′foid), *n.* an infectious disease similar to but less severe than typhoid fever, caused by a salmonella bacillus and spreading where hygiene is poor. Also **para-typhoid fever.**

par·a·vane (par**′**əvān), *n.* an apparatus towed by a ship, consisting of a pair of vanes at the ends of cables and used to cut the moorings of submerged mines so that they rise to the surface and can be destroyed.

par·a·vent (par**′**əvent), *n.* a screen against wind or drafts.

par·buck·le (pär**′**bukəl), *n.* ə device for raising and lowering casks and the like, consisting of a rope fastened by its center at the higher level so that the two ends can be passed round the item to be raised and hauled on or let out from the higher level.

par·ce·nar·y (pär**′**sənerē), *n.* the joint possession of an undivided inheritance, as land, by two or more heirs.

par·e·gor·ic (parəgôr**′**ik), *n.* any soothing or pain-killing medical preparation.

par·en·ter·al (paren**′**tərəl), *adj.* entering the body by a means other than absorption from the intestine, as a drug by injection; not intestinal.

pa·ren·ti·cide (pəren**′**tisīd), *n.* the act of killing one or both of one's parents.

pa·re·sis (pərē**′**sis), *n.* partial paralysis or weakening of muscular power affecting movement but not sensation. —**pa·ret′ic,** *adj.*, *n.*

par·es·the·sia, par·aes·the·sia (par**′**isthē**′**zHə), *n.* a form of interference with sensation in which numbness, tingling, prickling, etc., are felt, as in cases of injury to peripheral nerves, etc.

pa·re·ve (pär**′**əvə), *adj.* (in Judaism) able to be eaten with both meat and dairy meals because it contains neither meat nor milk, consistent with laws of diet. Also **parve.**

par·get (pär**′**jit), *n.* any of several kinds of rough plaster, esp. one used for lining chimneys.

parg·ing (pär**′**jiNG), *n.* a thin plaster or mortar coating used for sealing or smoothing over rough masonry.

pa·ri·ah (pərī**′**ə), *n.* a social outcast.

par·i·es (per**′**eēz), *n.*, *pl.* **pa·ri·e·tes**

(pərī**′**itēz). the wall of the body or of any of its hollow organs; a structural wall of a plant.

pa·ri·e·tal (pərī**′**itl), *adj.* **1.** relating to or situated near the two parietal bones at the top and sides of the skull. **2.** relating to a paries or to parietes. **3.** relating to or with authority over life within the bounds of a college, university, etc.

pa·ri pas·su (per**′**ē pas**′**o͞o), *Latin.* equally; fairly; without bias.

par·i·son (par**′**isən), *n.* molten glass in a partially shaped state. Also **paraison.**

Park·in·son's disease (pär**′**kinsənz), a medical disorder in which there is progressive rigidity of the muscles, and tremors. Also **Par′kin·son·ism, paralysis agitans, shaking palsy.**

par·lance (pär**′**ləns), *n.* idiom; the way of speaking proper to a particular subject, as *legal parlance.*

par·ley (pär**′**lē), *n.* a discussion of matters in dispute, esp. one among military leaders to arrange peace terms.

par·lous (pär**′**ləs), *adj.* difficult to escape from or deal with; perilous.

Par·men·tier (pär**′**mentyā**′**), *adj.* of a dish made from or garnished with potato. Also **Par·men·tière′.**

Par·me·san (pär**′**mizan), *n.* a hard, strongly flavored, skim-milk cheese usually grated to serve with pasta, soup, etc., originally made in Parma, N. Italy. Also **Parmesan cheese.**

par·mi·gia·na (pärməzHä**′**nə), *adj.* of an Italian dish containing or garnished with Parmesan cheese. Also **par′mi·gia·no.**

Par·nas·sus (pärnas**′**əs), *n.* **1.** a collection of poems or fine pieces of writing. **2.** poetry or poets considered as a lofty whole.

pa·ro·chi·al (pərō**′**kēəl), *adj.* of excessively narrow interests or views. —**pa·ro′chi·al·ism,** *n.*

parochial school, a school run and maintained by a religious body.

par·o·don·ti·um (parədon**′**sHēəm), *n.*, *pl.* **par·o·don·tia** (parədon**′**sHēə). See **periodontium.**

pa·roe·mi·ol·o·gy (pərē′mēol′əjē), *n.* the technique or practice of coining proverbs. —**pa·roe·mi·ol′o·gist,** *n.*

par·o·no·ma·sia (par′ənōmā′zHə), *n.* punning; word-play.

par·o·nych·i·a (parənik′ēə), *n.* inflammation of the tissue around a fingernail or toenail, usually through infection, causing pus to form. Also **perionychia.**

par·o·nych·i·um (parənik′ēəm), *n.,* *pl.* **par·o·nych·i·a.** See **perionychium.**

pa·ro·tic (pərō′tik), *adj.* near the ear.

pa·rot·id (pərot′id), *n.* a salivary gland, in man the largest of three, at the base of and in front of the ear.

par·o·ti·tis (parətī′tis), *n.* mumps. Also **pa·rot·i·di′tis.**

par·ox·ysm (par′əksizm), *n.* any fit or outburst, as of action or emotion.

par·pen (pär′pən), *n.* See **perpend.**

par·ri·cide (par′isīd), *n.* the act of murdering one's father. Also **patricide.**

par·sec (pär′sek), *n.* a unit used in astronomy in the measurement of stellar distances, equivalent to 3.26 light years.

Par·see (pär′sē), *n.* an Indian who belongs to the Zoroastrian religion.

par·si·mo·ny (pär′səmōnē), *n.* excessive carefulness in using money, food, etc.; stinginess. —**par·si·mo′ni·ous,** *adj.*

par·the·no·car·py (pär′thənōkär′-pē), *n.* the formation of fruit without fertilization, as can occur in the banana and pineapple, resulting in seedless but otherwise normal fruits. —**par·the·no·car′pic, par·the·no·car′pous,** *adj.*

par·the·no·gen·e·sis (pär′thənōjen′-isis), *n.* development of an individual from an unfertilized ovum, normal in aphids and rotifers and able to be artificially induced in many animals.

par·tic·u·late (pärtik′yəlit), *adj.* relating to, consisting of, or of the nature of particles.

par·ti·tive (pär′titiv), *adj.* forming or acting as a partition; serving to separate into parts.

par·tu·ri·ent (pärtŏŏr′ēənt), *adj.* about to give birth; in labor.

par·tu·ri·fa·cient (pärtŏŏr′əfā′-sHənt), *adj.* bringing on or hastening labor.

par·tu·ri·tion (pär′tŏŏrisH′ən), *n.* childbirth; the act of giving birth.

pa·rure (pərŏŏr′), *n.* a matched set of jewels, jewelry, or other personal ornaments.

par·ve (pär′və), *n.* See **pareve.**

par·ve·nu (pär′vənŏŏ), *n.* a person who has lately or suddenly become wealthy or important but has not yet acquired the appropriate social refinements, as in dress, manners, etc.; an upstart.

pa·se·o (päsā′ō), *n.,* *pl.* **pa·se·os.** an area or path for public strolling; a promenade.

pas·quil (pas′kwil), *n.* a pasquinade.

pas·quin·ade (paskwənād′), *n.* a lampoon or satire, originally one displayed in a public place.

passe·ment (pas′mənt), *n.* a trimming for garments, made of thread of gold, silver, silk, etc. Also **pass′a·ment.**

passe·men·terie (pasmen′trē), *n.* a trimming of gold or silver braid, lace, cord, or of beads or the like.

passe-par·tout (pas′pärtŏŏ′), *n.* **1.** a decorative mat for framing a picture. **2.** a universal pass or means of entry; a master key.

pas·ser·ine (pas′ərin), *adj.* belonging or relating to the biological order comprising the birds with feet adapted for perching, having one toe pointing backward and the other three forward.

pas·si·ble (pas′əbəl), *adj.* capable of sensation or emotion; with easily roused or influenced feelings.

pas·sim (pas′im), *adv. Latin.* here and there; throughout; everywhere, usually of the occurrences of a particular phrase, allusion, topic, name, etc., in a work or the works of an author when these are too frequent to mention or index separately.

pas·sus (pas′əs), *n.,* *pl.* **pas·sus, pas·sus·es.** one of the major parts or sections into which a literary work of prose or poetry is divided.

pas·ta (pä′stə), *n.* any one or all of the many forms of egg and flour paste, Italian in origin, formed into various sized strips, rolls, tubes, shells, etc., for cooking in boiling water and serving with sauces of meat, tomato, etc.; a dish based on such an egg and flour paste.

paste (pāst), *n.* an unleavened dough made from flour and shortening for use as pie crust, flan cases, and in other pastry dishes.

pas·tic·cio (pastē′CHō), *n., pl.* **pas·tic·ci** (pastē′CHē). a pastiche.

pas·tiche (pastēsH′), *n.* a musical or literary work or a painting composed of a mixture of borrowed themes, motifs, etc., from another's work; a piece of music or literature or a painting executed in the style of another, usually well known, composer, writer, or painter; an incongruous mixture of items or themes from various sources.

pas·to·ral (pas′tərəl), *adj.* relating to the country or rural life; having or evoking the virtues, as peacefulness, simplicity, of country life.

pas·to·ral·ism (pas′tərəlizm), *n.* the rearing of herds of sheep, cattle, or the like, as the chief activity in the economy of a community.

pas·tose (pastōs′), *adj.* of painting in which the paint is laid on thickly.

pas·tra·mi (pəsträ′mē), *n.* beef, usually shoulder, highly seasoned and smoked or pickled.

pâ·té de foie gras (pätä′ də fwä grä′), *pl.* **pâ·tés de foie gras** (pätäz′ də fwä grä′). a paste made from the liver of fatted geese, a prized culinary delicacy.

pa·tel·la (pətel′ə), *n., pl.* **pa·tel·lae** (pətel′ē). the bone forming the kneecap.

pa·tel·li·form (pətel′əfôrm), *adj.* having the shape of a shallow cup or saucer.

pa·ter·fa·mil·i·as (pā′tərfəmil′ēəs), *n., pl.* **pa·ter·fa·mil·i·as·es.** the male head of a household, usually the father.

pa·ter·nal·ism (pətur′nəlizm), *n.* the exercise of control over a nation, employees, a social group, etc., in the manner of a father over his children.

pathetic fallacy, the attributing of human emotions or characteristics to inanimate objects or parts of nature, as *the brave snowdrops.*

path·o·bi·ol·o·gy (path′ōbīol′əjē), *n.* the study of abnormal or diseased conditions in living things; pathology.

path·o·cure (path′əkyo͞or), *n.* the termination of a neurosis occurring in conjunction with the appearance of a physical disease.

path·o·for·mic (pathəfôr′mik), *adj.* relating to the symptoms occurring in the initial stages of a disease, esp. of a mental illness.

path·o·gen (path′əjən), *n.* any organism that gives rise to disease. Also **path′o·gene.**

path·o·gen·e·sis (pathəjen′isis), *n.* the origin and mode of development of a disease. Also **pa·thog′e·ny.**

path·o·gen·ic (pathəjen′ik), *adj.* capable of causing disease.

path·o·ge·nic·i·ty (path′ōjənis′itē), *n.* the capacity of an organism for causing disease.

pa·thog·no·my (pəthog′nəmē), *n.* the study of diagnosis; the study of the symptoms and characteristics particular to specific diseases. —**pa·thog·no·mon′ic,** *adj.*

pa·thog·ra·phy (pəthog′rəfē), *n.* a scientific description of a disease and its pathogenesis, often in the form of a published treatise.

path·o·log·i·cal (pathəloj′ikəl), *adj.* 1. relating to pathology. 2. resulting from or concerning disease. Also **path·o·log′ic.**

pa·thol·o·gy (pəthol′əjē), *n.* 1. the scientific study of physical diseases, their causes, symptoms, courses, and treatment. 2. any unhealthy or abnormal physical condition.

path·o·morph·ism (pathəmor′fizm), *n.* abnormality in form or structure.

path·o·neu·ro·sis (path′əno͞orō′sis), *n.* an abnormally excessive preoccupation with a real disease being suffered or with a part of the body affected by disease.

pa·thos (pā′thos), *n*. the quality in any event, work of art, etc., that arouses pity or sorrow.

pa·tho·sis (pathō′sis), *n*. any diseased state or condition.

pat·i·na (pat′ənə), *n*. a filmy layer, usually green, formed on old bronze by oxidation and thought to add to its ornamental value.

pat·ois (pat′wä), *n*., *pl*. **pat·ois**. a form of speech used by the ordinary people of a particular district and different from the standard form of the language; local dialect; jargon.

pa·tri·arch (pā′trēärk), *n*. the male head of a family or tribe.

pa·tri·ar·chy (pā′trēär′kē), *n*. a form of organization of a community in which the father or male head of the family, tribe, or the like, holds authority, descent is through the male line, and children become members of their father's family or tribe. See also **matriarchy**.

pa·tri·cian (pətrisн′ən), *n*. **1.** a person of aristocratic or other high social rank. —*adj*. **2.** of high social rank; aristocratic; befitting an aristocrat.

pa·tri·ci·ate (pətrisн′ēit), *n*. the aristocracy; the patrician class of society.

pat·ri·cide (pa′trisīd), *n*. See **parricide**.

pat·ri·lat·er·al (patrəlat′ərəl), *adj*. related on the father's side of the family. See also **matrilateral**.

pat·ri·lin·e·age (patrəlin′ēij), *n*. descent traced through the male line of a family.

pat·ri·lin·e·al (patrəlin′ēəl), *adj*. inheriting or descending through the male line of a family. Also **pat·ri·lin′ e·ar**.

pat·ri·li·ny (pat′rəlīnē), *n*. the tracing of family descent through the male line.

pat·ri·lo·cal (patrəlō′kəl), *adj*. living with or situated near the husband's family; relating to such living or situation. Also called **virilocal**. See also **matrilocal**.

pat·ri·mo·ny (pat′rəmōnē), *n*. heritage; any inherited trait, quality, etc.

pat·ri·po·tes·tal (pat′rəpōtes′tl), *adj*. relating to the authority held by a father or his side of a family.

pa·tris·tic (pətris′tik), *adj*. relating to the fathers of the Christian Church or to their writings or the study of them. Also **pa·tris′ti·cal**.

pa·trol·o·gist (pətrol′əjist), *n*. one who studies or is learned in patrology.

pa·trol·o·gy (pətrol′əjē), *n*. the study of the teachings of the fathers of the Christian Church. Also **pa·tris′tics**.

pat·ro·nym·ic (patrənim′ik), *adj*. relating to or denoting a name derived from the father or ancestor in the male line.

pat·sy (pat′sē), *n*. (in slang usage) a scapegoat; a person blamed for something, often wrongfully.

pat·ten (pat′n), *n*. a wooden sole held on the foot by a leather strap and often raised from the ground on a metal ring so as to keep the wearer's foot clear of mud, puddles, etc.; any similar footwear designed for the same purpose.

pat·u·lous (pacн′ələs), *adj*. open; spreading, as a tree, etc.

pau·ci·ty (pô′sitē), *n*. smallness of number or of quality; insufficiency.

pav·o·nine (pav′ənīn), *adj*. relating to or resembling the peacock.

pawl (pôl), *n*. a short bar pivoted at one end to a support and engaging at the other end with a toothed wheel or bar so as to prevent recoil or to allow slight forward movement, as of a rope.

Pax Ro·ma·na (paks′ rōmä′nə), harsh peace terms imposed by a powerful nation on nations too weak to dispute them and against their will, esp. the peace enforced on its dominions by the Roman Empire.

pax vo·bis·cum (paks′ vōbis′kəm), *Latin*. peace be with you.

peace pipe, a calumet.

pe·an (pē′ən), *n*. See **paean**.

pearl·ized (pur′līzd), *adj*. made to look like mother-of-pearl.

peau de soie (pō′ də swä′), a smooth

heavy silk or rayon fabric with a soft texture and grained, dull satiny surface on both sides, used for dresses, coats, etc. See also **paduasoy, poult-de-soie.**

pebble dash, a finish to an exterior wall made of mortar into which small pebbles are pressed while it is still wet.

pec·ca·ble (pek′əbəl), *adj.* liable to sin, error, or fault.

pec·ca·dil·lo (pekədil′ō), *n., pl.* **pec·ca·dil·loes, pec·ca·dil·los.** a small sin; a minor fault or offense.

pec·cant (pek′ənt), *adj.* guilty of sin; erring morally.

pec·ca·vi (pekā′vē), *n., pl.* **pec·ca·vis.** a confession of having sinned or done wrong.

Peck·sniff·i·an (peksnif′ēən), *adj.* hypocritically professing to be benevolent or of high morals. [after Mr Pecksniff in Charles Dickens's *Martin Chuzzlewit*]

pec·ti·nate (pek′tənāt), *adj.* forming or having close-set toothlike projections; like a comb.

pec·tize (pek′tīz), *v.* to make or become set like a jelly; to gel.

pec·to·ral (pek′tərəl), *adj.* in, on, or relating to the chest.

pec·u·late (pek′yəlāt), *v.* to embezzle; to appropriate fraudulently money or property held or controlled on behalf of another. —**pec·u·la′tion,** *n.* —**pec·u·la′to·ry,** *adj.*

pe·cu·li·um (pikyōō′lēəm), *n.* a private or exclusive possession; private property.

ped·ant (ped′nt), *n.* **1.** one who shows off his knowledge excessively. **2.** one who adheres strictly to petty rules or details or to theoretical knowledge, ignoring common sense. —**pe·dan′ti·cism, ped′ant·ry,** *n.*

ped·ate (ped′āt), *adj.* having or resembling a foot or feet.

pe·dat·i·fid (pədat′əfid), *adj.* having palmate divisions with each division cleft to resemble toes, as a leaf; pedately divided.

pe·dat·i·lob·ate (pədat′əlō′bāt), *adj.* having palmate lobes with each lobe cleft to resemble toes, as a leaf; pedately lobed. Also **pe·dat′i·lobed.**

ped·er·ast, paed·er·ast (ped′ərast), *n.* a man who has sexual relations with another male, esp. with a boy.

ped·er·as·ty, paed·er·as·ty (ped′ərastē), *n.* sexual relations between two males, esp. between a man and a boy.

pe·des·tri·an (pədes′trēən), *adj.* unimaginative; ordinary; dull; prosaic.

pe·di·at·rics, pae·di·at·rics (pē′dēat′riks), *n. sing.* the study and treatment of the diseases of children. —**pe·di·a·tri′cian, pae·di·a·tri′cian, pe·di·at′rist, pae·di·at′rist,** *n.*

ped·i·cel (ped′isəl), *n.* a small, subordinate, stalk-like structure in a plant or animal. —**ped·i·cel′late,** *adj.*

ped·i·cle (ped′ikəl), *n.* a pedicel; a peduncle.

pe·dic·u·lar (pədik′yələr), *adj.* relating to lice.

pe·dic·u·li·cide (pədik′yəlisīd), *adj.* having the capacity to kill lice. Also **pe·dic·u·li·ci′dal.**

pe·dic·u·lo·sis (pədik′yəlō′sis), *n.* infestation with lice; the state of being lice-ridden. —**pe·dic′u·lous,** *adj.*

ped·i·form (ped′əfôrm), *adj.* having the form of a foot.

pe·do·bap·tism, pae·do·bap·tism (ped′ōbap′tizm), *n.* the act or practice of baptizing young children or infants. —**pe·do·bap′tist, pae·do·bap′tist,** *n.*

pe·do·don·tics (pēdədon′tiks), *n. sing.* the dental care and treatment of children's teeth. Also **pe·do·don′tia.** —**pe·do·don′tist,** *n.*

pe·do·phil·i·a (pēdəfil′ēə), *n.* sexual desire felt by an adult for a child.

pe·dun·cle (piduNG′kəl), *n.* a stalk, esp. a main supporting stalk, as of a flower, fungus, organ, etc. —**pe·dun′cu·late,** *adj.*

peign·oir (pānwär′), *n.* a loose dressing gown worn by women.

pej·o·ra·tion (pejərā′sHən), *n.* a worsening; a lowering of worth; depreciation. See also **melioration.**

pe·jo·ra·tive (pijôr′ətiv), *adj.* depreciatory; disparaging; making lower in worth or quality.

pel·age (pel′ij), *n.* the hair, fur, wool, or the like covering the skin of an animal.

pe·lag·ic (pəlaj′ik), *adj.* relating to the open sea or ocean.

pe·lec·y·pod (pəles′əpod), *n.* any bivalve mollusk, as the oyster, the mussel, etc.

pel·er·ine (pel′ərēn), *n.* a woman's fur or cloth close-fitting cape or tippet, usually waist-length in back and with long ends in front.

Pe·le's hair (pā′lāz), threads of glass solidified from ejected volcanic lava. [from Hawaiian *Pele*, goddess of Kilauea volcano]

Pele's tears, globules of volcanic glass solidified from ejected lava.

pe·lisse (pəles′), *n.* 1. a fur-lined or fur-trimmed knee-length coat or cloak for women. 2. an ankle-length, narrow woman's cloak with slit armholes.

pel·la·gra (pəlā′grə), *n.* a disease caused by the deficiency of nicotinic acid in the diet and leading to skin, digestive, and nervous disorders.

pel·li·cle (pel′ikəl), *n.* a thin skin or film; scum.

pel·lu·cid (pəlo͞o′sid), *adj.* transparent; translucent; clear to the sight or mind.

pel·oid (pel′oid), *n.* mud used in medical treatment.

pel·vis (pel′vis), *n.*, *pl.* **pel·vis·es, pel·ves** (pel′vēz). the bony girdle formed by the hip bones and sacrum.

pem·mi·can (pem′əkən), *n.* powdered dried meat mixed with fat and dried fruits and formed into a loaf or small cakes.

pen·chant (pen′CHənt), *n.* a leaning toward; an inclination; a strong liking.

pend·ent (pen′dnt), *adj.* hanging; suspended from above.

pe·ne·plain, pe·ne·plane (pē′nəplān), *n.* an area of land made almost level by erosion.

pen·e·tra·li·a (penətrā′lēə), *n. pl.* the innermost parts of a place or thing.

pen·e·trom·e·ter (pen′itrom′itər), *n.* an instrument to measure the power of penetration of x-rays and other types of radiation. Also **pen·e·tram′ e·ter, qualimeter.**

pen·i·cil (pen′isil), *n.* a small bristly tuft, as on a caterpillar.

pen·na (pen′ə), *n.*, *pl.* **pen·nae** (pen′ē). one of the stiff-shafted, firm-vaned feathers of a bird appearing on the surface of the plumage and giving the body, wings, and tail their characteristic shape; a contour feather.

pen·na·ceous (pənā′sHəs), *adj.* with the firm texture of a penna.

pen·nate (pen′āt), *adj.* having feathers or wings. Also **pen′nat·ed.**

pen·non (pen′ən), *n.* 1. a long, tapering or swallowtail flag; any flag or banner. 2. a bird's wing or the terminal part of it.

Penn·syl·va·ni·an (pensəlvā′nēən), *adj.* relating to or denoting a geological period within the Paleozoic era (but sometimes considered an epoch within the Carboniferous period), lasting from about 300,000,000 years ago to 270,000,000 years ago and characterized by warm climate, swamps, and the advent of large reptiles.

pen·sile (pen′sil), *adj.* 1. suspended, as some birds' nests. 2. that constructs a hanging nest, used of birds.

pen·ta·cle (pen′təkəl), *n.* See **pentagram.**

pen·tad (pen′tad), *n.* a group of five, as a five-year period; the number five.

pen·ta·dac·tyl (pentədak′təl), *adj.* with five digits to each hand or foot; with five fingerlike parts.

pen·ta·dec·a·gon (pentədek′əgon), *n.* a polygon with fifteen sides and containing fifteen angles.

pen·tag·o·noid (pentag′ənoid), *adj.* five-sided; pentagon-shaped.

pen·ta·gram (pen′təgram), *n.* a star with five points. Also called **pentacle.**

pen·ta·he·dron (pentəhē′drən), *n.*, *pl.* **pen·ta·he·drons, pen·ta·he·dra.** a five-faced solid.

pen·tam·er·ous (pentam′ərəs), *adj.* having or divided into five parts.

pen·tap·tych (pen′taptik), *n.* a work of art, as a painting, carving, etc., consisting of five panels hinged side by side, each bearing a part of the whole picture or bearing a separate picture. See also **diptych, polyptych, triptych.**

pen·tar·chy (pen′tärkē), *n.* government by a group of five people.

pen·to·bar·bi·tal (pentəbär′bital), *n.* a barbiturate drug used chiefly as a sedative and hypnotic.

pen·tose (pen′tōs), *n.* the name given to a group of sugars resembling glucose but having only five carbon atoms in the molecule.

pe·nul·ti·ma (pinul′təmə), *n.* the next to the last syllable of a word. Also **pe′nult.** See also **ultima.**

pe·nul·ti·mate (pinul′təmit), *adj.* last but for one; next to last.

pe·num·bra (pinum′brə), *n., pl.* **pe·num·brae** (pinum′brē), **pe·num·bras.** a partial shadow round an area of total shadow, as round the total shadow of the moon or earth or the sun during an eclipse.

pen·u·ry (pen′yərē), *n.* destitution; utter poverty; scarcity; lack. —**pe·nu′ri·ous,** *adj.*

pep·lum (pep′ləm), *n.* a short flounce attached to a garment round the waist and sometimes long enough to cover the hips.

pep·sin, pep·sine (pep′sin), *n.* a stomach enzyme that breaks down proteins, manufactured commercially to ferment cheese, for use in digestive aids, etc.

pep·tic (pep′tik), *adj.* relating to or aiding digestion.

per·ad·ven·ture (purədven′CHər), *n.* **1.** chance or possibility. **2.** a conjecture. —*adv.* **3.** maybe; perhaps. **4.** by chance or at random.

per·cale (pərkāl′), *n.* a plain- and close-woven, smooth, plain or printed cotton fabric.

per·ca·line (purkəlēn′), *n.* a light, shiny-surfaced cotton fabric, usually in a plain color and used for lining.

per cap·i·ta (pər kap′itə), by the person; for each; a method of dividing the estate of a person who leaves no will, whereby all related equally to the decedent receive equal shares. See also **per stirpes.**

per·cen·tile (pərsen′tīl), *n.* (statistics) one of the class of values of a variable that divides the total frequency of a sample or population into 100 equal parts. See also **quantile, quartile.**

per·cept (pur′sept), *n.* the result of, as distinct from the act of, perceiving; the thing perceived.

per·cip·i·ent (pərsip′ēənt), *adj.* in the act of perceiving; having powers of perception or insight.

per·cuss (pərkus′), *v.* to strike with resulting shaking or shock in the person or thing struck.

per·di·tion (pərdisH′ən), *n.* utter ruin of the spirit or soul; eternal damnation.

per·du, per·due (perdY′), *adj. French.* hidden; out of sight.

per·dur·a·ble (pərdŏŏr′əbəl), *adj.* permanently durable; everlasting.

per·dure (pərdŏŏr′), *v.* to last for ever; to endure permanently.

per·e·gri·nate (per′əgrənāt), *v.* to make a journey, esp. on foot. —**per·e·gri·na′tion,** *n.*

per·e·grine (per′əgrin), *adj.* from abroad; alien.

per·emp·to·ry (pəremp′tərē), *adj.* allowing no refusal or argument; dictatorial.

peremptory challenge, an objection to a juror that requires no cause to be shown.

per·fer·vid (pərfur′vid), *adj.* extremely ardent or intense.

per·fi·dy (pur′fidē), *n.* treachery; intentional breaking of faith. —**per·fid′i·ous,** *adj.*

per·func·to·ry (pərfuNGk′tərē), *adj.* performed as routine duty; done superficially or mechanically.

per·fuse (pərfyŏŏz′), *v.* to spread liquid, color, or the like over something. —**per·fu′sion,** *n.*

per·gel·i·sol (pərjel′isôl), *n.* permafrost.

per·go·la (pur′gələ), *n.* an arbor or covered walk of climbing plants growing on horizontal trelliswork held overhead on posts or columns.

per·i·anth (per′ēanth), *n.* the calyx and corolla of a flower.

per·i·apt (per′ēapt), *n.* a lucky charm for wearing on the person as a bracelet, etc.; an amulet.

per·i·ar·ter·i·tis (per′ēär′tərī′tis), *n.* inflammation around the outside of an artery.

pe·rib·o·los, pe·rib·o·lus (pərib′ələs), *n.*, *pl.* **pe·rib·o·loi** (pərib′əloi). a wall around sacred ground.

per·i·car·di·al (perəkär′dēəl), *adj.* relating to the pericardium. Also **per·i·car′di·ac.**

per·i·car·di·tis (per′əkärdī′tis), *n.* inflammation of the pericardium.

per·i·car·di·um (perəkär′dēəm), *n.*, *pl.* **per·i·car·di·a** (perikär′dēə). the thin membrane that encloses the heart.

per·i·carp (per′əkärp), *n.* the vessel containing a ripe seed, as a husk, nut, or berry.

per·i·chon·dri·um (perəkon′drēəm), *n.*, *pl.* **per·i·chon·dri·a** (perəkon′drēə). the membrane that covers cartilages, except at joints.

Per·i·cle·an (perəklē′ən), *adj.* of outstanding intellect, power, and wealth. [after Pericles, *c.* 490–429 B.C., the leader under whom Athens attained its highest power]

pe·ric·o·pe (pərik′əpē), *n.*, *pl.* **pe·ric·o·pes, pe·ric·o·pae** (pərik′əpē). a short, selected passage from a book.

per·i·gee (per′ijē), *n.* that point in the orbit of a planet or artificial satellite which is nearest the earth. See also **apogee.**

per·i·he·li·on (perəhē′lēən), *n.*, *pl.* **per·i·he·li·a** (perəhē′lēə). that point in the orbit of a heavenly body which is nearest the sun. See also **aphelion.**

per·i·o·don·tics (per′ēədon′tiks), *n. sing.* the branch of dentistry concerned with the surroundings of the teeth. Also **per·i·o·don′tia.**

per·i·o·don·tium (per′ēədon′sнəm), *n.*, *pl.* **per·i·o·don·tia** (per′ēədon′sнə). the gum, tissue, and bone surrounding and holding the teeth. Also **parodontium.**

per·i·o·nych·i·a (per′ēōnik′ēə), *n.* See **paronychia.**

per·i·o·nych·i·um (per′ēōnik′ēəm), *n.*, *pl.* **per·i·o·nych·i·a** (per′ēōnik′ēə). the tissue around a fingernail or toenail. Also **paronychium.**

per·i·o·tic (per′ēō′tik), *adj.* denoting, relating to, or near the bony capsule protecting the inner ear.

per·i·pa·tet·ic (per′əpətet′ik), *adj.* going from place to place; itinerant.

pe·riph·ra·sis (pərif′rəsis), *n.*, *pl.* **pe·riph·ra·ses** (pərif′rəsēz). roundabout speech or an instance of it. —**per·i·phras′tic,** *adj.*

per·i·stal·sis (perəstal′sis), *n.*, *pl.* **per·i·stal·ses** (perəstal′sēz). rhythmic contractions progressing in one direction along a muscular tube, as the intestine, and propelling the contents along it. —**per·i·stal′tic,** *adj.*

per·i·to·ne·um (per′ətənē′əm), *n.*, *pl.* **per·i·to·ne·ums, per·i·to·ne·a** (per′ətənē′ə). the serous membrane forming the lining of the abdomen and surrounding the viscera.

per·i·to·ni·tis (per′ətənī′tis), *n.* inflammation of a part of the peritoneum.

per·i·vis·cer·al (perəvis′ərəl), *adj.* around or near the viscera.

per·ma·frost (pur′məfrôst), *n.* the permanently frozen condition of soil, subsoil, and bedrock in arctic and subarctic regions. Also called **pergelisol.**

per·me·a·ble (pur′mēəbəl), *adj.* capable of being passed through or pervaded; allowing the passage of fluid.

per·me·ant (pur′mēənt), *adj.* penetrating throughout; pervading.

per·mute (pərmyo͞ot′), *v.* to alter, esp. a sequence. —**per·mu·ta′tion,** *n.* —**per·mu·ta′tion·al,** *adj.*

per·ni·cious (pərnisн′əs), *adj.* harmful; fatal.

per·o·rate (per′ərāt), *v.* to make a speech, often a lengthy one; to make a summing up at the end of a formal speech.

per·pend (pur′pənd), *n.* a large stone built into a wall so that it passes through the entire thickness. Also

parpen, per·pent. Also **through stone.**

per·qui·site (pur′kwizit), *n.* a casual profit or fee coming in addition to the regular revenue or income.

per·si·flage (pur′səfläzH), *n.* light banter.

per·so·na·li·a (pursənā′lēə), *n. pl.* personal effects; a person's belongings.

per·so·na non gra·ta (pərsō′nə nōn grä′tə), *pl.* **per·so·nae non gra·tae** (pərsō′nē nōn grä′tē). *Latin.* an unwelcome or unacceptable person.

per·spi·ca·cious (purspəkā′sHəs), *adj.* having keen insight; discerning. —**per·spi·cac′i·ty,** *n.*

per·spi·cu·i·ty (purspəkyōō′itē), *n.* clarity to the mind; lucidity of expression. —**per·spic′u·ous,** *adj.*

per stir·pes (pər stur′pēz), a method of dividing the estate of a deceased person, whereby if one of the legatees is already dead, his share shall pass to his children. See also **per capita.**

per·ti·na·cious (purtənā′sHəs), *adj.* holding firmly, as to an intention or opinion; obstinate. —**per·ti·nac′i·ty,** *n.*

per·vi·ca·cious (purvəkā′sHəs), *adj.* extremely stubborn; dogged.

per·vi·ous (pur′vēəs), *adj.* allowing entry or passage; accessible, as to reason, etc.

pet·al (pet′l), *n.* one of the ring of conspicuous, usually brightly colored parts of a flower immediately within the calyx and surrounding the reproductive organs.

pe·tard (pitärd′), *n.* a small explosive device, as one used formerly to breach a gate, etc.

pet·i·ole (pet′ēōl), *n.* **1.** the stalk attaching a leaf to a stem. **2.** a stalk-like structure in animals, as that joining the abdominal and thoracic segments of the wasp. —**pet′i·o·late,** *adj.*

pe·tit bour·geois (pətē′ bŏŏrzHwä′), *pl.* **pe·tits bour·geois** (pətē′ bŏŏrzHwä′). a member of the lower middle class.

pe·tite bour·geoi·sie (pətēt′ bŏŏrzHwäzē′), the section of the middle class with the least wealth and lowest social standing.

pe·tite mar·mite (pətēt′ mär′mīt), a thin meat and vegetable broth, usually served in its cooking pot.

pe·tit mal (pətē′ mal′), a mild form of epilepsy, in which only brief loss of consciousness occurs. See also **grand mal.**

pet·ro·glyph (pet′rəglif), *n.* a prehistoric or primitive carving or drawing on rock. Also **pet′ro·graph.**

pet·rous (pet′rəs), *adj.* rocky; hard as stone. Also **pe·tro′sal.**

pet·ti·fog (pet′ēfog), *v.* to operate a small, inferior, or rascally law practice.

pet·tish (pet′isH), *adj.* peevish; apt to sulk.

pet·u·lant (pecH′ələnt), *adj.* given to or exhibiting sudden irritability; peevish over trifles. —**pet′u·lance,** *n.*

pe·yo·te (pāō′tē), *n.* a cactus of the southwestern U.S. and Mexico, containing the narcotic drug mescaline.

phag·e·de·na, phag·e·dae·na (fa′-jidē′nə), *n.* an ulcer causing severe erosion.

phag·o·cyte (fag′əsīt), *n.* a colorless blood cell that engulfs and destroys foreign particles in the blood, as dead cells and bacteria.

phag·o·cy·tol·y·sis (fag′əsītol′isis), *n.* the destruction of phagocytes. Also **pha·gol′y·sis.**

phag·o·cy·to·sis (fag′əsītō′sis), *n.* the ingestion and destruction of foreign particles by phagocytes.

pha·lan·ge·al (fəlan′jēəl), *n.* relating to a phalanx or the phalanges.

pha·lanx (fā′laNGks), *n., pl.* **pha·lang·es** (fəlan′jēz). any bone in the fingers or toes. Also **phal′ange.**

phan·tasm, fan·tasm (fan′tazm), *n.* a ghost; an illusion; an illusive likeness or vision of something real. —**phan·tas′mal, phan·tas′mic,** *adj.*

phan·tas·ma·go·ri·a (fantaz′məgôr′-ēə), *n.* **1.** a shifting series of real or illusory figures and scenes, as in a dream. **2.** a dreamlike series of shifting, merging images produced by a magic lantern or the like.

phar·i·sa·ic (far′isā′ik), *adj*. observing the outward forms of religion or accepted behavior without sincerely believing in the spirit behind them; hypocritical. —**phar′i·sa·ism**, *n*.

phar·i·see (far′isē), *n*. a sanctimonious hypocrite; a self-righteous person.

phar·ma·col·o·gy (fär′məkol′əjē), *n*. the scientific study of the effects of chemical substances on the human body and esp. of the nature and action of those used as drugs to treat disease.

phar·ma·co·poe·ia (fär′məkəpē′ə), *n*. an officially published book listing drugs and giving detailed information on them, as their formulas, uses in medicine, and the like.

phar·ma·co·psy·cho·sis (fär′məkō-sīkō′sis), *n*. a psychosis resulting from taking a drug.

pha·ryn·ge·al (fərin′jēəl), *adj*. relating to or near the pharynx.

phar·yn·gec·to·my (far′injek′təmē), *n*. the surgical removal of a part or all of the pharynx.

phar·yn·gi·tis (far′injī′tis), *n*. inflammation of the pharynx.

phar·yn·gol·o·gy (far′iNGgol′əjē), *n*. the scientific study of the pharynx and diseases that affect it.

pha·ryn·go·scope (fəriNG′gəskōp), *n*. an apparatus used to carry out a medical examination of the pharynx.

phar·ynx (far′iNGks), *n*., *pl*. **phar·yn·ges** (fərin′jēz), **phar·ynx·es**. the cavity behind the nose and mouth and the muscle and membrane enclosing it, communicating with the nose, mouth, and, at the lower end, the larynx, and partially divided by the soft palate into the upper or nasal section and lower or oral section.

phe·no·bar·bi·tal (fē′nōbär′bital), *n*. a drug used chiefly as a sedative and hypnotic.

phe·nol·o·gy (finol′əjē), *n*. the scientific study of the part played by climate in annually recurring natural phenomena, as bird migration, flowering time in plants, etc.

phe·no·type (fē′nətīp), *n*. the sum of the characteristics exhibited by an organism resulting from the interaction of inherited genes and environment. See also **genotype.**

pher·o·mone (fer′əmōn), *n*. any of several hormonelike substances important in insect physiology, influencing the growth and behavior of individuals and acting from one individual to another, and thus thought to be an integrating factor among social insects.

phi·lan·der (filan′dər), *v*. (of a man) to flirt, court, or make love merely for amusement with no serious intention.

phi·lip·pic (filip′ik), *n*. a speech denouncing a person or thing with bitter invective.

phi·lis·tine (phil′istēn), *n*. an uncultured person; a person of commonplace interests.

phi·log·y·ny (filoj′ənē), *n*. love of women; liking for women.

phi·lol·o·gy (filol′əjē), *n*. the study of written records to establish their meaning, authenticity, etc.

phil·o·pro·gen·i·tive (fil′ōprōjen′-itiv), *adj*. bearing many offspring; relating to or having typically a love of one's own or any children.

phi·los·o·phas·ter (filos′əfas′tər), *n*. a pretender to knowledge of philosophy; a person with superficial knowledge of philosophy.

phil·ter, phil·tre (fil′tər), *n*. a love potion; any magic potion.

phil·trum (fil′trəm), *n*., *pl*. **phil·tra** (fil′trə). the hollow running down from the septum dividing the nostrils to the upper lip.

phle·bi·tis (fləbī′tis), *n*. inflammation of the veins.

phleb·o·scle·ro·sis (fleb′ōsklirō′sis), *n*. thickening or hardening of the walls of veins.

phleb·o·throm·bo·sis (fleb′ōthrom-bō′sis), *n*. the condition of having a blood clot in a vein, but without inflammation of the wall of the vein. See also **thrombophlebitis.**

phleb·o·tome (fleb′ətōm), *n*. a surgical instrument for cutting open a vein.

phle·bot·o·my (fləbot′əmē), *n*. the cutting open of a vein for blood-letting, a medical treatment no longer used. —**phleb·o·tom′ic**, *adj.* —**phle·bot′o·mist**, *n.* —**phle·bot′o·mize**, *v.*

phleg·mat·ic (flegmat′ik), *adj.* not easily roused to act or to feel emotion; sluggish.

pho·bi·a (fō′bēə), *n.* an abnormally excessive fear; an irrationally obsessive aversion or dread.

pho·cine (fō′sīn), *adj.* relating to seals, esp. the earless or hair seals.

phon (fon), *n.* a unit used in measuring the apparent loudness of a noise, being, for a given sound, equal in number to the decibel intensity of a pure note at a frequency of 1000 cycles per second which has been adjusted until in the opinion of a group of listeners the two sounds are equally loud.

pho·net·ics (fənet′iks), *n. sing.* the scientific study of the sounds of spoken language, including their production, classification, transcription, etc.

pho·ni·at·rics (fō′nēat′riks), *n. sing.* the study and treatment of disorders affecting the voice. Also **pho·ni′a·try.**

phon·ics (fon′iks), *n. sing.* a method of teaching reading and writing through phonetics.

phos·phate (fos′fāt), *n.* a salt or ester of phosphoric acid; an ingredient of some detergents that is not biodegradable and hence causes pollution.

phos·pho·res·cence (fosfəres′əns), *n.* the property of shining after exposure to light or other radiation. See also **fluorescence.** —**phos·pho·res′cent,** *adj.*

phot (fot, fōt), *n.* a unit used in measuring illumination, equal to one lumen per square centimeter.

pho·tics (fō′tiks), *n. sing.* the scientific study of light. —**pho′tic,** *adj.*

pho·tism (fō′tizm), *n.* a form of synesthesia in which a visual sensation is produced by a stimulus to a different sense, as hearing, touch, etc.

pho·to·bath·ic (fōtəba*th*′ik), *adj.* relating to that layer of the sea that sunlight can penetrate.

pho·to·bi·ot·ic (fō′tōbīot′ik), *adj.* requiring light to live or thrive.

pho·to·chem·is·try (fō′tōkem′istrē),

n. the scientific study of the chemical effects of light.

pho·to·com·pose (fō′tōkəmpōz′), *v.* to use a photocomposer. —**pho·to·com·po·si′tion,** *n.*

pho·to·com·po·ser (fō′tōkəmpō′zər), *n.* a machine that uses photographic techniques to set up type for printing.

pho·to·gram·me·try (fōtəgram′itrē), *n.* the process of mapping and surveying by means of photography.

pho·to·he·li·o·graph (fōtəhē′lēəgraf), *n.* a camera combined with a modified telescope, used for taking photographs of the sun. Also **heliograph.**

pho·to·ki·ne·sis (fō′tōkinē′sis), *n.* movement of a cell or organism in response to the stimulus of light and varying according to the intensity of the stimulus.

pho·tol·y·sis (fōtol′isis), *n.* the breakdown of substances due to the presence of light.

pho·to·mac·ro·graph (fōtəmak′rəgraf), *n.* a photograph taken through a microscope capable of only low magnification.

pho·tom·e·ter (fōtom′itər), *n.* an optical instrument used to measure light intensity, flux, color, etc., by comparing light from one source with light from another source of which the characteristics are standardized.

pho·tom·e·try (fōtom′itrē), *n.* the measuring of light intensities; the scientific study, as analysis, comparison, etc., of light intensities. —**pho·to·met′ric,** *adj.*

pho·to·mi·cro·graph (fōtəmī′krəgraf), *n.* a microphotograph.

pho·to·mul·ti·pli·er (fōtəmul′təplīər), *n.* a device for greatly amplifying light and other radiation.

pho·ton (fō′ton), *n.* a light quantum; the smallest indivisible quantity of light or other radiant energy; the elementary particle by which such energy is transmitted from a source. See also **quantum.**

pho·top·a·thy (fōtop′əthē), *n.* **1.** the movement of a cell or organism in response to the stimulus of light and usually away from it. **2.** a disease caused by excessive amounts of light.

pho·to·pe·ri·od·ism (fōtəpēr'ēədizm), *n.* the response of plants and animals to the relative length of day and night. Also **pho·to·pe·ri·o·dic'i·ty.**

pho·toph·i·lous (fōtof'ələs), *adj.* thriving in light, esp. strong light.

pho·to·pho·bi·a (fōtəfō'bēə), *n.* an abnormally excessive fear of light.

pho·to·pi·a (fōtō'pēə), *n.* normal, full vision in bright daylight. See also **scotopia.**

pho·to·sphere (fō'təsfēr), *n.* the shallow layer of ionized gases forming the visible surface of the sun.

pho·to·syn·the·sis (fōtəsin'thisis), *n.* the forming of organic compounds using light energy, esp. the forming in plants of carbohydrates from carbon dioxide and water under the stimulus of light and with chlorophyll acting as a catalyst.

pho·to·tax·is (fōtətak'sis), *n.* the movement of a cell or organism in response to light and orientated in relation to the direction of the light. Also **pho'to·tax·y.**

pho·to·the·od·o·lite (fō'tōthēod'-əlīt), *n.* an instrument for tracking and filming a rocket or missile in flight. See also **the·od'o·lite.**

pho·to·ther·a·peu·tics (fō'təther'ə-pyōo'tiks), *n. sing.* the study and use of light rays to treat disease.

pho·to·ther·a·py (fōtəther'əpē), *n.* the treating of disease by light rays.

pho·to·ther·mic (fōtəthur'mik), *adj.* **1.** relating to heat produced by light. **2.** relating to both light and heat.

pho·to·troph (fō'tətrof), *n.* a microorganism for which light is the energy source.

pho·to·trop·ic (fōtətrop'ik), *adj.* exhibiting phototropism.

pho·tot·ro·pism (fōtot'rəpizm), *n.* growth or tendency of an organism, as a plant or sedentary animal, in response to light and orientated according to the direction of the light.

pho·to·vol·ta·ic cell (fō'tōvoltā'ik),

an electric cell generating electromotive force through the action of electromagnetic radiation on the junction of two dissimilar materials, which causes a potential difference to be developed between them.

pho·tu·ri·a (fōto͞or'ēə), *n.* a medical disorder in which phosphorescent urine is passed.

phra·try (frā'trē), *n.* a grouping of social units, as clans, within a tribe.

phren·o·gas·tric (fren'ōgas'trik), *adj.* relating to both the diaphragm and the stomach.

phre·nol·o·gy (frinol'əjē), *n.* the study of the external contours of an individual's skull as a supposed indication of his mental capabilities and character.

phro·ne·sis (frōnē'sis), *n.* wisdom in deciding aims and the ways of achieving them.

phthis·ic (tiz'ik), *n.* **1.** a disease causing wasting away of the lungs; phthisis. —*adj.* **2.** relating to or characterized by phthisis.

phthi·sis (*thī'*sis), *n.* consumption; pulmonary tuberculosis. —**phthis'i·cal,** *adj.*

phy·col·o·gy (fīkol'əjē), *n.* the scientific study of algae.

phy·let·ic (fīlet'ik), *adj.* relating to race, species, tribe, or clan; relating to the development or history of such a group.

phyl·loid (fil'oid), *adj.* resembling a leaf.

phy·log·e·ny (filoj'ənē), *n.* the history of the development of a race or of a plant or animal type. Also **phy·lo·gen'e·sis.** See also **ontogeny.**

phy·lum (fī'ləm), *n., pl.* **phy·la** (fī'lə). the first division in biological classification of animals, each consisting of one or more related classes.

phy·ma (fī'mə), *n., pl.* **phy·mas, phy·ma·ta** (fī'mətə). a small skin tumor; a nodule of the skin.

phys·i·at·rics (fiz'ēat'riks), *n. sing.* **1.** the diagnosis and treatment of medical disorders by physical means, as manipulation, massage, application of heat, etc. **2.** physiotherapy.

phys·i·at·rist (fiz ′ēat′rist), *n.* a doctor who specializes in physiatrics.

physical anthropology, the scientific study of the evolution and biology of man and closely related species.

physical chemistry, the scientific study, description, and interpretation physical and chemical properties of substances.

physical geography, the scientific study, description, and interpretation of the natural features and phenomena of the earth's surface, as land forms, climate, vegetation, etc.

physical science, the scientific study of natural phenomena except those relating to living things, as physics, astronomy, etc.

phys·i·og·no·my (fiz ′ēog′nəmē), *n.* 1. the face, esp. regarded as a reflection of character. 2. Also called **anthroposcopy.** the art of reading a person's character from his bodily, esp. facial, features.

phys·i·og·ra·phy (fiz ′ēog′rəfē), *n.* physical geography.

phys·i·ol·o·gy (fiz ′ēol′əjē), *n.* the scientific study of the parts and normal functioning of living things. Also called **bionomy.** —**phys·i·o·log′i·cal,** *adj.*

phys·i·om·e·try (fiz ′ēom′itrē), *n.* the science of measuring the human body's physiological functions.

phys·i·o·path·ol·o·gy (fiz ′ēəpəthol′əjē), *n.* the scientific study of abnormalities occurring in physiological functions as a result of disease.

phys·i·o·ther·a·py (fiz ′ēəther′əpē), *n.* the treatment of medical disorders by physical means only, as exercise, massage, heat, etc., rather than by drugs.

phy·sis (fī′sis), *n., pl.* **phy·ses** (fī′sēz). (in Greek philosophy) the single fundamental reality underlying and unifying the seeming diversity of nature and the material from which all objects stem with individual variation in properties or forms to differentiate them; the principle of growth or development in nature; that which develops or results.

phy·to·bi·ol·o·gy (fī ′tōbīol′əjē), *n.* the scientific study of plants; botany.

phy·to·cide (fī′təsīd), *n.* a chemical agent for killing plants.

phy·to·cli·ma·tol·o·gy (fī ′tōklī′mətol′əjē), *n.* the study of the local climatic conditions in which individual plants and plant communities live.

phy·to·coe·no·sis (fī ′tōsēnō′sis), *n., pl.* **phy·to·coe·no·ses** (fī ′tōsēnō′sēz). the entire plant life of any given area.

phy·to·gen·e·sis (fī ′tōjen′isis), *n.* the origin and evolution of plants. Also **phy·tog′e·ny.** —**phy·to·gen′ic,** *adj.*

phy·to·ge·og·ra·phy (fī ′tōjēog′rəfē), *n.* plant geography; the scientific study of the range and distribution of plants over the globe, on land and in water, both as biological units such as families, species, etc., and as communities such as forest plants, grassland plants, etc., and the summation of results by descriptive analysis and in tables and maps.

phy·tog·ra·phy (fītog′rəfē), *n.* the scientific description of plants; descriptive botany.

phy·to·hor·mone (fītəhôr′mōn), *n.* any hormone present in plants.

phy·to·pa·thol·o·gy (fī ′tōpəthol′əjē), *n.* the scientific study of plant diseases; plant pathology.

phy·toph·a·gous (fītof′əgəs), *adj.* plant-eating; herbivorous.

phy·to·plank·ton (fītəplaNGk′tn), *n.* the plant organisms of plankton. See also **zooplankton.**

phy·to·plasm (fī′təplazm), *n.* plant protoplasm.

phy·to·so·ci·ol·o·gy (fī ′tōsō ′sēol′əjē), *n.* the study of the relationships of plant communities with their environment and of relationships between plants in a community; the ecology of plant communities.

phy·to·suc·civ·o·rous (fī ′tōsəksiv′ərəs), *adj.* feeding on the sap of plants, as some insects.

phy·to·tox·in (fītətok′sin), *n.* any poison produced by a plant. —**phy·to·tox′ic,** *adj.*

pi·ac·u·lar (pīak′yələr), *adj.* amending for sin or wrong; expiatory.

pi·a ma·ter (pī'ə mā'tər), the inner-most of the three delicate coverings protecting the brain and spinal cord. See also **dura mater, arachnoid.**

pi·a·nism (pē'ənizm), *n.* the technical and artistic skill of a pianist.

pi·broch (pē'brokн), *n.* a dirge or military piece played on the bagpipe.

pi·ca (pī'kə), *n.* an abnormal desire to eat something not usually considered as food, as soil, chalk, etc.

pi·ca·dor (pik'ədôr), *n., pl.* **pi·ca·dors.** a mounted assistant to a mata-dor who goads the bull in the earlier stages of a bullfight and weakens it by putting lances in its shoulder mus-cles.

pic·a·resque (pikəresk'), *adj.* rog-uish; relating the adventures of a lik-able rogue, as a novel.

pic·a·yune (pik'eyoon'), *adj.* of small amount or importance; paltry.

pic·e·ous (pis'ēəs), *adj.* relating to or like pitch; inflammable.

Pick·wick·i·an (pikwik'ēən), *adj.* un-usual or strange, either by design or by accident, esp. relating to the use of words. [after Charles Dickens's char-acter Mr. Pickwick in *The Pickwick Papers*]

pi·co·cu·rie (pī'kəkyoorē), *n.* a unit of radioactivity equal to one trillionth of a curie. *Abbrev.:* **pCi, pc.**

pi·co·far·ad (pī'kōfar'əd), *n.* a unit of electrical capacity equal to a micro-farad. *Abbrev.:* **pF, pf.**

pi·co·me·ter (pī'kōmē'tər), *n.* a unit of length in the metric system, equal to a micromicron.

pi·co·sec·ond (pī'kōsek'ənd), *n.* a unit of time equal to one trillionth of a second. *Abbrev.:* **psec.**

pi·cot (pē'kō), *n.* one of a row of small loops of twisted thread used to deco-rate embroidery, a ribbon edge, etc.

pi·co·watt (pē'kəwot), *n.* a unit of electric power equal to one trillionth of a watt. *Abbrev.:* **pW, pw.**

pic·ric acid (pik'rik), a bitter, poison-ous acid used principally as an ex-plosive.

pic·to·graph (pik'təgraf), *n.* **1.** a writ-ten record using stylized pictorial symbols to stand for the thing depic-ted, as in some primitive writing, a pictorial graph. **2.** a pictorial symbol. —**pic·tog'ra·phy,** *n.*

pie·bald (pī'bôld), *adj.* **1.** with irregu-lar patches of different colors, esp. black and white. **2.** an animal, esp. a horse, with such coloring.

pièce de ré·sis·tance (pēes' də rizē-stäns'), *pl.* **pièces de ré·sis·tance** (pēes' də rizēstäns'). *French.* **1.** the most important dish or course of a meal. **2.** the most important item, as in a series of events, achievements, etc.

pied-à-terre (pyädater'),*n.,pl.* **pieds-à-terre** (pyädater'). *French.* a dwell-ing for staying in for short periods, as an apartment for overnight stays in a city.

Pi·er·rette (pēəret'), *n.* the female equivalent of and companion of a Pierrot.

Pi·er·rot (pēərō'), *n.* a male character in French pantomime, with whitened face and loose white costume.

pi·e·tism (pī'itizm), *n.* fervent reli-gious devotion; exaggeratedly pious feeling or behavior.

pi·e·ty (pī'itē), *n.* a dutifully reverent attitude to God; an earnest and de-vout fulfillment of religious obliga-tions.

pi·e·zo·e·lec·tric·i·ty (pīē'zōilek-tris'itē), *n.* electricity generated by pressure on certain nonconducting asymetric crystals, as quartz.

pi·e·zom·e·ter (pī'izom'itər), *n.* any of various kinds of instrument for measuring the pressure of a fluid or the compression caused by a fluid in another substance.

pi·e·zom·e·try (pī'izom'itrē), *n.* the measurement of pressure or of capa-city for being compressed.

pig·gin (pig'in), *n.* a wooden pail of which the handle is formed by a con-tinuation of one of its staves.

pi·gno·li·a (pēnyō'lēə), *n.* the edible seed contained in cones of the south-ern European nut pine.

pi·las·ter (pilas'tər), *n.* a rectangularly sectioned projection running up a wall and made in imitation of a column.

pile (pīl), *n.* the lower of the two dies used in minting coins by hand. See also **trussell.**

pi·le·at·ed (pī'lēātid), *adj.* having a feathered crest, as the American woodpecker.

pi·lif·er·ous (pīlif'ərəs), *adj.* with hair; bearing or producing hair.

pil·i·form (pil'əfôrm), *adj.* like hair or a hair.

pi·lose (pī'lōs), *adj.* with a covering of hair or fur. Also **pi'lous.**

pil·u·lar (pil'yələr), *adj.* relating to or like a pill or pills.

pil·ule (pil'yōōl), *n.* a small pill.

pi·lus (pī'ləs), *n.*, *pl.* **pi·li** (pī'lī). a hair; a structure resembling a hair.

Pi·ma cotton (pē'mə), a kind of Egyptian cotton, used for shirts, ties, etc.

pim·o·la (pimō'lə), *n.* a stuffed olive, usually one stuffed with sweet red pepper.

pinch·beck (pincH'bek), *n.* something which is not genuine; a counterfeit; a sham.

pin·e·al (pin'ēəl), *adj.* having the shape of a pine cone.

pineal body, a small conical glandular body situated in the midbrain of all vertebrates with a cranium and of unknown function but thought to secrete a hormone and perhaps to represent a vestigial sense organ.

pin·guid (piNG'gwid), *adj.* oily; fat. —**pin·guid'i·ty,** *n.*

pin·ion (pin'yən), *n.* **1.** the terminal segment of a bird's wing. —*v.* **2.** to remove the pinions of or bind a bird's wings to prevent the bird from flying.

pin·na (pin'ə), *n.*, *pl.* **pin·nae** (pin'ē), **pin·nas.** a feather; a wing; a part resembling a wing.

pin·nate (pin'āt), *adj.* arranged or made like a feather with similar parts ranged along both sides of a central axis, as the leaf of an ash tree. —**pin·na'tion,** *n.*

pin·nat·i·ped (pinat'əped), *adj.* of birds with a membranous flap along each side of each toe.

pin·nat·i·sect (pinat'isekt), *adj.* divided in pinnate form, usually of a leaf.

pin·ni·grade (pin'əgrād), *adj.* using flippers or fin-like structures to effect movement, as seals.

pin·ni·ped (pin'əped), *adj.* belonging to the aquatic suborder of carnivores that includes the seals and walruses.

pin·nu·la (pin'yələ), *n.*, *pl.* **pin·nu·lae** (pin'yəlē). a pinnule.

pin·nule (pin'yōōl), *n.* a part or organ resembling a small wing, as a fin, the barb of a feather, etc. —**pin'nu·late,** *adj.*

pin·tle (pin'tl), *n.* a kind of pin on which something, as a rudder, hinge, etc., turns.

pinx·it (piNGk'sit), *Latin.* (he or she) painted it: formerly used after the artist's name in his signature to a painting, engraving, etc.

pi·pette (pīpet'), *n.* a glass tube, often graduated and used mainly in chemistry for taking up, usually by being sucked like a drinking straw, small quantities of liquid for transferring to another vessel.

pi·quant (pē'kənt), *adj.* with a pleasantly sharp or spicy flavor.

pique (pēk), *v.* to cause resentful irritation or a wound to a person's pride.

pi·rosh·ki (pirôsH'kē), *n. pl.* a Russian dish consisting of small pies or turnovers made of yeast dough or puff pastry with a sweet or savory filling. Also **pi·ro·gen** (pirō'gən).

pis al·ler (pē zalā'), *French.* the final resort; a makeshift; a course followed because of the lack of any better one.

pis·ca·tor (piskā'tər), *n.* a fisherman.

pis·ca·to·ry (pis'kətôrē), *adj.* relating to fishermen or fishing; depending on or addicted to fishing. Also **pis·ca·to'ri·al.**

pis·ci·cul·ture (pis'ikulcHər), *n.* the farming of fish; the rearing of fish in artificial conditions.

pis·ci·form (pis'əfôrm), *adj.* fish-shaped.

pis·cine (pis'īn), *adj.* relating to or like a fish or fishes.

pis·civ·o·rous (pisiv'ərəs), *adj.* living on fish; fish-eating.

pisiform

pi·si·form (pī′səfôrm), *adj.* pea-shaped.

pis·mire (pis′mīr), *n.* an ant.

pis·til (pis′til), *n.* See **gynoecium**.

pis·tol·o·gy (pistol′əjē), *n.* a branch of theology, concerned with faith.

pitch (piCH), *v.* to deviate from a stable course because of oscillation about the vertical axis. See also **yaw**.

pit·tance (pit′əns), *n.* an inadequate salary, wage, or living allowance.

pi·tu·i·tar·y gland (pitoo′iterē), a small ductless endocrine gland at the base of the brain, which secretes hormones which regulate many functions of the body, as growth and hormone production in other endocrine glands, as the thyroid, the gonads, etc. Also **hypophysis**.

pit·u·ri (piCH′ərē), *n.* a small Australian tree whose leaves and twigs contain nicotine and are dried by the aborigines to use as a narcotic.

pit·y·roid (pit′əroid), *adj.* scaly; bran-like.

pix·i·lat·ed (pik′səlātid), *adj.* amusingly prankish; eccentric; crazy.

plac·age (plak′ij), *n.* a thin outer layer of material put on the front of a building for decoration or protection and different from the building material it covers.

pla·ce·bo (pləsē′bō), *n.*, *pl.* **pla·ce·bos, pla·ce·boes.** a substance having no pharmacological effect but given as a medicine either to a patient who insists he needs one or to people acting as the control in an experiment where another group is given a drug that is being tested.

pla·cen·ta (pləsen′tə), *n.* a structure formed of fetal and maternal tissues, attached to the wall of the uterus, developing with the fetus which is attached to it by the umbilical cord, and acting as a channel through which the fetus is given nourishment and freed of its waste products until parturition, when it is expelled after the fetus. —**pla·cen′tal**, *adj.*

plack·et (plak′it), *n.* an opening at the top of a skirt or in another garment to make it easier to put on and take off.

plac·oid (plak′oid), *adj.* plate-shaped.

pla·ga (plā′gə), *n.*, *pl.* **pla·gae** (plā′jē). a stripe, streak, or spot of color. —**pla′gate**, *adj.*

pla·gia·rism (plā′jərizm), *n.* the taking and using of another's writings, ideas, inventions, etc., and passing off of them as one's own. —**pla′gia·rize**, *v.* —**pla′gia·ry**, *n.*

pla·gi·o·trop·ic (plā′jēətrop′ik), *adj.* relating to, denoting, or showing growth in a direction away from the vertical to a greater or lesser degree. —**pla·gi·ot′ro·pism**, *n.*

plain text, a message transcribed from code or cipher. Also **clear text.** See also **cryptography.**

plain·tiff (plān′tif), *n.* the party who brings a suit in a court of law.

plain·tive (plān′tiv), *adj.* expressing sorrowfulness; mournful.

pla·nate (plā′nāt), *adj.* having a level or plane surface; flat-topped.

pla·na·tion (plānā′sHən), *n.* the leveling of a surface by erosion.

planch, planche (planCH), *n.* a tray for use in an enameling oven, as one of stone or metal.

plan·e·tes·i·mal (plan′ites′iməl), *n.* one of those innumerable minute bodies which originally revolved around the sun and gradually joined to form the solar system, according to one theory of the origin of the universe.

plan·et·oid (plan′itoid), *n.* an asteroid; one of the many thousands of minor planets in the solar system, mostly in the region between Mars and Jupiter.

plan·e·tol·o·gy (plan′itol′əjē), *n.* the scientific study of the physical features of the planets.

plan·gent (plan′jənt), *adj.* having a loud, vibrating, lamenting sound, with a wave-like beat or surge.

pla·ni·form (plā′nəfôrm), *adj.* of flattened form.

pla·nim·e·ter (plənim′itər), *n.* a mechanical device for measuring the area of irregular plane figures.

pla·nim·e·try (plənim′itrē), *n.* the measurement of plane surfaces.

plan·ish (plan′isH), *v.* to flatten out to a smooth finish by hammering or passing through rollers, as sheet metal, paper, etc.

plan·i·sphere (plan′isfēr), *n.* a device for showing that part of a map of the celestial sphere which is visible at a given time and place; projection or other representation on a plane of a sphere or a part of one.

plank·ter (plaNGk′tər), *n.* any organism in plankton.

plank·ton (plaNGk′tən), *n.* all of the mostly minute, drifting or floating organisms in the sea or a stretch of fresh water. See also **phytoplankton, zooplankton.**

pla·no-con·cave (plā′nōkon′kāv), *adj.* relating to or denoting a lens with one side flat and the other concave.

pla·no-con·vex (plā′nōkon′veks), *adj.* relating to or denoting a lens with one side flat and the other convex.

pla·no·graph (plā′nəgraf), *v.* to print from a flat surface, directly or by offset. —**pla·nog′ra·phy,** *n.*

plan·tar (plan′tər), *adj.* relating to the sole of the foot.

plan·ti·grade (plan′təgrād), *adj.* that uses the whole underside of the foot when walking, as man, bears, etc.

plaque (plak), *n.* **1.** an ornamental tablet of metal or the like fixed on a wall or set into a piece of wood. **2.** the mixture of bacteria and saliva that accumulates in a jelly-like deposit on the teeth. **3.** a small flat mass, mark, or spot on the skin or other part of the body.

pla·quette (plaket′), *n.* a small metal panel with a design in relief, often set into the cover of books made in France in the 15th and 16th centuries.

plas·ma (plaz′mə), *n.* **1.** the clear liquid part of blood or lymph in which the other parts are suspended. **2.** a highly ionized gas with nearly equal numbers of positive and negative charges. Also **plasm.**

plas·ma·pher·e·sis, plas·ma·phaer·e·sis (plazməfer′isis), *n., pl.* **plas·ma·pher·e·ses** (plazməfer′isēz). a medical procedure for obtaining blood plasma by centrifuging blood to separate out the corpuscles which can then be returned to the bloodstream of the donor. Also **plas·ma·phor′e·sis.**

plas·mo·di·um (plazmō′dēəm), *n., pl.* **plas·mo·di·a** (plazmō′dēə). any parasitic protozoon that causes malaria in man.

plas·mo·ma (plazmō′mə), *n., pl.* **plas·mo·mas, plas·mo·ma·ta** (plazmō′mətə). a tumor consisting of plasma cells.

plastic bomb, a putty-like, sticky mixture of explosives used as a bomb chiefly by guerrilla fighters and terrorists.

plas·ti·queur (plastēkoōr′), *n., pl.* **plas·ti·queurs** (plastēkoōr′), *French.* someone who makes or uses plastic bombs.

plas·tom·e·ter (plastom′itər), *n.* a device used to measure the plasticity of a substance.

plate·let (plāt′lit), *n.* a small, oval or round body resembling a plate, esp. such a body in blood.

plat·i·tude (plat′itoōd), *n.* a commonplace, dull remark, esp. one delivered as if it were original or significant. —**plat·i·tu′di·nous,** *adj.* —**plat·i·tu′di·nous·ly,** *adv.*

Pla·ton·ic (pləton′ik), *adj.* **1.** relating to or typical of Plato or his philosophy. **2.** (*usually lower case*) free from sensual desire, as *platonic love.*

Platonic year, the time required for a complete revolution of the equinoxes, about 26,000 years. See also **precession of the equinoxes.**

plat·yr·rhine (plat′irīn), *adj.* having a broad flat nose in which the nostrils point forward and are divided by a wide septum.

pleas·ance (plez′əns), *n.* a place arranged as a pleasure garden or promenade.

ple·be·ian (pləbē′ən), *adj.* relating to or belonging to the common people; common; coarse.

pledg·et (plej′it), *n.* a small wad of lint, absorbent cotton, etc., for putting on a cut, etc.

plein air (plān′ er′), the open air; broad daylight out of doors.

plei·o·tax·y (plī′ətaksē), n. an increase in the usual number of parts, as may occur in a plant. Also **plei·o·tax′is.**

Pleis·to·cene (plī′stəsēn), adj. relating to or denoting the geological epoch immediately preceding the present epoch, forming the earlier part of the Quaternary, originating about one million years ago, and characterized by the Ice Ages and the evolution of early man.

ple·na·ry (plē′nərē), adj. **1.** full; complete; absolute; not subject to limitation, as *plenary pardon.* **2.** fully constituted; with all members present, as *a plenary assembly.*

ple·nip·o·tent (plənip′ətnt), adj. having full powers.

plen·i·po·ten·ti·ar·y (plen′ēpəten′-sнēer′ē), n. a person invested with full powers to act on behalf of another, as an ambassador on behalf of his sovereign.

plen·i·tude (plen′itood), n. fullness; sufficiency; abundance.

ple·o·mor·phism (plēəmôr′fizm), n. the state or condition of being polymorphous; polymorphism. Also **ple′o·mor·phy.**

ples·sor (ples′ər), n. See **plexor.**

pleth·o·ra (pleth′ərə), n. an excess; glut; superabundance. —**ple·thor′ic,** adj.

pleu·ra (ploor′ə), n., pl. **pleu·rae** (ploor′ē). a serous membrane surrounding each lung in mammals and lining the thorax.

pleu·ri·sy (ploor′isē), n. inflammation of the pleura, sometimes with liquid forming between the lung and the thorax.

pleu·ro·dy·ni·a (ploorədī′nēə), n. pain affecting the chest or side.

pleu·ro·pneu·mo·ni·a (ploor′onoo-mō′nēə), n. pleurisy and pneumonia combined.

plex·i·form (plek′səfôrm), adj. relating to or like a plexus; intricate.

plex·or (plek′sər), n. a small hammer used by doctors to strike or tap for diagnostic purposes. Also **plessor.**

plex·us (plek′səs), n., pl. **plex·us·es, plex·us.** a network, as of nerve fibers or blood vessels. —**plex′al,** adj.

pli·cate (plī′kāt), adj. folded; pleated like a fan. Also **pli′cat·ed.** —**pli·ca′tion,** n.

Pli·o·cene (plī′əsēn), adj. relating to or denoting a geological epoch, the last of the Tertiary period, lasting from ten million years ago to one million years ago and characterized by a cooling climate, the formation of mountains, and the advent of larger mammals such as the mastodon.

ploy (ploi), n. a maneuver or trick to gain an advantage.

plu·mate (ploo′māt), adj. like a feather; feathered, as a bristle from which small hairs grow.

plum·ba·go (plumbā′gō), n., pl. **plum·ba·gos.** graphite, a form of carbon used for pencil leads, as a solid lubricant, etc.

plum·be·ous (plum′bēəs), adj. containing lead; lead-like, esp. in color.

plum·bif·er·ous (plumbif′ərəs), adj. lead-bearing; containing or yielding lead.

plu·mose (ploo′mōs), adj. with or like feathers or plumes.

plu·mu·la·ceous (ploomyəlā′sнəs), adj. having a downy texture.

plu·mule (ploom′yool), n. a down feather.

plu·mu·lose (ploom′yəlōs), adj. with the shape of a down feather or a bud inside a plant embryo.

plu·ral·ism (ploor′əlizm), n. a philosophical theory that there is more than one basic substance or ultimate principle. See also **dualism, monism.**

plu·toc·ra·cy (plootok′rəsē), n. rule by the wealthy; the power of wealth. —**plu′to·crat,** n. —**plu·to·crat′ic,** adj.

Plu·to·ni·an (plootō′nēən), adj. relating to or like Pluto or his kingdom of the lower world; infernal. Also **Plu·ton′ic.**

plu·vi·al (ploo′vēəl), adj. relating to rain; rainy.

plu·vi·om·e·ter (ploo′vēom′itər), n.

a rain gauge; an instrument for measuring rainfall.

plu·vi·ous (plōo′vēəs), *adj.* rainy; relating to rain.

pneu·drau·lic (nōodrô′lik), *adj.* relating to a mechanical device using both pneumatic and hydraulic action.

pneu·ma (nōo′mə), *n.* the soul; the essential spirit.

pneu·mat·ics (nōomat′iks), *n. sing.* the science of the mechanical properties of elastic fluids, as air and other gases. Also **pneu·mo·dy·nam′ics.** —**pneu·mat′ic,** *adj.*

pneu·ma·tol·o·gy (nōomətol′əjē), *n.* the theological teaching or belief that beings have a spirit or soul.

pneu·ma·tom·e·ter (nōomətom′-itər), *n.* a device used to measure the quantity of air breathed in or out at a single breath, or the force of a single breath in or out.

pneu·ma·to·ther·a·py (nōo′mətō-ther′əpē), *n.* the treatment of disease by compressed or rarefied air.

pneu·mo·coc·cus (nōoməkok′əs), *n., pl.* **pneu·mo·coc·ci** (nōoməkok′sī). the bacterium which causes lobar pneumonia, and is also associated with meningitis, pericarditis, etc.

pneu·mo·co·ni·o·sis (nōo′məkō′nē-ō′sis), *n.* a group of diseases in which there is progressive lung damage resulting from the inhalation of abrasive dust during industrial procedures, as silicosis in stonecutters and coalminers. Also **pneu·mo·no·co·ni·o′sis, pneu·mo·no·ko·ni·o′sis.**

pneu·mo·graph (nōo′məgraf), *n.* a device used in medicine to make a graphic record of the movements of the thorax during breathing. Also **pneu′ma·to·graph.**

pneu·mog·ra·phy (nōomog′rəfē), *n.* the recording of chest movements during breathing.

pneu·mon·ic (nōomon′ik), *adj.* relating to the lungs.

pneu·mo·no·ul·tra·mi·cro·scop·ic·sil·i·co·vol·ca·no·co·ni·o·sis, pneu·mo·no·ul·tra·mi·cro·scop·ic·sil·i·co·vol·ca·no·ko·ni·o·sis (nōo′mənoul′trəmī′krəskop′iksil′-əkō′volkā′nōkō′nēō′sis), *n.* a lung disease resulting from inhaling very fine particles of siliceous dust.

pneu·mo·tho·rax (nōoməthôr′aks), *n.* the presence of air or another gas between the pleura surrounding the lung and that lining the thorax, an abnormal condition in this pleural cavity causing displacement and sometimes collapse of a lung.

pocket veto, a veto on a bill resulting from the President's failure to sign it within ten days of the adjournment of Congress.

po·co·cu·ran·te (pō′kōkŏoran′tē), *n., pl.* **po·co·cu·ran·ti** (pō′kōkŏoran′tē). someone who is careless, or shows little concern or interest.

poc·u·li·form (pok′yələfôrm), *adj.* with the shape of a cup.

po·dag·ra (pōdag′rə), *n.* gout, esp. affecting the feet.

po·dal·gi·a (pōdal′jə), *n.* pain affecting the foot. Also **pod·o·dyn′i·a.**

po·dal·ic (pōdal′ik), *adj.* relating to the foot or feet.

po·di·a·try (pōdī′ətrē), *n.* the study and treatment of foot disorders.

pod·sol (pod′sol), *n.* an infertile, very acid forest soil with an ashy-gray top layer from which basic salts, as iron, aluminum, etc., have been leached into the well-defined brownish lower layer, found across northern N. America, Europe, and Asia. Also **pod′zol.**

po·et·as·ter (pō′itastər), *n.* a writer of inferior verse.

pog·a·mog·gan (pogəmog′ən), *n.* a wooden club with a knob at the head, used by the Algonquins and other American Indian peoples.

po·grom (pəgrum′), *n.* an organized massacre, esp. of Jews, originally in Russia and Poland.

poi (poi, pō′ē), *n.* a Hawaiian dish of baked taro root pounded and fermented.

poign·ant (poin′yənt), *adj.* affecting sharply, esp. the mind or emotions.

poi·ki·lo·ther·mal (poi′kəlōthur′-məl), *adj.* with body temperature varying with that of its surroundings; cold-blooded.

poin·tel, poin·tal (poin′tl), *n.* a mosaic pavement of abstract design.

point·til·lism (pwan′təlizm), *n.* a technique of the Neo-Impressionist painters to reproduce the effects of light in a scientific way by juxtaposing spots of primary colors, which merge to give the correct color impression at a distance.

poise (pwäz), *n.* a unit used in measuring viscosity, equal to the viscosity of a fluid which requires a force of one centimeter per square centimeter to maintain a difference of one centimeter per second in velocity between two parallel planes one centimeter apart in the fluid and lying in the direction of flow. *Abbrev.:* **P, p.** [named after the French physician Poiseuille (1799–1869)]

po·lar·im·e·ter (pōlərim′itər), *n.* a device for measuring the quantity of polarized light in light from a particular source.

po·lar·i·scope (pōlar′iskōp), *n.* a device for measuring or exhibiting the properties of polarized light, for studying the effects of various agencies on light of known polarization, and for inspecting substances under polarized light.

po·lar·i·za·tion (pō′lərizā′sHən), *n.* **1.** a state in which light rays or other radiations have all the vibrations of one type in the same plane; the production of such a state. **2.** the giving of unity and direction, as to a project. —**po′lar·ize,** *v.*

po·lem·ics (pəlem′iks), *n. sing.* the art of controversial discussion. —**po·lem′ic,** *adj.* —**pol′e·mist, po·lem′i·cist,** *n.*

pol·i·clin·ic (pol′ēklin′ik), *n.* the outpatients' department of a hospital.

po·li·o·en·ceph·a·li·tis (pō′lēōensef′əlī′tis), *n.* an acute virus infection causing inflammation of the gray matter in the brain. Also **po·li·en·ceph·a·li′tis.**

po·li·o·en·ceph·a·lo·my·e·li·tis (pō′lēōensef′əlōmī′əlī′tis), *n.* an acute virus infection causing inflammation of the gray matter of the brain and spinal cord. Also **po·li·en·ceph·a·lo·my·e·li′tis.**

po·li·o·my·e·li·tis (pō′lēōmī′əlī′tis), *n.* an acute virus infection causing inflammation of the gray matter of the spinal cord, sometimes leading to permanent paralysis and deformity. Also called **po′li·o,** infantile paralysis.

Polish sausage. See **kielbasa.**

pol·i·tesse (pol′ites′), *n.* politeness; refined or courteous behavior.

pol·i·tic (pol′itik), *adj.* sagacious; expedient; scheming; political.

pol·i·ty (pol′itē), *n.* any given system of civil government, as civil, ecclesiastical, etc.

pol·lard (pol′ərd), *n.* a tree whose top has been cut off so as to produce a close round head of young shoots.

pollen count, the amount of pollen in the atmosphere, usually given as the average number of pollen grains collecting in a given time on slides in the open air.

pol·lex (pol′eks), *n., pl.* **pol·li·ces** (pol′isēz). the thumb or the corresponding digit in certain other vertebrates, as mammals and amphibians.

pol·li·ce ver·so (pol′isē vur′sō), *Latin.* thumbs down; with thumbs turned down to indicate failure, as ancient Romans asking for a gladiator to be put to death after a poor performance in a combat.

pol·lic·i·ta·tion (pəlis′itā′sHən), *n.* an offer made by one party to a lawsuit but not yet accepted by the other.

pol·ter·geist (pōl′tərgīst), *n.* a noisy ghost or other spirit supposed to show its presence by breaking crockery, banging doors, etc.

pol·troon (poltrōōn′), *n.* a coward. —**pol·troon′er·y,** *n.*

pol·y·an·dry (pol′ēən′drē), *n.* the practice or fact of a woman's having more than one husband at a time. See also **monandry; polygamy, monogamy, bigamy.** —**pol·y·an′drist,** *n.* —**pol·y·an′drous,** *adj.*

pol·y·ar·chy (pol′ēär′kē), *n.* a government by a group of people, usually more than three.

pol·y·ar·tic·u·lar (pol′ēärtik′yələr), *adj.* relating to several joints.

pol·y·chro·mat·ic (pol′ēkrōmat′ik), *adj.* many-colored. Also **pol·y·chro′mic**.

pol·y·chrome (pol′ēkrōm), *adj.* consisting of or decorated with many colors. —**pol′y·chro·my,** *n.*

pol·y·cy·the·mi·a, pol·y·cy·thae·mi·a (pol′ēsīthē′mēə), *n.* a blood disorder in which red blood cells are present in abnormally large numbers.

pol·y·dac·tyl (pol′ēdak′tl), *adj.* with several or many digits.

pol·y·dae·mon·ism, pol·y·de·mon·ism (pol′ēdē′mənizm), *n.* belief in the existence and power of many devils or evil spirits.

pol·y·dip·si·a (pol′ēdip′sēə), *n.* abnormally excessive thirst.

po·lyd·o·mous (pəlid′əməs), *adj.* living as a colony but inhabiting more than one nest, as certain colonies of ants. See also **monodomous.**

pol·y·don·tia (pol′ēdon′SHə), *n.* the condition of having more teeth than is usual.

pol·y·eth·nic (pol′ēeth′nik), *adj.* relating to, consisting of, or inhabited by a people or group of many ethnic origins.

po·lyg·a·my (pəlig′əmē), *n.* the practice or fact of having more than two marriage partners at the same time. See also **bigamy, monogamy; polyandry, monandry.** —**po·lyg′a·mist,** *n.* —**po·lyg′a·mous,** *adj.*

po·lyg·e·nism (pəlij′ənizm), *n.* the theory that man is descended from more than one ancestral type.

pol·y·glot (pol′ēglot), *adj.* multilingual; knowing or consisting of several languages.

pol·y·gon (pol′ēgon), *n.* a figure with more, often many more, than four sides and usually in one plane.

pol·y·graph (pol′ēgraf), *n.* a lie detector.

po·lyg·y·ny (pəlij′ənē), *n.* the practice or fact of having more than one wife at the same time. See also **monogyny.** —**po·lyg′y·nist,** *n.* —**po·lyg′y·nous,** *adj.*

pol·y·he·dron (pol′ēhē′drən), *n., pl.* **pol·y·he·drons, pol·y·he·dra** (pol′-ēhē′drə). a many-sided solid, usually one with more than six faces. —**pol·y·he′dral,** *adj.*

pol·y·his·tor (pol′ēhis′tər), *n.* a person learned in a variety of subjects; a great scholar. Also **pol·y·his·tor′i·an.**

pol·y·math (pol′ēmath), *n.* a master of many subjects.

pol·y·mor·phism (pol′ēmôr′fizm), *n.* the condition or fact or being polymorphous.

pol·y·mor·phous (pol′ēmôr′fəs), *adj.* occurring in any of a number of varied forms, as a species of butterfly some individuals of which mimic other species in their coloring.

po·ly·no·mi·al (pol′ēnō′mēəl), *adj.* having several or many names.

pol·y·nu·cle·ar (pol′ēnōō′klēər), *adj.* with several or many nuclei. Also **pol·y·nu′cle·ate.**

pol·y·pet·al·ous (pol′ēpet′ələs), *adj.* many-petaled; having more than one petal; with petals separated from one another.

pol·y·pha·gi·a (pol′ēfā′jēə), *n.* an abnormally excessive desire for food; the habit of feeding on a wide variety of foods.

pol·y·phon·ic (pol′ēfon′ik), *adj.* having more than one sound or voice, as music, a letter of the alphabet, etc. —**pol′y·phone, po·lyph′o·ny,** *n.*

pol·y·phy·let·ic (pol′ēfīlet′ik), *adj.* having been descended from quite different ancestors but now classified biologically in the same phylum.

pol·y·ploid (pol′ēploid), *adj.* with three or more times the haploid number of chromosomes.

pol·yp·ne·a, pol·yp·noe·a (pol′-ipnē′ə), *n.* panting; rapid breathing.

pol·yp·tych (pol′iptik), *n.* a painting or carving consisting of several panels hinged side by side, each bearing a part of the whole picture or bearing a separate picture. See also **diptych, pentaptych, triptych.**

pol·y·rhythm (pol′ēriTHəm), *n.* the use of several different rhythms at the same time in a musical composition.

pol·y·se·my (pŏl'ēsē'mē), *n*. a variety of meanings or senses. —**po·lys'e·mous**, *adj*.

pol·y·sper·mi·a (pol'ēspur'mēə), *n*. the abnormally excessive production of semen.

pol·y·style (pol'ēstīl), *adj*. having many pillars or columns.

pol·y·sty·rene (pol'ēstī'rēn), *n*. a stiff plastic foam, used for insulating and packing.

pol·y·syl·lab·ic (pol'ēsilab'ik), *adj*. of words having three or more syllables; of a written piece or a language characterized by having many such words. Also **pol·y·syl·lab'i·cal.**

pol·y·tech·nic (pol'ētek'nik), *adj*. relating to or devoted to scientific, technical, and industrial subjects.

pol·y·the·ism (pol'ēthēizm), *n*. the doctrine or belief that there is more than one god.

po·lyt·o·my (pəlit'əmē), *n*. the dividing of something into three or more parts.

pol·y·un·sat·u·rat·ed (pol'ēunsaCH'ərātid), *adj*. relating to or denoting a class of fats, as corn oil, cottonseed oil, etc., whose molecules contain many double bonds unsaturated by hydrogen atoms, a feature associated with a low production of cholesterol in the blood.

pol·y·u·ri·a (pol'ēyo͞or'ēə), *n*. the abnormally excessive formation of urine, as in diabetes, etc.

pom·ace (pum'is), *n*. the pulp remaining when fruit has been crushed and the juice pressed out, as apple pulp after cider-making.

po·ma·ceous (pōmā'sHəs), *adj*. relating to or like apples.

po·man·der (pō'mandər), *n*. a mixture of sweet-smelling substances, as herbs, petals, etc., in a bag, decorative metal case, etc., formerly carried by someone in front of himself to ward off infection.

pom·e·lo (pom'əlō), *n., pl.* **pom·e·los.** 1. a grapefruit. 2. See **shaddock.**

po·mi·cul·ture (pō'məkulcHər), *n*. fruit-growing; the raising and tending of fruit crops.

po·mif·er·ous (pōmif'ərəs), *adj*. bearing fruits of or similar to the apple family.

po·mol·o·gy (pōmol'əjē), *n*. the science of fruit-growing.

ponce (pons), *n*. (in slang usage) a pimp.

pon·ceau (ponsō'), *n*. a bright orange-red color.

pon·gee (ponjē'), *n*. a soft Chinese or Japanese fabric of wild silk in the natural tan color and of uneven weave. See also **shantung, tussah.**

pon·iard (pon'yərd), *n*. a slender dagger.

po·no·graph (pō'nəgraf), *n*. a medical instrument for making a graphic record of fatigue.

pon·tif·i·cate (pontif'əkāt), *v*. to speak pompously; to act or speak as if infallible.

pont·lev·is (pontlev'is), *n*. a drawbridge; a bridge hinged at one end or in the middle so that it can be drawn up to permit tall shipping to pass beneath or to prevent anyone from crossing.

Pop Art, a style of the 1960's in the fine arts, esp. painting, characteristically using very large images usually from commercial art sources, as comics, advertisements, food wrappings, etc.

pop·in·jay (pop'injā), *n*. a vain, showy, foppish, empty-headed person.

pop·lit·e·al (poplit'ēəl), *adj*. relating to the back of the knee.

pop·ple (pop'əl), *v*. to tumble about; to move irregularly to and fro, as water below a waterfall or when boiling.

por·cine (pôr'sīn), *adj*. relating to or resembling swine; hog-like.

po·rif·er·ous (pôrif'ərəs), *adj*. having pores.

po·ri·form (pôr'əfôrm), *adj*. pore-shaped.

pork barrel, (in slang usage) government money, legislation, or policy promoting local improvements whereby the local member of the legislature hopes to win votes and influence.

por·rect (pərekt′), *adj.* stretching out horizontally.

por·ta·tive (pôr′tətiv), *adj.* portable; capable of or relating to carrying.

porte-co·chere, porte-co·chère (pôrt′kōsHer′), *n.* an entrance for carriages leading through the house to a courtyard; a porch to shelter people stepping into or out of carriages.

por·tend (pôrtend′), *v.* to foreshadow; to give warning of. —**por′tent,** *n.* —**por·ten′tous,** *adj.*

por·ti·co (pôr′təkō), *n., pl.* **por·ti·coes, por·ti·cos.** an imposing porch consisting of a roof supported by columns.

por·tiere, por·tière (pôrtyer′), *n.* a curtain hung over a door or instead of a door.

port·man·teau (pôrtman′tō), *n., pl.* **port·man·teaus, port·man·teaux** (pôrtman′tōz). a suitcase or traveling trunk, esp. one hinged along the back to open into two halves.

po·seur (pōzur′), *n.* a person who affects ideas, a style of living, etc., to impress other people.

pos·i·grade rocket (poz′əgrād), a rocket, in a missile with several stages, which fires in the direction of flight, as to cause the stages which are to continue to draw away from stages no longer required.

pos·it (poz′it), *v.* to put in place; to assume as fact or truth.

po·sol·o·gy (pəsol′əjē), *n.* the branch of pharmacology concerned with finding out what amount of a drug should be prescribed.

pos·set (pos′it), *n.* a drink made of sweetened hot milk curdled with ale, wine, etc., and usually flavored with spices.

post-bel·lum (pōstbel′əm), *adj.* postwar, esp. after the American Civil War.

post·di·lu·vi·an (pōst′dilōō′vēən), *adj.* in or of the period after the Flood. See also **antediluvian.**

pos·ter·i·ad (postēr′ēad), *adv.* toward the posterior of a living creature.

pos·te·ri·or (postēr′ēər), *adj.* at the rear or hind end. See also **anterior.**

pos·tern (pō′stərn), *n.* a back or side entrance; a private door or gate.

post hoc, er·go prop·ter hoc (pōst hōk′ er′gō prop′tər hōk′), *Latin.* it happened after this, therefore it happened because of this; a phrase to point up the error in logic of confusing sequence with consequence.

pos·tiche (postēsH′), *adj.* relating to an ornament added to a work, as of sculpture, already finished, esp. a superfluous or unsuitable ornament; artificial; false.

pos·ti·cous (postī′kəs), *adj.* posterior; esp., of flowers, relating to the part nearest the main axis.

pos·til·ion, pos·til·lion (postil′yən), *n.* the man who rides the horse on the left of the pair, or on the left of the leading pair where four or more are used, drawing a carriage.

post·or·bit·al (postôr′bitl), *adj.* lying behind the eye socket.

post par·tum (pär′təm), relating to or denoting the period of time immediately following childbirth. Also **post·par′tal.** See also **ante partum.**

post·pran·di·al (postpran′dēəl), *adj.* after-dinner; after a meal.

pos·tre·mo·gen·i·ture (postrē′mōjen′icHər), *n.* the right of inheritance or succession by the last-born son. Also called **ultimogeniture.** See also **primogeniture.**

pos·trorse (pos′trôrs), *adj.* turned or bent backward.

pos·tu·lant (pos′cHələnt), *n.* **1.** a person demanding or applying for something. **2.** a candidate, esp. for admission into a religious order.

pos·tu·late (pos′cHəlāt), *v.* **1.** to ask for or demand. **2.** to assume without proof. **3.** to assume a fact or principle as a basis for discussion. **4.** to lay down as indisputable.

po·ta·ble (pō′təbəl), *adj.* fit to drink; in a drinkable form.

po·tage (pôtazH′), *n. French.* soup.

po·tam·ic (pōtam′ik), *adj.* relating to rivers.

po·ta·tion (pōtā′sHən), *n.* drinking, esp. the drinking of alcoholic beverages; a drink, usually alcoholic.

po·ta·to·ry (pō'tətôrē), *adj.* relating to drinking; habitually taking strong drink.

pot-au-feu (pôtōfōō'), *n.* a French dish consisting of stewed meat and vegetables with the broth from them served separately.

po·ten·ti·ate (pəten'sнēāt), *v.* to endow with the power or ability to do something; to make more effective; to make possible.

po·ten·ti·om·e·ter (pəten'sнēom'-itər), *n.* an instrument for making accurate measurements of electromotive force or differences in electrical potential by balancing that to be measured against that produced by a current of known voltage.

poth·er (potн'ər), *n.* commotion; agitation; fuss.

pot·latch (pot'lacн), *n.* a festival among American Indian peoples of the N. Pacific coast, with great display of wealth, as by lavish presentation of gifts and competition to outdo all others in destroying one's own belongings to show that one can afford it.

pot liquor, pot-liquor, the liquid in which meat or vegetables have been cooked and containing flavorsome juices from them.

po·tom·e·ter (pətom'itər), *n.* a device for measuring the amount of water lost by a plant through transpiration, consisting of a vessel holding a known quantity of water and entirely sealed around the emerging plant so that moisture can leave only through the plant.

pot·pour·ri (pō'pōōrē'), *n., pl.* **pot·pour·ris** (pō'pōōrēz'). **1.** a mixture of dried petals, spices, and essential oils, kept in a dish or pierced container for their fragrance. **2.** a medley of musical or literary pieces; any mixture of unrelated items.

pot·sherd (pot'sнərd), *n.* a broken piece of earthenware, usually one of archaeological interest.

pou·lard, pou·larde (pōōlärd'), *n.* a hen spayed to make it more fleshy, tender, and tasty for the table; a fat hen.

poult (pōlt), *n.* a young fowl or game-bird.

poult-de-soie (pōōdəswä'), *n.* a strong, finely corded silk fabric used for dresses. See also **paduasoy, peau de soie.**

poul·tice (pōl'tis), *n.* **1.** a paste of breadcrumbs, starch, meal, linseed oil, herbs, etc., usually spread between layers of muslin and applied to the skin to soothe inflammation, etc. —*v.* **2.** to apply a poultice.

pour·boire (pōōrbwar'), *n., pl.* **pour·boires** (pōōrbwar'), *French.* a tip; a gratuity.

prac·ti·cum (prak'təkəm), *n.* that part of a course of study spent on practical work.

prae·cip·i·ta·ti·o (prēsip'itā'sнēō), *n.* rain, hail, or snow that reaches the earth's surface. See also **virga.**

prae·di·al, pre·di·al (prē'dēəl), *adj.* relating to land that is owned or farmed and to its products; attached to the land, as slaves.

prag·mat·ic (pragmat'ik), *adj.* relating to the practical aspect of any matter. Also **prag·mat'i·cal. —prag'ma·tism, prag'ma·tist,** *n.*

pran·di·al (pran'dēəl), *adj.* relating to dinner or to any meal.

prate (prāt), *v.* to talk too much; to keep up a stream of meaningless chatter.

pra·tique (pratēk'), *n.* a certificate showing that a ship presents no health hazard and therefore permitting it to use a particular port.

prat·tle (prat'l), *v.* to talk in a childish manner; to utter foolish chatter.

prax·is (prak'sis), *n., pl.* **prax·is·es, prax·es** (prak'sēz). the practical application of theory, knowledge, or skill.

Pre·cam·bri·an (prēkam'brēən), *adj.* relating to or denoting the earliest era of geological time, lasting from about 4,500,000,000 years ago to 600,000,000 years ago and characterized by the formation of the earth's crust and supposedly by the appearance of the first forms of life although no fossils remain.

prec·a·to·ry (prek′ətôrē), *adj.* relating to or expressing a request or entreaty; supplicatory. Also **prec′a·tive.**

pre·cent (prisent′), *v.* to perform the duties of a precentor.

pre·cen·tor (prisen′tər), *n.* a person appointed to lead the singing in church.

pre·cept (prē′sept), *n.* a command giving a rule of conduct or action; an instruction or exhortation as to morals or behavior. —**pre·cep′tive,** *adj.* —**pre·cep′tor,** *n.*

pre·ces·sion (prēsesн′ən), *n.* the motion of a rotation axis when a torque disturbs it so that it describes a cone, as the spindle of a spinning top.

precession of the equinoxes, the slow change in the direction of the earth's axis, due to gravitational forces, so that the celestial North Pole describes a circle once in 26,000 years and in consequence the equinoxes describe a circle round the ecliptic during the same period. See also **Platonic year.**

pré·cieuse (prā′sēo͞oz′), *n., pl.* **pré·cieus·es** (prā′sēo͞oz′iz). **1.** one of the women who frequented the literary salons of 17th-century Paris and aimed at or affected a refined delicacy of language and taste, usually carried to ridiculous extremes. **2.** any woman with an affected manner, esp. in speech.

pré·cieux (prā′sēo͞o′), *adj.* (of a man) too fastidious; affected.

pre·ci·os·i·ty (presн′ēos′itē), *n.* an affected refinement; excessive fastidiousness, esp. in the use of language.

pre·cip·i·tant (prisip′itnt), *adj.* hurried; rushing or falling headlong; rash; abrupt.

pre·cip·i·tate (prisip′itit), *adj.* headlong.

pre·cip·i·tous (prisip′itəs), *adj.* extremely steep; like a precipice.

pré·cis (prāsē′), *n., pl.* **pré·cis.** a summary.

pre·ci·sian (prisizн′ən), *n.* a person who strictly observes rules or accepted forms of behavior.

pre·ci·sive (prisī′siv), *adj.* cutting off, separating, or defining one person or thing from another or others.

pre·clude (priklo͞od′), *v.* to prevent or exclude from.

pre·co·cial (prikō′sнəl), *adj.* relating to or denoting birds which at the time of hatching are covered with down and able to move about freely.

pre·co·cious (prikō′sнəs), *adj.* forward or premature in development, esp. of the mind or faculties. —**pre·coc′i·ty,** *n.*

pre·cog·ni·tion (prē′kognisн′ən), *n.* knowledge of an event or state before it comes about.

pre·co·nize (prē′kənīz), *v.* **1.** to proclaim, announce, or extol in public. **2.** to summon by name; to call upon publicly.

pre·con·scious (prēkon′sнəs), *adj.* not in the conscious mind but capable of being readily made conscious, as of ideas, memories, etc.

pre·cur·sor (prikur′sər), *n.* a forerunner; someone or something preceding another, as in office, a building, etc. —**pre·cur′so·ry,** *adj.*

pre·da·cious, pre·da·ceous (pridā′-sнəs), *adj.* predatory; grasping; extortionate.

pre·da·tion (pridā′sнən), *n.* the act of preying upon or plundering.

pred·a·tor (pred′ətər), *n.* a person or animal living by or habitually preying upon others. —**pred′a·to·ry,** *adj.*

pre·di·al (prē′dēəl), *adj.* See **praedial.**

pred·i·ca·ble (pred′əkəbəl), *adj.* that can be stated as true or asserted.

pred·i·cant (pred′əkənt), *adj.* **1.** preaching. —*n.* **2.** a preacher.

pred·i·cate (pred′əkāt), *v.* to state as true; to assert as a fact; to proclaim or declare.

pre·di·lec·tion (predəlek′sнən), *n.* a liking or preference for; a partiality to.

pre·dis·pose (prē′dispōz′), *v.* to make liable to or inclined to. —**pre·dis·po·si′tion,** *n.*

pre·dor·mi·tion (prē′dôrmisн′ən), *n.* the period of semiconsciousness before sleep.

pre·em·i·nent, pre-em·i·nent, pre·ëm·i·nent (prēem′ənənt), *adj.* distinguished beyond or excelling all others. —**pre·em′i·nence, pre-em′i·nence, pre·ëm′i·nence,** *n.*

preen gland. See **uropygial gland.**

pre·for·ma·tion (prē′fôrmā′sHən), *n.* the theory held formerly that a complete individual is contained in the germ and grows to normal size during the embryonic period. See also **epigenesis.**

pre·hen·sile (prihen′sil), *adj.* adapted for or capable of grasping something or wrapping around something, as a hand, a monkey's tail, etc. —**pre·hen′sion,** *n.*

pre·pos·sess (prēpəzes′), *v.* to prejudice, usually favorably; to impress favorably beforehand or immediately. —**pre·pos·ses′sion,** *n.*

pre·pos·sess·ing (prēpəzes′iNG), *adj.* arousing a favorable impression.

pre·po·tent (prēpō′tnt), *adj.* powerful above all others; predominant.

pre·pran·di·al (prēpran′dēəl), *adj.* before dinner; before a meal.

pre·rog·a·tive (prirog′ətiv), *n.* a right or privilege exclusive to a particular person, group, office, rank, etc.

pres·age (pres′ij), *v.* **1.** to give or have a forewarning of. **2.** to forecast; to make a prediction. —*n.* **3.** an augury; a portent or forewarning.

pres·by·cu·sis (prezbəkyōō′sis), *n.* deterioration of hearing caused by old age. Also **pres·by·cou′sis, pres·by·a·cu′sia, pres·by·a·cou′sia.**

pres·by·o·pi·a (prez′bēō′pēə), *n.* deterioration of vision with old age due to the inability to alter the focal length of the lens, with consequent difficulty in seeing near objects. —**pres′by·ope,** *n.*

pre·sci·ence (prē′sHēəns), *n.* foreknowledge; foresight.

pre·sid·i·o (prisid′ēō), *n., pl.* **pre·sid·i·os.** a garrisoned fort or post.

pre·sid·i·um (prisid′ēəm), *n.* a permanent committee, esp. in communist organizations, exercising the full powers of the parent assembly when this is in recess.

pres·ti·dig·i·ta·tion (pres′tidij′itā′-sHən), *n.* conjuring; legerdemain.

pre·ter·hu·man (prētərhyōō′mən), *adj.* beyond what is human; more than human.

pret·er·i·tion (pretərisH′ən), *n.* disregard; omission; an act of omission.

pre·ter·mit (prētərmit′), *v.* **1.** to disregard; to leave undone. **2.** to suspend or discontinue for a time.

pre·ter·nat·u·ral (prētərnacH′ərəl), *adj.* beyond what is normal; supernatural.

pre·var·i·cate (privar′əkāt), *v.* to make evasive or deliberately misleading statements. —**pre·var′i·ca·tor,** *n.*

pre·ven·ient (privēn′yənt), *adj.* occurring before; previous; anticipating.

price-earnings ratio, the ratio between the market price of a share and its earnings.

price index. See **consumer price index.**

prie-dieu (prē′dyōō′), *n., pl.* **prie-dieus, prie-dieux** (prē′dyōōz′). a piece of furniture for kneeling on during prayer, resembling a chair with a rest for a book at the top and a low seat for kneeling on.

prig (prig), *n.* a self-righteous person exaggeratedly proper in conduct, fussy about minor details, and demanding similar behavior from others. —**prig′gish,** *adj.*

pri·ma·cy (prī′məsē), *n.* the state of being above all others, as in rank, authority, etc.

pri·ma don·na (prē′mə don′ə), *pl.* **pri·ma don·nas, pri·me don·ne** (prē′me don′e). **1.** the principal singer, as in an operatic company. **2.** a temperamental and difficult person.

pri·ma fa·ci·e (prī′mə fā′sHēē), apparent; self-evident.

pri·me·val, pri·mae·val (prīmē′vəl), *adj.* relating to, belonging to, or as if belonging to the first age of the world. as *primeval forests, primeval instincts.*

pri·mi·ge·ni·al (prī′mijē′nēəl), *adj.* primitive; primordial. Also **pri·mo·ge′ni·al.**

pri·mip·a·ra (prīmip′ərə), *n., pl.* **pri·**

mip·a·rae (prīmip′ərē). a woman who has given birth only once or is giving birth for the first time.

pri·mo·gen·i·tor (prīməjen′itər), *n.* the earliest ancestor; an ancestor.

pri·mo·gen·i·ture (prīməjen′iСНər), *n.* **1.** the right of inheritance or succession by the first-born son. See also **postremogeniture. 2.** the state or fact of being the first-born of the children of the same parents.

pri·mor·di·al (prīmôr′dēəl), *adj.* relating to, existing in or since the beginning; original; initial; primitive.

pri·mor·di·um (prīmôr′dēəm), *n., pl.* **pri·mor·di·a** (prīmôr′dēə). the earliest recognizable stage of an organ during its development.

principal plane, a plane at right angles to the axis of a lens, mirror, or the like, and at which rays parallel to the axis start to converge and rays diverging from a focal point become parallel to the axis.

prin·ci·pate (prin′səpāt), *n.* supreme authority or office.

prin·cip·i·um (prinsip′ēəm), *n., pl.* **prin·cip·i·a** (prinsip′ēə). a principle.

prin·ta·nier (praNtanyā′), *adj.* served with a garnish of diced spring vegetables. Also **prin·ta·nière** (praNtanyer′).

print-out (print′out′), *n.* the printed material put out by a computer, usually on a continuous roll of paper.

pris·tine (pris′tēn), *adj.* relating to early or the earliest time; retaining its original form or purity.

priv·a·tive (priv′ətiv), *adj.* denoting or marked by the absence, lack, or taking away of something; causing deprivation.

priv·y (priv′ē), *adj.* sharing private or secret knowledge; private; confidential. —**priv′i·ly,** *adv.* —**priv′i·ty,** *n.*

prix fixe (prē′ fiks′), *pl.* **prix fixes** (prē′fiks′). a set price for a meal chosen from a restaurant's menu.

prob·a·bil·i·ty (probəbil′itē), *n.* (in statistics) the likelihood of something occurring measured by the ratio of actual occurrences to the total of possible occurrences.

pro·ba·tive (prō′bətiv), *adj.* acting or designed as a test; giving proof. Also **pro′ba·to·ry.**

pro·bi·ty (prō′bitē), *n.* honesty; incorruptibility.

pro bo·no pu·bli·co (prō bō′nō pub′likō), *Latin.* for the public good; for the benefit of the public.

pro·bos·ci·date (prōbos′idāt), *adj.* having a proboscis.

pro·bos·cid·e·an (prōbəsid′ēən), *adj.* **1.** relating to or like a proboscis. **2.** having a proboscis.

pro·bos·cid·i·form (prōbəsid′əfôrm), *adj.* proboscis-shaped.

pro·bos·cis (prōbos′is), *n., pl.* **pro·bos·cis·es, pro·bos·ci·des** (prōbos′idēz). any elongated snout or snoutlike part used for feeding, as an elephant's trunk.

proc·e·leus·mat·ic (pros′əlo͞osmat′ik), *adj.* arousing to action or animation; putting life into; encouraging.

pro·cel·lous (prōsel′əs), *adj.* stormy, tempestuous.

pro·ces·sive (prəses′iv), *adj.* going on or forward; proceeding; progressive.

pro·cès-ver·bal (prōsā′vərbäl′), *n., pl.* **pro·cès-ver·baux** (prōsā′vərbō′). minutes; a detailed written report of the proceedings at a meeting, etc.

pro·chro·nism (prō′krənizm), *n.* the assigning through error of a date earlier than the true one to a person, happening, etc. Also **prolepsis.** See also **anachronism, parachronism.**

proc·li·nate (prok′lənāt), *adj.* bent or directed forward.

pro·cliv·i·ty (prōkliv′itē), *n.* a natural inclination toward or tendency to.

pro·cre·ate (prō′krēāt), *v.* to beget offspring; to generate; to bring into being. —**pro′cre·ant,** *adj.*

pro·cryp·tic (prōkrip′tik), *adj.* giving an animal concealment from its predators. See also **anticryptic.**

proc·tol·o·gy (proktol′əjē), *n.* the study and treatment of disorders of the rectum.

proc·to·scope (prok′təskōp), *n.* a medical instrument passed through the anus to facilitate inspection of the inside of the rectum.

pro·cum·bent (prōkum′bənt), *n.* lying face down; prostrate.

pro·cur·ance (prōkyŏŏr′əns), *n.* the bringing about of or obtaining of something for another or for oneself.

proc·u·ra·tion (prokyərā′sHən), *n.* the act of procurance. —**proc′u·ra·tor,** *n.*

prod·i·gal (prod′əgəl), *adj.* recklessly extravagant; wastefully lavish, as of money; agreeably lavish, as with gifts. —**prod·i·gal′i·ty,** *n.*

pro·di·gious (prədij′əs), *adj.* extraordinary or amazing by reason of size, force, ability, etc.

prod·i·gy (prod′ijē), *n.* a person, esp. a child, endowed with an extraordinary talent or skill.

pro·drome (prō′drōm), *n.* a warning symptom.

pro·em (prō′ēm), *n.* a preface; an introduction.

prof·fer (prof′ər), *v.* to offer.

pro·fi·lom·e·ter (prōfəlom′itər), *n.* an instrument for measuring the roughness of a surface.

prof·li·ga·cy (prof′ləgəsē), *n.* **1.** shameless immorality. **2.** wild extravagance.

prof·li·gate (prof′ləgit), *adj.* **1.** thoroughly immoral; licentious. **2.** wildly extravagant. —*n.* **3.** a profligate person.

prof·lu·ent (prof′lōōənt), *adj.* flowing out freely, abundantly, or smoothly.

pro for·ma (prō fôr′mə), *Latin.* as a matter of form; done according to or for the sake of form.

pro·fu·sive (prəfyōō′siv), *adj.* lavish; extravagant; prodigal.

prog·e·ny (proj′ənē), *n.* children; offspring; issue; outcome.

pro·ges·ter·one (prōjes′tərōn), *n.* a female hormone secreted by the ovary, responsible for preparing the reproductive organs for pregnancy, and during pregnancy, when it is also secreted by the placenta, responsible for maintaining the uterus.

prog·na·thous (prog′nəthəs), *adj.* with projecting jaw.

prog·nose (prognōs′), *v.* to make a medical prognosis.

prog·no·sis (prognō′sis), *n., pl.* **prog·no·ses** (prognō′sēz). a forecast of the likely progress and result of a disease. —**prog·nos′tic,** *adj.*

prog·nos·ti·cate (prognos′təkāt), *v.* to predict from present signs; to foresee; to foreshadow or betoken. —**prog·nos·ti·ca′tion,** *n.*

pro·gram (prō′gram), *n.* the sequence of detailed instructions fed into a computer in accordance with which it deals with problems given to it. —**pro′gram·mer,** *n.*

pro·jec·tile (prəjek′til), *n.* a missile or any body projected by force, as from a gun.

pro·jet (prōzHā′), *n.* a project; a draft, as of a treaty.

pro·lapse (prōlaps′), *n.* the downward displacement of an organ, as the uterus. Also **pro·lap′sus.**

pro·late (prō′lāt), *adj.* elongated in the direction of the polar diameter, as a spheroid described by an ellipse revolving about its longer axis. See also **oblate.**

pro·leg (prō′leg), *n.* one of the thick, jointless appendages on the abdomen of caterpillars, etc., used as a leg.

pro·le·gom·e·non (prōləgom′ənon), *n., pl.* **pro·le·gom·e·na** (prōləgom′ənə). an introductory passage or discussion; a preface or prologue. —**pro·le·gom′e·nous,** *adj.*

pro·lep·sis (prōlep′sis), *n., pl.* **pro·lep·ses** (prōlep′sēz). See **prochronism.**

pro·le·tar·i·at (prō′liter′ēət), *n.* the poorest class in a society, esp. the wage-earning laboring class having little or no property.

pro·li·cide (prō′lisīd), *n.* the killing or the crime of killing one's own or other children.

pro·lif·er·a·tion (prōlif′ərā′sHən), *n.* rapid growth or increase.

pro·lif·ic (prōlif′ik), *adj.* producing much; fertile; fruitful.

pro·line (prō′lēn), *n.* an amino acid present in all proteins and recently discovered in a meteorite.

pro·lix (prōliks′), *adj.* unnecessarily or tediously wordy; of such a speaker or writer.

pro·loc·u·tor (prōlok′yətər), *n.* a chairman.

pro·lu·sion (prōloo′zHən), *n.* an introductory essay or article. —**pro·lu′so·ry**, *adj.*

Pro·me·the·an (prəmē′*th*ēən), *adj.* creative; daringly original.

prom·ul·gate (prom′əlgāt), *v.* to make public by proclaiming or publishing; to put into force, as a new law, etc.

pro·na·tion (prōnā′sHən), *n.* a movement in which the hand or forearm is turned so that the palm faces downward or backward; the position resulting from such a turn. See also **supination.** —**pro′nate**, *v.*

pro·nun·ci·a·men·to (prənun′sēəmen′tō), *n., pl.* **pro·nun·ci·a·men·tos.** a proclamation; a manifesto, as of rebels.

pro·pae·deu·tic (prō′pidoo′tik), *adj.* relating to or like introductory instruction, as to some art or science. Also **pro·pae·deu′ti·cal.**

prop·a·ga·ble (prop′əgəbəl), *adj.* that can be propagated.

pro·pag·u·lum (prōpag′yələm), *n., pl.* **pro·pag·u·la** (prōpag′yələ). a propagating part, as a bud. Also **prop′a·gule.**

pro·phy·lac·tic (prōfəlak′tik), *adj.* preventive; protecting, as against disease.

pro·phy·lax·is (prōfəlak′sis), *n.* the prevention of disease; a measure designed to prevent a particular disease, as inoculation, etc.

pro·pin·qui·ty (prōpiNG′kwitē), *n.* closeness; nearness; affinity.

pro·pi·ti·ate (prəpisH′ēāt), *v.* to make well disposed toward; to win forgiveness or tolerance for. —**pro·pi·ti·a′tion**, *n.* —**pro·pi′ti·a·to′ry**, *adj.*

pro·pi·tious (prəpisH′əs), *adj.* favorable, as *propitious conditions for sailing.*

propjet engine. See **turbo-propeller engine.**

pro·pound (prəpound′), *v.* to put forward; to propose, as a plan, a question, etc.

pro·pri·o·cep·tor (prō′prēəsep′tər),

n. a sense organ which detects position, movement, pain, pressure, and other changes caused by stimuli within the body. —**pro·pri·o·cep′tive**, *adj.*

pro·pri·o mo·tu (prō′prēō mō′too), *Latin.* of one's own accord; at one's own will or initiative.

prop·ter hoc (prop′tər hok′), *Latin.* because of this.

pro·rogue (prōrōg′), *v.* to postpone; to discontinue for a period.

pro·scribe (prōskrīb′), *v.* to forbid; to denounce as dangerous, etc. —**pro·scrip′tion**, *n.*

pro·sect (prōsekt′), *v.* to dissect for demonstration purposes.

pros·e·lyt·ize (pros′əlitīz), *v.* to convert a person from one opinion, religion, etc., to another. —**pros′e·lyte**, *n.*

pros·o·dem·ic (prosədem′ik), *adj.* relating to or denoting a disease spread by personal contact.

pros·o·dy (pros′ədē), *n.* the study of verse form and poetic meter. —**pros′o·dist**, *n.*

pro·so·po·poe·ia, pro·so·po·pe·ia (prōsō′pəpē′ə), *n.* the rhetorical device of personifying inanimate things or making imagined or dead people speak or act.

pros·tate (pros′tāt), *adj.* relating to or denoting the prostate gland.

pros·ta·tec·to·my (pros′tətek′təmē), *n.* the surgical removal of a part or all of the prostate gland.

prostate gland, a muscular gland at the base of the bladder in male mammals which contributes substances to semen and through which the urethra passes. Also **pros′tate.**

pros·the·sis (pros*th*ē′sis), *n., pl.* **pros·the·ses** (pros*th*ē′sēz). the attachment of an artificial part or device to the body to replace a missing part, for functional or cosmetic purposes; the part or device so added. Also **proth′e·sis.**

pros·thet·ics (pros*th*et′iks), *n., sing.* the branch of surgery or dentistry concerned with restoring and maintaining function by supplying artifi-

prosthodontics

—**pros′the·tist**, n.

pros·tho·don·tics (prosthədon′tiks),
n. sing. dental prosthetics. Also **pros·
tho·don′tia**. —**pros·tho·don′tist**, n.

prot·a·nom·a·ly (prōtənom′əlē), n. a
sight defect in which the retina has an
abnormally weak response to the
color red.

prot·an·o·pi·a (prōtənō′pēə), n. a
sight defect in which the retina makes
no response to the color red.

prot·a·nope (prō′tənōp), n. a person
who suffers from protanopia.

prot·a·sis (prot′əsis), n., pl. **prot·a·ses**
(prot′əsēz). 1. the conditional clause,
usually beginning "if" in a conditional sentence. See also **apodosis**. 2.
the introductory part of an ancient
drama. See also **catastasis, catastrophe, epitasis**.

pro·te·an (prō′tēən), adj. able to
change form or character easily; variable; versatile.

pro·tec·tion·ism (prətek′sHənizm),
n. market and price protection ac-
corded domestic producers by measures such as high tariffs and quota
restrictions on imported goods.
—**pro·tec′tion·ist**, n.

pro·tein (prō′tēn), n. any of a group
of organic compounds of high molecular weight, synthesized by plants
and animals; the chief nitrogen-
containing compounds in their tissue,
consisting of amino acids which are
the essential tissue-building elements
for animals.

pro·tha·la·mi·on (prōthəlā′mēən), n.,
pl. **pro·tha·la·mi·a** (prōthəlā′mēə). a
song or poem written for the occasion
of a marriage. See also **epithalamion**.

proth·e·sis (proth′isis), n. 1. the adding of a sound or syllable at the beginning of a word, as Spanish escena,
espectador from Latin scena, spectator.
2. See **prosthesis**.

pro·thon·o·tar·y (prōthon′ətərē), n.
the chief official in certain lawcourts,
as the chief clerk, etc.

pro·tho·rax (prōthôr′aks), n., pl. **pro·
tho·rax·es, pro·tho·ra·ces** (prōthôr′-
əsēz). the front one of the three seg-

ments of the thorax of an insect,
bearing legs but no wings.

pro·throm·bin (prōthrom′bin), n. a
protein formed in the liver from vitamin K and necessary for normal
blood-clotting. Also **thrombogen**.

Pro·tis·ta (prətis′tə), n. pl. all single-
celled organisms considered as a
group.

pro·to·lith·ic (prōtəlith′ik), adj. pertaining to or denoting stones used as
tools because of their shape but not
shaped by the user.

pro·to·mor·phic (prōtəmôr′fik), adj.
of primitive type or structure.

pro·ton (prō′ton), n. the nucleus of a
hydrogen atom; the fundamental
particle that is a constituent of the
nucleus of all atoms, having a positive electrical charge equal in magnitude to that of an electron.

pro·to·path·ic (prōtəpath′ik), adj. relating to or denoting response to pain
or temperature. See also **epicritic**.

pro·to·plasm (prō′təplazm), n. a
colorless fluid, the substance of which
all animal and vegetable cells mainly
consist, and thus the essential matter
of all life. —**pro·to·plas′mic**, adj.

pro·to·troph·ic (prōtətrof′ik), adj. (of
certain microorganisms) 1. requiring
only inorganic substances for growth.
2. with no nutritional requirements
other than those of the majority of its
species.

pro·to·type (prō′tətīp), n. a thing or
person serving as the original or
model for or typifying something.

pro·to·zo·an (prōtəzō′ən), adj. belonging to or relating to the phylum
comprising single-celled organisms.
Also **pro·to·zo′ic**. —**pro·to·zo′al**,
adj.

pro·to·zo·ol·o·gy, pro·to·zo·öl·o·gy
(prō′tōzōōl′əjē), n. the scientific
study of protozoa.

pro·to·zo·on (prōtəzō′on), n., pl. **pro·
to·zo·a**. a protozoan organism.

pro·tract (prōtrakt′), v. 1. to make
longer in time. 2. to extend or stick
out. 3. to plot and draw to scale using
a protractor, as a diagram, plan, etc.
—**pro·trac′tion**, n.

pro·trac·tile (prōtrak′til), *adj*. able to be protracted; that can be protracted.

pro·tru·sile (prōtrōō′sil), *adj*. able to be thrust or extended forward, as a frog's tongue.

pro·tru·sive (prōtrōō′siv), *adj*. that projects forward, sticks out, or bulges.

pro·tu·ber·ate (prōtōō′bərāt), *v*. to form a rounded prominence; to bulge.

prov·e·nance (prov′ənəns), *n*. place of origin; source. Also **pro·ve′ni·ence**.

pro·vi·so (prəvī′zō), *n*., *pl*. **pro·vi·sos, pro·vi·soes**. a condition or stipulation, as a limiting clause in a contract, etc.

pro·vo·lo·ne (prōvəlō′nē), *n*. a hard, smoked, full-flavored Italian cheese.

prox·i·mal (prok′səməl), *adj*. situated toward the center or point of attachment, as of a limb. See also **distal**.

prox·i·mate (prok′səmit), *adj*. next or nearest, as in sequence, place, time, etc.; immediately before or after; close. —**prox·im′i·ty**, *n*.

prox·y (prok′sē), *n*. 1. the power or function of someone authorized to act for another. 2. a document authorizing someone to act for another.

pru·i·nose (prōō′ənōs), *adj*. with a bloom or powdery coating, as a grape, certain species of cacti, etc.

pru·nelle (prōōnel′), *n*. 1. a sweet French liqueur made from plums. 2. Also **pru·nel′la, pru·nel′lo**. a lightweight worsted twill fabric for women's and children's clothes; a smooth fabric of wool or mixed fibers formerly used for clerical robes, etc.

pru·ri·ent (prōōr′ēənt), *adj*. 1. having, given to, or causing lewd thoughts. 2. full of changing desires, itching curiosity, or an abnormal craving.

pru·ri·go (prōōrī′gō), *n*. a skin disease characterized by violently itching papules. —**pru·rig′i·nous** (prōōrij′ənəs), *adj*.

pru·ri·tus (prōōrī′təs), *n*. an itching sensation or other irritation of the skin.

Prze·wal·ski's horse (psHəväl′skēz). See **tarpan**.

psel·lism (sel′izəm), *n*. stuttering.

pse·phol·o·gy (sēfol′əjē), *n*. the study, esp. statistical analysis, of elections.

pseud·e·pig·ra·phy (sōōdəpig′rəfē), *n*. the false attribution of an article, novel, poem, etc., to a certain writer.

pseu·do·a·quat·ic (sōō′dōəkwat′ik), *adj*. native to a wet or moist habitat but not aquatic.

pseu·do·de·men·tia (sōō′dōdimen′-shə), *n*. temporary insanity due to extreme emotion.

pseu·do·her·maph·ro·dite (sōō′dō-hurmaf′rədīt), *n*. an individual whose internal reproductive organs are of one sex but whose external genitals resemble those of the opposite or both sexes.

pseu·dom·o·nas (sōōdom′ənəs), *n*., *pl*. **pseu·do·mon·a·des** (sōōdəmon′-ədēz). any of various species of rod-shaped bacteria, some of which cause diseases in plants and animals.

pseu·do·morph (sōō′dəmôrf), *n*. an irregular form which cannot properly be classified.

pseu·do·nym (sōō′dənim), *n*. a pen name; a name other than one's own used to conceal identity, esp. by an author.

pseu·do·pa·ral·y·sis (sōō′dōpəral′-isis), *n*. a state which is not true paralysis but in which a person is unable to move a part of the body because of pain, shock, etc.

pseu·do·phone (sōō′dəfōn), *n*. a device which changes the relationship between the direction of a sound and the receptor so as to produce the illusion that the sound comes from a different place or source.

pseu·do·po·di·um (sōōdəpō′dēəm), *n*., *pl*. **pseu·do·po·di·a** (sōōdəpō′dēə). a temporary protrusion of the protoplasm of a cell, occurring in protozoa, white blood cells, etc., and used in movement, feeding, etc. Also **pseu′do·pod**.

pseu·do·scope (sōō′dəskōp), *n*. an optical instrument which produces an image in reverse relief by means of two adjustable reflecting prisms. —**pseu·dos′co·py**, *n*.

psi·lan·thro·pism (sīlan′thrəpizm), *n.* the doctrine or belief that Christ was an ordinary human being. Also **psi·lan′thro·py.**

psi·lo·sis (sīlō′sis), *n.* loss of hair; falling hair.

psit·ta·cism (sit′əsizm), *n.* repetitious and meaningless speech; parrotlike speech.

psit·ta·co·sis (sitəkō′sis), *n.* parrot fever; a contagious disease affecting birds, esp. parrots, causing diarrhea and weight loss, and communicable to man when it also causes fever and bronchial pneumonia.

pso·ri·a·sis (sərī′əsis), *n.* a chronic skin disease causing round red patches covered with white scales. Also **pso′ra.**

psy·chas·the·ni·a (sī′kasthē′nēə), *n.* a neurosis marked by anxiety and acute fear.

psy·cha·tax·i·a (sīkətak′sēə), *n.* inability to concentrate.

psy·che (sī′kē), *n.* the soul, spirit, or mind; the principle of mental and emotional life.

psych·e·del·ic (sīkədel′ik), *adj.* relating to or denoting a state of heightened mental awareness producing intensified sensual perception and enjoyment and increased creativeness; denoting a drug which produces such an effect, as LSD, mescaline, etc. Also **psy·cho·del′ic.**

psy·cho·bi·ol·o·gy (sī′kōbīol′əjē), *n.* the scientific study of the interrelation of body and mind, as in the nervous system, etc.

psy·cho·di·ag·nos·tics (sī′kōdī′əgnos′tiks), *n. sing.* the study of personality through behavior and mannerisms, as posture, facial expression, etc. —**psy·cho·di·ag·no′sis,** *n.* —**psy·cho·di·ag·nos′tic,** *adj.*

psy·cho·dra·ma (sī′kōdrä′mə), *n.* a method of group psychotherapy in which patients dramatize and act out their various problems in the form of a play.

psy·cho·dy·nam·ics (sī′kōdīnam′iks), *n. sing.* the study of personality through examining past and present experiences and the motivation that produced them.

psy·cho·gal·van·ic (sī′kōgalvan′ik), *adj.* relating to electric changes in the body due to mental or emotional stimuli.

psy·cho·gal·va·nom·e·ter (sī′kōgal′vənom′itər), *n.* a type of galvanometer adapted for measuring psychogalvanic currents.

psy·cho·gen·e·sis (sī′kōjen′isis), *n.* **1.** the origin and development of the psyche. **2.** the origin of any physical or psychological state in the interaction of the conscious and unconscious mind.

psy·cho·gen·ic (sī′kōjen′ik), *adj.* originating in the mind.

psy·cho·graph (sī′kəgraf), *n.* a graph showing the relative strengths of a person's various personality traits. —**psy·chog′ra·pher,** *n.*

psy·cho·lin·guis·tics (sī′kōliNGgwis′tiks), *n. sing.* the study of the interrelation of language and the behavioral pattern of its users.

psy·chol·o·gism (sīkol′əjizm), *n.* the giving of great weight to psychological factors in forming a theory (used as a term of disparagement implying that too much weight has been given to psychological factors).

psy·cho·man·cy (sī′kōman′sē), *n.* communication with or between spirits.

psy·chom·e·try (sīkom′itrē), *n.* the measurement of mental characteristics. Also **psy·cho·met′rics.**

psy·cho·mo·tor (sī′kōmō′tər), *adj.* relating to movement induced by mental processes.

psy·cho·neu·ro·sis (sī′kōnoŏorō′sis), *n.* a functional disorder of the mind in which patients show insight into their condition but have personalities dominated variously by anxiety, depression, obsessions, compulsions, and physical complaints with no evidence of organic disease, all of which are symptoms which can be relieved by psychotherapy without cure of the root cause. —**psy·cho·neu·rot′ic,** *adj.*

psy·cho·path (sī′kəpa*th*), *n.* a mentally deranged or unstable person; a person with a psychopathic personality. —**psy·cho·path′ic**, *adj.*

psychopathic personality, a personality type characterized by outbursts of violence, antisocial behavior, inability to form meaningful relationships, and extreme egocentricity.

psy·cho·pa·thist (sīkop′ə*th*ist), *n.* one who specializes in treating psychopathy.

psy·cho·pa·thol·o·gy (sī′kōpa*th*ol′-əjē), *n.* the scientific study of mental disease.

psy·chop·a·thy (sīkop′ə*th*ē), *n.* mental disease, esp. severe disease disturbing the moral sense or character.

psy·cho·phar·ma·col·o·gy (sī′kōfär′məkol′əjē), *n.* the study of the psychological effects of drugs.

psy·cho·phys·ics (sī′kōfiz′iks), *n. sing.* a field of study within psychology concerned with measuring the relations between the physical aspects of stimuli and the sensations they produce.

psy·cho·phys·i·ol·o·gy (sī′kōfiz′ēol′-əjē), *n.* a field of study within physiology concerned with the relations between physical and mental phenomena. —**psy·cho·phys·i·o·log′i·cal,** *adj.*

psy·cho·pomp (sī′kōpomp), *n.* someone who conducts the souls of the dead to the next world, as Charon in classical mythology.

psy·cho·pro·phy·lax·is (sī′kōprō′fəlak′sis), *n.* a method of preparing pregnant women for childbirth by their studying the labor process and training in breathing exercises, rhythm, and relaxation. Also **Lamaze technique.**

psy·cho·sex·u·al (sī′kōsek′sнo͞oəl), *adj.* relating to the relationship of mental and sexual phenomena.

psy·cho·sis (sīkō′sis), *n., pl.* **psy·cho·ses** (sīkō′sēz). a severe mental illness which may cause alteration of the entire personality.

psy·cho·so·mat·ic (sī′kōsəmat′ik), *adj.* relating to or denoting a physical disorder caused or greatly influenced by emotional stress.

psychosomatic medicine, the use of psychological techniques and principles in treating physical illness. Also **psy·cho·so·mat′ics.**

psy·cho·sur·ger·y (sī′kōsur′jərē), *n.* the use of brain surgery to treat mental illness.

psy·cho·tech·nics (sī′kōtek′niks), *n. sing.* the use of psychological techniques and theories for controlling human behavior for practical purposes.

psy·cho·tech·nol·o·gy (sī′kōteknol′-əjē), *n.* the study of psychotechnics.

psy·cho·ther·a·peu·tics (sī′kōther′-əpyo͞o′tiks), *n. sing.* the remedial treatment of disease by psychic influence, as mental suggestion, etc.

psy·cho·ther·a·py (sī′kōther′əpē), *n.* the science or technique of treating mental disorders by psychological methods.

psy·chrom·e·ter (sīkrom′itər), *n.* a type of thermometer used to measure relative atmospheric humidity, consisting of two thermometers mounted side by side one of which has its bulb wrapped in damp material dipping in water so that there is evaporation from the wick, with consequent cooling of the bulb, at a rate dependent on the relative humidity of the air, which can then be measured by comparing the reading from the wet thermometer with that from the dry one.

psy·chrom·e·try (sīkrom′itrē), *n.* the scientific measurement of atmospheric humidity.

psy·chro·phil·ic (sīkrəfil′ik), *adj.* able to grow at a temperature at or near 0°C., esp. of bacteria.

pter·i·dol·o·gy (ter′idol′əjē), *n.* the scientific study of ferns, horsetails, clubmosses, etc.

pte·rid·o·phyte (tərid′əfīt), *n.* any plant of the division that includes ferns, horsetails, clubmosses, etc.

pter·o·car·pous (terəkär′pəs), *adj.* having winged fruit, as the sycamore tree.

pte·ryg·i·um (tərij′ēəm), *n., pl.* **pte·**

ryg·i·ums, pte·ryg·i·a (tərij′ēə). a triangular thickened mass of the membrane that covers the eye, stretching from the inner eye-corner to the pupil.

pter·y·goid(ter′əgoid),adj.wing-like.

pter·y·gote (ter′əgōt), adj. relating to the biological subclass comprising the winged insects. Also pte·ryg′o·tous.

pter·y·la (ter′ələ), n., pl. pter·y·lae (ter′əlē). any of the feathered portions of the skin of a bird. Also feather-tract. See also apterium.

pter·y·lol·o·gy (terəlol′əjē), n. the study of pterylosis.

pter·y·lo·sis (terəlō′sis), n. the distribution of birds' feathers in definite areas on the skin.

pti·lo·sis (tilō′sis), n. a disorder characterized by falling out of the eyelashes.

pti·san (tiz′ən), n. barley water; a nourishing preparation originally made from water in which barley had been boiled, supposedly of some medicinal benefit.

Ptol·e·ma·ic system (toləmā′ik), a conception of the universe elaborated by Ptolemy, in which the earth was thought to be central and stationary, with the sun, moon, and other planets moving around it. [after Ptolemy, Greek astronomer, geographer, and mathematician of the 2nd century A.D.]

pto·maine (tō′mān), n. any of a group of basic nitrogenous compounds, as cadaverine, muscarine, etc., some of which are highly poisonous, formed during the putrefaction of plant or animal protein, and having a characteristic appearance and smell.

pto·sis (tō′sis), n. the downward displacement of an organ, esp. the upper eyelid.

pty·a·lism (tī′əlizm), n. the abnormally excessive production of saliva.

pu·bes (pyōō′bēz), n., sing. and pl. 1. the lower part of the abdomen. 2. the hair which appears on this part at puberty. 3. See pubis.

pu·bes·cent (pyōōbes′ənt), adj. 1. at or reaching the age of puberty. 2. with a covering of soft, downy hair, as insects, leaves, etc.

pu·bis (pyōō′bis), n., pl. pu·bes (pyōō′bēz). in man the projecting part at the lower end of either side of the pelvic girdle, forming its front wall, and the corresponding part in four-legged animals.

pub·li·can (pub′ləkən), n. (in Britain) a person who owns or manages a pub or tavern.

public domain, the legal status of works on which copyright has expired or never been granted.

puce (pyōōs), adj. purplish-brown in color; of the color of a flea. [from the French word for flea]

pu·den·cy (pyōō′dənsē), n. modesty; sensitivity to feelings of shame; shyness.

pu·den·dum (pyōōden′dəm), n., pl. pu·den·da (pyōōden′də). Usually in pl. the external genital organs, esp. of the female.

pu·er·ile (pyōō′əril), adj. relating to a child; immature; childish; trivial. —pu·er·il′i·ty, n.

pu·er·il·ism (pyōō′ərəlizm), n. childish behavior in an adult.

pu·er·per·al (pyōōur′pərəl), adj. relating to childbirth or women during childbirth.

puerperal fever, a fever that may occur after childbirth, usually due to infection.

pu·er·pe·ri·um (pyōōərpēr′ēəm), n. the state of a woman during childbirth and the period immediately following when the uterus returns to normal size and lactation begins.

puffer fish, one of several related spiny fishes that are able to inflate themselves into a prickly ball when threatened.

puff paste, a dough rich in shortening, folded and rolled many times to make it rise in flaky layers when cooked.

pug·na·cious (pugnā′sHəs), adj. given to fighting; belligerent.

pu·is·sance (pyōō′isəns), n. great power, might, or influence. —pu′is·sant, adj.

puk·ka sa·hib (puk′ə sä′hēb), a real gentleman, used as a respectful term of address by Indians to British colonial officials in India.

pul·chri·tude (pul′kritōōd), *n.* physical beauty. —**pul·chri·tu′di·nous,** *adj.*

pule (pyōōl), *v.* to cry weakly; to whine in a thin tone.

pul·let (pōōl′it), *n.* a young hen from the time it begins to lay until its first moult; other domestic fowl in this phase.

pul·lu·late (pul′yəlāt), *v.* to sprout or germinate; to breed or multiply rapidly; to exist in large numbers.

pul·mo·nar·y (pul′mənerē), *adj.* relating to the lungs.

pul·mon·ic (pulmon′ik), *adj.* **1.** pulmonary. **2.** relating to pneumonia.

pul·que (pōōl′kē), *n.* a Mexican fermented drink made from the sap of certain species of agave.

pul·sa·tile (pul′sətil), *adj.* throbbing; pulsating; beating, as a pulse, percussion music, etc.

pul·sim·e·ter (pulsim′itər), *n.* an instrument for measuring the strength or rapidity of the pulse.

pul·ver·u·lent (pulver′yələnt), *adj.* consisting of or covered with dust or powder; crumbling to a fine powder.

pul·vi·nate (pul′vənāt), *adj.* shaped like a cushion.

pun·cheon (pun′CHən), *n.* a heavy rough slab of timber used as a floorboard, or upright as a short support or piece of framing.

punc·tate (puNGk′tāt), *adj.* marked or studded with dots, points or depressions. Also **punc′tat·ed.** —**punc·ta′tion,** *n.*

punc·ti·form (puNGk′təfôrm), *adj.* like a dot or point.

punc·til·i·o (puNGktil′ēō), *n., pl.* **punc·til·i·os.** a fine point, as of ceremony, honor, conduct, etc.

punc·til·i·ous (puNGktil′ēəs), *adj.* observing all the punctilios; showing great attention to details.

pun·dit (pun′dit), *n.* an authority or expert on some matter (often used jocularly).

pu·ni·tive (pyōō′nitiv), *adj.* punishing; intended to punish; relating to punishment. Also **pu′ni·to·ry.**

pun·kah (puNG′kə), *n.* a very large cloth fan hung from the ceiling and swung to and fro by machinery or a servant, esp. in India.

pu·pa (pyōō′pə), *n., pl.* **pu·pae** (pyōō′pē), **pu·pas.** an insect in the stage between the larva and the imago when it does not move or feed but develops greatly.

pu·pate (pyōō′pāt), *v.* to become a pupa.

pu·pip·a·rous (pyōōpip′ərəs), *adj.* relating to or denoting insects that bear larvae which are already so far developed that they are ready to pupate.

pur·dah, pur·da (pur′də), *n.* (in India, Pakistan, etc.) a curtain, screen, or veil used or worn to conceal women of rank from men or strangers; the system of so concealing women.

pu·rée (pyōōrā′), *n.* cooked and sieved food, esp. fruit or vegetables.

pur·fle (pur′fəl), *v.* **1.** to edge with a decorative border. **2.** to use miniature architectural forms to decorate a shrine, canopy, etc. —**pur′fling,** *n.*

pur·lieu (pur′lōō), *n.* **1.** a district or area at the edge of a town, forest, etc. **2.** a place where one has the right to come and go at will and wander freely; a place one habitually frequents; a haunt; one's limits.

pur·loin (pərloin′), *v.* to steal; to take dishonestly.

pur·port (pərpôrt′), *v.* **1.** to profess; to intend to seem, usually falsely. —*n.* **2.** the meaning or sense, either apparent or real.

pur·pu·ra (pur′pyōōrə), *n.* a disease in which the blood is forced from the blood vessels and diffuses through the surrounding tissue causing purplish spots on the skin.

pur sang (pyr säN′), *French.* genuine beyond question; full-blooded. [lit., pure blood]

pur·su·ant (pərsōō′ənt), *adj.* following; pursuing. —**pur·su′ance,** *n.*

pur·sui·vant (pur'swivənt), *n.* a follower; an attendant.

pur·sy (pur'sē), *adj.* short of breath, esp. from being too fat.

pu·ru·lence (pyŏŏr'ələns), *n.* the condition of forming, containing, or discharging pus. —**pu'ru·lent,** *adj.*

pu·ru·loid (pyŏŏr'əloid), *adj.* like pus.

pur·vey (pərvā'), *v.* to supply or provide as a trade, esp. provisions. —**pur·vey'ance,** *n.* —**pur·vey'or,** *n.*

pur·view (pur'vyŏŏ), *n.* the scope or province, as of authority, concern, subject, etc.

pu·sil·la·nim·i·ty (pyŏŏ´sələnim'-itē), *n.* faintheartedness; lack of spirit; timidity; cowardliness. —**pu·sil·lan'i·mous,** *adj.*

pus·tu·late (pus'cHəlāt), *adj.* 1. covered with pustules. —*v.* 2. to cause to break out in pustules. —**pus'tu·lant,** *adj.*

pus·tule (pus'cHŏŏl), *n.* a small swelling on the skin containing pus; any pimple-like or blister-like swelling on the skin. —**pus·tu·la'tion,** *n.* —**pus'tu·lar, pus'tu·lous,** *adj.*

pu·ta·tive (pyŏŏ'tətiv), *adj.* reputed; supposed; generally regarded as.

pu·tre·fac·tion (pyŏŏtrəfak'sHən), *n.* the act or process of decomposition of living matter by bacteria and fungi with resulting foul-smelling products; rotting.

pu·tres·cent (pyŏŏtres'ənt), *adj.* in process of putrefaction; becoming rotten.

pu·tres·ci·ble (pyŏŏtres'əbəl), *adj.* liable to putrefaction.

pu·tri·lage (pyŏŏ'trəlij), *n.* matter which has become or is becoming putrid.

Putsch (pŏŏtsH), *n. German.* a sudden and speedy uprising or takeover of government.

P wave, the first major shock wave radiating from the center of an earthquake. Also **primary wave.** See also **L wave, S wave.**

pyc·nom·e·ter (piknom'itər), *n.* an instrument for ascertaining the density of a liquid or solid by comparing it under the same conditions of temperature and pressure with an equal volume of a liquid or solid whose density is known.

py·e·li·tis (pīəlī'tis), *n.* inflammation of the pelvis or the kidney outlet.

py·e·lo·gram (pī'ələgram), *n.* an x-ray photograph produced by pyelography. Also **py'e·lo·graph.**

py·e·log·ra·phy (pīəlog'rəfē), *n.* the science or technique of photographing the kidneys, renal pelves, and ureters by injecting a radiopaque solution before taking x-ray photographs.

py·e·lo·ne·phri·tis (pī'əlōnəfrī'tis), *n.* inflammation of the kidney and the adjoining part of the urinary tract caused by bacterial infection spread back from the urethra and bladder.

py·e·lo·ne·phro·sis (pī'əlōnəfrō'sis), *n.* any disease affecting the kidney and the area immediately surrounding it.

py·e·mi·a, py·ae·mi·a (pīē'mēə), *n.* a diseased condition characterized by the growth of abscesses in various organs owing to the presence in the blood of bacteria which cause formation of pus.

pyk·nic (pik'nik), *adj.* relating to or denoting a physical type characterized by a short, stocky build, bulky muscles, and often excessive fat. See also **athletic, asthenic, leptosome.**

py·lo·rec·to·my (pīlərek'təmē), *n.* surgical removal of the pylorus.

py·lo·rus (pīlôr'əs), *n., pl.* **py·lo·ri** (pīlôr'ī). the small opening leading from the stomach into the duodenum.

py·o·der·ma (pī'ōdur'mə), *n.* any skin disease marked by the formation of pus.

py·o·gen·e·sis (pīəjen'isis), *n.* the formation of pus; the process by which pus is formed. —**py·o·gen'ic,** *adj.*

py·oid (pī'oid), *adj.* relating to or like pus.

py·o·ne·phri·tis (pī'ōnəfrī'tis), *n.* inflammation of the kidney associated with discharge of pus.

py·o·per·i·car·di·um (pī'ōper'əkär'-dēəm), *n.* the presence of pus in the pericardium.

py·oph·thal·mi·a (pī'ofthal'mēə), *n.* inflammation of the eye with associated discharge of pus. Also **py·oph·thal·mi/tis.**

py·o·pneu·mo·tho·rax pī'ōnoō'-mōthôr'aks), *n.* the presence of pus and gas in the cavity between the pleura.

py·or·rhe·a (pīərē'ə), *n.* infection of the gums around the teeth, and in its more severe form the formation of pus between the roots of the teeth and the tissue surrounding the roots leading to loosening and loss of teeth. Also **pyorrhea al·ve·o·lar/is.**

py·o·sis (pīō'sis), *n.* the formation of pus.

py·o·tho·rax (pī'ōthôr'aks), *n.* an abscess in the cavity between the pleura ; empyema.

py·re·thrum (pīrē'*th*rəm), *n.* the dried flower heads of certain chrysanthemums, used as an insecticide and sometimes to treat certain skin diseases.

py·ret·ic (pīret'ik), *adj.* relating to, affected by, or causing fever.

pyr·e·tol·o·gy (pir'itol'əjē), *n.* the study and treatment of fevers.

pyr·e·to·ther·a·py (pir'itō*th*er'əpē), *n.* treatment of a disease or disorder by raising the body temperature, as by inducing fever or by electric currents, etc.

py·rex·i·a (pīrek'sēə), *n.* fever; raised body temperature.

pyr·he·li·om·e·ter (pīr'hēlēom'itər), *n.* an instrument for measuring the rate at which heat energy is received from the sun by means of the rate of rise in temperature of a black surface exposed to the sun.

pyr·i·form (pir'əfôrm), *adj.* pear-shaped.

py·ro·con·duc·tiv·i·ty (pī'rəkon'-duktiv'itē), *n.* electrical conductivity created by applying heat, esp. in solids that are not conductors at lower temperatures.

py·ro·e·lec·tric·i·ty (pī'rōilektris'-itē), *n.* an electromagnetic force developed between the opposite faces of certain crystals, as tourmaline, when the crystal is heated. —**py·ro·e·lec/tric,** *adj.*

py·ro·gen (pī'rəjen), *n.* any substance which causes a raised body temperature when it enters the bloodstream of man or an animal. Also **pyrotoxin.** —**py·ro·gen/ic,** *adj.*

py·rog·e·nous (pīroj'ənəs), *adj.* produced by the action of heat, as certain rocks, chemical substances, etc.

py·rog·nos·tics (pīrəgnos'tiks), *n. pl.* those properties that a mineral exhibits when heated by blowpipe, as fusibility, coloration of the flame, etc.

py·rog·ra·phy (pīrog'rəfē), *n.* the process of making designs with a heated tool, as on wood, leather, etc. Also **py·ro·gra·vure'.**

py·ro·lig·ne·ous (pīrəlig'nēəs), *adj.* distilled from wood as, formerly, acetone. Also **py·ro·lig/nic.**

py·rol·y·sis (pīrol'isis), *n.* the decomposition of an organic compound by exposure to extremely high temperature.

py·ro·man·cy (pī'rəmansē), *n.* divination by fire.

py·ro·ma·ni·a (pīrəmā'nēə), *n.* a form of madness characterized by the compulsion to set fire to things. —**py·ro·ma/ni·ac,** *n.*

py·ro·met·al·lur·gy (pīrəmet'əlurjē), *n.* the process or technique of refining ores by applying heat.

py·ro·met·ric bead (pīrəmet'rik), a ball of material set in a kiln to show when a certain temperature has been reached by changing color.

pyrometric cone, a triangular piece of material set in a kiln to show when a certain temperature has been reached by melting or changing shape.

py·ro·pho·bi·a (pīrəfō'bēə), *n.* an abnormally excessive dread of fire.

py·ro·phor·ic (pīrəfôr'ik), *adj.* capable of igniting on exposure to air.

py·ro·pho·tom·e·ter (pī'rōfōtom'-itər), *n.* an instrument for measuring high temperatures by optical or photometric means.

py·ro·sis (pīrō'sis), *n.* heartburn.

py·ro·stat (pī'rəstat), *n.* a device that triggers off an alarm if fire breaks out near it.

py·ro·tech·nics (pīrətek′niks), *n. sing.* the art of making fireworks. —**py·ro·tech′nic,** *adj.* —**py·ro·tech′nist,** *n.*

py·ro·tox·in (pīrətok′sin), *n.* See **pyrogen.**

Pyr·rhic (pir′ik), *adj.* relating to or denoting a costly victory. [after Pyrrhus, the king of Epirus, who in the 3rd century B.C. defeated the Romans but lost most of his army]

Pyr·rho·nism (pir′ənizm), *n.* extreme skepticism. [after Pyrrho, *c*360–270 B.C., Greek philosopher]

pyth·o·gen·ic (pīthəjen′ik), *adj.* originating in decomposing matter or filth. Also **py·thog′e·nous.**

py·thon·ic (pīthon′ik), *adj.* oracular; prophetic. [after Pythia, priestess of the Delphic oracle in classical mythology]

py·u·ri·a (piyo͞or′ēə), *n.* the presence of pus in the urine.

Q clearance, (in the Atomic Energy Commission) the highest level of security clearance, which gives a person access to all secret information.

Q.E.D. See **quod erat demonstrandum.**

Q-fever (kyōō′fēvər), *n.* a fever characterized by symptoms like those of pneumonia, caused by Rickettsiae transmitted to man by insects.

qua (kwā, kwä), *adv.* as; considered as; as being; *the role of parent* qua *moral teacher is much diminished.*

quack·sal·ver (kwak′salvər), *n.* an unqualified person practicing medicine; a quack doctor.

quad·ra·ge·nar·i·an (kwod′rəjəner′-ēən), *adj.* **1.** between 40 and 50 years old. —*n.* **2.** a person aged 40 or between 40 and 50.

quad·rant (kwod′rənt), *n.* a quarter of a circle.

quad·rate (kwod′rit), *adj.* rectangular; square.

quad·ra·ture (kwod′rəcHər), *n.* the process or act of squaring.

quad·rel (kwod′rəl), *n.* a stone or brick that is square.

quad·ren·ni·um (kwodren′ēəm), *n.*, *pl.* **quad·ren·ni·ums, quad·ren·ni·a** (kwodren′ēə). a period of four years. —**quad·ren′ni·al,** *adj.*

quad·ri·cen·ten·ni·al (kwod′risenten′ēəl), *adj.* **1.** of or relating to a period of 400 years. —*n.* **2.** a period of 400 years; the celebration or anniversary marking such a period.

quad·ril·lion (kwodril′yən), *n.* a number represented by the figure one followed by 15 zeros (but in the United Kingdom and Germany by the figure one followed by 24 zeros).

qua·drille (kwədril′), *n.* a game of cards for four persons.

quad·ri·ple·gi·a (kwodrəplē′jēə), *n.* paralysis affecting all four limbs. Also **tetraplegia.** —**quad′ri·pleg′ic,** *n.*

quad·ri·sect (kwod′risekt), *v.* to cut or divide into four, usually equal parts.

quad·riv·i·al (kwodriv′ēəl), *adj.* having four roads which meet in a point.

quad·riv·i·um (kwodriv′ēəm), *n., pl.* **quad·riv·i·a** (kwodriv′ēə). the higher division of the seven liberal arts studied in medieval schools, consisting of arithmetic, geometry, astronomy, and music. See also **trivium.**

quad·ru·mane (kwod′rōōmān), *n.* an animal which can use all four feet as hands, as the monkey. —**quad·ru′ ma·nous,** *adj.*

quad·rum·vi·rate (kwodrum′vərit), *n.* joint rule by four men. See also **triumvirate.**

quad·ru·plex (kwod′rōōpleks), *adj.* fourfold; in four parts; four times as large.

quag·gy (kwag′ē), *adj.* like a marsh or quagmire; boggy.

quag·mire (kwag′mīr), *n*. a bog, esp. one which quakes under the tread.

qua·lim·e·ter (kwəlim′itər), *n*. See **penetrometer.**

qualm (kwäm), *n*. a momentary feeling of apprehension or unease; a pang of conscience. —**qualm′ish,** *adj.*

quan·da·ry (kwon′dərē), *n*. a state of uncertainty as to what action to take; a practical dilemma.

quand même (käN mem′), *French.* even so; nevertheless; all the same.

quan·ti·fy (kwon′təfī), *v*. to express as or determine a quantity.

quan·tile (kwon′tīl), *n*. (in statistics) any value of a variate that divides the total frequency of a sample into equal quantities. See also **percentile, quartile.**

quan·ti·ta·tive (kwon′titā′tiv), *adj.* relating to, measured by, or based on quantity.

quan·tum (kwon′təm), *n*., *pl*. **quan·ta** (kwon′tə). **1.** a quantity; amount. **2.** the smallest quantity of radiant energy.

quantum mechanics, the branch of mechanics dealing with systems at the atomic and nuclear levels.

qua·qua·ver·sal (kwäkwəvur′səl), *adj.* (relating to a rock formation) sloping down in every direction from a tip.

quark (kwôrk), *n*. any of the three types of particle which some physicists believe are the basis of all matter.

quar·rel (kwôr′əl), *n*. a square or rhomboidal pane of glass.

quar·tan (kwôr′tn), *adj.* of a fever marked by paroxysms recurring every third (or by inclusive reckoning every fourth) day, as in some kinds of malaria. See also **tertian, quintan, sextan.**

quar·ter·age (kwôr′tərij), *n*. the provision or cost of accommodation for troops.

quar·ter·fi·nal (kwôrtərfī′nl), *adj.* relating to that round of a sports tournament which precedes the semifinal. —**quar·ter·fi′nal·ist,** *n*.

quarter horse, one of a breed of horses bred to run quarter-mile races.

quar·tic (kwôr′tik), *adj.* of or relating to the fourth algebraic degree.

quar·tile (kwôr′tīl), *adj.* (in statistics) the value of a variable that divides the distribution of the variable into four groups with equal frequencies. See also **quantile, percentile.**

quar·to (kwôr′to), *n*., *pl*. **quar·tos.** a book size of approximately $9\frac{1}{2} \times 12$ inches; a size of paper obtained by folding a sheet in half twice.

qua·sar (kwā′sär), *n*. a celestial object emitting powerful radio energy from a distance of four to ten billion light-years; quasi-stellar radio source.

quash[1] (kwosH), *v*. to suppress; to put an end to.

quash[2] (kwosH), *v*. to annul or set aside as not valid, esp. a legal decision.

qua·si (kwā′zī, kwä′sē), *adj.* seeming; as if; having the semblance of, as *a quasi judicial role.*

qua·ter·nar·y (kwä′tərnerē), *adj.* **1.** having or consisting of four parts. **2.** relating or belonging to the present geological period, which began approximately one million years ago. See also **Neocene.**

qua·ter·nate (kwä′tərnāt), *adj.* consisting of or in groups of four, as some leaves.

qua·ter·ni·on (kwətur′nēən), *n*. a group or set of four.

quat·re·foil (kat′ərfoil), *n*. a four-lobed leaf.

quat·tro·cen·to (kwo′trōcHen′tō), *n*. the 15th century, with reference to the Italian art of that period.

quat·tu·or·de·cil·lion (kwot′ōōôr′disil′yən), *n*. a number represented by the figure one followed by 45 zeros (but in the United Kingdom and Germany by the figure one followed by 84 zeros).

qua·ver (kwā′vər), *v*. to shake; to tremble, esp. a voice or musical note.

quean (kwēn), *n*. an ill-behaved woman; a hussy; a prostitute.

que·nelle (kənel′), *n*. a dish consisting of pounded meat or fish bound with eggs or breadcrumbs, shaped into a ball, boiled, and served with a sauce.

quer·cine (kwur′sin), *adj.* relating to the oak tree.

quer·u·lous (kwer′ələs), *adj.* of a complaining tone or nature.

quiche (kēsH), *n.* a dish consisting of an open tart of unsweetened pastry filled with beaten eggs and cream of milk mixed with cheese, bacon, or the like, and baked in the oven.

quid·di·ty (kwid′itē), *n.* **1.** the essence of a thing which makes it unique. See also **haecceity. 2.** a trivial distinction in argument; a quibble.

quid·nunc (kwid′nuNGk), *n.* a newsmonger; a gossip.

quid pro quo (kwid′ prō kwō′), *pl.* **quid pro quos, quids pro quo.** something given in return, as for a favor; tit for tat.

qui·es·cent (kwēes′ənt), *adj.* being at rest; silent; motionless.

qui·e·tus (kwīē′təs), *n.*, *pl.* **qui·e·tus·es.** anything that settles or ends something, as an argument.

quill (kwil), *n.* a hollow stem used as a bobbin on which to wind yarn; any bobbin so used.

qui·na·ry (kwī′nərē), *adj.* relating to the number five; consisting of five.

qui·nate (kwī′nāt), *adj.* in groups of five.

quin·cunx (kwiNG′kuNGks), *n.* an arrangement of five objects with one at each corner of a square and the other at its center. —**quin·cun′cial,** *adj.*

quin·dec·a·gon (kwindek′əgon), *n.* a polygon with 15 angles and 15 sides.

quin·de·cen·ni·al (kwin′dicen′ēəl), *adj.* **1.** relating to a period of 15 years or to a 15th anniversary. —*n.* **2.** a 15th anniversary.

quin·de·cil·lion (kwin′disil′yən), *n.* a number represented by the figure one followed by 48 zeros (but in the United Kingdom and Germany by the figure one followed by 90 zeros).

quin·qua·ge·nar·i·an (kwiNG′kwəjəner′ēən), *adj.* **1.** between 50 and 60 years old. —*n.* **2.** a person aged 50 or between 50 and 60.

quin·quag·e·nar·y (kwinkwä′jənerē), *n.* a 50th anniversary.

quin·que·fid (kwin′kwəfid), *adj.* split into five parts or lobes.

quin·que·foil (kwin′kwəfoil), *n.* See **cinquefoil.**

quin·quen·ni·al (kwinkwen′ēəl), *adj.* **1.** relating to or lasting for five years. —*n.* **2.** a five-year period.

quin·quen·ni·um (kwinkwen′ēəm), *n.*, *pl.* **quin·quen·ni·ums, quin·quen·ni·a** (kwinkwen′ēə). a five-year period. Also **quin·quen′ni·ad.**

quin·sy (kwin′zē), *n.* an abscess on a tonsil, usually occurring as a complication of tonsillitis.

quin·tal (kwin′tl), *n.* **1.** a unit of weight in the metric system, equal to 100 kilograms. **2.** a hundredweight equal to 100 lb. (but 112 lb. in the United Kingdom).

quin·tan (kwin′tn), *adj.* of a fever marked by paroxysms occurring every fourth (or by inclusive reckoning every fifth) day. See also **tertian, quartan, sextan.**

quinte·foil (kwint′foil), *n.* See **cinquefoil.**

quin·tes·sence (kwintes′əns), *n.* the purest essence of anything; the most perfect embodiment of something.

quin·tic (kwin′tik), *adj.* (in mathematics) of the fifth degree.

quin·til·lion (kwintil′yən), *n.* a number represented by the figure one followed by 18 zeros (but in the United Kingdom and Germany by the figure one followed by 30 zeros).

quire (kwīr), *n.* a set of 24 equal-sized sheets of paper.

quirk (kwurk), *n.* a mannerism; a peculiarity of behavior. —**quirk′y,** *adj.*

quirt (kwurt), *n.* a riding whip with a short handle and braided leather lash.

quis·ling (kwiz′liNG), *n.* one who collaborates with an invading enemy; a fifth columnist. [after Major Vidkun *Quisling* (1887–1945) who in 1940 aided the German invaders of his native Norway]

quit·tance (kwit′ns), *n.* **1.** recompense. **2.** release from a debt or obligation.

qui vive (kē viv′), *French.* **1.** who goes there? **2. on the qui vive,** on the alert.

quix·ot·ic (kwiksot′ik), *adj.* extremely romantic or chivalrous; pursuing lofty but impractical ideals. Also **quix·ot′i·cal.** —**quix′ot·ism,** *n.*

quiz·zi·cal (kwiz′ikəl), *adj.* **1.** odd; amusing. **2.** puzzled; questioning. **3.** mockingly questioning; making fun of.

quod e·rat de·mon·stran·dum (kwod er′at demənstran′dəm), *Latin.* which was to be demonstrated or proved. *Abbrev.* : **Q.E.D.**

quod·li·bet (kwod′ləbet), *n.* a subtle argument, esp. on a theological or scholastic topic.

quod·li·betz (kwod′ləbets), *n.* a painted decorative motif, as a playing card, letter of the alphabet, or similar small object, used on ceramics and the like.

quoin (koin, kwoin), *n.* the external angle of a building; the stone or brick forming it; a cornerstone.

quon·dam (kwon′dam), *adj.* former; previous; of earlier times.

quo·rum (kwôr′əm), *n.* the number or percentage of members of any board, society, or the like needed to constitute a valid assembly for transacting business.

quo·tid·i·an (kwōtid′ēən), *adj.* **1.** everyday; ordinary. **2.** occurring daily, as paroxysms of some fevers.

quo·tient (kwō′sHənt), *n.* the result of a division. See also **dividend, divisor.**

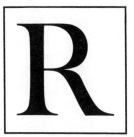

R

Rab·e·lai·si·an (rabəlā′zēən), *adj.* broadly or coarsely humorous, satirical, etc.

ra·bies (rā′bēz), *n.* a contagious infection causing madness in dogs, cats, and other animals and usually fatal to man if transmitted by the bite of an infected animal.

ra·chi·tis (rəkī′tis), *n.* rickets.

ra·ci·nage (rasənäzH′), *n.* the technique of treating leather with acid to produce a decorative effect.

rack-rent, rack rent (rak′rent′), *n.* exorbitant rent whose annual amount is equal, or almost equal, to the value of the property.

ra·dar (rā′där), *n.* a device for detecting the location and direction of an object, as an aircraft, by reflecting radio waves off it.

rad·i·cel (rad′isəl), *n.* a tiny root; a rootlet.

rad·i·cle (rad′ikəl), *n.* a small rootlike structure. —**ra·dic′u·lar,** *adj.*

ra·dic·u·li·tis (rədik′yəlī′tis), *n.* inflammation of the root of a spinal nerve.

ra·dic·u·lose (rədik′yəlōs), *adj.* having many radicels.

ra·di·o·ac·tive (rā′dēōak′tiv), *adj.* relating to, connected with, stemming from, or exhibiting radioactivity.

radioactive decay. See **decay.**

ra·di·o·ac·tiv·i·ty (rā′dēōaktiv′itē), *n.* the spontaneous emission of radiation

resulting from the disintegration of atomic nuclei.

ra·di·o·bi·ol·o·gy (rā′dēōbīol′əjē), *n.* the branch of biology dealing with the effects of radiation on living organisms.

ra·di·o·car·bon (rā′dēōkär′bən), *n.* a radioactive isotope of carbon, esp. carbon 14.

radiocarbon dating, the process and technique by which the age of ancient organic matter is estimated from the radioactivity of its carbon content.

ra·di·o·chem·is·try (rā′dēōkem′istrē), *n.* the branch of chemistry dealing with radioactive phenomena.

radio compass, a direction-finding radio receiver used in determining the bearing of a radio transmitter.

ra·di·o·di·ag·no·sis (rā′dēōdī′əgnō′-sis), *n.* diagnosis by means of x-rays.

ra·di·o·el·e·ment (rā′dēōel′əmənt), *n.* a radioactive chemical element.

ra·di·o·gen·ic (rā′dēōjen′ik), *adj.* produced by decay of radioactivity, as certain isotopes.

ra·di·o·gram (rā′dēōgram′), *n.* a telegram sent by radio.

ra·di·o·graph (rā′dēōgraf′), *n.* an image produced on a photographic plate by x-rays. —**ra·di·og′ra·phy,** *n.*

ra·di·o·i·so·tope (rā′dēōī′sətōp), *n.* an artificially produced, radioactive isotope.

ra·di·o·lo·ca·tion (rā′dēōlōkā′sHən),

n. the determination of the location and speed of objects by use of radar.

ra·di·ol·o·gy (rā′dēol′əjē), *n.* the study of the application of x-rays and other forms of radiant energy to medical diagnosis, therapy, etc. — **ra·di·o·log′i·cal,** *adj.*

ra·di·o·lu·cent (rā′dēōlōō′sənt), *adj.* offering little or no resistance to the passage of x-rays or other forms of radiant energy. See also **radiopaque, radiotransparent.**

ra·di·o·lu·mi·nes·cence (rā′dēōlōō′mənes′əns), *n.* luminescence induced by radioactivity.

ra·di·o·me·te·or·o·graph (rā′dēōmē′tēərəgraf), *n.* radiosonde.

ra·di·om·e·ter (rā′dēom′itər), *n.* a device consisting of a four-bladed fan mounted on a vertical axis in an evacuated glass bulb, with successively alternate sides of the blades blackened and mirror-like, used for demonstrating and detecting the presence of radiant energy and of its conversion to mechanical energy.

ra·di·o·mi·crom·e·ter (rā′dēōmī-krom′itər), *n.* a device for measuring minute emissions of radiant energy.

ra·di·o·paque (rā′dēōpāk′), *adj.* not allowing the passage of x-rays; visible in x-ray photographs. See also **radiolucent, radiotransparent.**

ra·di·o·phare (rā′dēōfer′), *n.* a navigational beacon that broadcasts a radio signal for use by ships to determine their positions.

ra·di·o·phone (rā′dēōfōn′), *n.* a radiotelephone.

ra·di·o·pho·to·graph (rā′dēōfō′təgraf), *n.* a photographic image transmitted by radio. Also **ra′di·o·pho·to, ra·di·o·pho′to·gram.**

radio range beacon, a radio transmitter designed to transmit signals enabling an aviator to determine his approximate position without a radio compass.

ra·di·os·co·py (rā′dēos′kəpē), *n.* the direct internal examination of opaque objects by the use of x-rays or other forms of radiant energy.

ra·di·o·sen·si·tive (rā′dēōsen′sitiv),

adj. of or pertaining to organisms or tissue sensitive or susceptible to destruction by x-rays or other forms of radiant energy.

ra·di·o·sonde (rā′dēōsond′), *n.* a radio transmitter and meteorological instruments carried to great heights by balloon. Also **radiometeorograph.**

ra·di·o·sur·ger·y (rā′dēōsur′jərē), *n.* the surgical insertion of radioactive substances for therapeutic purposes.

ra·di·o·tech·nol·o·gy (rā′dēōteknol′əjē), *n.* the application of radiation to industry.

ra·di·o·tel·e·gram (rā′dēōtel′ə-gram), *n.* a radiogram.

ra·di·o·tel·e·graph (rā′dēōtel′əgraf), *n.* a telegraph using radio waves rather than wires or cables. — **ra·di·o·te·leg′ra·phy,** *n.*

ra·di·o·tel·e·phone (rā′dēōtel′əfōn), *n.* a telephone transmitting speech by radio waves. — **ra·di·o·te·leph′o·ny,** *n.*

radio telescope, a radio antenna or an array of antennae designed to intercept radio waves from celestial sources.

ra·di·o·ther·a·py (rā′dēōther′əpē), *n.* the treatment of disease by the use of x-rays or other radiant energy.

ra·di·o·trac·er (rā′dēōtrā′sər), *n.* a tracer making use of isotope.

ra·di·o·trans·par·ent (rā′dēōtrans-per′ənt), *n.* not opaque to radiation; not seen in x-ray photographs. See also **radiolucent, radiopaque.**

ra·dix (rā′diks), *n., pl.* **rad·i·ces** (rad′-isēz). a root.

ra·dome (rā′dōm), *n.* a dome-shaped housing for a radar antenna.

raff·ish (raf′ish), *adj.* cheap; tawdry; in bad taste; discreditable.

ra·ga (rä′gə), *n.* any of the traditional melody patterns of Hindu music, with characteristic intervals, rhythms, and embellishments.

ra·gout (ragōō′), *n.* a spicy stew of meat or fish and vegetables.

rail·ler·y (rā′lərē), *n.* banter; good-natured pleasantry.

rai·son d'être (rā′zōn de′trə), *pl.* **rai·**

sons d'être (rā′zōnz de′trə). *French.* a reason for existence.

rai·son·né (rezônā′), *adj. French.* ordered; organized, as *a catalogue raisonné.*

rale (ral), *n.* an abnormal rattling or bubbling sound accompanying breathing, usually indicating a diseased condition of the lungs.

ram·e·kin (ram′əkin), *n.* **1.** a lidless ceramic baking dish for individual service. **2.** any preparation baked and served in a ramekin.

ra·men·tum (rəmen′təm), *n., pl.* **ra·men·ta** (rəmen′tə). a thin shaving or scraping.

ram·i·form (ram′əfôrm), *adj.* branched or branch-like.

ram·i·fy (ram′əfī), *v.* to separate into branches or branch-like divisions. —**ram·i·fi·ca′tion,** *n.*

ra·mose (rā′mōs), *adj.* bearing many branches.

ra·mous (rā′məs), *adj.* **1.** ramose. **2.** branch-like.

ram·pa·geous (rampā′jəs), *adj.* with uncontrolled vigor and energy; raging; unruly.

ram·u·lose (ram′yəlōs), *adj.* with many small branches. Also **ramulous** (ram′yələs).

ra·mus (rā′məs), *n., pl.* **ra·mi** (rā′mī). a branch or branch-like part, as of a capillary, etc.

ran·cid (ran′sid), *adj.* having a bad smell or taste; spoiled. —**ran·cid′i·ty,** *n.*

ran·cor (raNG′kər), *n.* bitter hatred or resentment; deep spite; malice. —**ran′cor·ous,** *adj.*

rand·y, ran·die (ran′dē), *adj.* lascivious; lustful; lecherous.

range·find·er (rānj′fīndər), *n.* an instrument for determining the distance of a target or object from the observer, or from a gun, camera, etc.

ran·kle (raNG′kəl), *v.* to continue to cause long-lasting anger, resentment, irritation, etc., within the mind.

rap (rap), *v.* (slang) to discuss; have a bull session.

ra·pa·cious (rəpā′sHəs), *adj.* disposed to taking by force; plundering; predacious.

ra·phe (rā′fē), *n., pl.* **ra·phae** (rā′fē). a seam-like joining between two halves of an organ, as of the tongue.

rap·port (rapôr′), *n.* sympathetic relationship; harmony. See also **en rapport.**

rap·proche·ment (raprôsHmäN′), *n.* a reconciliation; restoration of good relations.

rap·to·ri·al (raptôr′ēəl), *adj.* **1.** of or like a bird of prey; predacious. **2.** equipped for seizing prey.

ra·ra a·vis (rer′ə ā′vis), *n., pl.* **ra·rae a·ves** (rer′ē ā′vēz). an unusual or rare person or thing.

rar·e·fy (rer′əfī), *v.* to thin out or make less dense; to refine. —**rar·e·fac′tion,** *n.*

ra·so·ri·al (rəsôr′ēəl), *adj.* characteristically scratching the ground for food, as a chicken.

ras·ter (ras′tər), *n.* the device in a cathode-ray tube that creates a pattern of scanning lines over the area onto which the image is projected.

ra·ti·oc·i·nate (rasH′ēos′ənāt), *v.* to reason, esp. by using formal logic. —**ra·ti·oc·i·na′tion,** *n.*

ra·tion·ale (rasHənal′), *n.* **1.** reasons or principles; the fundamental reasons for something. **2.** the ultimate excuse for a certain action.

rau·cous (rô′kəs), *adj.* (of a sound) harsh; grating; hoarse.

raun·chy (rôn′cHē), *adj.* (slang) slovenly; of poor appearance; sloppy.

rau·wol·fi·a (rôwŏŏl′fēə), *n.* a medicinal extract from the roots of the rauwolfia tree yielding various alkaloids, esp. reserpine.

ra·vi·gote (ravēgôt′), *n.* a spicy sauce of white wine, vinegar, butter, cream, and mushrooms, usually served hot with meats and poultry.

ra·win·sonde (rā′winsond), *n.* meteorological observations conducted by means of a radar-tracked radiosonde.

re·al·ism (rē′əlizm), *n.* **1.** a style in art that attempts to recreate reality. **2.** (in literature) the representation of the ordinary or mundane aspects of life matter-of-factly, in an attempt to reflect life as it actually is. See also **naturalism.**

real time, the actual time used by a computer in solving a problem, the result being required to control a process going on at the same time.

re·ap·por·tion·ment (rēəpôr′sHən-mənt), *n.* a redistribution or change in the proportions, esp. of the proportional representation in a congressional body.

re·a·ta (rēä′tə), *n.* See **riata.**

Ré·au·mur (rā′əmyōōr), *adj.* of or pertaining to a temperature scale in which 0° represents the freezing point and 80° the boiling point of water at sea level.

re·bar·ba·tive (rēbär′bətiv), *adj.* repellent; unattractive; forbidding.

reb·o·ant (reb′ōənt), *adj.* loudly echoing or reverberating.

re·bo·zo, re·bo·so (ribō′zō), *n.* (in Spain and Latin America) a long scarf worn by women over the head and shoulders. Also **rebosa, riboza.**

re·bus (rē′bəs), *n., pl.* **re·bus·es.** the representation of a word or phrase by pictures, letters, symbols, etc., sometimes used in heraldry to represent a surname. See also **canting arms.**

re·ca·lesce (rēkəles′), *v.* to appear to increase temporarily in temperature.

re·cant (rikant′), *v.* to withdraw a statement formally; retract.

re·cen·sion (risen′sHən), *n.* a revision of a text on the basis of detailed study of the sources used.

re·cep·ti·ble (risep′təbəl), *adj.* appropriate for reception.

re·cep·tor (risep′tər), *n.* a nerve ending or group of nerve endings, specialized for the reception of stimuli.

re·ces·sion (risesH′ən), *n.* a temporary decrease in business activity during a period of general increase.

re·ces·sive (rises′iv), *adj.* tending to recede or move back.

ré·chauf·fé (rāsHōfā′), *n., pl.* **ré·chauf·fés** (rāsHōfā′). a reheated dish of food.

re·cher·ché (rəsHer′sHā), *adj.* uncommon; choice; rare.

re·cid·i·vate (risid′əvāt), *v.* to relapse, esp. into crime.

re·cid·i·vism (risid′əvizm), *n.* habitual relapse, as into crime or antisocial behavior.

re·cip·i·ence (risip′ēəns), *n.* the act of receiving. —**re·cip′i·ent,** *n.*

re·ci·sion (risizH′ən), *n.* a rescinding or voiding; cancellation.

reck (rek), *v.* to have care or concern for.

ré·clame (rāklam′), *n.* publicity; notoriety; talent for getting publicity.

rec·li·nate (rek′lənāt), *adj.* bending downward, as a leaf or beak.

rec·li·vate (rek′ləvāt), *adj.* shaped like the letter 'S' or 'C'; sigmoid.

rec·luse (rek′lōōs), *n.* a hermit; one who sequesters himself from the society of others.

re·clu·sion (riklōō′zHən), *n.* the state of being a recluse.

re·cog·ni·zance (rikog′nizəns), *n.* responsibility for behavior, esp. under guarantee or obligation of a bond.

rec·on·dite (rek′əndīt), *adj.* concerning or involved with abstruse or difficult subjects; esoteric; little known, obscure.

rec·re·ant (rek′rēənt), *adj.* **1.** cowardly. **2.** traitorous. —*n.* **3.** a coward. **4.** an apostate or traitor.

rec·re·ment (rek′rəmənt), *n.* a bodily secretion that is reabsorbed, as saliva.

re·crim·i·nate (rikrim′ənāt), *v.* to accuse in turn; revile.

re·crim·i·na·tion (rikrim′ənā′sHən), *n.* mutual accusation or reproach; countercharge.

re·cru·desce (re′krōōdes′), *v.* to break out anew after lying inactive, as a sore. —**re·cru·des′cence,** *n.* —**re·cru·des′cent,** *adj.*

rec·ti·tude (rek′titōōd), *n.* moral or religious uprightness; integrity.

rec·trix (rek′triks), *n., pl.* **rec·tri·ces** (rektrī′sēz). any of the large tail feathers of a bird.

rec·tus (rek′təs), *n., pl.* **rec·ti** (rek′tī). any of various straight muscles, as of the eye, neck, or thigh.

re·cum·bent (rikum′bənt), *adj.* reclining; lying down.

reify

re·cur·vate (rikur′vāt), *adj.* recurved; bent back.

re·curve (rikurv′), *v.* to curve or bend backward.

rec·u·sant (rek′yəzənt), *adj.* refusing to obey, comply, etc.; obstinate in opposition. —**rec′u·san·cy,** *n.*

re·demp·tion (ridemp′sHən), *n.* a redeeming or being redeemed; deliverance. —**re·demp′tive,** *adj.* —**re·demp′to·ry,** *adj.*

red·hi·bi·tion (red′ibisH′ən), *n.* the nullification of a sale because of a defect in the article sold.

red·in·te·grate (redin′təgrāt), *v.* to make whole or perfect again; restore; renew. —**red·in·te·gra′tion,** *n.*

red·i·vi·vus (redəvī′vəs), *adj.* revived; living again; reborn.

red·o·lent (red′ələnt), *adj.* giving out a pleasing odor; fragrant.

re·doubt (ridout′), *n.* a breastwork built for defense around a prominent point.

re·doubt·a·ble (ridou′təbəl), *adj.* formidable; commanding respect.

re·dress (rē′dres, ridres′), *n.* the remedying of a wrong; relief from or reparation for a wrong or injury done.

red tide, a reddish discoloration of sea waters by large numbers of red protozoan flagellates.

re·duct (ridukt′), *n.* a small area partitioned off from a room for the sake of balance with a fireplace, etc.

re·duc·ti·o ad ab·sur·dum (riduk′-sHēō ad absur′dəm), *Latin.* a reduction to an absurdity; the disproof of a proposition by showing its consequences to be impossible or absurd when carried to a logical conclusion.

reef·er (rē′fər), *n.* a cigarette containing marijuana, usually hand-rolled.

re·fec·to·ry (rifek′tərē), *n.* a dining hall in a monastery, convent, college, etc.

ref·er·en·dum (refəren′dəm), *n.*, *pl.* **ref·er·en·dums, ref·er·en·da** (refəren′də). the referral to a public vote of a bill or issue before a legislative body.

ref·er·ent (ref′ərənt), *n.* the object, concept, etc., referred to by a term or symbol. —**ref·er·en′tial,** *adj.*

re·flate (riflāt′), *v.* to restore a former price structure by increasing the amount of currency in circulation. —**re·fla′tion,** *n.*

re·flet (rəflā′), *n.* luster or iridescence, as on glazed pottery.

ref·lu·ent (ref′lōōənt), *adj.* running out; ebbing, as the tide to the sea.

re·flux (rē′fluks), *n.* a flowing back; ebb.

re·frac·tion (rifrak′sHən), *n.* the bending of rays of light, heat, sound, etc., when passing from one medium to another of different density. —**re·fract′,** *v.* —**re·frac′tive,** *adj.*

re·frac·to·ry (rifrak′tərē), *adj.* **1.** hard to manage; resisting conventional treatment. **2.** hard to melt or work, as an ore or metal. —*n.* **3.** a heat-resistant material.

re·fran·gi·ble (rifran′jəbəl), *adj.* that can be refracted, as light rays.

re·frin·gent (rifrin′jənt), *adj.* refracting; refractive.

re·ful·gent (riful′jənt), *adj.* shining; resplendent.

re·fute (rifyōōt′), *v.* to prove a person, argument, opinion, etc., to be wrong; confute. —**ref·u·ta′tion,** *n.* —**re·fut′a·tive,** *adj.*

re·ge·late (rē′jəlāt), *v.* to cause to freeze by regelation.

re·ge·la·tion (rējəlā′sHən), *n.* the melting of ice and freezing of water at the same temperature by changing the pressure.

Re·gen·cy (rē′jənsē), *adj.* **1.** of or designating the style of architecture prevalent during the period 1811–20 in Britain, characterized by simplicity of appearance and often imitating ancient Greek forms. **2.** of or designating the style of furnishings or decoration of the British Regency, similar to French Empire styles and often imitating ancient Greek and Egyptian forms, typically with columns and pilasters, ornamented with ormolu, decorating furniture, the use of marble for flat horizontal surfaces, etc.

reg·i·cide (rej′isīd), *n.* the killing of a monarch.

re·i·fy (rē′əfī), *v.* to make concrete

something abstract; concretize. —re·
i·fi·ca′tion, n.

re·jec·ta·men·ta (rijek′təmen′tə), n.
pl. things rejected as valueless.

re·ju·ve·nate (rijoo′vənāt), v. to make
young or youthful once more. Also
re·ju′ve·nize.

re·ju·ve·nes·cent (rijoo′vənes′ənt),
adj. making or becoming young
again.

re·late (rilāt′), v. (usually followed by
to) to establish a sympathetic relationship with a person or thing.

rel·a·tiv·i·ty (relətiv′itē), n. the theory
of the relative, rather than absolute,
character of motion, velocity, mass,
etc., and the interdependence of matter, time, and space, as formulated
by Albert Einstein.

rel·ic (rel′ik), n. an object that has
survived or been kept because it
represents the past, esp. a fragment
of something associated with a person
much venerated in the history of certain religions.

re·lict (rel′ikt), n. someone or something extant or surviving.

re·li·gi·ose (rilij′ēōs), adj. being religious; pious; excessively religious.
—re·lig·i·os′i·ty, n.

rel·i·quar·y (rel′əkwerē), n. a small
box or receptacle for relics.

re·luc·tance (riluk′təns), n. the resistance offered to magnetic flux by a
magnetic circuit.

rem (rem), n. a unit dose of ionizing
radiation whose biological effect is
equal to that produced by one roentgen of x-rays. [r(oentgen) e(quivalent
in) m(an)]

rem·a·nent (rem′ənənt), adj. remaining; leftover.

re·mex (rē′meks), n., pl. rem·i·ges
(rem′ijēz). one of the flight feathers
of a bird's wing.

rem·i·form (rem′əfôrm), adj. oar-
shaped.

rem·i·grant (rem′əgrənt), n. that
which or one who returns.

rem·i·ped (rem′əped), adj. having
feet adapted for use as oars.

re·miss (rimis′), adj. neglectful of an
obligation.

re·mis·sion (rimisH′ən), n. 1. pardon
or absolution, as for sins. 2. decrease
or reduction in power or vigor, as of
a disease. 3. release from an obligation.

re·mis·sive (rimis′iv), adj. 1. decreasing; tending to abate. 2. pardoning.

re·mon·strate (rimon′strāt), v. to say
or plead in protest, complaint, etc.
—re·mon′strance, n. —re·mon′
strant, adj.

ré·mou·lade (rāməläd′), n. a cold
sauce of spices, herbs, chopped
pickle, etc., with a mayonnaise base.
Also re·mo·lade′.

Ren·ais·sance (ren′isäns′), adj. of
or designating the style of architecture, furnishing, and decoration developed in Italy in the 15th and 16th
centuries, typified by an imitation of
classical Roman motifs and an ad-
herence to symmetry and mathematical proportions.

re·nas·cent (rinas′ənt), adj. acquiring or showing new life or vigor;
being reborn. —re·nas′cence, n.

ren·coun·ter (renkoun′tər), n. a conflict or contest of any kind. Also ren·
con·tre (renkon′tər).

ren·i·fleur (renəflur′), n. one who is
sexually stimulated or gratified by
odors.

ren·i·form (ren′əfôrm), adj. kidney-
shaped.

re·ni·tent (rinī′tnt), adj. resisting
pressure; opposing stubbornly.

ren·voi (renvoi′), n. 1. the expulsion
of an alien, esp. a diplomat, from a
country. 2. the referral of a jurisdic-
tional dispute involving international
law to a law other than the local one.

rep·li·cate (rep′ləkit), adj. folded
back on itself. Also rep′li·cat·ed.

rep·li·ca·tion (repləkā′sHən), n. 1. a
reply or answer. 2. a reply to an
answer. 3. duplication.

re·pos·it (ripoz′it), v. 1. to replace. 2.
to deposit or store.

rep·re·hend (rep′rihend′), v. to find
fault with; reprimand; rebuke.
—rep·re·hen′si·ble, adj. —rep·re·
hen′sion, n.

rep·ro·bate (rep′rəbāt), n. 1. a depraved or unprincipled person. **2.** a person rejected by God and excluded from salvation. —**rep·ro·ba′tion,** *n.* —**rep′ro·ba·tive,** *adj.*

re·pu·di·ate (ripyōō′dēāt), *v.* to deny the authority of; disown; reject with condemnation; reject with denial. —**re·pu·di·a′tion,** *n.*

re·pugn (ripyōōn′), *v.* to oppose or resist. —**re·pug′nance,** *n.* —**re·pug′nant,** *adj.*

req·ui·es·cat (rek′wēes′kat), *n.* a prayer for the repose of the dead, the beginning of *Requiescat in pace* . . .

re·qui·es·cat in pa·ce (re′kwēes′kät in pä′CHe), *Latin.* may he (or she) rest in peace.

req·ui·site (rek′wizit), *adj.* required or necessary for some purpose.

re·quit·al (rikwī′tl), *n.* a return, reward, repayment, etc., for a kindness or service; something as reward, punishment, etc., in return.

rere·dos (rēr′dos), *n.* **1.** an ornamental screen or partition wall behind an altar in a church. **2.** the back of a fireplace.

re·scind (risind′), *v.* to revoke, retract, or cancel; to invalidate, repeal.

re·scis·si·ble (risis′əbəl), *adj.* rescindable.

re·scis·sion (risizH′ən), *n.* the act of rescinding.

re·scis·so·ry (risis′ərē), *adj.* acting or tending to rescind.

re·script (rē′skript), *n.* a written order or answer to a petition presented in writing; any official decree or edict.

re·seau (räzō′), *n.*, *pl.* **re·seaux** (rä-zōz′, räzō′), **re·seaus.** **1.** a network; a netted or meshed foundation in lace. **2.** a reticle on a glass plate, used in photographic telescopes to produce a grid on photographs of stars, for purposes of location.

res·er·pine (res′ərpin), *n.* an alkaloid obtained from the root of the rauwolfia tree, used in the treatment of hypertension and as a sedative.

res ges·tae (rēz jes′tē), acts; deeds.

re·sid·u·um (rizij′ōōəm), *n.*, *pl.* **re·sid·u·a** (rizij′ōōə). the residue or remainder.

re·sile (rizīl′), *v.* to spring back; recoil.

re·sil·ient (rizil′yənt), *adj.* elastic; returning to the original shape after being bent, stretched, etc.; recovering readily from illness, adversity, etc. —**re·sil′ience,** *n.*

res·in·ate (rez′ənāt), *v.* to impregnate or treat with resin.

res·in·if·er·ous (rezənif′ərəs), *adj.* yielding resin.

res·in·oid (rez′ənoid), *adj.* like resin.

res·in·ous (rez′ənəs), *adj.* containing resin; resembling, pertaining to, or having the characteristics of resin.

re·spect·er (rispek′tər), *n.* a person or thing influenced by social standing, importance, power, etc. (usually in negative constructions) as, *sickness is no respecter of rank or position.*

res·pi·rom·e·try (respərom′itrē), *n.* the science of measurement of respiration.

re·su·pine (rē′sōōpīn′), *adj.* prone; prostrate; supine.

re·sur·gence (risur′jəns), *n.* the rising again from virtual extinction; revival. —**re·sur′gent,** *adj.*

re·tard·ate (ritär′dāt), *n.* a mentally retarded person.

re·te (rē′tē), *n.*, *pl.* **re·ti·a** (rē′sHēə). a network, as of nerve fibers.

re·ti·ar·y (rē′sHēer′ē), *adj.* **1.** using a net. **2.** net-like.

ret·i·cle (ret′ikəl), *n.* a network of fine lines, wires, etc., in the focus of the objective of a telescope. —**re·tic′u·lar,** *adj.* —**re·tic′u·late,** *adj.*, *v.* —**re·tic·u·la′tion,** *n.*

re·tic·u·lo·en·do·the·li·al (ritik′yə-lōen′dōthē′lēəl), *adj.* designating or of the system of macrophages found in certain tissues and organs that help maintain resistance and immunity to infection.

re·tic·u·lum (ritik′yələm), *n.*, *pl.* **re·tic·u·la** (ritik′yələ). **1.** any system or structure resembling a network. **2.** the second of the four stomachs of a ruminant. See also **rumen, omasum, abomasum.**

re·ti·form (rē′təfôrm), *adj.* net-like in form; reticulate.

ret·i·ni·tis (retəni′tis), *n.* inflammation of the retina.

ret·i·no·scope (ret′ənəskōp), *n.* skiascope; a device for determining the refractive power of the eye.

ret·i·nos·co·py (retənos′kəpē), *n.* a method of measuring the refraction of an eye by observing the movements of light and shadow on the pupil with a skiascope.

re·trad (rē′trad), *adv.* to the back; backward.

re·tral (rē′trəl), *adj.* at, near, or to the back; posterior.

ret·ro·bul·bar (re′trōbul′bər), *adj.* behind the eyeball.

ret·ro·cede (retrəsēd′), *v.* to go back; recede.

ret·ro·ces·sion (ret′rəsesHən), *n.* a restoration, in American Indian reservations, of police power to a Federal agency.

ret·ro·len·tal fi·bro·pla·sia (re′trōlen′tl fībrəplā′zHə), a disease resulting in blindness found in premature infants, caused by abnormal growth of fibrous tissue behind the lens of the eye.

re·torse (ritrôrs′), *adj.* bent or turned backward.

ret·rous·sé (re′trōōsā′), *adj.* turned up, as *a retroussé nose.*

ret·ro·ver·sion (retrəvur′zHən), *n.* a turning toward the back; the resulting state or condition.

re·trude (ritrōōd′), *v.* (in dentistry) to produce retrusion in.

re·tru·sion (ritrōō′zHən), *n.* displacement of the teeth toward the back of the mouth.

ret·si·na (ret′sənə), *n.* a white or red wine of Greece flavored with resin.

re·tuse (ritōōs′), *adj.* having a blunt or rounded tip with a small notch, as some leaves.

re·vanche (rivänCH′), *n.* the policy that moves a defeated nation aggressively to seek restoration of its original territory. —**re·vanch′ist,** *n.*

rev·e·nant (rev′ənənt), *n.* one who returns; a ghost.

re·vers (rivēr′), *n., pl.* **re·vers.** a part of a garment turned back to show the reverse side or facing, as a lapel. Also **re·vere′.**

re·vet (rivet′), *v.* to face, as the side of a trench or embankment, with masonry, sandbags, etc., for protection.

re·vet·ment (rivet′mənt), *n.* **1.** a facing of masonry, sandbags, etc., for the protection of a wall or bank of earth. **2.** an ornamental facing of marble, tiles, etc.

re·vile (rivīl′), *v.* to attack with abusive or contemptuous language.

re·viv·i·fy (riviv′əfī), *v.* to put new life into; revive.

rev·i·vis·cence (revəvis′əns), *n.* the state of being revived; revival.

rev·o·lute (rev′əlōōt), *adj.* curled back at the edge, as some leaves.

re·vul·sant (rivul′sənt), *adj.* **1.** causing revulsion. —*n.* **2.** a medicinal agent that draws blood from one part of the body to another.

re·vul·sion (rivul′sHən), *n.* **1.** extreme distaste, repugnance, or loathing. **2.** the lessening of action of a disease in one region of the body by irritation in another. —**re·vul′sive,** *adj.*

rhab·do·man·cy (rab′dəmansē), *n.* divination by rod or wand, esp. in finding underground water; dowsing.

rhab·do·my·o·ma (rab′dōmīō′mə), *n., pl.* **rhab·do·my·o·ma·ta** (rab′dōmīō′mətə). a tumor composed of striated muscular fibers.

rha·thy·mi·a (rəthī′mēə), *n.* carefree, indifferent behavior; light-heartedness.

rhe·mat·ic (rimat′ik), *adj.* pertaining to word formation; of or derived from a verb.

rhe·ol·o·gy (rēol′əjē), *n.* the study of the change in flow and form of matter.

rhe·om·e·ter (rēom′itər), *n.* an instrument for measuring fluid flow, as of circulating blood.

rhe·o·re·cep·tor (rē′ōrisep′tər), *n.* nerve endings stimulated by water currents.

rhe·o·scope (rē′əskōp), *n.* a device for detecting the presence of an electric current.

rhe·o·stat (rē′əstat), *n.* a device for varying the resistance of an electric circuit without breaking the circuit, used for regulating the brightness of electric lights, etc.

rhe·o·tax·is (rēətak′sis), *n.* the tendency of an organism to move in response to a current of water.

rhe·ot·ro·pism (rēo′trəpizm), *n.* the tendency of a plant to respond to the stimulus of a current of water by some change in its direction of growth.

rhet·o·ric (ret′ərik), *n.* the effective use of language to persuade or impress; a style that aims to arouse emotion.

rhe·tor·i·cal (ritôr′ikəl), *adj.* used for or concerned with style or effect rather than with content or meaningfulness. —**rhe·tor′i·cally,** *adv.*

rheum (rōōm), *n.* **1.** a watery discharge from the mucous membrane. **2.** a cold. —**rheum′y,** *adj.*

rhex·is (rek′sis), *n.*, *pl.* **rhex·es** (rek′- sēz). a break, as of a blood vessel, organ, etc.

Rh factor, a group of inherited antigens present in the red blood cells of most persons (who are said to be Rh positive), which may cause hemolytic reactions during pregnancy or after transfusion of blood containing this factor into someone lacking it (said to be Rh negative).

rhi·nal (rī′nl), *adj.* of the nose; nasal.

rhi·nar·i·um (rīner′ēəm), *n.*, *pl.* **rhi· nar·i·a** (rīner′ēə). the naked, glandular skin surrounding the nostrils of some mammals.

rhi·nen·ceph·a·lon (rī′nensef′əlon), *n.* the part of the brain concerned with the sense of smell.

rhi·ni·tis (rīnī′tis), *n.* inflammation of the nasal mucous membrane.

rhi·noc·e·rot·ic (rīnos′ərot′ik), *adj.* concerned with or like a rhinoceros.

rhi·nol·o·gy (rīnol′əjē), *n.* the branch of medicine dealing with the nose and its diseases.

rhi·no·plas·ty (rī′nōplas′tē), *n.* plastic surgery of the nose.

rhi·nor·rhe·a, rhi·nor·rhoe·a (rī′-

nōrē′ə), *n.* an excessive mucous discharge from the nose.

rhi·no·scope (rī′nəskōp), *n.* an instrument for examining the internal passages of the nose; nasoscope.

rhi·nos·co·py (rīnos′kəpē), *n.* the examination of the nasal passages.

rhi·zo·gen·ic (rī′zōjen′ik), *adj.* producing roots. Also **rhi·zog′e·nous.**

rhi·zoid (rī′zoid), *adj.* rootlike.

rhi·zo·mor·phous (rī′zōmôr′fəs), *adj.* formed like a root; root-shaped. Also **rhi·zo·mor′phoid.**

rhi·zoph·a·gous (rīzof′əgəs), *adj.* normally eating roots.

Rh negative, having or denoting blood that lacks the Rh factor.

rhom·bic (rom′bik), *adj.* of or having the form of a rhombus.

rhom·bo·he·dron (rombəhē′drən), *n.*, *pl.* **rhom·bo·he·drons, rhom·bo· he·dra** (rombəhē′drə). a six-sided three-dimensional figure, each side of which is a rhombus.

rhom·boid (rom′boid), *n.* a parallelogram with oblique angles and only the opposite sides equal.

rhom·bus (rom′bəs), *n.*, *pl.* **rhom· bus·es, rhom·bi** (rom′bī). an equilateral parallelogram with oblique angles.

rhon·chus (rong′kəs), *n.*, *pl.* **rhon·chi** (rong′kī). a rattling sound in the bronchial tubes caused by a partial bronchial obstruction.

rho·ta·cism (rō′təsizm), *n.* excessive use of the sound ‘r ’ or the substitution of some other sound for it.

Rh positive, having the Rh factor.

ri·a (rē′ə), *n.* a long, narrow inlet, widening and deepening toward the sea.

ri·ant (rī′ənt), *adj.* laughing; smiling; cheerful.

ri·a·ta (rēä′tə), *n.* a lariat. Also **reata.**

rib·ald (rib′əld), *adj.* coarse or vulgar in speech, language, etc. —**rib′ald· ry,** *n.*

ri·bo·fla·vin (rī′bōflā′vin), *n.* a factor of the vitamin B complex found in milk, eggs, meat, leafy vegetables, etc., used in vitamin preparations, etc. Also **ri·bo·fla′vine.**

ribo·nu·cle·ic acid (rī′bōnōōklē′ik). See **RNA.** Also **ribose nucleic acid.**

ri·bose (rī′bōs), *n.* a sugar obtained from RNA.

ri·bo·zo (ribō′zō), *n.* See **rebozo.**

rick·ets (rik′its), *n.* a children's disease of the skeletal system, characterized by a softening and, often, bending of the bones, usually caused by a vitamin D deficiency.

rick·rack, ric·rac (rik′rak), *n.* flat, zigzag braid for trimming clothing, linens, etc.

ri·cot·ta (rikot′ə), *n.* a soft Italian cheese made from whey.

rictal bristle, a feather resembling a bristle which grows from the base of a bird's bill.

ric·tus (rik′təs), *n., pl.* **ric·tus, ric·tus·es.** the opening produced by the gaping of the mouth. —**ric′tal,** *adj.*

rid·dle (rid′l), *v.* **1.** to make many holes in; puncture throughout, as *to riddle with gunshot.* —*n.* **2.** a sieve.

ri·dent (rī′dnt), *adj.* laughing; riant.

Rie·man·ni·an geometry (rēmä′nēən), a form of non-Euclidean geometry in which there are no parallel lines and every pair of straight lines intersects. Also **elliptic geometry.** See also **Euclidean geometry, hyperbolic geometry.**

ri·fa·ci·men·to (rifä′CHimen′tō), *n., pl.* **ri·fa·ci·men·ti** (rifä′CHimen′tē). an adaptation or reworking, as of a piece of music or literature.

rig·a·to·ni (rigətō′nē), *n.* (in Italian cookery) small, ribbed casings of pasta, usually stuffed with ground meat, tomatoes, cheese, etc., and cooked.

rig·or·ism (rig′ərizm), *n.* extreme strictness or severity.

rig·or mor·tis (rig′ər môr′tis), the progressive stiffening of the body after death.

ri·mose (rī′mōs), *adj.* full of cracks or chinks. Also **ri·mous** (rī′məs).

rim·ple (rim′pəl), *n.* a wrinkle; rumple; crease.

rin·ceau (raNsō′), *n., pl.* **rin·ceaux** (raNsō′). an ornamental motif of flowers, leaves, or leafy branches.

rin·gent (rin′jənt), *adj.* agape; open.

ri·par·i·an (riper′ēən), *adj.* of, adjacent to, or living on the bank of a river or other body of water.

ri·poste (ripōst′), *n.* a sharp, often witty response in speech or action. Also **ri·post′.**

rip·rap (rip′rap), *n.* broken stone, usually in flat pieces, used for constructing foundations, embankments, etc.

rip·tide (rip′tīd′), *n.* a tide opposing another tide or current thus causing a violent turbulence.

ris·i·ble (riz′əbəl), *adj.* **1.** able or inclined to laugh. **2.** connected with laughing; laughable. —**ris·i·bil′i·ty,** *n.*

ri·sot·to (risô′tō), *n.* (in Italian cookery) a rice dish cooked with broth and flavored with grated cheese, etc.

ris·qué (riskā′), *adj.* close to being improper or indecent; off-color, as *a risqué joke.*

ris·sole (risōl′), *n.* a small pastry filled with meat or fish, eggs, bread crumbs, etc., and deep-fried.

ris·so·lé (ris′əlē), *adj.* (in cooking) browned in deep fat.

riv·er·ine (riv′ərīn), *adj.* of, like, or near a river.

ri·vière (riv′ēer′), *n.* a necklace, often in more than one strand, of diamonds or other precious stones.

RNA, any of the ribose-containing nucleic acids present in the cytoplasm of the cell. Also **ribonucleic acid, ribose nucleic acid.** See also **DNA.**

rob·o·rant (rob′ərənt), *adj.* tending to make stronger.

ro·bus·tious (rōbus′CHəs), *adj.* rough; boisterous; coarse.

ro·caille (rōkī′), *n.* rock, shell, and foliage forms combined with artificial shapes used for decorative effect in Rococo designs.

rock·a·bil·ly (rok′əbilē), *n.* a type of music resulting from a combination of rock-'n'-roll and hillbilly music.

rock-'n'-roll (rok′ənrōl′), *n.* a form of music characterized by a strong and regular beat, evolved in part from blues and folk music.

ro·co·co (rəkō′kō), *n.* **1.** a style of architecture and decoration developed in 18th-century France from the baroque and characterized by elaborate rocaille ornamentation. —*adj.* **2.** of or like a style of painting of this period characterized by smallness of scale, delicacy of color and playfulness of theme.

ro·den·ti·cide (rōden′tisīd), *n.* a poison used for killing rodents.

rod·o·mon·tade (rod′əmontād′), *n.* arrant, arrogant boasting or braggadocio; ranting, blustering talk.

roent·gen (rent′gən), *n.* the unit of radiation.

roent·gen·o·gram, rönt·gen·o·gram (rent′gənəgram), *n.* (old-fashioned) an x-ray photograph. Also **roent′gen·o·graph, rönt′gen·o·graph.**

roent·gen·ol·o·gy (rentgənol′əjē), *n.* the study and use of x-rays in diagnosis and therapy.

roent·gen·om·e·ter (rentgənom′itər), *n.* a device for measuring the intensity of x-rays.

roent·gen·o·paque (rent′gənōpāk′), *adj.* radiopaque to x-rays.

roent·gen·o·par·ent (rent′gənōper′ənt), *adj.* made visible by means of x-rays.

roent·gen·o·scope, rönt·gen·o·scope (rent′gənəskōp), *n.* a fluoroscope.

roent·gen·o·ther·a·py (rent′gənəther′əpē), *n.* the treatment of disease by x-rays.

rog·a·to·ry (rog′ətôrē), *adj.* concerning or denoting the process of asking or querying.

roil (roil), *v.* **1.** to cloud or muddy a liquid by stirring up sediment. **2.** to stir up; agitate; irritate.

roil·y (roi′lē), *adj.* muddy; turbid.

rois·ter (roi′stər), *v.* to boast or swagger; revel boisterously.

Ro·man·esque (rō′mənesk′), *adj.* designating the European style of architecture from the 9th to the 12th centuries, characterized by thick, load-bearing walls, round arches, the barrel vault, etc.

ron·dure (ron′jər), *n.* a circle or sphere; roundness.

rönt·gen·o·gram (rent′gənəgram), *n.* See **roentgenogram.**

rood (rōōd), *n.* a crucifix, esp. one in a medieval church set over the entry to the chancel.

roor·back (rōōr′bak), *n.* a report, usually of damaging effect, distributed for political reasons.

Roque·fort (rōk′fərt), *n.* a strong cheese veined with a bluish mold, made of sheep's or goat's milk and ripened in caves at Roquefort, in France.

ro·sa·ce·a (rōzā′sHeə), *n.* a form of acne characterized by red lesions on the face.

ro·se·o·la (rōzē′ələ), *n.* measles; rubella.

ros·in (roz′in), *n.* the brittle, yellowish to amber residue after oil has been distilled from turpentine; used for rubbing on violin bows, and in making varnish, inks, soaps, etc.

ross (rôs), *n.* **1.** the rough exterior of bark. —*v.* **2.** to remove ross from in milling.

ros·tel·late (ros′təlāt), *adj.* with a rostellum.

ros·tel·lum (rostel′əm), *n., pl.* **ros·tel·la** (rostel′ə). a small, beak-like process or part.

ros·trum (ros′trəm), *n., pl.* **ros·tra** (ros′trə), **ros·trums.** any platform, stage, etc., for public speaking; a pulpit. —**ros′tral,** *adj.* —**ros′trate,** *adj.*

ro·ta·tive (rō′tātiv), *adj.* turning on its own axis; rotating or causing rotation; occurring regularly in succession.

ro·te·none (rō′tənōn), *n.* a substitute for DDT. See also **malathion.**

ro·ti·form (rō′təfôrm), *adj.* shaped like a wheel.

rou·é (rōōā′, rōō′ā), *n.* a dissipated man; debauchee; rake.

rou·lade (rōōläd′), *n.* a rolled slice of meat filled with chopped meat and cooked.

rou·leau (rōōlō′), *n., pl.* **rou·leaux, rou·leaus** (rōōlōz′). a roll of coins stacked in a paper wrapper.

roun·del (roun′dəl), *n.* something round or circular in form, as a disk.

roup (ro͞op), *n.* hoarseness; huskiness. —**roup′y,** *adj.*

royal jelly, a nutritious mixture secreted by the pharyngeal glands of worker honeybees, fed to all larvae at first and then only to those chosen to be queens.

rub·bing (rub′iNG), *n.* the reproduction of a raised design by laying paper on it and rubbing it with a pencil, crayon, charcoal, or the like. See also **frottage.**

ru·be·fa·cient (ro͞obəfā′sHənt), *adj.* causing redness, as of the skin.

ru·be·fac·tion (ro͞obəfak′sHən), *n.* the act or process of making red, as with a rubefacient.

ru·bel·la (ro͞obel′ə), *n.* German measles.

ru·be·o·la (ro͞obē′ələ), *n.* 1. measles. 2. German measles.

ru·bi·fy (ro͞o′bəfī), *v.* to make red; redden.

ru·big·i·nous (ro͞obij′ənəs), *adj.* rust-colored; reddish-brown.

ru·bi·ous (ro͞o′bēəs), *adj.* ruby-colored; red.

ru·bri·cate (ro͞o′brəkāt), *v.* to mark, color, or illuminate (a book, etc.) with red.

ruc·tion (ruk′sHən), *n.* a noisy disturbance, quarrel, or uproar.

ru·der·al (ro͞o′dərəl), *adj.* (of a plant) growing in waste places, in rubbish, or along the wayside, etc.

ru·fes·cent (ro͞ofes′ənt), *adj.* having a red tinge; rufous.

ru·fous (ro͞o′fəs), *adj.* reddish; brownish-red; rust-colored.

ru·ga (ro͞o′gə), *n., pl.* **ru·gae** (ro͞o′jē). a wrinkle, fold, or ridge.

ru·gate (ro͞o′gāt), *adj.* having wrinkles; rugose.

ru·gose (ro͞o′gōs), *adj.* wrinkled; ridged; ribbed.

ru·gu·lose (ro͞o′gyəlōs), *adj.* having many small wrinkles; finely rugose.

ru·men (ro͞o′min), *n., pl.* **ru·mi·na** (ro͞o′mənə). the first of the four stomachs of a ruminant. See also **reticulum, omasum, abomasum.**

ru·mi·nant (ro͞o′mənənt), *n.* a hoofed mammal that chews its cud and has four stomachs, as the camel, cow, giraffe, etc.

ru·mi·nate (ro͞o′mənāt), *v.* 1. to chew the cud, as a cow does. 2. to meditate; ponder. —**ru·mi·na′tion,** *n.*

run·ci·ble spoon (run′səbəl), a fork with two broad tines and one sharp tine, for serving hors d'oeuvres.

run·ci·nate (run′sənit), *adj.* irregularly saw-toothed, with the teeth curved back, as some leaves.

run·dle (run′dl), *n.* 1. a rung of a ladder. 2. a rotating object, as a wheel or the drum of a capstan.

rune (ro͞on), *n.* a character from an early medieval Indo-European alphabet. —**ru′nic,** *adj.*

run·nel (run′l), *n.* a small stream; little brook or rivulet.

rusk (rusk), *n.* a piece of sweet, raised bread dried and baked a second time until brown and crisp; zwieback.

rus·ti·cate (rus′təkāt), *v.* 1. to go to or remain in the country. 2. to make or finish (a wall surface) in a rustic style. —**rus·ti·ca′tion,** *n.* —**rus·tic′i·ty,** *n.*

ruth (ro͞oth), *n.* pity or compassion; sorrow or remorse.

rut·i·lant (ro͞o′tələnt), *adj.* glittering or glowing with reddish or golden light.

sab·u·lous (sab′yələs), *adj.* sandy; gravelish; gritty.

sac·cad·ic (sakä′dik), *adj.* jerky; twitching.

sac·cate (sak′it), *adj.* saccular; having a sac.

sac·cha·rif·er·ous (sakərif′ərəs), *adj.* bearing sugar.

sac·cha·rim·e·ter (sakərim′itər), *n.* an optical instrument for measuring the concentration of sugar in a solution.

sac·cha·rim·e·try (sakərim′itrē), *n.* the measuring of sugar concentrations in substances.

sac·cha·rine (sak′ərin), *adj.* excessively or deceitfully sweet in facial expression or in speech.

sac·cha·rize (sak′ərīz), *v.* to convert into sugar.

sac·cha·rom·e·ter (sakərom′itər), *n.* a type of hydrometer used to measure the density of sugar solutions.

sac·cu·lar (sak′yələr), *adj.* of sac-like form; saccate.

sac·cu·late (sak′yəlāt), *adj.* having, or having the form of, a sac or saccule.

sac·cule (sak′yōōl), *n.* a small sac.

sac·cu·lus (sak′yələs), *n.*, *pl.* **sac·cu·li** (sak′yəlī). a saccule.

sac·er·do·tal (sasərdō′tl), *adj.* of priests or priesthood; priestly.

sac·er·do·tal·ism (sasərdō′təlizm), *n.* the system, practices, or principles underlying the priesthood.

sa·cral (sā′krəl), *adj.* of or relating to the sacrum.

sac·ra·ment (sak′rəmənt), *n.* **1.** the consecrated bread and wine of the Eucharist. **2.** something considered to have sacred or mysterious significance or influence. —**sac·ra·men′tal**, *adj.* —**sac·ra·men′tal·ist**, *n.*

sac·ris·tan (sak′ristən), *n.* an official keeper of the sacred vessels, etc., of a religious house or church. Also **sac′rist.**

sac·ris·ty (sak′ristē), *n.* the room or building where the sacred vessels and vestments of a church or religious house are kept.

sac·ro·il·i·ac (sak′rōil′ēak), *n.* the joint where the ilium joins the sacrum.

sac·ro·sanct (sak′rōsaNGkt), *adj.* secured by religious sanction against violation; especially sacred.

sac·ro·sci·at·ic (sak′rōsīat′ik), *adj.* relating to the sacrum and the ischium.

sac·rum (sak′rəm), *n.*, *pl.* **sac·ra** (sak′rə). a composite triangular bone consisting, in man, of five fused vertebrae, forming the posterior wall of the pelvic girdle.

sad·ism (sad′izm), *n.* **1.** a sexual perversion in which pleasure is derived from inflicting pain and humiliation. **2.** enjoyment in inflicting cruelty on others. See also **masochism.**

sad·o·mas·o·chism (sad´ōmas´-əkizm), *n.* a psychiatric disorder in which both sadism and masochism are exhibited.

sa·gac·i·ty (səgas´itē), *n.* acuteness of mind allied to practical wisdom. —**sa·ga´cious,** *adj.*

sage (sāj), *n.* **1.** a man of great wisdom. —*adj.* **2.** wise; of sound judgment.

sag·it·tal (saj´itl), *adj.* relating to or resembling an arrow or arrowhead.

sag·it·tate (saj´itāt), *adj.* shaped like an arrowhead.

sa·ke (sä´kē), *n.* a Japanese fermented liquor made from rice.

sa·la·cious (səlā´sHəs), *adj.* lustful; lecherous; obscene.

sal·e·ra·tus (salərā´təs), *n.* baking soda; sodium bicaronate.

sa·li·ent (sā´lēənt), *adj.* **1.** conspicuous; most noticeable. **2.** jutting out; pointing outwards. —**sa´li·ence, sa´li·en·cy,** *n.*

sa·lif·er·ous (səlif´ərəs), *adj.* salt-bearing, as of rocks.

sal·i·fy (sal´əfī), *v.* to form into or combine with a salt.

sa·li·na (səlī´nə), *n.* a salt lake, spring, marsh, etc.; a saltworks.

sa·line (sā´līn), *adj.* containing, relating to, or resembling common salt.

sal·i·nom·e·ter (salənom´itər), *n.* an instrument for determining the concentration of salt in a solution. Also **sal·im´e·ter.**

sal·low (sal´ō), *adj.* of a sickly yellow or yellowish-brown color.

sal·ma·gun·di (salməgun´dē), *n.* a mixture; a miscellaneous collection.

sal·mi (sal´mē), *n.* a highly seasoned dish of gamebirds partially roasted and then cut into pieces and stewed in wine and butter.

sal·mo·nel·la (salmənel´ə), *n., pl.* **sal·mo·nel·lae** (salmənel´ē). any of the large group of rod-shaped microorganisms of the genus *Salmonella* which cause many forms of enteritis, including food poisoning and typhoid fever, and hog cholera.

sal·pin·gi·tis (salpinjī´tis), *n.* inflammation of a Fallopian tube or Eustachian tube.

sal·pinx (sal´piNGks), *n., pl.* **sal·pin·ges** (salpin´jēz). a trumpet-shaped tube.

sal·tant (sal´tnt), *adj.* leaping; dancing; jumping.

sal·ta·tion (saltā´sHən), *n.* a leaping or jumping; a dancing movement; a sudden movement or change. —**sal·ta·to´ri·al, sal´ta·to·ry,** *adj.*

salt·ern (sôl´tərn), *n.* a saltworks; a series of pools made for the natural evaporation of sea water so as to produce salt.

sal·ti·grade (sal´təgrād), *adj.* moving by leaps.

salt·pe·ter, salt·pe·tre (sôltpē´tər), *n.* a salt-like substance, the naturally occurring form of potassium nitrate, used chiefly in making gunpowder and fireworks and to preserve meat. Also called **niter.**

sa·lu·bri·ous (səloo´brēəs), *adj.* promoting good health; health-giving.

sal·u·tar·y (sal´yətər´ē), *adj.* promoting good health; producing good effect.

sal·u·tif·er·ous (salyətif´ərəs), *adj.* salutary.

san·a·tive (san´ətiv), *adj.* of or able to bring about healing.

sanc·tion (saNGk´sHən), *n.* **1.** something operating to enforce a rule of conduct, an oath, etc. **2.** action by states to bring about another state's compliance with an international law or agreement, as by withholding economic aid, reducing trade, etc. **3.** the confirmation or approval of an action.

sanc·tion·a·tive (saNGk´sHənā´tiv), *adj.* relating to or tending toward sanction.

sanc·ti·tude (saNGk´titōōd), *n.* saintliness; sacred character.

sanc·tum (saNGk´təm), *n., pl.* **sanc·tums, sanc·ta** (saNGt´ə). a holy place; a person's private retreat, as a study.

sang·froid (säNfrwä´), *n.* composure; calmness in face of danger or annoyance.

san·gri·a (saNGgrē´ə), *n.* an iced drink made from diluted red wine mixed with sugar, spices, and sometimes fruit juices.

san·guic·o·lous (saNGgwik′ələs), *adj.* living in the blood.

san·guif·er·ous (saNGgwif′ərəs), *adj.* blood-carrying, as an artery.

san·gui·fi·ca·tion (saNG′gwəfəkā′-sHən), *n.* the formation of blood corpuscles; hematopoiesis.

san·gui·nar·y (saNG′gwəner′ē), *adj.* full of or delighting in bloodshed; bloody; bloodthirsty.

san·guine (saNG′gwin), *adj.* 1. of cheerful and courageous disposition. 2. blood-red; of reddish color.

san·guin·e·ous (saNGgwin′ēəs), *adj.* containing or of the color of blood. Also **san′gui·nous.**

san·guin·o·lent (saNGgwin′ələnt), *adj.* of or relating to blood; bloody.

san·guiv·or·ous (saNGgwiv′ərəs), *adj.* blood-eating; feeding on blood.

sa·ni·es (sā′nēez), *n.* a watery fluid, often of greenish color, discharged from a wound or open sore. —**sa′ni·ous,** *adj.*

sans-cu·lotte (sanz′kyo͞oŏlot′), *n.* a person of extreme republican views; a revolutionary.

sans gêne (säN zHen′), *French.* without regard for conventional forms; free of restraint or embarrassment.

sans sou·ci (sänso͞oosē′), *French.* without care; carefree; unconcerned.

sa·phe·nous (səfē′nəs), *adj.* of, relating to, or in the region of a saphenous vein.

saphenous vein, either of two large superficial veins running up the foot, leg, and thigh, one on the inner side and one on the outer side. Also **sa·phe·na.**

sap·id (sap′id), *adj.* tasty; savory; palatable.

sa·pi·ent (sā′pēənt), *adj.* wise; of fancied wisdom.

sa·pi·en·tial (sā′pēen′sHəl), *adj.* containing or characterized by wisdom.

sap·o·dil·la (sapədil′ə), *n.* a large evergreen tree native to tropical America, yielding chicle and bearing edible fruit.

sap·o·na·ceous (sapənā′sHəs), *adj.* of, resembling, or containing soap.

sa·pon·i·fy (səpon′əfī), *v.* to convert fat or oil into soap by boiling it with an alkali.

sa·por (sā′pər), *n.* the taste of a substance; that property of a substance that affects the sense of taste; the sensation of taste.

sap·o·rif·ic (sapərif′ik), *adj.* giving flavor.

sap·o·rous (sap′ərəs), *adj.* flavorsome; tasty.

sa·pre·mi·a (səprē′mēə), *n.* a type of blood poisoning.

sap·ro·gen·ic (sap′rōjen′ik), *adj.* causing putrefaction.

sa·proph·a·gous (saprof′əgəs), *adj.* feeding on dead or decaying organic matter.

sap·ro·phyte (sap′rəfīt), *n.* any organism living on decayed organic matter. —**sap·ro·phyt′ic,** *adj.*

sar·co·ad·e·no·ma (sär′kōad′ənō′-mə), *n., pl.* **sar·co·ad·e·no·mas, sar·co·ad·e·no·ma·ta** (sär′kōad′ənō′mə-tə). See **adenosarcoma.**

sar·co·car·ci·no·ma (sär′kōkär′sə-nō′mə), *n., pl.* **sar·co·car·ci·no·mas, sar·co·car·ci·no·ma·ta** (sär′kōkär′-sənō′mətə). See **carcinosarcoma.**

sar·coid (sär′koid), *n.* 1. a sarcoma-like growth. 2. sarcoidosis or one of the lesions caused by it. —*adj.* 3. fleshy; flesh-like.

sar·coid·o·sis (sär′koidō′sis), *n.* a disease characterized by the appearance of minute grainy, inflamed, ulcerating protruberances in the lungs and liver and less often in the kidneys, bones, eyes, on the skin, etc.

sar·co·lem·ma (sär′kōlem′ə), *n., pl.* **sar·co·lem·mas, sar·co·lem·ma·ta** (sär′kōlem′ətə). the thin sheath of membrane around a muscle fiber.

sar·co·ma (särkō′mə), *n., pl.* **sar·co·mas, sar·co·ma·ta** (särkōmətə). a variety of malignant growth that arises in bones and in the connective tissues lying beneath the skin and between and around muscles and organs.

sar·co·ma·to·sis (särkō′mətō′sis), *n.* a condition characterized by the development of large numbers of sarcomas throughout the body.

sar·coph·a·gous (särkof**ˈ**əgəs), *adj.* living on flesh; carnivorous.

sar·coph·a·gus (särkof**ˈ**əgəs), *n., pl.* **sar·coph·a·gi** (särkof**ˈ**əjī). **1.** a coffin made of stone, usually with inscriptions, reliefs, etc. **2.** a stone thought by the ancient Greeks to consume the remains of corpses.

sar·co·phile (sär**ˈ**kəfīl), *n.* any flesh-eating creature.

sar·cous (sär**ˈ**kəs), *adj.* composed of or relating to flesh or skeletal muscle.

sar·don·ic (särdon**ˈ**ik), *adj.* of bitter or scornful character.

sar·men·tose (särmen**ˈ**tōs), *adj.* (in botany) having runners, as a strawberry. Also **sar·men**ˈ**tous.**

sar·men·tum (särmen**ˈ**təm), *n., pl.* **sar·men·ta** (särmen**ˈ**tə). a stem put out along the ground from the base of a plant, as in the strawberry. Also **sar**ˈ**ment.**

sa·ros (ser**ˈ**os), *n.* the period of years after which eclipses are repeated but are 120° toward the west from the previous series, equivalent to 233 synodic months or 6585.32 days.

sar·to·ri·al (särtôr**ˈ**ēəl), *adj.* of or relating to dress, esp. to men's clothing.

sa·ti·e·ty (sətī**ˈ**ətē), *n.* the state of having had too much; a surfeit.

sa·trap (sā**ˈ**trap), *n.* a subordinate ruler, esp. one enjoying great luxury or practising tyranny. —**sa**ˈ**tra·py,** *n.*

sat·u·rate (saCH**ˈ**ərāt), *v.* **1.** to cause a substance to combine with or dissolve the maximum quantity it can of another substance. **2.** to cause to absorb or hold the maximum possible amount of anything, as electric charge, moisture, etc. **3.** to bomb a target so heavily that defenses are powerless and the target is completely destroyed.

sat·u·rat·ed (saCH**ˈ**ərāˈtid), *adj.* (of fats) containing no double bonds and so unable to accept any additional atoms of hydrogen; such fats, which are hard at room temperature, raise the level of cholesterol in the blood. See also **monounsaturated, polyunsaturated.**

sat·ur·na·li·a (satərnā**ˈ**lēə), *n., pl.* **sat·**

ur·na·li·a, sat·ur·na·li·as. a period or scene of wild revelry.

Sa·tur·ni·an (sətur**ˈ**nēən), *adj.* prosperous and peaceful, as in the supposedly golden age of Saturn's reign.

sat·ur·nine (sat**ˈ**ərnīn), *adj.* **1.** of cold, gloomy, sluggish temperament or of an appearance suggesting such a temperament. **2.** of, suffering from, or due to lead poisoning.

sa·ty·ri·a·sis (sātərī**ˈ**əsis), *n.* abnormally excessive and uncontrollable sexual desire in males.

sa·tyr·o·ma·ni·ac (sāˈtərōmā**ˈ**nēak), *n.* a lustful man.

sau·ri·an (sôr**ˈ**ēən), *adj.* **1.** belonging to or relating to a group of reptiles that includes the lizards. **2.** lizardlike.

sau·té (sōtā**ˈ**), *adj.* **1.** lightly browned by being fried in oil or fat over heat. —*v.* **2.** to cook by frying in a small amount of fat or oil over heat.

sau·toir (sōtwär**ˈ**), *n.* **1.** a chain, scarf, ribbon, etc., fastened around the neck with the ends crossing at the front. **2.** a chain or ribbon bearing a pendant for wearing around the neck.

sauve qui peut (sōvkēpoͦˈ), *French.* a disorderly flight in which everyone looks only to his own safety; each man for himself.

sa·van·na (səvan**ˈ**ə), *n.* a great plain, esp. in subtropical regions, of coarse grasses and scattered trees and having seasonal rainfall.

sa·vant (səvänt**ˈ**), *n.* a man of great learning.

save-all (sāv**ˈ**ôl), *n.* any device or means for stopping loss or reducing waste.

sa·voir-faire (savˈwärferˈ), *n.* the quality of seeing and doing the right thing in any situation.

sa·voir-vi·vre (savˈwärvēˈvrə), *n.* the quality of knowing the ways of and being at home in polite society.

sa·vor (sā**ˈ**vər), *n.* **1.** a distinctive taste, smell, or quality; that part of any substance that affects the sense of taste or smell. —*v.* **2.** to perceive or appreciate the taste or smell of something.

saw·yer (sô′yər), *n.* a man who makes his living by sawing timber.

sax·a·tile (sak′sətil), *adj.* living or growing on rocks or in rocky places.

sax·ic·o·line (saksik′əlin), *adj.* living or growing in rocky places. Also **sax·ic′o·lous.**

scab·i·cide (skab′isīd), *adj.* of any substance used or able to destroy the parasitic mite that causes scabies.

sca·bies (skā′bēz), *n.* a contagious skin disease caused by a parasitic mite burrowing under the skin, occurring in cattle, sheep, and man.

sca·bi·ous (skā′bēəs), *adj.* composed of or covered with scabs; relating to or like scabies.

scab·rous (skab′rəs), *adj.* **1.** having a surface covered with tiny projections. **2.** full of difficulties. **3.** obscene; indecent.

sca·lar (skā′lər), *n.* a mathematical quantity that has only magnitude. See also **vector.**

sca·lene (skālēn′), *adj.* of a triangle with no two sides equal.

sca·le·no·he·dron (skālē′nəhē′drən), *n.,pl.* **sca·le·no·he·drons, sca·le·no·he·dra** (skālē′nəhē′drə). a solid with 8 or 12 faces, each one of which forms a scalene triangle.

scal·pri·form (skal′prəfôrm), *adj.* chisel-shaped.

scan·dent (skan′dənt), *adj.* of climbing habit, as a plant.

scan·so·ri·al (skansôr′ēəl), *adj.* (in zoology) adapted for climbing; given to climbing.

scaph·oid (skaf′oid), *adj.* shaped like a boat.

scap·u·lar (skap′yələr), *adj.* of or relating to the shoulders.

scap·u·lo·hum·er·al (skap′yəlōhyo͞o′mərəl), *adj.* of or relating to the shoulder blade (scapula) and the bone of the upper arm (humerus).

scarce·ment (skers′mənt), *n.* a ledge or foothold formed in a wall by one portion being set back from the rest.

scar·i·fy (skar′əfī), *v.* to make superficial cuts or scratches; to wound with harsh words. —**scar·i·fi·ca′tion, scar′i·fi·ca·tor,** *n.*

scar·i·ous (sker′ēəs), *adj.* dry, papery, and membranous, as a grass bract.

scar·la·ti·na (skärlətē′nə), *n.* scarlet fever. **scar·la·ti′noid,** *adj.*

scarlet fever, a contagious disease caused by streptococci and characterized by a scarlet rash on the skin and in the mouth and throat.

scarp (skärp), *n.* a line of cliffs or steeply sloping ground formed by a fracture and vertical separation in the earth's crust; escarpment.

scathe (skāTH), *v.* **1.** to injure, esp. by fire. **2.** to hurt by invective or satire.

sca·tol·o·gy (skətol′əjē), *n.* **1.** the study of or excessive interest in excrement or obscenity. **2.** the study of fossil excrement. Also called **coprology.**

sca·to·ma (skətō′mə), *n., pl.* **sca·to·mas, sca·to·ma·ta** (skətō′mətə). a tumor-like mass of feces in the rectum or large intestine.

sca·toph·a·gy (skətof′əjē), *n.* the religious practice of or psychiatric disorder characterized by eating excrement. —**sca·toph′a·gous,** *adj.*

sca·tos·co·py (skətos′kəpē), *n.* the medical examination of feces to diagnose certain conditions.

scat singing, singing, usually in jazz, in which the singer improvises nonsense words to fit the music and also makes sounds in imitation of musical instruments.

scau·per (skô′pər), *n.* an engraving tool with a flattened or hollowed blade. Also **scorper.**

sce·nog·ra·phy (sēnog′rəfē), *n.* the graphic representation of objects following the rules of perspective.

sche·ma (skē′mə), *n., pl.* **sche·ma·ta** (skē′mətə). a diagram; an outline; a scheme.

schism (sizm), *n.* a separation into opposing groups because of a difference of opinion; a group formed by the separation. —**schis·mat′ic,** *adj.*

schis·to·sis (SHistō′sis), *n.* fibrosis of the lungs due to prolonged inhalation of slate dust.

schis·to·some (SHis′təsōm), *n.* a type of blood-fluke, including the parasite which causes bilharzia.

schis·to·so·mi·a·sis (sнisˈtəsōmīˈə-sis), *n.* any of several serious illnesses caused by infestation with parasitic blood-flukes.

schiz·o·gen·e·sis (skizəjenˈisis), *n.* reproduction by the splitting of cells. —**schiz·o·ge·net′ic, schi·zog′e·nous,** *adj.*

schiz·oid (skitˈsoid), *adj.* of, resembling, having, or tending toward schizophrenia.

schiz·o·phre·ni·a (skitsəfrēˈnēə), *n.* a severe mental illness, often recurring and sometimes progressive, in which the behavior becomes withdrawn and out of character, the intellect and emotions deteriorate, and hallucinations may occur. —**schiz·o·phren′ic,** *adj.*

schiz·o·phyte (skizˈəfīt), *n.* any of a group of plants characterized by reproduction by cell-splitting.

schiz·o·thy·mi·a (skitsəthīˈmēə), *n.* the exhibiting of the features that distinguish schizophrenia but within normal limits.

schle·ma·z·zle, schle·ma·zel (sнləmäˈzl), *n.* a particularly stupid and awkward person.

schle·miel, schle·mihl (sнləmēlˈ), *n.* a poor fool who is always the victim of others.

schlepp (sнlep), *v.* to drag about, esp. unnecessarily or burdensomely.

schlie·ren (sнlērˈən), *n. pl.* **1.** streaks in a fluid having a density and index of refraction different from that fluid. **2.** streaks of differently colored or textured rock in an igneous rock.

schlock (sнlok), *adj.* (colloquial) cheap and trashy. Also **schlock′y.**

schmaltz (sнmälts), *n.* (colloquial) exaggerated, sickly sentimentality. —**schmaltz′y,** *adj.*

schneck·en (sнnekˈən), *n. pl., sing.* **schnecke.** sweet rolls of snail-like spiral shape made from raised dough mixed with chopped nuts, cinnamon, and butter.

schnor·rer (sнnôrˈər), *n.* (colloquial) a beggar; a sponger.

scho·li·ast (skōˈlēast), *n.* any of the ancient grammarians who wrote explanatory comments on passages in a classical author's work.

schuss (sнōos), (in skiing) *n.* **1.** a run directly down the steepest line of a slope with no attempt to control speed. —*v.* **2.** to perform a schuss.

sci·am·a·chy (sīamˈəkē), *n.* the act of or an instance of fighting an imaginary foe. Also **sci·om′a·chy.**

sci·at·ic (sīatˈik), *adj.* of, relating to, near, or affecting the ischium or lowest part of the pelvic girdle where it connects with the hip.

sci·at·i·ca (sīatˈikə), *n.* pain and soreness in parts of or near the sciatic nerve, which runs from the pelvis down the back of the leg to the foot.

sci·en·tial (sīenˈsнəl), *adj.* of, relating to, or having knowledge.

sci·en·tism (sīˈəntizm), *n.* the belief that the methods applicable to physics and biology are equally appropriate to all other disciplines including the humanities and social sciences.

scil·i·cet (silˈiset), *adv.* namely; that is to say.

scin·til·la (sintilˈə), *n.* a spark, a shred, a minute particle, as *not a scintilla of evidence.*

scin·til·late (sinˈtəlāt), *v.* to give out sparks; to sparkle; to twinkle. —**scin′til·lant,** *adj.* —**scin·til·la′tion,** *n.*

sci·o·lism (sīˈəlizm), *n.* superficial knowledge.

sci·os·o·phy (sīosˈəfē), *n.* knowledge of natural or supernatural phenomena based on astrology, phrenology, or the like.

scir·rhus (skirˈəs), *n., pl.* **scir·rhi** (skirˈī), **scir·rhus·es.** a hard, painless tumor; a hard cancer.

scis·sel (sisˈəl), *n.* the metal strip from which coin blanks have been cut.

scis·sile (sisˈil), *adj.* capable of being cut or split.

scis·sion (siZHˈən), *n.* a cutting; a division; a split.

sci·u·roid (sīyŏōrˈoid), *adj.* resembling a squirrel's tail.

scle·re·ma (sklirēˈmə), *n.* hardening or sclerosis, esp. affecting the skin.

scle·ro·der·ma (sklērədurˈmə), *n.* a

disease causing all the layers of skin to harden and become rigid. Also **scle·ri·a·sis** (sklərī′əsis).

scle·ro·der·ma·ti·tis (sklēr′ōdur′-mətī′tis), *n.* a disease causing hardening and inflammation of the skin. Also **scle·ro·der·mi′tis.**

scle·ro·der·ma·tous (sklērədur′-mətəs), *adj.* having a covering of hardened tissue such as scales.

scle·rog·e·nous (sklirōj′ənəs), *adj.* giving rise to hardened tissue.

scle·roid (sklēr′oid), *adj.* hard or hardened.

scle·ro·ma (sklirō′mə), *n., pl.* **scle·ro·mas, scle·ro·ma·ta** (sklirō′mətə). a tumor-like mass of hardened tissue.

scle·rom·e·ter (sklirom′itər), *n.* any device for making an accurate measure of the hardness of a substance.

scle·ro·phyl·ly (sklēr′əfil′ē), *n.* a normal development in foliage which results in it becoming thickened and hardened. —**scle′ro·phyll,** *adj., n.*

scle·rosed (sklirōst′), *adj.* thickened or hardened by sclerosis.

scle·ro·sis (sklirō′sis), *n., pl.* **scle·ro·ses** (sklirō′sēz) the replacement of normal tissue by increased fibrous or supporting tissue, with a resulting thickening and hardening leading to loss of function. —**scle·rot′ic,** *adj.*

scle·ro·ti·tis (sklērətī′tis), *n.* inflammation of the sclera, the external covering of the eyeball. Also **scle·ri′tis.**

scle·rous (sklēr′əs), *adj.* hard; thick; firm; bony.

scoff·law (skôf′lô), *n.* (colloquial) one who shows contempt for the law in word or deed.

sco·li·o·sis (skō′lēō′sis), *n.* sideways curvature of the spine.

sco·pol·a·mine (skəpol′əmēn), *n.* a drug used chiefly to increase the effect of narcotics in bringing about twilight sleep, as a sedative, and to produce dilatation of the pupil of the eye.

sco·po·phil·i·a (skōpəfil′ēə), *n.* a psychiatric disorder in which sexual gratification is obtained exclusively by looking at nude bodies, erotic photographs, and the like.

scop·u·late (skop′yəlāt), *adj.* broomlike; in the shape of a brush.

scor·bu·tic (skôrbyōō′tik), *adj.* of, relating to, resembling, or affected with scurvy.

scor·per (skôr′pər), *n.* See **scauper**

scor·pi·oid (skôr′pēoid), *adj.* curved back on itself at the end like the tail of a scorpion.

scotch (skoch), *v.* to wound without killing so as to render harmless.

sco·to·ma (skōtō′mə), *n., pl.* **sco·to·mas, sco·to·ma·ta** (skōtō′mətə). a loss of sight affecting only part of the visual field; a blind spot.

sco·to·pi·a (skətō′pēə), *n.* the ability to see in dim light. See also **photopia.**

scourge (skurj), *n.* **1.** a whip for chastising or torturing; a person or thing administering punishment or harsh criticism. **2.** that which brings about affliction or disaster. —*v.* **3.** to whip.

screed (skrēd), *n.* **1.** a long and tedious letter, essay, discourse, or the like. **2.** a wooden or metal strip for leveling a concrete or similar surface as it is made.

scrim (skrim), *n.* **1.** a thin cotton or linen open-weave fabric resembling fine canvas. **2.** a piece of such fabric used as a stage drop to appear solid when lit from the front and almost transparent when lit from behind.

scro·bic·u·late (skrōbik′yəlit), *adj.* having a furrowed or pitted surface.

scrof·u·la (skrof′yələ), *n.* a name formerly used for a tubercular condition characterized by swelling and degeneration of the lymphatic glands and joints. —**scrof′u·lous,** *adj.*

scru·ple (skrōō′pəl), *n.* a unit used in measuring very small weights, equal to 20 grains or 1/3rd dram.

scru·ta·ble (skrōō′təbəl), *adj.* able to be understood after detailed examination or study.

sculp·sit (skōōlp′sit), *Latin.* (this person) carved, sculptured, or engraved (this work).

scum·ble (skum′bəl), *v.* **1.** to lay a thin coat of opaque or semiopaque color over parts of a painted area with an almost dry brush to soften the color or line. —*n.* **2.** an effect so achieved.

scun·ner (skun′ər), *n.* a dislike taken with no reason.

scurf (skûrf), *n.* any scaly incrustation on a surface. —**scurf′y,** *adj.*

scur·ril·ous (skur′ələs), *adj.* grossly or obscenely abusive. —**scur·ril′i·ty,** *n.*

scu·tate (skyoo′tāt), *adj.* having the form of or furnished with a scute or scutes.

scute (skyoot), *n.* an oblong or round bony or horny plate or large scale forming a defensive covering in creatures such as crocodiles and turtles.

scu·tel·late (skyootel′it), *adj.* having the form of or furnished with scutes or scutella. —**scu·tel·la′tion,** *n.*

scu·tel·li·form (skyootel′əfôrm), *adj.* scutellum-shaped.

scu·tel·lum (skyootel′əm), *n.*, *pl.* **scu·tel·la** (skyootel′ə). a small plate, scale, or shield-like part.

scu·ti·form (skyoo′təfôrm), *adj.* shield-shaped.

scu·tum (skyoo′təm), *n.*, *pl.* **scu·ta** (skyoo′tə). a scute.

scy·phate (sī′fāt), *adj.* cup-shaped.

scy·phi·form (sī′fəfôrm), *adj.* having the shape of a cup or goblet.

scy·pho·zo·an (sīfəzō′ən), *n.* any animal of the class comprising the jellyfishes.

scy·phus (sī′fəs), *n.*, *pl.* **scy·phi** (sī′fī). a cup-shaped part.

sea·dog (sē′dôg), *n.* See **fogbow.**

sea eagle, any of various large species of eagle that feed mainly on fish.

sea·mount (sē′mount), *n.* an underwater mountain reaching a height of several hundred feet above the sea bed but with its peak well below sea level.

se·ba·ceous (sibā′sнəs), *adj.* relating to, resembling, or of the same nature as tallow or fat; fatty.

se·bif·er·ous (sibif′ərəs), *adj.* containing or secreting fat or fatty matter.

seb·or·rhe·a, seb·or·rhoe·a (sebərē′ə), *n.* excessive or otherwise abnormal secretion by the sebaceous glands. —**seb·or·rhe′ic,** *adj.*

se·cern (sisurn′), *v.* to distinguish or be distinguished in thought.

se·cern·ent (sisur′nənt), *adj.* secreting.

se·clu·sive (sikloo′siv), *adj.* tending to retire into privacy.

sec·o·bar·bi·tal (sek′ōbär′bital), *n.* a sedative and hypnotic drug.

secondary boycott, a boycott operated by members of a union against their employer intended to force him to exercise his influence on another employer who is in dispute with members of the same union in his employ.

se·cre·to·ry (sikrē′tərē), *adj.* relating to or capable of secretion.

sec·tile (sek′til), *adj.* that can be cut easily with a knife.

sec·to·ri·al (sektôr′ēəl), *adj.* adapted for cutting, esp. of a carnivore's tooth.

sec·u·lar (sek′yələr), *adj.* of or relating to the things of this world; lay; temporal as opposed to sacred, spiritual, and religious. —**sec′u·lar·ism, sec·u·lar′i·ty,** *n.*

sec·u·lar·ize (sek′yələrīz), *v.* to separate from religious or spiritual controls or connections.

sed·en·tar·y (sed′nter′ē), *adj.* sitting; characterized by or requiring a sitting position.

sed·i·men·tol·o·gy (sedəməntol′əjē), *n.* the scientific study of rocks formed of consolidated sediment.

se·di·tion (sidisн′ən), *n.* any incitement to unlawful action against the authority of government. —**se·di′tious,** *adj.*

sed·u·lous (sej′ələs), *adj.* diligent and persevering; persistently and unremittingly kept up. —**se·du′li·ty,** *n.*

se·gue (sā′gwā), *v.* to continue without interruption or blend in with the next part or item, usually of a musical performance.

sei·cen·to (sāchen′tō), *n.* the sixteen hundreds, that is the 17th century, referring esp. to the art or literature of Italy at that time.

seiche (sāsн), *n.* sudden oscillation in the surface of a lake or other large stretch of water caused occasionally by changes in atmospheric pressure, wind direction, earth tremor, etc.

seism (sī′zəm), *n.* an earthquake. —**seis′mic,** *adj.*

seis·mic·i·ty (sīzmis′itē), *n.* the factors in a given area that relate to earthquakes, including frequency of occurrence, force, distribution, and the like.

seis·mism (sīz′mizm), *n.* the natural phenomena associated with an earthquake.

seis·mo·gram (sīz′məgram), *n.* a record made by a seismograph.

seis·mo·graph (sīz′məgraf), *n.* any instrument for recording and measuring tremors in the earth's crust.

seis·mog·ra·phy (sīzmog′rəfē), *n.* the recording and measuring of earthquake tremors. —**seis·mog′ra·pher,** *n.*

seis·mol·o·gy (sīzmol′əjē), *n.* the scientific study of earthquakes and the natural phenomena associated with them.

seis·mom·e·ter (sīzmom′itər), *n.* a type of seismograph that measures the actual movement of ground during an earthquake and records the direction, duration, and force of the movement.

seis·mo·scope (sīz′məskōp), *n.* an instrument that records earthquake activity.

sel·e·nod·e·sy (selənod′isē), *n.* the branch of astronomy concerned with measuring the surface of the moon and its gravitational field.

se·le·no·dont (silē′nədont), *adj.* having crescent-shaped ridges on the crowns of the teeth.

sel·e·nog·ra·phy (selənog′rəfē), *n.* the branch of astronomy concerned with the physical geography of the moon and the irregularities of its surface.

sel·e·nol·o·gy (selənol′əjē), *n.* the branch of astronomy concerned with the physical characteristics of the moon and the origin of its surface features.

se·le·no·tro·pism (silē′nətrō′pizm), *n.* a response, such as growth or movement, to the stimulus of moonlight.

sel·vage (sel′vij), *n.* the edge of fabric woven so that the weft will not ravel, and often different from the weave of the rest of the fabric.

se·man·tics (siman′tiks), *n.* **1.** the branch of linguistics concerned with meanings. **2.** See **general semantics.** —**se·man′tic,** *adj.*

se·ma·si·ol·o·gy (simā′sēol′əjē), *n.* the branch of linguistics concerned with meanings and their changes.

se·mat·ic (simat′ik), *adj.* giving warning to enemies or attracting attention, as the markings of poisonous animals.

se·mei·ol·o·gy (sē′mīol′əjē), *n.* the study of or a system of signs. Also **semiology.**

sem·i·ab·stract (sem′ēab′strakt), *adj.* relating to or denoting a style of art in which the representation is not naturalistic but the subject remains recognizable.

sem·i·breve (sem′ēbrēv), *n.* (in musical notation) a whole note; the longest note in general use, equal to half the length of a breve.

sem·i·cen·ten·ni·al (sem′ēsenten′ēəl), *adj.* **1.** of or relating to a 50th anniversary. —*n.* **2.** a 50th anniversary. Also **sem·i·cen′te·nar·y.**

sem·i·con·duc·tor (sem′əkənduk′tər), *n.* a material, used in diodes, whose conductivity is less than that of a metal and more than that of an insulator.

sem·i·de·tached (sem′ēditacĦt′), *adj.* of or relating to a house joined to another by a party wall on one side.

sem·i·di·ur·nal (sem′ēdīur′nl), *adj.* relating to, consisting of, or taking half a day; occurring once in each 12 hours.

sem·i·fi·nal (sem′ēfīn′l), *adj.* of or relating to the round preceding the final in a contest whose losers are eliminated. —**sem·i·fi′nal·ist,** *n.*

sem·i·nal (sem′ənl), *adj.* **1.** that originates something, as an idea, a style, etc., and influences future development. **2.** containing, composed of, or relating to semen.

sem·i·na·tion (semənā′sнən), *n.* a sowing of, impregnation with, or spreading of seed.

sem·i·nif·er·ous (semənif′ərəs), *adj.* containing, carrying, or producing seed or semen.

sem·i·niv·or·ous (seməniv′ərəs), *adj.* seed-eating, as certain birds.

se·mi·ol·o·gy (sē′mēol′əjē), *n.* See **semeiology.**

se·mi·ot·ic (sē′mēot′ik), *adj.* **1.** relating to signs. **2.** of or relating to medical symptoms. —*n.* **3.** Also **semiotics,** a comprehensive philosophical theory of signs and languages.

sem·i·o·vip·a·rous (sem′ēōvip′ərəs), *adj.* bearing partially developed young, as the kangaroo.

sem·i·pal·mate (sem′epal′māt), *adj.* partially palmate; half-webbed, as the feet of certain birds.

sen·a·ry (sen′ərē), *adj.* of or relating to the number six.

se·nes·cent (sənes′ənt), *adj.* aging; becoming old.

sen·e·schal (sen′əsнəl), *n.* a steward in charge of all domestic arrangements and order in a great medieval household.

sen·sate (sen′sāt), *adj.* endowed with or perceived by physical sensation.

sen·sil·lum (sensil′əm), *n., pl.* **sen·sil·la** (sensil′ə). a simple sense organ composed of one or a small number of cells at the end of a sensory nerve fiber.

sen·so·ri·mo·tor (sen′sərēmō′tər), *adj.* of, having, or relating to both sensory and motor functions or parts; of or relating to motor activity in response to a sensory stimulus.

sen·so·ri·um (sensôr′ēəm), *n., pl.* **sen·so·ri·ums, sen·so·ri·a** (sensôr′-ēə). the brain, or a particular part of it, regarded as the seat of all sensation.

sen·so·ry (sen′sərē), *adj.* of or relating to sensation or the senses; of a bodily structure, esp. a nerve, that conveys impulses that cause sensation.

sen·ten·tious (senten′sнəs), *adj.* full of pithily expressed truths; given to self-righteous moralizing.

sen·tience (sen′sнəns), *n.* the power of or capacity for perception through the senses. —**sen′tient,** *adj.*

se·pal (sē′pəl), *n.* one of the small, often green, leaf-like parts covering the buds of certain flowers and forming the outermost ring when the flower has opened.

se·pal·oid (sē′pəloid), *adj.* like a sepal.

sep·a·ra·trix (sep′ərā′triks), *n., pl.* **sep·a·ra·tri·ces** (sepərā′trisēz), **sep·a·ra·trix·es.** something that separates or marks off one part from another, as a line, decimal point, punctuation mark, etc.

sep·sis (sep′sis), *n.* the condition of having, the location of, or the presence of dead and decomposing tissue caused by bacterial infection.

sept (sept), *n.* a group of people who believe themselves to be descended from a common ancestor.

sep·tal (sep′tl), *adj.* of or relating to a septum.

sep·tate (sep′tāt), *adj.* having a septum or septa.

sep·tem·vir (septem′vər), *n., pl.* **sep·tem·virs, sep·tem·vi·ri** (septem′-vərī). one of a ruling body of seven men. —**sep·tem′vi·ral,** *adj.*

sep·tem·vi·rate (septem′vərit), *n.* a ruling body composed of seven men.

sep·te·nar·y (sep′tənər′ē), *adj.* **1.** of, relating to, or based on the number seven. **2.** septennial. —*n.* **3.** a group or set of seven.

sep·ten·de·cil·lion (sep′tendisil′-yən), *n.* a number represented by the figure one followed by 54 zeros (but in the United Kingdom and Germany by the figure one followed by 102 zeros).

sep·ten·nial (septen′ēəl), *adj.* of, for, or every seven years.

sep·ten·tri·o·nal (septen′trēənl), *adj.* northern. See also **meridional.**

sept·foil (sept′foil), *n.* a seven-lobed ornament or decorative motif.

sep·tic (sep′tik), *adj.* relating to, of the nature of, or infected by sepsis.

sep·ti·ce·mi·a (sep′tise′mēə), *n.* the spread of septic matter through the blood; blood-poisoning.

sep·til·lion (septil′yən), *n.* a number

represented by the figure one followed by 24 zeros (but in the United Kingdom and Germany by the figure one followed by 42 zeros).

sep·tu·a·ge·nar·i·an (sep′CHOO̅o̅ojə-ner′ēən), *adj.* **1.** aged between 70 and 80 years. —*n.* **2.** a person of this age.

sep·tum (sep′təm), *n., pl.* **sep·ta** (sep′-tə). a dividing wall, partition, layer, membrane, etc., as between the nostrils, the ventricles of the heart, etc.

sep·ul·cher, sep·ul·chre (sep′əlkər), *n.* a tomb or burial place, esp. one cut in rock or made of stone. —**se·pul′-chral,** *adj.*

sep·ul·ture (sep′əlcHər), *n.* burial; the placing of a body in a sepulcher.

se·qua·cious (sikwā′sHəs), *adj.* following smoothly or logically; coherent.

se·que·la (sikwē′lə), *n., pl.* **se·que·lae** (sikwē′lē). any abnormal condition present as a result of some disease.

se·quent (sē′kwənt), *adj.* **1.** following; following logically or as a matter of course. **2.** in continuous succession; consecutive.

se·ques·ter (sikwes′tər), *v.* to put into solitude; to seclude. —**se·ques·tra′ tion,** *n.*

se·ques·trec·to·my (se′kwestrek′tə-mē), *n.* the surgical removal of dead splinters or pieces, esp. of bone.

se·ques·trum (sikwes′trəm), *n., pl.* **se·ques·tra** (sikwes′trə). a bone fragment that has died through disease or injury and separated from the normal bone.

sere (sēr), *n.* the succession of changes in the composition of a plant population from the initial colonization by plants to the final state of vegetation.

se·rein (səran′), *n.* a fine rain falling after sunset from an apparently cloudless sky.

ser·en·dip·i·ty (serəndip′itē), *n.* the faculty of accidentally making fortunate discoveries. —**ser·en·dip′i· tous,** *adj.*

se·ri·ate (sēr′ēit), *adj.* in series.

se·ri·a·tim (sēr′ēā′tim), *adv.* singly in succession; one after another.

se·ri·ceous (sirisH′əs), *adj.* silky;

with a covering of silky down. Also **ser′i·cate.**

ser·i·cul·ture (ser′əkul′cHər), *n.* silkworm-breeding to produce raw silk.

ser·i·graph (ser′əgraf), *n.* a print made by the silk-screen process.

se·ri·o·com·ic (sēr′ēōkom′ik), *adj.* partly serious and partly comic.

se·rol·o·gy (sirol′əjē), *n.* the scientific study of the constitution, properties, and functions of blood, esp. of blood serum.

se·ro·mu·cous (sēr′ōmyoo̅′kəs), *adj.* relating to or consisting of serum and mucus.

se·ro·si·tis (sīrōsī′tis), *n.* inflammation of one of the thin membranes that line certain body cavities and exude a serous fluid.

se·ro·ther·a·py (sēr′ōther′əpē), *n.* medical treatment by injections of a serum from an immune animal or person.

se·rot·i·nal (sirot′ənl), *adj.* in or relating to late summer.

ser·o·tine (ser′ətin), *adj.* late in occurring or achieving full development, esp. of late-flowering plants.

ser·o·to·nin (serətō′nin), *n.* a compound crystalline substance that occurs in the brain, intestines, and platelets, and brings about narrowing of blood vessels and contraction of muscles.

se·rous (sēr′əs), *adj.* **1.** serum-like. **2.** of, containing, producing, or relating to serum.

ser·pi·go (sərpī′gō), *n.* any spreading skin disease.

ser·rate (ser′it), *adj.* having a notched edge like a saw, esp. of leaves. —**ser· ra′tion,** *n.*

ser·ri·form (ser′əfôrm), *adj.* notched like the edge of a saw.

ser·ru·late (ser′yəlit), *adj.* with finely toothed edges. —**ser·ru·la′tion,** *n.*

ser·ry (ser′ē), *v.* to crowd together closely.

se·rum (sēr′əm), *n., pl.* **se·rums, se· ra** (sēr′ə). **1.** the clear yellow fluid that remains when blood has clotted. **2.** such fluid obtained from an animal immune to some disease and used as an antitoxic or therapeutic agent against that disease. **3.** the portion of milk left after removal of butterfat, casein, and albumin, or after cheese-making.

ser·vi·ette (sur'vēet'), *n.* a table napkin.

ser·vo·mech·an·ism (sur'vōmek'ə-nizm), *n.* a closed-cycle electronic control system in which a large-output mechanism is actuated and controlled by a small-input signal, as the movement of a gun turret by a small knob.

ses·qui·cen·ten·ni·al (ses'kwisen-ten'ēəl), *adj.* relating to or celebrating a 150th anniversary.

ses·qui·pe·da·li·an (ses'kwipidā'-lēən), *adj.* given to the use of long words.

ses·sile (ses'il), *adj.* fixed and stationary, as certain animals or cells.

ses·tet (sestet'), *n.* a group of six musical performers; a piece of music for such a group.

se·ta (sē'tə), *n., pl.* **se·tae** (sē'tē). a bristle or bristle-like process.

se·ta·ceous (sitā'sʜəs), *adj.* having or resembling bristles. Also **se·ti·form** (sē'təfôrm).

se·tig·er·ous (sitij'ərəs), *adj.* bearing bristles or bristle-like processes.

se·tose (sē'tōs), *adj.* having or covered with setae.

set·u·la (secʜ'ələ), *n., pl.* **set·u·lae** (secʜ'əlē). a short, blunt bristle or bristle-like process.

set·u·lose (secʜ'əlōs), *adj.* having or covered with setulae.

sève (sev), *n. French.* the distinctive fineness and strength of flavor of a particular wine.

seven deadly sins. See **deadly sins.**

sex·a·ge·nar·i·an (sek'səjənər'ēən), *adj.* **1.** aged between 60 and 70 years. —*n.* **2.** a person of this age.

sex·ag·e·nar·y (seksaj'əner'ē), *adj.* of or relating to the number 60.

sex·a·ges·i·mal (seksəjes'əməl), *adj.* relating to or based on the number 60.

sex·cen·te·nar·y (seksen'tnər'ē), *adj.* **1.** relating to the number 600 or a period of 600 years; celebrating a 600th anniversary. —*n.* **2.** a 600th anniversary; the celebration of a 600th anniversary.

sex·de·cil·lion (seks'disil'yən), *n.* a number represented by the figure one followed by 51 zeros (but in the United Kingdom and Germany by the figure one followed by 96 zeros).

sex·e·nar·y (sek'səner'ē), *adj.* **1.** of or relating to the number 6. **2.** consisting of six parts. **3.** based on the number 6.

sex·en·ni·al (seksen'ēəl), *adj.* of, for, or every 6 years.

sex·ol·o·gy (seksol'əjē), *n.* the scientific study of sexual behavior.

sex·tan (seks'tən), *adj.* of a fever recurring every fifth (or by inclusive reckoning sixth) day. See also **tertian, quartan, quintan.**

sex·til·lion (sekstil'yən), *n.* a number represented by the figure one followed by 21 zeros (but in the United Kingdom and Germany by the figure one followed by 36 zeros).

shad·dock (sʜad'ək), *n.* the largest citrus fruit, that of the tree *Citrus grandis,* with pale-yellow skin and edible flesh of a lighter color, esp. the larger, coarser, pear-shaped varieties, the smaller, rounder varieties being known as grapefruit.

shadow cabinet, (in the British Parliament) the appointees made by the leadership of the nonincumbent party to posts of responsibility corresponding to those of the cabinet of the party in power.

sha·green (sʜəgrēn'), *n.* **1.** a kind of untanned leather with a rough grainy surface made from the skin of a horse, ass, seal, shark, etc., and often dyed green. **2.** the rough skin of certain sharks, rays, etc., covered with minute hard protuberances and used as an abrasive.

sha·man (sʜä'mən), *n.* a priest and witch-doctor exercising supposed powers over the supernatural in the primitive religion of northern Asia or any similar religion. —**sha'man·ism,** *n.*

shan·dy (sʜan'dē), *n.* a drink of mixed beer and lemonade.

shan·dy·gaff (SHan'dēgaf), *n.* a drink of mixed beer and gingerbeer.

shan·tung (SHan'tuNG'), *n.* a soft, heavy, usually undyed fabric of thick strands of raw silk; a cotton or rayon imitation of such fabric. See also **pongee.**

shash·lik (SHäSHlik'), *n.* a dish of cubed, seasoned meat broiled or roasted on a skewer. Also **shish kebab.**

sherd (SHurd), *n.* **1.** a piece of broken earthenware. **2.** a scale or shell. **3.** the hard wing-case of a beetle. Also **shard.**

shib·bo·leth (SHib'əli*th*), *n.* **1.** a password or favorite phrase of a party or sect. **2.** a word, opinion, style of dress, way of behaving, etc., peculiar to and distinguishing one type or group of persons.

shin·gles (SHiNG'gəlz), *n.*, *sing.* and *pl.* a virus infection of the nerves of the skin causing a rash of clustering blisters and severe pain. Also **herpes zoster, zoster.**

ship biscuit. See **hardtack.**

shirr (SHur), *v.* **1.** to gather fabric or the like with three or more parallel threads. **2.** to bake, esp. eggs, in a shallow dish.

shish ke·bab (SHiSH' kəbob'). See **shashlik.**

shiv·a·ree (SHivərē'), *n.* See **charivari.**

shock therapy, a method of psychiatric treatment by injecting drugs or administering electric or icepack shocks so as to induce convulsions which are usually followed by coma.

shot-peen (SHot'pēn), *v.* to bombard (steel) with hard steel shot so as to increase its durability.

shrive (SHrīv), *v.* **1.** to assign a penance. **2.** to absolve; to grant absolution.

shut·tle·cock (SHut'lkok), *n.* any idea, object, or person pushed back and forth between opposing parties or sides, as *The refugees' plight became a political shuttlecock.*

shy·lock (SHī'lok), *v.* (colloquial) to lend money at exorbitant interest rates.

si·a·lad·e·ni·tis (sī'əlad'ənī'tis), *n.* inflammation of one or more salivary glands.

si·al·a·gog·ic (sī'ələgoj'ik), *adj.* promoting the production of saliva. Also **si·al'a·gogue.**

si·a·loid (sī'əloid), *adj.* saliva-like.

si·am·oise (sē'amwoz'), *n.* an S-shaped sofa.

sib[1] (sib), *adj.* **1.** related by blood. —*n.* **2.** a blood relative.

sib[2] (sib), *n.* a group descended through either the male line only or the female line only.

sib·i·lant (sib'ələnt), *adj.* of or denoting any speech sound with some resemblance to a hiss, as *s, sh, z,* etc.

sib·i·late (sib'əlāt), *v.* to hiss.

sib·ling (sib'liNG), *n.* a brother or sister; any child of the same two parents.

sic·ca·tive (sik'ətiv), *adj.* having drying properties; inducing or encouraging the absorption of moisture.

sickle cell, a red blood corpuscle with an abnormal shape, often like a sickle, because it contains an abnormal hemoglobin.

sic tran·sit glo·ri·a mun·di (sēk trän'sit glô'rēä' mo͞on'dē), *Latin.* thus passes away earthly glory.

side (sīd), *n.* the assumption of superiority; an affected manner; impudence.

side·man (sīd'man), *n.* one who plays an instrument in a band or orchestra.

si·de·re·al (sīdēr'ēəl), *adj.* of, relating to, or determined by the stars.

sid·er·og·ra·phy (sidərog'rəfē), *n.* the technique or art of steel engravings.

sid·er·o·lite (sid'ərəlīt), *n.* a meteorite composed of approximately half iron and half stone-like material.

sid·er·o·phile (sid'ərəfīl), *adj.* with an affinity for iron.

sid·er·o·scope (sid'ərəskōp), *n.* a device for finding iron or steel splinters in the eye.

sid·er·o·sis (sidərō'sis), *n.* a lung disease caused by the inhalation of particles of iron or of some other metal.

sid·er·o·stat (sid'ərəstat), *n.* an instrument for keeping the light from a star in a constant direction as viewed through a telescope, by using a mirror and clock mechanism to correct for the earth's rotation. See also **coelostat.**

sie·mens (sē'mənz), *n.* a unit used in measuring electrical conductance, equal to one mho. *Abbrev.: S.*

si·en·na (sēen'ə), *n.* earth containing iron or iron rust used as a pigment of either yellowish-brown or reddish-brown color according to whether it is raw or has been roasted in a furnace.

si·er·ra (sēer'ə), *n.* a continuous range of mountains or high hills with jagged peaks projecting like the teeth of a saw.

sig·il (sij'il), *n.* a small seal, sometimes one set in a finger ring.

sig·il·late (sij'əlāt), *adj.* with stamped decorations or markings suggesting sigil-like impressions.

sig·ma·tism (sig'mətizm), *n.* a speech defect in which sibilant sounds cannot be pronounced or are mispronounced.

sig·moid (sig'moid), *adj.* crescent- or S-shaped resembling the capital and noncapital signs for the Greek letter sigma. Also **sig'mate.**

sig·nal·ment (sig'nlmənt), *n.* a description in detail of a person's features for identification, esp. by police.

sig·nif·ics (signif'iks), *n.* semantics.

si·lage (sī'lij), *n.* green fodder for animals preserved without drying in a cylindrical structure above ground or a pit in the ground.

si·li·ceous (silisH'əs), *adj.* containing, composed of, or like silica.

sil·i·cif·er·ous (silisif'ərəs), *n.* containing or yielding silica.

si·lic·i·fy (silis'əfī), *v.* to convert or be converted into silica.

sil·i·cle (sil'ikəl), *n.* a short silique.

sil·i·co·sis (siləkō'sis), *n.* a chronic lung disease caused by the prolonged inhalation of siliceous rock dust, affecting stonecutters, coalminers, etc.

si·lic·u·lose (silik'yəlōs), *adj.* bearing or resembling a silicle.

si·lique (silēk'), *n.* a long, pod-like, two-valved seed vessel.

sil·i·quose (sil'əkwōs), *adj.* bearing siliques; having the appearance of a silique or silicle.

silkscreen process, a technique for making prints by rolling a squeegee over a tightly stretched screen of silk or similar material so as to force color through the mesh of portions not previously sized with glue.

sil·la·bub (sil'əbub), *n.* a dish of cream or milk whipped with wine, sweetened, and sometimes flavored, as with lemon.

sil·vic·o·lous (silvik'ələs), *adj.* belonging to a woodland habitat; growing in or inhabiting woodland.

sil·vi·cul·ture (sil'vəkulcHər), *n.* forestry; the growing and tending of forest trees.

sim·i·an (sim'ēən), *adj.* of, relating to, resembling, or characteristic of apes and monkeys.

sim·i·le (sim'əlē), *n.* a figure of speech explicitly comparing two apparently unlike things for the purpose of creating a heightened effect or emphasising a particular feature, as *He ran like the wind.*

si·mil·i·tude (simil'itoōd), *n.* **1.** likeness, as *their similitude of dress.* **2.** a facsimile; that which bears a likeness to another, as *He is a similitude of his father.* **3.** a guise; a semblance, as *It was given a similitude of legality.* **4.** a simile, a comparison, an allegory, as *He illustrated by similitudes.*

si·mo·ni·ac (simō'nēak), *n.* one who practices simony.

si·mo·ny (sī'mənē), *n.* the act or practice of trading in sacred things.

sim·pa·ti·co (simpä'tikō), *adj.* agreeable by virtue of being in sympathy with ideas, manner, personality, etc.

sim·plex (sim'pleks), *adj.* simple; consisting of one substance, part, action, etc.

sim·plism (sim'plizm), *n.* oversimplification; the act or practice of choosing to regard, treat, or seize on only one aspect of something more complex.

sim·plis·tic (simplis'tik), *adj.* characterized by simplism.

sim·u·la·crum (simyəlā′krəm), *n.*, *pl.* **sim·u·la·cra** (simyəlā′krə). a supposed, superficial, or deceptive likeness or semblance.

sim·u·lant (sim′yələnt), *adj.* imitating; pretending.

si·mul·cast (sī′məlkast), *n.* a broadcast transmitted on television and radio at the same time.

sin·e·cure (sin′əkyŏŏr,sī′nəkyŏŏr),*n.* an office yielding honor or profit but entailing few or no duties.

sin·e di·e (sin′e dē′e), *Latin.* without a day having been set for resumption; indefinitely, as, *The meeting was adjourned* sine die.

sin·e qua non(si′nekwä nōn′),*Latin.* an indispensable requirement; an essential condition, as *His agreement was the* sine qua non *of the plan's being put into operation.*

sin·gul·tus (siNGgul′təs), *n.* a hiccup.

sin·is·ter (sin′istər), *adj.* **1.** threatening; of evil omen or appearance; wicked, unfavorable. **2.** on or relating to the left side.

sin·is·trad (sin′istrad), *adv.* to the left; leftward; sinistrally.

sin·is·tral (sin′istrəl), *adj.* **1.** of, relating to, or on the left; the left. **2.** left-handed. —**sin·is·tral′i·ty, sin·is·tra′tion,** *n.* —**sin′is·tral·ly,** *adv.*

sin·is·troc·u·lar (sin′istrok′yələr), *adj.* using the left eye rather than the right. See also **dextrocular.** —**sin·is·troc·u·lar′i·ty,** *n.*

sin·is·tro·dex·tral (sin′istrōdeks′-trəl), *adj.* moving from left to right.

sin·is·tro·gy·ra·tion (sin′istrō′jīrā′-sHən), *n.* the turning to the left of the plane of polarization of a ray of polarized light, as caused by certain chemical substances. Also called **levorotation.**

sin·is·trorse (sin′istrôrs), *adj.* with whorls rising to the left as viewed from inside the spiral, as in certain stems and shells. See also **dextrorse.**

sin·is·trous (sin′istrəs), *adj.* **1.** sinister; unfavorable; disastrous. **2.** sinistral.

sin·u·ate (sin′yŏŏit), *adj.* bending in and out; wavy; sinuous.

sin·u·a·tion (sin′yŏŏā′sHən), *n.* waviness; a bend.

sin·u·os·i·ty (sin′yŏŏos′itē), *n.* a curve or bend; sinuousness.

sin·u·ous (sin′yŏŏəs), *adj.* with many bends or curves. —**sin′u·ous·ness,** *n.*

si·nus (sī′nəs), *n.* **1.** a curving portion; a curved recess. **2.** a bend or curve. **3.** any cavity, recess, or passage in the bone or tissue of the body, as one of the cavities in the bone of the skull connecting with the nostrils.

si·nus·i·tis (sīnəsī′tis), *n.* inflammation of a sinus, usually of those connecting with the nostrils.

sip·id (sip′id), *adj.* with a pleasing taste, flavor, or character.

sip·pet (sip′it), *n.* a small piece; a piece of bread for dipping in gravy, milk, or other liquid food; a crouton.

si·re·ni·an (sīrē′nēən), *n.* any large, aquatic, vegetarian mammal of the order that includes manatees, dugongs, and seacows.

si·ren·ic (sīren′ik), *adj.* of or characteristic of a siren; melodious; irresistibly tempting; dangerously alluring.

si·ri·a·sis (sirī′əsis), *n.* sunstroke.

si·tol·o·gy (sītol′əjē), *n.* the medical field of study concerned with nutrition and dietetics.

si·to·ma·ni·a (sītəmā′nēə), *n.* an abnormal or neurotic craving for food.

si·to·pho·bi·a (sītəfō′bēə), *n.* an abnormal or neurotic aversion to food.

sit·u·a·tion·ism (sicH′ŏŏā′sHənizm), *n.* a theory of psychology that behavior is mainly the result of response to an immediate situation.

si·tus (sī′təs), *n.,* *pl.* **si·tus.** position; the original or proper position.

sitz·krieg (sits′krēg), *n.* warfare in which action is almost at a standstill and frequently stalemated.

skep (skep), *n.* a wicker or wooden basket or hamper, as frequently used on farms.

skep·to·phy·lax·is (skep′tōfilak′sis), *n.* See **tachyphylaxis.**

ski·a·graph (skī′əgraf), *n.* a photograph made by the exposure of a sensitive film or plate to x-rays passed through an object; shadowgraph.

ski·a·scope (skī'əskōp), *n.* an instrument for testing the refractive power of the eye by reflecting light on to it from a mirror and observing the movement of the shadow across the pupil. Also **retinoscope.**

ski·jor·ing (skējôr'iNG), *n.* a sport in which a skier is towed, usually by a horse or horse-drawn vehicle.

skim·ble-scam·ble (skim'bəlskam'-bəl), *adj.* jumbled; rambling; absurd.

skin·tle (skin'tl), *v.* to build unevenly with bricks and mortar so as to create a picturesque effect.

skip·dent (skip'dent), *n.* an open-weave appearance given to a fabric by not fixing some of the warp ends (the precise ones depending on the effect desired) to the loom, so that they are not held taut during the weaving.

skip·pet (skip'it), *n.* a small, round, wooden box to preserve a seal affixed to a document, or to protect sealed documents.

skive (skīv), *v.* to split or pare into layers, esp. leather.

skul·dug·ger·y (skuldug'ərē), *n.* dishonorable conduct; underhand or rascally trickery.

skulk (skulk), *v.* **1.** to lurk or avoid observation, esp. with sinister or cowardly motive. **2.** to move stealthily.

slake (slāk), *v.* **1.** to relieve or diminish by satisfying, as thirst, desire, etc. **2.** to cool or freshen, as *She slaked his fevered brow with a cold, damp cloth.*

sla·lom (slä'ləm), *n.* a downhill ski-race with a zig-zag course between artificial obstacles such as poles or gates.

slat·tern (slat'ərn), *n.* a slut; a slovenly or immoral woman; a prostitute.

slav·er (slav'ər), *v.* to let saliva trickle from the mouth; to slobber.

slav·oc·ra·cy (slāvok'rəsē), *n.* government or domination by slave-holders.

sleave (slēv), *v.* **1.** to separate a thread into filaments. —*n.* **2.** anything raveled or entangled.

slea·zy (slē'zē), *adj.* of thin or poor texture; flimsy.

sleeping sickness, 1. a disease, often fatal, characterized by fever, weight loss, and extreme lethargy, prevalent in parts of W. and S. Africa and caused by a parasite transmitted by the bite of a tsetse fly; African trypanosomiasis. **2.** a virus disease causing inflammation of the brain accompanied by drowsiness, apathy, muscular degeneration, and impairment of vision; encephalitis lethargica.

sliv·o·vitz (sliv'əvits), *n.* plum brandy, esp. from eastern Europe.

sloe (slō), *n.* the fruit of the blackthorn, small, ovate, bluish-black, and with a sour taste.

slough¹ (slou), *n.* a swamp; a muddy area.

slough² (sluf), *n.* **1.** an outer layer of skin shed periodically, as by a snake, etc.; layer of dead tissue cast off from the surface of a wound, ulcer, etc. —*v.* **2.** to cast off or be cast off, as a slough.

slov·en (sluv'ən), *n.* a person who is habitually slipshod or negligent in appearance, behavior, or work.

slub·ber (slub'ər), *v.* to do hastily and without due care.

slum·gul·lion (slumgul'yən), *n.* **1.** a dish of stewed meat and vegetables. **2.** any weak, watered-down soup or beverage.

slur·ry (slur'ē), *n.* a suspension consisting of particles of a solid in a liquid, esp. a watery mixture of clay used in ceramic work for decoration, etc.

slur·vi·an (slur'vēən), *adj.* of or related to slurred speech. —**slur'vi·an·ism,** *n.*

smack (smak), *n.* (slang) heroin.

small-scale (smôl'skāl'), *adj.* small in relation to the original, as of a map, model, or other representation.

smarm·y (smär'mē), *adj.* fulsomely flattering, ingratiating, or fawning.

smaze (smāz), *n.* smoke and haze mingled together.

smeg·ma (smeg'mə), *n.* a thick, sebaceous secretion collecting around the clitoris in females or under the foreskin of the penis in males.

smog (smog), *n.* smoke and fog mingled together.

smutch (smuch), *v.* **1.** to smudge, dirty, or stain. —*n.* **2.** a smudge or stain.

snail·ing (snā'liNG), *n.* a spiraling or circular pattern made on watch or clock parts by means of abrasive disks.

sniff·ish (snif'ish), *adj.* contemptuous; disdainful.

snol·ly·gos·ter (snol'ēgos'tər), *n.* (colloquial) a clever, unprincipled person.

snoop·er·scope (snōō'pərskōp), *n.* a device that allows one to detect objects in the dark by transmitting infrared rays which are reflected if they strike a solid object, received by the device, and formed into an image on a fluorescent screen.

snor·kel (snôr'kəl), *n.* **1.** a funnel-like device on submarines consisting of tubes reaching above the water to take in air and expel foul air and fuel exhaust so that the submarine can remain below water for long periods. **2.** a tube held in the mouth by persons swimming just below the surface of the water and reaching above the water to permit breathing.

snow (snō), *n.* (colloquial) cocaine or heroin.

snow·bird (snō'burd), *n.* (colloquial) a person addicted to cocaine or heroin.

snow blindness, a dimming of vision, usually temporary, caused by the glare of sun on snow. Also **niphablepsia.**

snow·blink (snō'bliNGk), *n.* a white brilliance on the bottom of clouds caused by light reflected up from a snow-covered surface. See also **iceblink.**

snow bunny, a woman or girl who goes to ski resorts in the hope of meeting men.

so·a·ve (sōä'vā), *n.* a dry, white wine from the district round Verona, Italy.

so·bri·quet (sō'brəkā), *n.* a nickname.

Social Democratic party, any of several political parties of continental Europe that advocate a gradual change by democratic processes to socialism or a system approaching it.

social disease, a disease that is spread by close contact of people, esp. a venereal disease.

so·cial·ism (sō'sHəlizm), *n.* the organization of society so that the community as a whole owns and controls all sources of wealth and means of production and distribution.

social pathology, any feature of society which tends to disorganize it or inhibit normal development in its members, as poverty, crime, unemployment, etc.

social science, any of several sciences, or fields of study treated scientifically, concerned with an aspect of society, as politics, economics, anthropology, etc.

so·ci·o·ge·net·ic (sō'sēōjənet'ik), *adj.* relating to or affecting social development.

so·ci·o·gen·ic (sō'sēōjen'ik), *adj.* having its origin in or being affected by social factors.

so·ci·ol·o·gism (sō'sēol'əjizm), *n.* an interpretation, notion, etc., in the context of social factors and esp. emphasizing social factors to the exclusion of other factors concerned. —**so·ci·ol·o·gis'tic,** *adj.*

so·ci·om·e·try (sō'sēom'itrē), *n.* the measurement of social attitude by means of preferences expressed by members of the society.

so·ci·o·path (sō'sēəpath), *n.* one who is hostile to society.

Socratic method, a method of instruction and inquiry by posing a series of questions so as to develop a latent idea in a pupil or lead an opponent to make admissions that tend to establish the proposition he opposes.

so·dal·i·ty (sōdal'itē), *n.* **1.** companionship; comradeship. **2.** a guild, association, or society.

sodium ben·zo·ate (ben'zōit), a chemical used mainly as a food preservative and also as an antiseptic.

sodium bicarbonate, a chemical used mainly in making baking powder, soft drinks, and sodium salts, and as an antacid and a fire extinguisher.

sodium carbonate, 1. soda ash, a chemical used in making glass, soaps, paper, petroleum, and as a cleanser and bleach. **2.** common washing soda, the decahydrated form of sodium carbonate.

sodium citrate, a chemical used in the manufacture of soft drinks, in photography, and as a blood anticoagulant.

sodium cyc·la·mate (sī′klə̄mit), a chemical used mainly as a sweetening agent, esp. in low-calorie foodstuffs.

sodium fluoride, a chemical used in water fluoridation and for killing insects and rodents.

sodium glutamate. See **monosodium glutamate.**

sod·om·y (sod′əmē), *n.* unnatural, esp. anal, sexual intercourse with a man, woman, or animal.

sof·frit·to (sōfrē′tō), *n.* a mixture of hot fat, browned onion or garlic, and sometimes other vegetables or herbs, used in Italian cookery for lightly frying or browning meat, etc., before stewing it.

soft goods, items of purchase that wear out, as furnishing fabrics, carpets, clothes. See also **hard goods.**

soft sell, an advertising or merchandising technique employing subtle or indirect persuasion. See also **hard sell.**

soi-di·sant (swadēzäɴ′), *adj. French.* self-styled; alleging himself to be.

soi·gné (swänyā′), *adj.* arranged or performed with care and elegance; well-groomed.

soi·ree, soi·rée (swärā′), *n.* an evening social gathering, esp. for a particular purpose, as listening to a musical performance, or a talk, or holding a discussion on a specific topic.

so·lan·der (səlan′dər), *n.* a container for maps, photographs, and the like, made in the form of a book with the front and an edge hinged for ease of access.

solar wind, a mass of protons thrown out from the sun by a solar storm and disturbing the magnetic fields of the planets.

sol·dier (sōl′jər), *n.* (slang) a lower-echelon member of the Mafia.

sol·e·cism (sol′isizm), *n.* any mistake, breach of propriety, or inconsistency, esp. a grammatical error.

so·lic·i·tous (səlis′itəs), *adj.* anxious; concerned, as for or about the welfare or health of a person. —**so·lic′i·tude,** *n.*

sol·i·dar·y (sol′ider′ē), *adj.* distinguished by or relating to joint or like interests and obligations.

solid-state, *adj.* relating to or denoting electronic devices capable of controlling current without moving parts, vacuum gaps, or filaments, as transistors, piezoelectric devices, etc.

sol·id·un·gu·late (soliduɴɢ′yəlit), *adj.* having an undivided hoof on each foot, as a horse.

sol·i·fid·i·an (soləfid′ēən), *n.* one who believes that salvation can be won by faith alone without performing good works.

so·lil·o·quize (səlil′əkwīz), *v.* to talk while or as if alone, often done in drama to reveal a character's thoughts.

so·lil·o·quy (səlil′əkwē), *n.* the act of or an instance of soliloquizing; the words so uttered.

sol·ip·sism (sol′ipsizm), *n.* a philosophical theory that the self is the only thing that exists or can be proved to exist.

sol·stice (sol′stis), *n.* the time when the sun is at its farthest distance from the equator, occurring twice a year, once on about June 21 (**summer solstice**), when it reaches its northernmost point (marked on maps by the Tropic of Cancer), and once on about December 22 (**winter solstice**), when it reaches its southernmost point (marked on maps by the Tropic of Capricorn). —**sol·sti′tial,** *adj.*

sol·ute (sol′yōōt), *n.* the substance dissolved in any solution.

sol·vent (sol′vənt), *adj.* **1.** able to pay all one's debts. **2.** having the power to dissolve another substance.

so·ma (sō′mə), *n., pl.* **so·ma·ta** (sō′-

məta), **so·mas.** a body cell as opposed to a germ cell, i.e. one of those cells forming the tissues, organs, etc., of an organism as opposed to those specialized for reproduction.

so·mat·ic (sōmat′ik), *adj.* of the body; corporeal; physical.

so·ma·tist (sō′mətist), *n.* a psychiatrist who believes that all mental illnesses are physical in origin.

so·ma·tol·o·gy (sōmətol′əjē), *n.* the scientific study of the physical characteristics of mankind.

so·ma·to·to·ni·a (sō′mətətō′nēə), *n.* the personality pattern usually associated with the mesomorphic body type, characterized by aggressiveness and physical energy. See also **cerebrotonia, viscerotonia.**

som·me·lier (sumalyā′), *n.* a wine-waiter.

som·nam·bu·late (somnam′byəlāt), *v.* to walk or carry out other actions while asleep. —**som·nam·bu·la′ tion, som·nam′bu·lism,** *n.*

som·ni·fa·cient (somnəfā′sHənt), *adj.* causing sleep.

som·nif·er·ous (somnif′ərəs), *adj.* bringing sleep.

som·nif·ic (somnif′ik), *adj.* causing sleep.

som·nil·o·quy (somnil′əkwē), *n.* the act or habit of speaking in one's sleep.

som·no·lent (som′nələnt), *adj.* sleepy; drowsy. —**som′no·lence,** *n.* —**som′no·lent·ly,** *adv.*

so·nant (sō′nənt), *adj.* having sound; sounding. —**so′nance,** *n.*

so·nar (sō′när), *n.* **1.** a method of detecting and locating objects under water by picking up the sound waves they transmit or reflect. **2.** the apparatus used for such detection and location.

sonde (sond), *n.* a balloon, rocket, or similar device used to observe atmospheric phenomena.

sone (sōn), *n.* a unit of subjective loudness, equal to the loudness produced by a tone at 40 decibels above a reference tone which has been adjusted to the minimum audible threshold of a group of listeners.

sonic boom, a sharp bang heard on the ground when an aircraft moves overhead at a speed just below or above the speed of sound and caused by the shock wave created.

son·ics (son′iks), *n.* the science dealing with sound in its practical applications.

so·nif·er·ous (sənif′ərəs), *adj.* carrying or making sound.

so·no·rous (sənôr′əs), *adj.* producing or capable of producing sound, esp. a rich, deep sound. —**so·nor′i·ty,** *n.*

soo·gee (sōō′jē), *n.* **1.** a soapy or detergent solution for cleaning decks and paintwork. —*v.* **2.** to clean the decks, bulkheads, etc., of a vessel.

sop (sop), *n.* a piece of bread or similar solid food dipped or soaked in liquid food.

soph·ism (sof′izm), *n.* a deceptive or fallacious argument or belief. —**soph′ ist, soph′ist·er,** *n.* —**soph′ist·ry,** *n.* —**so·phis′tic,** *adj.*

so·phis·ti·cat·ed (səfis′təkātid), *adj.* not simple; complex; complicated; of many parts, as a machine or an organization.

soph·o·mor·ic (sofəmôr′ik), *adj.* resembling or reminiscent of a sophomore, esp. in pretending to know more than he does, in being childishly overconfident, or the like.

so·phros·y·ne (səfros′ənē), *n.* self-control; moderation; prudence.

so·por (sō′pər), *n.* an unnatural state of deep sleep or lethargy.

sop·o·rif·er·ous (sopərif′ərəs), *adj.* bringing sleep.

sop·o·rif·ic (sopərif′ik), *adj.* producing or tending to produce sleep.

sop·o·rose (sop′ərōs), *adj.* abnormally sleepy; characterized by abnormally deep sleep; comatose.

sor·did (sôr′did), *adj.* dirty; squalid; extremely poor and shabby.

so·ror·ate (sôr′ərāt), *n.* marriage of one man with two sisters, either consecutively or concurrently.

so·ror·i·cide (sərôr′isīd), *n.* one who kills his or her sister.

sor·rel (sôr′əl), *n.* a light reddish-brown color.

sor·ti·lege (sôr′təlij), *n*. divination by drawing lots; the drawing of lots for divination.

sot·to vo·ce (sot′ō vō′CHē), in a whisper or undertone; in a quiet voice to avoid being overheard.

sou·bise (sōōbēz′), *n*. a white or brown sauce containing puréed onions, served with various meats.

sou·brette (sōōbret′), *n*. a vivacious, pert, or coquettish young woman.

souf·fle (sōōflā′), *n*. (in medicine) a low murmur or blowing sound such as is listened for with the aid of a stethoscope.

sough (sou), *v*. to make a sighing, rushing, or rustling sound, as of a wind blowing through trees.

sou mar·qué (sōō′ märkā′), *pl*. **sous mar·qués** (sōō′ märkā′). something of little or no value.

sound spectrogram, a record made by a sound spectrograph.

sound spectrograph, an electronic device for making a graphic record of the frequency, intensity, duration, and variation of a sound or succession of sounds.

soup·çon (sōōpsôN′), *n*. a trace; a flavor; a hint or suspicion.

sou·tache (sōōtasH′), *n*. narrow, flat, ornamental braid, usually made of mohair, silk, or rayon.

sou·ter·rain (sōōtərän′), *n*. an underground passage or building; a grotto.

south·paw (south′pô), *n*. (colloquial) a left-handed person.

space-time (spās′tīm′), *n*. a philosophical concept of a fusion of space and time regarded as a four-dimensional continuum in which all physical entities exist and can be located.

spa·do (spā′dō), *n*., *pl*. **spa·do·nes** (spādō′nāz). a castrated man or animal.

spaetz·le (sHpet′slə), *n*. a dish of small dumplings or thread-like pieces made from a batter of flour, milk, eggs, and salt poured through a coarse colander into boiling water before being drained to serve tossed in butter or in a soup, sauce, or stew.

spall (spôl), *n*. **1.** a splinter or chip, esp. of stone or metal ore. —*v*. **2.** to break or split into small pieces or chips.

spa·ne·mi·a (spənē′mēə), *n*. anemia.

Spanish fly, powder made from certain brilliant green beetles found abundantly in Spain and used medicinally as a skin irritant, diuretic, and aphrodisiac. Also **cantharides.**

sparge (spärj), *v*. **1.** to sprinkle. —*n*. **2.** a scattering.

spar·ver (spär′vər), *n*. a tent-shaped canopy or curtain over a bed.

spasm (spaz′əm), *n*. a sudden, violent, involuntary contraction of a muscle.

spas·mod·ic (spazmod′ik), *adj*. relating to or similar in nature to a spasm; characterized by spasms.

spas·mo·phil·i·a (spazməfil′ēə), *n*. an abnormal condition in which spasms, convulsions, or tetany are brought on by only a little mechanical or electrical stimulation. —**spas·mo·phil′ic,** *adj*.

spas·tic (spas′tik), *adj*. **1.** relating to, of the same nature as, or characterized by involuntary muscular contractions, esp. the long-continued contractions known as tonic spasms. —*n*. **2.** a person afflicted by such spasms; a person suffering from cerebral palsy.

spastic paralysis, an abnormal condition in which muscles are affected by tonic spasm and alteration in reflexes.

spate (spāt), *n*. a sudden rush or outburst, as of water, words, customers, etc.

spathe (spāTH), *n*. a single bract or a pair of bracts, frequently brightly colored, borne on the same axis as and enveloping a flower spike or cluster. —**spa·tha′ceous, spa′those,** *adj*.

spa·ti·og·ra·phy (spā′sHēog′rəfē), *n*. the study of outer space, esp. of phenomena likely to affect missiles and spacecraft.

spat·ter·dash (spat′ərdasH), *n*. a long gaiter or legging to protect the clothing on the legs from rain, splashing mud, etc.

spav·ined (spav′ind), *adj*. in a worn-out or broken-down condition.

spay (spā), *v.* to remove the ovaries of a female animal.

spé·cia·li·té de la mai·son (spesyä-lētā′ də la mäzôN′), *French.* a dish for which a restaurant is noted; a restaurant's speciality.

spe·ci·a·tion (spē′sHēā′sHən), *n.* the origination of a species; the process by which new species originate.

spe·cie (spē′sHē), *n.* coined money.

spe·cies (spē′sHēz), *n.* a group of things or individuals having some characteristics in common; a sort or kind.

spe·cious (spē′sHəs), *adj.* superficially good or right but inwardly false; plausible.

spec·tro·bo·lom·e·ter (spektrōbō-lom′itər), *n.* an instrument combining a spectroscope and a bolometer, used for finding accurately the distribution of radiant energy in a spectrum.

spec·tro·chem·is·try (spek′trōkem′-istrē), *n.* the branch of chemistry concerned with analyzing substances by means of the light spectra they absorb or produce. —**spec·tro·chem′i·cal,** *adj.*

spec·tro·col·o·rim·e·try (spek′trō-kul′ərim′itrē), *n.* the measuring of color quantities by means of a spectrophotometer.

spec·tro·gram (spek′trəgram), *n.* a photograph or other representation of a light spectrum.

spec·tro·graph (spek′trəgraf), *n.* a device for producing a light spectrum and making a photograph or other representation of it.

spec·tro·he·li·o·gram (spek′trōhē′-lēəgram), *n.* a photograph produced by a spectroheliograph.

spec·tro·he·li·o·graph (spek′trōhē′-lēəgraf), *n.* a photographic apparatus that can be set so that only light of a certain wavelength reaches the photographic plate and which is used for making photographs of the sun in a given monochrome so that the details of the sun's surface appear as they would if the sun emitted only that given monochrome.

spec·tro·he·li·o·scope (spek′trōhē′-lēəskōp), *n.* a spectroheliograph or a form of it that produces a visual instead of photographic image.

spec·trol·o·gy (spektrol′əjē), *n.* the study of ghosts or other apparitions.

spec·trom·e·ter (spektrom′itər), *n.* an optical instrument for producing light spectra and making measurements of them, as of their wavelength, amount of refraction, etc.

spec·tro·mi·cro·scope (spek′trō-mī′krəskōp), *n.* a combined spectroscope and microscope.

spec·tro·pho·to·e·lec·tric (spek′trō-fō′tōilek′trik), *adj.* relating to the connection between the wavelength of the radiation striking and the number of electrons set free by a substance during photoelectric effect.

spec·tro·pho·tom·e·ter (spek′trōfō-tom′itər), *n.* an instrument for measuring and comparing the light intensity of different parts of a spectrum.

spec·tro·po·lar·im·e·ter (spek′trō-pō′lərim′itər), *n.* a combined spectroscope and polarimeter used for measuring the amount by which different solutions cause plane-polarized light of various wavelengths to rotate.

spec·tro·po·lar·i·scope (spek′trōpō-lar′iskōp), *n.* a combined spectroscope and polariscope.

spec·tro·ra·di·om·e·ter (spek′trō-rä′dēom′itər), *n.* a combined spectroscope and radiometer, used for determining the distribution of radiant energy in a light spectrum.

spec·tro·scope (spek′trəskōp), *n.* an optical instrument for producing and examining visible spectra, i.e. spectra of light and radiation, by passing the light or radiation through a slit, arranging it in parallel rays by means of a collimator, and separating it into its component elements by means of a prism.

spec·tros·co·py (spektros′kəpē), *n.* the science concerned with the use of the spectroscope and with analyzing bodies and substances by means of the spectra they produce.

spec·trum (spek′trəm), *n., pl.* **spec·tra** (spek′trə). **1.** the effect produced when electromagnetic radiations are resolved into their component waves which are then arranged according to their wavelength and range. **2.** any part of the entire electromagnetic spectrum, as the audio spectrum, but esp. the spectrum of light, which appears as bands of violet, indigo, blue, green, yellow, orange, and red in order of increasing wavelength.

spec·u·lar (spek′yələr), *adj.* of or having the properties of a mirror.

spec·u·lum (spek′yələm), *n., pl.* **spec·u·la** (spek′yələ), **spec·u·lums. 1.** a mirror, usually made of polished metal, esp. one on or in an optical instrument. **2.** a surgical instrument for dilating an inaccessible body cavity or passage to make inspection possible.

spe·lae·an, spe·le·an (spilē′ən), *adj.* of, relating to, or living in caves.

spe·le·ol·o·gy, spe·lae·ol·o·gy (spē-lēol′əjē), *n.* the scientific exploration and study of caves. —**spe·le·ol′o·gist,** *n.*

spe·lunk (spiluNGk′), *v.* to explore caves. —**spe·lun′ker,** *n.*

Spen·ce·ri·an (spensēr′ēən), *adj.* relating to or characteristic of a handwriting style in which the letters are clear, rounded, and slope to the right.

sper·ma·cet·i (spurməset′ē), *n.* a white, waxy substance obtained from the head of the sperm whale and used mainly in making soap, cosmetics, candles, in glazing fabrics, and as an emollient in certain medical preparations. Also **cetaceum.**

sper·ma·ry (spur′mərē), *n.* an organ for generating sperm; a testis.

sper·mat·ic (spurmat′ik), *adj.* of, relating to, or similar to sperm; seminal. Also **sper′mic.**

sper·mat·o·gen·e·sis (spurmat′-əjen′isis), *n.* the formation and development of spermatozoa. —**sper·ma·tog′e·nous,** *adj.*

sper·ma·toid (spur′mətoid), *adj.* sperm-like.

sper·ma·tor·rhe·a (spur′mətərē′ə), *n.* abnormally frequent involuntary ejaculation of semen.

sper·ma·to·zo·on (spur′mətəzō′ən), *n., pl.* **sper·ma·to·zo·a** (spur′mətə-zō′ə). one of the mature male reproductive cells in semen, which may fertilize the female's ovum.

sper·mi·o·gen·e·sis (spur′mēōjen′-isis), *n.* the final process in the development of spermatozoa from male germ cells.

sperm oil, a thin, yellow liquid obtained from the sperm whale and used mainly as a lubricant for watches, scientific apparatus, and other intricate light machinery.

sper·mous (spur′məs), *adj.* relating to or having the properties of sperm.

sperm whale, a large whale of warm oceans, having a large cavity in its head containing sperm oil, which is valued in itself and from which spermaceti is obtained. Also **cachalot.**

sphac·e·late (sfas′əlāt), *v.* to become or cause to become affected with sphacelus.

sphac·e·lus (sfas′ələs), *n.* a mass of gangrenous tissue.

sphag·num moss (sfag′nəm), *n.* any of a large number of soft mosses comprising a genus, growing on swamps and bogs and used mainly for surgical dressings, packing of plants and the like, and potting of plants.

sphe·nic (sfē′nik), *adj.* shaped like a wedge. Also **sphe′noid.**

sphe·no·gram (sfē′nəgram), *n.* any of the wedge-shaped characters in cuneiform writing.

sphe·nog·ra·phy (sfēnog′rəfē), *n.* the art of or study of cuneiform writing.

spher·al (sfer′əl), *adj.* of, pertaining to, or having the form of a sphere.

spher·ics[1] (sfer′iks), *n.* the geometry and trigonometry of figures described in or on the surface of a sphere.

spher·ics[2] (sfer′iks), *n.* a branch of meteorology in which electronic devices are used to study the atmosphere and in particular those aspects relating to weather forecasting.

sphe·rom·e·ter (sfirom′itər), *n.* an

instrument used to measure the curvature of spheres and of curved surfaces such as lenses.

spher·ule (sfer'ōōl), *n.* a small sphere or globe.

sphinc·ter (sfiNGk'tər), *n.* a ring of voluntary or involuntary muscle encircling the orifice of a hollow organ or the wall of a tubular organ and able to close or narrow it, as *oral*, *anal*, or *cardiac sphincter*.

sphra·gis·tic (sfrəjis'tik), *adj.* of or relating to seals or signet rings.

sphra·gis·tics (sfrəjis'tiks), *n.* the study of or knowledge of seals or signet rings.

sphyg·mic (sfig'mik), *adj.* of or relating to the pulse.

sphyg·mo·gram (sfig'məgram), *n.* a record made by a sphygmograph.

sphyg·mo·graph (sfig'məgraf), *n.* an instrument for making a graphic record, as a tracing or diagram, of the strength and rapidity of, and any variations in the arterial pulse.

sphyg·moid (sfig'moid), *adj.* resembling an arterial pulse.

sphyg·mo·ma·nom·e·ter (sfig'mōmənom'itər), *n.* an instrument which is used in conjunction with a stethoscope for measuring blood pressure and which consists of a manometer and an inflatable cuff to constrict an artery.

sphyg·mom·e·ter (sfigmom'itər), *n.* an instrument for measuring the strength of the arterial pulse.

spi·cate (spī'kāt), *adj.* with points or spikes, as a plant.

spic·u·late (spik'yəlāt), *adj.* small and needle-like in shape.

spic·ule (spik'yōōl), *n.* a small, needle-like body, part, process, or the like. Also **spic'u·lum,** *pl.* **spic'u·la.**

spiel (spēl), *n.* (colloquial) a high-flown, extravagant speech or story, esp. to attract people to buy or to attend some performance. —**spiel' er,** *n.*

spike·nard (spīk'nərd), *n.* See **nard.**

spile (spīl), *n.* 1. a wooden peg or plug, esp. for stopping up an opening. —*v.* 2. to stop up with a peg or plug.

spil·li·kin (spil'əkin), *n.* a jackstraw; one of a heap of small rods of wood, plastic, etc., used in a game in which the object is to remove each rod without disturbing the rest.

spin·drift (spin'drift), *n.* spray blown along the surface of the sea.

spi·nes·cent (spīnes'ənt), *adj.* with a spiny end; spine-bearing; becoming or being spine-like.

spi·nif·er·ous (spīnif'ərəs), *adj.* bearing or covered with spines.

spin·ner·et (spin'əret), *n.* an organ of insects such as spiders or a device on a machine making synthetic yarn through which a fine thread is extruded.

spi·nose (spī'nōs), *adj.* bearing, covered with, or armed with spines, thorns, or sharp projections, as a plant or animal; resembling a spine. Also **spi'nous.**

spin·thar·i·scope (spinthar'iskōp), *n.* an instrument used to observe alpha particles by making them visible as flashes on a fluorescent screen.

spi·nule (spī'nyōōl), *n.* a small spine.

spi·ra·cle (spī'rəkəl), *n.* 1. a hole giving access to air. 2. openings on the side of an insect's body through which it breathes.

spi·rif·er·ous (spīrif'ərəs), *adj.* having a spire or spiral appendages.

spi·ril·lum (spīril'əm), *n., pl.* **spi·ril·la** (spīril'ə). any of various corkscrew-shaped species of bacteria several of which cause disease in man.

spir·it·ism (spir'itizm), *n.* a doctrine or practice based on spiritualism.

spiritual incest, sexual intercourse between persons baptized or confirmed together.

spi·ri·tu·el (spir'iCHŌōel'), *adj.* having or exhibiting refinement and grace in mind, wit, or movement.

spi·ri·tus fru·men·ti (spir'itəs frōōmen'tī), whiskey.

spi·ro·chete (spī'rəkēt), *n.* any of several species of long spiral bacteria many of which cause disease in man and one of which causes syphilis.

spi·ro·che·to·sis (spī'rəkētō'sis), *n.* any disease caused by a spirochete.

spi·ro·graph (spī′rəgraf), *n*. an instrument for recording the movements concerned with respiration.

spi·roid (spī′roid), *adj*. nearly spiral; resembling a spiral.

spi·rom·e·ter (spīrom′itər), *n*. an instrument used to measure lung capacity.

spitch·cock (spicH′kok), *n*. an eel split or cut up and broiled or fried.

splanch·nic (splaNGk′nik), *adj*. of or relating to the viscera.

splanch·nol·o·gy (splaNGknol′əjē), *n*. the branch of medicine concerned with the viscera.

spleen (splēn), *n*. **1.** a ductless gland, in mammals situated at the left side under the diaphragm, of which the main functions are to form antibodies, to destroy red blood cells at the end of their life, and to store red blood cells. **2.** ill-nature; peevishness.

splen·dif·er·ous (splendif′ərəs), *adj*. (colloquial) magnificent; splendid.

splen·dent (splen′dənt), *adj*. shining; brilliant; lustrous.

sple·nec·to·my (splinek′təmē), *n*. the surgical removal of part or all of the spleen.

sple·net·ic (splinet′ik), *adj*. of, relating to, or affecting the spleen; ill-natured; irritable; spiteful.

splen·ic (splē′nik), *adj*. of, relating to, or affecting the spleen.

sple·ni·tis (splinī′tis), *n*. inflammation of the spleen.

spon·dy·li·tis (spondəlī′tis), *n*. a medical disorder in which the vertebrae are inflamed.

spon·sion (spon′sHən), *n*. a promise, esp. an engagement to act as surety for another person.

spon·son (spon′sən), *n*. a structure projecting from a ship's or other vessel's side, as a gun platform, the edge of a paddle box, a buoyancy tank, or a canoe.

spoor (spoͦr), *n*. a track or trail, esp. of a person or animal being pursued or hunted.

spo·rad·ic (spôrad′ik), *adj*. recurring at irregular intervals of time.

spo·ri·cide (spôr′isīd), *n*. a substance or preparation used to kill spores.

spo·rif·er·ous (spôrif′ərəs), *adj*. bearing or capable of bearing spores.

spo·ro·gen·e·sis (spôrəjen′isis), *n*. the formation and development of spores.

Sprach·ge·fühl (sHpräkH′gəfyl), *n*. *German*. an instinctive grasp of the spirit of a language, esp. consciousness of what is acceptable usage in a particular language's grammar or idiom.

spritz·er (sprit′sər), *n*. a drink made from wine and soda water and served chilled in tall glasses.

sprue (sprо̄о̄), *n*. a chronic condition in which inability to absorb certain food constituents, esp. fats, leads to diarrhea and ulceration of the lining of the digestive tract, the condition being caused by malnutrition and occurring most often in the tropics.

spu·mes·cent (spyoͦomes′ənt), *adj*. foaming; frothy.

spu·ri·ous (spyoͦor′ēəs), *adj*. not genuine; of counterfeit origin; bastard; of illegitimate birth.

spu·tum (spyoͦo′təm), *n*., *pl*. **spu·ta** (spyoͦo′tə). spittle, esp. that mixed with mucus or pus expectorated by persons with diseases of the throat or lungs.

squa·ma (skwā′mə), *n*., *pl*. **squa·mae** (skwā′mē). a scale or scale-like part, as of skin or bone.

squa·mate (skwā′māt), *adj*. furnished with or covered with squamae. —**squa·ma′tion**, *n*.

squa·mi·form (skwā′məfôrm), *adj*. in the shape of a squama.

squa·mo·sal (skwəmō′səl), *adj*. of or relating to the thin, scale-like portion of skull behind the ear which articulates with the bones of the lower jaw.

squa·mous (skwā′məs), *adj*. covered with, composed of, or resembling squamae.

squam·u·lose (skwam′yəlōs), *adj*. having or covered with small squamae.

square mile, a unit used in measuring area, equal to the area contained by a square whose sides each measure one mile. *Abbrev.* : **sq. mi., mi**^{2}.

square millimeter, a unit used in measuring area, equal to the area contained by a square whose sides each measure one millimeter. *Abbrev.* : **sq. mm., mm**^{2}.

squar·rose (skwar′ōs), *adj.* with a rough or ragged surface.

squas·sa·tion (skwosā′sHən), *n.* a form of or device for torture or punishment in former times, in which the victim had his arms bound behind, his feet heavily weighted and was jerked up and down on a rope passing under his arms. See also **strappado**.

squib (skwib), *n.* **1.** a short, witty composition or saying. **2.** a short item of news used as a filler in a newspaper.

squint (skwint), *n.* strabismus.

sta·bile (stā′bil), *adj.* **1.** fixed; stable. —*n.* **2.** a piece of sculpture consisting of immobile pieces attached to supports. See also **mobile**.

stac·ca·to (stəkä′tō), *adj.* sharply disconnected; composed of abruptly disjointed words, notes, movements, or the like.

stac·tom·e·ter (staktom′itər), *n.* an instrument for finding the number of or the weight of individual drops in a volume of liquid. Also **stalagmometer**.

sta·dim·e·ter (stədim′itər), *n.* an instrument for measuring the angle subtended by an object of known height and from it determining the distance of the object from the observer.

sta·di·om·e·ter (stādēom′itər), *n.* an instrument that runs a toothed wheel over curves, dashed lines, and the like to measure their length.

stag·ing (stā′jiNG), *n.* scaffolding; a temporary support.

staid (stād), *adj.* sedate or steady in character or bearing.

sta·lac·ti·form (stəlak′təfôrm), *adj.* shaped like or similar to a stalactite.

sta·lac·tite (stəlak′tīt), *n.* an icicle-like formation of crystalline calcium carbonate built up by the dripping of water through overlying limestone and hanging from the roof or wall of a cave or the like.

sta·lag·mite (stəlag′mīt), *n.* a deposit on the floor of a cave or the like, resembling an inverted stalactite and formed in the same way.

stal·ag·mom·e·ter (staləgmom′itər), *n.* See **stactometer**.

sta·men (stā′mən), *n.* the male reproductive organ of a flowering plant, consisting of the anther, which has two lobes each with two pollen sacs, borne at the apex of the slender filament.

stam·inate (stam′ənit), *adj.* of or denoting a flower with stamens but no pistil, and therefore male.

stam·i·nif·er·ous (stamənif′ərəs), *adj.* bearing or capable of bearing stamens.

stam·i·no·dy (stam′ənō′dē), *n.* the transformation into a stamen of some other part of a flower, as a petal.

stanch (stônCH), *v.* to check the flow, as of blood, from a leak.

stanch·less (stônCH′lis), *adj.* unstoppable; incessant.

standard of living, the degree of material comfort enjoyed in everyday life by a community, class, or person.

stan·na·ry (stan′ərē), *n.* a tin-mining area.

stan·num (stan′əm), *n.* tin.

sta·pes (stā′pēz), *n.*, *pl.* **sta·pes, sta·pe·des** (stəpē′dēz). a small stirrup-shaped bone in the middle ear of mammals.

staph·y·lo·coc·cus (staf′ələkok′əs), *n.*, *pl.* **staph·y·lo·coc·ci** (staf′ələkok′-sī). any of several species of bacteria, globular in form and tending to cluster, certain of which cause severe but localized infections in man, as abscesses, carbuncles, etc.

staph·y·lo·ma (stafəlō′mə), *n.* an abnormal localized bulge on the eyeball, from a variety of causes.

staph·y·lor·rha·phy (stafəlôr′əfē), *n.* a surgical operation to join a cleft palate.

Star Chamber, 1. (in Tudor England) the Privy Council sitting to try civil and criminal cases, especially those affecting Crown interests, until its abolition in 1641 for being arbitrary in its judgments. **2.** any tribunal, committee, or the like whose methods are unfair.

starve·ling (stärv′liNG), *adj.* starving; underfed.

sta·sis (stā′sis), *n.* the state of balance or inactivity brought about by opposing equal forces or powers.

stat·ics (stat′iks), *n.* the branch of physics dealing with the action of forces on bodies at rest. See also **dynamics.**

stat·ism (stā′tizm), *n.* the belief in or policy of putting the control of economic, political, and other such matters in the hands of the state instead of the individual. —**stat′ist,** *n.*

sta·tis·tics (stətis′tiks), *n.* the branch of study concerned with collecting, classifying, analyzing, and interpreting facts, esp. numerical facts.

stat·o·cyst (stat′əsist), *n.* an organ of balance present in certain invertebrates such as flatworms and crustaceans and consisting of a sac containing sensory cells and granules of sand, lime, etc., the granules stimulating the cells as the animal moves.

stat·o·lith (stat′əli*th*), *n.* **1.** one of the granules present in a statocyst. **2.** a solid inclusion, frequently a starch grain, in a plant cell, free to change position under the influence of gravity and assumed to cause corresponding change in the position of the plant.

sta·tor (stā′tər), *n.* a stationary or fixed part of an electrical machine, esp. of a generator.

sta·tus quo (stā′təs kwō′), the existing or previous state of affairs. Also **sta′tus in quo′.**

steady state theory, the theory that the universe is constantly expanding and can continue to do so without limit. See also **big bang theory.**

steal·age (stē′lij), *n.* **1.** stealing. **2.** loss due to stealing.

steamboat Gothic, a style of architecture in the 19th century United States characterized by elaborate ornamentation around windows and

doors and on beams and rails, etc., in imitation of river steamboats.

ste·a·tite (stē′ətīt), *n.* soapstone, a grayish-green or brown variety of talc with a waxy feel used in cosmetics and as a pigment in ceramics.

ste·a·to·py·gi·a (stē′ətōpī′jēə), *n.* a large deposit of fat on and around the buttocks, esp. of women, as among Hottentots, Bushmen, and other peoples of southern Africa.

ste·a·tor·rhe·a (stē′ətərē′ə), *n.* the presence of an abnormal amount of fat in the feces causing diarrhea with consequent weight loss and due to disease of the pancreas or intestine, to malnutrition, and other causes. Also **ste·ar·rhe′a.**

steel·yard (stēl′yärd), *n.* a lever with unequal arms used as a balance, the item to be weighed hanging from the shorter arm and a movable counterpoise being pushed along the calibrated longer arm to give a reading of weight.

steeve (stēv), *n.* **1.** a long derrick or boom used to lift and lower cargo into a ship's hold. —*v.* **2.** to pack tightly, as cargo in a ship's hold.

ste·le (stē′lē), *n.*, *pl.* **ste·les, ste·lai** (stē′lī). an upright slab or pillar of stone bearing a sculptured design or inscription used as a gravestone or other marker.

stel·late (stel′it), *adj.* star-shaped.

stel·lif·er·ous (stelif′ərəs), *adj.* having, esp. many, stars.

stel·li·form (stel′əfôrm), *adj.* star-shaped.

St.-É·mi·li·on (sāntəmē′lēən), *n.* a dry claret from the parish of St. Emilion, Bordeaux, France.

stem turn, a ski-turn in which the skier pushes the heel of one ski outward, so that it glides over the snow at an angle to the direction of movement and points in the direction to be turned to, and then shifts weight and brings the other ski parallel.

sten·o·cho·ric (stenəkôr′ik), *adj.* not widely distributed, as of a plant or animal. See also **eurychoric.**

sten·o·graph (sten′əgraf), *n.* a machine resembling a typewriter for writing in one of various shorthand systems.

sten·o·ha·line (stenəhā′lĭn), *adj.* able to tolerate only a slight variation in the salinity of its environment. See also **euryhaline.**

sten·o·pe·ic (stenəpē′ik), *adj.* **1.** having or relating to a narrow slit or other minute opening. —*n.* **2.** an appliance worn over the eyes for keeping out bright sunlight and consisting of a piece of cardboard, metal, wood, or the like with a narrow horizontal slit.

sten·o·pet·al·ous (sten′ōpet′ələs), *adj.* having narrow petals.

ste·noph·a·gous (stinof′əgəs), *adj.* able to live on a narrow range of foodstuffs. See also **euryphagous.**

sten·o·phyl·lous (sten′ōfil′əs), *adj.* narrow-leaved.

ste·nosed (stinōst′), *adj.* exhibiting stenosis; of abnormal narrowness.

ste·no·sis (stinō′sis), *n.* a medical condition of abnormal narrowness of an opening, tube, or vessel, as of an artery, etc.

sten·o·ther·mal (stenəthur′məl), *adj.* able to tolerate only a narrow variation in the surrounding temperature. See also **eurythermal.**

sten·o·ther·mo·phile (stenəthur′-məfīl), *n.* an obligate bacterium growing best at temperatures not lower than 60°C. —**sten·o·thur·mo·phil′ic,** *adj.*

sten·o·top·ic (stenətop′ik), *adj.* able to withstand only narrow variation in environmental conditions, as temperature, humidity, etc. See also **eurytopic.**

sten·o·typ·y (sten′ətīpē), *n.* shorthand in which the shortened forms of words or groups of words consist of written or typed alphabetic letters, as distinct from phonetic or other symbols.

sten·to·ri·an (stentôr′ēən), *adj.* with a very loud or powerful voice or sound. Also **sten·to′ri·ous.**

steppe (step), *n.* a vast, grassy, largely treeless plain in the temperate zone, as across Eurasia.

ster·co·ra·ceous (sturkərā′sHəs), *adj.* of, like, or relating to dung or feces.

ster·co·ric·o·lous (sturkərik′ələs), *adj.* inhabiting dung.

stere (stēr), *n.* a unit of the metric system for solid measures, equal to one cubic meter, and used chiefly in measuring blocks of timber. *Abbrev.*: **s.**

ster·e·og·no·sis (ster′ēognō′sis), *n.* the faculty of recognizing similarities and differences in the size, weight, shape, and texture of objects by touching or lifting them.

ster·e·o·gram (ster′ēəgram), *n.* a picture or diagram conveying an impression of the solidity of the object represented.

ster·e·o·graph (ster′ēəgraf), *n.* one or both of the two pictures required to produce a stereoscopic picture.

ster·e·og·ra·pher (ster′ēog′rəfər), *n.* a person who takes stereoscopic photographs.

ster·e·og·ra·phy (ster′ēog′rəfē), *n.* **1.** the art of drawing solid bodies on a plane. **2.** a branch of geometry, concerned with the construction of regularly defined solids.

ster·e·om·e·try (ster′ēom′itrē), *n.* the measurement of solids; geometry as applied to solids.

ster·e·o·phon·ic (ster′ēəfon′ik), *adj.* of a system of sound reproduction using more than one microphone or loudspeaker, separately placed, to enhance the realism of the reproduction, used esp. in high-fidelity recordings and for wide-screen motion pictures. See also **monophonic.** —**ster·e·oph′o·ny,** *n.*

ster·e·o·pho·tog·ra·phy (ster′ēōfə-tog′rəfē), *n.* the production of stereoscopic photographs.

ster·e·op·sis (ster′ēop′sis), *n.* stereoscopic vision.

ster·e·op·ter (ster′ēoptər), *n.* an ophthalmic instrument for measuring the eye's perception of three-dimensionality.

ster·e·op·ti·con (ster′ēop′təkən), *n.* a projector that makes one picture dissolve as the next forms, usually by having two complete lanterns.

ster·e·o·scope (ster′ēəskōp), *n.* an optical instrument for showing two pictures of the same object, made from slightly different points of view, one to one eye and one to the other, producing the effect of a single image with the illusion of three-dimensionality.

ster·e·o·scop·ic (ster′ēəskop′ik), *adj.* denoting or relating to three-dimensional vision or any process or device that produces an illusion of three-dimensionality from two-dimensional images.

ster·e·os·co·py (ster′ēos′kəpē), *n.* three-dimensional vision; the study of the stereoscope.

ster·e·o·tax·is (ster′ēətak′sis), *n.* movement of an organism resulting from the stimulus of contact with a solid. See also **thigmotaxis.**

ster·e·ot·o·my (ster′ēot′əmē), *n.* the technique of precision-cutting of solids such as stones.

ster·e·o·type (ster′ēətīp), *n.* **1.** a process of making a metal printing plate by taking a papier maché or similar mold of a form of type and then casting the mold in metal. Also **ster′e·o·ty·py. 2.** a plate so made. **3.** a hackneyed form; something perpetuated in unchanged form.

ster·ling (stur′liNG), *adj.* **1.** of or relating to the money of the United Kingdom. **2.** having the standard fineness of $92\frac{1}{2}$ per cent silver and $7\frac{1}{2}$ per cent copper; formerly the standard fixed by law for silver coin and now used for jewelry, utensils, etc.

sterling bloc, the group of countries, mostly in the British Commonwealth, between which payment is freely made in sterling, for which institutions in the City of London act as bankers, and whose currency value tends to vary directly with that of the pound sterling. Also **sterling area.**

ster·nal (stur′nl), *adj.* of or relating to the sternum.

ster·no·cos·tal (stur′nōkos′tl), *adj.* of, relating to, or between the sternum and the ribs.

ster·num (stur′nəm), *n., pl.* **ster·na** (stur′nə), **ster·nums.** the breastbone; a bone or series of bones along the middle and ventral side of the chest of vertebrates and having the ribs and shoulder girdle attached to it.

ster·nu·ta·tion (sturnətā′sHən), *n.* the act of or an instance of sneezing.

ster·nu·ta·tor (stur′nyətātər), *n.* a poison gas causing coughing and irritation of the nose.

ster·nu·ta·to·ry (stərnōō′tətôrē), *adj.* causing or able to cause sneezing.

ster·oid (ster′oid), *n.* any of a large group of organic chemical compounds, similar chemically but diverse biologically, having important and specific physiological function, and including bile acids, vitamin D, some sex hormones, some carcinogens, etc.

ster·ol (ster′ōl), *n.* any of a group of unsaturated fat-soluble organic chemical compounds, as cholesterol, ergosterol, present in all animal and plant cells.

ster·tor (stur′tər), *n.* an abnormally heavy rasping sound that accompanies breathing in some illnesses.

ster·to·rous (stur′tərəs), *adj.* accompanied by stertor or snoring.

stet (stet), *v.* to let stand, used as an imperative to a printer to retain a letter, word, passage, etc., canceled on a manuscript or proof, and marked by a row of dots under the part affected.

ste·thom·e·ter (stethom′itər), *n.* an instrument for measuring the movements of the chest walls and abdomen during breathing.

steth·o·scope (steth′əskōp), *n.* a medical instrument used for listening to sounds in the body, esp. in the chest, and consisting of a piece to be applied to the body, to receive and amplify the sound, connected by rubber tubing to closely fitting earpieces. —**steth·o·scop′ic,** *adj.*

sthe·ni·a (sthənī′ə), *n.* a medical condition of abnormal strength or energy.

sthen·ic (sthen′ik), *adj.* sturdy or strong in build.

stich (stik), *n.* a line, a verse, or a stanza of poetry. —**stich'ic**, *adj.*

sti·chom·e·try (stikom'itrē), *n.* the practice of setting out prose in lines divided according to the sense and indicating the phrasing.

stig·ma (stig'mə), *n., pl.* **stig·ma·ta** (stig'mətə), **stig·mas. 1.** a mark of disgrace; a stain on one's good name; a mark characterizing a defect or disease. **2.** a spot on the skin, esp. one that bleeds spontaneously, as during hysteria. **3.** See **carpel. 4.** (*pl.*) marks resembling wounds on the crucified body of Christ, said to have developed on the bodies of some saints or other holy people.

stig·mat·ic (stigmat'ik), *adj.* **1.** of or relating to a stigma. **2.** converging to a point, as of light, the effect of lenses, etc.; free of astigmatism.

stig·ma·tism (stig'mətizm), *n.* the property of converging or causing convergence to a point; the medical condition of having stigma (def. 2).

stig·ma·tize (stig'mətīz), *v.* to mark, as with a sign or brand; to mark with or describe in terms of disgrace.

still hunt, a hunt for game by stealth, as by stalking or by ambush from cover.

stil·li·form (stil'əfôrm), *adj.* drop-shaped; spherical.

stim·u·lus (stim'yələs), *n., pl.* **stim·u·li** (stim'yəlī). something that rouses or spurs on activity of body or mind; something that rouses an organism or tissue to specific activity.

stipe (stīp), *n.* a stalk; a stalk-like part.

sti·pend (stī'pend), *n.* a fixed periodical payment from public funds, as to a teacher, student, public official, or esp. clergyman; a salary.

sti·pen·di·a·ry (stīpen'dēer'ē), *adj.* **1.** relating to, similar to, receiving, working for, or paid for by a stipend. —*n.* **2.** a person who receives a stipend, esp. as opposed to one who gives services freely.

stip·i·tate (stip'itāt), *adj.* bearing or borne by a stipe.

stip·i·ti·form (stip'itəfôrm), *adj.* of stipe-like form.

stir·pi·cul·ture (stûr'pəkul'CHər), *n.* the raising of special stocks or strains by selective breeding.

stirps (sturps), *n., pl.* **stir·pes** (stur'pēz). a stock; a breed; a family; a line of descent.

stith·y (stiTH'ē), *n.* an anvil; a forge; a smithy.

sti·ver (stī'vər), *n.* the smallest value or amount, as *I would not give a stiver for it; not a stiver of effort.*

sto·chas·tic (stəkas'tik), *adj.* of or relating to a process of the science of statistics, concerned with the behavior of systems evolving in time in accordance with probalistic laws and in particular with the effect of such evolution on random variables in a system.

stock car, a standard production automobile adapted for racing.

stock·pot (stok'pot), *n.* a pot in which is made and kept a liquid derived from stewed meat, bones, or vegetables and used for soups and sauces.

stodge (stoj), *v.* to eat greedily; to gorge; to stuff, esp. with food.

stodg·y (stoj'ē), *adj.* dull; heavy; too full of facts or details; tedious, as a person, book, style, etc.

sto·i·cal (stō'ikəl), *adj.* impassive; self-controlled; courageous in the face of pain; austere in the face of temptation.

stoi·chi·om·e·try (stoi'kēom'itrē), *n.* the branch of chemistry concerned with the quantitative and other relationships among the elements of a compound substance.

stol·id (stol'id), *adj.* not easily excited; slow to feel or show feeling; unemotional.

sto·ma (stō'mə), *n., pl.* **sto·ma·ta** (stō'mətə), **sto·mas.** a small or simple mouth-like aperture in lower animals and plants, acting as a mouth, pore, or the like.

sto·mat·ic (stōmat'ik), *adj.* relating to the mouth.

sto·ma·ti·tis (stōmətī'tis), *n.* inflammation of the tissues and mucous membranes of the mouth.

sto·ma·tol·o·gy (stōmətol'əjē), *n.* the

scientific study of the mouth and its diseases.

stone·ware (stōn'wer), *n*. a hard, dense kind of pottery made from clay containing or mixed with flint or sand particles.

stope (stōp), *n*. the working face of a mine; any excavation of ore made accessible by shafts and drifts.

stop·ple (stop'əl), *n*. a stopper or plug for a bottle, etc., usually made of the same material as the bottle.

stoup (stoop), *n*. a container for holy water, usually a stone basin set in the wall near or standing near the door of a church.

stra·bis·mus (strəbiz'məs), *n*. a squint; a visual condition in which one or both eyes are turned from the normal position so that they cannot reach a focus jointly.

stra·bot·o·my (strəbot'əmē), *n*. a surgical operation on one or more eye muscles to correct strabismus.

strafe (strāf), *v*. to attack from aircraft with machine-gun fire.

strait·en (strāt'n), *v*. **1.** to place in difficulty, esp. financial. **2.** to narrow or restrict in income, amount, scope, extent, etc.

stra·min·e·ous (strəmin'ēəs), *adj*. of or like straw; straw-colored.

strap·pa·do (strəpā'dō), *n., pl.* **strap·pa·does** (strəpā'dōz). a form of punishment or torture in former times in which the victim was hoisted by a rope, usually by his hands tied behind him, and allowed to fall to the length of the rope, which did not reach the ground and so caused a painful jerk. See also **squassation.**

strass (stras), *n*. a glass-like composition with a high lead content used to make imitation gems.

strat·a·gem (strat'əjəm), *n*. a plan, trick, or device to attain an objective or deceive or gain advantage over an adversary.

stra·te·gic (strətē'jik), *adj*. **1.** (of a military operation) intended to make the enemy incapable of warfare, as a bombing mission to destroy materials, the economy, or morale. **2.** es-

sential to the conduct of warfare, as of particular materials, industries, etc. See also **tactical.**

stra·tig·ra·phy (strətig'rəfē), *n*. the study, description, classification, and interpretation of the order and succession of rock strata; historical geology.

stra·toc·ra·cy (strətok'rəsē), *n*. government by the army.

stra·to·cu·mu·lus (strā'tōkyoō'myələs), *n. sing.* and *pl.* a type of heavy cloud lying below 8000 feet and consisting of round gray masses of water vapor in lines, waves, or groups within a continuous sheet. Also **cumulo-stratus.**

strat·o·sphere (strat'əsfēr), *n*. the region of the atmosphere lying above the tropopause, extending from about 10 miles above the equator and 4 miles above the poles to about 15 miles above the earth, and within which the temperature remains comparatively stable.

stra·tus (strā'təs), *n. sing.* and *pl.* a cloud or a class of cloud lying horizontally with a uniform base, heavy and gray in appearance, usually below 8000 feet, and often giving persistent drizzle.

strep·i·tous (strep'itəs), *adj*. noisy; noisily rough.

strep·to·coc·cus (streptəkok'əs), *n., pl.* **strep·to·coc·ci** (streptəkok'sī). any of a group of spherical or oval, chain-forming bacteria causing many common infections esp. of the throat, with a more generalized effect than is caused by a staphylococcus but less violent at the source of infection, as scarlet fever, tonsillitis, endocarditis, puerperal fever.

strep·to·my·ces (streptəmī'sēz), *n. sing.* and *pl.* any of several species of aerobic bacteria which produce antibiotics.

strep·to·my·cin (strep'tōmī'sin), *n*. an antibiotic produced by a mold-like bacteria found in soil and used chiefly as a highly effective treatment for tuberculosis.

streu·sel (SHtroi'zəl), *n*. a crumbly

mixture of sugar, cinnamon, flour, butter, and chopped nuts used as a topping for cakes, esp. for coffeecake.

stri·a (strī′ə), *n., pl.* **stri·ae** (strī′ē). a slight ridge, furrow, score, stripe, or similar linear mark, esp. one of several arranged in parallel fashion.

stri·ate (strī′āt), *v.* **1.** to mark with striae. —*adj.* **2.** marked with striae. —**stri·a′tion,** *n.*

strick·le (strik′əl), *n.* a rod for leveling off heaped-up grain, etc., in line with the top of a measuring container.

stric·tion (strik′sнən), *n.* the act of pulling tight or constricting.

stric·ture (strik′cнər), *n.* **1.** a comment, esp. one of adverse criticism. **2.** an abnormal narrowing of a passage or tube of the body, as the rectum, urethra.

stri·dent (strīd′nt), *adj.* having or making a harsh or grating sound.

stri·dor (strī′dər), *n.* a loud, harsh, grating sound.

strid·u·late (strij′əlāt), *v.* to make a shrill grating noise by rubbing together hard parts of the body, as does a grasshopper. —**strid′u·lous,** *adj.*

strig·i·form (strij′əfôrm), *adj.* of, relating to, or belonging to the order consisting of the owls.

stri·gose (strī′gōs), *adj.* bristly or hairy; finely ridged or grooved; with close-set, fine points.

strin·gent (strin′jənt), *adj.* rigorous or binding, as of laws, regulations, etc.; compelling; urgent.

string·piece (striNG′pēs), *n.* a long horizontal timber connecting and supporting parts of a framework.

strob·i·la·ceous (strobəlā′sнəs), *adj.* cone-like.

stro·bo·scope (strō′bəskōp), *n.* **1.** a device for studying the motion of a rapidly vibrating or revolving object by illuminating it periodically with a flash of the same frequency as the vibration or revolution, or by revealing it through widely spaced openings on a revolving disk, so that the object appears to slow down or stop. **2.** a photographic device for illuminating a rapidly moving object such as a

bullet for a very brief period and synchronizing the illumination with a rapid shutter-opening of a camera so as to produce a still photograph; a photograph produced by such a device.

stro·bo·tron (strō′bətron), *n.* a lamp used in a stroboscope to produce a brilliant flash of light in response to a pulsing voltage.

stro·ga·noff (strô′gənôf), *adj.* denoting a way of serving meat, usually beef, cut into thin strips, sautéed with onion and mushroom in butter, and with sour cream stirred into the mixture to form a sauce.

stro·phe (strō′fē), *n.* **1.** a part of an ancient Greek choral ode during which the chorus moved to its left as it sang. **2.** any of the separate sections of a poem that does not have a regularly recurring pattern. —**stroph′ic,** *adj.*

stru·del (strōōd′l), *n.* a pastry consisting of a roll of extremely thin flaky pastry filled with a fruit or cheese mixture.

stru·ma (strōō′mə), *n., pl.* **stru·mae** (strōō′mē). **1.** goiter. **2.** a scrofulous swelling. —**stru′mous,** *adj.*

stru·thi·ous (strōō′thēəs), *adj.* like or of the same family as the ostriches.

strych·nine (strik′nin), *n.* a poison extracted from certain plants, esp. nux vomica, and having a highly stimulative effect on the nervous system, used mainly as an antidote for poisoning by depressant drugs.

strych·nin·ism (strik′ninizm), *n.* a medical condition caused by an overdose, perhaps accumulated, of strychnine.

stuffed derma. See **kishke.**

stul·ti·fy (stul′təfī), *v.* to make foolish; to show up in a ridiculous light; to render futile or worthless.

stum (stum), *n.* **1.** unfermented or incompletely fermented grapejuice. **2.** wine to which stum has been added and which has therefore undergone further fermentation.

stump·age (stum′pij), *n.* standing timber with reference to its value; the right to cut timber standing on another's land.

stu·pa (stōō′pə), *n.* a dome-shaped or pyramidal monument, of earth or other materials, built over relics of or at a place associated with Buddha.

stupe (stōōp), *n.* layers of flannel or similar material soaked in hot water and put on the skin as a counter-irritant.

stu·pe·fa·cient (stōōpəfā′sHənt), *adj.* causing stupor; stupefying; stunning.

stu·pe·fac·tion (stōōpəfak′sHən), *n.* the act of producing or the state of being in a stupor. —**stu·pe·fac′tive,** *adj.*

sty·lar (stī′lər), *adj.* like a stylus, pen, needle, or similar pointed instrument.

style (stīl), *n.* (in a flower) See **carpel.**

sty·let (stī′lit), *n.* a slender dagger.

sty·li·form (stī′ləfôrm), *adj.* resembling a stylus in shape.

sty·lo·graph (stī′ləgraf), *n.* a type of fountain pen with a fine tube forming the writing point. —**sty·lo·graph′ic,** *adj.*

sty·log·ra·phy (stīlog′rəfē), *n.* the art of using a stylus.

sty·loid (stī′loid), *adj.* stylus-like; slender and pointed.

sty·lus (stī′ləs), *n., pl.* **sty·li** (stī′lī), **sty·lus·es.** an ancient writing implement made of metal, bone, or similar material, with one end sharp for cutting the letters in a waxed tablet and the other end blunt for obliterating letters and smoothing the wax; any implement similar in form or function.

styp·sis (stip′sis), *n.* the use of or application of a styptic agent or substance.

styp·tic (stip′tik), *adj.* having the property of contracting organic tissue or checking bleeding.

sua·sion (swā′zHən), *n.* the act of attempting to convince or impel by reason or advice, as opposed to compulsion by force.

sub·al·i·men·ta·tion (sub′aləmen-tā′sHən), *n.* See **hypoalimentation.**

sub·al·tern (subôl′tərn), *adj.* of lower rank; subordinate.

sub·cla·vate (subklā′vāt), *adj.* nearly or to some degree club-shaped.

sub·con·tig·u·ous (subkəntig′yōōəs), *adj.* nearly touching.

sub·cu·ta·ne·ous (sub′kyōōtā′nēəs), *adj.* under the skin, as tissue, an injection, or certain parasites.

sub·fe·brile (subfē′brəl), *adj.* slightly fevered.

sub·fusc (subfusk′), *adj.* dusky; dingy; somber. Also **sub·fus′cous.**

sub·in·flu·ent (subin′flōōənt), *n.* an organism that has a subordinate effect on the ecology of its community. See also **influent.**

sub·ja·cent (subjā′sənt), *adj.* underlying.

subjective idealism, a philosophical theory that all experience consists of ideas that originate in or are distorted in the mind of the observer. See also **objective idealism.**

sub·lim·i·nal (sublim′ənl), *adj.* below the threshold of consciousness; perceived unconsciously. See also **supraliminal.**

sub·lux·a·tion (sub′luksā′sHən), *n.* partial dislocation of a joint due to stretching of the ligaments by injury; sprain.

sub·merse (səbmurs′), *v.* to submerge.

sub·min·i·a·tur·ize (submin′ēəcHə-rīz′), *v.* to make or design in an extremely small size, as electronic equipment.

sub·orn (səbôrn′), *v.* to bribe or to induce by unlawful or underhand means to commit a crime or misdeed. —**sub·or·na′tion,** *n.*

sub·rep·tion (səbrep′sHən), *n.* a misleading or mistaken representation; a conclusion drawn from such representation.

sub·ro·gate (sub′rōgāt), *v.* to substitute.

sub ro·sa (sub rō′zə), in confidence; secretly.

sub·se·rous (subsēr′əs), *adj.* under a serous membrane.

sub·serve (səbsurv′), *v.* to be instrumental in furthering; to serve as a means toward.

sub·ser·vi·ent (səbsur′vēənt), *adj.* servile; cringing; obsequious.

sub·struc·tion (substruk′shən), *n.* a foundation or structure acting as the foundation of a building or other construction.

sub·sume (səbsoom′), *v.* to take into or consider as part of a larger whole, as one idea, instance, principle into a theory, rule, class, etc.

sub·tend (səbtend′), *v.* to act as, contain in, or define an outline.

sub·ter·fuge (sub′tərfyooj), *n.* an evasion, trick, or device used to avoid or conceal something.

sub·ter·rane (sub′tərān), *n.* a cave; a room under ground.

sub·to·pi·a (subtō′pēə), *n.* suburban paradise, used ironically of the spread of commonplace houses and narrowly conventional attitudes.

sub·tra·hend (sub′trəhend), *n.* a number or quantity to be subtracted from another. See also **minuend.**

su·bu·late (soo′byəlit), *adj.* shaped like an awl.

sub·ur·bi·car·i·an (səbur′bāker′- ēən), *adj.* near Rome.

sub·vene (səbvēn′), *v.* to serve as a support or relief.

sub·ven·tion (səbven′shən), *n.* **1.** a grant of money, esp. by a government, to support or help an enterprise or institution; a subsidy. **2.** the supplying of support or help.

sub·ver·sive (səbvur′siv), *adj.* tending to subvert.

sub·vert (səbvurt′), *v.* to overthrow; to bring about the ruin of; to corrupt.

suc·ce·da·ne·um (suk′sidā′nēəm), *n., pl.* **suc·ce·da·ne·a** (suk′sidā′nēə). a substitute, frequently an inferior one.

suc·cinct (səksiNGkt′), *adj.* concise; brief in verbal expression.

suc·cor (suk′ər), *n.* **1.** aid or relief in time of need. —*v.* **2.** to give help or relief in time of need; to come to the aid of.

suc·cu·bus (suk′yəbəs), *n., pl.* **suc· cu·bi** (suk′yəbī). a female demon

supposed to have sexual intercourse with men while they are asleep. Also **succuba.** See also **incubus.**

suc·cumb (səkum′), *v.* to give way to a superior force, as disease, old age, etc.

suc·cur·sal (səkur′səl), *adj.* subsidiary; subordinate to another, esp. of a religious foundation.

suc·cuss (səkus′), *v.* to shake up. —**suc·cus′sion,** *n.*

su·da·to·ri·um (soodətôr′ēəm), *n., pl.* **su·da·to·ri·a** (soodətôr′ēə). a room where hot air baths are taken to induce sweating; such a bath.

su·da·to·ry (soo′dətôrē), *adj.* relating to or inducing sweating.

su·dor·if·er·ous (soodərif′ərəs), *adj.* containing or secreting sweat.

su·dor·if·ic (soodərif′ik), *adj.* causing or promoting sweating.

su·dor·ip·a·rous (soodərip′ərəs), *adj.* producing or secreting sweat.

suf·fice (səfīs′), *v.* to be enough; to meet the needs of.

suf·frage (suf′rij), *n.* the right of voting at elections, esp. political elections.

suf·fra·gist (suf′rəjist), *n.* an advocate of granting voting rights.

suf·fru·tes·cent (suf′rootes′ənt), *adj.* partly or to some degree woody.

suf·fu·mi·gate (səfyoo′məgāt), *v.* to subject to fumes or smoke esp. from below.

suf·fuse (səfyooz′), *v.* to overspread with or as if with a fluid, a color, light, etc.

sug·gest·i·ble (səgjes′təbəl), *adj.* capable of being influenced or easily influenced by suggestion.

sug·ges·tive (səgjes′tiv), *adj.* that suggests; full of suggestions; evocative; suggesting something indecent.

su·i ju·ris (soo′ī joor′is), of full age and capacity to manage one's affairs or take legal responsibility.

su·ki·ya·ki (soo′kēyä′kē), *n.* a Japanese dish of pieces of beef, chicken, or pork, green vegetables, and bean curd, usually flavored with soy sauce and cooked at the table in a chafing dish.

sul·cate (sul′kāt), *adj.* furrowed; grooved; cleft, as certain plant stems or animal hoofs.

sul·cus (sul′kəs), *n.* a furrow; a groove; a fissure, esp. between brain convolutions.

sul·fa·di·a·zine (sulfədī′əzēn), *n.* a drug derived from sulfanilamide and used mainly to treat infections caused by pneumococci, staphylococci, streptococci, and gonococci.

sulfa drug. See **sulfonamide.**

sul·fa·mer·a·zine (sulfəmer′əzēn), *n.* a drug derived from sulfadiazine and used mainly to treat infections caused by meningococci.

sul·fa·nil·a·mide (sulfənil′əmīd), *n.* a synthetic organic chemical compound used mainly to arrest infections caused by hemolytic bacteria such as staphylococci, gonococci, etc.

sul·fa·pyr·a·zine (sulfəpēr′əzēn), *n.* a drug derived from sulfonamide and used to treat infections caused by staphylococci or gonococci.

sul·fa·pyr·i·dine (sulfəpēr′idēn), *n.* a drug derived from sulfanilamide and used chiefly to treat one form of dermatitis but formerly to treat pneumococcal infections.

sulf·ars·phen·a·mine (sulf′ärsfen′-əmēn), *n.* a drug formerly used to treat syphilis.

sul·fa·thi·a·zole (sulfəthī′əzōl), *n.* a drug derived from sulfanilamide and used formerly to treat pneumonia and infections caused by staphylococci but now little used because of its toxic side effects.

sul·fi·sox·a·zole (sulfisok′səzōl), *n.* a drug derived from sulfanilamide and used mainly to treat infections of the urinary tract.

sul·fon·a·mide (sulfon′əmīd), *n.* any of a certain group of drugs, the first effective antibacterial drugs to be discovered, which have the effect of arresting the development of bacteria and are still widely used to treat various bacterial diseases, infections, burns, wounds, and the like, although partly superseded by antibiotics. Also **sul·phon′a·mide.** Also **sulfa drug.**

sulfur dioxide, a suffocating gas formed when sulfur burns and used mainly as a bleach, a disinfectant, a fumigating agent, in preserving fruit and vegetables, and in the production of sulfuric acid.

sul·lage (sul′ij), *n.* sewage; sediment deposited by running water.

sul·ly (sul′ē), *v.* to soil or stain; to pollute or defile.

su·mi (soo′mē), *n.* a black ink much used by calligraphers and painters, made by a Japanese method of mixing plant soot and glue and letting the mixture solidify into cakes or sticks which are then powdered into water to form the ink.

sum·ma cum lau·de (soom′ə koom lou′dā), with highest praise; the highest of the three special grades of honor granted to above-average graduates. See also **cum laude, magna cum laude.**

sum·mand (sum′and), *n.* an item to be added in a sum.

sum·ma·ry (sum′ərē), *n.* **1.** a brief but comprehensive account of previous statements; a résumé. *—adj.* **2.** concise; performed with prompt directness; done without formality or due ceremony.

su·mo (soo′mō), *n.* a form of Japanese wrestling, usually between tall, heavy, hereditary participants, in which the aim is to force the opponent out of the ring or to make him touch the ground with any part other than his feet.

sump (sump), *n.* a pit, well, or other such reservoir for collecting liquid.

sump·tu·ary (sump′CHŌōer′ē), *adj.* regulating expenditure or expense.

sump·tu·ous (sump′CHŌōəs), *adj.* costly; splendidly luxurious.

su·per·an·nu·at·ed (soopəran′yooā′-tid), *adj.* **1.** retired because of old age or infirmity, esp. with a pension. **2.** discarded as too old; outdated.

su·per·bomb (soo′pərbom), *n.* a bomb of unusually great destructive power, as a hydrogen bomb.

su·per·cil·i·ous (soopərsil′ēəs), *adj.* showing haughty contempt.

su·per·con·duc·tiv·i·ty (sōō′pər-kon′dəktiv′itē), *n.* the property possessed by some substances at very low temperatures of having no resistance to the flow of electric current.

su·per·cool (sōōpərkōōl′), *v.* to cool a liquid below its freezing point without bringing about its solidification or crystallization.

su·per·e·go (sōōpərē′gō), *n.* that part of the mind, part conscious and part unconscious, that mediates between the desires of the ego and social ideals.

su·per·er·o·gate (sōōpərer′əgāt), *v.* to do more than is required by duty or circumstances. —**su·per·e·rog′a·to·ry**, *adj.*

su·per·fi·ci·es (sōōpərfisʜ′ēēz), *n. sing.* and *pl.* the surface; the outside; the outward appearance.

su·per·flu·id (sōōpərflōō′id), *n.* a fluid that exhibits abnormally low viscosity and frictionless flow (so that it flows easily through small openings or long narrow tubes), and also has extremely high heat conductivity, the only known example being liquid helium at a temperature lower than 2.19°K.

su·per·gene (sōō′pərjēn), *adj.* formed by waters percolating down through rocks, as mineral and ore deposits. See also **hypogene.**

supergiant star, a star of exceptional brightness and enormous size, being more than 100 times greater in diameter than the sun, as Antares.

su·per·graph·ics (sōōpərgraf′iks), *n. pl.* decorative graphic designs in oversized patterns or panels.

su·per·in·cum·bent (sōō′pərin-kum′bənt), *adj.* lying on or overhanging something else.

su·per·ja·cent (sōōpərjā′sənt), *adj.* lying on or above something else.

su·per·max·il·la (sōō′pərmaksil′ə), *n., pl.* **su·per·max·il·lae.** the upper jaw.

su·per·mun·dane (sōō′pərmun-dān′), *adj.* above or superior to earthly or worldly matters.

su·per·nal (sōōpur′nl), *adj.* belonging or relating to a higher state of existence than on earth; heavenly; in or of the skies; celestial; lofty in powers or position.

su·per·no·va (sōōpərnō′və), *n., pl.* **su·per·no·vae** (sōōpərnō′vē), **su·per·no·vas.** a nova of extreme brilliance, giving out ten million to a hundred million times more light than the sun, leaving behind some permanent change, as the patch of gas known as the Crab Nebula, and of such rare occurrence that only three have been recorded in our galaxy and about 50 more in other galaxies.

su·per·nu·mer·ar·y (sōōpərnōō′-mərer′ē), *adj.* **1.** in excess of the usual or necessary number; extra. **2.** of or denoting an actor employed in addition to the regular company and appearing on stage but having no lines to speak.

su·per·sat·u·rate (sōōpərsacʜ′ərāt), *v.* to increase the concentration, as of a solution, a vapor, etc., beyond saturation point.

su·per·son·ic (sōōpərson′ik), *adj.* with or at a speed greater than the speed of sound.

su·per·vene (sōōpərvēn′), *v.* to occur as something in addition or unrelated to the matter in hand.

su·pi·na·tion (sōōpənā′sʜən), *n.* the movement of the hand or forearm so that the palm faces forward or upward; the position resulting from such a turn. See also **pronation.**

su·pine (sōōpīn′), *adj.* lying front or face upward; inactive, esp. from laziness or indifference.

sup·ple·to·ry (sup′litôr′ē), *adj.* added to fill a deficiency; supplementary.

sup·pli·ant (sup′lēənt), *n.* a person who supplicates.

sup·pli·cate (sup′ləkāt), *v.* to pray, ask, or beg for humbly. —**sup·pli·ca′tion,** *n.*

sup·po·si·tious (supəzisʜ′əs), *adj.* assumed; based on hypothesis or supposition; suppositious.

sup·pos·i·ti·tious (səpoz′itisʜ′əs), *adj.* substituted for the real, esp. fraudulently; not genuine.

sup·pu·rate (sup′yərāt), *v.* to pro-

duce, secrete, or discharge pus.
—**sup·pu·ra'tion**. *n.* —**sup'pu·ra·tive**, *adj.*

su·pra (soo'prə), *adv.* above, as referring to a previous part of a text. See also **infra**.

su·pra·lim·i·nal (soo̅prəlim'ənl), *adj.* above the threshold of consciousness or sensation, thus within normal consciousness. See also **subliminal**.

su·pra·ra·tion·al (soo̅prərasʜ'ənl), *adj.* above or beyond the power of reason or comprehension.

su·ral (soor'əl), *adj.* of or relating to the calf of the leg.

sur·cease (surses'), *v.* to cease; to desist.

sure·ty (sʜoor'itē), *n.* a thing pledged as a security against loss or damage, or for the fulfillment of a promise or debt.

surface-active agent (sur'fisak'tiv ā'jənt), any substance that affects the surface tension or interfacial tension of water or water-based solutions, usually reducing it so that the wetting or spreading capability of the liquid is increased. Also **surfactant**.

surface boundary layer, the thin layer of air immediately above the surface of the earth and usually no more than 300 feet in height. Also **ground layer, friction layer, atmospheric boundary layer**.

sur·fac·tant (sərfak'tənt), *n.* See **surface-active agent**.

sur·feit (sur'fit), *n.* an excess.

sur·mise (sərmīz'), *v.* **1.** to form an opinion on slight evidence; to guess. —*n.* **2.** a guess; an opinion formed on slight evidence.

sur·ro·gate (sur'əgāt), *n.* **1.** a person appointed to act or be deputy for another. —*v.* **2.** to appoint a deputy or successor.

sur·tax (sur'taks), *n.* a tax levied in addition to normal tax on incomes above a certain level. See also **normal tax**.

sur·tout (sərtoo'), *n.* a man's overcoat; a hooded cape for a woman.

sur·veil·lance (sərvā'ləns), *n.* a close guard or watch, as over a prisoner,

suspect premises, or the like. —**sur·veil'lant,** *adj.*

sus·pi·ra·tion (suspərā'sʜən), *n.* a heavy sigh.

sus·ten·ta·tion (sus'tentā'sʜən), *n.* the sustaining or maintaining of life or activity; the providing of support, maintenance, or money for upkeep.

sus·ten·tion (səsten'sʜən), *n.* the act of sustaining; the condition of being sustained.

su·sur·rant (soosur'ənt), *adj.* whispering; gently rustling. —**su·sur·ra'tion,** *n.*

su·sur·rus (soosur'əs), *n.* a whisper; a gentle rustle or murmur. —**su·sur'rous,** *adj.*

sut·ler (sut'lər), *n.* a person who follows an army to sell food and other provisions to the soldiers.

su·ze·rain (soo'zərin), *n.* a sovereign or state holding political control over another. —**su'ze·rain·ty,** *n.*

swale (swāl), *n.* a depression in a stretch of land, frequently damper and with coarser vegetation than its surroundings.

sward (swôrd), *n.* the short grass covering a lawn or open land; turf.

swarf (swôrf), *n.* a mass of small pieces and shavings of metal, plastic, or the like, removed by grinding or cutting tools during machining operations.

swarth·y (swôr'ᴛʜē), *adj.* dark in color, usually of the complexion. Also **swart**.

swas·ti·ka (swos'tikə), *n.* a figure consisting of a cross with four equal arms, each arm having an extension at right angles to it and all extensions pointing clockwise or all pointing anti-clockwise, the figure having been universally used since prehistoric times as a symbol and ornament and, with clockwise extensions, as the symbol of the Nazi party in Germany.

swath (swoᴛʜ), *n.* the area covered by one stroke of a scythe or one passage of a mower.

swathe (swoᴛʜ), *v.* to bind or envelop with strips of linen, bandage, rope, or the like.

S wave, secondary wave, the second

major shock wave radiating from an earthquake. See also **L wave, P wave.**

sweetheart contract, (in colloquial usage) a contract agreed by collusion between representatives of management and labor to pay union employees low wages.

swindle sheet, (colloquial) an account drawn up of expenses incurred in carrying out one's job and to be repaid in addition to salary; an expense account.

syb·a·rite (sib′ərīt), *n.* a person who practices luxurious and sensuous self-indulgence. —**syb·a·rit′ic,** *adj.*

syc·o·phan·cy (sik′əfənsē), *n.* excessive flattery and servility to a superior, esp. to hold or gain a position.

syc·o·phant (sik′əfənt), *n.* a person practicing or in the habit of practicing sycophancy. —**syc·o·phan′tic,** *adj.*

syl·la·bar·y (sil′əber΄ē), *n.* a system of symbols representing syllables and used for writing a particular language, as several ancient West Semitic, Aegean, and Mesopotanian languages, and Japanese.

syl·lo·gism (sil′əjizm), *n.* **1.** (in logic) a form of reasoning in which a conclusion is drawn from two premises which have a term in common, as *All rivers flow to the sea; This is a river: Therefore, this flows to the sea.* **2.** a subtle or specious argument. —**syl·lo·gis′tic,** *adj.*

sylph (silf), *n.* a slender, graceful woman.

syl·van (sil′vən), *adj.* of, relating to, or living in woodlands.

syl·vi·cul·ture (sil′vəkulcHər), *n.* See **silviculture.**

sym·bi·ont (sim′bīont), *n.* a symbiotic organism.

sym·bi·o·sis (simbīō′sis), *n.*, *pl.* **sym·bi·o·ses** (simbīō′sēz). an association of two dissimilar organisms living either attached each to the other or one as tenant of the other, usually when the association benefits both organisms. —**sym·bi·o′tic,** *adj.*

sym·met·al·ism (simmet′əlizm), *n.* the use of more than one metal as a monetary standard with each having

its value fixed in relation to the other(s). See also **bimetallism.**

sym·pa·thet·ic (simpəthet′ik), *adj.* pertaining to the major part of the motor nerve supply to smooth muscles and glands which consists of nerves and ganglia running from the thoracic and lumbar regions of the spinal cord to all of the skin, the limbs, and the internal organs, in many of which they act antagonistically to parasympathetic nerves, as in stimulating the heartbeat, dilating the pupil of the eye, inhibiting peristalsis in the gut, etc. See also **parasympathetic.**

sym·pat·ric (simpa′trik), *adj.* from or in the same locality or region, as of biological species.

sym·phy·sis (sim′fisis), *n.*, *pl.* **sym·phy·ses** (sim′fisēz). a fusion of bones or a joint allowing only slight or no movement, as that of the lower jawbone or of the pubis in man.

sym·po·si·arch (simpō′zēärk), *n.* the director or chairman of a symposium.

sym·po·si·um (simpō′zēəm), *n.*, *pl.* **sym·po·si·ums, sym·po·si·a** (simpō′zēə). a conference where lectures are given or discussions (esp. before an audience) held by several speakers on a particular subject.

symp·to·sis (simptō′sis), *n.* local or general wasting away of the body.

syn·ar·thro·sis (sin΄ärthrō′sis), *n.*, *pl.* **syn·ar·thro·ses** (sin΄ärthrō′sēz). a fixed joint, as of the bones of the skull or the teeth sockets.

sync (siNGk), *n.* (colloquial) synchronization; synchronism.

syn·chro·nism (siNG′krənizm), *n.* the state of occurring at, existing in, or occupying the same space of time. —**syn·chron′ic,** *adj.*

syn·cre·tism (siNG′kritizm), *n.* the reconciling of or attempt to reconcile diverse or opposite beliefs, practices, or groups, esp. in religion or philosophy.

syn·dac·tyl (sindak′til), *adj.* having some fingers or toes joined together completely or partially.

syn·de·re·sis (sindərē′sis), *n.* an inborn moral sense. Also **syn·te·re′sis.**

syn·des·mo·sis (sin′desmō′sis), *n.*, *pl.* **syn·des·mo·ses** (sin′desmō′sēz). a linkage of bones by ligaments or similar connective tissue other than at a joint and allowing little possibility of movement in relation to each other.

syn·det (sin′det), *n.* a synthetic detergent.

syn·det·ic (sindet′ik), *adj.* serving to link or join.

syn·dic (sin′dik), *n.* a person who officially represents and transacts business for a university or other corporate body. —**syn′di·cal,** *adj.*

syn·di·cal·ism (sin′dikəlizm), *n.* a movement, originally French, seeking to transfer the control and ownership of the means of production and distribution, and ultimately the control of society, to workers' unions. —**syn′di·cal·ist,** *n., adj.*

syn·drome (sin′drōm), *n.* a group of medical symptoms which when they occur together indicate a particular condition or disease.

syn·e·chism (sin′əkizm), *n.* a philosophical inclination in thought to emphasize continuity, first recognized and recommended by the American philosopher C. S. Peirce (1839–1914).

sy·ne·cious, sy·noe·cious (sinē′- sHəs), *adj.* See **synoicous.**

syn·e·col·o·gy (sinəkol′əjē), *n.* the ecology of a community of plants and animals as opposed to that of an individual species. See also **autecology.**

syn·ec·tics (sinek′tiks), *n.* the study of creativity, esp. creativity generated among a group of people and applied to solving problems.

synectics group, a group of diverse individuals who meet to try to find creative solutions to problems by the free play and interplay of their imaginations.

syn·er·get·ic (sinərjet′ik), *adj.* working together. Also **syn·er·gis′tic.**

syn·er·gism (sin′ərjizm), *n.* the combined activity of two or more drugs, hormones, muscles, stimuli, or the like, which work toward the same end

and produce an effect greater than the sum of effects of each acting alone.

syn·er·gy (sin′ərjē), *n.* cooperative activity, esp. of two or more muscles, nerves, drugs, hormones, or the like.

syn·es·the·sia, syn·aes·the·sia (sin′- isthē′zHə), *n.* a sensation produced in one part of the body by a stimulus in another part; an effect on one of the senses produced by a stimulus to another, as a mental impression of a particular smell produced by the stimulus of a particular sight.

syn·ga·my (siNG′gəmē), *n.* the fusion of male and female gametes in fertilization.

syn·gen·e·sis (sinjen′isis), *n.* reproduction by fusion of male and female gametes; sexual reproduction.

syn·od (sin′əd), *n.* any convention or council.

syn·od·ic (sinod′ik), *adj.* relating to similar positions of the moon or a planet relative to an imaginary line from the center of the sun through the center of the earth, and hence relating to the time between two instances of the moon or a planet apparently lying on this line.

sy·noet·ic, sy·net·ic (sinet′ik), *adj.* in community or association with others.

syn·oi·cous (sinoi′kəs), *adj.* having male and female flowers on the same flower head, as in many composites such as the daisy and dandelion. Also **sy·ne′cious.**

syn·op·tic (sinop′tik), *adj.* of, relating to, taking, or giving a condensed but comprehensive statement or view of a subject.

syn·os·to·sis (sin′ostō′sis), *n.* the fusion of separate bones to form one bone.

syn·o·vi·a (sinō′vēə), *n.* a viscous fluid secreted by membranes lining certain joints and sheathing certain tendons and having the function of lubrication.

syn·tal·i·ty (sintal′itē), *n.* the mental and behavioral features of a group corresponding to the personality of an individual.

synthetic philosophy, a philosophical system formulated and expounded by the English philosopher Herbert Spencer (1820–1903), and intended to comprehend and unify all knowledge on the basis of the evolutionary principle.

Syn·the·tism (sin*'th*itizm), *n.* a style of painting developed in the late 19th century making use of flat areas of strong color in the manner of cloisonné enamel to convey abstract ideas in a simplified symbolic way. Also **Cloisonnisme.** See also **Nabi.**

sy·pher (sī*'*fər), *v.* to join edge to edge to form an even surface, as of slant-edged boards.

syr·inx (sir*'*iNGks), *n., pl.* **sy·rin·ges** (sərin*'*jēz), **syr·inx·es.** the sound-producing organ of birds situated at the point where the trachea divides to form the bronchi.

sys·sar·co·sis (sis*'*ärkō*'*sis), *n., pl.* **sys·sar·co·ses** (sis*'*ärkō*'*sēz). the joining together of bones by intervening muscle, as the shoulder blade to ribs and vertebrae.

sys·tal·tic (sistôl*'*tik), *adj.* contracting, esp. of rhythmic contraction alternating with dilatation.

sys·tem·a·tol·o·gy (sis*'*təmətol*'*əjē), *n.* the scientific study of systems and their development.

sys·tem·ic (sistem*'*ik), *adj.* relating to or affecting the whole body or one of the body's sytems of organs.

sys·to·le (sis*'*təlē), *n.* that phase of the heart-beat when the ventricles contract, forcing the blood into the arteries. See also **diastole.**

syz·y·gy (siz*'*ijē), *n.* the point in orbit at which a heavenly body is in conjunction with or in opposition to the sun.

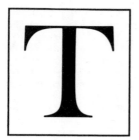

ta·bes (tā′bēz), *n.* a wasting away, usually resulting from chronic disease.
ta·bes·cent (təbes′ənt), *adj.* wasting away; becoming emaciated.
tab·o·ret (tab′ərit), *n.* **1.** a stool. **2.** a stand or frame for embroidery.
ta·chis·to·scope (təkis′təskōp), *n.* an apparatus used to present various stimuli to the eye for a very brief period.
ta·chom·e·ter (takom′itər), *n.* **1.** a device for measuring speed. **2.** a device for measuring revolutions per minute made by a piece of machinery.
tach·y·aux·e·sis (tak′ēôgzē′sis), *n.* the growth of part of an organism at a faster rate than the whole. See also **isauxesis, bradyauxesis.**
tach·y·car·di·a (takəkär′dēə), *n.* abnormally rapid beating of the heart.
ta·chym·e·ter (takim′itər), *n.* an instrument used in surveying for the rapid calculation of distances, directions, and differences in height.
ta·chym·e·try (takim′itrē), *n.* the technique of measuring distance, etc. with a tachymeter.
tach·y·phy·lax·is (tak′əfilak′sis), *n.* temporary resistance to the effects of an injection of poison achieved by previous small injections of the poison. Also **skeptophylaxis.** See also **mithridatism.**
tach·yp·ne·a, tach·yp·noe·a (tak′-ipnē′ə), *n.* abnormally fast breathing.

tach·y·tel·ic (tak′itel′ik), *adj.* relating to an abnormally fast rate of evolution. See also **horotelic, bradytelic.**
tal·i·on (tal′ēən), *n.* See **lex talionis.**
tac·it (tas′it), *adj.* expressed without words; implied; unspoken.
tac·i·turn (tas′iturn), *adj.* disinclined to talk; avoiding conversation. —**tac·i·turn′i·ty,** *n.*
ta·co (tä′kō), *n.* a tortilla rolled or folded over a filling.
tac·ti·cal (tak′tikəl), *adj.* relating to a maneuver or plan to achieve a desired purpose or temporary gain. See also **strategic.**
tac·tile (tak′til), *adj.* relating to the sense of touch.
tac·tion (tak′sHən), *n.* contact; touch.
tac·tu·al (tak′cHŌŌəl), *adj.* relating to or arising from the sense of touch.
tae·ni·a·cide (tē′nēəsīd), *n.* any substance for destroying tapeworms.
tae·ni·a·fuge (tē′nēəfyŌŌj), *n.* any substance used to drive out tapeworms from the body.
tae·ni·a·sis (tēnī′əsis), *n.* infestation with tapeworms.
taille (tāl), *n.* the waist or bodice of a dress, robe, etc.
tail·leur (täyur′), *n.* a woman's tailored suit or costume.
tal·i·grade (tal′əgrād), *adj.* putting the weight on the outer side of the foot when walking.

tal·i·ped (tal′əped), *adj.* **1.** distorted or twisted in the foot. **2.** clubfooted.

tal·i·pes (tal′əpēz), *n.* **1.** a clubfoot. **2.** clubfootedness.

tal·is·man (tal′ismən), *n.* a lucky charm.

ta·lus (tā′ləs), *n.* the anklebone; astragalus.

ta·ma·le (təmä′lē), *n.* a Mexican dish of meat wrapped in cornmeal dough and steamed.

ta·ma·sha (təmä′shə), *n.* (in the East Indies) a show; a spectacle; an entertainment.

tam·pon (tam′pon), *n.* a plug of lint, cotton wool, etc., to stop bleeding from an orifice.

tam·pon·ade (tampənād′), *v.* **1.** the application of a tampon to stop bleeding. **2.** compression of the heart by fluid accumulated in the cavity surrounding it.

tan·ge·lo (tan′jelō), *n.* a hybrid between the tangerine and the grapefruit.

tan·gi·ble (tan′jəbəl), *adj.* that can be touched; actual; substantial; real.

tan·go·re·cep·tor (taNG′gōrisep′tər), *n.* a receptor responsive to touch.

tan·ta·mount (tan′təmount), *adj.* equal in value, meaning, or effect to, as *His absence was tantamount to an admission of guilt.*

tan·tiv·y (tantiv′ē), *adv.* **1.** at the gallop; swiftly. —*adj.* **2.** fast; swift.

ta·pa (tä′pə), *n.* a cloth made from bark used in the Pacific Islands.

tape·worm (tāp′wûrm), *n.* any of various parasitic flatworms inhabiting the intestines of vertebrate animals.

taph·e·pho·bi·a (tafəfō′bēə), *n.* an abnormally excessive fear of being buried alive.

tap·is (tap′ē), *n.* a carpet or tapestry.

tap·ping (tap′iNG), *n.* See **paracentesis.**

tar·an·tel·la (tarəntel′ə), *n.* a lively, whirling dance of southern Italy.

tar·ant·ism (tar′əntizm), *n.* a nervous disorder producing an irresistible urge to dance.

tar·boosh (tärbōōsh′), *n.* a brimless cap with a tassel, worn by Muslim men and sometimes surrounded by a turban.

tar·di·grade (tär′dəgrād), *adj.* having a slow movement.

tare (ter), *n.* the weight of the receptacle, wrapping, etc., in which goods are packed.

tarn (tärn), *n.* a small lake in a mountainous region.

ta·rot (tarō′), *n.* a special set of playing cards used in fortunetelling.

tar·pan (tärpan′), *n.* a variety of wild horse of eastern Europe and central Asia. Also **Przewalski's horse.**

tar·sal (tär′səl), *adj.* relating to the tarsus.

tar·si·a (tär′sēə), *n.* See **intarsia.**

tar·sus (tär′səs), *n.* the group of bones forming the heel and ankle in humans and the corresponding part in other vertebrates.

ta·sim·e·ter (təsim′itər), *n.* an electrical apparatus for recording very small changes in temperature and the like by means of pressure changes caused by expanding solids.

ta·ta·mi (tətä′mē), *n.* a kind of straw mat used in Japanese dwellings to partition off the interior.

tat·ter·de·mal·ion (tat′ərdimāl′-yən), *n.* a person dressed in ragged clothing.

tau·ri·form (tôr′əfôrm), *adj.* having the form of a bull.

tau·rine (tôr′īn), *adj.* relating to or resembling a bull.

tau·rom·a·chy (tôrom′əkē), *n.* the art of bullfighting.

tau·tol·o·gy (tôtol′əjē), *n.* unnecessary repetition of an idea in different words.

taw (tô), *v.* to dress a raw material, as an animal skin, for use.

tax·is (tak′sis), *n.* the response of an organism to an external stimulus by movement in a particular direction. See also **tropism.**

tax·on (tak′son), *n.* a taxonomic species, group, etc.

tax·on·o·my (takson′əmē), *n.* the scientific classification of living things. —**tax·o·nom′ic,** *adj.*

Tay-Sachs disease, a rare disease characterized by gradual blindness and weight loss, and invariably fatal, usually affecting children of Jewish or eastern European origin.

teaching machine, an automatic device for presenting an item of information to a pupil and extracting a correct response before presenting further items.

tea·poy (tē′poi), *n.* a three-legged stand, esp. one used in serving tea.

tea·sel (tē′zəl), *v.* to raise a nap on cloth by brushing it with the prickly flowerhead of the teasel.

tech·noc·ra·cy (teknok′rəsē), *n.* government by those skilled in the uses of technology, as engineers, technical experts, etc.

tech·nog·ra·phy (teknog′rəfē), *n.* the description and study of the history and distribution of the arts and sciences.

tech·nol·o·gy (teknol′əjē), *n.* applied science; the industrial arts.

tec·ton·ic (tekton′ik), *adj.* relating to building or architecture.

tec·ton·ics (tekton′iks), *n.* the art or science of construction, as of buildings, furniture, etc.

ted (ted), *v.* to spread out cut grass and the like to dry.

te·di·um (tē′dēəm), *n.* the quality of being irksome or wearisome. —**te′di·ous,** *adj.*

teg·men (teg′mən), *n.* a top layer or covering.

teg·u·lar (teg′yələr), *adj.* relating to or consisting of tiles.

teg·u·ment (teg′yəmənt), *n.* a covering of skin.

tek·non·y·my (teknon′əmē), *n.* the primitive custom of giving a child's name to its parent.

tek·tite (tek′tīt), *n.* a small, glassy body supposedly of meteoric origin.

tel·aes·the·sia (telisthē′zHə), *n.* See **telesthesia.**

tel·e·gen·ic (teləjen′ik), *adj.* having an appearance or personality that shows to advantage on television. Also **videogenic.**

tel·eg·no·sis (telənō′sis), *n.* knowl-

edge acquired by supernatural means. —**tel·eg·nos′tic,** *adj.*

te·leg·o·ny (təleg′ənē), *n.* the supposed continuation of the influence of a sire upon the offspring born to the mother after matings with subsequent sires.

tel·e·ki·ne·sis (tel′əkinē′sis), *n.* the causing of objects to move without physical contact or other normal force.

te·lem·e·ter (təlem′itər), *n.* an apparatus for measuring the value of a quantity and transmitting the results over a distance, usually by a radio device.

tel·en·ceph·a·lon (tel′ensef′əlon), *n.* the anterior part of the forebrain.

tel·e·ol·o·gy (tel′ēol′əjē), *n.* the doctrine that all things in nature are designed to fulfill a purpose.

te·lep·a·thy (təlep′əthē), *n.* communication of ideas, feelings, etc., by means other than the normal senses. —**te·lep′a·thist,** *n.*

te·leph·o·ny (təlef′ənē), *n.* the transmission of sounds by telephone or similar equipment.

tel·e·plasm (tel′əplazm), *n.* the supposed emanation from a medium's body used to produce telekinesis.

Tel·e·prompt·er (tel′əpromptər), *n.* the trade name of a device for enabling a speaker on television to read his script while apparently speaking spontaneously.

tel·e·ran (tel′əran), *n.* a system of aerial navigation which transmits information by television to airplanes.

tel·es·the·sia, tel·aes·the·sia (telisthē′zHə), *n.* sensation received from a distance without normal use of the senses.

tel·ic (tel′ik), *adj.* tending toward a particular end.

tell·er (tel′ər), *n.* one entrusted with the counting of votes, money, etc.

tel·lu·ric (teloŏr′ik), *adj.* relating to the earth; terrestrial.

tel·lu·ri·on (təloŏr′ēon), *n.* an apparatus for demonstrating how the rotation of the earth causes day and night and seasonal changes.

tel·o·dy·nam·ic (tel′ōdīnam′ik), *adj.* relating to the transmission of power over a long distance.

tel·o·tax·is (telətak′sis), *n.* movement of an organism in response to any of a number of simultaneous stimuli.

tel·pher, tel·fer (tel′fər), *n.* a car, etc., carried by means of telpherage.

tel·pher·age, tel·fer·age (tel′fərij), *n.* a transportation system in which cars are suspended from or run on aerial cables.

tem·blor (tem′blər), *n.* an earth tremor; an earthquake.

tem·er·ar·i·ous (temərer′ēəs), *adj.* rash; reckless; impetuous.

te·mer·i·ty (təmer′itē), *n.* recklessness; daring; boldness.

tem·per·a (tem′pərə), *n.* a medium for painting consisting of powdered colors mixed with a natural or artificial emulsion, as egg yolk, oil, gum, etc., and the commonest painting medium before the invention of oil paint.

tem·plet (tem′plit), *n.* a wooden or metal mold used as a guide in shaping or cutting wood, stone, or the like.

tem·po·ral (tem′pərəl), *adj.* 1. relating to time. 2. relating to or concerning earthly life. 3. temporary; not eternal.

tem·po·rize (tem′pərīz), *v.* to avoid making a decision; be evasive.

tem·pu·ra (tem′pōōrä), *n.* a Japanese dish of seafood or vegetables coated with batter and fried.

ten·a·ble (ten′əbəl), *adj.* that can be maintained, occupied, possessed, etc.

te·na·cious (tənā′sHəs), *adj.* having a firm hold or grip.

te·nac·i·ty (tənas′itē), *n.* the quality of being tenacious.

te·nac·u·lum (tənak′yələm), *n.* a small hook used by surgeons for holding parts, such as arteries, in operations.

Ten Commandments. See **Decalogue.**

ten·den·tious (tenden′sHəs), *adj.* having a bias; lacking impartiality; not fair or just.

ten·e·brif·ic (tenəbrif′ik), *adj.* causing darkness.

ten·e·brous (ten′əbrəs), *adj.* gloomy; dark.

ten·ent (ten′ənt), *adj.* adapted for holding on or clinging with.

te·nes·mus (tənez′məs), *n.* an urge to evacuate the bowels or bladder but without the ability to do so.

ten·et (ten′it), *n.* a belief or doctrine held to be true.

te·nor·rha·phy (tənôr′əfē), *n.* the surgical stitching of a tendon.

te·not·o·my (tənot′əmē), *n.* the surgical cutting of a tendon.

ten·seg·ri·ty (tenseg′ritē), *n.* (in architecture) the efficient use of continuous tension members and discontinuous compression members in skeleton structures.

ten·si·ble (ten′səbəl), *adj.* that may be pulled or stretched.

ten·sile (ten′səl), *adj.* 1. relating to tension. 2. capable of being stretched.

tensile strength, the maximum longitudinal stress which a material can support without rupture.

ten·sim·e·ter (tensim′itər), *n.* an instrument which measures the pressure of vapor or gas.

ten·si·om·e·ter (ten′sēom′itər), *n.* 1. a device for measuring tensile stress in wires, beams, etc. 2. an instrument which measures the surface tension of liquids.

ten·sor (ten′sər), *n.* a muscle that stretches any part of the body.

ten·ta·tion (tentā′sHən), *n.* the perfection of a mechanical apparatus or the like by means of a series of tests of its functioning.

ten·u·i·ty (tənōō′itē), *n.* the quality or state of being tenuous.

ten·u·ous (ten′yōōəs), *adj.* thin in form or consistency; rarefied; flimsy.

ten·ure (ten′yər), *n.* the act or right of holding or possessing something.

ter·a·tism (ter′ətizm), *n.* 1. See **teratosis.** 2. adoration of the monstrous.

ter·a·to·gen·e·sis (ter′ətōjen′isis), *n.* the production of biological monstrosities or abnormal formations. Also **ter·a·tog′e·ny.**

ter·a·toid (ter'ətoid), *adj.* of monstrous or abnormal biological form.

ter·a·tol·o·gy (terətol'əjē), *n.* the study of malformations or monstrosities in organisms.

ter·a·to·sis (terətō'sis), *n.* a biological freak; a monstrosity. Also **ter'a·tism.**

ter·cen·te·nar·y (tursen'təner'ē), *n.* 1. a 300th anniversary. —*adj.* 2. relating to a 300th anniversary.

te·rete (tərēt'), *adj.* slender and cylindrical with tapering ends.

ter·gi·ver·sate (tur'jivərsāt'), *v.* to equivocate; to vacillate; to change one's opinions repeatedly.

ter·ma·gant (tur'məgənt), *n.* a violent, overbearing, or shrewish woman.

ter·mi·na·tor (tur'mənātər), *n.* the dividing line between the lit and the unlit part of a planet.

ter·na·ry (tur'nərē), *adj.* 1. involving or relating to three; triple. 2. third in order or rank. 3. using the number three as a base.

ter·nate (tur'nit), *adj.* having three parts; arranged in groups of three.

terne metal, an alloy of lead and tin.

terp·si·cho·re·an (turp'səkərē'ən), *adj.* relating to dancing.

terra cotta, a hard earthenware, brownish in color and usually unglazed.

ter·rane (tərān'), *n.* a connected group of rock formations.

ter·ra·que·ous (terā'kwēəs), *adj.* comprising both land and water.

ter·rar·i·um (tərer'ēəm), *n., pl.* **ter·rar·i·ums, ter·rar·i·a.** 1. a vivarium for terrestrial animals. 2. a glass container in which plants are grown.

ter·rene (terēn'), *adj.* 1. worldly; earthly; mundane. 2. earthy.

ter·ric·o·lous (terik'ələs), *adj.* living on or in the ground.

ter·rig·e·nous (terij'ənəs), *adj.* 1. produced by the earth. 2. relating to sediment caused by the erosive action of tides, currents, etc., or to rocks formed from such sediment.

ter·rine (tərēn'), *n.* 1. an earthenware casserole. 2. a delicacy of meat or fish cooked in such a casserole.

terse (turs), *adj.* concise; using few words.

ter·tian (tur'sHən), *adj.* of a fever marked by paroxysms which recur every second (or by inclusive reckoning every third) day, as some kinds of malaria. See also **quartan, quintan, sextan.**

ter·ti·ar·y (tur'sHēer'ē), *adj.* 1. third in rank or importance. 2. (in geology) (*cap.* **T-**), relating to the earlier part of the Cenozoic era. See also **Neocene, Paleocene.**

ter·ti·um quid (tûr'sHēəm kwid'), something related to two things but distinct from each.

tes·sel·late (tes'əlāt), *v.* to pave with small blocks or squares, as a floor or pavement. —**tes·sel·la'tion,** *n.*

tes·sel·lat·ed (tes'əlātid), *adj.* relating to or having the appearance of a mosaic; checkered.

tes·ser·a (tes'ərə), *n., pl.* **tes·ser·ae.** 1. a small piece used in mosaic work. 2. a piece of bone or wood used by the ancients as a voucher, tally, ticket, etc.

tes·ta (tes'tə), *n., pl.* **tes·tae.** the hard external covering of a seed; integument.

tes·ta·cean (testā'sHən), *adj.* having a shell, as certain invertebrates.

tes·ta·ceous (testā'sHəs), *adj.* relating to shells; having a hard covering such as a shell.

tes·ta·men·ta·ry (testəmen'tərē), *adj.* 1. relating to a will or testament. 2. bequeathed by means of a will.

tes·tate (tes'tāt), *adj.* having left a valid will.

tes·ta·tor (tes'tātər), *n.* one who has made a will.

tes·ta·trix (testā'triks), *n., pl.* **tes·ta·tri·ces** (testā'trisēz), a female testator.

test ban, an agreement between nations not to test nuclear weapons or to test them only under certain prescribed conditions.

tes·ter (tes'tər), *n.* a canopy over a bed, pulpit, etc.

tes·ti·fi·ca·tion (tes'təfəkā'sHən), *n.* the act of testifying; testimony.

tes·tu·di·nal (testōōd'ənl), *adj.* relating to or resembling a tortoise or tortoise shell.

tes·tu·di·nate (testōōd′ənit), *adj.* shaped like a tortoise shell.

tes·ty (tes′tē), *adj.* irritable; easily annoyed.

tet·a·nus (tet′ənəs), *n.* **1.** an infectious disease caused by a particular bacterium entering open wounds and producing violent tonic spasms. See also **lockjaw. 2.** a condition in which muscles are contracted for a prolonged period.

tet·a·ny (tet′ənē), *n.* a medical condition marked by severe tonic spasms.

tête-à-tête (tāt′ətāt′), *n.* **1.** a close conversation or private interview, esp. between two people. **2.** a siamoise.

tet·rad (te′trad), *n.* a set, group, or arrangement of four.

tet·ra·gon (te′trəgon), *n.* a figure with four angles and four sides. —**te·trag′o·nal,** *adj.*

tet·ra·gram (te′trəgram), *n.* a word of four letters.

Tet·ra·gram·ma·ton (tətrəgram′əton), *n.* the Hebrew word for God, written with four consonants usually transliterated as YHVH.

tet·ra·he·dral (tetrəhē′drəl), *adj.* relating to or having the form of a tetrahedron.

tet·ra·he·dron (tetrəhē′drən), *n.* a solid contained by four plane faces.

tet·ra·ple·gia (tetrəplē′jēə), *n.* See **quadriplegia.**

tet·ra·pod (te′trəpod), *n.* an object or device with four projections radiating from a central point at an angle of 120° to one another, so that if any three of the projections touch the ground, the fourth will point upward. See also **caltrop.**

thal·a·mus (thal′əməs), *n.* the middle part of the posterior subdivision of the forebrain.

tha·las·sic (thəlas′ik), *adj.* relating to, growing in, or living in the smaller seas, gulfs, etc.

thal·as·sog·ra·phy (thaləsog′rəfē), *n.* the branch of oceanography dealing with coastal or smaller bodies of sea water.

thal·weg (täl′veg), *n.* a line joining the lowest points of a valley.

than·a·to·pho·bia (thanʹətəfō′bēə), *n.* an abnormally excessive dread of death.

than·a·top·sis (thanətop′sis), *n.* speculation about or contemplation of death.

thau·ma·tol·o·gy (thômətôl′əjē), *n.* the study of miracles.

thau·ma·trope (thô′məturjcard with a different picture on each side, which when rotated swiftly causes the two pictures to appear combined as one.

thau·ma·turge (thô′məturj), *n.* one who performs miracles. —**thau·ma·tur′gic,** *adj.*

thau·ma·tur·gy (thô′mətur′jē), *n.* the performance of miracles.

the·an·throp·ic (thēanthrop′ik), *adj.* relating to both god and man; divine and human.

the·an·thro·pism (thēan′thrəpizm), *n.* **1.** the union of the divine and human; the incarnation of God as man in Christ. **2.** the attributing of human characteristics to gods.

theater of war, the whole area in which military forces are deployed and may be used in direct military action. See also **zone of interior.**

the·ba·ine (thē′bəēn), *n.* a substance obtained from opium but having poisonous effects similar to those of strychnine rather than narcotic effects.

the·ca (thē′kə), *n.* a cover or receptacle; sac.

the·ine (thē′ēn), *n.* caffeine, esp. as it occurs in tea.

the·ism (thē′izm), *n.* **1.** belief in the existence of one god as the creator of the universe. See also **deism. 2.** belief in the existence of a god or gods. See also **atheism.**

the·lyt·o·ky (thilit′əkē), *n.* parthenogenesis resulting in the birth of female offspring only. Also **thel·y·ot′o·ky.** —**the·lyt′o·kous,** *adj.*

the·nar (thē′när), *n.* **1.** the fleshy ball of the thumb. **2.** the fleshy outer side of the palm.

the·o·cen·tric (*th*ēəsen′trik), *adj.* having God as the center of all thoughts, feelings, etc.

the·oc·ra·cy (*th*ēok′rəsē), *n.* a form of government in which the rulers, usually priests, claim to have or are regarded as having divine guidance.

the·oc·ra·sy (*th*ēok′rəsē), *n.* a mixture of religious forms and deities as the object of worship by believers.

the·od·o·lite (*th*ēod′əlīt), *n.* a surveying instrument for checking gradients, angles, etc.

the·og·o·ny (*th*ēog′ənē), *n.* a genealogy of the gods; an account of or poem dealing with the origin of the gods.

the·ol·a·try (*th*ēol′ətrē), *n.* worship of a god.

the·om·a·chy (*th*ēom′əkē), *n.* a conflict against or among the gods.

the·o·ma·ni·a (*th*ē′ōmā′nēə), *n.* a form of madness in which the sufferer believes himself to be God or especially chosen by God.

the·o·mor·phic (*th*ēəmôr′fik), *adj.* resembling a god in appearance.

the·op·a·thy (*th*ēop′əthē), *n.* strong emotion aroused by the contemplation of God.

the·oph·a·ny (*th*ēof′ənē), *n.* the visible manifestation of God or a god to man.

the·os·o·phy (*th*ēos′əfē), *n.* any religious belief or philosophy claiming mystical insight into the divine nature. —**the·o·soph′i·cal,** *adj.*

Ther·a·va·da (therəvä′də), *n.* See **Hinayana.**

ther·blig (*th*ur′blig), *n.* any element in an operation or procedure that can be subjected to time and motion study. [anagram of F. B. *Gilbreth* (1868–1924), U.S. engineer]

the·ri·ac (*th*ēr′ēak), *n.* **1.** treacle; molasses. **2.** an antidote to snake bites and other poisons, made of numerous drugs mixed with honey.

the·ri·an (*th*ēr′ēən), *adj.* relating to marsupial and placental mammals.

the·ri·an·throp·ic (*th*ēr′ēanthrop′ik), *adj.* partly animal and partly human in form.

the·ri·o·mor·phic (*th*ēr′ēəmôr′fik),

adj. having the form of an animal, esp. of gods.

ther·mae (*th*ur′mē), *n. pl.* hot springs.

therm·al·ge·si·a (*th*urm′alijē′zēə), *n.* pain caused by heat.

therm·an·es·the·sia, therm·an·aes·the·sia (*th*urm′anis*th*ē′zHə), *n.* inability to feel heat or cold. Also **ther·mo·an·es·the′sia.**

therm·es·the·sia, therm·aes·the·sia (*th*urm′is*th*ē′zHə). the ability to feel heat or cold.

therm·i·on (*th*urm′īən), *n.* an electrically charged particle, as an ion, emitted by an incandescent body. —**therm·i·on′ic,** *adj.*

therm·i·on·ics (*th*urm′īon′iks), *n. sing.* the scientific study of thermionic phenomena.

ther·mis·tor (*th*ərmis′tər), *n.* a resistor whose resistance varies with changes in temperature.

ther·mo·cline (*th*ur′məklīn), *n.* a layer of water in a sea, lake, etc., marked by greater variations in temperature than the layers above and below it. See also **epilimnion, hypolimnion.**

ther·mo·cou·ple (*th*ur′məkup′əl), *n.* a device used to ascertain the temperature of a substance by measuring its electromotive force. Also **thermel, thermoelectric couple, thermoelectric thermometer.**

ther·mo·dur·ic (*th*urmədŏŏr′ik), *adj.* resistant to high temperatures, as certain microorganisms.

ther·mo·dy·nam·ics (*th*ur′mōdīnam′iks), *n.* the study of the relation between heat and mechanical energy and the conversion of one into the other. —**ther·mo·dy·nam′ic,** *adj.*

ther·mo·gen·e·sis (*th*ur′mōjen′isis), *n.* the production of heat in an animal body. —**ther·mo·ge·net′ic,** *adj.*

ther·mo·gen·ic (*th*urmōjen′ik), *adj.* relating to or causing the production of heat.

ther·mog·e·nous (*th*ərmoj′ənəs), *adj.* heat-producing.

ther·mo·ge·og·ra·phy (*th*ur′mōjēog′rəfē), *n.* the study of variations in temperature according to geographical distribution.

ther·mog·ra·phy (thərmog′rəfē), n. a printing process in which the printed matter is dusted with powder and heated to make the letters stand out in relief.

ther·mo·lu·mi·nes·cence (thur′-mōlōō′mənes′əns), n. phosphorescence induced by the action of heat. Also **ther·mo·phos·pho·res′cence.** —**ther·mo·lu·mi·nes′cent,** adj.

ther·mol·y·sis (thərmol′isis), n. the dissipation of heat from the body.

ther·mom·e·try (thərmom′itrē), n. the science dealing with the measurement of temperature.

ther·mo·mo·tive (thur′məmō′tiv), adj. relating to motion caused by heat.

ther·mo·nu·cle·ar (thur′mōnōō′-klēər), adj. relating to or involving a thermonuclear reaction.

thermonuclear reaction, a nuclear reaction between the atomic nuclei of a substance heated to a temperature of several million degrees.

ther·mo·phile (thur′məfīl), n. an organism, as certain bacteria, that grows best in comparatively high temperatures, esp. between 50° and 60°C. —**ther·mo·phil′ic,** adj.

ther·mo·pile (thur′məpīl), n. an apparatus consisting of a series of thermocouples joined together and used to generate electric current or to measure radiant energy.

ther·mo·plas·tic (thurməplas′tik), adj. having properties of softness and plasticity when heated.

ther·mo·re·cep·tor (thur′mōrisep′-tər), n. a receptor sensitive to changes in temperature.

ther·mo·scope (thur′məskōp), n. a device for measuring changes in temperature of a substance by noting the accompanying changes in its volume.

ther·mo·sen·si·tive (thur′mōsen′si-tiv), adj. easily affected by a change, esp. a rise in temperature.

ther·mo·set·ting (thur′mōset′iNG), adj. having the property of setting hard when heated and being incapable of remolding.

ther·mo·sphere (thur′məsfēr), n. the region in the earth's atmosphere which lies above the mesosphere and in which temperature increases with altitude.

ther·mo·sta·ble (thurməstā′bəl), adj. retaining its characteristic properties when subjected to moderate heat.

ther·mo·stat (thur′məstat), n. a device for regulating a heating apparatus so as to maintain a constant temperature.

ther·mo·tax·is (thurmətak′sis), n. **1.** movement of an organism in response to a source of heat. **2.** the regulation of body temperature.

ther·mot·ro·pism (thərmo′trəpizm), n. growth of an organism in a direction determined by a source of heat. —**ther·mo·trop′ic,** adj.

the·roid (thēr′oid), adj. having the characteristics or tendencies of an animal.

the·ro·phyte (thēr′əfīt), n. a plant whose lifetime covers only one growing season.

ther·sit·i·cal (thərsit′ikəl), adj. abusive; foul-mouthed.

the·sis (thē′sis), n. a proposition put forward for discussion; a lengthy dissertation supporting such a proposition.

thes·pi·an (thes′pēən), adj. relating to the drama or to acting.

the·ur·gy (thē′urjē), n. **1.** a system of magic or supernatural practices by those claiming to have the help of beneficent deities. **2.** the operation of divine or supernatural agency in human affairs.

thews (thyōōz), n. pl. sinew; muscle; muscular strength.

thi·a·sus (thī′əsəs), n. (in ancient Greece) a group holding a celebration or ceremony in honor of a patron god.

thig·mo·tax·is (thigmətak′sis), n. **1.** the movement of an organism in response to an object providing a mechanical stimulus. **2.** See **stereotaxis.**

thig·mo·tro·pism (thigmo′trəpizm), n. growth of an organism in which the direction is determined by mechanical contact.

thill (*th*il), *n.* either of the two shafts of a vehicle which is drawn by one animal.

thim·ble·rig (*th*im'bəlrig), *n.* a game of deception in which a pea or the like, supposedly concealed under one of three thimbles, is palmed by one player while the other player guesses and lays bets on which thimble it is under.

thi·o·u·ra·cil (*th*ī'ōyŏŏr'əsil), *n.* a crystalline powder used to reduce overactivity of the thyroid gland.

thix·ot·ro·py (*th*ikso'təpē), *n.* the characteristic of certain gels to become liquid when stirred.

tho·rac·ic (*th*ôras'ik), *adj.* of or relating to the thorax.

thrall (*th*rôl), *n.* one held in bondage; a slave.

thra·son·i·cal (*th*rāson'ikəl), *adj.* boastful; bragging.

threm·ma·tol·o·gy (*th*remətol'əjē), *n.* the breeding of animals and plants under domestication.

thren·o·dy (*th*ren'ədē), *n.* a lament; funeral song; dirge. Also **thre'node.**

throe (*th*rō), *n.* a sharp spasm; a pang of emotion.

throm·bin (*th*rom'bin), *n.* a substance that facilitates coagulation of the blood.

throm·bo·cyte (*th*rom'bəsīt), *n.* a nucleate cell that facilitates coagulation of blood in those vertebrates without blood platelets.

throm·bo·gen (*th*rom'bəjen), *n.* See **prothrombin.**

throm·bol·y·sis (*th*rombol'isis), *n.* the dissolution of a thrombus. Also **throm·boc'la·sis.**

throm·bo·phle·bi·tis (*th*rom'bōflibī'tis), *n.* inflammation of a vein with resulting occurrence of thrombosis in the affected part. See also **phlebo-thrombosis.**

throm·bo·sis (*th*rombō'sis), *n.* the clotting of blood in any part of the circulatory system.

throm·bus (*th*rom'bəs), *n.* a clot of blood which forms in a blood vessel.

throw·ster (*th*rō'stər), *n.* a person who carries out the textile operation of twisting filaments, as of silk or synthetic fiber, into yarn without stretching them, an operation known as throwing.

thrum (*th*rum), *n.* one of the fringe of unwoven warp threads left on a loom after the web of fabric is cut off.

thug·gee (*th*ug'ē), *n.* (formerly in India) murder, usually by strangulation, and robbery by professional thugs.

thun·der·stone (*th*un'dərstōn), *n.* any of various stones, as meteorites, etc., once believed to have fallen as thunderbolts.

thu·ri·ble (*th*ŏŏr'əbəl), *n.* a vessel used for the burning of incense; censer.

thu·ri·fer (*th*ŏŏr'əfər), *n.* a person who carries a thurible in religious services.

thurm (*th*urm), *v.* to shape or carve (wood) across the grain so as to make it appear to turn.

thy·la·cine (*th*ī'ləsīn), *n.* a carnivorous, tan-colored, black-striped, wolf-like marsupial of Tasmania.

thy·roid (*th*ī'roid), *n.* a ductless two-lobed endocrine gland situated in the neck of vertebrates, whose secretions regulate metabolism and growth. Also **thyroid gland.**

thy·ro·tox·i·co·sis (*th*ī'rōtok'səkō'sis), *n.* an abnormal condition caused by excessive activity of the thyroid gland and characterized by enlargement of the thyroid, weight loss, protruding eyes, tremors, rapid pulse, etc.

tib·ia (tib'ēə), *n.* the inner of the two bones between the knee and the ankle.

tic dou·lou·reux (tik'dŏŏ'lŏŏrŏŏ'), a form of neuralgia producing paroxysmal pain and muscular twitching in the face. Also **facial neuralgia.**

Tiffany glass. See **Favrile glass.**

ti·glon (tī'glən), *n.* the offspring of a mating between a tiger and a lioness.

ti·ki (tē'kē), *n.* a carved image of an ancestor, supernatural power, etc., worn as an amulet in some Polynesian cultures.

til·ak (til′ək), *n.* a colored mark worn on the forehead by Hindu men and women.

til·de (til′də), *n.* **1.** a mark (˜) placed over a letter, as over *n* in Spanish, to indicate a change in the sound of a letter. **2.** a similar mark used to indicate the omission of a syllable or word, as a sign of negation in logic and mathematics, etc.

tim·bal, tym·bal (tim′bəl), *n.* **1.** a kettledrum. **2.** a vibrating membrane found in certain insects.

tim·bre (tim′bər), *n.* the distinctive quality of a sound, as of a voice or of music produced by a particular instrument.

time-binding (tīm′bīndiNG), *n.* the preservation of memories and experiences by one generation for the use of succeeding generations.

tim·or·ous (tim′ərəs), *adj.* fearful; timid.

tim·pa·ni, tym·pa·ni (tim′pənē), *n. pl.* a set of kettledrums as used by an orchestra.

tinc·to·ri·al (tiNGktôr′ēəl), *adj.* relating to colors, dyeing, or staining.

tin·ni·ent (tin′ēənt), *adj.* having a ringing sound.

tin·ni·tus (tinī′təs), *n.* a sensation of ringing in the ears.

tin·tin·nab·u·lar (tintinab′yələr), *adj.* relating to bells or their sounds. Also **tin·tin·nab′u·lar·y, tin·tin·nab′u·lous.**

tin·tin·nab·u·la·tion (tin′tinab′-yəlā′sHən), *n.* the sound of bells ringing.

tint·om·e·ter (tintom′itər), *n.* a colorimeter for comparing a color with a range of standard tints or colors.

tin·type (tin′tīp), *n.* a photograph in the form of a positive made on a sensitized sheet of enameled tin or iron.

tip·pet (tip′it), *n.* a cape or scarf of fur or wool worn with the two ends hanging loose in front.

tip·ple (tip′əl), *v.* to drink repeated small quantities of intoxicating liquor.

ti·rade (tī′rād), *n.* a protracted speech of denunciation or abuse.

ti·ro (tī′rō), *n.* See **tyro.**

ti·tan·o·saur (tītan′əsôr), *n.* any herbivorous dinosaur of the genus *Titanosaurus* which belonged to the Cretaceous period.

tithe (tīTH), *n.* **1.** a tenth part of income or of agricultural produce paid to a church or religious institution. **2.** any one-tenth tax or levy.

tit·i·vate[1] (tit′əvāt), *v.* to dress up; to make smart; to adorn.

tit·i·vate[2] (tit′əvāt), *v.* to titillate; to tickle; to excite agreeably, as by stroking or flirtation.

ti·trate (tī′trāt), *v.* to determine the quantity of a constituent in a compound by adding a precise amount of a reagent.

tit·tle (tit′l), *n.* **1.** a small dot in printing or writing. **2.** a very small part of anything; a minute quantity.

tit·u·ba·tion (ticH′ōōbā′sHən), *n.* a disorder in bodily equilibrium causing an unsteady gait and trembling. **—tit′u·bant,** *adj.*

tit·u·lar (ticH′ələr), *adj.* **1.** relating to or of the nature of a title. **2.** existing only in title; without the duties of office; nominal.

tme·sis (təmē′sis), *n.* the separation of parts of a compound word by the interposition of one or more other words, as *what deeds soever.*

TNT, a solid, highly explosive but not affected by normal friction or shock, used chiefly in explosive devices such as shells, and in the making of dyes and photographic chemicals. Also **trinitrotoluene, methyltrinitrobenzene.**

toc·ca·ta (təkä′tə), *n., pl.* **toc·ca′te.** a musical composition intended to show the performer's technique.

to·col·o·gy, to·kol·o·gy (tōkol′əjē), *n.* obstetrics.

toc·sin (tok′sin), *n.* a warning signal; an alarm sounded by a bell.

to·gat·ed (tō′gātid), *adj.* peaceful. [from Latin: literally, wearing a toga]

to·hu·bo·hu (tō′hōōbō′hōō), *n.* disorder; chaos. [from Hebrew]

to·ko·dy·na·mom·e·ter, to·co·dy·na·mom·e·ter (tō′kōdī′nəmom′itər), *n.* a device for measuring pressure within the uterus during labor. Also **tocometer.**

tom·al·ley (tom′alē), *n.* the liver of a lobster, as used in cookery.

tom·bo·lo (tom′bəlō), *n., pl.* **tom·bo·los.** a spit or bar of sand linking one island with another or with the mainland.

tome (tōm), *n.* a separate volume forming part of a set or a larger work; any learned or serious book.

to·men·tose (təmen′tōs), *adj.* densely covered with down or matted hair.

to·mo·gram (tō′məgram), *n.* a photograph obtained by using tomography.

to·mo·graph (tō′məgraf), *n.* an apparatus for making tomograms.

to·mog·ra·phy (təmog′rəfē), *n.* the technique of making x-ray photographs of a selected plane of the body.

to·net·ics (tōnet′iks), *n. sing.* the study of linguistic tones.

ton·neau (tunō′), *n., pl.* **ton·neaus, ton·neaux** (tunō′). **1.** the rear compartment of an automobile with passenger seating. **2.** See **millier.**

to·nom·e·ter (tōnom′itər), *n.* **1.** a device for measuring tonal frequency. **2.** any of several measuring instruments, as one for measuring tension inside the eyeball, one for finding blood pressure, etc.

ton·sil·lec·to·my (tonsəlek′təmē), *n.* the surgical excision of one or both tonsils.

ton·sil·li·tis (tonsəlī′tis), *n.* inflammation of one or both tonsils.

ton·so·ri·al (tonsôr′ēəl), *adj.* relating to a barber or to shaving.

ton·sure (ton′shər), *n.* the shaven part, usually the crown, of the head of a cleric.

ton·tine (ton′tēn), *n.* a form of annuity in which the amount left to each subscriber increases as other subscribers die.

to·nus (tō′nəs), *n.* a normal condition of moderate tension in muscle tissue.

tope (tōp), *v.* to drink any alcoholic beverages habitually in excessive quantities. —**top′er,** *n.*

to·pec·to·my (təpek′təmē), *n.* the surgical removal of a section of the cerebral cortex in order to relieve pain, etc.

to·phus (tō′fəs), *n., pl.* **to·phi** (tō′fī). a calcareous deposit in soft tissue around joints or on bone, esp. as a result of gout.

to·pi·ar·y (tō′pēer′ē), *n.* the art of clipping shrubs into ornamental shapes.

top·i·cal (top′ikəl), *adj.* **1.** relating to things of current or local interest. **2.** (in medicine) relating to a particular part of the body.

to·pog·ra·phy (təpog′rəfē), *n.* the detailed description or representation of the features of a particular region or district, esp. on a map or chart. —**to·pog′ra·pher,** *n.*

to·pol·o·gy (təpol′əjē), *n.* the branch of geometry that deals with those properties of forms which remain unchanged under conditions of deformation or transformation.

top·o·nym (top′ənim), *n.* a name which is derived from the name of a place.

to·pon·y·my (təpon′əmē), *n.* **1.** the etymological study of place names. **2.** the classification of the names of the various parts of the body.

toque (tōk), *n.* a woman's close-fitting hat without a brim.

tor (tôr), *n.* a rocky hill; a mass of rock reaching to a peak.

tor·chère (tôrsHer′), *n.* a holder or stand for a candelabrum.

tor·e·a·dor (tôr′ēədôr), *n.* a bullfighter, usually mounted.

to·re·ro (tərer′ō), *n.* a bullfighter, esp. a matador.

to·reu·tics (tərōō′tiks), *n. sing.* the technique of embossing or chasing metal or the like. —**to·reu′tic,** *adj.*

tor·ic (tôr′ik), *adj.* relating to a lens having a surface forming part of a torus.

to·roid (tôr′oid), *n.* a surface generated by a plane closed curve rotated about an axis lying in its plane. —**to·roi′dal,** *adj.*

tor·pid (tôr′pid), *adj.* sluggish; lethargic; dull; dormant.

tor·por (tôr′pər), *n.* a state of mental and physical inactivity; inertia; dormancy.

tor·por·if·ic (tôrpərif′ik), *adj.* producing torpor.

tor·quate (tôr′kwit), *adj.* having markings, distinctive feathers, etc., in a band around the neck.

torque (tôrk), *n.* a force or movement which causes rotation.

tor·ques (tôr′kwēz), *n. sing.* a marking or formation encircling the neck.

tor·re·fy (tôr′əfī), *v.* to parch or scorch; to dry with heat.

tor·sade (tôrsād′), *n.* a twisted cord, esp. as used for ornamentation.

tor·si·bil·i·ty (tôrsəbil′itē), *n.* the capability of being twisted.

tor·sion (tôr′sнən), *n.* the act of twisting.

tort (tôrt), *n.* a legal wrong in breaching a duty or infringing a right and for which the remedy lies in a civil action, as negligence, defamation. —**tor′tious,** *adj.*

torte (tôrt), *n.* a rich cake made of eggs, cakecrumbs, sugar, and ground nuts.

tor·ti·col·lis (tôrtəkol′is), *n.* a condition in which the neck is twisted and the head carried in an abnormal position. Also **wryneck.**

tor·tile (tôr′til), *adj.* twisted.

tor·til·la (tôrtē′ə), *n.* a Mexican thin, flat cake of corn meal baked on a hot iron or earthenware plate.

tor·til·lon (tôr′tēon′), *n.* a lump of paper twisted to a point.

tor·tu·ous (tôr′cнooəs), *adj.* full of twists; winding; indirect; deceitful. —**tor·tu·os′i·ty,** *n.*

to·rus (tôr′əs), *n.* **1.** (in architecture) a large convex molding, commonly found at the base of a column. **2.** Also **anchor ring.** a doughnut-shaped surface described by the revolution of a conic section, esp. a circle, about an axis in its plane. —**to·roi′dal,** *adj.*

toss·pot (tôs′pot), *n.* a drunkard.

to·tal·i·tar·i·an·ism (tōtal′iter′ēən-izm), *n.* a system of government in which the state exerts absolute control over its citizens and does not tolerate differing opinions.

totem pole, a pole or post set up in front of a North American Indian dwelling, bearing carved or painted representations of the objects or creatures adopted as the emblems of the family or group.

to·ti·pal·mate (tōtəpal′mit), *adj.* having all toes fully webbed, as certain birds.

tour·bil·lion (toorbil′yən), *n.* a whirlwind or something resembling one, as a firework giving out spirally rising sparks.

tour de force (toordəfôrs′), *pl.* **tours de force.** an outstanding achievement that is unlikely to be equaled or repeated.

tour·ne·dos (toor′nidō), *n., sing.* and *pl.* thickly sliced fillet of beef served with any of several sauces.

tower of silence, a raised stone platform on which Parsees leave their dead to be eaten by vultures. Also **dakhma.**

tox·e·mi·a, tox·ae·mi·a (toksē′mēə), *n.* a diseased condition caused by the presence in the bloodstream of a poison of animal or vegetable origin. —**tox·e′mic, tox·ae′mic,** *adj.*

tox·i·co·gen·ic (tok′səkōjen′ik), *adj.* producing poisonous substances.

tox·i·col·o·gy (toksəkol′əjē), *n.* the scientific study of poisons, their effects, and problems connected with them.

tox·i·co·sis (toksəkō′sis), *n.* an abnormal bodily condition resulting from the action of a poison.

tox·in·an·ti·tox·in (tok′sinan′titok′-sin), *n.* a mixture of toxin and antitoxin formerly used to provide immunity against certain diseases.

tox·i·pho·bia (toksəfō′bēə), *n.* an abnormally excessive fear of being poisoned.

tox·oid (tok′soid), *n.* a toxin which has been treated to make it nontoxic, used to induce immunity against a specific disease by causing the formation of antibodies.

tra·be·at·ed (trā′bēā′tid), *adj.* designed or constructed with beams.

tra·bec·u·la (trəbek′yələ), *n.* a part of

a botanical or other structure resembling a bar, rod, or small beam.

trac·er·y (trā′sərē), *n.* ornamentation consisting of a decorative interlacing of lines, bars, ribs, etc., esp. in architecture.

tra·che·a (trā′kēə), *n.*, *pl.* **tra·che·ae** (trā′kēē). the windpipe in man and other vertebrates, carrying air to and from the lungs.

tra·che·ot·o·my (trā′kēot′əmē), *n.* the surgical operation of making an incision in the trachea.

tra·cho·ma (trəkō′mə), *n.* a form of contagious conjunctivitis marked by granulations.

trac·tate (trak′tāt), *n.* a tract; treatise.

trac·tile (trak′til), *adj.* capable of being drawn out lengthwise. See also **ductile, malleable.**

trac·tive (trak′tiv), *adj.* serving to pull; exerting traction.

trade-last (trād′last′), *n.* a complimentary remark about a person repeated to him by a person who heard it in return for the repeating of a similar compliment paid to that person.

trade wind, the wind that blows almost constantly from the high-pressure areas of the subtropics to the low-pressure equatorial areas and, being deflected westward by the earth's rotation, comes from a north-easterly direction in the northern hemisphere and a south-easterly direction in the southern hemisphere. Also **trade winds, trades.**

trad·i·tor (trad′itər), *n.*, *pl.* **trad·i·to·res** (traditôr′ēz). an early Christian who betrayed his co-religionists under Roman persecution.

tra·duce (trədoos′), *v.* to slander, malign, or blacken the reputation of.

tra·du·cian·ism (trədoo′sHənizm), *n.* the doctrine that the soul as well as the body is born of one's parents. See also **creationism.**

trag·a·canth (trag′əkanth), *n.* a kind of gum obtained from certain Asian plants and used to bind powders into pills, stiffen fabrics, etc. Also **gum tragacanth.**

trag·i·com·e·dy (trajikom′idē), *n.* a play, novel, etc., containing both tragic and comic elements.

tra·gus (trā′gəs), *n.*, *pl.* **tra·gi** (trā′jī). a prominence in front of the external opening of the ear.

train oil, a thick oil obtained from marine animals, as whales, seals, etc.

tra·jec·to·ry (trəjek′tərē), *n.* the path of a missile, as a shell, rocket, arrow, etc., through the air.

tram·mel (tram′əl), *n.* **1.** (usually *pl.*) something that impedes action or progress; a restraint or check. **2.** an instrument for describing ellipses.

tra·mon·tane (trəmon′tān), *adj.* located or being beyond the mountains. Also **transmontane.**

tran·quil·ize, tran·quil·lize (traNG′kwəlīz), *v.* to calm or soothe; to become calm.

tran·quil·iz·er (traNG′kwəlīzər), *n.* a drug which calms; a sedative.

trans·ca·lent (transkā′lənt), *adj.* allowing the passage of heat.

trans·ceiv·er (transē′vər), *n.* a radio set which combines a transmitter and a receiver.

tran·scend·ent (transen′dənt), *adj.* surpassing the normal limits; lying outside ordinary experience. —**tran·scend′ence,** *n.*

tran·scen·den·tal (tran′senden′tl), *adj.* **1.** transcendent. **2.** abstract; abstruse. **3.** idealistic; exaggerated.

trans·duc·er (transdoo′sər), *n.* a device that transfers energy from one system to another, often in a different form.

tran·sect (transekt′), *v.* to cut across.

trans·el·e·ment (transel′əmənt), *v.* to transmute; change the nature of. Also **trans·el′e·ment·ate.**

trans·em·pir·i·cal (trans′empir′ikəl), *adj.* outside the limits of what can be learned by experience.

trans·fig·ure (transfig′yər), *v.* to change the form or appearance of; transform.

trans·form·er (transfôr′mər), *n.* an apparatus which transforms electrical energy from one set of one or more circuits to another set of one or more circuits at the same frequency but usually at a different voltage. See also **converter**.

trans·hu·mance (transhyōo′məns), *n*. the seasonal movement of livestock and those who tend them.

tran·sil·i·ent (transil′ēənt), *adj*. moving rapidly from one state to another.

trans·il·lu·mi·nate (transilōo′mənāt), *v*. to make light pass through.

tran·sis·tor (tranzis′tər), *n*. a very small electronic device which utilizes a semiconductor in order to control current flow between two terminals and is much used in electronic circuits in place of electronic tubes.

tran·si·to·ry (tran′sitôr′ē), *adj*. not lasting; short-lived; temporary.

trans·lit·er·ate (translit′ərāt), *v*. to represent the (letters, words, etc.) of one language in the alphabet of another.

trans·lu·cent (translōo′sənt), *adj*. permitting the partial passage of light. Also **trans·lu′cid**.

trans·mi·grate (transmī′grāt), *v*. **1**. to go from one place to another, esp. to another country in order to settle there. **2**. (of the soul) to be reborn in another body after death. —**trans·mi·gra′tion**, *n*.

trans·mog·ri·fy (transmog′rəfī), *v*. to change appearance, esp. with a weird or grotesque effect.

trans·mon·tane (transmon′tān), *adj*. See **tramontane**.

trans·mun·dane (trans′mundān′), *adj*. beyond the visible world.

tran·spic·u·ous (transpik′yōoəs), *adj*. transparent.

tran·spon·der (transpon′dər), *n*. a radio or radar set which automatically emits information on receipt of a certain signal.

trans·po·ni·ble (transpō′nəbəl), *adj*. able to be transposed.

tran·sub·stan·ti·ate (tran′səbstan′-sHēāt), *v*. **1**. to change into another substance. **2**. to change (bread and wine) in essence, but not in appearance into the body and blood of Christ.

trans·u·ran·ic (trans′yōoran′ik), *adj*.

having an atomic number greater than that of uranium.

trans·vec·tion (transvek′sHən), *n*. the conveyance of a witch by supernatural agency through the air.

tra·pe·zi·um (trəpē′zēəm), *n*., *pl*. **tra·pe·ziums**, **tra·pe·zia**. **1**. a quadrilateral figure in which no two sides are parallel. **2**. (in Euclidian geometry) a trapezoid.

trap·e·zoid (trap′izoid), *n*. a quadrilateral figure with only two parallel sides.

tra·pun·to (trəpōon′tō), *n*., *pl*. **tra·pun·tos**. a type of quilting bearing a raised design made by outlining the design in running stitch and padding it underneath.

trau·ma (trou′mə), *n*., *pl*. **trau·ma·ta** (trou′mətə), **trau·mas**. **1**. an injury; a condition caused by injury. **2**. a severe and lasting emotional shock caused by an unpleasant or alarming experience. —**trau·mat′ic**, *adj*.

tra·vail (trəvāl′), *n*. work of a difficult or irksome nature; anguish; suffering.

trav·erse (trav′ərs), *v*. to travel or pass along or through.

trav·er·tine, **trav·er·tin** (trav′ərtin), *n*. a light-colored limestone deposited around mineral springs, esp. hot springs, and used as a building material.

trav·es·ty (trav′istē), *n*. **1**. a ludicrous or ridiculous distortion; caricature or parody. —*v*. **2**. to make ridiculous by grotesque distortion.

tre·cen·to (trācHen′tō), *n*. the 14th century in Italian art, literature, etc.

tre·en·ware (trē′ənwer), *n*. kitchen utensils, household vessels, etc., made of wood.

tre·foil (trē′foil), *n*. an ornamental motif or structure resembling a clover leaf.

treil·lage (trā′lij), *n*. a trellis; latticework.

trem·u·lant (trem′yələnt), *adj*. trembling; shaking.

trem·u·lous (trem′yələs), *adj*. affected with trembling as a result of nervousness, fear, etc.

trench·ant (tren′CHənt), *adj.* **1.** incisive; sharp; cutting. **2.** energetic; vigorously effective.

tre·pan (tripan′), *n.* a tool for gouging out cores so as to form small holes.

tre·phine (trifīn′), *n.* a circular saw with a guiding center pin, used in surgery for cutting out circular sections of bone.

trep·i·da·tion (trepidā′sHən), *n.* a state of fear or alarm; anxiety.

trep·o·ne·mi·a·sis (trep′ənəmī′əsis), *n.* syphilis or a related disease.

tret (tret), *n.* an allowance of extra weight formerly given to a purchaser to make up for deterioration or waste of goods during transportation.

tri·ad (trī′ad), *n.* a group of three closely associated persons or things.

tri·ar·chy (trī′ärkē), *n.* government or rule by three persons; a triumvirate.

Tri·as·sic (trīas′ik), *adj.* relating to the earliest period of the Mesozoic era, from about 220 million to 180 million years ago, distinguished by volcanic activity and the appearance of marine and amphibious reptiles.

trib·ade (trib′əd), *n.* a female homosexual.

trib·a·dism (trib′adizm), *n.* homosexuality in females.

trib·u·la·tion (tribyəlā′sHən), *n.* suffering; distress; affliction.

tri·bu·nal (trībyo͞on′l), *n.* a court of justice; a judicial assembly.

trib·une (trib′yo͞on), *n.* one who represents the ordinary people and defends their rights.

trice (trīs), *n.* a very short space of time; an instant; a moment.

trich·oid (trik′oid), *adj.* resembling hair.

tri·chol·o·gy (trikol′əjē), *n.* the study of hair and its diseases.

tri·chot·o·my (trikot′əmē), *n.* a division into three.

tri·chro·ma·tism (trīkrō′mətizm), *n.* the condition of normal vision in which all the basic colors are perceived. Also **tri·chro·ma·top′si·a.** See also **monochromatism, dichromatism.**

tri·corn, tri·corne (trī′kôrn), *n.* a hat having the brim turned up to form three sides.

tri·dent (trīd′nt), *n.* a three-pronged spear.

tri·fid (trī′fid), *adj.* divided into three.

tri·fur·cate (trīfûr′kāt), *v.* to branch or fork into three parts.

trig·o·nal (trig′ənl), *adj.* relating to or shaped like a triangle.

trig·o·nous (trig′ənəs), *adj.* having three angles; triangular.

tri·he·dral (trīhē′drəl), *adj.* having three surfaces meeting in a point.

tri·he·dron (trīhē′drən), *n.* the figure formed by three surfaces meeting in a point.

tri·lem·ma (trīlem′ə), *n.* a situation in which there are three unpleasant alternatives. See also **dilemma.**

tri·ma·ran (trī′məran), *n.* a sailing vessel with three separate hulls.

trine (trīn), *adj.* triple; threefold.

trin·gle (trinG′gəl), *n.* a relatively narrow, straight, square-sectioned architectural molding.

tri·ni·tro·tol·u·ene (trīnī′trōtol′yo͞oēn), *n.* See **TNT.** Also **tri·ni·tro·tol′u·ol.**

tripe (trīp), *n.* the first or second stomach of a ruminant mammal, used as food.

tri·phib·i·an (trīfib′ēən), *adj.* adept at or equipped for operations, warfare, etc., on land, sea, and in the air. Also **tri·phib′i·ous.**

triph·thong (trif′thônG), *n.* a combination of three differing vowel qualities to form one sound.

trip·tych (trip′tik), *n.* a picture, carving, etc., on three panels side by side, esp. one in which the side panels fold over the central one. See also **diptych, pentaptych, polyptych.**

tri·que·tra (trīkwē′trə), *n.* a geometrical figure contained within three points, esp. one composed of three intersecting arcs, lobes, or ellipses. —**tri·que′trous,** *adj.*

tri·reme (trī′rēm), *n.* a war galley with three rows of oars on each side.

tri·sect (trīsekt′), *v.* to divide into three, esp. three equal, parts.

trumeau

tris·kel·i·on (triskel′ēon), *n.*, *pl.* **tris·kel·i·a.** a figure composed of three branches, arms, or legs radiating from a center. Also **tris′kele.**

tris·mus (triz′məs), *n.* an involuntary contraction of the jaw muscles.

tris·oc·ta·he·dron (trisok ′təhē′-drən), *n.*, *pl.* **tris·oc·ta·he·drons, tris·oc·ta·he·dra.** a solid having 24 equal faces, a group of three corresponding to each face of an octahedron.

triste (trēst), *n. French.* mournful; sad.

tris·tesse (trēstes′), *n. French.* sadness; melancholy.

trit·an·ope (trīt′ənōp), *n.* one who suffers from tritanopia.

trit·an·o·pi·a (trītənō′pēə), *n.* a defect in perception of color in which the eye fails to distinguish properly blue and yellow.

trit·u·rate (triCH′ərāt), *v.* to grind to a fine powder; to pulverize. —**trit·u·ra′tion,** *n.*

tri·um·vi·rate (trīum′vərit), *n.* government by three men sharing power jointly. See also **quadrumvirate.**

tri·une (trī′yōōn), *adj.* **1.** three in one constituting a unity. —*n.* **2. Triune,** the Trinity.

triv·et (triv′it), *n.* a stand with short legs placed under a hot dish to protect a table surface.

triv·i·um (triv′ēəm), *n.*, *pl.* **triv·ia.** the lower division of the seven liberal arts studied in medieval schools, consisting of grammar, rhetoric, and logic. See also **quadrivium.**

tro·che (trō′kē), *n.* a medicinal tablet, usually circular in shape.

trof·fer (trof′ər), *n.* a trough, usually fixed on a wall, for holding and reflecting upward the light of fluorescent lamps.

trog·lo·dyte (trog′lədīt), *n.* a cave dweller; a recluse; one who shuns the society of others.

troi·ka (troi′kə), *n.* a Russian carriage drawn by three horses harnessed abreast.

trol·lop (trol′əp), *n.* a slovenly or loose-living woman.

trom·mel (trom′əl), *n.* a screen used for sifting ores, coal, gravel, etc., according to size.

trompe l'oeil (trômp′ lā′), the attempt to deceive the eye into taking a painting of an object for real by means of perspective, foreshortening, and fine detail; a painting intended to create such an illusion.

trope (trōp), *n.* the use of a word or phrase in a figurative sense; a figure of speech.

tro·pism (trō′pizm), *n.* the response of an organism to an external stimulus by growing toward or away from it. See also **taxis.**

tro·pol·o·gy (trōpol′əjē), *n.* the use of figurative language in speech or writing.

trop·o·pause (trop′əpôz), *n.* the upper boundary layer of the troposphere, separating it from the stratosphere.

tro·poph·i·lous (trōpof′ələs), *adj.* adapted to a climate which has alternating periods favoring growth and dormancy.

trop·o·phyte (trop′əfīt), *n.* a tropophilous plant.

trop·o·sphere (trop′əsfēr), *n.* that part of the atmosphere in which temperature decreases with height, lying below the stratosphere, separated from it by the tropopause, and extending about 6 to 12 miles above the surface of the earth.

Trot·sky·ism (trot′skēizm), *n.* the theories advocated by the Russian revolutionary and writer Leon Trotsky (1879–1940), including the concept of immediate worldwide revolution. —**Trot′sky·ite,** *n.*

trou·blous (trub′ləs), *adj.* disturbed; full of troubles; agitated.

truck·le (truk′əl), *v.* to submit abjectly or tamely; to be servile.

truc·u·lent (truk′yələnt), *adj.* **1.** cruel; brutal; harsh. **2.** defiant or hostile.

truf·fle (truf′əl), *n.* a kind of edible subterranean fungus.

tru·meau (trōōmō′), *n.*, *pl.* **tru·meaux.** a carved or painted panel set together with a mirror, above or below it, in a frame.

trun·cate (truNG′kāt), *v.* to cut the top off; to shorten by cutting. —**trun·ca′tion**, *n.*

trun·cheon (trun′CHən), *n.* a short thick stick or club carried by a policeman.

trun·nion (trun′yən), *n.* one of a pair of bar-like projections on the sides of a cannon, supporting it on its carriage and enabling it to swivel.

trus·sell, trus·sel (trus′əl), *n.* the upper die used in making coins by hand. See also **pile.**

truth serum, any drug, as scopolamine and some barbiturates, used in psychiatric treatment and criminal investigation to diminish a person's conscious or unconscious resistance to recalling experiences. Also **truth drug.** See also **narcoanalysis.**

tryp·a·no·some (trip′ənəsōm), *n.* any of a genus of parasitic flagellate protozoans causing various kinds of disease in man and animals and usually transmitted by insects.

tryp·a·no·so·mi·a·sis (trip′ənōsō-mī′əsis), *n.* any disease caused by trypanosomes.

tryp·sin (trip′sin), *n.* an enzyme produced by the pancreas and able to convert proteins into peptone.

tryst (trist), *n.* an agreement to meet at a certain time and place, esp. one made secretly between lovers.

tsar·e·vitch (zär′əviCH), *n.* See **czare-vitch.**

tsa·rev·na (zärev′nə), *n.* See **czarev-na.**

tsa·ri·na (zärē′nə), *n.* See **czarina.**

tsu·na·mi (tsōōnä′mē), *n.* a very large sea wave caused by a submarine earth movement or volcanic shock.

tu·ber·cle (tōō′bərkəl), *n.* a small swelling, excrescence, or growth on the body or in an organ of an animal, on a plant, etc.

tubercle bacillus, the bacterium, *Mycobacterium tuberculosis,* which causes tuberculosis.

tu·ber·cu·lin (tōōbur′kyəlin), *n.* a sterile liquid prepared from the tubercle bacillus and used in diagnosing and treating tuberculosis.

tu·ber·os·i·ty (tōōbəros′itē), *n.* a large prominence or protuberance on a bone, usually serving to attach ligaments or muscle.

tu·fa (tōō′fə), *n.* a porous limestone deposited round mineral springs. Also **calcareous tufa, calc-tufa.**

tuff (tuf), *n.* rock composed of fine volcanic ash. Also **volcanic tuff.**

tuft·hun·ter (tuft′huntər), *n.* one who seeks to ingratiate himself with important people; a sycophant or toady.

tu·la·re·mi·a, tu·la·rae·mi·a (tōōlə-rē′mēə), *n.* a bacterial disease of rabbits and other rodents, capable of being transmitted to man in the form of a fever of several weeks' duration. Also **deer fly fever, rabbit fever.**

tulle (tōōl), *n.* a fine net fabric of silk or nylon used for dresses, veils, etc.

tum·brel (tum′brəl), *n.* a cart in which condemned persons were carried to the guillotine during the French Revolution.

tu·me·fa·cient (tōōməfā′sHənt), *adj.* swelling; causing to swell.

tu·me·fac·tion (tōōməfak′sHən), *n.* the action or process of making or becoming tumid.

tu·me·fy (tōō′məfī), *v.* to cause to swell; to become swollen.

tu·mes·cent (tōōmes′ənt), *adj.* becoming tumid; somewhat swollen.

tu·mid (tōō′mid), *adj.* swollen; bloated; enlarged.

tum·mel·er, tum·mul·er (tōōm′əl-ər), *n.* a person employed as entertainer and entertainment organizer by certain resorts.

tu·mul·tu·ar·y (tōōmul′CHōōer′ē), *adj.* turbulent; lawless; disorderly.

tu·mu·lus (tōō′myələs), *n., pl.* **tu·mu·lus·es, tu·mu·li.** **1.** an artificial mound or hillock, esp. over a grave. **2.** a rounded mound in congealed lava. —**tu′mu·lar, tu′mu·lous,** *adj.*

tun (tun), *n.* **1.** a large cask for holding wine, beer, etc. **2.** a unit of liquid capacity, esp. one equal to 252 wine gallons.

tur·ba·ry (tur′bərē), *n.* a piece of ground from which turf or peat may be taken.

353 typology

tur·bid (tur'bid), *adj.* opaque; muddy; clouded; dense; confused.

tur·bi·nate (tur'bənit), *adj.* shaped like a scroll; spiraled. Also **tur'bi·nat·ed.**

tur·bo·fan (tur'bōfan), *n.* a turbojet engine having a turbine-driven fan which supplies air for combustion, cooling, etc.

tur·bo·jet (tur'bōjet), *n.* **1.** an airplane equipped with turbojet engines. **2.** a turbojet engine.

turbojet engine, a jet-propulsion engine using a turbine-driven compressor to compress air from the atmosphere for fuel combustion. Also **turbojet.**

tur·bo·prop (tur'bōprop), *n.* **1.** an airplane using turbo-propeller engines. **2.** a turbo-propeller engine.

turbo-propeller engine, a jet engine fitted with a turbine-driven propeller, whose thrust is additional to that obtained by the thrust of the jet exhaust. Also **turboprop, turboprop engine, propjet engine.**

tur·di·form (tur'dəfôrm), *adj.* resembling a thrush in appearance.

tur·gent (tur'jənt), *adj.* turgid.

tur·ges·cent (turjes'ənt), *adj.* becoming swollen or turgid.

tur·gid (tur'jid), *adj.* bloated; swollen; pompous.

tur·gor (tur'gər), *n.* the state of being turgid.

turn·er·y (tur'nərē), *n.* **1.** the shaping of articles on a lathe. **2.** articles so made. **3.** a place where such articles are made.

tur·pi·tude (tur'pitōōd), *n.* wickedness of character; a wicked or depraved act.

tur·ri·cal (tur'ikəl), *adj.* relating to or resembling a turret.

tur·ric·u·late (tərik'yəlit), *adj.* resembling or having a turret or turrets.

turt·let (turt'lit), *n.* a young turtle.

tusche (tŌŌSH), *n.* a greasy substance used in lithography for its receptivity to lithographic ink and in etching and silk-screen printing as a resist.

tus·sah (tus'ə), *n.* a coarse brownish silk from India. Also **tus'sore.** Also

wild silk. See also **pongee, shantung.**

tus·sis (tus'is), *n.* a cough. —**tus'sal,** *adj.*

tu·te·lar·y (tōōt'əler'ē), *adj.* serving as a guardian or protector of a person or place.

tu·toy·er (tōō'twäyā'), *v.* to address or treat (a person) with familiarity, esp. where no familiarity exists.

tu·tu (tōō'tōō), *n., pl.* **tu·tus.** a short skirt of layers of stiffened tulle, worn by female ballet dancers.

tweet·er (twē'tər), *n.* a small loudspeaker which reproduces only high-frequency sounds. See also **woofer.**

tweet·er-woof·er (twē'tərwŏŏf'ər), *n.* a loudspeaker in which the tweeter is placed in front of the cone of the woofer.

tweeze, tweese (twēz), *n.* (formerly) a case holding surgical or similar instruments.

twi·bill (twī'bil), *n.* a mattock with one end of the head like an adz-head and the other like an ax-head.

twit (twit), *v.* to tease or taunt; make fun of.

Ty·burn tree (tī'bərn trē'), the gallows. [after the site of the gallows near Marcle Arch, London]

ty·chism (tī'kizm), *n.* the philosophical theory that chance plays an active part in the universe.

ty·cho·po·tam·ic (tī'kōpətam'ik), *adj.* living or growing mainly in fresh and usually still rather than flowing water.

tym·bal (tim'bəl), *n.* See **timbal.**

tym·pa·ni (tim'pənē), *n. pl.* See **timpani.**

tym·pa·nist (tim'pənist), *n.* one who plays the timpani or other percussion instruments in an orchestra.

typh·lol·o·gy (tiflol'əjē), *n.* the body of scientific knowledge about blindness.

typh·lo·sis (tiflō'sis), *n.* blindness.

ty·pog·ra·phy (tīpog'rəfē), *n.* the art of printing with type; the work of designing and setting type and printing.

ty·pol·o·gy (tīpol'əjē), *n.* the theory or study of types or symbols; the systematic classification of objects according to type.

ty·poth·e·tae (tīpo*th*′itē), *n. pl.* an association of master printers.

ty·ro, ti·ro (tī′rō), *n.* a beginner.

ty·ro·thri·cin (tī′rō*th*rī′sin), *n.* a powdered antibiotic obtained from any of several soil bacilli and used for external treatment of localized bacterial infections.

u·bi·e·ty (yo͞obī'itē), *n.* the state of being in a definite place.

u·biq·ui·tous (yo͞obik'witəs), *adj.* omnipresent; being everywhere at once. —**u·biq'ui·tous·ly,** *adv.*

u·biq·ui·ty (yo͞obik'witē), *n.* **1.** the state of being everywhere or in many places, esp. at the same time. **2.** (in theology) the omnipresence of God.

u·dom·e·ter (yo͞odom'itər), *n.* an instrument for measuring rainfall; a rain gauge.

UHF, uhf. See **ultrahigh frequency.**

u·kase (yo͞o'kās), *n.* a proclamation or edict given by an absolute authority. See also **fiat.** [from Russian]

u·lig·i·nous (yo͞olij'ənəs), *adj.* growing in mud or swamps. Also **u·lig'i·nose.**

ul·lage (ul'ij), *n.* the amount by which contents, usually liquids, fall short of filling their container.

u·lot·ri·chous (yo͞olo'trəkəs), *adj.* belonging to a woolly-haired group of mankind.

u·lot·ri·chy (yo͞olo'trəkē), *n.* the condition of having woolly or very curly hair.

ul·ti·ma (ul'təmə), *n.* the last syllable in a word. See also **penultima.**

ul·ti·mo·gen·i·ture (ul'təmōjen'-iCHər), *n.* See **postremogeniture.**

ul·tra·high frequency (ul'trəhī), any radio frequency between 300 and 3000 megahertz. *Abbrev.:* **uhf, UHF.**

ul·tra·ism (ul'trəizm), *n.* extremism; any manifestation of extremism.

ul·tra·ma·rine (ul'trəmərēn'), *adj.* **1.** beyond the sea. **2.** deep blue.

ul·tra·mon·tane (ul'trəmontān'), *adj.* situated beyond the mountains.

ul·tra·mon·ta·nism (ultrəmon'tə-nizm), *n.* the policy of one group within the Roman Catholic Church that favors increased authority for the pope. See also **Gallicanism.**

ul·tra·mun·dane (ultrəmun'dān), *adj.* **1.** beyond the earth or the solar system. **2.** beyond the limits of physical existence; otherworldly.

ul·tra·son·ic (ultrəson'ik), *adj.* of or denoting a sound frequency too high to be perceived by the human ear.

ul·tra·son·ics (ultrəson'iks), *n. sing.* the scientific study of ultrasonic phenomena.

ultra vi·res (vī'rēz), exceeding the powers granted by law, esp. to a corporation or one of its officers.

ul·tra·vi·rus (ultrəvī'rəs), *n., pl.* **ul·tra·vi·rus·es.** a virus so small that it can pass through the finest bacterial filters and can be seen only under a microscope specially adapted for viewing the minutest objects.

ul·u·late (yo͞ol'yəlāt), *v.* **1.** to howl like a dog or hoot like an owl. **2.** to lament; wail, esp. shrilly. —**ul'u·lant,** *adj.*

um·bo (um'bō), *n., pl.* **um·bos, um·bo·nes** (umbō'nēz). a boss on a shield,

often at the center. —**um′bo·nal,
um′bo·nate,** *adj.*

um·bra (um′brə), *n.*, *pl.* **um·brae**
(um′brē). shadow; shade. See also
penumbra.

um·brage (um′brij), *n.* a sense of
slight or injury; the giving or taking
of offense. —**um·bra′geous,** *adj.*

um·brif·er·ous (umbrif′ərəs), *adj.*
giving or throwing shade.

uncertainty principle, a concept of
wave mechanics, formulated in 1927
by Heisenberg, that the precise position and the precise momentum of a
particle in a given instant cannot both
be known, and the more accurately
the one is known the less accurately
is the other known.

un·ci·al (un′sHēəl), *adj.* pertaining to
or written in a type of majuscule writing used in Latin and Greek manuscript between the 3rd and 9th centuries A.D. having more curves than
monumental capitals and some as-
cending and descending strokes.

un·ci·form (un′səfôrm), *adj.* **1.**
shaped like a hook. —*n.* **2.** See **ha-
mate.**

un·ci·nate (un′sənit), *adj.* shaped like
or furnished with a hook or hooks.

unc·tion (uNGk′sHən), *n.* the act of
anointing, for medical or ritual purposes.

unc·tu·ous (uNGk′cHōōəs), *adj.* **1.** of
the nature of ointment; greasy. **2.** with
an excessively moralizing, smooth,
or complacent manner.

un·de·cil·lion (un′disil′yən), *n.* a
number represented by the figure one
followed by 36 zeros (but in the
United Kingdom and Germany by
the figure one followed by 66 zeros).

un·der·croft (un′dərkrôft), *n.* an
underground room or vault.

un·der·fur (un′dərfur), *n.* the fine fur
under the coarser outer fur in certain
animals, as seals.

un·der·glaze (un′dərglāz), *n.* a layer
of color applied to ceramic ware before it is glazed.

un·der·set (un′dərset), *n.* an under-
current in water, flowing in the opposite direction to the surface current.

un·du·late (un′jəlāt), *v.* **1.** to move or
cause to move with a wavelike or
winding motion. **2.** to give a wavelike
form to. **3.** to have a wavy shape or
surface. —*adj.* **4.** wavy; winding.
—**un′du·lat·ed, un′du·lant, un′du·
la·tor·y,** *adj.* —**un·du·la′tion,** *n.*

un·ex·cep·tion·a·ble (un′iksep′-
sHənəbəl), *adj.* beyond criticism;
with which no fault can be found.

un·ex·cep·tion·al (un′iksep′sHənl),
adj. ordinary; not unusual.

un·gual (uNG′gwəl), *adj.* relating to,
shaped like, or furnished with a nail,
claw, or hoof.

un·guent (uNG′gwənt), *n.* a soft or
liquid ointment for wounds, etc.

un·guic·u·late (uNGgwik′yəlit), *adj.*
furnished with or resembling a nail
or claw. Also **un·guic′u·lat·ed.**

un·gui·nous (uNG′gwinəs), *adj.* consisting of or like oil or fat; greasy.

un·guis (uNG′gwis), *n.*, *pl.* **un·gues**
(uNG′gwēz). a nail, claw, or hoof.

un·gu·late (uNG′gyəlit), *adj.* hoofed.

u·ni·cam·er·al (yōō′nəkam′ərəl),
adj. having only one (legislative)
chamber.

u·ni·cos·tate (yōōnəkos′tāt), *adj.* with
one rib or ridge.

u·nip·ar·ous (yōōnip′ərəs), *adj.* producing offspring or eggs only one at
a time.

u·ni·pla·nar (yōōnəplā′nər), *adj.* restricted to one plane or two-dimensional continuum, as movement.

u·ni·tive (yōō′nitiv), *adj.* able or serving to unite; involving union.

un·sat·u·rat·ed (unsacH′ərā′tid), *adj.*
denoting oils, esp. fish and vegetable
oils, that are liquid at room temperatures, that are able to accept additional hydrogen atoms, and that do
not raise cholesterol levels. See also
**monounsaturated, polyunsatura-
ted.**

un·sa·vor·y (unsā′vərē), *adj.* **1.** lacking flavor; having an unpleasant flavor or smell. **2.** causing social or moral
distaste or offense.

un·scram·bler (unskram′blər), *n.* a
device to render scrambled telecom-
munications signals intelligible.

un·ten·a·ble (unten′əbəl), *adj.* indefensible, as an argument, etc. —**un·ten′a·bly,** *adv.*

un·touch·a·ble (untuсн′əbəl), *n.* a person below the lowest social division of Hindu society, whom a caste man may not touch for fear of being defiled.

u·pas (yōō′pəs), *n.* the poisonous sap of a Javanese tree, used on poison arrows.

up·per (up′ər), *n.* all that part of a boot or shoe which is above the sole.

up·stage (up′stāj′), *adv.* **1.** at or toward the back of the stage. —*v.* **2.** to force another actor to turn his back to the audience and so overshadow his performance.

u·rae·us (yōōrē′əs), *n.*, *pl.* **u·rae·us·es.** the sacred asp or snake of ancient Egypt, used as an emblem of gods and rulers.

u·ra·nog·ra·phy (yōōrənog′rəfē), *n.* the branch of astronomy devoted to describing and mapping the heavens, esp. fixed stars. Also **uranology.**

u·ra·nol·o·gy (yōōrənol′əjē), *n.* **1.** See **uranography. 2.** a treatise on stars.

u·ra·nom·e·try (yōōrənom′itrē), *n.* **1.** a chart showing the positions and sizes of stars on the celestial sphere. **2.** the measurement of distances between stars.

ur·bi·cul·ture (ur′bəkul′снər), *n.* the way of life in cities.

ur·ce·o·late (ur′sēəlit), *adj.* pitcher-shaped.

u·re·mi·a, u·rae·mi·a (yōōrē′mēə), *n.* the presence in the blood of matter normally excreted in the urine, caused by malfunction of the kidneys. —**u·re′mic, u·rae′mic,** *adj.*

u·re·thra (yōōrē′thrə), *n.*, *pl.* **u·re·thrae** (yōōrē′thrē), **u·re·thras.** the tube which carries urine from the bladder out of the body and which in males also discharges semen.

ur·ic·ac·id·e·mi·a (yōōr′ikas′idē′-mēə), *n.* See **lithemia.**

u·rol·o·gy (yōōrol′əjē), *n.* the medical study of urine and the genitourinary tract and of diseases affecting them.

u·ro·pyg·i·al gland (yōōrəpij′ēəl),

a gland opening at the base of a bird's tail which secretes a fluid used in preening or cleaning the feathers. Also **oil gland, preen gland.**

u·ro·pyg·i·um (yōōrəpij′ēəm), *n.* the terminal part of a bird's body, to which the tail feathers are attached.

ur·si·form (ur′səfôrm), *adj.* bear-shaped.

ur·sine (ur′sīn), *adj.* bearlike; of or relating to the bear.

ur·ti·car·i·a (urtəker′ēə), *n.* a skin rash caused by an allergy, with raised pale areas on the skin and severe itching such as is caused by nettle stings; hives.

ur·ti·cate (ur′təkāt), *v.* **1.** to sting with or as if with nettles. **2.** to whip with nettles or so as to cause a stinging sensation. —**ur′ti·cant,** *adj.* —**ur·ti·ca′tion,** *n.*

us·tu·late (us′снəlit), *adj.* of scorched appearance. —**us·tu·la′tion,** *n.*

u·su·fruct (yōō′zōōfrukt), *n.* the right to use or benefit from something which belongs to another, short of destroying or harming it. —**u·su·fruc′tu·ar·y,** *n.*

u·surp (yōōsurp′), *v.* **1.** to seize power illegally or by force. **2.** to use without right. —**u·sur·pa′tion,** *n.*

u·su·ry (yōō′zнərē), *n.* **1.** an extortionate, esp. illegally high, rate of interest. **2.** the practice of lending money at such a high rate of interest. —**u′su·rer,** *n.* —**u·su′ri·ous,** *adj.*

u·til·i·tar·i·an (yōōtil′iter′ēən), *adj.* **1.** relating to usefulness; useful rather than decorative. **2.** supporting the doctrine of utilitarianism.

u·til·i·tar·i·an·ism (yōōtil′iter′-ēənizm), *n.* the doctrine that promoting the greatest happiness for the greatest number of people should be the principal concern of morality, a doctrine expounded by Jeremy Bentham and J. S. Mill.

u·ti pos·si·de·tis (yōō′tī pos′idē′-tis), the principle of international law that at the conclusion of a war each side may claim as its own territory it actually occupies.

u·tri·cle (yōō′trikəl), *n.* **1.** a small, air-filled sac, as in a seaweed. **2.** the larger of two sacs in the internal ear. —**u·tric′u·lar, u·tric′u·late,** *adj.*

u·tric·u·li·tis (yo͞otrik ′yəlī′tis), *n.* inflammation of the utricle of the inner ear.

u·vu·la (yo͞o′vyələ), *n.*, *pl.* **u·vu·las, u·vu·lae** (yo͞o′vyəlē). the conical flap of flesh that hangs down from the soft palate at the back of the mouth.

ux·o·ri·al (uksôr′ēəl), *adj.* of or befitting a wife.

ux·o·ri·cide (uksôr′isīd), *n.* **1.** the act of killing one's wife. **2.** a man who kills his wife.

ux·o·ri·lo·cal (uksôr ′əlō′kəl), *adj.* See **matrilocal.**

ux·o·ri·ous (uksôr′ēəs), *adj.* excessively fond of or submissive to one's wife.

vac·il·late (vas′əlāt), *v.* **1.** to sway unsteadily; to fluctuate. **2.** to waver between different opinions; to be indecisive. —**vac′il·lant, vac′il·la·to·ry,** *adj.* —**vac·il·la′tion,** *n.*

va·cu·i·ty (vakyōō′itē), *n.* **1.** the state of being empty. **2.** a void; a vacuum. **3.** an absence of thought; something unintelligent or senseless.

vac·u·ous (vak′yōōəs), *adj.* empty; without ideas, intelligence, or purpose.

va·de me·cum (vā′dē mē′kəm), *pl.* **va·de me·cums.** something carried about the person constantly or frequently, esp. a book for reference.

va·gar·y (vəger′ē), *n.* **1.** an erratic or unpredictable occurrence or action. **2.** a whimsical, odd, or unusual idea. —**va·gar′i·ous,** *adj.*

vag·ile (vaj′əl), *adj.* able to move; having freedom of movement.

va·gi·na (vəjī′nə), *n., pl.* **va·gi·nas, va·gi·nae** (vəjī′nē). **1.** the passage leading from the womb to the exterior of most female mammals. **2.** a part or organ resembling a sheath, as that formed by the base of some leaves around a stem.

vag·i·nis·mus (vajəniz′məs), *n.* a painful involuntary contraction of the vagina.

val·e·tu·di·nar·i·an (val′ətōōd′ə-ner′ēən), *n.* **1.** an invalid. **2.** someone obsessed with his poor health.

val·gus (val′gəs), *n., pl.* **val·gus·es.** an abnormal position of part of the human bone structure, as a bowleg or a knock-knee, etc.

val·ine (val′ēn), *n.* an amino acid, obtained by hydrolysis of plant or animal protein, used chiefly in medical nutrition and laboratory production of bacteria. Found in a meteorite in 1970.

val·late (val′āt), *adj.* surrounded or bordered by a ridge.

val·la·tion (vəlā′sHən), *n.* a rampart; the technique of building ramparts.

val·lec·u·la (vəlek′yələ), *n., pl.* **val·lec·u·lae** (vəlek′yəlē). a furrow; a hollow.

val·lec·u·late (vəlek′yəlāt), *adj.* having furrows or hollows.

val·or·ize (val′ərīz), *v.* (of a government) to fix and maintain the price of a commodity by buying it at a fixed price. —**val·or·iz·a′tion,** *n.*

va·lu·ta (vəlōō′tə), *n.* the value of any currency expressed as its exchange-rate with another currency.

Van·sit·tart·ism (vansit′ərtizm), *n.* the doctrine that Germany is an aggressive country and should be demilitarized and undergo corrective education to prevent future aggression.

vap·id (vap′id), *adj.* insipid; dull; lifeless.

va·po·ret·to (vapəret′ō), *n., pl.* **va·po·**

359

ret·tos, va·po·ret·ti (vapəret′ē). a small steamboat used as part of a passenger transport service, esp. in Venice, Italy.

var·i·cel·la (varisel′ə), *n.* chicken pox. —**var·i·cel′loid,** *adj.*

var·i·cel·late (varisel′it), *adj.* having longitudinal ridges showing the former positions of the rim of the aperture of a shell.

var·i·cel·la·tion (var′isəlā′sHən), *n.* inoculation with chicken pox virus.

var·i·ces (ver′isēz), *n. pl.* See **varix.**

var·i·e·gate (ver′ēəgāt), *v.* **1.** to vary the appearance of something, as by adding colors. **2.** to diversify; to make varied. —**var·i·e·ga′tion,** *n.*

va·ri·o·la (vərī′ələ), *n.* smallpox. —**var′i·o·late,** *adj.*

var·i·ole (ver′ēōl), *n.* **1.** a small depression resembling the marks left on the skin by smallpox. **2.** any of the light-colored small spheres that resemble pock-marks found in several igneous rocks known as variolite.

var·i·o·rum (ver′ēôr′əm), *adj.* containing various versions of a text; containing many notes made by various critics or scholars.

var·is·tor (varis′tər), *n.* an electrical resistor, the resistance of which varies automatically in proportion to the voltage passing through it.

var·ix (ver′iks), *n., pl.* **var·i·ces** (ver′-isēz). **1.** a permanent abnormal dilatation and lengthening of a vein or artery, usually accompanied by the development of many twists. Also **var·i·cos′i·ty. 2.** a longitudinal ridge on a shell marking the former position of the rim.

var·let (vär′lit), *n.* a rascal; a scoundrel.

vas·o·con·stric·tion (vas′ōkən-strik′sHən), *n.* constriction of the blood vessels. —**vas·o·con·stric′tive,** *adj.*

vas·o·con·stric·tor (vas′ōkənstrik′-tər), *adj.* **1.** causing constriction of blood vessels. —*n.* **2.** a drug or nerve that causes constriction of blood vessels.

vas·o·di·la·tor (vas′ōdīlā′tər), *adj.* **1.**

causing blood vessels to relax or dilate. Also **vas·o·de·pres′sor.** —*n.* **2.** a nerve or drug causing dilatation of the blood vessels.

vas·o·in·hib·i·tor (vas′ōinhib′itər), *n.* anything that inhibits the performance of the vasomotor nerves, as a drug.

vas·o·mo·tion (vas′ōmō′sHən), *n.* a change in diameter of a blood vessel.

vas·o·mo·tor (vas′ōmō′tər), *adj.* controlling the diameter of blood vessels so as to regulate the flow of blood.

va·so·pres·sor (vas′ōpres′ər), *n.* a chemical, as adrenalin, that causes the muscular walls of arteries to contract, thus narrowing the arteries and increasing the blood pressure.

vas·o·stim·u·lant (vas′ōstim′yə-lənt), *adj.* stimulating the vasomotor nerves.

vas·o·ton·ic (vas′ōton′ik), *adj.* relating to or controlling the muscular tone of the blood vessels.

vas·sal (vas′əl), *n.* a subject; retainer; subordinate. —**vas′sal·age,** *n.*

vat·ic (vat′ik), *adj.* of, relating to, or of the nature of a prophet. Also **vat′i·cal.**

vat·i·cide (vat′isīd), *n.* **1.** someone who murders a prophet. **2.** the act of murdering a prophet.

va·tic·i·nal (vətis′ənl), *adj.* of, relating to, or of the nature of prophesy; prophetic.

va·tic·i·nate (vətis′ənāt), *v.* to prophesy; to foretell the future. —**vat·i·ci·na′tion,** *n.*

vaunt (vônt), *v.* **1.** to boast of; to brag about. —*n.* **2.** a boast.

vaunt·ed (vôn′tid), *adj.* praised to excess; boastfully praised.

vec·tion (vek′sHən), *n.* the passing on of a disease from one person to another.

vec·tor (vek′tər), *n.* **1.** a mathematical quantity having both magnitude and direction, represented by an arrow of a length proportional to the magnitude and made in the appropriate direction. See also **scalar. 2.** the direction followed by a missile, airplane, etc. **3.** an organism, as an insect, that carries disease and transmits it from one host to another.

vec·tor·car·di·og·ra·phy (vek ′tər-kär ′dēog′rəfē), *n.* a method of finding the direction of the electrical forces of the heart and measuring their magnitude.

vegetable sponge. See **luffa.**

veld, veldt (velt), *n.* an area of open grassland characteristic of parts of South Africa, as on the plateau, and sometimes having scattered shrubs or trees.

vel·i·ta·tion (velitā′sHən), *n.* a minor argument or conflict.

vel·le·i·ty (vəlē′itē), *n.* a very weak volition prompting no action; wishfulness.

vel·li·cate (vel′əkāt), *v.* **1.** to twitch or cause to twitch. **2.** to pinch; to nip. **3.** to move convulsively.

ve·lou·té (vəlōōtā′), *n.* a smooth white sauce made with any meat or fish stock.

ve·lu·ti·nous (vəlōōt′ənəs), *adj.* having a velvety surface, as some plants.

ve·na ca·va (ve′nə kā′və), *pl.* **ve·nae ca·vae.** either of the two large veins discharging blood into the right atrium of the heart.

ve·nal (vē′nl), *adj.* able to be bribed; willing to use influence or authority improperly for mercenary gain. —**ve·nal′i·ty,** *adj.*

ve·nat·ic (vēnat′ik), *adj.* relating to hunting. Also **ve·nat′i·cal.**

ve·na·tion (vēnā′sHən), *n.* the arrangement of veins, as in an insect's wing or in a leaf.

ven·due (vendōō′), *n.* a public auction.

ven·e·nose (ven′ənōs), *adj.* poisonous.

ve·ni·al (ve′nēəl), *adj.* able to be pardoned or overlooked, as a sin or fault.

ven·in (ven′in), *n.* any of various poisonous substances present in snake venom. Also **ven′ene, ven′ine.**

ve·ni·re·man (vinī′rēmən), *n., pl.* **ve·ni·re·men.** someone summoned to act as a juror in a trial.

vent·age (ven′tij), *n.* a small outlet giving on to a confined space, as a

fingerhole in some wind instruments.

ven·ter (ven′tər), *n.* **1.** (in zoology) the abdomen or belly; a bellylike protuberance or concave part, as of bone. **2.** (in law) the womb, a wife, or a mother, as a source of progeny.

ven·tose (ven′tōs), *adj.* windy; given to empty talking.

ven·tral (ven′trəl), *adj.* relating to the abdomen or belly; on or relating to the front side or surface of the body.

ven·tri·cle (ven′trikəl), *n.* **1.** one of various hollow organs or parts of an animal body. **2.** either of the two lower chambers of the heart, which pump blood into the arteries. **3.** one of a series of communicating cavities in the brain. —**ven·tric′u·lar,** *adj.*

ven·tri·cose (ven′trəkōs), *adj.* **1.** swollen, esp. on one side. **2.** with a large abdomen.

ven·ue (ven′ōō), *n.* the place where an event or action occurs.

ven·ule (ven′yōōl), *n.* a minute vein. —**ven′u·lose, ven′u·lous,** *adj.*

ver·ba·tim (vərbā′tim), *adv.* word for word; in precisely the same words.

ver·bi·age (vur′bēij), *n.* wordiness; an unnecessary abundance of words.

ver·bose (vərbōs′), *adj.* wordy; using too many words. —**ver·bos′i·ty,** *n.*

ver·dant (vur′dnt), *adj.* covered with or green with vegetation.

ver·di·gris (vur′dəgrēs), *n.* a green or greenish-blue deposit formed on copper, brass, or bronze through prolonged exposure to air. Also called **aerugo.**

ver·dure (vur′jər), *n.* greenness, esp. of a mass of new vegetation; any green vegetation, as grass. —**ver′dur·ous,** *adj.*

ver·e·cund (ver′əkund), *adj.* diffidently embarrassed; shy; modest.

ve·rid·i·cal (vərid′ikəl), *adj.* truthful; true; genuine.

ver·i·si·mil·i·tude (ver′isimil′itōōd), *n.* the appearance of truth or fact; probability. —**ver·i·sim′i·lar,** *adj.*

ver·ism (vēr′izm), *n.* the theory that reality must be represented in art and literature, and therefore the ugly and vulgar must be portrayed.

ver·juice (vur′jo͞os), *n.* **1.** the acid juice of crab apples, unripe grapes, etc., used in cooking. **2.** sourness, as of disposition, etc.

ver·meil (vur′mil), *n.* any gilded metal, as silver gilt.

ver·mi·cide (vur′misīd), *n.* any substance used to kill worms, esp. parasitic intestinal worms.

ver·mic·u·lar (vərmik′yələr), *adj.* **1.** relating to or done by worms. **2.** marked with wavy lines resembling worms or their tracks.

ver·mic·u·late (vərmik′yəlāt), *adj.* worm-eaten; of worm-eaten appearance.

ver·mi·form (vur′mifôrm), *adj.* wormlike in form.

vermiform appendix, a small, wormlike blind tube extending from the cecum in man and some other mammals, having no known purpose, and situated in man in the lower right-hand part of the abdomen.

ver·mi·fuge (vur′məfyo͞oj), *adj.* having the effect of driving out parasites, as worms, from the intestines.

ver·nac·u·lar (vərnak′yələr), *adj.* native; local; not of foreign or learned origin, esp. of language.

ver·nal (vur′nl), *adj.* relating to, occurring in, or coming in spring; springlike.

ver·nal·ize (vur′nəlīz), *v.* to accelerate the blossoming or seed bearing of a plant by chilling the seed or bulb.

ver·ru·ca (vəro͞o′kə), *n., pl.* **ver·ru·cae** (vəro͞o′sē). a wart or wartlike formation. —**ver′ru·cous,** *adj.*

ver·ru·cose (ver′əkōs), *adj.* warty; wartlike growths.

ver·sant (vur′sənt), *n.* the slope of a mountain or range of mountains; the general slope of a region or country disregarding interrupting features.

ver·so (vur′sō), *n., pl.* **ver·sos.** the back of a book or a manuscript leaf; a left-hand page of a book. See also **recto.**

ver·te·brate (vur′təbrāt), *adj.* **1.** having a backbone. —*n.* **2.** any animal with a backbone.

ver·tig·i·nous (vərtij′ənəs), *adj.* **1.**
whirling round. **2.** affected with or liable to affect with vertigo.

ver·ti·go (vur′təgō), *n., pl.* **ver·ti·goes, ver·tig·i·nes** (vərtij′ənēz). dizziness; a disorder in which a person feels himself or his surroundings to be whirling round and often loses his balance.

ver·tu (vərto͞o′), *n.* See **virtu.**

verve (vurv), *n.* enthusiasm; animation; vivaciousness, as of literature, art, personality, etc.

ve·si·ca (vəsī′kə), *n., pl.* **ve·si·cae** (vəsī′sē). a bladder. —**ves′i·cal,** *adj.*

ves·i·cate (ves′əkāt), *v.* to blister; to cause to blister. —**ves′i·cant,** *adj., n.* —**ves′i·ca·to·ry,** *adj., n.*

ves·i·cle (ves′ikəl), *n.* a small bladder-like sac or cyst. —**ve·sic′u·lar,** *adj.*

ves·per·tine (ves′pərtin), *adj.* relating to or taking place in the evening.

ves·pi·ar·y (ves′pēer′ē), *n.* a nest of wasps.

ves·pid (ves′pid), *n.* any insect of the wasp family.

ves·pine (ves′pīn), *adj.* relating to or resembling a wasp.

ves·tal (ves′tl), *adj.* vowed to chastity as the virgins who tended the temple of the Roman goddess Vesta; pure; chaste; virgin.

ves·ti·ar·y (ves′tēer′ē), *adj.* relating to garments or official vestments.

ves·tige (ves′tij), *n.* a lingering trace of some thing, practice, or state no longer in existence. —**ves·tig′i·al,** *adj.*

ves·tig·i·um (vestij′ēəm), *n., pl.* **ves·tig·i·a** (vestij′ēə). a vestigial anatomical structure or any other vestige.

ves·ture (ves′cHər), *n.* all that grows on and covers the land, with the exception of trees.

vet·i·ver (vet′əvər), *n.* the long aromatic roots of an East Indian grass used for screens and the like and in perfumery.

vi·and (vī′ənd), *n.* any item of foodstuff.

vi·at·i·cum (vīat′əkəm), *n., pl.* **vi·at·i·ca** (vīat′əkə), **vi·at·i·cums.** anything essential for a journey, as money, provisions, etc.

vi·a·tor (vīā′tôr), *n.*, *pl.* **vi·a·to·res** (vīətôr′ēz). a traveler; a voyager.

vi·bra·tile (vī′brətil), *adj.* relating to or like vibration; vibrating; capable of vibration.

vi·bris·sa (vībris′ə), *n.*, *pl.* **vi·bris·sae** (vībris′ē). one of the stiff hairs about the mouth of many animals, as rabbits, mice, etc.

vi·car·i·ous (vīker′ēəs), *adj.* acting, done, or suffered for another; experienced in the imagination through the words or deeds of another.

vice·ge·rent (vīsjēr′ənt), *n.* a deputy appointed by a ruler or supreme chief. —**vice·ge′ren·cy,** *n.*

vic·e·nar·y (vis′əner′ē), *adj.* consisting of or relating to 20.

vi·cen·nial (vīsen′ēəl), *adj.* relating to, lasting for, or happening every 20 years.

vice-re·gent (vīs′rē′jənt), *n.* one acting in place of a regent, sovereign, or governor.

vice·reine (vīs′rān), *n.* the wife of a viceroy.

vice·roy (vīs′roi), *n.* a person appointed to act in the name of or in place of the sovereign in a dependent province or country.

vic·i·nage (vis′ənij), *n.* **1.** a neighborhood or surrounding district or its people. **2.** nearness.

vic·i·nal (vis′ənl), *adj.* **1.** belonging to or relating to a district. **2.** near; adjoining.

vi·cis·si·tude (visis′itōōd), *n.* **1.** a change during the course of something. **2.** *pl.* the ups and downs of fortune; successive changes or alternations of condition.

vic·to·rine (viktərēn′), *n.* a fur tippet.

vic·tress (vik′tris), *n.* a female victor.

vic·trix (vik′triks), *n.*, *pl.* **vic·tri·ces.** (vik′trisēz). a victress.

vict·ual (vit′l), *n.* **1.** *pl.* food; provisions. Also **vict′ual·age.** —*v.* **2.** to supply with victuals. —**vict′ual·er,** *n.*

vid·e·o·gen·ic (vid′ēōjen′ik), *adj.* See **telegenic.**

vi·du·i·ty (vidōō′itē), *n.* widowhood or its duration.

vi·ges·i·mal (vījes′əməl), *adj.* relating to or based on 20; 20th; in 20s.

vi·gi·a (vijē′ə), *n.*, *pl.* **vi·gi·as.** **1.** a warning mark on a navigational chart to indicate a likely hazard. **2.** an unknown feature sighted at sea and considered a likely hazard.

vig·or·ish (vig′ərisн), *n.* (in slang usage) **1.** a charge on a bet, payable to a bookie or the like. **2.** interest paid to a moneylender on a loan.

vi·gou·reux printing (vēgərōō′), a method of printing worsted fibers with color before they are made into yarn, producing a multicolored yarn.

vil·i·fy (vil′əfī), *v.* to speak ill of; to defame.

vil·i·pend (vil′əpend), *v.* **1.** to consider or treat as of little importance. **2.** to defame or slander.

vil·li·form (vil′əfôrm), *adj.* **1.** shaped like a villus. **2.** with fine close-set projections giving an appearance of velvet, as the teeth of some fishes.

vil·los·i·ty (vilos′itē), *n.* a villus; a group of or a covering of villi.

vil·lus (vil′əs), *n.*, *pl.* **vil·li** (vil′ī). a slender hairlike small projection on certain membranes, as on the lining of the small intestine. —**vil′lose, vil′lous,** *adj.*

vi·men (vī′men), *n.*, *pl.* **vim·i·na** (vim′inə). a long pliable plant shoot.

vi·min·e·ous (vimin′ēəs), *adj.* relating to, resembling, made of, or producing long pliable shoots or twigs.

vin·ci·ble (vin′səbəl), *adj.* conquerable.

vin·cu·lum (vinG′kyələm), *n.*, *pl.* **vin·cu·la** (vinG′kyələ). a bond or tie indicating unity, as over two numbers.

vi·nic (vī′nik), *adj.* relating to, in, or from wine.

vin·i·cul·ture (vin′əkul′cнər), *n.* the study of winemaking.

vi·nif·er·ous (vīnif′ərəs), *adj.* suitable for or giving a heavy yield for winemaking.

vin·om·e·ter (vinom′itər), *n.* a device for measuring the alcoholic content of wine, usually as a percentage.

vi·nos·i·ty (vīnos'itē), *n.* the characteristics of a wine considered as a whole.

vi·nous (vī'nəs), *adj.* relating to or like wine; due to, showing, or given to habitual wine-drinking.

vin·tag·er (vin'təjər), *n.* a helper at the grape harvest.

vi·o·la·ble (vī'ələbəl), *adj.* capable of being broken or infringed upon, as a promise, a code of behavior, etc.

vi·o·les·cent (vīəles'ənt), *adj.* of a near-violet color; becoming violet in color.

vi·ra·go (virā'gō), *n., pl.* **vi·ra·goes, vi·ra·gos.** a fiercely ill-tempered woman.

vi·re·mi·a, vi·rae·mi·a (vīrē'mēə), *n.* the presence of viruses in the blood.

vi·res·cent (vīres'ənt), *adj.* becoming green. —**vi·res'cence,** *n.*

vir·ga (vur'gə), *n. sing.* and *pl.* a streak of rain, hail, or snow which evaporates before it reaches the ground. See also **praecipitatio.**

vir·gate (vur'git), *adj.* rod-shaped; long, thin, and straight.

vir·gu·late (vur'gyəlit), *adj.* shaped like a rod.

vir·gule (vur'gyōōl), *n.* a short oblique stroke between two alternative words, as *Dear Sir/Madam.* Also **solidus, shilling mark.**

vir·i·des·cent (vir'ides'ənt), *adj.* tinged with or somewhat green. —**vir·i·des'cence,** *n.*

vi·rid·i·ty (vərid'itē), *n.* 1. greenness, esp. of vegetation. 2. mental or bodily inexperience or innocence; youth.

vir·i·lo·cal (virəlō'kəl), *adj.* See **patri-local.**

vi·rol·o·gy (vīrol'əjē), *n.* the scientific study of viruses and the diseases they cause.

vi·ro·sis (vīrō'sis), *n.* any infection caused by a virus.

vir·tu, ver·tu (vərtōō'), *n.* 1. excellence in objects of art. 2. *pl.* objects of art; antiques, or the like. 3. a knowledge of or a taste for such objects.

vi·ru·cide (vī'rəsīd), *n.* a substance used for or capable of killing viruses.

vir·u·lent (vir'yələnt), *adj.* 1. powerfully poisonous. 2. intensely hostile, bitter, or malignant.

vi·rus (vī'rəs), *n., pl.* **vi·rus·es.** an organic particle, by far the smallest living organism known, existing only in animal and plant cells, and capable of causing various diseases.

vis-à-vis (vēzəvē'), *adj.* face to face.

vis·cer·a (vis'ərə), *n. pl., sing.* **vis·cus** (vis'kəs). the internal organs of the principal body cavities, esp. the abdominal cavity. —**vis'cer·al,** *adj.*

vis·cer·o·to·ni·a (vis'ərətō'nēə), *n.* the personality pattern usually found in persons of endomorphic body type, exhibiting extroversion and love of comfort. See also **cerebrotonia, somatotonia.**

vis·cer·o·trop·ic (vis'ərətrop'ik), *adj.* attracted to or affecting the viscera, esp. of a virus.

vis·cer·o·tro·pism (vis'ərətrō'pizm), *n.* infection of or attraction to the viscera.

vis·cid (vis'id), *adj.* of a thick, sticky consistency.

vis·co·e·las·tic (vis'kōilas'tik), *adj.* relating to a substance which is both viscous and elastic.

vis·coid (vis'koid), *adj.* slightly or tending to be viscous. Also **vis·coi'dal.**

vis·cos·i·ty (viskos'itē), *n.* 1. the condition or property of being viscous. 2. the property of a fluid of resistance against flowing.

vis·cous (vis'kəs), *adj.* of a sticky consistency or nature; thick in consistency.

vi·tal·ism (vīt'əlizm), *n.* the doctrine that phenomena are in essence self-determining and only partly controlled by mechanical forces. See also **dynamism, mechanism.**

vi·tel·line (vitel'in), *adj.* relating to the egg yolk; resembling an egg yolk, in color, shape, or the like.

vi·ti·ate (vɪsH'ēāt), *v.* to impair; to corrupt; to invalidate in law. —**vi'ti·a·ble,** *adj.*

vit·i·cul·ture (vit'əkulcHər), *n.* the scientific study or the cultivation of grapevines.

vit·i·li·go (vitəlē′gō), *n.* an abnormality of skin pigmentation producing a piebald appearance, affecting the forearm principally. Also **leukoderma, piebald skin.**

vit·re·ous (vi′trēəs), *adj.* resembling glass in appearance and nature, as in luster, composition, etc.

vi·tres·cent (vitres′ənt), *adj.* becoming, tending to become, or capable of becoming glass. Also **vi·tres′ci·ble.**

vit·ric (vi′trik), *adj.* relating to, resembling, or of the nature of glass.

vit·rics (vi′triks), *n. sing.* and *pl.* 1. *sing.* the technique or art of making glassware. 2. *pl.* glassware or other vitreous articles.

vit·ri·form (vi′trəfôrm), *adj.* glasslike in form or appearance.

vit·ri·fy (vi′trəfī), *v.* to convert or be converted into glass or a glasslike substance. —**vit·ri·fi·ca′tion,** *n.*

vi·trine (vitrēn′), *n.* a glass-fronted and often glass-sided display cabinet.

vit·ri·ol (vi′trēəl), *n.* 1. concentrated sulfuric acid. 2. something severely hurtful in effect, as scathing sarcasm. —**vit·ri·ol′ic,** *adj.*

vit·ta (vit′ə), *n., pl.* **vit·tae** (vit′ē). a stripe or streak, as of color on a plant or animal.

vit·tate (vit′āt), *adj.* having one or more longitudinal stripes.

vit·u·line (vɪCH′əlīn), *adj.* relating to or resembling a calf or veal.

vi·tu·per·ate (vītōō′pərāt), *v.* to find fault with in harsh language; to speak to abusively or harshly. —**vi·tu′per·a·tive,** *adj.*

vi·var·i·um (vīver′ēəm), *n., pl.* **vi·var·i·ums, vi·var·i·a** (vīver′ēə). a place for keeping living wild animals under conditions as near natural as possible, esp. for scientific purposes.

vi·va vo·ce (vī′və vō′sē), orally; by word of mouth.

vi·ver·rine (vīver′īn), *adj.* relating to an Asiatic and African family of small catlike carnivores including civets, palm cats, etc.

viv·i·fy (viv′əfī), *v.* to give life to; to enliven.

vi·vip·ar·ous (vivip′ərəs), *adj.* giving birth to live young in a developed state rather than in eggs. See also **oviparous.**

viv·i·sect (viv′əsekt), *v.* to dissect or make surgical experiments on live animals. —**viv·i·sec′tion,** *n.*

vi·zier, vi·zir (vizēr′), *n.* a minister of state or other high official in various Muslim countries, esp. formerly.

vo·ca·ble (vō′kəbəl), *n.* 1. a word or term. 2. a word considered only as a form without regard to its meaning.

vo·cal·ic (vōkal′ik), *adj.* relating to, resembling, or rich in vowels.

vo·cif·er·ate (vōsif′ərāt), *v.* to utter noisily; to shout. —**vo·cif′er·ance, vo·cif·er·a′tion,** *n.* —**vo·cif′er·ant, vo·cif′er·ous,** *adj.*

vo·coid (vō′koid), *adj.* 1. resembling a vowel. —*n.* 2. a sound resembling a vowel. See also **contoid.**

voile (voil), *n.* a fine, semitransparent dress fabric of silk, cotton, wool, etc., with a plain open weave.

voir dire (vwär′ dēr′), 1. an oath swearing a prospective juror or witness to tell the truth during questioning to ascertain his competence. 2. such questioning.

vo·lant (vō′lənt), *adj.* 1. flying or capable of flying. 2. nimble in movement.

vo·lar[1] (vō′lər), *adj.* relating to the palm of the hand or sole of the foot.

vo·lar[2] (vō′lər), *adj.* relating to or for flight.

volcanic tuff. See **tuff.**

vol·can·ol·o·gy (volkənol′əjē), *n.* the scientific study of volcanoes and phenomena associated with them. Also **vulcanology.**

vole (vōl), *n.* the winning of all possible tricks in a deal by one player in a card game.

vol·i·tant (vol′itnt), *adj.* 1. in the act of or capable of flying. 2. moving; engaged in action.

vol·i·ta·tion (volitā′sHən), *n.* the act of or capacity for flying.

vo·li·tion (vōlisH′ən), *n.* the act or power of willing; a decision made by the will.

vol·i·tive (vol′itiv), *adj.* relating to or involving the will.

vol·plane (vol′plān), *v.* to glide earthward in an unpowered airplane or one with the power cut off.

volt (vōlt), *n.* the unit used in measuring electric current, equivalent to the force or potential difference that will produce a steady flow of one ampere through a resistance of one ohm. *Abbrev.:* **V, v.** —**volt′age,** *n.*

volte-face (voltfäs′), *n. sing.* and *pl.* a complete reversal, as of opinion, policy, or the like.

vol·u·ble (vol′yəbəl), *adj.* with a ready flow of words; talkative.

vol·u·met·ric (volyəme′trik), *adj.* relating to measurement of or by volume.

vo·lup·tu·ar·y (vəlup′cHo͞oer′ē), *n.* one devoted to a life of luxurious and sensual self-indulgence.

vo·lute (vəlo͞ot′), *n.* a spiral or coiled object or form.

vom·i·to·ry (vom′itôr′ē), *n.* **1.** an emetic. **2.** an opening, esp. one through which large numbers of people can enter or leave, as in a stadium. Also **vom·i·to′ri·um.**

voo·doo (vo͞o′do͞o), *n.* a religious and ritual system centered on magic and several gods, practiced mainly by West Indian Negroes.

vo·ra·cious (vōrā′sHəs), *adj.* wanting or eating a large amount of food; eager, esp. excessively eager, to absorb or obtain. —**vo·rac′i·ty,** *n.*

vor·tex (vôr′teks), *n., pl.* **vor·tex·es, vor·ti·ces** (vôr′tisēz). a whirling, often suctional, mass of water, air, or fire. —**vor′tic·al, vor′ti·cose, vor·tig′i·nous,** *adj.*

vo·ta·ry (vō′tərē), *n.* a person bound by vows to religious life, as a nun.

vo·tive (vō′tiv), *adj.* given, consecrated, etc., in fulfillment of a vow.

vouch·safe (voucHsāf′), *v.* to give or allow as a favor or by condescension.

vox bar·ba·ra (voks′ bär′bərə), a questionable word formation or usage, esp. of pseudo-classical elements, as a Neo-Latin scientific term.

vo·yeur (vwäyur′), *n.* one who practices voyeurism.

vo·yeur·ism (vwäyur′izm), *n.* the deriving of sexual gratification by looking at, esp. in secret, sexual organs, objects, or acts. —**voy·eur·is′tic,** *adj.*

voy·euse (vwayo͞oz′), *n. French.* a chair formerly used at gaming tables, with a padded rail across the top for spectators to lean on.

V/STOL(vē′stôl), *abbrev.* for *V*ertical *S*hort *T*ake-*O*ff and *L*anding.

V/TOL(vē′tôl), *abbrev.* for *V*ertical *T*ake-*O*ff and *L*anding.

vul·can·ism (vul′kənizm), *n.* the phenomena associated with the origin and movement of molten rock material.

vul·can·ol·o·gy (vulkənol′əjē), *n.* See **volcanology.**

vul·gate (vul′gāt), *n.* **1.** any generally recognized version of a work. —*adj.* **2.** generally accepted or used.

vul·gus (vul′gəs), *n.* the common mass of people; the populace.

vul·ner·ar·y (vul′nərer′ē), *adj.* **1.** useful in healing wounds, as a drug, herb, etc. —*n.* **2.** any preparation or drug used to heal or promote healing of wounds.

vul·pec·u·lar (vulpek′yələr), *adj.* foxlike; relating to the fox.

vul·pi·cide, vul·pe·cide (vul′pisīd), *n.* the act of killing a fox other than by hunting.

vul·pine (vul′pīn), *adj.* relating to or characteristic of the fox; foxlike.

vul·tur·ine (vul′cHərīn), *adj.* vulture-like in behavior, as in rapacity, etc.

vul·va (vul′və), *n., pl.* **vul·vae** (vul′vē), **vulvas.** the external female genital organs, including the clitoris, the openings of the urethra and vagina, and the labia majora and labia minora.

wad·dy (wod′ē), *n.* a heavy club used in war by the Australian aborigines.

wa·di, wa·dy (wä′dē), *n.*, *pl.* **wa·dis.** a northern African watercourse that is dry except during the rainy season; the stream flowing through such a watercourse.

waf·ture (waf′cHər), *n.* the act of wafting; a thing that is wafted.

wain (wān), *n.* a farm cart.

wald·glas (väld′gläs), *n.* a type of unrefined Medieval and Renaissance glassware, greenish in color.

wal·lah, wal·la (wä′lä), *n. Anglo-Indian.* a person in charge of, or connected with, a particular thing or function, as *a newspaper wallah, a government wallah.*

walled plain, a circular or nearly circular area on the moon, partially enclosed by walls that are usually lower than those of a crater. Also **ringed plain.**

wam·ble (wom′əl), *v.* to move unsteadily; to stagger; to twist or roll about.

wam·pus (wom′pəs), *n.* a strange or disagreeable person; a lout.

wa·mus (wô′məs), *n.* a heavy, loosely knit cardigan jacket with a belt.

wan·i·gan (won′əgən), *n.* **1.** a lumber camp's trunk, chester, etc., for storing supplies. **2.** a small office or shelter on wheels used in temporary lumber camps.

want·age (won′tij), *n.* that which is lacking, desired, or needed.

wap·pen·shaw, wap·in·shaw (wop′-ənsHô), *n.* a periodic review or muster of persons under arms formerly held by chiefs in certain areas of Scotland. Also **wap′pen·shaw·ing, weapon-shaw.**

war·i·son (war′isən), *n.* a note sounded to start an attack.

war·lock (wôr′lok), *n.* a person who practices black magic; a sorceror.

warp (wôrp), *n.* the set of threads running lengthwise in a loom and crossed by and interlaced with the weft or woof.

war·ren (wôr′ən), *n.* a place where rabbits breed or are numerous.

wash sale, an illegal share transaction by buying and selling simultaneously through different brokers so that the shares appear to change ownership (but in reality do not) and trade in that stock appears active.

was·sail (wos′əl), *n.* **1.** a celebration with much drinking of healths. **2.** spiced ale or other liquor for drinking healths at festivities, as on Christmas Eve and Twelfth-night.

water hammer, the thumping sound caused by sudden stopping of a moving volume of water in a pipe.

wa·ter·proof (wô′tərproof), *adj.* impervious to water.

wa·ter·re·pel·lent (wô′tərripel′ənt),

adj. able to repel water but not impervious to it.

wa·ter·re·sist·ant (wô′tərrizis′tənt), *adj.* able to resist water but not entirely prevent its penetration.

watt (wot), *n.* the unit of measurement of power, esp. electric power, equal to one joule per second or the energy expended per second by a steady electric current of one ampere flowing in a circuit across a potential difference of one volt. *Abbrev.:* **W, w.** [named after Scottish engineer and inventor James *Watt* (1736–1819)]

weal (wēl), *n.* well-being; welfare, as *the public weal.*

wea·sand (wē′zənd), *n.* **1.** the throat. **2.** the esophagus. **3.** the trachea.

web press, a rotary press into which paper is fed from a large roll. Also **web-fed press.**

web·ster (web′stər), *n.* a weaver.

weft (weft), *n.* the yarns interwoven by a shuttle back and forth across the warp in weaving. Also **woof.**

weir (wēr), *n.* a small dam in a river.

welfare state, a state in which the welfare of its citizens with regard to employment, health and education, social security, etc., is the responsibility of the government.

Welt·an·schau·ung (velt′änsHou′-ŌONG), *n. German.* a comprehensive philosophy or conception of the universe and of human life in relation to it.

wel·ter·weight (wel′tərwāt), *n.* a boxer of the class between light welterweight and light middleweight in amateur boxing, lightweight and middleweight in professional boxing, and weighing 148 lb. or less if an amateur, 147 lb. or less if a professional.

Welt·po·li·tik (velt′pōlitēk′), *n. German.* the policy of a nation toward the world.

Welt·schmerz (velt′sHmerts), *n. German.* sentimental pessimism or melancholy over the state of the world.

weth·er (weth′ər), *n.* a castrated male sheep.

wet·land (wet′land′), *n., usually pl.* a region of swamps, marshes, or bogs.

wharf·in·ger (hwôr′finjər), *n.* a person who owns or is in charge of a wharf.

wheal (hwēl), *n.* a small itching or burning swelling on the skin, as from an insect bite.

wheel·a·brate (hwēl′əbrāt), *v.* to harden the surface of steel by means of a rotating shot-peening device.

whelk (hwelk), *n.* a pimple or pustule.

whelm (hwelm), *v.* to submerge or engulf; to overcome.

whelp (hwelp), *n.* **1.** the young of the dog, or of the lion, tiger, bear, leopard, wolf, etc. —*v.* **2.** to bring forth young, usually of a dog, lion, etc.

wher·ry (hwer′ē), *n.* a light rowboat used on rivers; skiff.

whick·er (hwik′ər), *v.* to neigh or whinny.

whif·fet (hwif′it), *n.* a small dog.

whif·fle (hwif′əl), *v.* **1.** to blow in puffs or gusts, as the wind. **2.** to shift or veer about; to vacillate.

whif·fler[1] (hwif′lər), *n.* a person who frequently shifts his opinions, interests, etc.; a person who vacillates or is evasive in an argument.

whif·fler[2] (hwif′lər), *n.* an attendant, usually carrying a staff or sword, formerly employed to clear the way for a procession.

Whig (hwig), *n.* **1.** (in American History) **a.** a member of the party that supported the Revolution. **b.** a member of the party (c1834–1855) formed in opposition to the Democratic party and supporting a loose construction of the Constitution and tariff protection of industry. **2.** (in British Politics) **a.** a member of a political party which championed reform and held liberal principles, and later became the Liberal Party. **b.** one of the more conservative members of the Liberal Party.

whig·ma·lee·rie (hwigməlēr′ē), *n.* a fanciful idea; a whim.

whi·lom (hwī′ləm), *adj.* former; erstwhile, as *their whilom friends.*

wise

white·a·cre (hwīt′ākər), *n*. a fanciful name for a hypothetical piece of land, esp. in lawbooks to distinguish one piece of land from another. See also **blackacre.**

whited sepulcher, something or someone evil with the outward appearance of something good; a hypocrite. [Matt. 23: 27]

white man's burden, the alleged duty of the white race to look after the subject people of other races in its colonies.

white paper, an official report by a government.

white paternoster, an incantation used to ward off evil spirits and black magic. See also **black paternoster.**

white plague, tuberculosis, esp. of the lungs.

white primary, a primary election formerly held among the Democrats in those southern States of the U.S. in which only white people could vote.

white rainbow. See **fogbow.**

white sauce, a sauce made of butter or the like, flour, milk or stock, and seasoning.

white slave, a woman enticed or forced into prostitution.

white-smith (hwīt′smith′), *n*. a tinsmith.

white water, foaming water, as in rapids, etc.

whit·low (hwit′lō), *n*. an inflammation of a finger or toe, often with a discharge of pus. Also **agnail.**

Whiz Kid, (in colloquial usage) a young and extremely intelligent, powerful, or successful executive, advisor, etc.

wid·der·shins (wid′ərsHinz), *adv*. See **withershins.**

wid·get (wij′it), *n*. **1.** a knob, switch, or other similar small mechanism, esp. one such of which the name is not known or has been forgotten. **2.** a typical or representative thing, as of a manufacturer's products.

widow's cruse, a supply that is inexhaustible. [I Kings 17: 10–16 and II Kings 4: 1–7]

wig·an (wig′ən), *n*. a canvas-like cloth for stiffening hems, lapels, etc.

wild·ing (wīl′diNG), *n*. any plant that grows wild.

wild silk. See **tussah.**

will-o'-the-wisp (wil′əTHəwisp′), *n*. See **ignis fatuus.**

willow pattern, a design for china, originated in England in 1780 and picturing a willow tree, small bridge, pagodas, etc., derived from Chinese sources and usually blue and white in color.

wim·ble (wim′bəl), *n*. **1.** a device for extracting the rubbish from a bored hole, as in mining. **2.** any of various tools for boring.

wind·age (win′dij), *n*. the deflection of a projectile by the influence of the wind.

win·dow (win′dō), *n*. (in military usage) See **chaff.**

wind rose, a map symbol that shows for a particular place the frequency and strength of wind from different directions.

wind·row (wind′rō), *n*. a row of hay, sheaves of grain, etc., raked or stacked together to dry.

wind shake, a flaw in wood supposedly caused by strong winds deforming the tree trunk. Also **cup shake.**

wind·ward (wind′wərd), *adv*. **1.** toward the side from which the wind blows. —*n*. **2.** the side facing into the wind.

win·kle·hawk (wiNG′kəlhôk), *n*. an L-shaped tear in cloth.

win·now (win′ō), *v*. **1.** to separate grain from chaff, esp. by tossing it up so that the lighter chaff blows away and the grain falls back. **2.** to analyze critically; to separate or distinguish useful from useless parts.

win·some (win′səm), *adj*. attractive in an engaging way; charming.

winter lamb, a lamb born in the fall or winter and sold for slaughter before May 20.

wise (wīz), *n*. (in combination or certain phrases) way; manner, as *lengthwise, in nowise,* etc.

wi·sent (vē′zənt), *n.* the European bison, now nearly extinct.

wist·ful (wist′fəl), *adj.* characterized by longings or yearnings; pensive, esp. in a melancholy way.

witch ball, a ball of many mirrored facets hanging from the ceiling of a ballroom and rotated so that it sparkles in bright light.

with·al (wiтнôl′), *adv.* in addition; as well; in spite of all.

withdrawal symptom, any of the physiological and mental disturbances, as sweating, depression, etc., experienced by a narcotics addict deprived of drugs.

withe (wiтh, wiтн), *n.* a tough, flexible twig of willow, osier, or the like used for binding things together.

with·er·shins (wiтн′ərsнinz), *adv.* in a direction contrary to the natural one, as counterclockwise, and supposed to bring bad luck. Also **widder-shins.**

with·y (wiтн′ē), *n.* a flexible twig or stem; a withe.

wit·ling (wit′linG), *n.* one who affects wittiness.

wit·tol (wit′əl), *n.* a man who knows of his wife's adultery and tolerates it. See also **cuckold.**

wi·vern (wī′vərn), *n.* See **wyvern.**

wiz·ened (wiz′ənd), *adj.* dried up; shriveled, as *a wizened old face.*

wold (wōld), *n.* a high, open tract of land.

wom·er·a (wom′ərə), *n.* a spear-throwing device used by Australian aborigines. Also **woo′mer·a.**

wood·wind (wŏŏd′wind), *n.* any of the group of musical instruments played by blowing and traditionally made of wood, as the flute, oboe, etc., and usually the saxophone.

wood-wool (wŏŏd′wŏŏl′), *n.* fine wood shavings used in insulation, for packing breakable objects, as a binder in plaster, etc.

woof (wŏŏf), *n.* See **weft.**

woof·er (wŏŏf′ər), *n.* a large loud-speaker for reproducing low-frequency sounds. See also **tweeter, tweeter-woofer.**

wool·fell (wŏŏl′fel), *n.* the pelt of a wool-bearing animal with the wool still on it.

wort[1] (wurt), *n.* a malt infusion, which after fermenting, becomes beer or mash.

wort[2] (wurt), *n.* (in combination) a plant, vegetable, or herb, as *pearl-wort, hornwort, navelwort.*

wrack (rak), *n.* a wreck; ruin; the remains or a vestige of something that has been destroyed.

wraith (rāth), *n.* an apparition of a person, supposed to foretell his death.

wran·gle (ranG′gəl), *v.* **1.** to argue noisily. **2.** to herd or round up, as livestock.

wreak (rēk), *v.* to inflict or give vent to, as harm, punishment, vengeance, etc.

wrick (rik), *v.* **1.** to sprain or wrench. —*n.* **2.** a sprain or wrench.

wrig·gle·work (rig′əlwurk′), *n.* decorative zigzags engraved on metal.

write-down (rīt′doun′), *n.* (in accounting) the reducing of the recorded value of an asset.

write-off (rīt′ôf′), *n.* a cancellation from accounts as a loss.

wroth (rôth), *adj.* angry; incensed, as *He was wroth to discover the theft of his documents.*

wry·neck (rī′nek), *n.* See **torticollis.**

wurst (wurst, wŏŏrst), *n.* sausage, esp. in combination as *liverwurst, brat-wurst.*

wy·vern (wī′vərn), *n.* a heraldic winged dragon with two legs like an eagle's and a barbed tail. Also **wivern.**

xan·thic (zan′th*i*k), *adj.* yellow or yellowish; relating to such a color.

Xan·thip·pe (zantip′ē), *n.* a shrewish wife or woman.

xan·tho·chroid (zan′th*ə*kroid), *adj.* belonging to or relating to those peoples of the white races with fair skin or hair.

xan·thous (zan′th*ə*s), *adj.* yellow or yellowish.

xat (кнät), *n.* a totem pole.

X chromosome, a sex chromosome containing numerous genes including those which produce female characteristics, and usually found in pairs in females but in males singly or with a Y chromosome. See also **Y chromosome.**

xen·o·gen·e·sis (zen*ə*jen′isis), *n.* the procreation of offspring with biological characteristics completely different from those of the parents, formerly but no longer thought possible.

xen·o·pho·bi·a (zeb*ə*fō′bē*ə*), *n.* **1.** an abnormally excessive dread or dislike of foreign or strange people or things. **2.** an unreasonable dislike of foreigners. —**xen′o·phobe,** *n.*

xe·rarch (zēr′ärk), *adj.* (of a sere) arising in a dry habitat.

xe·ric (zēr′ik), *adj.* of, relating to, or adapted to very dry conditions.

xe·rog·ra·phy (zirog′r*ə*fē), *n.* a process for copying material from film or paper by means of charging with static electricity those areas of a plain paper corresponding to the printed areas of the original so that powdered resin carrying an opposite charge adheres to them and is then fused.

xe·roph·i·lous (zirof′*ə*l*ə*s), *adj.* living or growing in very dry, and usually hot, conditions.

xe·roph·thal·mi·a (zēr′ofthal′mē*ə*), *n.* abnormal dryness of the eyeball, a symptom of certain diseases, as conjunctivitis.

xe·ro·phyte (zēr′*ə*fīt), *n.* a plant adapted to a very dry habitat.

xe·ro·sere (zēr′*ə*sēr), *n.* a sere arising under dry conditions.

xe·ro·sis (zirō′sis), *n.* **1.** a medical condition of abnormal dryness, as of the skin. **2.** the hardening of body tissues normal in old age.

x-height (eks′hīt), *n.* (in typography) the height of the letter x in lower case of a given typeface.

x-high (eks′hī′), *adj.* (in typography) of a height equal to that of a lower-case x of the same type face and body.

xiph·oid (zif′oid), *adj.* sword-shaped.

xy·lem (zī′l*ə*m), *n.* the woody fiber or tissue of a tree.

xy·lo·graph (zī′l*ə*graf), *n.* a design carved in wood; a print made from such a carving.

xy·log·ra·phy (zīlog′r*ə*fē), *n.* the art of carving on wood or of making prints from such carving.

xy·loid (zī′loid), *n.* woody; resembling wood.

xy·lo·phage (zī′ləfāj), *n.* an insect that feeds on wood.

xy·loph·a·gous (zīlof′əgəs), *adj.* wood-eating. Also **hylophagous.**

xy·lot·o·mous (zīlot′əməs), *adj.* wood-boring or wood-cutting, as various insects.

xy·lot·o·my (zīlot′əmē), *n.* the technique of cutting thin slices of wood for examination under a microscope.

xys·ter (zis′tər), *n.* a surgical instrument used to scrape bones.

ya·hoo (yä′hōō), *n.*, *pl.* ya·hoos. a bestial or coarse person.

Yang (yaNG), *n.* See Yin.

yare (yer, yär), *adj.* quick; agile; easily handled, as a boat.

yar·mul·ke (yär′məlkə), *n.* a skullcap worn by Orthodox Jewish men and boys, esp. for prayer and religious study.

yar·o·vize (yär′əvīz), *v.* See iarovize.

yash·mak (yäsHmäk′), *n.* the veil worn by Muslim women in public to conceal the face below the eyes.

yaul (yôl), *v.* (in rocketry) to deviate from a stable course because of oscillation about the longitudinal axis. See also pitch.

yaws (yôz), *n.* a contagious tropical disease caused by a particular bacterial species and characterized by warty red eruptions on the skin followed by the ulceration of tissue and destruction of bones. Also frambesia.

Y chromosome, a sex chromosome carrying the genes which produce male characteristics, occurring only in males, where it is paired with an X chromosome, and determining sex by its presence or absence. See also X chromosome.

yean (yēn), *v.* to give birth, as of ewes, she-goats, or the like.

yean·ling (yēn′liNG), *n.* a newborn lamb, kid, or the like.

yegg (yeg), *n.* (in colloquial usage) a traveling petty burglar; a vicious ruffian.

yellow-dog contract, a contract by which an employer agrees to employ a worker who in return agrees to leave or remain outside a labor union.

yellow fever, a severe, often fatal, virus infection occurring in tropical climates, transmitted by a mosquito, and characterized by fever, jaundice, vomiting, and hemorrhages. Also yellow jack.

yen·ta (yen′tə), *n.* (in colloquial usage) an unpleasant scandalmongering woman.

ye·shi·va (yəsHē′və), *n.*, *pl.* ye·shi·vahs, ye·shi·voth (yəsHē′vōt). an elementary school for Orthodox Jewish children; a school of higher education in Orthodox Jewish religious teaching, esp. for students intending to become rabbis.

yi (yē), *n.* the fulfillment of the particular obligations to society specified in Chinese philosophy.

Yin and Yang (yin; yaNG), the two universal forces held in Chinese philosophy to be responsible for the harmonious balance of nature and to pervade and control the nature and destiny of all things, Yin being dark, cold, solid, and still, Yang being bright, warm, and active.

y·lem (ī′ləm), *n.* the primordial entity conceived in philosophy as the source from which all things in the universe have derived.

Yo·ga (yō'gə), *n.* union with the supreme spirit or any of the methods of attaining such union, esp. a Hindu system of ascetism, concentration, meditation, and exercise.

yo·gi (yō'gē), *n.* a person who practices or embraces Yoga.

young·ling (yuNG'liNG), *n.* a young person or animal; a beginner.

Young Turk, a rebellious member or adherent of a political party, usually agitating for more liberal policies.

youn·ker (yuNG'kər), *n.* a youngster.

yurt (yōort), *n.* a portable circular hut or dwelling of the native tribes of northern and central Asia.

za·ba·glio·ne (zäbəlyō′nē), *n.* an Italian dessert made of egg yolks, sugar, and Marsala whipped to a thick foam in a bain-marie and served either hot or cold.

zaf·tig (zäf′tig), *adj.* (of a woman) desirably plump and shapely.

zai·bat·su (zī′bätsoo′), *n. sing.* and *pl. Japanese.* the large Japanese industrial or financial combines.

za·mar·ra (zəmär′ə), *n.* a coat made from sheepskin and resembling those worn by Spanish shepherds.

zap·ti·ah (zuptē′ə), *n.* a Turkish policeman.

za·re·ba (zərē′bə), *n.* a stockade, usually of growing thorn bushes, to protect a camp or village in the Sudan and neighboring areas.

zarf (zärf), *n.* a decorative, usually metal, holder used in the Levant for handling coffee cups made without handles.

zar·zue·la (zärzwā′lə), *n.* a Spanish drama with music, frequently satirical and topical.

zax (zaks), *n.* a type of ax for making holes in slate through which nails can be driven.

zeal·ot (zel′ət), *n.* **1.** an enthusiastic or excessively enthusiastic supporter of a cause or person. **2.** a member of a fiercely patriotic Jewish resistance group which opposed the occupying heathen Romans in Judea before and for some time after the fall of Jerusalem in 70 A.D.

ze·na·na (zenä′nə), *n.* the part of an Indian or Persian house where the females of the family were or are secluded; the females so secluded.

ze·nith (zē′nith), *n.* the point on the celestial sphere directly above any observer or given location; the highest point. See also **nadir.**

zero gravity, the state in which there is no gravitational force, as in orbit outside the earth's atmosphere.

zib·el·ine (zib′əlin), *adj.* **1.** of or relating to the sable. —*n.* **2.** the dressed skin of the sable used as a fur for trimmings or garments.

zig·gu·rat (zig′ŏŏrat), *n.* a pyramidal temple of the ancient civilizations of Mesopotamia consisting of several superimposed stages, each smaller than the lower one, giving a terraced appearance, with a sanctuary at the top, or in the Assyrian version having a broad ramp winding around and up the pyramid to the sanctuary at the top.

zin·cog·ra·phy (ziNGkog′rəfē), *n.* the technique of making a printing plate of zinc by etching away the unwanted parts of its surface, leaving the part to be printed standing in relief.

zo·an·thro·py (zōan′thrəpē), *n.* a mental illness in which the patient believes he is an animal.

zo·e·trope (zō′ētrōp), *n.* a device consisting of a drum inside which is placed, opposite slits, a series of images representing successive positions of a moving object so that when the drum is rotated rapidly the images seen through the slits give an illusion of motion.

zo·gan (zō′gän), *n.* Japanese inlaid metalwork used for decoration.

zone melting, a technique used to purify various metals and other minerals by passing a bar of the material through an induction coil to cause momentary melting of each part of the bar with consequent movement of impurities from the molten area to the area still to pass through the coil. Also **zone refining.** See also **cage zone melting.**

zone of interior, the entire area of a theater of war except for the combat zone and its immediate communications zone.

zo·o·chem·is·try (zōəkem′istrē), *n.* chemistry as it relates to the animal body.

zo·o·chore (zō′əkôr), *n.* a plant so adapted in structure that it is spread by animals.

zo·o·ge·og·ra·phy (zō′əjēog′rəfē), *n.* the scientific study of animal distribution and its causes and effects.

zo·og·ra·phy (zōog′rəfē), *n.* the scientific description of animals.

zo·oid (zō′oid), *n.* any organism capable of separate existence from the parent organism and either capable of spontaneous movement or produced by asexual reproduction.

zo·ol·a·try (zōol′ətrē), *n.* the worship of animals.

zo·om·e·try (zōom′itrē), *n.* the scientific measurement and comparison of measurements of the parts of animals.

zo·o·mor·phic (zōəmôr′fik), *adj.* attributing animal form or nature to something, esp. to a deity. —**zo·o·mor′phism,** *n.*

zo·on·o·sis (zōon′əsis), *n.* an animal disease that can be passed on to man.

zo·oph·i·lous (zōof′ələs), *adj.* adapted to be pollinated by some animal that has been in contact with pollen.

zo·o·pho·bi·a (zōəfō′bēə), *n.* an abnormal dread of animals.

zo·o·phyte (zō′əfīt), *n.* any of various low forms of animal life, usually resembling a plant, as corals, sea-anemones, and the like.

zo·o·plank·ton (zōəplaNGk′tən), *n.* the minute animal organisms in plankton. See also **phytoplankton.**

zo·o·plas·ty (zō′əplastē), *n.* the transplanting into a human body of living tissue from another animal species.

zo·ot·o·my (zōot′əmē), *n.* the study of the bodily structure of animals, esp. by means of dissection; dissection for such a purpose.

zo·o·tox·in (zōətok′sin), *n.* a poisonous substance from an animal, as snake venom; a serum formed by the provocation of such a poison.

zo·ri (zôrē), *n., pl.* **zo·ri.** a flat-soled Japanese sandal held on by a thong passing to each side of the foot from between the big and second toes.

Zo·ro·as·tri·an (zôr′ōas′trēənizm), *n.* a believer in a religion founded in Persia in the 7th century B.C. by Zoroaster and surviving in the Parsees of India, teaching that there is a supreme divine being, Ahura Mazda, of whom all nature, wisdom, and truth are part, and that there is a constant cosmic battle between good and evil spirits in which magic plays a predominant part.

zos·ter (zos′tər), *n.* See **shingles.**

Zou·ave (zōōäv′), *n.* a member of a French infantry corps, originally of Algerian but now mainly of French soldiers, distinguished for their physique, dash, and picturesque uniform of baggy trousers, short open jacket, sash, and tasseled cap.

zuc·chet·to (zōōket′ō), *n.* a round skullcap worn by the Roman Catholic clergy, the Pope's being white, a cardinal's red, a bishop's violet, and a priest's black.

zug·zwang (tsōōk′tsfäNG), *n.* a situation in a game of chess where all the moves open to one player will cause damage to his position.

zwie·back (zwī′bak), *n.* a rusk made of a light bread containing eggs.

zyg·a·poph·y·sis (zigəpof′isis), *n., pl.* **zyg·a·poph·y·ses** (zigəpof′isēz). one of the projections serving as joints to interlock each vertebra with the ones above and below it.

zy·go·dac·tyl (zīgədak′til), *adj.* with the toes of each foot arranged in pairs, one pair pointing forward and one pair backward, as in a parrot.

zy·go·mat·ic bone (zīgəmat′ik), the cheekbone, forming the prominence of the cheek and the lower part of the eye socket.

zy·go·mor·phic (zīgəmôr′fik), *adj.* capable of being halved in one plane only to give two symmetrical halves, usually of flowers.

zy·mo·gen (zī′məjən), *n.* any substance capable of changing into an enzyme.

zy·mo·gen·e·sis (zīməjen′isis), *n.* the development of an enzyme from a zymogen.

zy·mol·o·gy (zīmol′əjē), *n.* the scientific study of enzymes and fermentation.

zy·mol·y·sis (zīmol′isis), *n.* the chemical reactions promoted by enzymes.

zy·mom·e·ter (zīmom′itər), *n.* an instrument for measuring the stage reached in fermentation, as in brewing, distilling, etc.

zy·mo·plas·tic (zī′mōplas′tik), *adj.* enzyme-producing.

zy·mo·sis (zīmō′sis), *n., pl.* **zy·mo·ses** (zīmō′sēz). any infectious or contagious disease.

zy·mos·then·ic (zīməsthen′ik), *adj.* bringing about greater enzyme activity.

zy·mot·ic (zīmot′ik), *adj.* relating to, caused by, or as if caused by fermentation.

zy·mur·gy (zī′murjē), *n.* the branch of applied chemistry that is concerned with fermentation, as in brewing, distilling, wine-making, and the like.